PARK CHUNG HEE
AND MODERN KOREA

PARK CHUNG HEE
AND MODERN KOREA

The Roots of Militarism
1866–1945

CARTER J. ECKERT

The Belknap Press of Harvard University Press
Cambridge, Massachusetts
London, England
2016

First printing

Library of Congress Cataloging-in-Publication Data
Names: Eckert, Carter J., author.
Title: Park Chung Hee and modern Korea : the roots of militarism 1866–1945 /
    Carter J. Eckert.
Description: Cambridge, Massachusetts : The Belknap Press of Harvard University
    Press, 2016. | Includes bibliographical references and index.
Identifiers: LCCN 2016015172 | ISBN 9780674659865 (alk. paper)
Subjects: LCSH: Park, Chung Hee, 1917–1979. | Militarization—Korea (South)—History. |
    Korea (South)—Politics and government—1960–1988. | Korea (South)—History—1960–1988.
Classification: LCC DS922.35 .E25 2016 | DDC 951.95/03092—dc23
LC record available at https://lccn.loc.gov/2016015172

In memory of
Yu Yangsu 柳陽洙
(1923–2007)

I have sought to pursue my philosophy of life solely within the military.
—Park Chung Hee

CONTENTS

ABBREVIATIONS

CCP   Chinese Communist Party

CIS   *Ch'in-Il inmyŏng sajŏn*

CTS   Central Training School (Chūo Rikugun Kunrensho), in Mukden

CWZ   *Changchun wenshi ziliao 2*

Dōtokudai   *Dōtokudai dai-shichikisei shi*

GGK   Government-General of Korea (Chōsen Sōtokufŭ)

IJA   Imperial Japanese Army

JMA   (Imperial) Japanese Military Academy (Rikugun Shikan Gakkō), also referenced in text as Sōbudai or Zama

JMAP   JMA Preparatory Academy (Rikugun Yoka Shikan Gakkō), in Asaka

JSDF   Japan Self-Defense Forces

Kiji   *Rikugun Shikan Gakkō kiji*

KMA   (ROK) Korean Military Academy (Yukkun Sagwan Hakkyo)

Kokoroe   *Rikugun Shikan Gakkō seito oyobi gakusei kokoroe*

MG   *Manshūkokugun*

MKJ   *Manjugukkunji*

MMA   (Imperial) Manchurian Military Academy (Dai
             Manshū Teikoku Gunkan Gakkō), also referenced in
             text as Dōtokudai or Lalatun

PLA   People's Liberation Army

ROK   Republic of Korea (Taehan Min'guk)

ROKA   Republic of Korea Army

RSG   *Rikugun Shikan Gakkō*

SA   Supreme Advisor (to Manchukuo Army Ministry)

Sakuyō   *Sakusen yōmurei*

SJ   *Nihon riku-kaigun sōgō jiten*

SJS   *Riku-kaigun shōkan jinji sōran*

Sōten   *Hohei sōten* (IJA *Infantry Manual*)

SSJ   *Nihon riku-kaigun no seidō soshiki jinji*

TNS   Taegu Normal School

Yomoyama   *Rikugun Shikan Gakkō yomoyama monogatori*

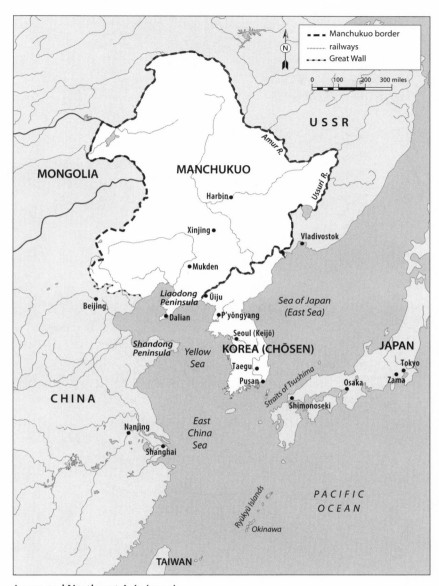

Japan and Northeast Asia (1944)

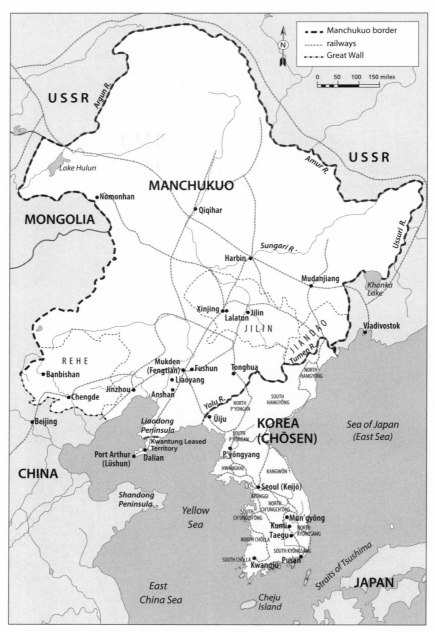

Manchukuo border --·--·--
railways ·········
Great Wall ─·─·─

0   50   100   150 miles

USSR

Argun R.

USSR

Lake Hulun

MANCHUKUO

Amur R.

Nomonhan

Qiqihar

MONGOLIA

Sungari R.

Harbin

Mudanjiang

Khanka Lake

Ussuri R.

Xinjing

Jilin

Lalatun

JIAND
AO

J I L I N

Vladivostok

REHE

Banbishan

Mukden
(Fengtian)

Fushun

Tonghua

Tumen R.

NORTH
HAMGYŎNG

Liaoyang

Jinzhou

Anshan

Yalu R.

NORTH
P'YŎNGAN

SOUTH
HAMGYŎNG

Chengde

Ŭiju

**KOREA
(CHŌSEN)**

*Sea of Japan
(East Sea)*

Beijing

*Liaodong
Peninsula*

SOUTH
P'YŎNGAN

**Kwantung Leased
Territory**

Port Arthur
(Lüshun)

Dalian

P'yŏngyang

CHINA

HWANGHAE

KANGWŎN

*Shandong
Peninsula*

Seoul (Keijō)

KYŎNGGI

*Yellow
Sea*

NORTH
CH'UNGCH'ŎNG

SOUTH
CH'UNGCH'ŎNG

Mun'gyŏng

Kumi

NORTH
KYŎNGSANG

Taegu

NORTH CHŌLLA

SOUTH KYŎNGSANG

*East
China Sea*

SOUTH CHŌLLA

Pusan

Kwangju

Straits of Tsushima

JAPAN

*Cheju
Island*

Korea (Chōsen) and Manchukuo (1944).

PARK CHUNG HEE
AND MODERN KOREA

INTRODUCTION

In a brief twenty-year span during the last century, from the early 1960s to the late 1970s, the Korean peninsula experienced the greatest socioeconomic transformation in its recorded history, and one of the most remarkable and rapid in the history of the world. For many in an older generation now passing as I write, which had known little more than poverty, colonialism, and civil war, it was in many ways the best of times, a period of growing affluence and national prominence. For others in a later generation, more attuned to a postcolonial and postwar world of democratic aspirations and social justice, it was the worst of times, a period of increasing political oppression and social inequity. Few in either generation, however, would deny the period's historical significance. Like any great historical shift, irreducible in its complexity, South Korea's transformation has beguiled scholars of many countries and disciplines from its inception. The focus of scholarly attention, moreover, has also ranged widely, beginning with an interest in the South Korean state and spreading out to encompass diverse aspects of Korean society and culture, both historical and contemporary, as well as key historical actors, both large and small, most especially Park Chung Hee (1917–1979). To a surprising extent, however, the accumulated scholarship of past decades, including my own earlier work, has tended to look past or through an enormous elephant in the room, so obvious, perhaps, as to be invisible. I refer here to the influence of the South Korean military, the army in particular. It was of course the army under the leadership of Park, a major general, that originally seized power in a coup d'état in May 1961 and established a political regime zealously dedicated to "modernization" (*kŭndaehwa*), a South Korean version of the paradigmatic "developmental state," or, as it is also frequently described in Korean scholarship, a "developmental dictatorship" (*kaebal tokchae*).[1] But the influence of the army went far beyond the mere seizure of power. In the course of its formation and expansion under Park (who continued to head the regime first as coup leader, then as elected president, and finally in effect as president for life until his assassination in 1979), the Korean state, as befitting its origins, consistently exhibited a distinctive military cast—martial aspects that it brought to bear on all its projects, economic and otherwise, and which over time also came to have far-reaching effects on Korean society. Indeed, so powerful and pervasive were these effects that by the time of Park's death, in 1979, it had become difficult to separate the overlay of the military from earlier tiers of Korean history, and even today features of South Korean army culture and practice continue to be ingrained in government, business, education, and virtually every other sphere of social activity, as well as in many facets of everyday Korean life. In no small way, then, it is the army that not only links Park to the state but also links the state to society. Furthermore, the army, as an institution rooted in history, allows us to connect some of the many still obscure dots of Korea's modern trajectory with a focus that is broad but also tapered. Without risk of exaggeration, one might say that the history of the South Korean army is not unlike the history of modern South Korea itself. From the beginning, both have been deeply intertwined with and shaped by martial forces: global and regional as well as national. The aim of this book, and a second volume to follow, is to illuminate and trace the genealogy and impact of these forces over time as they grew and strengthened, reaching their apogee in the 1970s state-led development under Park Chung Hee.

Here, four salient martial orientations of the Park modernization regime will serve as our guideposts as we weave our way through a century and more of Korean history. The first is political, as well as "militarist" in the classic, most basic definition of the term: a belief that in a national crisis of sufficient gravity, the army had not only a right but also a duty to intervene in the political system.[2] This sense of political entitlement was in turn a direct corollary of an outlook that idealized and privileged the military and military officers past and present as the locus of a pure and selfless national leadership that deplored the compromises and inefficiencies of Western democratic politics and was immune to the machinations of politicians, businessmen, and other groups in the society, which were seen as driven more by self-interest than concern for the nation.

A second orientation, focused on economy and society, in many ways followed from the first: a deep-seated distrust of capitalism in its most unfettered, laissez-faire form, and a corresponding sense that if it was to be countenanced at all, a capitalist economy would have to be scrupulously planned, implemented, and monitored by the state for the sake of increasing national wealth and power, and not permitted to serve merely as a system for private gain. Indeed, from this viewpoint all interests were to be subordinated to national interests, as defined by the state; in addition to directing the economy, the state was to play an active role in fostering and enforcing an overarching national unity and solidarity that transcended politics and in mobilizing the society by all means possible for economic and other national goals.

A third orientation was tactical and motivational: a commitment to bold, even risky action in pursuit of those same national goals, and a sense that unfailing willpower and confidence, even under the most extreme or adverse conditions, would in the end bring success. This can-do spirit, encapsulated in the Korean phrase *ha'myŏn toe nŭn kŏsida* (we can do [anything] if we try), frequently used by Park at the time in his writings and public pronouncements, became one of the hallmarks of the regime and remains a powerful national legacy even today, long after Park's assassination, democratization, and the growth of corporate influence and power have eroded other aspects of the original modernization state.

Finally, the Korean state under Park Chung Hee evinced a strong disciplinary character, seen as an essential concomitant to every undertaking. Ideally, in this orientation, the state and the society in all their parts and manifestations would function in tandem, with society engaged in a voluntary and active self-disciplining process in harmony with state goals. But the state also reserved the right to intervene anywhere and at any time, whenever it deemed it necessary, to implement its goals with force, impunity, and even violence.

Taken together, these orientations constituted a kind of technology of nation building and economic development. Or perhaps a more accurate term here would be "common sense," since in many cases the orientations were most likely unconscious, less an elaborately conceived design than an embedded psychical sense of what was "right," what "needed to be done." For Park and his associates those orientations were, one might say, templates of victory, based on internalized models of army life, but applied now to national governance, just as the military vocabulary of "battle," "no retreat," and "victory" itself found its way naturally and effortlessly into Park's speeches and other official documents. What gave the templates great power and reach was their extraordinary adaptability and elasticity. They could be applied to any specific state goal or policy decision, however different from others. At any given time a template might also wax or wane depending on internal or external circumstances, such as when the state was forced to adopt democratic politics for a time after 1963, including more corporatist labor policies; when it gradually took a more inclusive approach to business; or when it assumed a more overtly authoritarian character under the Yusin constitution in the last seven years of Park's rule.[3] But notwithstanding Park's own comments that the coup leaders had had "no clear plan for the state" when they took power, and despite notable political and policy shifts between 1961 and 1979, especially in 1972, I would argue that the basic templates, though always more visible and prominent in moments of perceived national emergency, held sway throughout, acting as a kind of unwritten, tacitly understood general framework of governance from beginning to end.[4]

That they did so bespoke a deep and layered history that antedated not just the coup in 1961 but even the establishment of the Republic of Korea (ROK) and the Republic of Korea Army (ROKA) more than a decade earlier. Central to this history were the culture and practices of the Imperial Japanese Army (IJA), especially as taught and inculcated in the IJA's premier officer training schools of Japan and Manchuria, from which Park Chung Hee and many of the early ROKA officers had graduated. Over the years I spent researching this work, time and again I would ask the men who had known Park best or worked with him most closely, including Kim Chŏngnyŏm, his presidential chief of staff for nine years, and O Wŏnch'ŏl, the architect of his regime's Heavy and Chemical Industry Plan, what they thought were the most formative influences in Park's approach to governing.[5] The unhesitating reply was always the same: Japanese army officer education (*Ilbonsik sagwan kyoyuk*).[6] One of the main goals of this work, therefore, and of this volume in particular, is to provide a "thick description" and analysis of that education using original sources and interviews, to reconstruct and transport readers back into the world of the 1940s at Lalatun and Zama, the respective sites of the Manchurian Military Academy (MMA) and the Japanese Military Academy (JMA)—not merely in general terms but, to the extent possible, as Park and other Koreans, including those who joined him in the coup, actually encountered it. There in the wartime classrooms, training areas, and barracks, a world of cadets and instructors, textbooks, lectures, diaries, drills, exercises, study trips, and, not least of all, regulations, rituals, traditions, and even songs associated with everyday academy communal life, one finds a multitude of micro-histories "embedded within a larger macro-story."[7] These are the historical threads and details of the foundational templates that would later significantly shape the South Korean development effort.[8]

In describing the IJA templates as "foundational" I of course in no way mean to imply any kind of teleology. History is fundamentally contingent, sometimes brutally so, and we are wise to keep in mind Foucault's warning about the "chimeras of the origin."[9] And ideology, as Carol Gluck has aptly noted, is not a thing but a process, subject to continual flux.[10] There is no inevitable cultural or historical path from Lalatun to Seoul between 1940 and 1961. On the other hand, the past often has a long reach, and continuity is also a real historical phenomenon. As William H. Sewell has put it: "History displays both stubborn durabilities and sudden breaks, and even the most radical historical ruptures are interlaced with remarkable continuities."[11] Moreover, even the inherent fragility of culture can be countered by "powerful institutional nodes," something Foucault himself made only too clear in his own historical studies.[12] It is one of the main arguments of this work that continuity and cultural coherence in the case of the IJA templates described above have been achieved and sustained not by some kind of invisible structure of inevitability, but by certain recurring and measurable historical "conditions of possibility," to borrow a phrase from Keith Michael Baker.[13] I would point especially to a changing but virtually unbroken century of militarization and attendant institution building in Korea that began in the late nineteenth century, even before Korea fell under Japanese control.[14] In that sense, as this volume explicitly tries to show, each of the foundational templates of the Japanese academies also had certain correspondences in Korean culture and society, endowing them for a generation of Koreans, and especially for the Korean cadets of that generation who matriculated there, with a certain familiarity and reasonableness that ultimately enhanced their overall social and institutional impact. Similarly, after 1945, in a very different political context, as a second volume will argue, these martial templates, whose lineages one might well have expected to come to an end with the collapse of Japan's empire and armies and Korea's consequent political liberation, were in fact revived and augmented in South Korea in a resurgent Cold War militarization under American hegemony, assuming somewhat new contours and connotations both before and after the May 1961 coup. Cold War militarization, which in the case of Korea also encompassed a horrific and traumatic civil war, provided in effect a temporal and institutional environment that enabled the culture and practices of the IJA and the Koreans who had most deeply imbibed and embraced them to flourish in new ways, especially within the ROK Army. In that sense it was not only fatigue from two hours of this author's questioning about IJA academy life that once led a group of Park Chung Hee's former Japanese classmates in Tokyo to suggest finally that I go back to Korea to continue my research. There, "in the ROK Army," they told me, I would still find the "IJA spirit" they had experienced as cadets.

Considering the centrality of the army to Korean economic development and nation building, it is surprising that relatively little scholarly work exists on the subject. Weber suggested long ago that "military discipline gives birth to all discipline," noting also that "military discipline is the ideal model for the modern capitalist factory."[15] And turning once again to Foucault, we are reminded how the disciplines of one domain, like the army, can "converge and gradually produce the blueprint of a general method" for another.[16] There is also a rich body of social science literature going back decades on the role of the military in economic development, and another corpus specifically on the "developmental state," some of which has dealt directly with Korea. But the former has often eschewed a historical approach, treating the "military" largely as a generic professional institution regardless of its origins and development, as in Huntington's well-known observation that as a matter of course in unstable political environments "the wealthy bribe; students riot; workers strike; mobs demonstrate, and the military coup."[17] The latter, on the other hand, has generally tended to focus on the structure and policies of the state, without necessarily connecting either to historically based patterns of culture and practice within the institution of the army itself, or exploring the spread of those patterns from state to society.[18] More recent scholarship has begun to examine some of these questions, and it is not uncommon today for scholars and laymen alike to speak or write of the "militarized" character of the Park Chung Hee state and era.[19] But precisely what this means—and, most important, what history lies behind it—are questions that still cry out for further research and study. To paraphrase Mark Twain's reputed comment on the weather, everyone talks about the militarism of the Park era, but few have done anything about it, at least in the form of a broad and systematic historical inquiry. Even the fascinating multivolume work on the life of Park Chung Hee by South Korean journalist Cho Kapche, an essential source for anyone working on the person or the period, is, as its title suggests, more of a personal biography of Park himself than a sustained historical analysis of South Korean militarism in the *longue durée*.[20]

Park was of course the central, dominant figure in the Korean modernization state. Indeed, it is impossible to understand, or even imagine, that state or the development it promoted without considering his character and intentions.[21] For that reason Park's personal experience, especially of army life, both before and after 1945, is a crucial and recurrent point of reference throughout this book. That positive or negative assessments of Park continue to serve as major fault lines in South Korean politics has also tended to concentrate much popular and scholarly attention on the man himself as an object of interest and study, often in a tone of either admiration or antipathy.[22] To dwell on Park in either mode, however—consumed with his virtues or vices, with Park as a great leader or a great oppressor—seems to me most unfulfilling, a highly subjective if not politicized exercise that runs the risk of turning into an apology or a polemic, and in either case "personalizing the historical process in extreme fashion," in the words of Hitler's eminent biographer, Ian Kershaw.[23] It is important here to recall Marx's dictum that while men make their own history, they make it "under circumstances directly found, given, and transmitted from the past." Even more to the point, perhaps, is what Marx wrote immediately after that: "And just when they seem engaged in revolutionizing themselves and things, in creating something entirely new, precisely in such epochs of revolutionary crisis they anxiously conjure up the spirits of the past to their service and borrow from them names, battle slogans and costumes in order to present the new scene of world history in this time-honored disguise and this borrowed language."[24] South Korea's distinguished academic and public intellectual Paek Nakch'ŏng (Nak-Chung Paik) has suggested that one of the challenges for the scholar of the Park Chung Hee era is "how to give him no more nor less than his due."[25] One way to do so, I would argue, is to see Park historically, as a product of his times, and most especially of the culture and practices of the military institution he so passionately admired, which he sought with great difficulty to join, and in which he ultimately excelled. If he was the spider that wove the web of Korean modernization, that web was interlaced with the battle slogans and language borrowed from an earlier militarism and armies past.

To understand Park as a product and emblem of this past is neither to glorify nor to excuse the achievements and failings of the man or the state he led, both of which were in ample evidence during the eight years I myself lived in Korea, five under the Yusin regime. And for those who suffered in those years I would also add, in a negative paraphrase of the famous French proverb, that to understand all is *not* necessarily to forgive all. But making the milieu as much as the man our focus leads us to larger questions about the historical and societal forces that made militarism and Park possible in South Korea, including how those forces came into existence, how they came to transcend the colonial/postcolonial political divide of 1945, how they worked to configure and transform South Korean modernity, and why they endured for so long.[26] Finally, in a certain sense it also helps to collapse a historiographical divide, still present in much writing on the Park regime, between those who would emphasize the regime's stunning economic achievements and those who would remind us of its darker sides, including the state's almost fanatical concentration on economic growth and its corresponding intolerance of those regarded as slackers and opponents. The truth is that the Park modernization regime was at once both extraordinarily optimistic and productive, with a single-minded and at times even reckless focus on achieving its goals, and also oppressive, especially in its later years, when Park felt those goals were in danger of being subverted by a combination of internal and external threats and challenges. And both faces of the regime, as of Park himself, can be traced back to a different time, when IJA culture and practice ruled, and where a template of "rushing headlong" and "joyously" into battle regardless of hazards was conjoined with a template of "absolute obedience," two complementary sides of a single fixation on victory at all costs.[27]

Our story, then, is a story of institutional and cultural evolution, power, and diffusion in Korea. It is exemplified most vividly in the figure of Park Chung Hee, but it is also a story that spans generations, encompassing not only Park's contemporaries but also many who lived before and after his time. Even Koreans alive today are not entirely free of its sway; in politics and other areas they often find themselves, like Fitzgerald's iconic Gatsby, moving forward only to be "borne back ceaselessly into the past."[28] Triumph and tragedy abound, but it is the double irony of the story that perhaps above all catches the eye of the historian. Behind Park Chung Hee and at the heart of Korea's modern transformation stands the army, an institution that in traditional form was for centuries disdained by the country's elite, and which in its modern form was profoundly shaped by the very forces that held the Korean people in thrall for forty years.

PART ONE

Contexts

ONE

MILITARIZING TIME
Waves of War

Are you not moved, when all the sway of earth
Shakes like a thing unfirm?
—William Shakespeare, *Julius Caesar*

The present time is clearly like the period of Warring States, with every
country contending for wealth and power.
—King Kojong, 1881

Looking at conditions today, both internal and external, we cannot help
but feel keenly a gravity and urgency beyond anything we have known
before.
—Park Chung Hee, October 1, 1961

On a warm spring day in 1958 a group of Korean men with their wives and
children posed for a photograph on the steps of Hwagyesa, a well-known
Buddhist temple and a popular tourist site in the northern part of Seoul. At
first glance there is nothing particularly unusual or striking about the picture that was taken—a memento of a relaxing excursion of friends and families, with some of the men dressed in short-sleeved shirts, some wearing
sunglasses, one with a large camera slung around his neck, and several
sporting the broad-rimmed fedoras popular in the United States and South
Korea at the time.

In retrospect, however, this is no ordinary photograph. Kneeling in front
is Park Chung Hee, who three years later, in May 1961, would lead an army
coup against the South Korean government and remain in power for the
next eighteen years, forever changing Korean history. In the last row, high
up on the steps of the temple, is Park's wife and later South Korea's first lady,
Yuk Yŏngsu, who would be killed in 1974 by a stray bullet meant for her hus-
band. Warily eyeing the camera and gently held in place for the photograph
by her father is Park's six-year-old daughter Kŭnhye (Geun-hye), who would
eventually go on to serve as president of the country some three decades

after her father's assassination in 1979. And surrounding Park in the picture are the key senior Republic of Korea Army (ROKA) officers who would support him in the coup: Kim Tongha, a marine major general who would furnish most of the troops deployed in the actual seizure of Seoul; Pak Imhang, a lieutenant general and commander of the Fifth Corps in 1961, who would forcibly take over the strategic First Field Army; Yi Chuil, who would assist the coup as major general and chief of staff of the Second Army; and Yun T'aeil, who would provide backing as a brigadier general within the ROKA headquarters. Also in the picture to Park's left is Pang Wŏnch'ŏl, a ROKA colonel who had arranged the spring outing and who, among other things, would play a role in helping to smooth over relations with American military forces in South Korea following the coup. Many years later, when he agreed to an interview and first showed me the photograph, Pang made a point of saying that it was precisely Park and the other men in the photograph, together with Park's nephew by marriage, Kim Chongp'il, who had "personified the May 16 coup and made it possible."[1]

But just as the 1958 visit to Hwagyesa was not the last meeting of these men, it was also not the first. The first meeting had in fact been eighteen years earlier in northeast China, when they had all been wearing the uniforms and insignia of the Manchurian Military Academy (MMA), a school for army officers in the new state of Manchukuo, which had been created in 1932 by the occupying Japanese Kwantung Army.[2] Park had just entered the second class of the academy (MMA 2), while the others were all one year ahead in the first (MMA 1). Though grainy and blurred, three older photographs, one of an inspection parade, another of a *kendō* match, and the third of an award ceremony, all from a Manchurian Japanese-language newspaper reporting the MMA 1 graduation ceremony from the school's preparatory course (*yoka*) in March 1941, capture something of that earlier time when the two classes were together.[3] And it is here in the 1940s, in the schools of the Imperial Japanese Army (IJA) that traversed both metropole and empire, and in the Koreans who attended them, Park Chung Hee above all, that one finds the first formations of what would later become the natal officer corps of the South Korean army and the first clustering of those foundational templates of military culture and practice that would later frame the Park state's modernization regime. In history, as in so much else, context is everything, and it is therefore with the broader contexts of these 1940s snapshots, temporal, discursive, spatial, and personal, that we begin.

Temporality

But how does one define historical context? Or, in the context of historical time, when? If it is true that to everything there is a season, then it falls to the historian to demarcate that season as precisely as possible. And it is certainly tempting to fix the temporal context of these first formations solely and squarely within the wartime militarization of Korea's late colonial period, between, say, the Japanese seizure of Manchuria in 1931 and the end of the war in 1945. Somewhat arbitrarily, one might even point to an actual season—the fall of 1934, for example, when, as the prominent Christian educator Yun Ch'iho noted in his diary, the colonial Government-General of Korea (GGK) had "with great importance" introduced military drill into the capital's two top Korean boys' higher common schools for the first time. This was a signal, as Yun presciently observed, "that Korean youths will certainly be asked to contribute their share of service and sacrifice to the warlike preparations of Japan."[4] Here without question we find a direct and immediate contextual link to Park Chung Hee and other Koreans standing in military formation in Manchuria less than six years later.

But both the season and the martial formations that sprang from it were in fact considerably longer than this, stretching back well before and beyond the 1940s, and even well before Park Chung Hee's birth in 1917. One might even say that the Japanese wartime colonial mobilization of the 1930s and 1940s represented a second wave of militarization that was preceded by an earlier wave antedating the colonial annexation and followed by a third after 1945. Indeed, it would not be an exaggeration to say that Korea has been in an almost continuous undulating state of militarization since the late nineteenth century, with each wave merging in various ways and degrees with the other, and with Koreans themselves taking the lead in the first and third. In recent years the second wave has been the subject of a number of studies in English, as well as Korean and Japanese, and a later volume of this study will deal with the third.[5] In this chapter, and in Chapters 2 and 3, our focus is on the first wave and its links to the second.

The Global Nexus

All three waves of Korean militarization in the nineteenth and twentieth centuries were embedded in larger global militarization processes that acted as catalysts. In the case of Korea's first wave, lasting roughly from the late nineteenth century to 1907, when the Chosŏn army was officially disbanded by a Japanese protectorate, the global process had been at work for centuries. In the late fourteenth century, for example, if a Korean army led by an able commander such as Yi Sŏnggye, the founder of the Chosŏn dynasty, had somehow encountered an army from either Britain or France, the dominant powers in Europe at the time, the two sides would not necessarily have been mismatched. Cavalry would have played a key role on both sides, and archery, swordsmanship, and the ability to wield spears and pikes would have been crucial, as would have been expertise in siege warfare, with its increasing use of gunpowder. Neither army at that time would have represented a mass mobilization by the state of its entire adult male population. And both sides would have been accustomed to battles that resembled more a general melee of hand-to-hand combat, featuring individual stamina and bravery, than a series of meticulously planned and coordinated tactical or strategic maneuvers.

Over the next five hundred years, however, military strength in Europe expanded dramatically. This remarkable development of military power was a reflection of numerous other related and overlapping economic, political, and ideological forces and changes in the West during this period, not least of all the industrial and French revolutions, but it was also the product of a virtually continuous period of warfare among the various countries of Europe. Indeed, in the mid-sixteenth century, Europe had already moved from more than a century of conflict in the long Hundred Years' War to another century of what one scholar has called "the most intense and unremitting warfare of any period in its history before or since."[6] This was soon followed by the military upheavals of the French revolution and Napoleonic era and later by an escalating arms race among the major European powers that led to conflict in the Crimea in 1854–1856, the Austro-Prussian War (1866), the Franco-Prussian War (1870–1871), and ultimately World War I (1914–1918).

In turn, industrialization, national state-building, and military escalation, all intertwined, gave birth to new military technologies, weapons, and tactics, as well as to large-scale armies recruited through universal conscription and commanded by a professionalized officer corps, enabling imperialistic European powers to extend their military reach across the globe and by the nineteenth century to subdue entire states in Africa and Asia with small detachments of troops. Only Japan was able fully to match the external challenge posed by European imperialism, in the end itself becoming a major industrial and imperialist power through the political changes and reforms of the 1868 Meiji Restoration, which had been kindled by the first Western incursions fourteen years earlier. As Japanese military power and ambitions grew in the region, moreover, Chosŏn Korea became a focal point of competing imperialist claims and interests, especially among Meiji Japan, Qing China, and tsarist Russia. The result was two victorious wars for Japan, first against China in 1894 and then against Russia ten years later. For Korea, however these wars meant foreign invasion, widespread destruction and human suffering, and finally occupation and colonization by Japan.[7]

The Chosŏn Military

To say that Chosŏn Korea was woefully unprepared for the global military onslaught it faced in this period of rampant imperialism would be an understatement. During the centuries of unprecedented European military change and expansion, Chosŏn's military had stagnated and eventually deteriorated. In part this decline was simply the ironic consequence of the dynasty's two-hundred-year peace. Following devastating invasions in the late sixteenth century by the Japanese warlord Toyotomi Hideyoshi and then by the Manchus several decades later, Korea suffered no further foreign military incursions until French warships sailed into the Han estuary and launched an attack on Kanghwa Island in 1866, finding the forts there deserted and empty and the once triumphant navy of Chosŏn's great admiral Yi Sunsin, who had famously routed Hideyoshi's ships, reduced to "a few useless junks lying idly along shore."[8] Over time, moreover, aristocratic exemptions from state financial levies and military duty, together with extensive corruption at the local level, had depleted the Chosŏn treasury and transformed military service into a regressive system of taxation that left the state conscription rosters filled with the names of nonexistent soldiers. By all accounts, the only military forces in the country remotely worthy of the name in the nineteenth century seem to have been a contingent of permanent, salaried units in the capital, better-trained and better-provisioned than any other units in the country, but also relatively small in number and prone to being a cat's-paw of Chosŏn factional politics and intrigues.[9]

Adding insult to injury in the case of the Chosŏn military, moreover, was the lower status that over time had come to be accorded to military practices and practitioners. If aristocratic power had worked to curtail and ultimately erode the financial and numerical strength of the military, aristocratic prestige had also served to undermine the social standing of the military and those associated with it. At the heart of the problem lay a conflation of traditional preference for civil rule with a deeply rooted Korean proclivity toward social organization based on hereditary status. Nevertheless, it is important to point out that before the Chosŏn dynasty the military had often enjoyed long periods of high prestige, and even during the first century or so of the Chosŏn period, the social position of the military officials remained high, as one might expect in a dynasty founded by a military officer. *Yangban,* the conventional term for the aristocratic class, originally meant simply the two traditional branches of officialdom, one civil (*munban*) and one military (*muban*). And in the early Chosŏn period, while the principle of civil rule tended to reward with higher bureaucratic posts those who had passed the civil examination, the same pool of aristocratic families that dominated the civil examinations also vied in the military competitions, and there was no clear status distinction drawn between civil and military examination passers.

In time, however, aristocratic status increasingly came to be disassociated from the military, and what emerged eventually as the core of the Chosŏn *yangban* aristocracy consisted primarily of family lineages in the capital associated largely with success in the civil examinations. The first step in this process may well have been the exempting of aristocratic families and relatives from the state's military service obligation in the early Chosŏn period, which helped foster the idea that military service was somehow incompatible with aristocratic status, an obligation to the state to be imposed only on commoners. Even more crucial in the lowering of military prestige, however, were the Hideyoshi invasions of the late sixteenth century, when the Chosŏn government, desperate for troops, abandoned its prohibition against slaves performing military service. Slaves were actively recruited for military duty, and even after the Japanese and Manchu invasions, they continued to be enlisted because of the increasing shortage of commoners available for service. Already by the early eighteenth century, slaves had come to constitute the bulk of the Chosŏn army's rank and file, and the military's earlier taint of commonness had been transformed into a stigma of baseness.

Low estimation of military service as a whole came to encompass even the military examinations and those associated with them. Again the process began with the Japanese invasions. The urgent demand for officers led a besieged government to lower the criteria for military degrees, in some cases awarding them to anyone who could produce a certain number of enemy heads. While such measures were clearly extreme, an exigency of war, degree qualifications tended to remain minimal thereafter, especially at the provincial level of the examination process. Lower standards also went hand in hand with a proliferation of special examinations called *mankwa* or "the military examinations of ten thousand passers," which also began during the Japanese invasions of the late sixteenth century. As the name suggests, an extraordinary number of candidates, usually thousands but at least in one case literally more than ten thousand, were permitted to pass the *mankwa* examination, thereby further degrading the military degree and the status of those who acquired it.

Perhaps most devastating to the status of the military degree holders, however, was the opening up of the military examinations to non-aristocratic candidates, even those of base background. The first such crack in the examination wall came in 1593, when King Sŏnjo permitted private and public slaves to stand for the examinations for the first time. This was of course another emergency act by an embattled state, but it set the stage for an increasing influx of lower-status groups into the military domain from the early seventeenth century on. To be sure, such limited social mobility was not without some benefit to the state. As Eugene Park suggests, the opening up of the military examinations in this way may have acted as a social leavening process, reducing potentially explosive social tensions and giving more stability to the dynasty.[10] But just as the admission of slaves into troop units had compromised the prestige of the army as an institution, so too was the prestige of the military officials diminished by association with a socially debased military examination. One eighteenth-century Korean *yangban* mother, exhorting her son to study, also cautioned him to "guard against indulging in shooting arrows and riding galloping horses." "This," she warned, "will coarsen your nature and stain and destroy the old and pure name of your family!"[11] By the nineteenth century military officials, even those of the higher three ranks, whose dress was emblazoned on the breast and back with two tigers to indicate their military affiliation, were forced to show obeisance to civil officials even if the latter were of equal or lower bureaucratic rank. [12] Military examination passers were often referred to in vulgar, pejorative terms as "ox horn benders" (*soe ppul hwigi*) or "dog legs graduates" (*kae tari ch'ulsin*).[13] Europeans, who were beginning to venture into Korea in larger numbers in this period, were always struck by the degree of disdain for the military profession. French missionaries, for example, noted that with respect to their civil counterparts, military officials were "almost on a level with the common people."[14]

The fall in social status of the Chosŏn military during the course of the dynasty had profound repercussions on military strength and morale. Among other things, it helped perpetuate the inefficient and inequitable system of military taxation by intensifying aristocratic resistance to any reform that might challenge, however weakly, the exemption from military service and thereby sully *yangban* honor. Commoners of course tried to avoid the army primarily because of its heavy financial burdens, but concerns about social position may also have played a part here. In a society so overwhelmingly dominated by considerations of status, and where exemption from military service carried a certain aristocratic cachet, commoners of some means and *yangban* pretensions were as likely as the *yangban* themselves to shun service. And even commoners without such means and pretensions did not relish interaction with the men of slave background who constituted the majority of troops. Indeed, in deference to commoner sensibilities, slaves and commoners were generally segregated in the military units.[15]

The importance that Chosŏn society placed on hereditary status also militated against the development of a professional officer corps. As the prestige of the military degree declined and the leading aristocratic capital lineages concentrated their efforts solely on the civil examinations, other capital lineages emerged to dominate the military examinations and the bureaucratic appointments that success in the examination made possible. Scholars differ on whether by the nineteenth century these *muban* families represented a substratum of a diverse and stratified ruling elite or a separate and discrete secondary elite, but their position in the social hierarchy seems clearly to have been below that of the civil lineages, as evidenced by the way in which they were treated by the latter.[16] There is also no doubt that, like their civil counterparts and indeed like most Chosŏn social aggregations, they constituted a closely knit hereditary group of families that generally intermarried and vigilantly defended their occupational terrain and status from penetration and pollution by outsiders, especially outsiders from lower-status groups.

As the numbers of such outsiders taking the military examinations increased in the late Chosŏn period, the capital *muban* families closed ranks and fought back in every way they could, even resorting to violence and fraud. The trenchant Chosŏn social critic Chŏng Yagyong writes of the capital military lineages hiring thugs to beat up and even cripple candidates from the provinces who had qualified for the second stage of the military examination in Seoul. Even if they survived such harassment and went on to take the examination, the provincials were often deliberately eliminated on some technicality during the examination itself by judges sympathetic to or bribed by the capital *muban* families. And even if some did manage to pass through the eye of this needle, the capital military lineages were still usually able to manipulate the system so that few if any outsiders ever actually received a bureaucratic post.[17]

Hereditary domination of the examination and appointment process by the capital *muban* lineages thus severely narrowed the pool of potential military officers, in effect closing it off to all but a few families generation after generation. Those kept out of the pool, moreover, were arguably among the most qualified candidates, natural soldiers tempered in the rougher, more physically demanding life of the countryside. The "effete" sons of the capital *muban* families, according to Chŏng Yagyong, were no match in physical prowess and the required martial arts such as archery for the provincial contenders, especially the "fearless fighters" of the northwest and the men of the southeast and southwest with their "outstanding skills."[18]

In their anxious attempts to protect themselves from such outside contamination, the capital military lineages also invariably stressed the importance of knowledge of classical military texts as opposed to actual military expertise and ensured that the military examinations would be weighted toward the former.[19] But that was not their only purpose in focusing on textual mastery. Fairbank suggests that in traditional China there was a "tendency to disesteem heroism and violence, not to glorify it," and the same might be said for Korea.[20] Both countries shared a common aphorism that "just as good iron should not be wasted on making nails, good men should not be wasted in making soldiers." One may appreciate how entrenched this view was in Chosŏn Korea by recalling how King Sŏnjo in 1595, at the height of the Japanese invasions, was forced to back down from his attempt to convert what he regarded as nonessential private academies to military training grounds by officials who insisted that "even in the midst of a war we must continue to nurture and train [scholars]. [Adhering to] the Way alone will sustain us, and now more than ever it is time to restore the Way."[21] Even Chŏng Yagyong, so critical of his country's neglect of the military in the nineteenth century, could not conceal a certain pride in Korea's customary "gentleness" and "prudence," which "took no pleasure in the military arts."[22]

In the Chosŏn context, moreover, these attitudes were infused with ideas of status, and both scholarly abilities and the scholar's disdain for the soldier became attributes commonly associated with aristocratic standing. By trumpeting their proficiency in classical military texts, the military families were not only able to distance themselves from their lower-status competitors, who were generally less accomplished in that area, but also able to partake in some way of the aristocratic aura that surrounded literacy in classical Chinese and an understanding of esoteric classical writings. Status fixations thus turned many military officers into what might be described as literati manqué, soldiers who were eager to demonstrate their social worth by eschewing soldierly virtues.[23]

The First Wave of Militarization

As the nineteenth century was drawing to a close, one Western observer, not at all unsympathetic to Chosŏn Korea's plight, expressed his astonishment that Koreans had not made "the faintest stand" against their recent aggressors.[24] Numerous scholars since have focused on the dynasty's military shortcomings and failures. The shortcomings and failures are undeniable; indeed, given the way foreign troops marched freely up and down the Korean peninsula in the late nineteenth and early twentieth centuries and the relative dearth of references in the conventional histories of this period to the Korean army, one might be tempted even today to conclude that the Chosŏn dynasty made little or no attempt to protect the country by reforming its decrepit military establishment.

The reality, however, was more complicated. War, Heraclitus once suggested, is the king and father of all. This is an exaggeration, to be sure, but the point is well taken. Centuries of neglect, combined with deeply rooted socioeconomic and political problems, had weakened and demoralized the Chosŏn military to a point that was perhaps unprecedented in Korean history, and military rejuvenation in the mid-nineteenth century seemed as elusive as it was essential. But the colossal inertia of the Chosŏn military system was at least in part the result of the absence of any serious outside military threat, and things were to change once such a danger was perceived. As early as the 1880s, long before the two great wars that would be waged on Korean soil in the twilight of the dynasty, Korean literati were already turning to the Chinese classics they knew so well to describe the unsettling new age in which they found themselves. They felt, many wrote, as if they were living in the ancient period of the Chinese "Warring States," famed for its brutal, unforgiving, and incessant warfare. The comparison, which King Kojong himself liked to use, seems only too apt.[25] Though the worst was still to come, it was already clear by the 1880s that the long Chosŏn peace had finally come to an end and Korea was entering a new and haz-ardous world of war and military power. As in Japan, a sense of anger and crisis provoked by foreign incursions would set Chosŏn Korea on its own course of militarization, and Meiji Japan would even provide a model for many of Korea's own military reforms. Although this first wave of mili-tarization in Korea would be far less comprehensive than in Japan and would ultimately do little to save the country from colonization, it would nevertheless have a profound effect on Korean institutions and thinking.

Early Militarization under the Taewŏn'gun

The military response of the Chosŏn dynasty to the first major foreign in-trusions in the 1860s was remarkably swift in view of the state of its armed forces. To no small degree the reason for this lay in the character of the king's father, the grand prince (Taewŏn'gun), who was in effect ruling the country during Kojong's minority. While, as a member of the capital aris-tocracy, he had grown up steeped in a knowledge of the personalities and workings of the court and bureaucracy, until his eleven-year-old son was unexpectedly elevated to the throne in 1864 he had lived the life of an inde-pendent nobleman, more or less free from the entanglements of court poli-tics and debates and beholden to no particular individual or faction. This deeply ingrained personal sense of independence, combined with a forceful, resolute, and essentially pragmatic temperament, quickly made him the most powerful figure in the young king's government, even though he tech-nically held no formal appointment. The very absence of any formal posi-tion actually enhanced his power, allowing him to bypass many of the more cumbersome institutional structures and even to issue direct orders on the spot. And, as a dutiful son faithful to the Chosŏn Neo-Confucian virtue of filial piety, Kojong more often than not acquiesced to his father's wishes, at least in the early years of his reign, when the American and French gun-boats began to encroach on Korean territory.

It was in fact the French fleet's invasion of 1866 that woke the Taewŏn'gun and the court to the threat of foreign attack and exposed the weaknesses of the Korean army in a dramatic and unnerving way. Although the fleet had finally withdrawn in the wake of fierce Korean opposition, the magnitude of the invasion had been a shock. That the government had also been forced in the struggle to rely largely on thousands of civilian volunteers and an advance guard of provincial native tiger hunters from the northern part of the peninsula also left no doubt that the military establishment was in need of urgent reform.

The Taewŏn'gun acted both quickly and decisively. Even before 1866 he had been moving toward a restructuring of the government to increase monarchical power, and in the wake of the invasion, he promulgated a variety of measures that by the early 1870s turned the country into a kind of garrison state. Under his leadership a centralized office for defense and military planning (Samgunbu) that had originally been proposed and approved in 1865 began to function in earnest and play an important role in building up the country's military strength. Separate from and equal in rank to the State Council (Ŭijŏngbu), the highest organ of government, the Samgunbu was made independent of the Ministry of War (Pyŏngjo), which was under the State Council. Although there were numerous concurrent appointments within the three agencies, the creation of the Samgunbu as an institutionally autonomous office was a clear indication of the government's heightened interest in military affairs. The commanding generals of the three capital-based forces, the Military Training Agency, the Forbidden Guards, and the Royal Command, were also given appointments within the Samgunbu, as were numerous other military officials who had the Taewŏn'gun's confidence and trust, thereby helping to coordinate command authority and imparting to the new office a distinctive military character that was unusual among high-level Chosŏn dynasty bureaucratic agencies.

In 1867, with the advice and assistance of Sin Kwanho, a gifted commanding general of the Military Training Agency who had once disparaged the capital troops under his command as a chaotic and undisciplined "murder of crows," the Taewŏn'gun began to implement a variety of military self-strengthening programs.[26] Over the next eight years the country saw the first serious attempt at a comprehensive augmentation of national defense since the Japanese and Manchu invasions in the late sixteenth and early seventeenth centuries. Fortresses and naval batteries were repaired or built throughout the country and manned with troops, especially in areas of strategic significance such as Kanghwa Island. There, for example, the Chinmu Camp (Chinmuyŏng), which on paper had been the island's key military unit since 1700 but had long since virtually ceased to exist, was reconstituted and raised in official importance. Decaying arsenals were replenished with new and better weapons and equipment, including artillery. Command effectiveness was fortified at the regional level by a reorganization and expansion of command zones. Following General Sin's recommendations, a major effort was also made to strengthen the combat efficacy of the capital troops by a revamping of the existing forces that involved retaining only the most promising soldiers, subjecting them to rigorous discipline and training, and rewarding the best with promotions and pay raises. General Sin, who had been impressed by the utility and potency of French firearms, was also responsible for the creation of what one scholar has called new "rifle units" in the army.[27]

The fruits of the Taewŏn'gun's efforts were visible during the invasion by an American expeditionary force in 1871 bent on opening Korea up to diplomatic intercourse. In stark contrast to 1866, the fortresses and batteries on Kanghwa Island and adjacent areas were well stocked with hundreds of weapons of various kinds, and thousands of Korean soldiers were stationed there and on alert when the Americans arrived. The Korean troops were aggressive, shelling and attacking the intruding ships at every opportunity, and they earned the respect of the American sailors for their bravery. It was in fact the Koreans' determined military opposition that in the end convinced the American force that the Chosŏn government was unlikely to agree to a treaty and led to the fleet's withdrawal.

In carrying out his military enhancement programs, the Taewŏn'gun also succeeded in expanding the sources of military revenue. In addition to drawing directly on the royal treasury for military expenditures and even minting new cash, he levied new taxes to support military strengthening, including a toll on all commercial goods passing through the main gates of Seoul and two other important trading localities, and a surtax on land to be paid by landowners in six of the country's eight provinces. He launched a vigorous campaign to curtail the corruption that was rampant throughout Chosŏn officialdom, siphoning off funds that could be used for national defense. Sumptuary laws were also put into effect to force the wealthy to reduce waste and extravagance in their dress and consumption.

Of all the Taewŏn'gun's defense funding measures, perhaps the most memorable and significant was his reform of the regressive military tax system. After centuries of opposition from the ruling elite, in 1870 the tax was finally extended to the aristocracy by abolishing the tax on individual commoners and substituting a general household tax that encompassed both *yangban* and commoner families. As James Palais notes, the change was not as revolutionary as might appear at first glance. *Yangban* families had in effect already been paying a portion of the military tax for some time, as the custom of holding whole villages responsible for the tax had proliferated throughout the country. The new household tax system also bowed to elite sensibilities by allowing *yangban* families to avoid the stigma of association with military service by paying the tax in the name of their household slaves.[28] Still, the reform of the basic military tax put military funding on a more rational footing than ever before, and in 1873 the minister of war was able to note with satisfaction a considerable increase in revenue as a result of the Taewŏn'gun's new policies.

That *yangban* families were permitted to save face by paying the new military household tax in the name of their slaves was a testimony to the continuing depth of disdain for the military profession in Chosŏn society, but the Taewŏn'gun's efforts to improve the quality of the army also helped give martial virtues a new prominence and cachet. In addition to elevating the Samgunbu to the level of the State Council and filling it with high-ranking military officials, the court paid special tribute to the soldiers who had died or been wounded in the struggle with the Americans in 1871, singling out several officers, as well as their wives and children, for recognition and material compensation. Honors and privileges were bestowed particularly on Ŏ Chaeyŏn, the deputy commander of the Chinmu Camp on Kanghwa, who had died leading the defense of the island. Soon after the fighting, the king granted Ŏ the posthumous title of *ch'ungjang,* meaning "loyal and brave," as well as posthumous promotions to war minister and a position on the Samgunbu, and the Finance Ministry was directed to spare no expense in giving him a lavish funeral. At the same time it was declared that his sons were to be given special treatment after their period of mourning, including official appointments by recommendation for those who had not yet taken the state examinations. Ŏ Chaeyŏn's younger brother, Chaesun, who had died with his brother in combat, was also given posthumous promotion, and the king declared that both brothers should be publicly honored for their service to the dynasty by having their names and virtues emblazoned on the gates of their homes or villages in the royal vermilion that was usually reserved for the king alone.

In a sense, however, the break with the past represented by such changes in the Chosŏn military was more apparent than real. For the most part the changes were innocent of any real knowledge of the extensive military developments that had taken place outside the country. Guns were a case in point. Although French guns may have convinced General Sin and the Taewŏn'gun of the superiority of contemporary Western firearms, Korea lacked the technology to produce them. During the American invasion in 1871, most of the Chosŏn army's artillery volleys, however aggressive and determined, were inaccurate or, as one American sailor noted, simply "fell short, a few striking our sides and falling back into the water, without doing any damage."[29]

The new "rifle units" referred to above, moreover, were not really rifle units at all. Korea was technically unable to produce real rifles, which had only recently come into general use even in Europe. Although there is some indication that Chosŏn Koreans, or at least the fearsome tiger hunters, had been exposed to the flintlock musket, perhaps through contacts in the border regions of the north, existing inventory records of weapons for the Chosŏn army during this period suggest that the Taewŏn'gun was pouring money into the production of some version of the old matchlock musket that had first been introduced into the army from Japan during the Hideyoshi invasions nearly three hundred years earlier, even before the invention of the bayonet. In addition to being saddled with complicated, cumbersome, and slow-firing guns with a limited range, the Chosŏn musketeers, lacking bayonets, still had to be protected during the loading and firing process by companies of pikemen. Quite apart from the obsolescence of their weapons, moreover, they had no knowledge of the Western drill that made such weapons so effective and had transformed the small-armed infantry into the key branch of the modern European army.

Like his guns, the Taewŏn'gun's other military improvement measures were cast in a similarly traditional mode. The establishment of the Samgunbu in fact represented a conscious resurrection of an institution that had existed at the beginning of the dynasty when military concerns had played a larger role in both domestic and foreign policy. Despite its military orientation, the new Samgunbu was still deeply embedded in the traditional bureaucratic structure and culture and very different from a modern professional army's general staff organization. It is not at all unlikely that the Taewŏn'gun envisioned it as a temporary office, as it had been created, like similar bureaucratic institutions in the past, to meet a specific military threat by bringing together in one organization those officials holding the top civil and military posts in the government.

Although it was considerably more ambitious and systematic than attempts by earlier rulers, the Taewŏn'gun's strengthening of the army was also a reform with precedents in Chosŏn history, most recently during the reigns of Kojong's two immediate predecessors. In addition to providing the soldiers with more and better weapons, it was, like earlier military reforms, focused largely on finding and cultivating men who were willing and able to fight rather than on a fundamental reexamination and overhaul of the existing system of military service. In time-honored Confucian fashion, General Sin also stressed the importance of civilian contributions to defense, whether in helping to construct coastal fortifications or in forming voluntary local militias. Even the Taewŏn'gun's new military household tax represented the culmination of a debate that had been going on for centuries. Although it required the aristocracy to participate indirectly in the financing of the military, the tax imposed no real obligation on *yangban* to actually serve in the army and can in no way be seen as a shift toward modern universal conscription. Essentially it was a practical financial measure that grew out of the Taewŏn'gun's need for new military revenue. The Taewŏn'gun's generous treatment of the fallen military defenders of Kanghwa and their families was also squarely within the tradition of honoring meritorious service to the dynasty and meshed well with the new policy of army improvement by encouraging and rewarding able and aggressive soldiers.

Able and aggressive soldiers, however, even armed with new matchlock muskets and supported by newly reinforced forts and batteries, could not carry the day against nineteenth-century gunboats and drilled troops with rifles. The Taewŏn'gun's failure to recognize this fact was due in part to the withdrawal of the American ships in 1871, which he incorrectly attributed to the success of his military strengthening effort rather than to the Americans' lack of sufficient commercial or strategic interest in Korea. But a deeper cause lay in his and his countrymen's lack of knowledge about the outside world, including the military developments that had taken place in the West and were rapidly spreading to Japan. Indeed, during his ten years of rule, the dynasty's long-standing seclusion policy was enforced with renewed strictness, and the Taewŏn'gun was particularly wary of what he regarded as the politically and culturally subversive ideas of barbaric Western missionaries and traders. But if Chosŏn Korea was to have any chance at all of defending itself, it was precisely these new military practices that it had to learn, a truth that became painfully clear when Japan finally forced the country to open its doors to international diplomatic and economic intercourse through the Kanghwa Treaty five years later.[30]

Influx of New Military Knowledge

With the opening of the country in 1876, knowledge of the many momentous changes, including in warfare, that had been occurring in western Europe during the past several centuries began to flow into Korea and take root. With respect to military as well as other ideas, there were many routes of entry. Undoubtedly the most palpable exposure to Western military practice for Koreans came in the form of gunboats and sailors, later followed by contingents of military guards at the major foreign legations in Seoul. Between 1876 and 1905, when Korea was forcibly turned into a Japanese protectorate, the country was also host, willingly or not, to thousands and sometimes tens of thousands of foreign troops, especially from China and Japan, but also to a lesser extent from Russia, and each of these three powers at various times sought to influence the development of Korea's military affairs.

It would be a mistake, however, to see Koreans in this period simply as averse or passive with respect to the new military knowledge that was becoming available. Indeed, one of the earliest and most effective channels of such information was the Chosŏn government itself, since 1873 under the direct rule of King Kojong. In the three decades after 1876, the government took an active role in searching out, securing, and helping to disseminate the new military knowledge by sponsoring official foreign observation and inspection missions, whose reports were widely circulated at court and in the bureaucracy; by hiring foreign military advisors; by purchasing foreign military weapons and equipment; and by sending Korean students abroad to study the new military technology or enroll in officer training schools. Of all these official attempts to learn from abroad, none was more important, especially in the early years after the opening of the country, than the government's inspection mission to Japan in 1881, officially designated as the Courtiers Observation Mission (Chosa Sich'altan), but commonly known in Korean history as the "Gentlemen's Sightseeing Mission" (Sinsa Yuramdan).

The Courtiers Observation Mission

To be sure, the Observation Mission was not the government's first dispatch of officials abroad since the opening of the ports. There had been two previous official trips, both also to Japan, one by Kim Kisu immediately after the conclusion of the Kanghwa Treaty in 1876, and another by Kim Hongjip in 1880.[31] Although both envoys, especially Kim Kisu, had brought back new information about the various changes that had been taking place in Japan since the Restoration, their visits were relatively brief and more in the nature of a diplomatic embassy than a formal inspection tour. The Observation Mission, in contrast, was a large-scale and extensive project. The common sobriquet, "Gentlemen's Sightseeing Mission," suggesting a pleasant recreational excursion, is an unfortunate misnomer; the mission was, in effect, nothing short of a serious, wide-ranging, systematic, and detailed effort on the part of the Chosŏn government to examine directly and make sense of the new modernizing world of Meiji Japan. In that sense it was not unlike the famous Iwakura Mission that the Meiji government itself had sent out a decade earlier to observe and report on the manifold aspects of European civilization.

The core of the Observation Mission consisted of twelve members of the bureaucratic elite ranging in age from their late twenties to their mid-fifties. The two highest-ranking members held vice ministerial positions carrying a second grade in the bureaucratic hierarchy, while all but one of the others were at the senior third grade. Even the lowest-ranking member was at the senior fourth grade. Accompanying each of the courtiers were various attendants, bringing the total number of people in the delegation to sixty-two. Each courtier was assigned a specific area or subject on which to report, which in practice largely corresponded to the Meiji government's key ministries or agencies: Interior, Culture, Justice, Industry, Foreign Affairs, Finance, Customs, and, of course, War. One courtier, Yi Wŏnhoe, who held the post of Right Naval Commander of Chŏlla Province, was also charged specifically with gathering information on Japanese military drill and training. In addition to meeting with high-ranking officials in the various ministries and other government organs in Tokyo, the members of the mission traveled throughout Japan during the course of their four-month residency there, visiting a wide variety of institutions, including arsenals and other military facilities. Upon their return to Korea, the courtiers all prepared lengthy reports on their observations, and they were subsequently summoned to the palace in three groups to present their findings directly to the king.

References to military issues are sprinkled throughout the reports submitted by the courtiers, particularly in the report of Ŏ Yunjung, who argued enthusiastically for the adoption of a Korean version of Meiji Japan's fundamental policy of "rich country, strong army." But the most substantive military information is contained in the reports submitted by Hong Yŏngsik, who had been dispatched to the Japanese Ministry of War, and by Yi Wŏnhoe. Hong's report, entitled "An Overview of the Japanese Military System," ran more than 400 handwritten pages in classical Chinese. Volume 1 began with several brief introductory chapters laying out the history, overall organization, numerical strength, and officer ranks of the Meiji army and then proceeded to describe in extraordinary detail the structure and functions of all the main institutions associated with the army, including the Ministry of War, the General Staff, and the Inspectorate General, the last of these responsible for overseeing military training in the various branches of the army. Special attention was also given to such subjects as army bands, military police, army courts and courts-martial, cavalry horses, army garrisons, the imperial guards, artillery and engineering units, and the three key Tokyo military schools: the Japanese Military Academy (JMA), for officer candidates; the Toyama School, specializing in marksmanship and physical training; and the Kyōdōdan, for noncommissioned officers.

Volumes 2 and 3 provided explicit and often lengthy descriptions of Japanese army procedures and practice: the system of universal conscription designed to supply the state with a regular, standing army and two tiers of reserves; the training of new inductees; annual military inspections; military law; promotions, decorations, dismissals, and pensions; and even military weddings and funerals. A great deal of information was included about the internal organization of the three military schools, together with a comprehensive outline of each school's course of study and training. A separate chapter in Volume 3 focused on the organizational changes necessary to shift the army to wartime status, including specific manpower increases in each branch, as well as personnel requirements at the brigade, division, and corps levels.

The fourth volume of Hong's report was devoted to a minute description of army expenditures, encompassing salaries, housing, food, uniforms, bedding, consumable items such as paper, and repairs. Each of these expenses was listed on both monthly and annual bases at the regimental, battalion, and platoon levels and for different branches of the regular army: infantry, cavalry, mountain artillery, field artillery, engineers, and transport corps. A similar breakdown of costs was separately provided for the imperial guard units. Salaries for commissioned and noncommissioned officers in both the regular army and imperial guards were noted for every branch and rank, as well as for retired officers and those awaiting appointments. There was also information on merit bonuses for noncommissioned officers, monthly and yearly pay increases in accord with rank and duty, military cadet allowances, and daily and yearly wages for different types of hired army laborers.

Yi Wŏnhoe's report was even more voluminous than Hong's, approaching 600 pages and covering six volumes. Although it offered general information about Japan's military establishment, including the conscription system, military schools, and other subjects that could also be found in Hong's report, it provided new details on all these topics. Moreover, while

Hong's report was essentially a survey of the entire Japanese military system, Yi's report was more narrowly focused on the army itself. Appropriately entitled "Drill Regulations of the Japanese Army," it was in fact a kind of textbook of army organization and training designed for practical use.

Yi began in Volume 1 by explaining how the Japanese army consisted of a regular standing army (*sangbi*) with first (*yebi*) and second (*hubi*) reserves and was divided into five branches (infantry, cavalry, artillery, engineers, and transport) totaling 43,229 officers and troops, as well as an imperial guard force consisting of 3,926 men divided into two infantry regiments, one cavalry company, one artillery battalion, and one company of engineers. For each of the five branches he also provided an explanation and description of basic army organizations and units, beginning with the squad (*pundae*) and continuing through the platoon (*sodae*), company (*chungdae*), battalion (*taedae*), and regiment (*yŏndae*), even including information about military bands, telegraph units, bugle and fife calls, banners, weapons, and army knapsacks. The heart of the report was contained in the subsequent five volumes, which laid out in precise detail and often with accompanying drawings the most important drills and training exercises for each branch of service. Not surprisingly, the main focus here was on the infantry. Yi in fact spent two entire volumes on infantry training, which covered everything from physical exercises to a wide variety of marching and rifle drills, as well as fifteen different drills at the company level and eighteen at the battalion level, all with diagrams.

One can hardly underestimate the significance of Hong's and Yi's reports. Within five years after the opening of the country, the Chosŏn government found itself in possession of a large fund of basic knowledge concerning the formation, structure, training, and even technical vocabulary of modern armies. The reports also provided extremely detailed practical intelligence on how such an army was being developed in Japan, a country that not only was located nearby but also shared certain perspectives stemming from a common cultural link to ancient China, and which, like Chosŏn Korea, was also grappling with the implications of its forced opening to the outside world. The information contained in these reports quickly found its way into the early government-sponsored newspapers of the 1880s, *Hansŏng sunbo* and *Hansŏng chubo,* as well as later publications.[32]

Knowing something and acting on that knowledge, of course, are two different things. Although the basic information about the modern military systems of the West and Japan was clearly available and in circulation in Korea by the 1880s, implementing it required the power of the Chosŏn state, and it was the king on whom that power ultimately devolved. But the monarch in the Chosŏn system was subject to multiple forces and checks from many quarters, not least of all from conservative *yangban* bureaucrats skeptical and wary of institutional changes based on foreign models. Especially in the early years after the opening of the country, for every enthusiastic supporter of reform there were scores of more powerful advisors who saw little merit in the new "barbarian" practices of Europe or Japan. Kim Kisu had in fact returned from his trip to Japan in 1876 arguing that to imitate Japan's policy of "rich country, strong army" would "poison" Korea, and despite the enthusiasm of Ŏ Yunjung and others in the Courtiers Observation Mission of 1881, the mission's majority opinion of the changes taking place in Meiji Japan had been largely negative.[33] The king was also buffeted in the decades after 1876 by a cacophony of advice and entreaty, to say nothing of pressure and even duress, from foreign powers with interests of one kind or another in Korea, all seeking to impose their own, often self-serving vision of reform on Korea. And even the advocates of reform were often sharply divided among themselves as to the proper program and pace of reform, some—including Kim Okkyun, Pak Yŏnghyo, and others inspired by Meiji models—actually frightening the king by their zealotry and willingness to resort to violence.

Nevertheless, at the beginning of Korea's tentative opening to the world in 1876, King Kojong, unlike his father and the conservative faction that tended to dominate the court, was clearly curious about and receptive to the new "enlightenment" (*kaehwa*) ideas swirling about in Korea in the late 1870s and 1880s. Indeed, the king, who was only twenty-three years old at the time of the Kanghwa Treaty, had in fact personally played a crucial role in the decision to negotiate and sign the agreement.[34] He was also particularly intrigued by the new military knowledge that was becoming available, and in the course of the next thirty years—despite a personality that was often feckless and capricious, and notwithstanding a growing disillusionment with many enlightenment projects, particularly those that in any way infringed upon his royal prerogatives—he would retain that interest and seek to develop the military by introducing a number of European reforms.[35] In doing so he would take the militarization begun by his father to an entirely new level.

State Militarization under Kojong in the 1880s

Korea's militarization in the decades after 1876 was directly reflected in the changing priorities and institutional restructuring of the late Chosŏn state. Before 1894 these changes were limited, in keeping with the conservative character of the government and a corresponding tendency to follow the kind of "self-strengthening" program being pursued at the time in China, where the focus was less on fundamental institutional innovation and more on the acquisition of Western skills and technology, including weapons. Within this circumscribed policy, however, the king quickly revealed his strong interest in military affairs and his determination to establish a hospitable institutional framework for acquiring and implementing the new military knowledge. In early 1881, even before the dispatch of the Courtiers Observation Mission—and, indeed, in anticipation of it and other official fact-finding and educational trips—a new office, the T'ongni Kimu Amun, was created as a central bureaucratic organ to lead the self-strengthening effort. As an indication of his interest in reform, the king gave the new office equal status with the State Council, appointing one of the state councilors as its president and filling it with officials of the highest rank.

Although the T'ongni Kimu Amun's responsibilities embraced several different areas, including post-Kanghwa foreign relations, the military functions of the new office were clearly axial. In that sense it represented a reformist version of the Taewŏn'gun's Samgunbu, which it replaced and whose actual offices it took over. Of the Amun's twelve departments, five were devoted exclusively to military concerns: general military affairs, border administration, ordnance, ships, and coastal surveillance. In January 1882, moreover, based on information contained in the Observation Mission's reports, the Department of General Military Affairs (Kunmusa) was subdivided into three sections. One section handled general administration and judicial, personnel, and financial matters, as well as the acquisition, repair, and manufacture of weapons. A second section functioned as a kind of incipient general staff organization, charged with such things as purchasing and printing maps, charts, and books; compiling information on foreign geography, governments, military systems, and military history; translating useful books on military issues; and carrying out other activities related to the accumulation, arrangement, and dispersal of military knowledge. A third section was concerned with the education of officers and troops, including the purchase, translation, publishing, and preservation of textbooks and the distribution and maintenance of training weapons. Appropriately, the two members of the Observation Mission who had authored its military reports, Hong Yŏngsik and Yi Wŏnhoe, were selected to head the department's first and third sections, respectively.

The life of the T'ongni Kimu Amun, however, proved to be short. Only six months after the Kunmusa's reorganization, the Amun was abolished by the Taewŏn'gun during his brief return to power in July 1882. To be sure, the office was reconstituted in slightly different form at the end of that year, with its original responsibilities apportioned to two separate offices, one of which, the T'ongni Kun'guksamu Amun, absorbed the Kunmusa. But the potency of this new Amun was further weakened following the enlighten-ment group's attempted coup in 1884, when it was placed under the juris-diction of the State Council, and during the subsequent decade, when the Qing representative Yuan Shikai wielded extraordinary power over Chosŏn state affairs. In retrospect, nevertheless, the short-lived T'ongni Kimu Amun, superimposed over the existing bureaucracy in 1881–1882, can be seen as the first significant step toward militarization of the Chosŏn state following the opening of the country in 1876 and an early sign of the king's resolution to revitalize the military with new ideas and approaches. It was, as it turned out, also a harbinger of even greater state militarization.[36]

State Militarization after 1894

After 1894 a number of events and changes worked together to further mil-itarization of the bureaucratic establishment. One was the political resur-gence that year of radical enlightenment reformers, who had been out of favor or in exile since the failed coup attempt in 1884. As a result of Japan's occupation of Korea during the Sino-Japanese War, many of these reform-ists, including Pak Yŏnghyo, were able with Japanese support to take power and form a new government in 1894. They were concerned, above all, to de-clare an end to what they perceived as Korea's pernicious and debilitating historical dependence on China and to establish a strong and independent new Korean state following the example of Meiji Japan. Openly adopting the Meiji slogan of "rich country, strong army," in 1894–1895 they enacted more than 200 pieces of sweeping new legislation based on enlightenment ideas. These became known in Korean history as the Kabo reforms, including laws creating a cabinet system of government with a prime minister and a new and more powerful Ministry of War (Kunbu), whose head was required by statute to be an active-duty military officer. Although their tenure of power was short-lived, collapsing in the wake of waning Japanese influence in Korea after pressure from Russia, France, and Germany,[37] and public outrage at the murder of Queen Min, their reform program became, as historian Yu Yŏngik (Lew Young Ick) has noted, the basic legal foundation for subsequent reforms until the end of the dynasty in 1910.[38]

Another factor that contributed to militarization after 1894 was King Kojong's own embrace of the "rich country, strong army" ideology in the wake of the Sino-Japanese War. There is no doubt that since 1884 the king had remained suspicious of the political ambitions of the enlightenment reformers, not least of all Pak Yŏnghyo, and he was equally resentful and fearful of Japan's political interference in Korea during the war. In order to escape such influences, he even took advantage of Japan's weakening international position in 1896 to seek refuge in the Russian legation, where he issued orders for the arrest of many of the reformist officials and criticized many of the reform measures.[39] Nevertheless, although he distrusted Japanese motives in Korea, the king—like the rest of the world—had been startled and impressed by Japan's unexpected and unambiguous victory in the war against Qing China, and this new recognition of Japanese military superiority led him to a more positive assessment of the Kabo policy of emulating Japan, at least with respect to building an independent state buttressed by a strong military.[40]

The king's renewed interest in militarization in this period was also profoundly affected by the direct experience and continuing threat of internal rebellion and foreign invasion. The Tonghak Rebellion in the southwest, the largest popular uprising in the dynasty's history, had in fact been a catalyst for the war between Japan and China in 1894, and the war itself had both devastated the peninsula and undermined the power of the throne.[41] Rural discontent and insurrection, moreover, continued to remain a concern even after 1894, as did the possibility of additional foreign invasions. In 1900, for example, the Boxer Uprising in China, with its denouement in the form of international military intervention, deeply disturbed the king, who feared that something similar might occur in Korea. And as relations worsened between Japan and Russia in the early years of the new century, the king followed that deteriorating situation with growing trepidation.[42]

One of the most important results of this conjunction of concerns and crises after 1894 was the proclamation by the king that the dynasty would be renamed and reestablished as the Great Han Empire (Taehan Cheguk). Around 2:00 p.m. on October 11, 1897, King Kojong and his son, the crown prince, proceeded with great pageantry from Kyŏngun (Tŏksu) Palace to a newly built altar to heaven as thousands of people watched from the streets and buildings. After inspecting the altar and the designated sacrificial animals—oxen, sheep, and pigs—the king and his party returned to the palace, where they remained until the early hours of the next morning. At 3:00 a.m. on October 12 the king went again to the altar, where the sacrifices were carried out, and two hours later he assumed the title of Great Han Emperor.

The imperial coronation was replete with meaning. At one level it represented an attempt to break away from the past and declare Korea's complete political independence from China by simultaneously using and subverting traditional symbols. For more than a millennium Korean kings had been formally invested by the Chinese emperor, and although the emperors had in fact seldom interfered in the internal politics of Korea so long as its kings ritually acknowledged the emperors' claim to suzerainty, the Korean kings had nevertheless been subordinate figures in the Sino-centric political cosmology that informed relations between the two countries. To the Chinese emperor alone, for example, had been reserved the right to wear the imperial yellow and sacrifice directly to heaven. The Korean kings had contented themselves with the royal red and had even eschewed naming their own personal reign era around which the calendar was ordered, instead following that of the emperor. The kings had also sent regular tribute missions to the emperor and had welcomed his envoys to Korea with all the pomp and circumstance befitting ambassadors from a great and superior political power. At the coronation ceremony in 1897, however, it was Kojong who donned the yellow silk robes and title of emperor and who performed the sacrifices to heaven and announced his personal reign era. The new altar, moreover, was not only modeled on the Temple of Heaven in Beijing but also quite deliberately built on the site of the former guesthouse of the Chinese emperor's envoys to emphasize the break with the past and the Korean ruler's new imperial status.

But the coronation was more than merely a break with the past. Despite its rich use of traditional language and ritual, it also signified a reaffirmation of the post-Kanghwa enlightenment effort to strive for equality with other countries by opening Korea to new ideas and promoting national prosperity and strength. In his first edict as emperor, Kojong, in a tone that was reminiscent of the Meiji emperor's Charter Oath of 1868, announced that "our desire is to abolish old abuses and to introduce what is new, making good government and wholesome customs prevail. We proclaim this to the world: let all hear and know."[43] Among other things Kojong was thinking of the Korean military, and on the day of the coronation, as he was carried through the city in a new gilded yellow chair on the shoulders of some fifty men, the entire length of the royal processional route from the palace to the altar of heaven was lined with Korean soldiers. While of course they were there primarily to protect the king during his movement through the city, their presence was also symbolic and adumbrative. A month earlier it had been announced that the soon-to-be emperor had selected as his new personal reign era the name "Kwangmu," which one Korean newspaper had translated into English as "Enlightenment and Power" but could also be rendered as "Brilliant and Martial."[44] And indeed, it would be under the flag of the Great Han Empire that the militarization of the Chosŏn state structure would reach its apogee.[45]

Militarization in the Great Han Empire

Intensified militarization at the bureaucratic level in this period was reflected above all in the creation and development of the Wŏnsubu or Supreme Military Council in the late 1890s. First established by the new emperor in 1899, it became the most important military organ in the government, gradually taking over most of the duties of the War Ministry, established several years earlier by the Kabo reformers. The War Ministry, in fact, shrank as a result in size and personnel to a mere shadow of its former self, becoming a kind of clerical appendage to the Wŏnsubu and dealing only with the artillery and engineering branches of the army, as well as with certain accounting matters. The Wŏnsubu, on the other hand, was not only given ultimate responsibility for all key military administrative and supervisory matters but also entrusted with all aspects of national defense and granted supreme command authority over all units of the armed forces. Combining in this way the dual functions of a war ministry and an army general staff organization, it represented the most radical centralization of military affairs of the late Chosŏn bureaucracy.

In addition to being more centralized than any of the earlier bureaucratic offices created to coordinate military matters, such as the Samgunbu, the T'ongni Kimu Amun, or even the new Kabo war ministry, the Wŏnsubu was also more powerful. It was, first of all, an office directly under imperial control and even situated within the palace. The emperor himself was the head of the Wŏnsubu, with the crown prince serving as his deputy. Under the crown prince were four chiefs (ch'ongjang), each presiding over one of the four main departments: military affairs, inspection, finance, and records. Of these four divisions, the Department of Military Affairs

(Kunmuguk), whose chief acted in effect as the emperor and crown prince's chief of staff, was the most important, for all practical purposes the executive center of the Wŏnsubu's activities. In addition to being responsible for all national defense planning and troop deployment, it was charged with the formation of new military units, troop mobilization, production, and provisioning during war; appointments and dismissals related to combat readiness; and the establishment and management of military schools. Furnished with daily reports from the War Ministry, the capital forces, and the Garrison Defense Forces, it kept the emperor regularly informed of the state of the military and in turn ratified and transmitted all imperial orders. Without the emperor's explicit command, conveyed through the Kunmuguk, no one in the central or local government or military establishment, including the minister of war, could order any military unit into action.

The other departments, though more limited in their reach, were also greatly privileged in both the military and civil bureaucracy. The Inspection Department (Kŏmsaguk) handled regular officer appointments, dismissals, promotions, punishments, and honors. It also served as the prosecutor in courts-martial and drafted regulations for military prisoners. The Finance Department (Hoegyeguk), in addition to managing all financial matters pertaining specifically to the Wŏnsubu, supervised the War Ministry's budget, approved all military expenditures, and distributed supplies and equipment to the War Ministry and military units. A special committee within the department also monitored the financial transactions and accounts of the various military units. The Records Department (Kirokkuk) acted as a clearinghouse for documents coming in and going out of the Wŏnsubu and maintained the office's archive. All of the Wŏnsubu chiefs, moreover, exercised wide-ranging and extraordinary authority that, in effect, turned the Supreme Military Council almost into a state within the state. Armed with an imperial command, chiefs were permitted to query and request reports from any of the cabinet ministers, to conduct unannounced inspections of the War Ministry as well as the capital and provincial forces, and to order army units into action without informing the minister of war in advance. In 1900 they were even given the authority to issue actual orders to the ministers and to interrogate the prime minister himself.

The Wŏnsubu's power was further enhanced by the fact that the new imperial government had made military development a priority and was devoting an increasing proportion of the national budget to that goal. Although we have reliable figures only for the period after 1894, when, as a

result of the Kabo reforms, a modern finance ministry with a national bud-
geting system was established, the increase in military expenditures is
nevertheless striking. In 1896, before the Wŏnsubu had been established,
expenditures on the military accounted for about 16 percent of national income. By 1898 that figure had risen to nearly 28 percent. In 1901 it jumped
again, to over 41 percent, and remained between 38 and 40 percent until
1905, when Korea became a Japanese protectorate. The preponderance of
military expenditures in the national budget was so great that it even occa-
sioned public criticism from reformers in the Independence Club (Tongnip
Hyŏphoe), which had been formed in the late 1890s to promote Korean independence and institutional change based on foreign models and was
otherwise well disposed toward the strengthening of the army.[46]

More centralized and powerful than its predecessors, the Wŏnsubu was
also in character and personnel the most unabashedly military of all post-
Kanghwa attempts to establish an effective bureaucratic agency for modern
military development. By law civilians were categorically excluded from
working in the Wŏnsubu; all employees had to be active-duty military officers. The four chiefs were lieutenant generals, who in turn were supported
by a staff of field, company, and noncommissioned officers, all clothed in
the new black European-style army uniforms of the Great Han Empire.
Even the emperor and the crown prince, as heads of the new office, assumed
the aspect of military figures during this period. Now in direct and personal
command of all the armed forces through the Wŏnsubu, they respectively
took the military titles of marshal commander in chief (Taewŏnsu) and field
marshal (Wŏnsu) that had been newly and expressly created for them, and
for the first time they began to appear in public and pose for official photographs dressed in imperial army uniforms. The emperor's new clothes and
titles were an unequivocal sign of the turn-of-the-century Chosŏn state's
growing military orientation.[47]

Building a New Army

Militarization of the state bureaucracy in this period was matched by a renewed interest in modernizing the Korean army itself. Efforts to develop a
new Korean army using the latest Western weapons and drill methods had
in fact begun as early as the spring of 1880, following an offer from the Japanese
ambassador, Hanabusa Yoshimoto, to provide an appropriate drill instructor
to train Korean troops. The result was the formation of the country's first

modern army unit, a company of about eighty infantry soldiers, carefully selected for their strength and skills from among the older, existing army units known as the Five Military Camps. The new company was attached to the palace guard, and training under a Japanese army captain, Horimoto Reizō, and other Japanese instructors began in May 1881, just as the Courtiers Observation Mission was arriving in Tokyo. That the new Western drill was still very much a novelty and an experiment for Koreans at the time was reflected in the designation of the new military unit as the Special Skills Force (Pyŏlgigun). Once the Courtiers Observation Mission had returned from Japan and Hong Yŏngsik and Yi Wŏnhoe were installed in key positions in the T'ongni Kimu Amun's Department of General Military Affairs, however, the Pyŏlgigun was given particular attention as a model unit on which to develop a new Korean army. Such preferential treatment helped precipitate the mutiny of the older army units that briefly brought the Taewŏn'gun back to power in 1882. In the ensuing violence Horimoto was killed and the Pyŏlgigun was subsequently disbanded.[48]

Between 1882 and 1894 the Korean army underwent numerous alterations, but most were superficial, involving a mere reconfiguration of the existing units, often accompanied by a change in name. During Yuan Shikai's political ascendancy in the 1880s and early 1890s, for example, the army was reorganized along the lines of the Qing army, and although Yuan was among the most capable young officers in China, neither he nor the Qing army, unlike their Japanese counterparts, had yet fully embraced the new military knowledge and technology of the West, a failure that would prove disastrous in 1894 when Chinese troops, 60 percent carrying some kind of unstandardized rifle and 40 percent armed only with pike, spear, or sword, encountered a completely modernized and uniformly drilled Japanese army.[49]

The relatively slow pace of Korean army development during this period was only too apparent in 1894 when the Chosŏn government experienced great difficulty in bringing the Tonghak rebellion to a quick and satisfactory conclusion. Although the rebels had no formal military training of any kind and were armed only with bamboo spears, they twice defeated the government's troops in major battles. During the Battle of Changsŏng the elite unit from the capital that had been sent to subdue them even fled the field like Sin Kwanho's notorious "murder of crows," abandoning 300 of their dead as well as artillery and rifles. After nearly two months the government troops finally succeeded in negotiating an armistice, but not before the rebels had occupied much of the southwestern province of Chŏlla, including the provincial capital, Chŏnju, and the government, worried that it would not be able to handle the situation on its own, had hastily called for foreign military assistance, thereby precipitating the Sino-Japanese War.[50]

Significant progress in the direction of building a new Korean army began only after the outbreak of the war in 1894 and the return of the enlightenment reformers to political power with Japanese backing. The changes thereafter were quick and dramatic. Soon after entering the capital, the occupying Japanese army selected about 300 Korean soldiers from the old army to create a new Training Company (Kyododae), which fought under Japanese officers at the Battle of P'yŏngyang in September of that year and subsequently assisted the Japanese in suppressing a renewed uprising by the Tonghak rebels. Even more important was the establishment four months later of a new force called the Drilled Troops (Hullyŏndae) on the recommendation of Japanese home minister Inoue Kaoru, who was then acting as an advisor to the new reform government. Like the earlier Pyŏl-gigun, the Hullyŏndae, trained and commanded by Japanese officers, was set up to serve as a model unit for the development of a new Korean army. It was considerably larger than its 1880s predecessor, however, comprising five battalions and totaling more than 2,000 troops, with each battalion divided into four companies of roughly 100 men each. In addition to having its main base in Seoul, where its first two battalions were housed, it also had a battalion-level presence in several other important cities, including P'yŏngyang.

With the formation of the Hullyŏndae, the old capital army was effectively superseded, and soldiers from the old capital units who were not selected for the Hullyŏndae were reorganized into a new reserve force. Although the Hullyŏndae did not have a long history—it was abolished in late 1895, when Japanese influence in Korea began to diminish following the end of the war and the queen's murder—it nevertheless marked the beginning of a new direction for the Korean army, and its legacy continued beyond 1895. Even though it was disbanded as a unit, its soldiers were reorganized into the first two battalions of what came to be called the Imperial Guards (Ch'inwidae). After the king had taken refuge in the Russian legation in 1896, moreover, about 1,000 of the Imperial Guard soldiers were chosen as the nucleus of a second new unit, the Attendant Guards (Siwidae), which was formed under Russian auspices for the initial purpose of protecting the king when he returned to the palace. It was these two military forces, the Imperial Guards and the Attendant Guards, that later came to constitute the core of the new army in the capital during the Great Han Empire.

The military establishment in the countryside also underwent funda-mental restructuring and development as a result of the Kabo reforms. The provincial army, such as it was, had remained virtually unchanged since before the opening of the country, but in June 1895 the new reform govern-ment issued a decree abolishing all existing provincial military forces and posts effective the following month. To reward and appease forced retirees, the government set up a commission within the new War Ministry to con-sider awards and honors for soldiers with good records. Moreover, about 2,500 of the strongest and most capable of the soldiers in the old system were retained for service in the new provincial army units that were being constructed. These units, called the Garrison Defense Forces (Chinwidae), would continue to expand in the next decade, and for the first time in centuries Korea would have a functioning standing army outside of Seoul.[51]

Military Expansion and Development 1895-1904

Between 1895 and 1905 the Chosŏn army was significantly transformed in a variety of ways. Among others things, the army grew in size and visibility. As Sŏ Chaep'il, the editor of the *Independent,* noted in an editorial in 1898, "One rarely goes upon the streets of Seoul without meeting sooner or later a squad of Korean soldiers tramping along and stopping here and there to execute their daily drill."[52] That such sights had become so "commonplace" as to be "monotonous," in Sŏ's words, was directly related to the expansion and development of the army in this period. Beginning in 1895 with the 2,000 troops of the Hullyŏndae, the army of the Great Han Empire doubled several times over, reaching a total of about 26,000 by the early 1900s, all trained in Western drill and firearms. About 8,000 of the soldiers were based in Seoul, where 4,000 served in the Imperial Guards, responsible for the defense of the capital city and government buildings; 3,400 in the At-tendant Guards, charged with the protection of the palace; and about 700 in a special unit called the Imperial Retinue (Howidae), which acted as a per-sonal bodyguard for the emperor and his family. The rest of the troops, which were assigned to the Garrison Defense Forces, were placed in strategic locations throughout the country from the northern boundary towns at the Yalu and Tumen Rivers to the southernmost reach of Chosŏn territory on Cheju Island, with regional headquarters in Kanghwa, Suwŏn, Taegu, P'yŏngyang, and Pukch'ŏng in North Hamgyŏng Province.

During this period the Korean army, which had hitherto been following Qing organizational models for the most part, also began to assume something of the shape and sophistication of the more modern armies of Europe and Japan. As the army grew larger, for example, it shifted from battalion- to regiment-sized administrative and tactical formations and began to develop new branches outside the original infantry units, including artillery, cavalry, and transport. By 1902, the Imperial Guards comprised two full infantry regiments, each with two battalions of five companies, and attached engineering and transport companies. The Attendant Guards also consisted of two regiments, each with two infantry battalions and one artillery battalion, and an attached cavalry battalion. In addition, the Attendant Guards boasted two military bands of platoon strength, one in the 1st Infantry Battalion and one in the Cavalry Battalion. Outside Seoul, the Garrison Defense Forces saw a similar development and by the turn of the century were divided into six regiments, each with three infantry battalions. Whether in the capital or provinces, moreover, the individual regiments were developing into large self-contained military forces, each with its own regimental banner, staff officers, clerks, physician, signalers, trumpeters, and other personnel. At the battalion level as well, there was considerable self-sufficiency. Such developments not only helped elevate a sense of regimental and battalion identity and pride but also created an organizational framework in which units could operate independently or in combination during actual combat.

A number of the differences and inconsistencies among individual units that had plagued the old Chosŏn army and limited its effectiveness as an efficient, unitary military force were also eliminated in the new army.[53] Among other things, the Kabo reformists declared a detailed and uniform military dress code, based on a similar code in effect in Japan. Later, during the Great Han Empire, the size, personnel, provisioning, and expenditures of each type of military unit—platoon, company, battalion, regiment—was regularized, and both capital and provincial forces were paid and promoted according to the same fixed scale and standards. With the inauguration of the Wŏnsubu, an unambiguous and unified chain of military command was also finally put in place, proceeding from the emperor as commander in chief through the crown prince to the Wŏnsubu's chief of military affairs, who held the imperial seals. In the capital all battalion heads were accountable to their regimental commanders, and the regimental commanders in turn reported directly to the emperor through the Wŏnsubu's chief of military affairs. Outside Seoul the commander of the P'yŏngyang regiment acted as the head of all the Garrison Defense Forces and also reported directly to the emperor through the Wŏnsubu.

The Korean army during this period was for the first time developing into a professional institution separate and distinct from the civilian bureaucracy and society. The statutory exclusion of non-military personnel from the Wŏnsubu and the requirement that the minister and vice minister of war be active-duty military officers were of course signs of this trend, but there were others as well, including the evolution of separate military legal, judicial, police, and penal systems. The process began in 1896 with the issuance by former Observation Mission courtier Ŏ Yunjung, then serving as acting war minister in the reformist government, of a set of disciplinary rules for the new Korean army that were adapted from existing Japanese regulations. This was followed in 1900 by the Wŏnsubu's promulgation of a full-fledged military law code and the subsequent establishment of Korea's first military court. At about the same time the Wŏnsubu also formed the country's first military police unit (hŏnbyŏngdae) and prison. Although the police and prison sometimes accommodated the needs of the civil authorities, as in the apprehension or incarceration of political criminals, like the court they were set up expressly to serve an expanding military organization that was beginning to differentiate itself from the civilian institutions in which it had been formerly embedded. The prison was accordingly managed by the military court, and the military police, like the court, were placed directly under the jurisdiction of the Wŏnsubu.[54]

The development of the Wŏnsubu and army in the decade between the Kabo reforms and the outbreak of the Russo-Japanese War in 1904 represented the apex of institutional militarization in the late Chosŏn period. To be sure, one must be careful not to exaggerate the extent and impact of this process. Even with much of the budget going to the military, the fundamental financial weakness of the state continued to be a major restraint, and one of the chief signifiers of a modern army, universal conscription, was never implemented.[55] And in the end Korean military expansion and the new army did nothing to stop Japan from occupying the peninsula and turning the country into a Japanese protectorate that would not only abolish the Wŏnsubu at the end of 1904 and disband the Korean army in 1907 but also bring an end to 518 years of Chosŏn dynastic rule by formally annexing Korea into its empire as a colony in 1910. Indeed, the army's effectiveness in defense of the country was never even tested. Maneuvering for political advantage between Russia and Japan in a war whose outcome was initially uncertain, and reportedly anxious about the overwhelming military odds against him, Kojong refrained from ordering the army into action in 1904, and Japanese troops entered Seoul and other Korean towns and cities unopposed.[56] But even if the emperor had commanded the army to resist, it is difficult to imagine that it would have fared well or lasted long against the Japanese forces. The superiority of the latter was simply too great, obvious from the moment Japanese troops began disembarking at the capital port of Chemulp'o (Inch'ŏn) in the opening days of the war. As one of the witnesses to that event, F. A. McKenzie, a Canadian journalist in Seoul and a courageous defender of Korea's interests against Japan in this period, later wrote: "Those of us who stood on the frozen shores on that cold February night, looking at the trim and alert Japanese infantry, their figures revealed by the glowing coal and paraffin fires on the landing-stage, knew that the old history of Korea was over and that a new era had begun."[57]

McKenzie's observation proved only too true, of course, but it is also important not to lose perspective here. That the Great Han military was ultimately unable to save the country from occupation should not blind us to the larger historical significance of the late Chosŏn militarization effort. For the first time since the early seventeenth century the military had again become a major focus of Korean attention and interest, especially at the state level. The state's endeavor to emulate Meiji Japan's achievement of "rich country, strong army" had introduced Koreans to contemporary European and Japanese military institutions and techniques and even produced a first generation of army officers trained in the new methods of warfare. And the state was not the only locus of militarization during this period. If invasion and occupation worked to militarize official Korean institutions, they also contributed to a certain militarization of Korean culture, giving birth to a new way of thinking about the military that would long outlive the ill-starred Great Han Empire itself.

TWO

MILITARIZING MINDS

New Ideas of Army and Nation

But I am armed,
And dangers are to me indifferent.
—William Shakespeare, *Julius Caesar*

Look around at this world! Why were the six great powers able so
triumphantly and willfully to overrun the heavens and the earth? The
answer is that their military power was strong.
—Sin Ch'aeho, February–March 1910

The army is the shield and defense of the state, and the mission of our
army on behalf of the state and nation is heavier and greater than that of
any other army in the world.
—Park Chung Hee, October 1, 1961

The great global wave of militarization that swept across East Asia and
Korea in the late nineteenth and early twentieth centuries also transformed
Korean ideas about the military. Behind the enlightenment slogan of "rich
country, strong army," for example, lay a new, more positive view of the military based on Western and Japanese models as an integral component and
symbol of modern nationhood, something to be developed and esteemed,
not neglected and derided, as had so long been the case in Korea. Although
the enlightenment reformers were a disparate group of people with differing
backgrounds, ambitions, and international orientations, as well as divergent
views of about the role and size of Korea's army, they all understood that
the country's survival and success in the new world in which Korea found
itself after the opening of the country in 1876 required a receptivity to new
knowledge and a willingness to make some institutional changes, not least
of all in the military. Indeed, from the beginning, modernization of the military was seen as an integral part of the enlightenment effort. Kim Ok-
kyun, one of the earliest and most radical of the reformers, who had led the
abortive coup in 1884 against the government in order to expedite the enlightenment program, told followers that there was no more urgent task

than strengthening the army for national defense, and he encouraged them to go to Japan and learn modern military skills.[1] Later enlightenment reformers also invariably included modernization of the military among their key goals, including two men whose writings and political activities were particularly influential in defining and promoting the enlightenment movement in Korea in the late Chosŏn period: Yu Kilchun and Pak Yŏnghyo.

Yu Kilchun (1856–1914)

Yu Kilchun was born in Seoul in 1856 and received an early education in the Chinese classics from his father and grandfather. In 1870, at the age of fourteen, he joined the circle of the famous scholar-official Pak Kyusu, who was one of the leading exponents of "northern studies" (*pukhak*), a school of thought within the critical, non-mainstream "practical learning" (*silhak*) movement of Chosŏn literati. The northern studies school stressed the importance of reforming the country by learning from abroad, and although at the time this meant learning primarily from Qing China, it was nevertheless a bold and unconventional idea in the Chosŏn context, where conservative Neo-Confucian scholars who dominated court politics still regarded the Manchu Qing rulers as barbarian usurpers. Pak's openness to foreign ideas and Qing connections also made him and his home a repository of Chinese knowledge and books about Europe, which he shared with his students, including Yu.

Yu's modern education took a giant leap when he was sent to Japan in 1881 as one of Ŏ Yunjung's attendants in the Courtiers Observation Mission. On Ŏ's recommendation he remained in Japan for about a year to study at the Keiō School (later Keiō University), founded by the intellectual leader of Meiji Japan's own enlightenment (*kaika*) movement, Fukuzawa Yukichi. In 1883 Yu accompanied Ambassador Min Yŏngik on Korea's first diplomatic mission to the United States, where he remained for about a year and a half, enjoying the patronage of the well-known Darwinian naturalist Edward Sylvester Morse, a friend of Fukuzawa's, and studying at the Governor Dummer Academy in Byfield, Massachusetts. Before returning to Korea in 1885, he also traveled through all the major countries of Europe.

By the mid-1880s, although barely thirty years old, Yu was unquestionably one of the Koreans most well informed and most experienced in the ways of the West and Japan. From that time forward he became, like his mentor Fukuzawa, a tireless advocate of enlightenment, writing and translating numerous books and articles to educate his countrymen about the outside world. His most important and influential book, patterned after and often directly drawing on similar work by Fukuzawa, was written in the 1880s after his return to Korea. Entitled *Observations on the West (Sŏyu kyŏnmun)*, it was a nearly 600-page exposition of Western politics, economy, society, institutions, and customs incorporating all that Yu had seen, heard, and read in the course of his travels to Japan, the United States, and Europe. The book was also a comprehensive manifesto of the Korean enlightenment movement, written to provide Koreans with a detailed understanding of the still unfamiliar new world in which they now found themselves and to offer contemporary models on which to base their own reforms.[2]

Two chapters in Yu's book dealt specifically with military issues. In one he explained and traced the development of modern European military organization down to the early nineteenth century, information that had not been included in the Japan-centered reports of the Courtiers Observation Mission. All the crucial historical European military changes were noted and described: the shift with the invention of the musket from a feudal emphasis on cavalry and individual physical prowess in hand-to-hand combat to a new accent on strategy and tactics; the consequent heightened role of the infantry and the emergence of hired standing armies, whose size was dependent on the amount of taxes a state could extract from its population; the gradual differentiation of military skills and evolution of specialized drills, as developed by Prince Maurice of Nassau in Holland, King Gustavus Adolphus in Sweden, and Frederick the Great in Prussia; and Napoleon's subsequent revolutionary transformation of military service from a mercenary occupation into a civic obligation through universal conscription, and his professionalization of the officer corps through strict promotion by merit. In what was one of Korea's earliest introductions to the great French general who a half century later would capture the imagination of a young Park Chung Hee, Yu wrote that "Napoleon was skillfully able to subdue the various countries of Europe, making all who heard his name tremble, and all the military systems in the West today have adopted his methods."[3]

In another chapter in his *Observations,* Yu presented the rationale and methods for developing a modern army as practiced in the West and Japan, covering in detail such areas as recruitment, training, conduct and discipline, officers, weapons, military medicine, and expenses. Here several points were given particular emphasis. First, Yu stressed at the very beginning of the chapter that the proper purpose of an army was defensive, whether the enemy was internal or external. Undoubtedly thinking of Korea's own recent experience of foreign incursions, he was passionate in denouncing countries who employed their armies for aggressive purposes: "Those who see themselves as strong and despise the weak or those who take pride in their size and mistreat the small are violating the fundamental purpose of establishing an army. This is truly the behavior of rapacious barbarians."[4]

Yu also placed great importance on training and discipline. Not only does each branch of service require its own specific and rigorous training, he wrote, but training itself must also be continuous. Perhaps with an eye to Korea's own military decline during the long Chosŏn peace, he insisted that "without the accumulated experience of training during peacetime, one will never be able to put aside concerns about things going wrong when war actually comes."[5] For that reason he strongly supported the idea of required annual field exercises involving the entire army and testing the readiness of each branch of service, a practice that also had been noted in the Observation Mission's reports.[6]

In developing an army, the most important element of all, according to Yu, was the cultivation of military officers, the "most outstanding exemplars" of military service.[7] Acutely aware of the conventional Chosŏn contempt for the military, Yu argued that being an officer was not a job for the unintelligent or uneducated. Military officers, he emphasized, required not only a general knowledge that encompassed subjects such as chemistry and foreign languages, but also a professional knowledge that covered many different areas and skills: military history; the principles of drill and warfare; the ability to sketch precisely the conditions of the battlefield and surrounding areas in military maps and drawings, and to judge the size and distance of the enemy force; an understanding of machinery and weapons; and a capacity for personal leadership. To educate and train such men, Yu continued, military schools with the highest and strictest standards of meritorious admission and performance had to be established. Once commissioned, officers had to begin their careers by serving in the lower grades and advance upward solely on the basis of their skills and record. The generals at the summit of command had to be exceptionally well-educated and talented officers, for they were the men who led all the other officers: "Although a commander without [sufficient] education may have the intelligence to deal with emergency situations and restrain an enemy, he will be lost when it comes to the principles of military drill and field warfare."[8]

Yu concluded his chapter on army development with a discussion of costs and size, providing contemporary figures for a diverse group of countries. He acknowledged that creating an effective army with men of high caliber was expensive. It would certainly consume the greatest share of national income, he suggested, but the goal was worth the price and the country should accept the burden: "If [the government] is too niggardly about this, the goal of developing an army will come to naught; while striving for moderation, it is entirely proper that the people should support such an effort with all their heart, because the government's effort to establish an army is for their benefit, and it is therefore on the people that the financial responsibility must lie."[9] Yu insisted that large countries had no monopoly on strong armies. Through universal conscription, "regardless of income or status," any country could mobilize its population effectively for military service. "Even a small country with sufficient resources," Yu wrote, "can be many times stronger militarily than a poor and lazy country."[10]

Yu's interest in military matters was also reflected in his numerous translations of foreign works, which included histories of both the Seven Years' War and the Crimean War, as well as the history of the Italian War of Independence and the history of the rise and fall of Poland. Such histories were meant not merely to inform Koreans about Europe's military past but also to serve as a warning to Koreans about the neglect of military matters in a world of "rapacious barbarians" and to provide encouragement and hope with respect to Korea's own situation.

Pak Yŏnghyo (1861-1939)

Another enlightenment reformist who deserves mention for his strong advocacy of military development is Pak Yŏnghyo. Although eight years Yu's junior, Pak had also studied with Pak Kyusu. His link though marriage to the royal family, moreover, not only secured him a princely title but also gave him close access to the king, and in 1882 he headed a three-month diplomatic mission to Japan to settle issues stemming from the anti-foreign mutiny led by supporters of the Taewŏn'gun earlier that year. Like Yu, Pak was inspired by the historic changes he saw taking place in Meiji Japan, and he, together with many of the young men who had accompanied him, returned to Korea to become some of the leading voices and practitioners of reform in the late Chosŏn period.

More a political activist than an intellectual, Pak did not leave behind a
large body of written work, as did Yu Kilchun. But his interest in military
affairs was already clear in the early 1880s, when, after returning from Japan,
he was appointed magistrate of Kwangju in Kyŏnggi province and immediately began to organize a modern army unit there under the direction of Sin
Pongmo, a Korean graduate of the Toyama School in Tokyo. In the late
1880s, while in exile in Tokyo as a result of his participation in the 1884
coup, he composed a long memorial to King Kojong that laid out his enlightenment program in considerable detail; military strengthening was
one of the document's main themes.[11]

Drawing on the popular "Warring States" simile and other classical al-
lusions, Pak warned the king that Korea was in a precarious position internationally. The country's military had decayed to a historic nadir at a time
when predatory "strong countries are swallowing up the weak" and independence was directly linked to military vigor.[12] The solution to this dilemma, according to Pak, was for Korea to follow Meiji Japan's example of
cultivating "wealth and power," and he proposed a number of immediate
reforms with that purpose in mind in a section of the memorial entitled
"Make Military Preparations to Protect the People and Defend the
Country."[13]

Pak recommended the establishment of an army of "several tens of thousands of troops, for the time being sufficient to subdue any internal threats,"
and suggested unifying the military chain of command, revamping the
country's old army laws and regulations as well as its traditional recruitment system, and restoring the arsenals with good weapons. Pak also
shared Yu Kilchun's concern about providing the military with a firm financial base. He proposed that military affairs should be carefully calculated,
planned, and budgeted as a percentage of regular annual state revenue to
avoid temporary shortfalls and confusion. He also paid special attention to
the navy, something Yu had mentioned only in passing. Given that Korea
was surrounded by the sea on three sides, a navy was crucial for the country's defense, Pak argued, and he called for a revitalization of the Korean
navy with warships that would recall the creativity and effectiveness of Admiral Yi Sunsin's famous ironclad turtle boats.[14]

Like Yu, Pak emphasized the importance of a trained and disciplined
army, writing that this was directly tied to the continued existence or collapse of the country. Also like Yu, he was passionate about the importance
of training outstanding Korean military officers, and he was pointedly
scornful of royal advisors who were said to be recommending the hiring of

foreign generals. If Korean commanders did not have sufficient education and knowledge, he wrote, they would lose the trust and control of their troops and suffer inevitable defeat in battle. The first priority, he argued, should therefore be the establishment of a military academy open to talented young men of all social backgrounds, whether from the royal family and aristocracy or from more humble families, to train men to lead troops in battle. In addition, Pak suggested, some young men could be also be sent abroad to study in foreign military schools.[15]

The writings of enlightenment reformists such as Yu and Pak, as well as the reports of the Courtiers Observation Mission, provide unequivocal evidence of the link that reformist Koreans were making between military institutions and modern national development in the early decades after the opening of the country in 1876. Indeed, one of the striking aspects of Pak's memorial, written in 1888, was its implicit assumption of a shared understanding of the fundamentals of the new military knowledge. He was making an argument to a king who was already familiar with the subject at hand, not to a complete novice to whom everything had to be explained.

Martial Virtues

In the discourse on military matters that accompanied the institutional militarization of the first wave, the army also came to be seen increasingly as a repository of martial virtues that were valuable, indeed indispensable, for personal character development and for the preservation and development of the nation, both conceived largely in hypermasculinized terms. Here again Korea found itself embedded in a larger context, the discursive side of the nineteenth-century global militarization process, centered in Europe and North America, where male-centered and frequently racist martial ideas, enthusiasms, and policies, often laced with and buttressed by social Darwinist concepts, had taken deep root. In their most radical manifestations, war itself was celebrated as a glorious and redemptive human ritual, the ultimate struggle for existence, and one that demanded a certain callousness toward the human suffering associated with social evolution, especially as Western imperialist ambitions reached their apogee in the late nineteenth century. During the three-year native insurrection against the United States following its acquisition of the Philippines from Spain in 1898, for example, one American newspaper, not at all atypical of the pro-imperialist element in the press at the time, editorialized: "There is no use dilly-dallying with these uncircumcised, uncivilized, unthankful and treacherous cutthroats; the sooner soldiers are sent there in sufficient numbers to finish up the business, the better it will be for Christianity and human progress."[16] Another was even more graphic in its call for action: "The struggle must continue til the misguided creatures there shall have their eyes bathed in enough blood to cause their vision to be cleared, and to understand that not only is resistance useless, but that those to whom they are now holding as enemies have no purpose toward them except to consecrate to liberty and to open for them a way to happiness."[17]

The most radical social Darwinists of this period made the American imperialist press seem almost mild. In an 1897 book called *Might Is Right or The Survival of the Fittest,* the pseudonymous author Ragnar Redbeard gloried in the idea of man as "the fiercest, most ferocious, most cunning, and most bloodthirsty of all the vertebrates ... the fighting, roving, pillaging, lusting, cannibalistic animal, par excellence—the King of the Great Carnivore," arguing that "conquering and masterful nations have ever been ravenous devourers of flesh-food," preferring, like any "normal" man, "to eat others than to be eaten."[18] He cursed the "white-livered and the meek" people of the world, saying, "May they 'earn' their bread (also that of their conquerors) by the slimy sweat of dishonored brows; and may they perish at last like abandoned curs."[19] He even condemned all forms of conventional morality, including the "sickly humanitarian ethics" of Christianity, calling Christ "this preacher of all eunuch-virtues—of self-abasement, of passive suffering," and acknowledged only what he termed the "higher law" of "might."[20] Toward the end of his book he included a long poem entitled "The Logic of Today," in which he exhorted the "fittest" to go forth and "prove your Right by deeds of Might," hunting down "weakling breeds" "like game": He continued: "The Strong must ever rule the Weak is grim Primordial Law/On earth's broad racial threshing floor, the Meek are beaten straw/Then ride to Power o'er foemen's neck let nothing bar your way/if you are fit you'll rule and reign is the logic of To-Day."[21]

Inspired like Redbeard by the writings of Nietzsche, who had written in *Twilight of the Idols* that "one has renounced great life when one renounces war," a British fringe journal called *The Eagle and the Serpent* also voiced many of these same sentiments.[22] Combining Nietzsche's philosophy of power with contemporary social Darwinist ideas, the journal railed against what it perceived as the "unfathomable stupidity" of altruism, a "deadly and poisonous" philosophy for "slaves or hypocrites" who sought for whatever reason to mitigate or deny the brutal struggle for life in which "the lamb is destined to lie down—inside the lion—so long as it cannot come before the lion with a power which the lion respects."[23] Deploring the "horrors of a universal peace," the London-based publication also expressed its "devout wish" for a "purifying and renewing" invasion of England "by a hostile enemy":

> Not for generations has England known the purifying and re-newing baptism of such a war—a war which would invest her own soil and scenery, her matchless vales, with the sacred mem-ories of patriot sons who had given for the dear homeland the last full measure of devotion. Such a war would reanimate the fires of patriotism in every breast, it would substitute actual for the present paper efficiency in the Army and Navy, and would give to our own generation living examples and parables of pa-triotism more potent than even the illustrious past or contests over lesser stakes can lend. . . . We can not, indeed, command other nations to invade our country, but we need not fear such an event, and personally, the writer believes that, for England's own sake, it is an event devoutly to be wished.[24]

While a fervent desire for a purifying war on native soil, to say nothing of cannibalism, were sentiments most Europeans and Americans undoubt-edly would have found excessive, war as an inevitable, even ennobling as-pect of human and national life was an idea that had wide currency at the time. In Prussia, where such thinking eventually reached its apex, philoso-phers from Kant to Hegel had commented on the vivifying and progres-sive effects of war.[25] General Helmuth von Moltke, the presiding genius of the nineteenth-century Prusso-German army general staff, had dismissed the idea of eternal peace as a "dream . . . and not even a pleasant one." "War," he continued, "is a part of God's world order. War develops man's noblest virtues, which otherwise would slumber and die out: courage, self-denial, devotion to duty, and willingness to make sacrifices. A man never forgets his experiences in war. They increase his capacity for all time to come."[26] Later General Friedrich von Bernhardi, head of the historical sec-tion of the German general staff, actually denounced efforts at world peace and argued in social Darwinist terms that war among nations was not only a "universal law of Nature" but a "biological necessity of the first importance," a "sanguinary struggle" that formed the "basis of all healthy development."[27]

Bernhardi's ideas, encapsulated in his 1912 book *Germany and the Next War,* were widely criticized, not least of all in England, where fear of German military competition and aggression was particularly acute. Nevertheless, the book was a bestseller and was translated into many languages, including Japanese.[28] One might argue, moreover, that although Bernhardi's views were extreme, the logic on which they were based found considerable resonance in a world infused with social Darwinist thinking. To be sure, some moderate social Darwinist writers such as Herbert Spencer and Benjamin Kidd regarded war as atavistic and looked forward to a future when Darwinian progress would see the end of war altogether. Others, however, such as the popular Yale sociologist William Graham Sumner, deplored war but also saw it as one of the "fundamental conditions of human existence," linked to the Darwinian "competition for life."[29] Most writers, moreover, including the staunchly pacifist Spencer, believed that warfare and what Spencer called "militancy" had contributed greatly to the evolutionary development of humanity. "War among men, like warfare among animals," Spencer wrote in *The Study of Sociology,* "has had a large share in raising their organizations to a higher stage."[30] "In the first epoch of social development," Kidd argued in *Principles of Western Civilization,* "the most potent type of organized society . . . would be, beyond doubt, that in which every element and interest had been subordinated to the end of military efficiency."[31] Even Sumner, while condemning the evils of an international arms race, paid homage to the legacy of the military in human civilization. "Military discipline educates," he wrote; "military interest awakens all the powers of men."[32]

Sumner's view was far from unique. In one of his most famous essays, "The Moral Equivalent of War," written in 1910, the American philosopher William James, who had strongly opposed "our squalid war with Spain" and placed himself "squarely in the anti-militarist party," nevertheless acknowledged the deep grounding of "military feelings . . . among our ideals" and argued that a "permanently successful peace economy" in fact required a promotion of the elements of army discipline. "Martial virtues," he declared, "must be the enduring cement: intrepidity, contempt of softness, surrender of private interest, obedience to command, must still remain the rock upon which states are built—unless, indeed, we wish for dangerous reactions against commonwealths fit only for contempt, and liable to invite attack whenever a centre of crystallization for military-minded enterprise gets formed in their neighborhood."[33]

At a more popular level, as James had noted, the enthusiasm for martial
virtues was even more straightforward and intense, as indicated by Thomas
Hughes's enormously popular novel *Tom Brown's School Days,* which became for generations of young men in England and the United States, including Theodore Roosevelt, a virtual primer of manhood and was also
widely read in translation in prewar Japan. The novel, first published in 1856,
idealized and celebrated the "muscular Christian" training of the late
nineteenth-century English public school system fostered by Thomas Ar-
nold, an educational reformer and Hughes's former headmaster at the
Rugby School. Crucial to Tom's masculine development in the novel was
learning to fight, and from time to time Hughes interrupted his narrative
to explicate for his readers the deeper lessons of Tom's experience: "After all,
what would life be like without fighting, I should like to know? From the
cradle to the grave, fighting, rightly understood, is the business, the real
highest, honestest business of every son of man."[34]

Victorian sentiments such as these led eventually to the inclusion of military drill in primary and secondary schools, especially in the anglophone
Protestant countries where "muscular Christianity" flourished, and also to
the emergence of nongovernmental youth organizations dedicated to cultivating perceived masculine and patriotic ideals in young men through
various forms of regimentation and sport, such as the Young Men's Christian
Association (YMCA) and the Boy Scouts. The Boy Scouts in particular,
founded in 1908 by a British colonist and soldier, Robert Baden-Powell,
exhibited from the beginning a strong military cast, complete with uniforms,
ranks, and a pledge of unquestioned obedience. On the obverse side of such
glorification of military manhood, moreover, was a widespread concern in
the late nineteenth century, especially in post–Civil War Protestant America,
that "overcivilization," defined as an "excessive, body-denying intellectualism,"
was emasculating American men.[35] As Theodore Roosevelt wrote, "An advanced state of intellectual development is too often associated with a certain
effeminacy of character."[36]

Martial Virtues in Late Chosŏn

Just as they were studying new military organizations in this period, late
Chosŏn reformists were also drawing on such foreign ideas in conjunction
with indigenous Korean critiques to construct a new edifice of respect for

military prowess and martial values. In his personal report to the king on the 1881 Courtiers Observation Mission to Japan, Ŏ Yunjung had bitterly attacked the Chosŏn tendency to esteem civil literati culture (*mun*) while looking down on all things associated with the military (*mu*), thus sounding a refrain that would be echoed again and again by a variety of enlightenment and nationalist writers over the next three decades and beyond.[37] When political power finally, if briefly, came into their hands in 1894–1895, it was thus no surprise that Kabo enlightenment reformers such as Yu Kilchun and Pak Yŏnghyo made changing Korean attitudes about the military one of their priorities. Not only did they reform the existing bureaucratic examination system with its inherent biases in favor of the civil aristocracy and literary accomplishment, a recommendation Ŏ Yunjung had in fact made in his report thirteen years earlier, but one of the first pieces of legislation they passed was a law abolishing the Chosŏn practice of treating all military officials, regardless of rank, as inferior to civil officials.[38] In the newly proclaimed Great Han Empire, military status was also enhanced by the central position of the Wŏnsubu in the bureaucracy and by the latter's direct association with the new imperial office (see Chapter 1).

With Korean national independence itself directly under siege after 1905, moreover, protectorate period nationalist writers such as Sin Ch'aeho (1880–1936) and Pak Ŭnsik (1859–1926) became ever more insistent and clamorous in their calls for Koreans to abandon their fixation on *mun* and learn to value *mu*. Both blamed the country's predicament on a failure to maintain sufficient military strength. The new century, Sin argued, had opened not only on a world of imperialism and nationalism but also on a "world of militarism" (*kun'guk segye*). However regrettable, Sin continued, militarism was a fact of twentieth-century life that nations ignored at their peril:

> Look around at this world! Why were the six great powers able so triumphantly and willfully to overrun the heavens and the earth? The answer is that their military power was strong. Why did the many countries of Asia and Africa passively submit to the lashes and the blows of outsiders? The answer is that their military power was weak. You who were born into this world of militarism—how can you not understand this?[39]

Korea's failure, in turn, was seen as deriving from the noxious effects of *munyak* (literally "a weakening by *mun*"), the Korean equivalent of "over-civilization." This pathological absorption in belles-lettres, Sin and Pak believed, had sapped the country of vitality and encouraged the development of an effete people unwilling to "gush righteous blood" for the nation's survival.[40] It was not that the cultivation of *mun* in itself was bad, Sin argued. Without *mun*, even states strong in *mu* could perish. What was pernicious in the case of Chosŏn Korea, Sin suggested, was the great imbalance between *mun* and *mu,* in which the former was exalted but the latter was neglected or even held in disdain—a recipe for extinction in a world where the "strong ate the weak and the great absorbed the small."[41]

Pak Ŭnsik was, if anything, even more enthusiastic than Sin about *mu* and critical of *munyak*. Like Sin, he noted the importance of cultivating both *mun* and *mu*. But if one had to choose between overindulgence in one or the other, it was better, he insisted, for a country to suffer from an excess of *mu:*

> A nation that reveres *mu* may invite the evils of savagery and cruelty, or even great disasters. But in such cases the whole country is not swallowed up by another, and once the disturbances are dealt with, national power is firm. But in the case of a nation that reveres *mun*, the evil is like a serious disease that lingers on and on, gradually enfeebling and weakening until the hundred veins and arteries all shrivel up and the entire body turns rotten. In the end, the whole nation cannot escape being swallowed up by another.[42]

It was precisely this "custom of revering *mun* and despising *mu,*" Pak argued, that had allowed Japan to "destroy our nation and cast our people into hell as slaves."[43] The Chosŏn prejudice against *mu* had over time intensified to the point where Koreans had come to regard "being enrolled as a soldier as more despicable than being listed as a slave."[44] And so great was the social stigma attached to the military, he lamented, that even the inhabitants of the country's northwest provinces, once famed for their military prowess and heroism, had eventually been shamed by the contemptuous civil *yangban* in the capital into forsaking their military expertise for a combination of "affected, trivial composition and empty ritual."[45] In the end, Pak noted bitterly, Japan's triumph was not its "relatively superior statecraft and somewhat advanced development through rapid assimilation of Western culture," nor was it the result of an "abundance of good fortune." What had ultimately given Japan mastery over Korea was simply its ability "to take advantage through its military strength of our *mun*-induced feebleness [*munyak*]."[46]

Thus in the final years of the Chosŏn dynasty, as Japan was tightening its grip on the peninsula ever more tightly and moving toward annexation, writers such as Sin and Pak clearly saw national salvation as lying in a new and more positive national attitude toward the military, a veneration of *mu*. For Sin in particular this meant developing a new understanding of Korean history that chronicled the country's military triumphs and celebrated its martial heroes, like Yi Sunsin, rather than its enfeebled and ineffectual literati,[47] who had regarded the soldiers whose function was to defend the country as "lumps of dirt," and talent in horsemanship and archery as "menial skills."[48] So when Sin did publish an account of Yi's life in 1908, putting him on a level with England's Nelson and other great historical military figures, even questioning whether Nelson in Yi's circumstances could have matched the Chosŏn hero's victory, he encouraged the "good men and faithful women" of Korea to "model" themselves on the admiral, writing in the final sentence of the biography that "Heaven awaits a second Yi Sunsin."[49] No less important for Sin, Pak, and many other Koreans writing at the time, moreover, was putting into practice a system of physical and mental "militarist education" (*sangmujŏk kyoyuk*), one that followed Japan's example and would rival even the thoroughgoing militarization of ancient Sparta at its peak, where, Pak wrote, the state had also taken the lead in inculcating its youth with martial virtues and abilities, and where mothers had been more concerned about victory in battle than the death of their sons.[50]

Post-Annexation Legacies and Continuities

With Japan's dissolution of the Chosŏn army in 1907 and the annexation of the peninsula three years later, Korea's first wave of militarization officially came to an end. Japan's own forces in Korea, the Chōsen Army (Chōsengun), had replaced the Great Han Empire's fledgling military, and after two expensive and bloody wars with China and Russia, even Japan itself was gradually moving in the direction of arms reduction. In the 1920s, following World War I and a widespread international revulsion against war and militarism in all its forms, the arguments in Japan for military retrenchment reached a peak, and the IJA was finally forced to reduce its budget and resources significantly in 1925. General Ugaki Kazushige, the war minister at the time, was criticized bitterly by many of his army peers for his actions, but in fact Ugaki had had little choice. He also made every effort to compensate for the reduction by using some of the savings to modernize Japan's weaponry. And most important for our purposes, in a quid pro quo agreement with the government for the ministry's cutbacks, he instituted a system of military training by active duty army officers in all the country's secondary schools and colleges, a program that during Korea's second wave of militarization between 1931 and 1945 would eventually be extended to the peninsula and have a profound impact on the recruitment of Korean officers for service in the Japanese and Manchukuo armies, including Park Chung Hee.[51]

In the 1920s, however, neither the Chōsen Army nor the colonial GGK had any interest in encouraging Koreans to think of themselves as potential soldiers, let alone in providing them with guns for military training. In addition to an abiding fear of arming a population that only a few years earlier had risen up en masse to protest Japanese rule and demand independence, the Japanese authorities felt there was no need to provide Koreans with such training, since they were not citizens and hence were ineligible for conscription duty.[52] Indeed, looking at the official elementary school textbooks for Korean schoolchildren in this period, it is all too clear that the GGK was encouraging its colonized populace to think of itself not so much as participating citizens in a modern nation but rather as simple farmers, productive and loyal to the state, and faithful to many of the more conservative Neo-Confucian values—almost as if Korea had experienced no significant change since the opening of the country fifty years earlier, or as if earlier Korean civics textbooks from the Great Han Empire had not explained and celebrated the army and universal conscription as critical constituents of national strength and development.[53]

But Korea had of course changed. And despite having lost both their army and their national sovereignty, the Korean colonial cultural elite, heirs to the Chosŏn enlightenment movement, continued to promote a positive view of military training and its attendant linkages to modernity and a masculinized nationalism. With a somewhat more liberal GGK in place and the rise of a Korean-language commercial press in the 1920s, such views proliferated, even cutting across growing Korean cultural and political divisions. While explicitly eschewing any direct connection with war or militarism, quasi-religious organizations such as the Korean YMCA, founded in 1903, and the Korean Boy Scouts, founded in 1922, promoted the development of the martial arts, including Japanese *kendō,* and argued also for the character-enhancing benefits of military drill.[54] Similarly, Korean nationalists, whether in Korea or elsewhere, and whatever their political orientation, from the "cultural nationalists" who accommodated themselves to

Japanese rule to the communists who sought to overthrow it, stressed the importance of military training as part of the nation-building process.[55] And "overcivilization" or "effeteness" continued to be denounced throughout this period as the bane of Korea's national existence, with one writer for a popular magazine, for example, decrying the history of the late Chosŏn dynasty as nothing more than "a history of *munyak*."[56]

Despite a worldwide surge of pacifism following the butchery of World War I, for many Koreans, not least of all the cultural nationalists who constituted the core of the colony's native publishing and entrepreneurial elite, the antidote to *munyak* continued to lie in emulating Japan's traditional respect for the military. Long before any incipient signs of a second wave of militarization on the peninsula, they combined their condemnations of *munyak* with admiration for the Japanese nation's martial qualities. These they associated not only with the country's traditional warrior culture, or *bushidō*, which Sin and Pak had also praised, but also with Japan's contemporary attention to the importance of modern military training in the public school system.[57]

That Korean students since the annexation were being denied such training infuriated many of Korea's cultural elite, who also treated the issue in the press as a touchstone of Japanese sincerity in implementing its avowed policy of "cultural rule" (*bunka seiji*) in the wake of the massive Korean demonstrations for independence in 1919 and a subsequent change of colonial regimes.[58] In 1923, when Japan was first looking into the possibility of instituting military training in Korea's secondary schools, the Korean-owned newspaper *Tonga ilbo* urged the GGK to move ahead immediately in an editorial entitled "Reform the Effete [*munyak han*] Character of Students!" The editorial is worth quoting at some length, as it captures the rationale and enthusiasm of the colonial Korean elite for military drill, as well as their frustration with the GGK failure to institute it earlier:

> Although we do not know the motivation behind the present intention to institute military training, we can only regard with regret any delay in this matter, and we unequivocally support implementation at the present time. Originally the inclusion of military training in the curriculum of secondary education grew out of the idea of national conscription. From the perspective of a radical pacifist, who regards all guns as evil instruments of murder, the institution of military training in secondary

schools can only be anathema. But the purpose of guns is by no means limited to the inhuman one of murder. On the contrary, one can also assert the sacred quality of guns in the sense of their positive value in warding off outside invasion and defending against disturbance of the peace. Given these different points of view, it is difficult to look at the problem in black-and-white terms. But a gun itself is nothing more than a tool. Whether it is used for good or evil in the end depends on the person using it. Whether it is turned into a practical tool for reforming the world or an evil instrument of irrationality that violates the principles of humanity is up to the person using it. Moreover, the military training in secondary schools is merely designed to foster a martial spirit [*sangmu ŭi chŏngsin*] and physical health. How can it be equated with general military training for war? A great concern of Korean educators is the general slackness of spirit among students in Korean secondary schools and, even worse, the evil of effeteness [*munyak*] at an early age. If we have inherited this evil habit of effeteness, so deeply rooted in our past way of life, how indeed can this not be a great problem that fills us with deep regret? Of course there is nothing to be gained by overstating the actual results of military training in secondary education. But we eagerly hope for the reform of our students' general feebleness of spirit through its zealous and rigorous implementation by the relevant authorities in every school.[59]

The newspaper's hopes were soon dashed, however. Later that month Vice Governor-General Ariyoshi Chūichi himself issued a blunt and unequivocal statement clarifying the GGK's position on military training. It was, he said, a matter related solely to conscription duty, and thus intended only for Japanese students. "Since there is no such necessity to provide military-style exercise for Koreans," he continued, "the issue of such exercise for Koreans was never even considered by the government. There is no reason to think that without military-style exercise, physical education is imperfect. Whatever hopes may exist, there is absolutely no intention to implement this for Koreans."[60]

During the next several years, with the unfolding of Ugaki's plans to put secondary school military training under the supervision of active-duty army officers, the Korean cultural nationalists continued to press their case to the GGK. At the same time, the GGK found itself struggling to implement a cumbersome discriminatory system of military training in the schools, especially in those schools that had both Korean and Japanese students. In such schools the GGK found it difficult to limit military training only to Japanese students, and compromises in the mixed schools simply encouraged advocates of military training for all Koreans to argue even more vociferously, if only on the grounds of consistency and fairness.[61] Finally, after years of what *Tonga ilbo* described as "divisive and noisy debate" within the colonial government, the GGK finally announced in the spring of 1928 that military training would be initiated for all Korean students at the secondary level. Yi Chinho, director of the GGK Education Bureau, himself a Korean and a supporter of the change, made the official announcement, adding in an interview: "I have been advocating military training for years to encourage the morale of Korean students, and now finally we see the prospect of having it instituted from this year."[62]

But once again such optimism proved premature. The "divisive and noisy debate" dragged on in the corridors of imperial power for several more years, with the IJA especially reluctant to begin sending its officers into Korean schools "because of the question of the advisability of military training for Koreans."[63] Only in the summer of 1934, as Korea's second wave of militarization was starting to build in the aftermath of Japan's seizure of Manchuria in 1931 and subsequent expansion on the continent, and as the GGK and IJA were slowly coming to the conclusion that Koreans might at some point be needed for military service, did the GGK begin to implement a full-scale program of military training for all Korean secondary school students.[64]

Even then, however, the army was cautious and deliberate. As noted in Chapter 1, Yun Ch'iho had recorded in his diary that military drill was introduced for the first time into the two best Korean boys' higher common schools in the fall of 1934. But the GGK had also announced at that time that the army was dispatching its officers there as test cases, and that expansion of the program to other schools would "depend on actual results."[65] Only after a year of trial did the GGK request permission from the War Ministry to expand the program.[66] And only after Colonel Kuroda Shigenori, chief of the ministry's recruitment section, personally visited Korea to inspect the schools in 1935 and pronounced the results "very good" did the program actually proceed.[67] It quickly gained speed thereafter as Korea's second wave of militarization billowed with the outbreak of hostilities with China in 1937, and as Yun's prediction of the eventual conscription of Korean men began taking ever more tangible form.

More than twenty years separated the first two waves of Korean militarization. The second wave was also very different in many respects. Compared to the first, there were few budgetary restraints, and the wartime colonial government, following metropolitan example, engaged in a total mobilization of resources and people that would have been unimaginable as well as impossible for the Great Han Empire. By the 1940s everything on the peninsula had in a sense been militarized to some degree. Even commercial advertising in the newspapers and magazines had turned to military themes to sell products as anodyne as lipstick, and Seoul (or Keijō, as the Japanese called the Korean capital city) was, like Tokyo itself, awash in uniforms and giant banners urging the populace to ever greater feats of sacrifice and heroism.[68]

Also unlike the first wave, the second was not generated or led by Koreans themselves. The cultural nationalists who had been pressuring the GGK to introduce military drill in the Korean schools had—perhaps naively, in retrospect—differentiated such drill from what the 1923 *Tonga ilbo* editorial had called a "general military training for war," seeing it instead primarily as a remedy for national "effeteness." In the end, however, it was precisely a "general military training for war," rather than pressure from the Korean press, that led the GGK and the army finally to extend military training to Korean students. Same bed at last, but different dreams.

Nevertheless, when the official call to participate in the second wave came as Yun Ch'iho had predicted, many Koreans responded positively. Elements of coercion notwithstanding, there was also active involvement at both the elite and mass levels. Cultural nationalists now used the *munyak* trope not to persuade the GGK to incorporate military drill in Korean schools but instead to persuade Korean young men to join the Japanese army.[69] And, as T. Fujitani has noted, "extraordinarily large numbers" of Korean young men did in fact apply for military service with the inauguration of a volunteer soldiers program in 1938.[70]

There were many reasons for such involvement, not least of all GGK promises of genuine civic equality once Japan had won the war, and new tangible opportunities for Korean advancement that the war had opened up.[71] But among these many reasons one must also point to the legacies of Korea's first militarization and the sea change it had wrought in Korean thinking about the military since the late nineteenth century. To Koreans such as Park Chung Hee, born after the annexation, in the teens and twenties of the new century, the military represented something entirely different from what it had in the past, something more positive and virtuous, a symbol fusing modernity and manhood with national strength and power. Japan had of course used that very strength and power to trample Korean sovereignty three decades earlier, but in the late 1930s and early 1940s imperial Japan was also "at its zenith," in Kenneth Ruoff's phrase, seemingly indestructible and growing larger and stronger with each year.[72] For a good number of Korean young men at the time, including even some who would oppose it, the Imperial Japanese Army was also the most visible and palpable incarnation of a martial vigor and power that their parents and teachers had been telling them they needed to cultivate, and toward which they themselves aspired, whether motivated by personal or nationalist desires or by some combination of the two.[73] And now, as its manpower needs multiplied with its expanding wars and territories, the Japanese army for the first time since the annexation had begun to open its military portal to Koreans, including the narrow gate of its officer corps and the institutions that sustained it.

THREE

MILITARIZING PLACES AND PERSONS

Academies and Cadets

Go to the gate; somebody knocks.
—William Shakespeare, *Julius Caesar*

The number of imposing and vigorous Korean officers is substantially
increasing.
—*Tonga ilbo,* March 2, 1940

Our national army . . . has continued to make great strides and today can
boast an elite world-class military force.
—Park Chung Hee, October 1, 1961

If to everything there is a season, so to every season are there places and
persons. Even for Michel Foucault, who famously stressed the diffuseness
of power, certain places such as prisons and hospitals were more important
than others, because such institutions were special repositories of discursive
knowledge, sustaining and reproducing it over time in ways and to degrees
that other places could or did not. By the late 1930s, nearly every institution
in Japan and its imperial possessions, including Korea, had been militarized to some extent by the continuing war in China, a process that would
only accelerate and deepen after Japan's 1941 attack on Pearl Harbor transformed the China conflict into World War II. Apart from the army itself,
among the most militarized places were the primary and secondary
schools, but even they paled in comparison to the military schools that were
being generated or augmented in the second wave of militarization between
1931 and 1945, especially the Japanese Military Academy (JMA) in Japan itself, and the Manchurian Military Academy (MMA) in the new state of
Manchukuo.[1] Just as Korea itself in the war years became for Japan an "advance military supply base" for its continental expansion, so too did the
academies ultimately serve as the forward bases of modern Korea's martial
lineages, militarizing and transforming the persons who passed through
their gates, not least of all men like Park Chung Hee, who would be the principal bearers of those lineages into the postcolonial Korean future.[2]

Colonial Korea's Schools in the Second Wave

Perhaps nothing better epitomizes the trend and scope of Korea's second wave of militarization than the revisions of official Korean elementary school textbooks in the late 1930s and 1940s, as the GGK prepared for Korean conscription and began a total mobilization of the Korean populace for war. Gone were the earlier Arcadian images of the simple Korean farmer. Now the textbooks concentrated on images and stories about Japan's great wars and military heroes, many of which had not been featured before. Most indicative of all was the appearance of Kiguchi Kohei in the morals textbooks (J: *shūshinsho*; K: *susinsŏ*) for Korean children. Kiguchi was a celebrated young bugler who had fought in Korea during the First Sino-Japanese War (1894–1895). It was said that even after having been mortally wounded in combat by an enemy bullet, he had continued to sound the battle charge, even as he died. Since the early 1900s, Kiguchi had been a standard figure in pre-1945 Japan's elementary school texts, an enduring example of "loyalty" (J: *chūgi*; K: *ch'ungŭi*) for Japanese students in their first years of school. The texts had featured a colored drawing of him at the moment of death, still clutching his rifle and pressing his lips tightly to his bugle, as he fell backward to the ground and his fellow soldiers continued to surge forward. Accompanying the drawing was a caption that read: "Kiguchi Kohei went bravely into battle; although struck by an enemy bullet, he did not take the bugle from his lips even as he was dying."[3] The message was clear. By following Kiguchi's example of self-sacrificing service and ultimate loyalty, even the most humble young man could become a great hero. With an eye now on Korean young men as well as Japanese, the GGK included the well-known drawing and caption as part of its 1939 textbook revisions.[4] As the twenty-third chapter of the first-year morals reader, Kiguchi's lesson in loyalty was subsequently taught by elementary school teachers throughout the peninsula, including by Park Chung Hee, who before joining the Manchukuo Army had spent three years as a primary school instructor in Mun'gyŏng, a small village in his home province, North Kyŏngsang. The Kiguchi story may well have struck a particular chord with Park, who was himself a bugler, famous among his classmates for his rapid, piercing, military-style blasts at Taegu Normal School (TNS), the teacher's college he had attended for five years before being posted to Mun'gyŏng.[5]

That TNS hours and activities were marked by bugle calls was in fact yet another telling sign of the second wave's reach into the colonial schools. Indeed, even before Park entered TNS as a student in April 1932, the normal school system was already the most militarized of the colonial educational institutions, a product of its inception in Japan in the late nineteenth century after the Restoration. In the 1880s Meiji Japan's first education minister, Mori Arinori, who was also the architect of the *shūshin* curriculum, had worked hand in glove with Yamagata Aritomo, the founder of the modern Japanese army, to create a state educational system that had a strong patriotic and military flavor. The normal schools had been a special focus of attention for Mori and Yamagata, as they were to be the training grounds for the teachers who would be the carriers and transmitters of their vision, and many of the first men who were appointed as normal school presidents had in fact been retired army officers. Even though in time the schools expanded into what were in effect five-year junior colleges, with a comprehensive range of academic and extracurricular activities, they never completely lost their quasi-military, ultra-patriotic character, which was reflected in the normal school system inaugurated on the peninsula as well, and intensified in both Japan and its overseas territories during the war years.[6]

Colonial Korea's first state-sponsored normal school was established in Seoul (Keijō) in 1922. Two additional schools were created in Taegu and P'yŏngyang in 1929, followed in subsequent years by several more in other parts of the country, as the need for primary education expanded during the war.[7] By the time Park Chung Hee graduated from TNS in late March 1937, the schools were already highly regimented along military lines.[8] After more than five years of military invasions and forays on the Asian continent, the IJA was in a tense holding position on the outskirts of Beijing, with war, as it turned out, only months away.

Since the early 1930s, moreover, the atmosphere of TNS in particular had become increasingly strict and militarized after the breakup and arrest of a Marxist study group at the school, which had been under the supervision of a popular Korean teacher (see Chapter 6). In 1934 the TNS had also seen the appointment of a new principal, Torikai Ikoma, an exacting and doctrinaire chauvinist who emphasized the importance of military training and who would later serve as dean of the GGK's Educational Research Institute, where he would work closely with the Chōsen Army to reshape the Korean educational system in accord with the army's needs and plans for Korean conscription. "In particular," he wrote while he was dean of the institute, "what is most necessary is a thorough penetration [into the schools] of military-style life and practice."[9]

Such penetration was already conspicuous during Torikai's five-year tenure at TNS between 1934 and 1939. According to Sŏ Pyŏngguk, a former student whose time at TNS overlapped with Park's and who shared sleeping quarters with Park at the school and recalled his enthusiastic bugling, the bugle calls were in fact only a small part of the military-style regimen. The dormitories were run much like Japanese army barracks, with reveille at 0600 and lights out at 2200. Student "room captains" (*silchang*) and aides (*pusilchang*) acted in effect as soldiers on duty, and supervising teachers (*sagam*) carried out nightly inspections much as duty officers did. Except for holidays and vacations, students in the dormitory could not leave the school without official permission.[10]

Such arrangements nicely complemented the actual military drills required by the school. Ugaki's program of military training under the supervision of active army officers had been in place in colonial Korea's normal and commercial schools since 1926, even before the second wave had begun to make itself felt.[11] In fact, TNS had opened three years later with the program already securely embedded in the physical education curriculum, which also included gymnastics and Japanese martial arts such as *kendō*.[12] Three hours a week were ordinarily devoted to military drill.[13] But as Park Chung Hee's TNS classmate Yi Sŏngjo noted, that time frame was often doubled or more on occasions when the whole school was assembled to drill together, and in the case of special events incorporating military drill, other classes at the school were canceled completely.[14] Students in their first two years were trained in infantry foot-marching drills, but starting in the third year they practiced with Japanese rifles and light machine guns as well. In their fourth year, moreover, all TNS students were required to complete seven to ten days of temporary military service in the main force of the 80th Infantry Regiment, based in Taegu, part of the Chōsen Army's 20th Infantry Division, where they honed their skills and experienced something of the everyday realities of military life.[15] While all these programs had been part of TNS's regimen since the school's establishment, they were significantly expanded or intensified under Principal Torikai, whose devotion to promoting "the Japanese spirit through gymnastics, drill, special events, and other activities" knew no bounds, and whose heavy hand led Korean students during his years at TNS to refer to the school among themselves as the "81st Infantry Regiment."[16]

Military Academies Past

While Torikai's buttoned-down TNS may well have seemed like an ersatz IJA regiment to Korean students at the time, it was of course still far from the real thing, and still far less militarized than the schools that were specifically designed to mold young men into army officers. As Korea's second wave of militarization swelled in the 1930s, short-term induction and training facilities had been set up for the special army volunteers program inaugurated by the GGK in 1938 with an eye to eventual Korean conscription (see Chapter 2). But no comprehensive officer-training institutions existed on the peninsula equivalent to the JMA in Japan.

Koreans were far from strangers to the idea of professional military academies, however, or to the JMA itself. During the first wave of militarization before the annexation, the Chosŏn state, after numerous abortive attempts in the previous two decades, had finally inaugurated the country's first full-scale officer-training school, the Great Han Empire Military Academy (Mugwan Hakkyo), by royal decree in early 1896.[17] Unfortunately, apart from the date of its founding and the fact that it did admit one class of 100 students several months later, a number of whom were subsequently given commissions in 1897, we know little of the school in its first two years of operation, a blank in the historical record that undoubtedly reflected the instability of the political situation during this period of King Kojong's refuge in the Russian embassy and of continuous jockeying for influence in Korea between Russia and Japan. Not surprisingly, Russian military advisors and instructors were in the ascendant while the king remained in their legation, but it was not long before reformists outside the government, especially in the newly formed Independence Club, were agitating for a new national defense policy that called for the expulsion of all foreign military advisors and the revitalization of the military academy under the new imperial banner. The result was the end of a foreign military advisory presence in Korea and a formal reinauguration of the Mugwan Hakkyo in July 1898.

Over the next six years, the academy gradually developed into the country's preeminent military educational institution, closely and consciously modeled on Japan's JMA (which had been created more than two decades earlier by the new Meiji government) and heavily dependent on translations of JMA textbooks. For the first time a Korean facility for the training of professional officers could boast a generous staff of administrators and teachers, all active-duty officers. In sharp contrast to its short-lived predecessors, the Mugwan Hakkyo had an extensive curriculum. Following JMA practice, its course of study was divided into two branches: an academic unit (*kyogwandan*) and a cadet corps (*haktodae*), the former responsible for general education and military science (*kyoyuk*) and the latter for military drill and moral or spiritual training (*hunyuk*).

The Mugwan Hakkyo was clearly envisioned by its promoters as a first-class professional institution where merit ruled and standards and expectations were high. Both an intensive, short-term program generally lasting about a year and a half and a long-term graduate program of five years were announced, and an admission process designed to select the best qualified young men between the ages of eighteen and twenty-seven regardless of social background was put into place. Applicants had to pass an entrance examination, including a physical check (all entrants had to be over five feet tall and in excellent health and condition). Together with their application form and a pledge that the information provided was correct, they also had to submit any previous school records, a recommendation from an active army officer or government official, a stamp from the relevant magistrate certifying that they were worthy of admission to the academy, and signed resumés from two "guarantors" (pojŭngin), who would share the burden for any fines or penalties imposed upon the cadet while in school. Once admitted, the cadets were by no means routinely passed. Emphasis in testing and evaluation was placed on the cadets' genuine understanding of the material at hand rather than on simple memorization, and practical application of knowledge rather than pure theory was stressed in the classroom and cadet corps exercises. Many students actually failed to make the required grade and were dismissed or left before finishing their course of study. Of the 100 cadets admitted to the first class in 1896, only 19 completed the program about a year later; 128 of 200 from the second class, which graduated in 1900; and 180 out of 350 finished the third class, in 1903.[18]

Although the Mugwan Hakkyo was Korea's only officer-training school in the last years of the Chosŏn dynasty, it was not the only place where Chosŏn officers were being trained. Some were learning their military skills abroad. While enlightenment reformers had been eager to see a military academy established in Korea itself, from the beginning they had also encouraged their younger followers with officer potential to go outside Korea and study at recognized military schools, and once the Korean government began to pursue a reformist agenda after 1876, it too promoted and even sponsored such foreign study.

Foreign military study for all practical purposes meant study in Japan. In 1893 the Korean government did in fact petition the United States to allow Korean students to attend West Point, but Washington ignored the request and nothing came of it.[19] Even if the United States had been more receptive, however, Japan would still have been the more natural magnet for such students. Not only did it have a number of excellent military schools, including the JMA, but Japan was also for Koreans and for Asians more generally the Asian center of the Western "new learning," and for Koreans in particular it was geographically, linguistically, and financially far more accessible than any Western country.[20] Unlike Washington, moreover, the government in Tokyo, at least in this period, seems to have been far more open to the idea of foreign students attending its military schools.

The first students to study military affairs in Japan had arrived in Tokyo in the fall of 1881, several months after the return of the Courtiers Observation Mission. Three in all, they had accompanied a Korean diplomatic envoy to Japan, afterward remaining in Tokyo, where two went on to attend the Toyama School and one the Kyōdōdan for noncommissioned officers.[21] The next year a sixteen-year-old named Pak Yugwoeng, who had also been selected to study in Japan as a Korean government scholarship student, went to Tokyo as a member of Pak Yŏnghyo's diplomatic mission following the anti-foreign mutiny of 1882, and after studying Japanese for several months at Fukuzawa Yukichi's Keiō school, became the first Korean student to attend the capital's Central Army Cadet School, the main feeder institution for the JMA, and later the first Korean to enter the JMA itself.[22] When Pak Yukwoeng was about six months into his course at the Cadet School, a large group of Korean students arrived in Tokyo in the early summer of 1883, all inspired by enlightenment ideas and personally encouraged by Kim Okkyun, who had helped arrange for the Korean government to pay their expenses with a loan floated in Japan. The entire group was welcomed by Fukuzawa, who temporarily put the students up in lodgings near his own home and through his assistant, Iida Sanji, helped direct them to specific schools and training programs based on their interests and abilities. As a result, fourteen of the students, including later Independence Club founder Sŏ Chaep'il, were sent to the army's Toyama School, where Sŏ enrolled in the regular officer's course and the others in the noncommissioned officer's program.[23]

Over the next twenty years numerous other Chosŏn students followed in the paths laid down by these first Japanese-trained Korean officers in the early 1880s. The exact numbers are not clear. Some went at government expense; others were privately funded. Some only matriculated and never completed their course of study; others became full-fledged graduates of their schools. After the first flush of students in the early 1880s, there was a noticeable drop-off in the numbers, owing to the king's unwillingness to sponsor such study in the wake of the 1884 coup attempt, in which the Toyama-trained followers of Kim Okkyun and Pak Yŏnghyo had been deeply involved. The next surge in numbers did not come until after 1894, when the Kabo reformers, including, of course, Pak Yŏnghyo, revived government scholarships for such study. The most complete record we have is of Korean students who attended the JMA, usually, like Pak Yugwoeng, after receiving a basic education in Japanese language and other academic areas at either the Army Cadet School or the Seijō Gakkō, one of the civilian middle schools geared toward the academy. Of the thirty-seven Korean students on the academy's rolls in this period, eight were in the eighth class, graduating in 1896 (JMA 8), twenty-one in the eleventh class, graduating in 1899 (JMA 11), and eight in the fifteenth class, graduating in 1903 (JMA 15).[24]

The Korean JMA graduates were undoubtedly among the best-trained Korean officers in the late Chosŏn period, and starting in about 1896 they began to return to Korea. For many their first posting was to the Mugwan Hakkyo, where they taught either in the academic unit or in the cadet corps. Because of their excellent education and positions of authority, they were quickly able to exert an influence that was far greater than their numbers, even despite resistance from some quarters of the government and military hierarchy that were more favorably disposed toward American or Russian training methods, or remained suspicious of Koreans with close Japanese connections.[25] In a 1930 memoir, Kim Hyŏngsŏp, a JMA 11 graduate who had joined the Mugwan Hakkyo's staff in 1901 along with many of his classmates, noted that this influence began to be felt immediately after their appointments.[26] By the time the JMA 15 graduates joined the Hakkyo as instructors three years later, one of Kim's classmates, Ŏ Tam, had become the superintendent's adjutant, and American and Russian pedagogical and training techniques that had characterized the Hakkyo in the late 1890s had more or less been replaced by methods Kim, Ŏ, and their fellow JMA graduates had learned in Japan.[27] Ironically, however, just as the Hakkyo was becoming increasingly more professionalized along the lines of the JMA, the Japanese protectorate abolished the Korean army, depriving the school of its purpose, and the Hakkyo itself was officially closed down two years later, in 1909.[28] Koreans would not have a military academy of their own again until after 1945.

Military Academies in the Second Wave

Following the annexation, thirty-three cadets in two classes still in training at the Mugwan Hakkyo (including a descendant of Yi Sunsin and others who would later constitute an important part of the founding officer corps of the Republic of Korea) were transferred to the JMA, receiving IJA commissions in 1914 and 1915, respectively. In the face of both educational and ethnic discrimination, as well as continuing Japanese concerns about Korean anti-Japanese feelings after the 1919 March First demonstrations, ordinary Koreans had little incentive or hope when it came to admission to Japan's most prestigious military institution, and for the next two decades only a handful of Korean men attended the school, mainly those of royal or aristocratic lineage, such as Emperor Kojong's son and heir, Crown Prince Ŭn, who graduated in the JMA 29 class of 1917. In the eleven JMA classes (JMA 31–41) that graduated between 1918 and 1930, there were no Korean students at all.[29]

The second wave changed everything. Even as early as the summer of 1932, following the Kwantung Army's seizure of Manchuria and continuing military ventures ever deeper into the continent, active duty army officers supervising military training in the mixed Japanese and Korean middle schools began to encourage their top Korean students to apply for JMA admission.[30] The ensuing conflict with China, the decision to accelerate plans to conscript Koreans as well as Japanese, and the increasing demand for officers as well as regular soldiers all sped the process, and by 1940 Minami Jirō, Korea's powerful governor-general, a high-ranking military figure in his own right, was beating the bushes of Korean officer recruitment, "fervently recommending to Korean young men," as one Korean magazine put it, "that they study at the JMA and become officers."[31] And, indeed, as *Tonga ilbo* reported proudly at the time, "the number of imposing and vigorous Korean officers is substantially increasing," including the "young men currently at the JMA who had surmounted the difficulties posed by the school."[32]

The number of Korean students in JMA graduating classes during this period was definitely higher, in some cases even reaching double digits.[33] But the "difficulties posed by the school," quite apart from the arduous training itself, were not insignificant. The greatest difficulty was in fact securing admission. Even though the Japanese authorities were now actively encouraging Korean young men to apply to the academy, and the academy itself was increasing its overall admissions quota, the vast majority of Koreans were greatly disadvantaged in the JMA's rigorous admissions process by the colonial school system, which was still largely separate and unequal, with the best primary and secondary schools reserved for Japanese and, in some cases, a limited number of Koreans. During the war years, however, the routes to an army commission proliferated, and the establishment of the state of Manchukuo on Korea's northern border in 1932 created new spaces and new institutions for Koreans to escape their colonial confines and pursue professional careers, including in the military.

The Manchukuo Army

As Kwantung Army officers overran Manchuria in 1931–1932 and eventually decided to set up a nominally autonomous state under their control, they also decided that the state should have a military of its own. From the perspective of the officers turned nation-builders, the existence of a national army not only lent credibility to what Prasenjit Duara has described as a quest for "sovereignty and authenticity."[34] It also gave the Kwantung Army increased strength and flexibility, as the new forces could concentrate primarily on internal dissent and rebellion while freeing up the IJA troops to focus on external threats, mainly from Chiang Kai-shek's (Jiang Jieshi's) Guomindang regime in Nanjing, and, even more important, from the Soviet Union, which army planners had identified as Japan's main enemy.

The prospects for a national army in 1932, however, were not very encouraging. The Japanese had inherited equipment and about 60,000 men from the defunct Northeastern Army of warlord Zhang Xueliang, who had allied himself with Chiang and fled to Nanjing after the Kwantung Army had routed his forces, and these were reorganized into several provincial "defense armies" (J: *keibigun;* C: *jingbeijun*) that were stationed throughout the country. But the quality of the officers and men in this makeshift new military left much to be desired. Zhang's army had been formed through a loose coalition of fellow warlords, whose troops were bound more by personal ties and a desire for the spoils of war than by any overarching sense of unity, national or otherwise, and they had little professional training. On one level the story of the Manchukuo Army is thus the story of the gradual retraining or replacement of these troops and the overall expansion of the army itself, both in terms of numbers and departments. By 1934, when the Kwantung Army installed Puyi (Aisin Gioro), the last ruler of the Qing dynasty, as the titular emperor of Manchukuo and carried out a major reorganization of both the government and military, the army had grown to about 79,000. General conscription for men was instituted in 1940, and by the end of the war five years later, the army had more than doubled to somewhere between 150,000 and 200,000 troops in eleven division-sized "district armies" (J: *gunkanku;* C: *junguanou*). In the meantime, branch (*heika*) development had expanded to include all the component arms of the IJA: infantry, cavalry, artillery, air, and transport, as well as an armored vehicle branch (*jidōsha*) found only in the Manchukuo Army.[35] The army had its own military police force as well, and under Kwantung Army tutelage and control an army ministry was established and expanded to supervise and administer all state military affairs. The new state's diverse population also led to the formation of a number of supporting ethnic army units, including a body of about 360 Korean troops, the Jiandao Special Force, which was set up in 1938 to fight Chinese communists and other anti-Japanese guerrillas (including other Koreans) in Manchukuo's southeast province of Jiandao, home to nearly a million ethnic Koreans.[36]

As the Manchukuo Army grew, so too did the need for officers. Naturally distrustful of the inhabitants of the land it had just invaded, especially Chinese with possible nationalist or communist ties, the Kwantung Army embarked on a major campaign to attract qualified Japanese men into the officer ranks of its new ancillary military force. No stone was left unturned. Through official military channels, as well as public notices and personal contacts, the Kwantung Army actively recruited from every possible group. These included not only retired IJA officers, who were often appointed to the top posts in the Manchukuo Army system, but also reserve officer candidates (*kanbu kōhosei*), senior noncommissioned officers who became candidates for commission (*shōi kōhosha*), and even former JMA cadets who had been unable for one reason or another to complete their officer education at the academy. Although such concerted efforts managed to draw in considerable numbers of applicants, as many as 6,000 for 300 slots at the height of the "Manchurian war fever" in 1933, by the end of the war only 3,000 Japanese officers had actually been commissioned. Given linguistic differences and the vast expanse of territory to be patrolled, moreover, it had in fact been clear from the beginning that native officers would also have to be deployed, and when the Kwantung Army had initiated its drive to recruit Japanese officers, it had simultaneously begun to recruit within the native population as well, from the Han Chinese, Manchus, Mongols, and Koreans, who together with the Japanese represented the "five races" in the new state's official ideology of "ethnic harmony" (*gozoku kyōwa*).[37]

Whatever their ethnic background, most of these new officer recruits required some form of military training, if only, as in the case of the Japanese officers from the IJA reserves, to be acclimated to their new positions in the Manchukuo Army. The Kwantung Army thus also began quickly to establish military instruction facilities once the new state had been formally proclaimed, and by the 1940s there was in place a substantial network of army educational institutions. In addition to schools for commissioned and noncommissioned army officers, the Manchukuo Army had a staff college, an air force academy, a medical college, a munitions school, a college of veterinary science, and even branch schools for engineers and experts in armored vehicles. And many of these schools had considerable numbers of Korean students, both from Manchuria and from Korea itself, including the two most prominent: the Chūo Rikugun Kunrensho, or Central Training School (CTS), and of course the MMA.[38]

The Central Training School (CTS)

The Central Training School opened in 1932 in Mukden (Fengtian) at a former battalion camp of Zhang's Northeastern Army. The following year it recruited about twenty Japanese instructors from the IJA reserves, largely of field officer rank, and hired another IJA reserve officer of major general rank, Mizumachi Takezō (JMA 10), to supervise the school's development.[39] The Kwantung Army also assigned two of its own officers as military advisors to the school, one of whom was Hong Saik, a Korean JMA 26 graduate, who had begun his career in the old Mugwan Hakkyo of the Great Han Empire and would later rise to lieutenant general rank in the IJA.[40] Thereafter the school was gradually reorganized and expanded into various divisions, including an administrative headquarters and research section, as well as departments devoted to infantry, cavalry, artillery, military police, communications, and other army branches and specialties. There were separate tracks for Japanese students, known as Nikkei, and for non-Japanese students, who regardless of ethnicity were labeled as "Manchurians" or Mankei, and by the time the CTS was restructured in the early 1940s, its original function having been superseded by the establishment of the MMA, it had produced ten classes of Nikkei officers and nine classes of Mankei.[41]

For the most part the Nikkei students were IJA senior noncommissioned officers who were eligible for commissioning on the basis of their service, or Japanese conscripts who had qualified for officer training. But some of the Nikkei students were also experienced company officers recruited from the IJA reserves. The first Mankei students were former Northeastern Army Chinese officers who had been absorbed into the new state's "defense armies" and needed to be retrained along Japanese lines, but later classes, although still largely Chinese, were composed of aspiring officer candidates drawn from the diverse population of the area, including Koreans.

Compared to the JMA, the CTS was something of an ad hoc training facility. The JMA was of course Japan's premier military school, through whose gates the IJA military elite had all passed since its establishment only a few years after the Meiji Restoration. With its two-year regular or main course (*honka*) preceded and buttressed by a two-year introductory course (*yoka*) at its affiliated feeder school, the JMA Preparatory Academy (JMAP), the JMA constituted in effect a four-year training continuum of two closely conjoined institutions, each with its own full range of facilities and staff, as well as nearly sixty years of accumulated military expertise, tradition, and lore. The CTS, on the other hand, had only a fraction of the JMA's resources, and was initially designed solely for the purpose of reeducating Japanese and Chinese officers for service in the Manchukuo Army, and for providing a modicum of basic training for new officer candidates. Given the pressing demand for officers in the fledgling army, the first class of Nikkei recruits had in fact graduated after only one month of training and were immediately posted to commands throughout the country, while the first Mankei graduates were given a slightly longer period of training of about five months. Subsequent classes of both Nikkei and Mankei were of somewhat greater duration. The Mankei CTS 5 class of Chŏng Ilgwŏn, for example, who would later hold many key posts in Park Chung Hee's eighteen-year regime, was trained at the school for only a year.[42] But even at its best, the CTS fell far short of offering the kind of full, sustained, two-level, four-year immersion in the culture and practices of IJA military life that was exemplified by the JMA. The MMA, however, would be founded precisely with that goal in mind.[43]

The Manchurian Military Academy (MMA)

From the beginning the Kwantung Army's officers in charge of the development of the Manchukuo Army had wanted to establish a Manchurian version of the JMA in the new country they were building.[44] Although military exigencies had forced them to settle in the early years for a smaller and more expedient facility in the form of the CTS, they never abandoned their vision or plans for a full-scale professional officer training institution that would be commensurate in size, quality, and prestige with the grandiose plans they harbored for the new nation. At the heart of those plans lay the idea of Manchukuo as a model for reforming Japan itself, a model founded above all on the values and practices of the IJA, and the establishment of the MMA, as the JMA of Manchuria, would ensure that those values and practices would be taught to succeeding generations of the new state's military elite.[45] An appropriate site was eventually secured on the outskirts of Changchun, which the Kwantung Army had set up as the new capital of the country and renamed Xinjing (J: Shinkyō), and the academy opened its doors to its first class of cadets in the spring of 1939. (See Chapter 4.)

In keeping with their image of the MMA as a comprehensive Manchurian JMA, the Kwantung Army established both a two-year *yoka* course and a two-year *honka* course within the school, so that cadets would receive the same full scope of professional training as offered by the JMA in combination with its preparatory affiliate in Japan. Except for the fact that they were now located in the same place, as had originally been the case in Japan itself, the two course regimens at the MMA, essentially schools within the school, were identical to their Japanese counterparts. The *yoka* focused on general education as well as military science, history, and tactics, while the *honka* specialized in training for a particular branch of service. After graduating from the *yoka,* cadets, now officially "officer candidates" (*kōhosei*), were dispatched to actual units in the army for three to six months of on-site training in what was known as "regimental attachment duty" (*taizuki kinmu*). Similarly, after graduation from the *honka,* the cadets were once again assigned to army units for about three months of apprenticeship as "probationary officers" (*minarai shikan*) before finally receiving commissions as second lieutenants. In both the MMA *yoka* and *honka* courses, moreover, most of the instructors were Japanese, the teaching materials used were more or less identical to those used in Japan, and Japanese was the school's official language. And special terms and practices that had over the years become linguistic and cultural conventions of IJA and JMA life also quickly found their way into the everyday life of the MMA cadets, either passed on naturally or consciously promoted by Japanese officers who served as the school's key administrators and instructors (and many of whom, especially at the senior level, were JMA graduates themselves).

In terms of its organization, the MMA adhered closely to the JMA system. Overseeing the entire school were a superintendent and vice superintendent, both of general rank. Below them was a broad hierarchy of officials, assigned, as in the case of the old Mugwan Hakkyo, either to the academic affairs unit (*kyōjubu*), headed by a dean (*kyōjubuchō*), who was also a general officer, or to the corps of cadets (*seitotai*), led by a corps commandant (*seitotaichō*), also of general rank. For the most part the academic affairs unit, staffed by both civilians and army officers, managed the general classroom instruction, while instructors in the cadet corps, who were active-duty army officers of company or field rank, were responsible for the cadets' "moral education" or *kun'iku,* which was deeply associated with barracks life and the actual physical drills and training supervised by the cadet corps officers. Each class in the corps was divided and barracked by company (*ren*) and section (*kutai*), with about four sections of thirty cadets to a company, and with officers attached to the cadet corps acting as company or section commanders (*renchō/kutaichō*).[46] Plus a number of senior noncommissioned officers were assigned to the school to assist the instructors and officers in their various tasks.[47]

Given its high expectations for the MMA and the crucial role of the superintendent in creating a proper regimen and atmosphere, the Kwantung Army took particular care in selecting the first Japanese officer for the top post, finally deciding on Major General Nagumo Shin'ichirō. In addition to being a JMA graduate himself (JMA 19), Nagumo had spent an unusually long time, about twelve consecutive years, as an officer attached to the cadet corps of the JMA, where he had served in a variety of capacities, including company commander, teacher, and academic division dean. In a newspaper interview at the time of his appointment, he emphasized that apart from a certain amount of instruction directly related to its special character as an institution of the Manchukuo Army, the MMA would be "in all respects exactly the same" (*mattaku dōitsu*) as the JMA, with even its textbooks "virtually unchanged" (*hotondo kawarazu*) from that of the Japanese school.[48]

Of course, one significant difference between the two schools lay in the ethnic composition of their cadets, since the MMA's primary mandate, like that of the CTS, was to recruit and train officers from the local, mainly Han Chinese, population. Again like the CTS, however, the MMA was envisioned as a school for Japanese as well, with separate Nikkei and Mankei tracks. In fact, the continuing presence of a substantial body of Japanese cadets was for the Kwantung Army an essential part of its overall plan for the MMA, seeing the Japanese as models for the other cadets, as well as the nucleus of the Manchukuo Army's new officer corps. Negotiations with Tokyo dragged on for years, however, as the Kwantung Army sought to make all the necessary arrangements for Nikkei recruitment and admission. Finally a deal was struck in 1939, whereby the Kwantung Army gave up its control of the admissions process for Japanese cadets to the IJA's Inspectorate General of Military Training in return for the right to dispatch all of its MMA Nikkei *yoka* graduates to Japan. There, according to the agreement, they would be enrolled in the JMA's International Corps of Cadets (Ryūgakuseitai) for their two years of *honka* training and graduate together with the regular JMA class of that year. Although the Kwantung Army was loath to relinquish its authority over its Japanese admissions, it accepted the arrangement as the only way to ensure a steady stream of high quality Japanese students for the school. It also welcomed the opportunity to forge a direct link with the JMA and to enhance the reputation of the MMA as a Manchurian extension of the esteemed institution on which the new school was being modeled.[49]

The MMA Classes

Between April 1941, when the first Japanese cadets arrived at the school, and the end of the war in August 1945, about 1,300 cadets in seven Nikkei classes attended the MMA. At the time of the Japanese surrender the Nikkei MMA 4 and MMA 6 classes were completing their training at the JMA in Japan, while the Nikkei MMA 7 was still only in its first year in Manchuria. (See the Conclusion.) The MMA *yoka* course for the Nikkei was one year instead of the usual two, and they initially slept in separate barracks, supervised by their own company and section commanders. They ate in the same mess hall as the Mankei cadets, however, and the two groups shared certain classes and participated together in all of the school's general activities and events, such as matriculations, commencements, and visits of dignitaries. In the second semester of the Nikkei MMA 6 class, moreover, which had entered in the spring of 1944, the Mankei cadets were gradually integrated into the Nikkei barracks, a pattern that would have continued had the war persisted and the academy continued to function. The number of cadets in the seven MMA Mankei classes between 1939 and 1945 totaled about 2,000 in all. The Kwantung Army had earlier set up a separate military academy expressly for Mongolians as part of its strategy to build up a Mongolian "independence" army that would support Japan against Chiang Kai-shek's Nanjing government, which had claimed sovereignty over Inner Mongolia, so most of the Mankei cadets were Han Chinese and Manchus. To encourage the non-Japanese at the school, the MMA chose a small number of the most outstanding cadets from each graduating Mankei *yoka* class to join their Nikkei counterparts for the *honka* at the JMA. Thus around the time of their *yoka* graduation, when they were also being assigned to a particular army branch for *honka* training and preparing for their regimental attachment duty, the selected Mankei were brought into the Nikkei group, where they remained until their graduation from the JMA and subsequent commissioning. Those Mankei not selected, the vast majority, remained at the MMA for the duration of their training.[50]

Among those Mankei sent to the JMA, the Korean cadets were especially prominent. In Park Chung Hee's MMA 2 Mankei class, for example, about half of those selected, which included Park himself, were Korean, an extraordinary number considering that the total number of Koreans in the class was only 11, while the non-Korean component was 240. In fact, of the forty-eight Koreans who attended the MMA, more than 60 percent were sent to Japan for the *honka,* or would have been had the war continued. From the beginning the performance of the Korean cadets at the MMA was overall so superior in relation to their numbers that in the final years of the school they were eventually moved from the Mankei category and enrolled directly in the Nikkei group.[51]

Embracing the Military

By the 1940s the second wave had enlarged and multiplied the places that were militarizing men into officers, and the outstanding record of the Koreans at the MMA underlined the degree to which they were successfully accommodating themselves to military life. But not all cadets, Chinese, Japanese, or Korean, came to the academy through the same door, or embraced the officer ethos and life with the same degree of enthusiasm, even though it would be fair to say that, unlike those who were forcibly conscripted into the ranks, they all aspired in one way or another to be officers and had committed to that goal more or less voluntarily. Nevertheless, the truth was that many different, often overlapping, forces had impinged to bring them to Xinjing, and once there, their reactions to their new environment also varied.

For the Japanese cadets in particular, patriotism in a time of war, encouraged by a constant drumroll of newspaper stories, novels, movies, banners, and school lectures, was often an important motivation in joining the officer corps. Nishikawa Nobuyoshi (MMA 7), for example, who had been a first-year middle school student when the Japanese navy bombed Pearl Harbor, was inspired by the heroic depiction of the attack in the media and wanted to defend Japan against what he saw as an inevitable counterattack from the United States. Even though his parents were of a liberal bent and argued against his volunteering, he went ahead anyway, thinking "it was completely natural to sacrifice myself for the sake of the nation."[52] For many Japanese men who faced imminent conscription, moreover, entering the army as an officer was more appealing than being drafted into the ranks, precisely the point the father of another Japanese cadet, Kaneko Tomio (MMA 2), made to his son, based on his own punishing experience as a private.[53]

In choosing to become officers, however, neither Nishikawa nor Kaneko, nor indeed any of the Nikkei cadets, imagined themselves going to Xinjing for their training. All had applied for admission to the JMA's affiliated preparatory school in Japan with the intention of completing their *yoka* course there and then going on to the JMA itself. In accordance with the confidential pact the MMA had made with IJA, however, the 150–200 Nikkei cadets in each class were selected for admission to the Xinjing school from among those applicants who had passed the qualifying exam for entrance to the Japanese preparatory school. Most had never even heard of the MMA, and when they received the notices of their test results, recommending them for admission to the Manchurian academy, they were often confused about what to do. In the end, however, the desire to be an officer, together with the promise of finishing up their final two years of training at the JMA, led most of them to accept the offer.[54]

For the Mankei cadets, especially the Chinese residents in Manchukuo, the new MMA was much better known. Indeed, according to interviews conducted with Chinese graduates of several different classes ranging over the six years of the school's existence, the MMA was regarded at the time as one of the best educational institutions in the country, equivalent or superior to the new state's "Nation-Founding" (Kenkoku) University, also located in Xinjing.[55] This reputation, in fact, was one of the main reasons for the MMA's large number of applicants, only a small fraction of which, between 200 and 300 per class, were actually admitted.[56] As many of the former graduates pointed out, it was free, so "even if you didn't have any money, you could go to the school, if you could get in."[57] Although there was no draft in Manchukuo until 1940, as in Korea the secondary school system in the 1930s had become increasingly militarized, and both the government and military drill instructors in the schools energetically fostered positive attitudes about martial life. In such an atmosphere the uniform of the MMA gave the young men who wore it a certain cachet—not least of all in the eyes of the opposite sex. Gao Qingyin (MMA 2), who had very much wanted to be admitted to the school and finally made it into the same class as Park Chung Hee as an alternate after another cadet had withdrawn, thought the MMA was the "number one school under the Japanese occupation," and particularly enjoyed the fact that "wherever we went, the girls liked us— they liked officers."[58]

The MMA was much less well known in Korea than in Manchuria itself, but Korean-language newspapers and magazines reported its opening and occasionally even featured articles on Koreans who were attending it and other Japanese-run officer training schools, including the CTS and the JMA.[59] Such media attention was of course part of Governor-General Minami's campaign in the late 1930s and 1940s to draw more Koreans into the Japanese army, both as officers and as enlisted men, and as the campaign intensified, local governments, communities, schools, and newspapers were brought into the effort, casting a deep, peninsula-wide net of encouragement and pressure that was difficult to ignore and brought rewards and prestige for the young men who responded to it and their families. As elsewhere in the empire, the active-duty IJA officers from the Chōsen Army who served as military drill instructors in the schools played a central role here, keeping a sharp eye out for bright young Korean middle school students who might qualify as officers; once they had identified a possible candidate, they left no stone unturned to persuade that young man to take the entrance exam for one of the officer programs or military schools. Koreans who might qualify for the JMA were a particular focus of the government officials and military instructors, and those few who managed to pass the exam and gain admission to the JMA preparatory school were treated in their hometowns like conquering young heroes, reminiscent in many respects of the adulation accorded in the Chosŏn dynasty to those returning sons of the local aristocracy who had succeeded in the government's civil service examination process.

One such young man was Chŏng Naehyŏk (JMA 58), who graduated from the JMA one year after Park Chung Hee, and who later joined the revolutionary military junta in May 1961 and subsequently served in numerous military and cabinet-level positions in Park's government, including superintendent of the Korean Military Academy and minister of defense. In the early 1940s, when Chŏng was a student at the ranking boys' middle school in Kwangju, the capital of southwestern Korea's South Chŏlla province, he caught the attention of both the Japanese school principal and the supervising

Japanese drill officer for his outstanding mental and physical abilities. Encouraged by his instructors to apply for the JMA preparatory academy, he studied assiduously and eventually took the entrance examination at the Chōsen Army's main headquarters in Seoul (Yongsan). Even though he walked out of the base thinking he had done well on the exam, he also knew the competition was fierce and assumed he would not be selected. For years, in fact, many of the top students in his middle school had been striving for admission to the JMA's *yoka* course, only to fail in the end. When his notification of admission came in early 1942, a first for his school, it created a celebratory uproar among the faculty and students and was heralded in the local newspaper as well. At the principal's insistence and with the principal at his side, Chŏng paid a visit to the provincial governor to inform him officially of the good news, and the principal also led the entire school to the local Japanese Shintō shrine, where Chŏng's admission to the academy was formally reported with accompanying ritualistic bows. When Chŏng left Kwangju soon thereafter to take up his new life as an IJA cadet, he was given a public send-off at the Kwangju train station, as well as another "grand farewell" (*kŏgukchŏgin hwansong*) a few days later in his hometown, Koksŏng, attended by·family and friends, elementary school teachers, and local government functionaries.[60]

The official regard lavished on a student such as Chŏng for his success in the JMA preparatory exam was not all that unusual at the time, and he might well never even have put himself forward had it not been for his school's initial encouragement. Behind Chŏng's decision, however, lay a number of other factors that were common to Koreans applying for a place in the Japanese or Manchurian officer corps. First, in a traditionally status-conscious and then colonized society such as Korea, where even those Koreans most favored by the Japanese suffered from various forms of discrimination, one cannot underestimate the empowering, masculinizing effect of a Korean man donning the uniform and insignia of a Japanese military officer, especially at a time when the military was ascendant in nearly all spheres of society. Although subtle, informal discrimination was never entirely absent in the colonial context (even, as we shall see, within the army itself), for the military and all that fell within its purview to function effectively, rank order had to take precedence over everything else. Even if it did not completely erase the stigma attached to a colonized subject, wearing an officer's uniform raised the Korean man who wore it to a new and exalted status that even Japanese officials, who might otherwise have looked down on him, could not ignore. As officers, Koreans could deal with Japanese from positions of power and authority that were virtually unimaginable in the everyday, civilian world of the colony.

A story by Chŏng Naehyŏk provides a vivid example of such empowerment. During his summer vacations from military training in Japan, Chŏng, like most Koreans traveling back and forth between Korea and Japan on the Pusan-Shimonoseki ferry, had to contend with the overbearing military policemen who monitored the passengers and were often deliberately intimidating and insulting to Koreans. But as a JMA cadet, Chŏng, unlike most of his fellow Koreans, was in a position to turn the tables on his tormentors. As Chŏng himself wrote:

> The military police on the Pusan wharf were extremely arrogant. At the point of embarkation there was also a nasty police officer who would single out Koreans for verbal abuse. Soldiers were not permitted to pick fights, but once I had acquired sergeant rank as a JMA cadet, I chewed out the Japanese military police numerous times for lack of courtesy. IJA military law elevated JMA cadets over other officers of equal rank, so we had the right to demand a salute from them even though they were the same rank, and I used the opportunity to blow up and vent my resentment.[61]

Status and power must always have figured to some extent in a Korean man's decision to join the officer corps, but there were other reasons as well. As noted above, the opportunity to expand one's education at no personal cost to oneself or one's family was certainly another attractive aspect of the academies, and for Chŏng Naehyŏk, whose family had lost much of its once considerable wealth, not wanting to be a family burden was also an important element in applying to the JMA.[62] Koreans already serving as officers in the IJA or Manchukuo Army, who were often featured in wartime newspapers or public rallies, were powerful recruitment magnets as well.[63] When, on top of that, the featured officer was a senior from the school the potential recruits were attending, the draw could be even more compelling. All but one of the thirteen Korean MMA 1 cadets, for example, including all of those in the Hwagyesa photograph with which this book begins, were from the same Korean middle school, Kwangmyŏng, located in the Jiandao region of Manchuria. According to Pang Wŏnch'ŏl, who was himself one of the former Kwangmyŏng students in the MMA 1 class, they had all been deeply affected by a visit to the school from Chŏng Ilgwŏn, who had graduated from the CTS and received a commission in the Manchukuo Army. Chŏng, in Pang's words, caught their attention, not only for his appearance in full dress uniform as a "handsome, impressive second lieutenant" but also because he was one of their seniors, having graduated from Kwangmyŏng only a few years earlier.[64] In the late 1930s, when Korean conscription was still several years away and the volunteer soldier program on the peninsula was only just being introduced, there were still many Koreans in middle schools who, as Chŏng Naehyŏk noted, "had no idea that Koreans could in fact become officers, let alone that their seniors were already serving as officers."[65] In such an environment, the return visit to his old school of an alumnus such as Chŏng Ilgwŏn, now transformed into a symbol of military authority, could have a potent impact on younger students still in the school.

Encouragement from teachers and government officials, empowerment as a Korean man, education without tuition, and emulation of seniors—all were elements that pulled Koreans into the officer corps in the late 1930s and 1940s. Another was simply personality. The military life attracted some men more than others, and for some it was even a cherished ambition. This was not initially the case with Chŏng Naehyŏk, who had not really considered a military career before being praised and cheered on by his middle school instructors. But other Korean men who went into the officer corps, including both Park Chung Hee and his MMA 2 classmate Yi Hallim, had been deeply influenced from adolescence, if not before, by heroic stories and images of Napoleon and Yi Sunsin that appeared frequently in Korean-language newspapers and magazines throughout the 1920s and 1930s. Today, thanks in no small part to official government promotion during the Park Chung Hee era, Yi Sunsin is well known to all schoolchildren in South Korea as an icon of Korean military genius and patriotism, and it is difficult to appreciate the astonishment and pride young Koreans in the colonial period experienced when hearing about Yi for the first time, not least of all those who, like Yi Hallim, were living in Manchuria, where Korean-language periodicals were often less accessible. In his autobiography, Yi wrote that he first learned of the admiral by reading the popular Seoul-based Korean-language magazine *Samch'ŏlli* and that the knowledge came as "no small shock." His admiration for Yi, as well as his "infatuation" with the "romantic elements" of Napoleon's brilliant military career, played a key role in bringing him to the gates of the MMA. The military, he felt, spoke to something deep in his psyche; he was certain that becoming an officer would "give life to my true self."[66]

The Question of Nationalism

That a Korean young man in the 1940s could find his "true self" in the IJA or Manchurian officer corps does not rest well today with a Korean nationalist sentiment that often tends to equate being true to one's Korean self at that time with being anti-Japanese, and joining the imperial officer corps equivalent to betraying the Korean nation. There is in fact a substantial body of contemporary Korean-language work on the colonial era that is sharply critical of Koreans who worked for or with the Government-General or other Japanese imperial institutions, including Koreans who had been enrolled in the IJA or Manchukuo Army as officers, and it is important to consider this perspective in trying to unravel the motivations and feelings of those Koreans who entered the JMA and MMA. At its most sweeping, such writing condemns as pro-Japanese or anti-nationalist all Koreans who served in some official occupation at a certain level or higher—company rank and above in the officer corps, for example—regardless of what they may actually have done in that capacity.[67]

On the one hand it is difficult to fault such writing, especially when it concerns the military, which was, after all, the chief engine of Japanese imperialism on the Asian continent and the ultimate enforcer of imperialist goals. To serve the Japanese army or its subsidiaries was in a very real sense to serve an institution that was literally and physically suppressing Korean nationalist political aspirations. The Jiandao Special Force mentioned above, for example, which was officered largely by Korean graduates of the CTS, specifically targeted Korean independence fighters in the area such as Kim Il Sung and others, often closely affiliated with the Chinese communists, as enemies to be tracked down and killed. And even though the vast majority of Korean officers in the IJA or Manchukuo Army were not deployed against other Koreans seeking to overturn Japanese colonial rule, their decision to join the officer corps seems to argue against their possessing a nationalist outlook, or at least one that had as its core the political goal of declaring and setting up a completely independent Korean nation, free of Japanese control.

But, as Yun Haedong and other scholars have suggested, colonial life was full of "gray areas," and nationalism also came in different forms and degrees.[68] Like most Koreans at the time, it is probable that the young officer candidates simply accepted Japanese rule as a fait accompli, at least for the foreseeable future, and that they followed their personal ambitions as best they could given the conditions under which they lived. As Kim Tonghun (MMA 6) put it to me when I posed the question of nationalism: "Unless you were committed to the independence movement, you just lived your life like an ordinary person."[69] At the same time, one should not forget that for the MMA cadets, as for other Koreans, the conditions of ordinary life, whatever else they were, were of course also the conditions of a colonized people. Even though the GGK at the time was actively promoting an official wartime policy of assimilation and equality between Koreans and Japanese, ethnic prejudice and discrimination against Koreans remained a fact of everyday life in the colony, as evinced by Japanese treatment of Koreans at the Pusan ferry landing even as late as 1944–1945, when Chŏng Naehyŏk was a cadet at the JMA. And even if Koreans joining the officer corps might not have been particularly nationalistic in a political sense, they were acutely aware of Koreans' second-place status in colonial society and certainly felt a keen sense of what might be called ethnic consciousness, or even ethnic (as opposed to political) nationalism. Indeed, as noted above, one of the attractions of the officer corps for Korean men in the late colonial period was the opportunity it offered to assert themselves as Koreans in a profession of great esteem that hitherto had been closed to them precisely because of their ethnicity.

As Chŏng's story shows, an officer's uniform did indeed empower the Koreans who wore it, but it is also important to note that racial bigotry was not entirely absent even in the army, or at the academies. The MMA in fact offered a prime example of the disparity between rhetoric and reality in that regard. Like the new state it served, the Manchukuo Army and its premier training facility were officially committed to a policy of "ethnic harmony," but as in the Manchurian government administration and bureaucracy, the ideal of "harmony" did not necessarily translate into "equality," at least in the minds of many Japanese officers and cadets.[70] Although in the army at least rank always took precedence over ethnicity in the chain of command, a Japanese attitude of condescension, sometimes blatant but more often subtle, nevertheless tended to color interethnic relations, exacerbating latent tensions and leading occasionally even to open clashes.

To be fair, the Japanese themselves, or at least the officers and cadets at the MMA, were conflicted if not actually confused on this issue. Here the extant diary of one of Park Chung Hee's MMA 2 Nikkei classmates, Hosokawa Minoru, is especially revealing. On the one hand, it catalogs countless lectures to the Nikkei from MMA officials in the corps of cadets to remember and observe the "harmony of the five races" in all their everyday relations with their Mankei counterparts. From Superintendent Nagumo on down there was in fact at the MMA a steady clarion call of "Nikkei and

Mankei as One," and section commanders emphasized over and over again that although the Nikkei were Japanese citizens (*kokumin*), they were also citizens (*kokumin*) of Manchukuo and should not let pride in being Japanese turn into a "sense of superiority" (*yūetsukan*) toward their Mankei classmates. They should, rather, in Nagumo's words, strive for "heart-to-heart, soul-to-soul" relations in all their Mankei contacts.[71] Following the outbreak of the Pacific War in 1941, such language took on an even greater urgency, with MMA corps commanders only hours after Japan's attack on Pearl Harbor stressing that it was now more important than ever for Nikkei and Mankei to be "of one mind" and for the Nikkei to "abandon any feelings of superiority."[72] Many of the Nikkei cadets, for their part, seem to have made a genuine effort to live up to the ideal of ethnic harmony. Hosokawa, for example, a dutiful cadet with a troubled conscience on this issue, frequently reminded himself that "I love my fatherland [*sokoku*], but I am also a citizen [*kokumin*] of Manchukuo" and that "I am in the Manchukuo Army."[73] He often berated himself for succumbing to the Japanese "sense of superiority," and whenever he encountered Mankei cadets or native Chinese, as he once did on a Sunday excursion to Xinjing to buy souvenirs for his family, he consciously tried to keep in mind the ideal of ethnic harmony.[74]

The problem, however, was that such exhortation and effort toward ethnic harmony existed side by side with contradictory impulses and encouragements. Even though the Nikkei cadets were formally under the rule of the Manchukuo emperor, many, such as Nishikawa Nobuyoshi (MMA 7), thought of themselves as serving primarily the Japanese emperor.[75] And although they served together with Mankei officers in the Manchukuo Army, because they were Japanese their role was considered special. Hosokawa had written that "I am in the Manchukuo Army," but in another entry he also declared, echoing the views of his instructors, that "the Manchukuo Army is the armored train; the track is the Imperial Way; and the engine is the Nikkei."[76] What this meant in terms of the Nikkei-Mankei relationship was that the former had a "duty to lead the Mankei like an elder brother [*chōkei*] and to serve as a model to other peoples."[77] "We must remember," Hosokawa noted, that "we have come to Manchuria as messengers of the Japanese emperor to imperialize [*kōka*] a foreign people."[78]

The Nikkei cadets' sense of their special mission, inculcated by their teachers, only strengthened the very feeling of superiority they were being asked to renounce, subverting efforts at ethnic harmony and instead provoking feelings of rivalry or antagonism on both sides. MMA athletic competitions or field exercises thus often simultaneously became ethnic competitions, with the Nikkei feeling especially disgraced if their prowess and performance did not match their self-image as models and leaders.[79] On a joint Nikkei-Mankei summer march with heavy backpacks in the Dalian area in 1941, for example, Mitsui Katsuo (MMA 2) barely managed to avoid passing out from the intense heat. That was embarrassing enough for a cadet whose instructors were constantly telling him that he should be able to surmount all such physical challenges, but as Mitsui wrote later in a memoir, the greater mortification for him would have been for him, a Nikkei, to collapse in the presence of the Mankei.[80]

Demonstrable evidence of Mankei abilities could often evoke a grudging Nikkei admiration and a resolve to work harder to develop their own strength and stamina to a "superior" level, even in such activities as skating, where, as Hosokawa wrote, the Mankei were very skilled, "as one might expect."[81] But the Nikkei's sense of latent, if not always apparent, superiority also led some to act in an arrogant manner toward their non-Japanese peers, especially the Chinese, referring to them even in public not as "Mankei" but as "Man-chan," an infantilizing ethnic slur comparable in English to something like "little Chinks."[82]

Such behavior naturally conspired to make the Mankei feel that there was a certain hollowness at the core of the vaunted ideal of ethnic harmony. And even when they were not being subjected to offensive language, Mankei sensitivities about Japanese discrimination were fueled by other factors as well. One was the MMA's mess hall policy of regularly serving white rice to the Nikkei cadets and the less desirable staple sorghum to the Mankei on the assumption that the unfamiliar sorghum would make the Nikkei sick.[83] Although the policy was applied only to entering Nikkei in their first six months and eventually abolished altogether during the MMA 6 class residency in 1944, it was a constant source of bitterness among the Mankei cadets, who regarded it as simply another sign of Japanese prejudice. And for many of the Chinese Mankei cadets, the memory of Japan's ruthless and humiliating invasion and occupation of Manchuria only a few years earlier also worked to bolster perceptions of Japanese arrogance and bias and to intensify feelings of resentment.

The Mankei gave expression to these perceptions and feelings in a variety of ways. Some simply shrugged them off and moved on with their training. Others vowed to excel in their endeavors, surpassing their Japanese counterparts and thus proving them wrong. But some took a more confrontational stance as well, using their authority of rank to challenge and discipline Nikkei underclassmen who failed to observe proper military etiquette or who for one reason or another had not performed well in a school activity. And among the Chinese cadets, there were also not a few whose more radical social consciousness and sense of nationalism led them to form links with the Chinese Communist Party. (See Chapter 6.)

The small number of Korean cadets in the MMA classes found themselves in an ambiguous and sometimes difficult position, hovering somewhere between the Mankei and Nikkei.[84] Koreans in the first four MMA classes, including those in Park Chung Hee's MMA 2 class, were assigned to the Mankei group, placed in Mankei companies and sections, and lodged in the Mankei barracks.[85] On the other hand, most, including Park, had taken Japanese names, spoke and wrote far better Japanese than most of their Chinese Mankei classmates, and were already relatively well acclimated to Japanese cultural life from their school years. In fact, according to Park's MMA 2 Chinese classmate Gao Qingyin, the Koreans seemed so much like the Japanese that many of the Chinese cadets, especially those who harbored strong resentments against the Japanese occupation, disliked and even feared them.[86]

But the Koreans, who suffered from something less than full acceptance in the Mankei group, also had to face the same assumption of superiority from the Nikkei that so angered their Chinese classmates. To be sure, their relatively high level of comfort with Japanese language and culture and often outstanding performance in academy tasks insulated them to a certain extent from the worst of Japanese condescension, and the derogatory "Man-chan" was of course directed not at them but at the Chinese. And once the Koreans were formally incorporated into the Nikkei group—whether, like Park Chung Hee, through special selection after the *yoka* course in the earlier MMA classes, or routinely from the time of matriculation, as was the case in the later classes—the insulation was even greater. Kim Tonghun, who, along with other Koreans in the MMA 6 class, had been fully incorporated into the Nikkei group, felt little sense of difference or alienation as a Korean: "We weren't Japanese, we weren't Chinese, but something in-between. We weren't rulers, but we also weren't as oppressed as the Chinese at that time, when Japan was still in the early stages of colonizing Manchuria."[87]

Bigotry, like beauty, however, lies to some extent in the eyes of the beholder, and even if they had never encountered the police at the Pusan ferry, as Chŏng Naehyŏk had, or any overt discrimination from officers or other cadets at the MMA, many Korean cadets had reason from their own earlier life experiences to feel that Japanese did not necessarily regard them as equals in any real sense. Hosokawa, struggling himself to overcome his Nikkei prejudices, was brought face-to-face with this reality of Korean everyday life in January 1942, when he took a train up the peninsula on return to the MMA from a winter break in Japan. Indignant at the differential treatment the police on the train were meting out to Koreans and Japanese, he lamented that "such was still the case after more than thirty years since the annexation." "I felt sad for the Korean people," he wrote, adding: "And they too of course were feeling the pressures keenly."[88] But even for the best-intentioned Nikkei cadets, such as Hosokawa, attitudes and emotions in the racially diverse academy context were complicated. In interviews years later other Nikkei cadets from Park Chung Hee's MMA 2 class told me their feelings were very mixed, "half sympathetic toward the Koreans and Chinese, half not."[89] And of course suspicious or less sympathetic feelings on the part of Japanese classmates and instructors could create problems, or even lead to tragedy, as occurred at Zama at the end of the war (see the Conclusion). It was not surprising, therefore, that many of the Nikkei sensed a strong ethnic nationalism from Park and other Korean classmates that was of course strengthened by such Nikkei ambivalence. "Thinking back," Kaneko Tomio (MMA 2) said, "the Koreans must have had a difficult time, must have had very complex ideas in their hearts."[90]

On occasion such difficult times and complex ideas led to bursts of Korean anger, not least of all when a Korean cadet felt a Japanese classmate was underestimating his ability or putting him down, as happened once during a live-ammunition artillery exercise at the JMA when Park Chung Hee's fellow 1961 coup conspirator Yi Chuil (MMA 1) exploded at a Japanese classmate for unfairly blaming him for a weapon misfiring.[91] But for the most part Korean ethnic nationalism at both the MMA and JMA took the form of a competitive striving for excellence that aimed at matching or exceeding the best efforts of the Japanese cadets. Korean upperclassmen even made a point of visiting their Korean juniors soon after they entered the academy to enjoin them never to "lose out" to their Japanese classmates.[92] Those in the MMA 1 class, who took their role as the first MMA Korean "seniors" very seriously, were especially severe with their MMA 2 juniors, including Park Chung Hee, not only encouraging them with words but also, according to Kim Muk (MMA 2), checking up on them on a regular basis and administering physical discipline if any of them failed to live up to expectations.[93] So deeply rooted was the Korean drive to outperform the Japanese in this quintessentially Japanese world that it might well be said that far from erasing or diminishing a sense of Korean identity, the experience of academy life may actually have strengthened it for most Korean cadets.[94]

Embracing Academy Life

But ethnic pride and competition notwithstanding, not all cadets performed at the same level or adjusted to academy life with equal ease. For some it was just a question of ability or experience. Before entering the MMA many of the non-Japanese cadets, for example, especially the Chinese, had acquired little or no familiarity with Japanese customs and practices, including *kendō*, which was at the core of the academy's martial arts curriculum.[95] Some, such as Korean cadet Kim Muk (MMA 2), just could not stay on a horse and kept falling off.[96] Personalities and attitudes were important as well. Even though all who came through the gates of the academy entered voluntarily and with their eyes fixed on an eventual commission, not all, whether Japanese or non-Japanese, were necessarily as earnest and conscientious in following the regimen as others. Although he desired the education and prestige the MMA could give him, for example, Park Chung Hee's Chinese classmate Gao Qingyin was often as indifferent as he dared to be to the rules and regulations of the school, and he was also not infrequently annoyed, like many of the less diligent cadets, at those classmates who made a point of taking everything with the utmost seriousness.[97] There was, in fact, a well-established jargon at both the MMA and the JMA to describe such unremittingly earnest cadets and officers, but the adjective most frequently heard was *majime*. A common Japanese word, widely used then and now in civilian life, especially in schools, *majime* carries the meaning of "serious" or "serious-minded." At the academies and in the officer corps more generally in the 1940s it conjured up the image of a sharp, critical, strong, and silent man of few words and resolute behavior, a difficult-to-approach and at times even frightening "true believer" who embraced the academy and military life with a conviction and commitment that were clearly demonstrated in his speech and behavior. For cadets such as Gao, the *majime* cadet or officer was someone to be avoided if at all possible, as the task or activity he would supervise was certain to be carried out with the utmost strictness and attention to detail. As a classmate or senior, moreover, the *majime* cadet, always a favorite of the instructors, could be the bane of existence for less able or less dedicated cadets, a vexing standard against which their own attitudes and actions would be judged

and graded.[98] Given what has already been said, it should come as no surprise that Koreans were generally regarded as among the most *majime* of
cadets at the MMA in the 1940s, not least of all by their Chinese Mankei
classmates.[99] And if there was one Korean who for many seemed to stand
out above all as an archetype of the *majime* cadet, especially within the
MMA 2 class, it was Park Chung Hee. Given his central role in both the
1961 coup and the subsequent shaping of the Korean modernization state, it
is crucial to understand the full extent of Park's devotion to the IJA's *majime* ideal.

Park Chung Hee as Aspiring Officer

In a speech at his official retirement ceremony from the army in late August 1963, as he was preparing to run for the South Korean presidency later
that year, Park Chung Hee told the assembled soldiers of the ROK Fifth
Corps that "I have sought to pursue my philosophy of life solely within the
military."[100] Indeed, his embrace of the institution was deep and genuine.
Perhaps the first thing to note is Park's long-standing desire and determination to become an officer. When Park was a child, admission to the JMA was
practically still all but impossible for most Koreans, let alone for someone
like Park, born in 1917 as the youngest son of a dirt-poor peasant family in
Kumi, a small village about fifty miles northwest of Taegu.[101] But he had been
drawn, like Yi Hallim and other young Korean boys at the time, to images
and stories of famous military figures. He had also been drawn to the sights
of actual soldiers from the Chōsen Army on maneuvers in his hometown
area, and he once told Yu Yangsu (Yoo Yangsoo), another ROKA officer who
would join the coup in 1961 and serve the Park government in many important capacities, that he had been captivated at the time by the Chōsen Army
officers in their uniforms and large, high-crowned hats.[102] "As a boy, I had a
profound yearning to be a soldier," he later wrote of those years:

> On occasion the Japanese 80th Infantry Regiment based in
> Taegu would come into the Kumi area for field exercises, and
> watching them, I thought how much I would like to be a soldier.
> As an elementary school student, I loved the great figures in
> Japanese history that we learned about in our Japanese-style ed-
> ucation. And then as a fifth-grader, I read Yi Kwangsu's biog-

raphy of Yi Sunsin and came to revere the admiral. As a sixth-grader, I read a biography of Napoleon, and he became an idol.[103]

Park's subsequent five years as a student at Taegu Normal School only cemented his fascination with soldiering and with Japanese military practice in particular. As noted earlier, the school, like the society, was becoming increasingly militarized from 1932, the year Park entered. And Park himself, who despite the privations of poverty had won a coveted tuition-free admission to the prestigious teacher's college after compiling an exceptional record at his elementary school and passing the TNS entrance exam, was gradually losing interest in his academic course of study while simultaneously discovering and reveling in all the school's military-related activities.[104] According to his TNS classmates, his zest for martial bugling was matched by his enthusiasm for the required military drills and exercises that were associated with it, exhausting activities that many of the other students disliked. Even outside of the scheduled drill periods, he could often be found lingering on the drilling grounds, or near the armory, where the school's rifles and machine guns and other military equipment used in training were stored.[105] Japanese sword fighting or kendō, another required activity unpopular with many TNS students, not least of all because of the physical pain it involved, was for Park a particular passion.[106] Sŏ Pyŏngguk, one of his dorm mates at the school in 1935–1936, remembered how Park, alone among all the students, would go each morning in kendō gear to practice his striking techniques with the bamboo sword (shinai) on a fence that separated TNS from the adjacent Taegu Commercial College, and how in the spring he would wield the shinai to slice off the blossoms on a cherry tree that stood on the commercial college's side of the fence.[107] In his final year, when each student was asked to choose a pose for the school graduation album that best reflected his personality and interests, Park elected to have a frontal photograph of himself taken in full kendō regalia, poised in the sport's classic "middle stance" (chūdan no kamae): right foot slightly forward, eyes fixed straight ahead, and shinai at the ready for attack or defense.[108]

Park's growing enchantment with the Japanese military at TNS was greatly deepened by his personal interaction for the first time with actual Japanese officers and soldiers. Some of this contact took place during the week or so of on-site military training at the Chōsen Army's 80th Infantry Regiment in Taegu that all TNS students were required to take, but the most sustained and important interface occurred during the drill sessions at the school, which were conducted by a team of by IJA officers from the regiment, including one lieutenant colonel, one second lieutenant, and one warrant officer. The ranking officer and chief instructor, Lieutenant Colonel Arikawa Shuichi, was the key figure here, not only singling Park out during drills as a model for the other students but also providing Park with a model he could emulate.[109] And that model, as Arikawa's friends, classmates, and fellow officers would later testify in a postwar tribute, was very much the epitome of a *majime* IJA commander—a term that they frequently used to describe Arikawa's personality and his performance in combat. Born into a rural samurai family (*gōshi*) with a long history of feudal ties to the illustrious Shimazu clan of the Kagoshima area on both his father's and his mother's side, he had been the first-ranking cadet in his JMA preparatory class in all subjects, including *kendō,* and had graduated from the JMA itself in 1913 in the upper echelon of the JMA 25 class.[110] At TNS he was a strict taskmaster, demanding the same high standards and supreme effort from his Korean students as from the small minority of Japanese who also attended the school, perhaps because he had directly observed the soldierly potential of Koreans when he was a cadet at the JMA.[111] In any case, it was a reputation that would follow Arikawa throughout his subsequent postings in Korea, China, and finally Okinawa, where, as a lieutenant general and brigade commander confronting hopeless odds, he would wrap his arms around a 10-kilogram (22.5 pounds) depth bomb in the unit headquarters and blow himself up in a suicide pact with his staff and men.[112]

While neither Park nor Arikawa himself could have imagined what lay ahead for the forty-four-year-old lieutenant colonel when he first appeared at TNS in 1935, Arikawa was for Park a living incarnation of a world and culture he was coming more and more to idealize and aspire toward. His classmates began to notice the seriousness with which Park approached all aspects of the school's military training—not only the bugling and the drills but even the required dress. Most of the TNS students paid minimal attention to the look of their uniforms, especially the calf-length cotton army puttees (*kyahan*) that had to be laboriously wound and strapped around their legs in typical IJA infantry fashion, and also frequently replaced, as they wore out very quickly. But Park took his cue from Arikawa's own attention to such details and always appeared on the training grounds looking like a smartly turned-out young cadet. As his TNS classmate Hwangbo Kyun told me, "You know, we would just tie those leggings on any which way, but not Park. He was meticulous—right up there at a level with JMA cadets. We suspected from that time that he was already thinking about becoming a soldier."[113]

Indeed he was, and that thinking only intensified after Park graduated from TNS in the spring of 1937 and was appointed to a teaching position (*kundō*) at Mun'gyŏng Elementary School (Mun'gyŏng Sŏbu Kongnip Simsang Sohakkyo), about seventy miles northwest of Taegu. Many if not most Koreans in colonial Korea would have looked upon such a job as a godsend, combining as it did the traditional prestige Koreans reserved for education and teachers with a steady and comfortable income.[114] But as Korea's second wave of militarization began to move into high gear with the fighting in China beginning in July 1937 and the GGK's establishment of a volunteer soldier system for Korean recruits in January 1938, Park became increasingly more intent on securing admission to a Japanese military academy and becoming an officer. Park's resolve to become an officer was undoubtedly reinforced by his unhappy personal situation at the time: an unwelcome arranged marriage essentially forced upon him in 1936 by his family to placate his aging and sick father. But there is no question that what was fundamentally driving him was his passion and ambition for a military career.[115] During the three months from May to the end of July 1938 that he roomed with another teacher at Mun'gyŏng, Yu Chŭngsŏn (Ryu Chungsun), sharing night service duty at the school, Park "talked almost continuously about becoming a soldier, how he could he fulfill all his ambitions only by becoming a soldier," according to Yu. "Never did he talk about his teaching career."[116]

Park also sought out Yu's advice on how to gain entrance to a military academy. Here Park's frustration was heightened by the fact that by 1938 he was past the age of admission for the JMA's affiliated preparatory school, the main gateway to the JMA itself. He knew, however, of the opening of the MMA in Xinjing, perhaps from a newspaper article that had appeared on the front page of *Tonga ilbo* on April 26, 1938, only a month before he and Yu had begun rooming together, and he told Yu that he thought the new school in Manchuria might be more flexible about age limits than the schools in Japan. But there was yet another stumbling block. Park had no connections in Manchuria, and he had no idea how to proceed. After much discussion with Yu, in the end Park decided to send a handwritten letter directly to the MMA explaining his situation and vowing to "to die for the greater good" (*isshi gohōkō*) of Manchukuo and Japan if the school would make an exception and permit him to join the officer corps. Together with his letter, Park enclosed a photograph and curriculum vitae, a copy of his family registry, a certification of his TNS military training, and a "blood pledge" (J: *kessho*; K: *hyŏlsŏ*), written and signed on a sheet of rice paper literally in his own blood, to reiterate and emphasize his willingness to serve to the death.

By the beginning of August Park and Yu had moved to separate lodgings, and Park waited in vain for a positive response from Manchuria. Whether he received a negative response or, indeed, any response at all is not clear, but in March 1939, about eight months after composing the original letter, Park, still not giving up hope, sent a second letter with a "blood pledge" that was received by the Manchukuo Ministry of War and found its way into the *Manshū shinbun,* one of the Japanese-language newspapers published in Xinjing. The resulting article, entitled "Blood Pledge from a Young Korean Teacher: Volunteers to be an Officer," excerpted parts of Park's letter and reported in its conclusion that the Ministry of War had "regrettably" and "politely" turned Park down because of the army's age restrictions.[117]

It is of course impossible to say, but postcolonial Korean history might well have taken a very different turn if Park's ambitions to follow in the footsteps of his first military mentor, Arikawa Shuichi, had ended at that moment, as one might well have expected, with the ministry's refusal to allow him to join the Manchukuo Army. But, as was so often the case in his life both before and after 1945, Park was lucky. Kang Chaeho, a Korean in Manchuria who shared Park's regional roots in the Kyŏngsang area of the peninsula, happened to read the *Manshū shinbun* article and was moved to act. More to the point, he was also in a position to act. Kang was a Manchukuo army captain who had graduated from the CTS (CTS 4) and was at that time one of the officers helping to organize and train the Jiandao Special Force in the southeastern Manchurian town of Yanbian. He wrote Park offering his assistance. And in October 1939, as one of the proctoring officers, he arranged for Park to bypass the regular application process and take the MMA 2 entrance examinations, both physical and written, at the Sixth District Army headquarters in Mudanjiang, about 180 miles from Yanbian. Six months later Park was at the MMA, finally wearing the uniform of an academy cadet.[118]

Park Chung Hee as Model Cadet

Once in uniform and free at last to pursue his true calling, Park's devotion to the *majime* ideal, already incipient in his Taegu and Mun'gyŏng years and explicitly stated in his letter to the MMA authorities, quickly began to manifest itself on the grounds of the academy. Even his MMA 2 Korean classmate Yi Hallim, who had *majime* aspirations of his own, was impressed by the "commanding" way in which Park from the beginning walked about with his shoulders stretched back and chest thrust forward, despite his small stature.[119]

And Park's actual performance at the academy proved to be a match for his swagger. All graduating cadets were graded and ranked at both the *yoka* and *honka* levels on the basis of their combined academic and *kun'iku* records, and although we do not have his academy transcripts or precise ranking, it is clear that Park excelled in his studies and training, especially at the MMA. Not only was he chosen as one of the few Mankei cadets who would be sent to Japan to complete his *honka* training at the JMA, but at the MMA 2 *yoka* graduation on March 23, 1942, he was one of only five cadets, and the only Korean, in a combined Mankei-Nikkei class of 418 graduates to be singled out as an honor cadet and given an imperial prize (*onshi shōkin*) by the Manchukuo emperor's aide-de-camp.[120] The prize was a telling indication of the spirit with which Park approached academy life and the army more generally. During the war years of the 1940s, the army had explicitly ordered the subordination of the academic division of the academies to its *kun'iku* counterpart, and most of the teaching positions even in the academic division came to be held by officers rather than civilians. Similarly, in the IJA's system of academy grading and ranking in this period a graduate's final class standing came to depend overwhelmingly on his *kun'iku* record, which the army regarded as the best indication of a cadet's level of seriousness with respect to IJA principles and practices—a measure, as it were, of his *majime* character.[121]

Park's high standing at the MMA actually went far beyond his class ranking. Just as Arikawa had often pointed to Park as a model for other students during military drills at TNS, so too did Park's section commander at the MMA often call on him to correct other cadets who had fumbled tactical and other problems being posed in training sessions, a pedagogical technique widely promoted in academy manuals of using outstanding cadets to teach and inspire their classmates. (See Chapter 8.) Park was in fact the type of cadet known in academy parlance as a *gomin*, a "model cadet" who was "superior in his studies and exemplary in his conduct," and who as an upperclassman was often selected to barrack in first-year sections and serve as a "counselor cadet" (*shidō seito*) for entering classes.[122] And while the *gomin* could indeed sometimes teach and inspire, he could also be a source of humiliation for classmates who for one reason or another were not as quick or accomplished. One of Park's MMA 2 Chinese section mates, Xu Shudong, who at first was able to understand only about half of what was being said in classes and training because of his imperfect Japanese, vividly remembered the embarrassment he felt on the numerous occasions when Park responded "correctly and clearly" to questions he had failed to answer.[123] And for many of the cadets, the *gomin*, always so serious and proper, was also a bit of a daunting figure—the kind of person, in the words of a Japanese cadet (JMA 57) who had overlapped with Park at the JMA, one could actually imagine "charging gloriously to death at the head of his unit in battle."[124]

But Park was not just a *gomin* at the MMA. He was a *gomin* among the *gomin*. Indeed, he was a special favorite of the superintendent himself, Nagumo Shin'ichirō. Such a relationship was not at all common. Time and again in interviews with former MMA cadets of all nationalities, I was told how little actual contact they had had with officers at the MMA or JMA apart from their section and company commanders, their immediate supervisors. The other officers were simply "too high," in the words of several of Park's Japanese classmates.[125] And Nagumo was of course the highest of them all. Gao Qingyin, Park's MMA 2 Chinese classmate and never one to mince words, described Nagumo as "too high, a big shot, short, and pompous." "At most," Gao recalled, "I saw him only two or three times."[126]

Park, however, saw Nagumo frequently, and not only at formal academy events. According to several of Park's MMA 2 Japanese classmates, Nagumo "liked Park" and "frequently invited him to his house."[127] And in a personal letter in response to queries about his father, Nagumo Katsurō (JMA 54), the superintendent's eldest son, related how he had met Park on one such occasion. The younger Nagumo had graduated in 1940 in the top 5 percent of his JMA infantry class, which had numbered more than a thousand cadets, and he had been dispatched to northeastern Manchuria as an officer with his home regiment.[128] During his deployment he had once stopped to visit his father at the MMA and joined an evening gathering at the superintendent's residence with a number of selected cadets. Before the cadets arrived, the elder Nagumo had told his son that he would seat him next to Park Chung Hee, a particularly "outstanding" cadet in the MMA 2 class, and in the course of the evening Park made a deep impression on the young officer, who himself had compiled an enviable academy record. Undoubtedly the younger Nagumo's view mirrored his father's and captured something of the way in which Park was perceived by the highest officials of the school at the time. "He and I were the same age," Nagumo Katsurō wrote, "and from his conversation, language, and attitude, I strongly sensed a fierce energy [*seikan na kihaku*] and brilliance."[129]

The superintendent's special fondness for Park and eagerness to have his son meet him takes on added significance with respect to Park's demeanor and performance at the academy when one considers Nagumo Shin'ichirō's stern reputation as a *majime* officer with a penchant for correctness. So formidable, in fact, was Nagumo's reputation as a disciplinarian that even the Kwantung Army initially had doubts about hiring him for the superintendency. Kagawa Yoshio (JMA 35), a Kwantung Army major general at the time who had interviewed Nagumo for the post, recalled fearing that after twelve years at the JMA and with his "extraordinary self-confidence and terrible temper," Nagumo might actually be too inflexible to adjust to the complicated environment of the MMA, with its mix of different ethnicities and large numbers of cadets such as Xu Shudong, who were far less prepared for academy life than anyone Nagumo had ever encountered in Japan. Indeed, it was only after Kagawa had spoken frankly and at length to Nagumo about the Kwantung Army's concerns and assured himself that Nagumo fully understood the situation that he finally recommended him for the job.[130] Clearly one of the main reasons Nagumo gave Park such special attention was that in Park he was certain he had found a cadet who was "in no way inferior" to the most *majime* cadets of the JMA, to whom he had so long been an exacting mentor.[131]

Park Chung Hee as Zealous Cadet

To appreciate the depth of Park's devotion to the *majime* ideal, it is necessary to understand that Park was not merely a model cadet. His blood pledge to the MMA authorities, his assumption of a masterful posture from the moment of matriculation, and the "fierce energy" that had so impressed Nagumo's son were all expressions of a passion for the culture and practices of the IJA that bordered on the zealous—what Kim Chongsin, who later served as Park's chief secretary for society and media in the 1960s and 1970s, when Park was in the Blue House, and who spent hours working closely with him on a variety of biographical and autobiographical materials, described as an "intoxication with the 'samurai spirit.'"[132]

Such zealousness undoubtedly reflected certain basic personality traits. Even in his early years Park was known as a man of intense, unqualified likes and dislikes. As Yu Chŭngsŏn, his colleague and roommate at Mun'gyŏng, put it: "If he disliked something, he disliked it absolutely; if he liked something, he liked it absolutely."[133] And such absolutist sensibility often led to behavior that others less intense or more equivocal found excessive, as in the case of Park's fastidiousness in dressing for TNS military drill, or his seemingly obsessive fixation on perfecting his *kendō* strikes. A particularly indicative example here, perhaps, was Park's way of expressing his admiration at the time for certain figures he regarded as heroes, whether historical or contemporary. In addition to Napoleon, Park was strongly drawn to both Benito Mussolini and Adolf Hitler, whose images filled the pages of 1930s Korean and Japanese newspapers and magazines, along with countless stories of Italian and German economic and military resurgence under their leadership.[134] To be sure, admiration for the two dictators as national saviors was not unusual at the time among TNS students, or more generally in Japan and Korea. While reading Mussolini's autobiography in 1929, for example, Yun Ch'iho had scarcely been able to contain his enthusiasm for the Italian leader. "What an ability, what an integrity, what a common sense, what an energy that man must have!" Yun had written in his diary in February that year.[135] But Park took such feelings to another level, turning admiration into something closer to veneration. As a fourth-year student at TNS in 1935–1936, he bought and studied on his own an early Japanese version of *Mein Kampf*.[136] He also kept two "very large" scrolled pictures in his dormitory, one of Mussolini and one of Hitler, which in a daily morning ritual of reverence he unrolled, hung up side by side, and bowed before, to the astonishment of his fellow students.[137] As this story suggests, Park's tendency toward zealous dedication seems to have been fueled by a strong sense of self—a self, moreover, that strove to be exceptional in its loyalties and devotions, a self that was willing to stand apart from peers, indeed, almost willfully bent on doing so. Zealousness in that sense seemed both an inner psychic drive toward total commitment and a visible assertion of separateness and difference.

Academy life gave Park full rein to develop and exercise such deeply rooted personal propensities. To be sure, his dedication to IJA norms and aloofness with peers was such that even many of his own MMA 2 classmates, whether Korean, Chinese, or Japanese, found it extreme. Often it was the little things that were most telling and long remembered. Xu Shudong (MMA 2) recalled how Park preferred to wear an official MMA summer hat even in the bitter cold of the Manchurian winter because it was more striking and imposing than its winter counterpart, and also how once when the cadets were given too little food on a visit to a mine, all except Park asked for more, even though he, like the others, was famished. "He was always alone," Xu continued. "He always acted superior to the other students. He thought he was different from the other students, and because of his actions, behavior, other cadets thought he was superior or proud. He was that way even with the other Korean cadets."[138] And Park's Korean class-mate Kim Muk (MMA 2) noted how Park preferred to spend his Sunday leaves not with his classmates but with senior Korean officers in Xinjing already commissioned in the Manchukuo Army, such as Wŏn Yongdŏk and Chŏng Ilgwŏn.[139]

To his peers Park was thus something of an enigma, brilliant and self-assured, but also generally silent when not explicitly addressed, and often alone with his own thoughts. And he was invariably earnest and correct to a fault in all aspects of academy life and training. Indeed, he exhibited a zeal that seemed so excessive to many of his classmates that, behind his back, according to Xu Shudong, he was given the nickname *baka-majime* or "crazy-serious."[140] But zealousness at the academy was of course no obstacle to be-coming an officer. Indeed, it was an attribute to be prized and praised, a *kun'iku* desideratum that also testified to a cadet's character as a potential commander. And here, one suspects, in this seamless match between person-ality and profession, lay the core of Park's devotion to the culture and prac-tices of the IJA.

The militarization of the 1930s and 1940s was a historical juggernaut, cre-ating or reshaping institutions and molding large numbers of Korean men into soldiers for the first time since the late Chosŏn dynasty. Apart from the army itself, the most militarized of the institutions were the officer acade-mies of Japan and Manchuria. And the exigencies of war, especially in the 1940s, had widened the gates of these schools for Koreans as well as Japa-nese, giving birth in the end to a small Korean professional officer corps that would later play a role in postcolonial history whose importance far out-weighed its numbers. For most if not all of these men, subjects of an impe-rium in which the IJA seemed to rule as well as to fight, their years at the academies were transformative and empowering, and they both strove and were exhorted to strive by their seniors to excel in their training. In time historical continuities and contingencies would combine to raise one of them, Park Chung Hee, above the rest, and Park's *baka-majime* seriousness would eventually come to shape and pervade South Korea's modernization state and society in the 1960s and 1970s.

But what exactly did it mean to be *majime*, let alone *baka-majime*, in the academy context of the 1940s? How did Park and other Korean cadets at the MMA actually experience the "samurai spirit" that had so captivated Park and later came to mark his approach to governing? The world of the acade-mies in the 1940s was in fact a crucible of conditioning in which military culture and practice were infused with particular political, socioeconomic, and behavioral perspectives, all as natural to the *majime* IJA officer as wearing a uniform or carrying a sword. It is time now to enter that world, to step through its gates and explore some of its most salient features. We begin with the political dimension.

Emperor Kojong in the military uniform of the Great Han Empire (1900). From *Sajin ŭro ponŭn tongnip undong* 1.

Park Chung Hee in
Taegu Normal School
graduation photo
(1937). Courtesy of
Yi Sŏngjo.

Park Chung Hee playing bugle at Taegu Normal School (1937). Park is the smallest
figure, at far right. Courtesy of Yi Sŏngjo.

Park Chung Hee in *kendō* uniform at Taegu Normal School (1937). Courtesy of Yi Sŏngjo.

有川先生

Lieutenant Colonel Arikawa Shuichi at Taegu Normal School (1937). Courtesy of Yi Sŏngjo.

後藤先生の教練

Military drill at Taegu Normal School (1937). Courtesy of Yi Sŏngjo.

Torikai Ikoma, Taegu Normal School principal 1934–1939.
Courtesy of Yi Sŏngjo.

Park Chung Hee (left) and Yu Chŭngsŏn (right) surrounded by their students at
Mun'gyŏng Elementary School (April 1939). Courtesy of Yu Chŭngsŏn.

Manchurian Military Academy main building. From *Dōtokudai*.

Grounds seen from Manchurian Military Academy main building. From *Dōtokudai*.

Manchurian Military Academy buglers. From *Dōtokudai*.

Manchurian Military Academy cadet barracks. From *Dōtokudai*.

Manchurian Military Academy cadet self-study room. From *Dōtokudai*.

Lieutenant General Nagumo Shin'ichirō, Manchurian Military Academy superintendent 1940–1943. From *MG*.

Manchukuo emperor Puyi formally opening Manchurian Military Academy (July 1941). From *Dōtokudai.*

Park Chung Hee receiving award at Manchurian Military Academy 2 graduation ceremony (March 23, 1942). From *Manshū nichi-nichi shinbun.*

Park Chung Hee during Manchurian Military Academy regimental attachment duty (*taizuki*) in the Kwantung Army's 30th Infantry Regiment in Harbin (July 1942). Park is the figure standing at far left. Hosokawa is the third figure from the right in the second row from the top. Courtesy of Hosokawa Akio.

Manchurian Military Academy 6 and 7 Korean cadets (Xinjing 1945). Kim Yun'gŭn (sitting) is in the front row at far left. Kim Kwangsik (sitting and wearing glasses) is in the same row, third from the right. Courtesy of Kim Kwangsik.

PART TWO

Academy Culture and Practice

FOUR

POLITICS AND STATUS

Special Favor

And this man is now become a god.
—William Shakespeare, *Julius Caesar*

The goal of this school's education . . . is to cultivate officers capable of
becoming the axle of well-being of the entire nation.
—General Ushijima Mitsuru, JMA superintendent, October 1, 1942

Officers must always be in the vanguard of their time . . . not only in the
army but also in the nation.
—Park Chung Hee, February 26, 1962

Early in the morning of May 16, 1961, Major General Park Chung Hee sent
a handwritten letter to ROK Army Chief of Staff Chang Toyŏng asking him
to take command of the military forces that Park and his associates had assembled to seize control of the South Korean government. Park's desire for
Chang to assume a leadership role was more likely a tactical maneuver to
secure the support of the army as a whole than a sincere desire to place
Chang at the head of the coup. Indeed, less than two months later, Chang
had been removed from that position and his place taken by Park himself.
Whatever Park's actual motives in seeking to involve Chang in the mutiny,
the brief letter he sent Chang that morning tersely encapsulated what is
perhaps the most fundamental element in the cluster of ideas, dispositions,
and practices that defined the Park Chung Hee modernization state: the sense
Park and his men had that they alone, as military officers, were uniquely
placed and equipped to save the country, and, moreover, that they had both
the obligation and the right to do so. As Park wrote in his letter to Chang: "We
have undertaken this decisive life-or-death action with an unshakeable sense
of national mission, and in the firm and unalterable belief that there is absolutely no other means to save the state and nation in its current extremity and
guarantee a prosperous tomorrow."[1]

It is hardly surprising that the military officers of national armies should
be imbued with a commitment to protect the state and nation. But the sense

of national mission expressed by Park in his letter went far beyond that, implying a privileged place and role for the military in political as well as military affairs. This orientation has a complicated lineage in Korea both before and after 1945, but here we explore its earlier pre-1945 traces, focusing particularly on the world of the military academies that Park and other Koreans attended in Manchuria and Japan in the 1930s and 1940s. In the highly militaristic atmosphere of the times, it was a world where repeated incantations of the cadets' "special favor" (*shugū*) and "singular duty" (*tokui no shokubun*) in the academies' *Regulations (Kokoroe)* and in the regular admonitory and morale-building lectures (*kunji* or *kunwa*) that the cadets had to memorize could easily be interpreted by both instructors and students as providing a moral basis for mutiny. Above all this was possible because of the IJA officer's sense that he occupied a special, even unique place of prestige and honor in 1940s Japanese imperial society. In fact, the officers were told that the "special favor" bestowed on them came directly from the emperor himself and gave them, as the *Regulations* explicitly stated, an "elite standing in society."[2] When Park and his MMA 2 classmates were formally matriculated at the JMA on October 1, 1942, for the regular or *honka* course of study, their final two years of officer training, the superintendent, Ushijima Mitsuru (JMA 20), personally addressed them (and the JMA 57 class with which they would henceforth be associated) in his welcoming *kunji* with yet another phrase, also in the *Regulations,* commonly used to describe the officer corps: "the axle of well-being of the entire nation."[3]

For Chosŏn-dynasty Koreans, such phrases exalting the status of military officers would have sounded strange, even bizarre, but for Park and other Koreans assembled on the JMA parade grounds listening to Ushijima on that early fall afternoon, they were no longer so. As we have seen, many of the negative traditional attitudes in Korea toward the military had undergone considerable change since the late nineteenth century, and Koreans of Park's generation in particular had grown up and been schooled in an atmosphere of hypermilitarism, where words of praise for the soldierly life rolled off the tongue of colonial instructors easily and frequently, and where military officers in particular were symbols of respect and authority.

Still, the academies were unique institutions, intense and relentless in pursuit of their goals. Even if cadets before entering had had some idea of the "special favor" that was associated with the military officer, and even if they might have been drawn to apply for admission for that very reason, academy training and life tended to reinforce, develop, and inscribe a sense of the differences of the officer's world from that of the civilian in very deep and personal ways. So profound were these cultural "distinctions," to borrow the term from Bourdieu, that the cadets invariably received a great "shock" on entering.[4] Indeed, it was not at all unusual for cadets to refer to life outside the academy as *shaba*, a Zen Buddhist term, originally from Sanskrit, denoting the mundane, earthly world they had left behind when they entered the MMA and JMA.[5]

Place

The distinctions of academy life began with the places themselves. As befitting what were essentially military bases, both the MMA and the JMA were physically separated from the society around them by walls and sentry gates. They were also both geographically set apart from the outside world by a buffer of time and space. In the Meiji period the preparatory (*yoka*) and main (*honka*) courses for the Japanese officer corps had originally been located together in the Ichigaya environs of Tokyo, when the reach of the capital city was far more limited and that area still consisted largely of rice fields. As Tokyo expanded both in area and population, especially after the Kantō earthquake of 1923, and the numbers of cadets increased dramatically following the outbreak of war in China, the *yoka* and *honka* courses were divided, each established as a separate school with its own facilities and personnel, including its own superintendent. The *yoka* institution, officially known as the Rikugun Yoka Shikan Gakkō or JMA Preparatory Academy (JMAP), remained at Ichigaya until 1941 when it was moved to the vicinity of Asaka in Saitama prefecture, northwest of Tokyo. The *honka* institution, the official JMA, was moved to the Zama area in Kanagawa prefecture even earlier, in September 1937, and it was here that all the Korean cadets sent by the MMA completed their academy training.[6]

The new school was about 40 kilometers (25 miles) southwest of Tokyo, about fifty minutes away by train on the then still relatively new Odakyū line from Shinjuku station. Zama at the time was still a small town (*machi*) with a population of about 6,000. The setting, on the plains of the Sagami River, surrounded by woods and mulberry fields stretching out toward the foothills of Mt. Ōyama and the Tanzawa mountain range, was rural and secluded. As if to emphasize further its separation from the civilian world, the precise site chosen for the new JMA, in keeping with Japanese military academy custom, was at a slightly higher elevation than the surrounding terrain, and it was given an honorary formal name by the emperor that included the suffix *dai* ("high place" or "heights"). Just as the old JMA had been commonly known as Ichigayadai, the new JMA at Zama was henceforth called Sōbudai.[7]

The MMA, which offered both *yoka* and *honka* courses, also had an imperial name, Dōtokudai, chosen by the Manchurian emperor to symbolize the "common virtue" (*dōtoku*) of Manchukuo and Japan.[8] It was located in Lalatun, a hilly area about 10 kilometers (6.25 miles) southeast of the new capital city of Xinjing.[9] The academy was set back from the road connecting Xinjing with Jilin to the east by a side road that ran about 300 meters (about 1,000 feet) to the main gate.[10] Even as late as the 1990s, when I was given a tour of the former MMA, then an elite tank technology school for the PRC's People's Liberation Army, the surrounding area was still virtually undeveloped, with thick forests and fields in every direction. In the spring of 1939, when the first class of cadets (MMA 1) entered, the city of Xinjing, a three-hour walk from the academy for the cadets, was still being built and was only a fraction of the size of its successor, Changchun, today.[11] In a private history of the MMA 1 class compiled by surviving classmates for their personal use and remembrance, one finds a description of the academy site that vividly captures its remoteness at the time:

The main road from Xinjing to Jilin was called Jilin Avenue or Kitsurin Kaidō in Japanese. Nanguan was the name of the eastern edge of the city of Xinjing. Crossing the Yitong river at Nanguan, and continuing east a bit along the Kitsurin Kaidō, one reached Erdaohezi. From the center of Xinjing to Nanguan, the streets had a modern look, but from Nanguan to Erdaohezi, the houses were traditional Chinese. Especially in Erdaohezi, with its lines of Tibetan-style homes and storehouses that looked like boiled fish cake loaves [*kamaboko*], one had a strong feeling of being in a foreign country. From Nanguan and Erdaohezi the road ran straight east, and except for two or three small villages scattered here and there, all one could see were fields and fields of sorghum [*gaoliang*], with the Kitsurin Kaidō running through the middle of them. About 8 kilometers [4.97 miles] from Erdaohezi, the road angled to the right, then followed a straight line for 2 kilometers [1.24 miles]. At that point the road bent sharply to the left in the direction of Jilin, entering an area of hills piled up on one another, with the Shibeiling peak visible on the right. It was in the rolling hills to the right of this sharp [left] crook in the Kitsurin Kaidō that our academy was located.[12]

Appearance

Once ensconced in the heights of Lalatun, where all the MMA attendees began their *yoka* course, including those such as Park who later went on to Zama for the *honka,* the new officer recruits began to take on the unique appearance and manners of the academy cadet or *seito.* The first thing to change was their hair. By the 1940s the once fashionable "modern boy" or *mobo* look, with its sleekly combed-back long locks, a style suited for the prewar *shaba,* had to a great extent disappeared even from civilian society, but the academies took the new wartime trend toward short-clipped male hair even further. Upon entering the *yoka,* the MMA cadets, like their counterparts at the JMAP in Asaka, were informed that they had to have their "heads replaced" (*sugekaeru*), and they soon found themselves completely shaved in the *bōzugari* manner of Buddhist monks, a style they were strictly required to maintain throughout their academy years.[13]

As with hair, so with dress. On entering the *yoka,* cadets also had to surrender their personal attire, which was stored away in a box tagged with their name.[14] In return they were provided with the distinctive uniforms of their school, including, in the case of the MMA, hats and caps emblazoned with a five-color, five-pointed star symbolizing the idealized harmony of the different ethnic groups that constituted the Manchukuo state and army.[15] Cadets were required to wear their new clothes outside the schools as well, where the uniforms tended to elicit respect and deference, thus confirming the cadets in their sense of themselves as a social elite.[16] As we saw in Chapter 3 in the case of the Korean cadet Chŏng Naehyŏk (JMA 58), even when encountering other military men the cadets came to expect such deference. This was especially so once they graduated from the *yoka,* where they had no official army rank, and entered the *honka* as officer candidates, where they began to receive periodic promotions in the noncommissioned grades. Hiruma Hiroshi, a member of the JMA 57 class, remembered angrily striking an elderly soldier near the Yasukuni Shrine and knocking off his hat because he had failed to salute. He also remembered confronting an older noncommissioned officer on horseback for the same reason, demanding that the man dismount and salute. As with Chŏng, military etiquette gave precedence to Hiruma as a JMA cadet. "Even though we were both corporals," Hiruma noted, "my rank of corporal as a JMA officer candidate was higher."[17]

Language

As new *seito,* the cadets were expected to cultivate a particular way of speaking and writing. Part of their instruction included what was called *gōrei chōsei,* or "command voice modulation," a daily outdoor group exercise after the evening meal that was designed to train them to shout orders in the blunt, stentorian style of commanding officers, essential for leading troops in the noise and chaos of battle.[18] Even forty years after his *seito* experience, one of Park Chung Hee's MMA 2 Japanese classmates, Wada Toshio, could still clearly hear in his mind the roar of young male voices reverberating throughout the Dōtokudai grounds at twilight as the MMA 1 and MMA 2 cadets attempted to outdo one another in shouting out the chopped Japanese verbs of command.[19] The cadets were also trained to write, even to their families, in an antiquated *sōrōbun* epistolary style favored by the officer corps and government officials, a formal and highly Sinicized form of correspondence that marked the writer as a person of dignity and authority.[20]

Language itself was a distinguishing marker of the academy cadet. Over time the schools had come to develop a special vocabulary that constituted one of their many layers of tradition, and the usage and mastery of this argot became part of the *seito* identity that cadets carried with them for the rest of their lives. So different in some cases was this new language from that of the outside world that entering cadets could not at first even understand what was being said to them.[21]

Much of the new language the cadets had to master was commonly used throughout the Japanese and Japanese-trained Manchukuo armies as a whole. In addition to a wide array of professional terms and expressions specifically concerned with army training and combat, there were also colloquial terms for army-related equipment and uniforms, including bayonets and regulation hats; for the martial arts, such as *kendō* and *jūdō;* and for various officer ranks, such as recently commissioned lieutenants, who were called *shinpin* or "new items."[22]

Most of the army branches had a nickname, often with an onomatopoeic twist; the infantry, for example, which Park Chung Hee would choose, was known as *bata,* from the "bata-bata" sound of boots fast-marching in unison, while the artillery branch was called *gara,* from the "gara-gara" clattering sound of heavy guns being rolled along. There were also slang terms for various kinds of food, drink, and cigarettes, such as the *busu mochi* (ugly rice cake) that was "pimpled" with beans, as well as terms for money, women, toilets, lunch boxes, notebooks, and various aspects of barracks life. Army wives were commonly called "adjutants" (*fukkan*) or "the big field train" (*daikōri*) by their officer husbands, who referred to their children as *shōkōri* or "the little field train." In army vernacular it was not unusual for quotidian Sinitic compound words to be reversed, so that *kantan,* for example, meaning "simple," became *tankan.*[23] In general, the army also favored the use of more formal verbal endings, such as *"dearimasu"* instead of *"desu"* in the case of the common verb "to be."[24] Perhaps the biggest difference from civilian speech, however, came in the army's use of the terms *ore* and *kisama* for "I" and "you," respectively, instead of the usual *boku* and *kimi* used by Japanese males. The use of *kisama* was a particularly distinguishing mark of the military man, as in everyday civilian speech it was rarely heard, and only then as a vulgar insult, not unlike the expression "you bastard" in English.[25] Within the army and the academies, however, it conveyed a certain sense of intimacy and comradeship among military men, not least of all among soldiers or cadets of the same unit.

In addition to words and expressions inherited from the army, the language of the cadets was further inflected with the special idioms of the academies themselves. There were of course numerous terms, both formal and colloquial, related to specific academy activities. These included such things as training exercises and written examinations, where, for example, the model response or correct answer was known as the *gen'an* or "basic plan," and a failing grade as an *akaten* or "red mark." They also included particular periods or events that were part of the regular or informal school calendar, such as the *oidashikai* or "expulsion party," which was customarily held for the graduating class by the class below. "Danger week" (*kiken shūkan*) referred to those periods when an especially strict rotating weekly duty officer was in charge, with the first few days after the new officer assumed his post, Sunday through Tuesday, being particularly "dangerous." There were time-honored colloquial terms for key academy personnel as well: the section commander (*kutaichō*) was informally known among the cadets of each section as the *kujō,* though the term was never uttered in the commander's actual presence—in that situation he was always addressed by full title and the polite suffix *dono.* There was even a long list of slang for different types of cadets: Thus there were "handsome cadets," "model cadets," "nearsighted cadets" (from too much studying), and "top-ranked cadets," as well as "ugly cadets," "stupid cadets," "sloppy cadets," and cadets deemed to be "drudges" or "slackers." Cadets who got sick and wound up staying in bed or the infirmary, thus missing training exercises, were called "bed-worms," while those who found themselves at a loss for words in the classroom, unable to come up with the *gen'an* when called upon, were called "fishcakes." As in the army more generally, the academies also had their own words for everyday things and places, including such things as textbooks, lecture halls, briefcases, and even slippers worn in the barracks.[26] And the MMA had some special words of its own, including the inexpensive soy sauce substitute made from sorghum served at meals, which the Japanese MMA cadets derogatively called "spindle oil."[27]

Body

Body mannerisms were as important as speech in distinguishing the aspiring military officer from his civilian peers. As a new cadet in the spring of 1940, Yi Hallim had been struck by the imposing shoulders-back, chest-out bearing of his MMA 2 classmate Park Chung Hee (see Chapter 3). But as Yi himself quickly discovered, such body language, which also featured a head that seemed embedded in the torso, arms swinging imperiously to and fro at the sides, thighs and toes turned outward, and goggle-like glaring eyes, was an externalized expression of the *majime* ideal the cadets were encouraged to cultivate, just as they were expected to acquire distinctive ways of speaking and writing.[28] The goal, according to one of the section commanders who worked with the MMA 1 and MMA 2 cadets who went on to the JMA, was for an officer to project a demeanor that made his subordinates "feel the weight of Mt. Fuji."[29]

Such body manners also pointed to a heightened sense of masculinity that the academies sought to cultivate. To no small extent the cadets were encouraged to measure their differences from other men in terms of their physical prowess and endurance, and the academies were the ultimate training grounds for such qualities. The arduous regimen and training of the schools, which on occasion even led cadets to commit suicide, will be discussed in detail later, but one may note here in passing that there was little sympathy for the weak or infirm, like the "bed-worms" who spent too much time in the infirmary.[30] Sugiyama Masayuki (MMA 1), for example, was sent to the infirmary with malaria as soon as he entered the JMA on August 15, 1941, even before checking into his assigned section in the barracks. Unfortunately for him, his section commander was Sakai Masao, nicknamed "Carbon" by the MMA 1 and MMA 2 cadets because of his dark complexion, and famous for his toughness with his charges. Ten days later, when he was released from sick bay and finally went to his section for the first time, Sugiyama introduced himself to Sakai and began to give him a full report about his health, still not completely back to normal. In response, the section commander thundered back at him: "Kisama! Why did you come to JMA?" Sugiyama, trembling and confused, had no idea what to say and simply blurted out an all-purpose "Yes, sir!" (*Hai!*) Sakai then said, "You will die in the gutter, I expect," meaning Sugiyama would die a meaningless death if he died of illness before he even reached the battlefront.[31]

Training at the academies could be dangerous too, as in the case of regular machine-gun exercises using real bullets.[32] On occasion it could even be fatal. Two former Chinese MMA cadets remembered classmates falling from their horses during riding practice and dying as a result.[33] On May 26, 1941, when both the MMA 1 and MMA 2 cadets were in residence at Lalatun, a Japanese MMA 1 engineering cadet named Furuyama Hiroshi was killed in a landslide during a trench-building "position-construction" exercise (*jinchi kōchiku*). A year later on the anniversary of his death, a monument was erected in his honor at the MMA to commemorate his "dying in the line of duty" (*junshoku*).[34] Similarly, a vertical stone slab engraved with the characters "Seven Lives," representing eternal patriotic sacrifice, was also erected at the new JMA Zama facility on December 30, 1943. The memorial paid homage to 2nd Lieutenant Kusabuka Hachirō and fifty-one other instructors and cadets who had died while in service at the school since its opening in 1937, and in the first of what was to intended to become an annual ceremony, its unveiling was accompanied by a ritual invocation and enshrinement of their "loyal spirits."[35] Such monuments were of course also a visible symbol and reminder to current and subsequent classes of cadets of the special challenges and hazards they faced even in the process of becoming a military officer.

Manchuria and the MMA were an especially grueling testing ground, requiring what Yi Hallim called a "fierce masculine vitality," a certain independence and toughness of character that Hosokawa Minoru (MMA 2) in his diary referred to as the mark of the "continental man" (*tairiku otoko*).[36] When the first two classes of cadets matriculated between 1939 and 1941, the school was still in the process of being built and lacked the more comprehensive, comfortable facilities of the new JMA at Zama. Conditions were sometimes even less than sanitary. An extant lecture from September 1940 by one of the MMA company commanders, Kanno Hiroshi, exhorts the cadets to pay special and close attention to their personal health and hygiene while on field exercises, but hygienic challenges abounded within the MMA itself.[37] Hard-shelled lice that could only be crushed with a mallet deposited their eggs in the cadets' underwear and left it in tatters, while bedbugs circled around their heads at night. In the warmer months the cadets had to compete at mealtimes with swarms of flies, which could also be found floating dead in the "spindle oil" or gestating as maggots among the pickled vegetables.[38] Tight schedules allowed for communal baths at most only twice a week, but cadets were often burned by poorly fitted, scalding underwater pipes in the hot tubs, and forced to bathe in dirty water, too infrequently changed, that filled the bathing room with a foul smell.[39] Even the annual summer swimming exercises at Dalian (Dairen) sometimes posed hygienic challenges, as in July 1941 when the cadets faced restrictions on their time in the water due to diarrhea and other health concerns.[40]

Weather was perhaps the greatest trial of all. Manchurian summers were hot and humid, followed by a brief autumn and spring. March brought howling Mongolian winds and yellow-dust storms that blocked visibility beyond 10 meters (about 33 feet) in any direction. The storms seeped through the MMA's double-sealed windows and completely coated the cadets' desks. Then came the spring rains and the great melting of the winter snow, which turned the ground into a thick stew of mud that collected on the cadets' boots and had to be continually cleaned off.[41]

Worst of all were the winters, long, icy, and brutal, epitomized by the title of Park Chung Hee's MMA 2 class memoir, *Sakufū banri* (The north wind of ten thousand leagues). Temperatures often dropped to levels that the Japanese or Korean cadets, even those Koreans from the northern part of the peninsula, had seldom experienced. As late as April in 1940, for example, when Park and other Koreans in the MMA 2 class arrived at the MMA, the chill of the Manchurian winter was still palpable, and ice and snow still covered the ground, but things were finally beginning to thaw.[42] Three months earlier, however, on January 16, when the MMA 1 Nikkei company had entered the school, the temperature had been recorded at −35°C (−31°F), and about a month later, on February 9, when they visited the Manchukuo Fourth District Army headquarters in Harbin, the temperature had been −45°C (−49°F)—so cold, one of the cadets later noted, that "a stream of piss would freeze on the ground before it went a full meter."[43] To harden cadets to such weather conditions, the MMA regularly took them outside in the bitterest months, usually February and March, for hours of "cold-endurance" (*taikan*) marches and exercises, often deliberately carried out at night when the temperatures plummeted and even the provisions and water being carried would freeze.[44]

But the ordeals of winter were not confined to special training exercises. Dealing with the cold was a daily struggle for the cadets during the winter months, and frostbite was a constant worry.[45] The buglers who signaled the rituals and regimens of the MMA day had to remove the mouthpieces from their instruments and warm them in their hands to keep them from freezing to their lips.[46] Cadets in bayonet practice or on their way to the baths had to move carefully to avoid the ice that formed on the floors of the martial arts building and the frigid bathroom changing rooms.[47] The cold even penetrated the classrooms, where the cadets spent most of their day sitting rigidly at attention. Especially in the upper-story rooms, which an inadequate heating system failed to reach, the cold was so severe that the ink used for writing froze, and cadets were sometimes given special permission to wear their overcoats to ward off the Arctic chill.[48] Kim Muk (MMA 2) also remembered donning his regulation fur hat on middle-of-the-night trips to the barracks toilets in the winter.[49]

The toilets in fact presented what was arguably the most hazardous daily winter trial for the cadets at the MMA. They were located in a separate, unheated section at one end of each of the company barracks and surrounded on the outside by a concrete wall. But since the academy was not connected to the Xinjing city sewer system, waste simply drained into a large hole that spanned the urinals and seats. Summer was not a particular problem, apart from inevitable reek of what was essentially an attached outhouse. But in the winter the waste would freeze and build up, forming stalagmites of hardened excrement that reached up and into the seats. Local Chinese workers were brought in to remove the waste when it rose to such high levels, but especially during the rushed morning and evening musters, when more than a hundred company members had to vie for only twenty seats, the cadets always had to remember to be on the lookout for the dangerous "pyramids" that threatened to stab them when they sat down on the toilets. One cadet from the MMA 7 class compared the experience to trying "to seat oneself on a steep mountain peak."[50]

Separation from the *Shaba*

While they were in residence at the academies, the cadets' sense of belonging to a separate, distinctive world was maintained by a strict monitoring of activities that brought them into contact with the outside world. Except for a single family photograph, which was to be kept tucked away in their self-study desk in the company barracks, cadets could have no private possessions.[51] They were also not allowed access to books and other reading materials apart from those assigned by instructors, unless the section commander gave his approval, in which case the approved items were expressly marked by stickers.[52] Cadets found in possession of books or other items without such stickers were reprimanded, as one of Park Chung Hee's MMA 2 Korean classmates, An Yŏnggil, quickly discovered when he was caught with a magazine from the outside.[53] News of the outside world was limited for the most part to newspaper articles and other information, mainly about the war, posted on public bulletin boards.[54] Cadets were forbidden to reproduce, print, distribute, or circulate any information, or to contribute to newspapers or magazines, without permission.[55]

Movies were shown from time to time, roughly one every six weeks, depending on the cadets' schedules, but these too were invariably films produced either in Manchuria or in Japan that glorified the Japanese war effort, such as the 1944 film *Rikugun (Army)* starring the famous actress Tanaka Kinuyo, or foreign films that served a similar propaganda purpose. MMA cadets were also regularly shown a 1942 documentary film celebrating the MMA itself produced by the government-run Manchurian Film Company (Man'ei), headed by Amakasu Masahiko.[56]

Music, like movies, was another potentially subversive medium that had to be controlled. With good reason Plato had banned certain types of music from the education of the warrior-guardians of his ideal republic, for, as he noted, "rhythm and harmony enter most powerfully into the innermost part of the soul and lay forcible hands upon it . . . making graceful him who is rightly trained, and him who is not, the reverse."[57] For Plato, the right training permitted only those modes of music that would "fittingly imitate the tones and accents of a man who is brave in battle."[58] This was precisely the pedagogical goal of the MMA and JMA, designed to keep the civilian world at bay while also serving to deepen the cadets' identities and loyalties as students of elite institutions and future military officers. Thus on entry to the academies, the cadets were given songbooks that contained a wide variety of military songs celebrating both general and historical military virtues and exploits, as well as the glories of specific units and branches of the military. Each academy had its own school song, as did each graduating class. In addition, the songbook at the MMA, called the *Hokushin* (North Star), combined all the songs in the JMA's famous *Otakebi* (War Cry) songbook with a special section of original songs devoted specifically to Manchuria, the Manchukuo state and army, and the MMA itself.[59] In time the cadets came to memorize most if not all of the songs, which they practiced, standing and without benefit of scores, virtually every night outside after dinner, led by their section commanders or upperclassmen, and which they also sang on marches and outings.[60] As one cadet wrote, the songs were sung on every imaginable occasion and became an "inseparable" part of the academy experience.[61] Indeed, by the time the cadets left the academies, many of the songs had become so familiar that decades later they were still indelibly inscribed on their minds, with the power to evoke even involuntarily a latent memory or mood, like Christmas carols or other holiday songs learned in childhood. "Even now, when I sing or hum to myself," one former MMA 6 cadet wrote more than twenty years after leaving the academy, "it is the songs of the *Hokushin* that give me courage and strength."[62] Similarly, Kim Kwangsik (Kim Kwangsic), a Korean cadet who had been in the MMA 7 class, enjoined me to "study the songs" to understand the ethos of 1940s academy life.[63]

Letters, the principal means for cadets to remain in contact with their families, were not prohibited, but all letters, messages, or packages, incoming as well as outgoing, had to be checked by the cadets' section or company commanders.[64] The sense of living in a separate, special, secret place was enhanced by an injunction against sharing with outsiders, even family members, any information about the academies, including photographs. The only sanctioned photographs of the academies were those taken by photographers directed and screened by the school authorities.[65] The heading on a map of the JMA grounds and facilities at Zama from the time said it all: "Secret: Internal Use Only."[66] Personal visits from the outside were also carefully supervised by the MMA and JMA. Cadets expecting visitors had first to request permission from their section commanders, and the visits were strictly regulated with respect to time, place, and length, even for family members.[67]

Even when for various reasons the cadets physically left the grounds of Sōbudai or Dōtokudai, the schools did their best to minimize outside contacts and to extend their influence beyond the gates. Thus for all official outside activities requiring long-distance movement the cadets traveled in special army trains, where they continued even on excursions to operate within the organizational units and perimeters of the academy system.[68] Leaves of course also opened the door for contact with the outside world, but here too there were constraints. Leaves had to be approved by the section commanders, and they were granted only on those Sundays and holidays when no official events or exercises were scheduled. The first leaves at the *yoka* were particularly long in coming, permitted only after the cadets had become sufficiently acculturated to academy regulations and life. According to Kim Muk, for example, the first leaves for his MMA 2 class were not granted until six months after matriculation.[69]

Leaves were limited to the day in question, beginning around 0800 following breakfast and inspection, and ending sharply with the 2100 evening roll call.[70] Cadets were not allowed to spend the night outside, and missing the evening roll call was a serious offense. To be sure, thirteen hours was not an insignificant allotment of free time, but for JMA cadets heading for Tokyo, the most popular leave destination, the round-trip train ride to and from Zama sliced off the time for exploring the city by about two hours. For MMA cadets the time loss was even greater. Although Xinjing, the main MMA leave destination, was far closer to the academy than the JMA was to Tokyo, the MMA cadets were forbidden to use vehicles of any kind. Forced to move everywhere on foot, they consequently could lose as much as six hours of their leave time simply getting to and from the capital city.

Cadets at both schools who were granted leaves were given strict orders as to where they could and could not go. The first leave for new cadets at the academies in fact always took the form of a guided tour by their instructional officers, where they were introduced to those sites favored by the authorities.[71] In general they were to avoid places that "damaged the dignity" of their high position as aspiring officers, such as restaurants and drinking places (except those establishments frequented by military officers or when accompanied by military officers), tearooms, movie houses, music halls, and theaters.[72] Given its proximity to Xinjing and the compactness of the city, the MMA was able more easily than the JMA to extend its watchful eye and enforce compliance with regulations on leave days by sending out patrols of duty officers and noncommissioned officers wearing identifying armbands. Since cadets were also required to wear their dress uniforms while on leave, they could be easily recognized.[73]

The watchful eye, whether of the MMA or the JMA, was inevitably weakened during the regular school breaks, generally in August and December, when the cadets were free to return home for about a month in summer and about three weeks in winter. Of the three summer vacation periods encompassing the preparatory and regular academy courses, however, the second was for all practical purposes consumed by one or more months of obligatory regimental attachment duty (*taizuki kinmu*) that followed graduation from the preparatory course. During the 1940s, moreover, when the academy courses were shortened to meet the increasing demand for new officers, vacations were sometimes cut back, both at the MMA and JMA. And vacations, as the most expendable element in the academy courses, could also be entirely canceled, depending on circumstances. In the summer of 1941, for example, when the Kwantung Army was staging special full-scale military maneuvers throughout the country, the MMA cadets, including Park Chung Hee's MMA 2 class, suddenly saw their vacation disappear.[74] Even when the vacations went on as scheduled, as at the MMA in the winter of 1941–42, the cadets were likely to be admonished on return to "leave aside the things of the world and return to being a soldier."[75]

Leaving aside the things of the world, however, did not mean separation from the greater outside world of the military. Quite the contrary. While the cadets were discouraged from close interaction with the civilian world, and personal visits from the outside were carefully monitored, the cadets were deliberately encouraged to think of themselves as part of an extensive martial universe that stretched far and wide outside the gates of the academies, and touched on other spheres of status and power to which the military was intimately linked. In the course of their roughly four years of training, cadets in both Manchuria and Japan, for example, were exposed to a staggering array of prominent military and political figures. Compiling a list of such figures for the years 1940–1944, when the MMA 1/JMA 56 and MMA 2/JMA 57 classes were in residence at Lalatun and Zama, one finds successive top-ranking military advisors to the Manchukuo government and numerous other well-known active and retired generals in the Japanese, Kwantung, and Manchukuo armies; government ministers; two prime ministers (Manchukuo, Japan); two heads of state (Republic of China, Burma), and various members of the Manchukuo and Japanese imperial families, including, of course, the two emperors themselves.[76] *Yoka* and *honka* commencements often brought the highest state and military figures together in a celebration of military life and purpose, as at Zama on April 20, 1944, when Park Chung Hee and other members of the MMA 2/JMA 57 graduating class were reviewed by the Japanese emperor and listened to a "grand farewell" speech by Prime Minister Tōjō Hideki.[77] Perhaps more than anything else, this continual flow of army and state luminaries in and out of the lives of the cadets served to highlight and maintain the special place or favor of the cadets in Japanese imperial society. However formalized and ritualized, such visits and occasions provided frequent and tangible confirmation to the cadets of their own elite standing in society. Above all, they pointed to the cadets' special role in the military and the state as the "pillars of the army" and the "limbs of the emperor," two commonly used terms that also peppered the *Hokushin* and *Otakebi* songbooks and whose connotations were reflected in a panoply of activities and monuments at both academies.

Pillars of the Army

Throughout the course of their training at both the *yoka* and *honka*, the cadets were continually reminded in various ways, directly and indirectly, of their unique place as the inheritors and successors in a long tradition and lineage of warriors and battles. For the cadets the most direct links in the lineage were of course recent academy graduates, their immediate seniors. In the case of the JMA, which had been physically moved from its original location in Tokyo in 1937, this link was reinforced and commemorated anew with the dedication at Sōbudai in 1938 of the school's Otakebi Shrine, honoring all JMA graduates who had died in battle or in service.[78]

Perhaps even more direct and immediate a link to academy seniors at both the MMA and JMA than the enshrined spirits of previous graduates was the flesh-and-blood presence of the military officers who lived and trained with the cadets on a daily basis. Most of these men were alumni of the schools, and many had also seen combat, most recently in the war in China that had broken out in 1937.[79] When the MMA 2 cadets were at Zama, for example, their section commanders or *kutaichō*, the officers with whom they had the most frequent daily contact and who were in many cases only a few years older than the cadets themselves, had often just arrived from one of the war zones and would be returning to combat duty after serving at the academy.[80] Park Chung Hee's two section commanders at Zama were a case in point. The first, Nishigaki Makoto (JMA 48), who had graduated from the JMA in 1936, had come back to the JMA directly from the front lines in China, where he had distinguished himself as a company commander, and to which he returned with a promotion to battalion commander after leaving the school in 1943.[81] His successor, Tahara Kōzō (JMA 52), who was even younger, had been serving as a company commander on the Soviet-Manchukuo border in the 31st Infantry Regiment before being transferred to the JMA, and in 1944 he was posted to the Philippines as a battalion commander on Luzon.[82] In the course of their close and extensive interaction with the cadets both on the training fields and in the barracks, section commanders such as Nishigaki and Tahara often shared their own combat experiences with the young men under their supervision, which not only provided the cadets with useful models and lessons but also linked them on a more personal and emotional level with the war in which they would soon be playing a leading role and with the officer corps as a whole.

The more senior officers serving at the academies in this period had generally been posted to Lalatun or Zama after or between assignments in the Manchurian, Chinese, or Pacific war theatres. Major Enami Shigeru (JMA 38), the company commander of the MMA cadets at the JMA, received his orders to report to the academy in 1941 while he was serving as a battalion commander with the newly established 235th Infantry Regiment on the front lines in China's Hubei province.[83] His immediate superior at the JMA was Colonel Kihara Yoshio (JMA 27), the commandant of the International Cadet Corps, of which the MMA company was a part.[84] Kihara had a long combat career in China beginning with the catalytic Marco Polo Bridge incident, where he had been a battalion commander, and he arrived at the JMA in 1941 after a year of successive military operations on the continent as commander of the 34th Infantry Regiment.[85] Before taking up their posts at the MMA and JMA, the two academy superintendents during this period, Major General Nagumo Shin'ichirō (JMA 19) and Lt. General Ushijima Mitsuru (JMA 20), had commanded combat divisions in north China and Manchuria, respectively: Nagumo had led an independent mixed brigade in Shanxi province and had been commander of the Beijing Defense Garrison, and Ushijima was given the top post at the JMA after serving on the front line of defense against the Soviets as commander of the 11th Infantry Division in northeast Manchuria.[86]

Links to Samurai Heroes

While the cadets naturally tended during these years of active war to identify closely with their more recent seniors and contemporary battles, they were encouraged to see themselves as part of an even older military tradition, in some cases stretching far back into the remote premodern past. Japan's centuries-long heritage of samurai culture, richly preserved in paintings, poetry, history, and actual artifacts, had in fact been part of every schoolchild's education before the war, in colonial Korea as well as in Japan itself, and during the late 1930s and 1940s, it was reinterpreted and reemphasized by a broad spectrum of government officials, educators, and artists, including filmmakers, to promote and popularize wartime policies and goals. But nowhere were the reminders of an ancient and glorious military past more deeply embedded in the system of teaching and training than at the military academies. Primers, lectures, and even earlier graduates' essays on *bushidō*, "the way of the warrior," as well as Yamamoto Tsunetomo's classic seventeenth-century *bushidō* manual, *Hagakure*, were all an integral part of the assortment of textual materials used at the academies, and one of their main purposes and effects was to give the cadets a sense of their special place and responsibility within a great, interconnected historical family of samurai who had commanded the great armies of the past.[87] Cadets were enjoined to meditate on and write about the most famous samurai "heroes" of medieval Japan, such as Takeda Shingen, Uesugi Kenshin, Oda Nobunaga, Toyotomi Hideyoshi, and Tokugawa Ieyasu, as if they were their spiritual ancestors, and in classes on Japanese history and classical literature the cadets studied their lives and battles and read and memorized the poetry that celebrated them. The very location of the JMA on the Sagami plain, not far from where Hideyoshi had defeated the great Hōjō clan and consolidated his power, and within easy traveling distance of many of the great castles and battlefields of that period, also helped bring to life the history they were studying.[88] The JMA, in fact, made a point of taking the cadets on excursions to such sites, especially those cadets in the International Cadet Corps who had not grown up in Japan. During the winter break in January 1943, for example, the International Corps commandant Kihara Yoshio escorted his non-Japanese cadets, including Park Chung Hee and the other MMA 2 Koreans, on a week-long study trip to the Ōsaka, Kōbe, and Kyūshū areas.[89] But even without such special trips the ancient warrior connections at Zama were palpable. Extended swimming exercises, for example, took the MMA 1 and MMA 2 cadets to the beaches of Kugenuma and Koshigoe, near the capital and battle sites of Japan's first shogunate at Kamakura.[90] And even on regular field maneuvers, the JMA cadets also frequently found themselves encamped in places that evoked the great figures and battles of the distant past, as did the MMA 1 *honka* cadets in September 1942, when for their second on-site tactical exercises they traveled to the area of the former castle town of Kōfu, the birthplace of Takeda Shingen.[91]

The example of Takeda Shingen in fact provides a fascinating and instructive illustration of the manifold ways in which the ancient samurai warlords were etched in the minds of the academy cadets of this period and continued to exert an imaginative power for years afterward. The wily Shingen's battles in the sixteenth century with his great adversary, Uesugi Kenshin, were well known to Japanese schoolchildren before the war. And even in colonial Korea the dramatic story of the battle at Kawanakajima in 1561, in which Kenshin's forces secretly crossed the Chikuma River at night, surprising Shingen's army and precipitating a subsequent hand-to-hand combat between the two rivals that Shingen in the end managed to ward off with his battle fan, was incorporated into Japanese-language readers for Korean elementary school students,[92] including the final two lines of the following classical Chinese poem about the battle by the Tokugawa scholar Rai Sanyō:

Sound of the horse whips, softly, softly, crossing the river at night.
At dawn the sight of a thousand soldiers protecting the great tusk.
A lasting regret! For ten years, polishing one sword
Beneath the light of a falling star, the long snake [Shingen]
    escapes.[93]

Thus even before they entered the academies, both Japanese and Koreans of the late 1930s and early 1940s were already acquainted with these two iconic samurai figures whom as cadets they were exhorted to study and emulate as part of their long professional lineage as warriors. In November 1941, moreover, three months after the MMA 1 arrived at the JMA, Japan's Tōhō film company released a new movie about the battle of Kawanakajima directed by Kinugasa Teinosuke and starring one of Japan's greatest *kabuki* performers, Ichikawa Ennosuke as Kenshin, and the popular actor Ōkōchi Denjirō in the role of Shingen.[94] Cadets entering the JMA in this period also found Rai Sanyō's poem, as well as a poem by Kenshin himself, in their *Otakebi* songbook as pieces to be memorized and chanted in the evening singing exercises, and on field trips and all the other many occasions when songs and poems were customarily sung.[95] Subsequent field training and mock battles in the Kōfu area where Shingen himself had once lived of course only deepened the cadets' identification with "the long snake" and his equally celebrated contender.

Just how deep and enduring such identification could be can be seen by jumping ahead in time and space to South Korea only months before the May 1961 coup, when Park Chung Hee was serving as deputy commander of the Second Army in Taegu. Yun Ch'idu, one of Park's former TNS classmates, then an elementary school principal in Taegu, had invited Park for an evening of drinking at one of his favorite watering holes in the city. In his usual dour way, Park sat in silence drinking glass after glass of sake talking neither to his friend nor to the hostess serving them until the hostess got up and left, and the concerned manager or "madam" of the bar came over and cajoled them into some turns of karaoke singing to liven up the atmosphere. When Park's turn came, he suddenly rose from his seat, intoxicated from the numerous rounds of sake, and to the astonishment of his friend and the madam, began to perform a Japanese sword dance. As he proceeded to move through the ritualistic steps and gestures of the piece, he also sang a Japanese poetic recitative to accompany his movements, beginning with the words "Beisei shuku yoru kawa o wataru." It was of course the opening line—"Sound of the horse whips, softly, softly, crossing the river at night"—of Rai Sanyō's poem about Kenshin's ambush and Shingen's escape at the battle of Kawanakajima.[96]

Heirs of the Meiji Restoration

In November 1961, less than a year after his drunken sword dance in Taegu, Park Chung Hee, now head of the military junta that was ruling South Korea, stopped off in Tokyo while on route to Washington, D.C., to meet with President John F. Kennedy, in effect a formal acceptance and recognition by the United States of the May 16 coup. Speaking about the coup in Japanese at a small luncheon in Akasaka hosted by former prime minister Kishi Nobusuke, he told the assembled guests, "We are young, and from the viewpoint of Japan, what we are doing must seem naïve, but in fact we are acting in the spirit of the men of high purpose [shishi] of the Meiji Restoration." "To that end," he added, "we are deeply studying Meiji history."[97] Later that same day when he met privately with Nagumo Shin'ichirō, his former superintendent at the MMA, he echoed these remarks and asked Nagumo to send him some "old books" on Meiji government, politics, foreign relations, military affairs, education, and economy.[98]

In this deep-seated admiration for the Meiji Restoration one can see yet another aspect of the ancestral warrior lineage to which cadets of Park's time felt linked. If they were encouraged to look to their immediate seniors as well as the legendary figures of the medieval past as part of that pedigree, they were also made to feel part of the greatest military endeavors of the more recent past, each with its respective pantheons of battles and heroes. In chronological order these included the Meiji Restoration of 1868, the Sino-Japanese War of 1894–1895, the Russo-Japanese War of 1904–1905, and the Manchurian Incident of 1931. Precisely because these events were temporally close enough to be seen as part of a continuum of military glory that was part of the modern Japanese imperial history in which they themselves were living, yet still sufficiently distant to evoke a sense of wonder and admiration, their power to inspire emulation and reinforce the cadets' sense of themselves as the "pillars of the army" was especially strong. Each had its own moments and leaders of greatness, but perhaps grandest of all in the minds of the cadets was the event that had given birth to modern Japan itself, the Meiji Restoration of 1868.

As the seminal event of modern Japanese history, the Meiji Restoration had been imprinted on the minds of the 1940s cadets, Koreans and Japanese alike, long before they entered the academies. Koreans in elementary schools were introduced to the Meiji emperor in ethics classes in some cases as early as the second year of the six-year curriculum, and from 1927 on, Meiji's birthday, November 3, was celebrated as a national holiday in both metropole and colony to honor, as the school textbooks stated, the former emperor's "benevolence" and the "glories of his reign."[99] As Koreans moved up the educational ladder, more and more information about the Meiji period and about the Restoration itself was included in the corresponding textbooks. In the 1939 textbook revision, Yoshida Shōin, the famous Chōshū mentor to many of the samurai leaders who toppled the Tokugawa shogunate and proclaimed the Restoration, was featured as the subject of the sixth-grade chapter on "imperial loyalty and patriotism."[100] Secondary school ethics texts in this period devoted even more space to the same theme, celebrating and quoting not only Yoshida but other late Tokugawa *shishi,* including Umeda Unpin, Takasugi Shinsaku, Hirano Kuniomi, Kido Kōin, and the monk Gesshō, a close friend of Saigō Takamori's.[101] Korean cultural nationalists writing in the 1930s also found much to admire in the Meiji Restoration. Hyŏn Sangyun's 1932 series of articles in *Tonga ilbo* praising and promoting *bushidō* featured pictures and commentary on both Saigō and Kido, as well as Ōkubo Toshimichi, together regarded as the three greatest figures of the Restoration; Hyŏn's serialized essay was in fact aptly entitled "The Motive Power of the Meiji Restoration."[102]

If the cadets were already attuned to Meiji "glories" even before they entered the academies, by the time they graduated they were thoroughly steeped in a hagiographic understanding of the Restoration, the era, and the men who had made it possible. In the *yoka* Japanese history curriculum, whether in Manchukuo or Japan, the Restoration and Meiji periods, only about ninety years in a national history that covered more than a millennium, accounted for as much as one-third of the total reading and class hours.[103] And even as the length of both the *yoka* and *honka* courses was shortened after the outbreak of war in China, the academies refused to reduce the time spent on this history, regarding it as the "foundation of state ideology."[104]

Restoration *shishi* such as Saigō were writ large in the cadets' education and imagination, appearing not only in the formal history texts but also in the songbooks, where pieces composed both about and by Saigō were prominent, and in the collections of essays by earlier graduates that the cadets were given to study.[105] Indeed, for the cadets, the history of this period was above all the history of the *shishi*. "What, I ask you, adorned the history of the late Tokugawa period so brilliantly with such wholehearted loyalty, such committed righteousness?" one essay by an earlier graduate queried in a flourish of rhetoric, only immediately and unhesitatingly to provide the answer: "It was the *shishi* of the Restoration!"[106] Another such essay, not atypically, focused on the inspirational quality of the Restoration and the senior-junior warrior bond linking the cadets to its leaders: "The deeds of those *shishi* who died as martyrs to construct a glorious new Japan fill us, their juniors [*kōhai*], with awe."[107]

Perhaps most revealing of the reverence in which the cadets of the 1940s held the Restoration and everything associated with it were the songs, pledges, and sayings that they themselves and their instructors composed or chose to emphasize. The official class songs of both the MMA 1 and the MMA 2 classes, written at the time by one or more of the cadets in those classes, honored the Restoration as an inspiring ideal that could be applied to Manchuria and, indeed, to wherever the ongoing "holy war" might extend the boundaries of empire. The songs also celebrated the role of the cadets as the heirs and new warriors in this infinitely expanding Restoration movement. Thus the MMA 1 cadets sang "We three hundred, grasping the shining sword of the Restoration and steadily advancing step by new step each day and month," and Park Chung Hee's fellow MMA 2 cadets sang of "Our Second Class now advancing . . . in fulfillment of its eternal mission, as the dawn heralds the Restoration in the endless ten-thousand leagues beneath the North Star."[108] The JMA 57 class, with which the MMA 2 Manchukuo cadets were officially associated and grouped in the JMA records, also had a class song that praised the Restoration as "that vast and far-reaching great ideal," to be spread throughout "the eight corners of the world."[109] The JMA 57 graduation album from 1944 contained frequent references to the Restoration too. On a page next to a photograph of the Seven Stars monument, for example, one finds the class "pledge" (*chikai*), in which the cadets vowed to be "true to the sacred Sōbudai name and lead the imperial army in the vanguard of the Restoration."[110] On another page featuring photographs of the members of the class's 5th Cadet Company (*chūtai*), Uchiyama Kazuya, the company commander, had penned his personal motto simply and boldly in large letters: "To die for the Restoration."[111]

Successors in a History of Victory

While no link in their ancestral warrior genealogy could quite match the unique connotations of the Meiji Restoration *shishi*, the cadets of the 1940s were also educated and trained to see themselves as the "pillars" of a great modern army whose history had already encompassed two great wars and several other major military expeditions, not least of all the Manchurian Incident of 1931. And this history, as Yamada Otozō, the inspector general of military training, pointedly reminded the cadets at the MMA 2/JMA 57 graduation ceremonies in April 1944—a time when Japan was steadily losing ground to U.S. air and naval forces in the Pacific—had been a "history of victory."[112]

The graduating cadets listening to Yamada that spring, Park Chung Hee among them, were in fact well acquainted with this "history of victory." The MMA 2 class had studied it at Lalatun at a general level, with an emphasis on diplomacy and international relations, as part of their regular Japanese history course. At the JMA, where the focus shifted specifically to military history, the cadets closely studied the major campaigns of each of Japan's major international conflicts beginning with the Sino-Japanese War (1894–1895) and continuing through the Boxer Rebellion (1900), the Russo-Japanese War (1904–1905), the seizure of German territory on the Shandong peninsula during World War I, the Siberian Expedition (1918–1922), military interventions in China in 1927–1928, and the Manchurian Incident (1931). Decisive engagements, especially in the wars with Qing China and Tsarist Russia, were individually examined and analyzed, and instructors supplemented the academy's military history textbooks with field diaries and battle reports, as well as memoirs, testimonies, and lectures by actual participants. In each case the cadets analyzed the combat readiness of the army in question, the particular arms employed, the use of fortifications, the communications system, the terrain, topography, and climate of the battleground, and the season, time, and degree of light or dark in which the battle was fought. Particular attention was given to the role and character of the cadets' "bold and brave seniors," the commanding officers in the battles—their ability to grasp all the necessary intelligence, tangible and intangible, and methodically decide, dispose, and execute commands that would determine the course and final result of the engagement.[113] In field exercises and term exams cadets were often tested on their mastery of this material, and even when they were not studying, training, or being tested, they were often reading essays by earlier cadets, or singing songs and poems from the *Otakebi* that celebrated one or another of the battles and the soldiers and seniors who had fought in them.

Of all the major military conflicts covered in the academy curriculum, the Sino-Japanese War with the Qing dynasty was for the cadets the most remote and unfamiliar. Still, as noted earlier, every Japanese schoolchild at least knew the famous story of the heroic bugler Kiguchi Kohei, who was said to have died in combat in that war with his bugle pressed firmly to his lips. Korean schoolchildren too had come to know the figure of Kiguchi by the late 1930s, and some of the most memorable military engagements of the Sino-Japanese War had of course taken place in Korea itself, including the Battle of Sŏnghwan in South Ch'ungch'ŏng province, where Kiguchi had been killed. (See also Chapter 3.) Indeed, a natural stone monument had been erected by Japanese residents in the area as early as 1914 to honor Kiguchi and his company officer, Captain Matsuzaki Naoomi, another casualty of the battle, and the surrounding area had become known as Seikan (Sŏnghwan) Park or Matsuzaki Park.[114]

At the academies, where the war was a formal subject of study, the IJA's siege of the old walled city of P'yŏngyang, which the Qing forces had occupied and settled in to defend after their defeat at Sŏnghwan, was one of the main battles singled out for instruction. Following the Qing occupation of the city, the Japanese had marched their troops northward from Seoul in a carefully coordinated three-pronged movement that kept the bulk of their force hidden from the Chinese and also deceived them as to the point from which the main attack would come. Having completely encircled the city by stealth and distracted the enemy with offensive feints, before daybreak on September 15, 1894, the Japanese finally launched their main attack, taking the Chinese by surprise and simultaneously assaulting the city from several directions. By early afternoon it was clear that the result had been a disaster for the Chinese, their panicked troops forced to escape from the city if they could by passing through a murderous gauntlet of Japanese fire. P'yŏngyang had been an early and crucial victory in the fighting, and its dramatic narrative also served to highlight the brilliance of the great imperial military legacy the cadets were said to be inheriting.[115]

In addition to studying this and other battles in the war, such as the Battle of the Yalu and the Battle of Weihaiwei, the cadets celebrated them in song. Indeed, twenty-four selections in the *Otakebi* were devoted to the Qing conflict, and the longest one, containing no fewer than twenty-three stanzas, was dedicated to the Battle of P'yŏngyang (Heijō no tatakai).[116] And of course among the twenty-four pieces on the war there was one about the Battle of Sŏnghwan, called "Crossing the Ansŏng" (Anjō no wataru).[117] Here as they sang in unison the cadets once again found themselves renewing their special common bond with the greatest popular hero of the war, the fallen but invincible bugler, Kiguchi Kohei, and by extension his infantry commander, Captain Matsuzaki, one of their own "bold and brave seniors," who was said to have been the first Japanese soldier to die in the war.[118]

However stirring the history of the Sino-Japanese War might have been to the cadets, nothing in Japan's modern "history of victory" as taught at the academies could quite compare in grandeur and glory to the Russo-Japanese War, which, as the JMA military history noted, "not only revealed to the whole world our empire's brilliant military power . . . but also placed [Japan] in the rank of the top nations of the world and brought a multitude of benefits and honors."[119] In countless ways the war provided a reference point and touchstone for the cadets' education and training as officers, and it also greatly exalted the cadets' sense of themselves as the heirs to a grand tradition of military leadership. (See Chapter 7.)

Precisely because the war was regarded as greatest martial triumph of Japan's modern era, cadets entering the academies in this period were already more familiar with it than they were with the Sino-Japanese War, despite the fact that, like the latter, it had occurred decades earlier, long before any of them had been born. Korean cadets were no exception here. Since elementary school they had been reading about the war, and so they were very familiar with the names and heroic acts of such military figures as the naval commander Hirose Takeo, killed at Port Arthur; cavalry captain Kobayashi Tamaki, who had died on return from a reconnaissance mission deep behind enemy lines; and, not least of all, army general Nogi Maresuke.[120] Middle or high school students were also routinely taken on required spring excursions to different parts of the colony and empire, where battle sites of the war were part of the regular itinerary. Such was the case, for example, in the spring of 1936, when Park Chung Hee's class at Taegu Normal School went to Manchuria.[121] Among the sites they visited was Port Arthur, including the famous Hill 203, where at least 16,000 Japanese soldiers had died or were wounded in repeated assaults under Nogi's command, including the younger of his two sons, before the Russians finally surrendered.[122]

Given the appalling costs of the conflict and the significance attached to it, it is not surprising that the Russo-Japanese War came to be deeply rooted in every cadet's consciousness. About 100 of the 191 pages in the 1942 military history text used by Park's MMA 2/JMA 57 class, for example, were devoted to it, with special attention to the key battles of Liaoyang, Port Arthur, and Mukden (Fengtian/Shenyang).[123] These battles also often formed the basis for instruction and testing in the "practical application" of JMA military tactics, as can be seen in the April 1944 issue of the *JMA Bulletin*, the JMA's internal journal for officers and cadets.[124] And of course songs and poems honoring the battles and heroes of the war were a prominent portion of the *Otakebi* collection.[125]

There and elsewhere, as in the model essays by former cadets, two figures in particular stood out. One was Tachibana Shūta, a major from Nagasaki who had died bravely at Fort Shuzan (Shuzanpo) in the Battle of Liaoyang in August 1904 and was posthumously elevated to lieutenant colonel. Over the years Tachibana had been deliberately promoted by the army as a model warrior or "war god" (*gunshin*) to counter the navy's apotheosis of Hirose Takeo, as well as Tōgō Heihachirō, the admiral whose forces had destroyed the Russian Baltic fleet in the Straits of Tsushima in 1905.[126] By the early 1940s a shrine to Tachibana had been established in Nagasaki Prefecture (Unzen), and he had entered the elementary school morals textbooks for both Japanese and Koreans.[127] No fewer than three of the eighteen songs in the *Otakebi* dealing directly with the Russo-Japanese War carried the title "Lieutenant-Colonel Tachibana," and two of them were included in the MMA's *Hokushin* songbook as well.[128] The three songs together constituted an epic war song of thirty-two stanzas, the longest such piece in the *Otakebi*, and took about fifteen minutes to sing in succession.[129]

It was General Nogi, however, who surpassed all other figures as the most renowned army officer of the war. Long before the 1940s he had already achieved a kind of mythical status for his relentless pursuit of victory at Port Arthur (Lüshun), and his ritual suicide eight years later following the death of the Meiji emperor had only enhanced his reputation and mystique, leading to the erection of no fewer than eight shrines to his memory, including the main shrine in Tokyo (Nogizaka), the site of his former residence.[130] The incorporation of this unrivaled *gunshin* into the cadets' martial genealogy as one of their "bold and brave seniors" was thus almost by itself an assurance of their illustrious status as the "pillars" of the army. If the cadets were not reading about him in their history texts or in the essays by former academy graduates, they were often singing about him, including a lengthy two-part "Song of General Nogi," altogether comprising twenty-four stanzas, as well as songs and poetry written by Nogi himself.[131] Nearly a half century later, when I asked two Chinese MMA graduates still living in Changchun (formerly Xinjing) what military figures in particular had been celebrated at the academy, both immediately mentioned Nogi. Without hesitation, one of them, Zhu Huan, then took out his pen and wrote down a poem by Nogi, reciting each line from memory as he drew the Chinese characters.[132]

To be able to include General Nogi and other heroes of the Russo-Japanese War as "bold and brave seniors" added a special luster to the military heritage that the cadets of the 1940s could claim as their own. But while Nogi and the war evoked an undeniable reverence, the great general was long dead and the battles long over. Not so the more recent military engagement studied at the academies: the Manchurian Incident.

The railroad explosion at Mukden that had precipitated the 1931 crisis, as well as Japan's subsequent invasion of Manchuria and building of the new Manchukuo client state, had all occurred not only within the cadets' lifetimes but within their living memories. In the decade before they entered the academies, these unfolding military and political events had been covered widely and often sensationally by their hometown press. In Korea, which shared a border with Manchuria, interest in the incident and its aftermath had been intense, no less so than in Japan, in part because of the large numbers of Koreans living in the southeastern region of Jiando (K: Kando), including all but one of the Korean members of the MMA 1 class. (See Chapter 3.) Many Koreans in business and other professions had also harbored great expectations about the benefits and opportunities that a Japan-controlled Manchuria on Korea's borders might bring.[133] Not surprisingly, therefore, the *Tonga ilbo,* in addition to following the Manchurian story closely in its regular morning and evening editions, had frequently published dramatic, up-to-the-minute newspaper flyers or "extras" (*hooe*) to keep up with the rapidly changing scene across the Yalu and Tumen Rivers.[134]

And the story, both military and political, was of course continuing to develop even as the MMA cadets were entering the academies. Manchukuo was still very much a work in progress in the late 1930s and early 1940s, with ongoing "pacification" campaigns, as well as sporadic encounters with Soviet troops focusing the Kwantung and Manchukuo armies' attention, most notably at Nomonhan in 1939.[135] As already seen, many of the instructors at the JMA had just come to Zama from postings in Manchuria, and the MMA itself, the key officer training school in the Manchurian military nexus, was of course a direct product of the 1931 incident. Thus if the Meiji Restoration and the Russo-Japanese War were the most imposing jewels in the 1940s cadets' genealogical crown, the Manchurian Incident was nevertheless the jewel that shone most brightly. It was the most direct, palpable, and emotionally charged link in the lineage, and precisely because it was still so close, so real, and so dazzling in its boldness and scope, it served as an unusually powerful elixir of martial inspiration and self-importance.

In addition to hearing personal stories from their section commanders and other instructors, the cadets' link to the army's Manchurian exploits was strengthened in much the same way as their links to the other wars. They studied in detail the major military engagements before and after the incident, read essays by former cadets dedicated (okuru) to "seniors in Manchuria" then and now fighting "on the front line of the Imperial Army" for the "glory of the national army and the peace of East Asia," and learned numerous songs in both the Otakebi and Hokushin songbooks.[136] The incident in all its dimensions, of course, held a special fascination and meaning for the MMA cadets, who were based in Manchuria itself, and whose martial lineage could thus be traced directly back to those seniors in the Kwantung Army who had played a pivotal role in the events that had transpired in the fall of 1931 and afterward.

Of all these seniors, none was held in greater esteem than Ishiwara Kanji (JMA 21). As operations officer of the Kwantung Army staff at the time, Ishiwara, together with another Kwantung staff member, Itagaki Seishirō (JMA 16), had planned and executed the spurious railway bombing that had led to Japan's invasion and occupation of Manchuria, as well as the establishment of Manchukuo. Although the details of the plot and Ishiwara's crucial role in it were not known to the general public until after the war, they were widely known within army circles. And particularly among the younger officers of the 1930s and 1940s, Ishiwara's exploits in Manchuria had become the stuff of legend, with he himself, in Mark Peattie's words, "the object of intense admiration."[137] Even after he was forced to retire from active duty in 1941 because of his outspoken criticism of the war in China, this admiration remained undiminished, and it was passed on to the cadets by their military superiors and instructors at the academies. On Saturday, August 1, 1942, for example, when the MMA 1 class at the JMA was finishing up several days of swimming exercises at Kugenuma Beach in Sagami Bay, Ishiwara made an unexpected appearance at the camp and spoke to the cadets. One of them, Sudō Tsukasa, who recorded the visit in his diary at the time, captured something of the feeling about Ishiwara in the junior officer corps at the time when he later wrote, "We had never ceased to revere General Ishiwara Kanji, and the fact that he had come in person expressly to honor us with a lecture [*kunwa*] made our impression of this particular exercise all the more profound."[138]

The MMA cadets' sense of connection to Japan's modern wars and of inclusion in a luminous professional pedigree of modern heroes such as Nogi and Ishiwara was fostered as well by their very proximity to the sites of martial valor and victory that they were studying and celebrating in classes, training maneuvers, and occasions of collective singing. With the exception of the Restoration, all the wars cited above were to a great extent Manchurian wars, and by the 1940s the new state of Manchukuo was dotted with commemorative parks and monuments honoring the battles that had been fought there and the men who had fought in them. Unlike their counterparts in Japan, who could only imagine Manchuria from a distance once wartime conditions had limited academy excursions there after 1937, the MMA cadets at Lalatun were literally surrounded on all sides by the vestiges and memorials of the wars of their Manchurian "seniors."

Of these sites, the nearest was Shibeiling, a roughly 1,000-foot-high hill, in effect a small mountain, only about 4 kilometers (2.5 miles) east-southeast of the MMA, and clearly visible from the grounds and barracks. There during the Russo-Japanese War Russian troops in retreat after the Japanese victory at Mukden in March 1905 had dug a series of trench fortifications to prepare for what was expected to be the next confrontation. Although that battle never ensued and the war itself ended shortly thereafter with the decisive Russian naval defeat at Tsushima, the remnants of the Shibeiling fortifications remained as a physical reminder of the war. For the MMA cadets living nearby, Shibeiling was both a historical site and a locus of continuing martial engagement, where they often mustered in double time for drills and camped out for field maneuvers, a familiar place that evoked a great and victorious war of the past with all its legends and heroes while simultaneously serving as a contemporary training ground for officers of present and future wars. Because of its many meanings and memories, Shibeiling was, in the words of one former cadet, "a difficult mountain to forget," and in both the *Hokushin* songbook used at the time and in reminiscences published by former cadets after 1945, it became almost a metonym for the MMA experience itself. One such volume of recollections begun by a cadet from the MMA 7 class (but never published) was entitled quite simply "Shibeiling."[139]

Somewhat farther away from the MMA and in the opposite direction from Shibeiling lay the city of Xinjing, which the cadets visited both on duty and on leave. Not merely a rapidly developing national capital of broad thoroughfares and imposing government buildings, Xinjing in the 1940s was also, in the apt words of David Vance Tucker, a burgeoning urban space of "ceremony and monument."[140] Walking south from the central railway station down Datong Avenue, the main boulevard of the city, cadets visiting the capital would first encounter the green expanse of Kodama Park on the right, named after General Kodama Gentarō, one of the founding figures of the Japanese Imperial Army, and, more to the point, the chief of staff of Japan's Manchurian army during the Russo-Japanese War. Inside the park they would find an imposing statue of the general on horseback, as well as a monument to the "loyal spirits" who had died in the war (chūkonhi).[141]

Further down on the right loomed the large walled compound of the Kwantung Army Headquarters, a massive white-walled building with an overhanging dark blue roof, built in the style of Japanese medieval castles.[142] Within the compound lay a number of other structures extending west for more than half a mile, including the residences of the Kwantung Army commander and his chief of staff. At the very end of the compound, on an enormous elevated site of more than 400,000 square feet, stood the Xinjing Chūreitō or Memorial Tower, designed in 1934 to commemorate the Manchurian Incident and to honor the thousands of Japanese soldiers who had died in the region or would give their lives for Manchukuo in the future. And as they walked farther toward the southern end of Datong Avenue, about three miles down from the main railway station, the cadets would find themselves looking east into a section of the city called Nanling (J: Nanryō), known also as the "National Cultural District" (kokuritsu bunka chiiki). There they would be facing not only a park and another war monument commemorating the Manchurian Incident but also the Kenkoku Chūreibyō or Nation-Founding Heroes Shrine. Built over the course of four years and opened on September 18, 1940, on the ninth anniversary of the incident, the shrine honored all soldiers, regardless of ethnicity, who had died in the course of the establishment of Manchukuo. Expressly constructed to be a counterpart to Japan's Yasukuni Shrine, it was regarded as the "most sacred place in Manchukuo."[143]

Visiting such commemorative sites was for the MMA cadets more than a casual exercise in tourism. On May 31 and September 19, both Manchukuo national holidays to honor the war dead, the Nation-Founding Heroes Shrine was the central locus of the state's celebrations, and the entire corps of cadets from the academy often attended the ceremonies held there, some-times, as in the fall of 1941, following their observances at the shrine with a field trip to the Nanling war memorial nearby. Also in 1941, as the shrine had only been opened the year before, the cadets participated on September 17 in the Chūreibyō's first anniversary of the enshrinement of its fallen soldiers.[144]

The Memorial Tower in the Kwantung Army Headquarters complex was a regular site of ritual observance for the cadets. There were in fact nine other such memorial towers throughout the country, and companies of cadets on school excursions to other cities would often be taken there to pay their respects, as in the winter of 1940, when the MMA 1 Japanese cadets visited Harbin, or in the summer of 1942, when the MMA 2 cadets were in Liaoyang.[145] And a trip to Harbin, as in 1940, frequently included a ritual stop at another "heroes" shrine, a monument to Yokokawa Shōzō and Oki Teisuke, two Japanese civilians who had been caught and executed by the Russian military in 1904 for working with the IJA to disrupt Russian supply routes.[146]

Ritual activities at the war shrines were only one of the ways by which the MMA sought to infuse its cadets with a sense of their Manchurian martial legacy. Official field trips for on-site study were another. In addition to its many other purposes, Shibeiling, ever close and convenient, was always a favorite such destination, and, as noted above, ritual visits to the Nation-Founding Heroes Shine could also easily be combined with a field trip to Nanling. But Xinjing and its environs were far from the only possible study sites in the country, and not even the most important; southern Manchuria in particular was filled with many famous battlegrounds, especially from the Russo-Japanese War, that could be used to enhance the cadets' understanding of Japan's modern wars and its "history of victory." Regular swimming and rowing exercises in July or August on the Dalian coast, for example, offered a perfect opportunity for day trips to such sites. Thus the MMA 1 cadets at Dalian in 1940 took time out to visit Port Arthur, to the south, while the following year the MMA 2 cadets on exercise there were taken north to Jinzhou and Nanshan.[147]

Special field trips directly to the sites were also part of the MMA curriculum. In early May 1941, a little more than a month after their graduation from the *yoka*, the MMA 1 Japanese, Korean, and Chinese cadets who would be going on to Zama for their *honka* course were led on a week-long study tour to southern Manchuria that incorporated on-site military history lectures by MMA officials and instructors, including Colonel Shi Weizhong, a

Chinese graduate of the Army War College in Japan, Major General Akiyama Hiizu from the MMA's head office, and even Superintendent Nagumo
himself.[148] The trip took them first to the Liaoyang battle site of Fort Shuzan.
There, after climbing what had become known in the Japanese military as
"Tachibana Mountain," they heard a lecture from Colonel Shi in front of a
monument that had been erected in honor of the young battalion commander and "war god," ate lunch, and took a brief rest. Before descending
the mountain back down to Liaoyang, they joined together in a forceful
singing of "Lieutenant-Colonel Tachibana," "reflecting as we sang," one of
the cadets, Andō Toyosaburō, later recalled, "on [that] distant battle of the
past between Russia and Japan." After Liaoyang, they traveled to two other
Russo-Japanese battle sites, first to Shaho, where General Akiyama laid out
the engagement in great detail, and then across the border to the Korean
city of Ŭiju, the site of the Battle of the Yalu, where Korean cadet Pak Imhang acted as an interpreter for the group with the local residents, and Superintendent Nagumo delivered an "impressive" lecture highlighting the
reasons for the Japanese victory.[149] The following year, at the end of July,
Park Chung Hee's MMA 2 class made a similar week-long trip to southern
Manchuria, where they visited Fort Shuzan as well as other sites, including
a museum in Mukden dedicated to the Manchurian Incident and located
on the very site in the city where Japanese troops had overrun local Chinese military forces following the fake bomb attack engineered by Ishiwara
and Itagaki.[150]

Once at Zama, the MMA cadets who were doing their *honka* at the JMA
were of course no longer physically steeped in the heady atmosphere of the
continent's martial past and present. But the JMA was no less keen than the
MMA to do what it could to intensify the psychic impact of Japan's victorious modern wars and to foster a sense of connection with famous battles
and heroes. Thus two large stone lions, taken as spoils in Japan's ongoing
war with China, were brought to Zama and strategically placed on either
side of the wide steps leading into the school's Great Lecture Hall, the most
imposing and prominent edifice in the JMA complex.[151] Even more important as a reminder of the school's martial heritage, however, was the special
"memorial hall" or *kinenkan* constructed in 1941, which cadets were encouraged to visit in their free time.[152] The hall was built of wood on two levels
and altogether comprised six main rooms. A couple of the rooms featured
Japanese military paintings, weaponry, and military utensils, as well as materials relating to foreign armies, but the first three rooms were devoted exclusively to Japan's modern wars. The first contained materials and artifacts

related to the Meiji Restoration and the wars with Qing China and tsarist Russia; the second focused largely on the Manchurian Incident and Japan's military involvement in the region before and after 1931; and the third was devoted to the "China Incident" at the Marco Polo Bridge in July 1937 that had expanded into full-scale conflict. Among the objects displayed the most important were the personal items and heirlooms of former cadets or "seniors" who had fought or perished as officers in the wars.

The hall, moreover, was built to be much more than a simple museum. Its true purpose was to serve as a "shrine of spiritual cultivation." Cadets entering it had to remove any headgear and boots, wear slippers, and refrain from touching any items (except books, which had to be handled carefully) and taking any photographs. Above all, the cadets were required to maintain a reverent attitude and absolute silence, respecting what was in effect meant to be a sacred space, not only one that evoked a vivid and graphic picture of the old battles but also one that in both a literal and psychological sense allowed the cadets of the past, many now long since dead, to "pass on their great achievement" to their "juniors" and successors. As an educative tool, a visit to the memorial hall was considered to be "more effective than a thousand lectures."[153]

Limbs of the Emperor

In addition to the war exhibition rooms, there was another room in the JMA memorial hall, a *tokubetsu shitsu* or "special room," that featured items related to the Japanese imperial household and family.[154] For the cadets it was a tangible indication of the ultimate source of their "special favor" and their unique position in imperial society, a sign that, as future officers, they were not only the "pillars of the army" but also the "limbs" (*kokō*: literally "arms and legs") of the emperor.

For the MMA cadets, of course, there were two emperors, the Kangde emperor of Manchukuo (*huangdi* in Chinese; *kōtei* in Japanese), in whose army they officially served, and the Shōwa emperor (*tennō*) of Japan, who was also a figure of ritualized worship. But any contradictions or conflicts that might have arisen from this peculiar dual loyalty were largely subsumed by the reality of Japanese power in Manchuria, and by the ideological edifice publicly embraced by Puyi, the Manchukuo emperor. In his imperial decrees, especially following his visits to Japan in 1935 and 1940, Puyi proclaimed that the two emperors and nations were "unified in virtue and

heart." He further stipulated that Manchukuo ultimately owed its foundation and protection to the Japanese sun goddess, Amaterasu Ōmikami, and
hence to her living descendant, the Shōwa emperor, and he thereafter began
to worship regularly at a Japanese-style National Foundation Shrine that
had been built within his palace grounds in Xinjing.[155] Another shrine, the
Genshinden, was later built at the MMA itself to reinforce the idea of two
countries' common roots.[156] Thus MMA cadets in the 1940s were able to
bask in the "special favor" of not one but two emperors and to claim a special relationship with both. Indeed, throughout the course of their academy
training, both in Manchuria and Japan, the cadets were continually reminded of this special relationship and by extension of the exalted position
they would soon occupy as military officers.

The Symbolic Presence

At one level the special relationship between emperor and cadets was symbolic, and the forms it took were in many respects not so different, except
perhaps in frequency and intensity, from what one could see at the time in
schools and other public institutions throughout the empire, including Korea
and Manchukuo: ritualized bowing to the imperial palace, and formal "reverential readings" (hōdoku) of important imperial rescripts, past and present.
At both the MMA and JMA in an area adjacent to the academy shrine, the
cadets routinely "bowed from afar" in the direction of the imperial palace, as
well as on special occasions such as imperial birthdays or celebrations, including the 2,600th anniversary of the founding of the Japanese Empire on
November 10, 1940.[157] Similarly, while still at Lalatun, the MMA cadets in a
formal ceremony "reverently accepted" (hōtai) Puyi's Rescript on the Con-
solidation of the Basis of the Nation, which the emperor had issued upon his
return from Japan, and on the morning of December 9, 1941, the MMA 1 cadets who had gone on to Zama for their honka course also "reverently accepted" Emperor Hirohito's declaration of war on the United States.[158]

Within the symbolic realm, however, what gave the relationship between
the emperor and cadets its special character was the army's emphasis on the
Meiji emperor's 1882 Imperial Rescript to Soldiers and Sailors (Gunjin
Chokuyu). Since the nineteenth century the rescript had functioned as a
kind of catechism for the IJA, especially the officer corps, laying out the five
key precepts that should guide the conduct of servicemen: loyalty (chūsetsu),
propriety (reigi), valor (buyū), righteousness (shingi), and simplicity (shisso).[159]

For our purposes here, however, what was most important about the rescript was that it represented a codified articulation by the emperor himself of the intimate personal bond between himself and the army, for the first time invoking the metaphor of imperial "limbs," which subsequently became a standard phrase in the academy manuals and songbooks:

> We are your supreme Commander-in-Chief. Our relations with you will be most intimate when We rely on you as Our limbs, and you look up to Us as your head. Whether We are able to guard the Empire, and so prove Ourself worthy of Heaven's blessings and repay the benevolence of Our Ancestors, depends on the faithful discharge of your duties as soldiers and sailors. If the majesty and power of Our Empire be impaired, do you share with Us the sorrow; if the glory of Our arms shines resplendent, We will share with you the honor. If you all do your duty, and being one with Us in spirit do your utmost for the protection of the state, Our people will long enjoy the blessings of peace, and the might and dignity of Our Empire will shine in the world.[160]

During the wartime period the rescript or sections of it were commonly taught as part of the required military training that had been introduced into the imperial school system for fourth-year middle school boys and above.[161] But at Lalatun and Zama in particular, where the rescript was generally read or recited every morning after the imperial bows and every night in the barracks at the end of evening study shortly before taps, the reading or recitation took on the quality of a sacred religious ritual that worked to underline and reinforce the special bond the cadets shared with the emperor. As one former MMA cadet described it: "We were required to hold up the rescript with the right hand to a point slightly above eye level and focus all attention on it, as if ceasing to breathe. Except when turning pages, our left hand remained fully extended at the side touching our trousers, and we stood at absolute attention with our legs fixed at a 90-degree angle."[162]

The Physical Presence

Ichigaya was chosen as the original site of the JMA in the nineteenth century not only because of its commanding elevation in central Tokyo but also because of its strategic location just across one of the bridges spanning the outer moat of the imperial palace. As the director of the Yasukuni Kaikō Archive, Daitō Shinsuke, himself a former military officer, told me in 2007, "The site of the academy was very important—it had to be physically close to the emperor."[163] When the JMA moved outside Tokyo to Zama in 1937, a new road, now Route 51, was expressly built for the emperor, providing a direct physical link between the palace and the academy.[164] Indeed, for the cadets of the 1940s, both in Manchuria and Japan, the emperor was both a powerful symbolic presence and an actual physical presence in their life at the academy, something that distinguished their relationship with him from his relationship with most of their civilian peers and gave substance to the *kokō* metaphor of the cadets as imperial "limbs."

On various occasions throughout the year, for example, the cadets were called upon to attend the emperor in person. Thus in June 1940 the MMA 1 cadets participated in a formal "send-off" (*hōsō*) ceremony for Emperor Puyi as he prepared to depart for Japan and a meeting with his Japanese counterpart.[165] And in April 1943 and again in January 1944 the MMA 2 cadets at Zama joined their fellow cadets from other JMA classes for a trip to Tokyo to be reviewed at Yoyogi Parade Grounds by the emperor on his birthday and on Army Day, respectively.[166]

The emperors returned the compliment by favoring the cadets with personal visits to the academies. The most important of these was of course commencement, which the emperors or one of their representatives always attended, presenting an imperial watch and other awards to the top-ranked cadets in the graduating class. Zama class albums, such as the one for Park Chung Hee's MMA 2/JMA 57 class, invariably featured pictures of Emperor Hirohito reviewing the graduating cadets.[167] There were also occasional special imperial visits. On June 20, 1941, for example, while the MMA 1 and MMA 2 cadets were both in residence, the Manchukuo emperor, Puyi, went by motorcade to Lalatun to bestow the imperial name of Dōtokudai on the academy and celebrate its formal inauguration.[168] The following year, in September, he visited again to commemorate the tenth anniversary of the establishment of Manchukuo.[169]

The presence or visits of imperial family members worked to reinforce the sense of the cadets' special physical bond with the emperors. No fewer than five members of Puyi's extended family served as instructors or administrators of the MMA during the early 1940s, including his brother-in-law, Zhao Guoqi, the descendant of a Mongolian prince, and his own younger brother Pujie, who at one point held the post of commandant of cadets for the *yoka* students. Three of Puyi's nephews also attended the MMA as cadets, including two in the MMA 2 class.[170]

And although Emperor Hirohito himself never went to Manchukuo, members of his family did. In May 1942 the MMA cadets participated in a military parade and review for the Shōwa emperor's younger brother Prince Takamatsu (Nobuhito), who had come to celebrate the tenth anniversary of the state's founding.[171] Two months later when yet another younger brother of Hirohito, Prince Mikasa (Takahito) came to Manchuria, he included Dōtokudai on his itinerary.[172] At Zama too there were more visits from the imperial clan, including even more distant relatives, as in February 1944, when Prince Higashikuni Toshihiko, the youngest son in one of the imperial branch families, toured the JMA with his classmates from the Peers School (Gakushūin).[173]

That the imperial families themselves were in a sense military families as well, with personal ties to the academies and sometimes even actual combat experience, undoubtedly strengthened the cadets' sense that they shared a special connection with the emperors they served. All five of Puyi's relatives with appointments at the MMA were JMA graduates and career officers, and Prince Takamatsu and Prince Mikasa were academy graduates and officers in the navy and army, respectively. In fact, it had been customary since the Meiji era for males in the Japanese imperial family to attend either the army or naval academy and pursue a career in one or the other of the services, and at Zama a special two-story residence had been built within the grounds of the school to accommodate imperial attendees and their families.[174] Academy instructors were eager to emphasize these imperial ties whenever the opportunity arose as a way of boosting professional morale and self-esteem among their charges. When General Akiyama delivered his long on-site lecture on the Russo-Japanese Battle of Shaho during the MMA 1 study tour in May 1941, for example, he was not only interested in describing the details and tactics of the Japanese victory; he was also intent on reminding the cadets that one of the heroes of that battle, Kan'in Kotohiko, a cavalry officer and one of their seniors, had been a *miya* or imperial prince, the adoptive brother of Emperor Meiji and the Shōwa emperor's great-uncle. Akiyama, himself a cavalry officer, emphasized to the cadets that the prince, a brigade commander, had not stood off on the sidelines but had been fully engaged in the battle "at the risk of his life," and the battleground had subsequently become known as "Miyanogahara," the "Prince's Field."[175]

All things considered, the imperial presence in the lives of the cadets was significant and palpable. That of the Shōwa emperor loomed especially large, perhaps, given that the entire structure, society, and ideology of the empire encompassing Japan, Taiwan, Korea, Manchukuo, and beyond was centered on his person, and thousands of officers and soldiers were dying in his name, as thousands before had died in the name of his grandfather. Indeed, for some cadets the imperial presence in their midst, especially a visit by the emperor himself or a member of his family, was so fraught with awe that they found themselves momentarily overwhelmed, a pressure the academies themselves only intensified by putting the cadets through a grueling regimen of preparation for such visits that interrupted regular classes and training and often went on for days, as in the case of Prince Takamatsu's visit to Xinjing in 1942 or Puyi's formal opening and naming of the MMA on June 20, 1941. In his diary entry for the latter day, Park Chung Hee's classmate, Hosokawa Minoru (MMA 2), described in detail the "long-awaited," "glorious" inaugural ceremony in which he, Park, and the other cadets in the first two academy classes had participated together with the emperor; in a prominent red-ink gloss, Hosokawa's section commander commented, "You will remember this day for the rest of your life."[176] Indeed, fifty years later another former MMA 2 Japanese cadet, Mitsui Katsuo, still recalled Puyi's visit with considerable emotion: "As a member of the first section of the fifth company, I was in the very front line of the ceremony for the MMA inauguration. Even today I clearly remember the Emperor and the Kwantung Army Commander Umezu standing on the dais. Being able to bow to such a great figure at such close distance made me enormously tense [*taihen kinchō*]."[177] Commencement at the JMA, in the presence of the Shōwa emperor, could be especially stressful, especially for the Japanese cadets, and it was not uncommon for a few upcoming graduates to experience panic attacks. According to Takayama Toshitake, a former section commander for the MMA *honka* course at Zama, one of the MMA 2 Japanese cadets under his authority initially refused to participate in the April 1944 commencement ceremonies because he deemed himself "unworthy" to attend and was filled with "dread"; in the end he was only persuaded to do so by the intervention of the company commander, Enami Shigeru, who, according to Takayama, was a "veteran" in such matters.[178]

To be sure, Koreans and Chinese seem to have been less susceptible than their Japanese counterparts to the religiosity of the imperial dignity, including even that of the Shōwa emperor. For Korean cadets, as academy officials noted at the time, an invitation to meet with Crown Prince Yi Ǔn, the head of the former Chosŏn royal family and also a JMA graduate (JMA 29), tended to stir considerable feeling, fueling an ethnic pride that Japanese instructors always worried might disrupt group solidarity.[179] Toward the Shōwa emperor, however, as Yi Hyŏnggŭn (JMA 56) would later write, the Koreans felt no such sentiment; from the beginning of his JMA experience, Yi felt somewhat "bewildered" by his instructors' assiduous attempts to instill a sense of supreme loyalty and devotion to the imperial personage.[180] Perhaps Yu Yangsu, a former Korean IJA officer who had commanded a platoon of mainly Japanese soldiers in China, put it best: for Japanese the imperial rituals and formalities had a certain "sacred" character, but for Koreans the emperor was not so much a hallowed figure of reverence as a "symbol of imperial rule and power."[181]

On the other hand, precisely because the emperor was the embodiment of imperial rule and power, his presence and that of members of the imperial family was not something the cadets, Koreans included, ever simply took for granted. Quite the opposite. For example, interviews and reminiscences of former MMA cadets, regardless of ethnicity, make it clear that they were all keenly aware of the impressive number of imperial family members at the MMA. In one such interview Kim Muk (MMA 2) brought up the subject entirely on his own, noting with pride that his company commander at the MMA had been the emperor's brother-in-law, the Mongol prince Zhao Guoqi, and that there were other members of the imperial family at the academy as well.[182] Memoirs by former Chinese cadets also highlight and detail the imperial family's involvement in the academy.[183]

Whatever range of meanings individual cadets might have attached to the two emperors, the imperial presence at the academies, both symbolic and personal, was for all the cadets who passed through the gates of the schools an unmistakable, indeed ultimate, sign and confirmation of the great esteem in which they and their chosen profession were held. When the Shōwa emperor appeared at Sōbudai on his white horse for the commencement review of the MMA 1/JMA 56 class on December 16, 1942, and again on April 20, 1944 for the MMA 2/JMA 57 class, all of the graduating cadets, Park Chung Hee and other Koreans included, knew that they were about to assume a unique status in imperial society, a "special favor" from on high that empowered them as men and as members of that society, and that also obligated them, should the times call for it, to perform "a singular duty."

FIVE

POLITICS AND POWER

A Singular Duty

We'll mutiny.
—William Shakespeare, *Julius Caesar*

Only we could shoulder this burden, and our duty as soldiers demanded it.
—Muranaka Takaji, February 26 Incident leader,
    from his prison diary, July 15, 1936

There is absolutely no other means to save the state and nation.
—Park Chung Hee, May 16, 1961

When the JMA *Regulations* spoke of the "singular duty" attendant upon military officers who by profession enjoyed the emperor's "special favor," the intention was not, of course, to provide a rationale for dissent from national policy, let alone for mutiny against the state. Indeed, the Meiji emperor's Imperial Rescript to Soldiers and Sailors had specifically enjoined the military from interfering in politics in any way.[1] But army interference was of course one of the hallmarks of 1930s Japanese political culture, and this activist idea of "singular duty" lingered on in the IJA and academy culture well into the 1940s and beyond, also finding its way into South Korean army culture. At the time of the coup in 1961, when Park Chung Hee wrote of his "firm and unalterable belief that there is absolutely no other means to save the state and nation in its current extremity and guarantee a prosperous tomorrow," he was echoing a radical view of military privilege and obligation that he and his fellow cadets had frequently encountered at Lalatun and Zama. Here we examine how an understanding of "singular duty" as mutiny came to be embedded in the academy culture of the 1940s, a lineage that arguably began with the Meiji Restoration itself.

The Meiji Restoration as Rebellion

In attempting to explain the politicization of the prewar Japanese military, scholars have often called attention to the Meiji constitutional structure.[2]

Without question, this was a crucial factor, and we will explore it in more detail below. But even before the constitutional structure was formally established in 1890, one might argue that the die was already cast by the very nature of the Meiji Restoration itself. In its simplest terms, the Restoration had been a coup d'état against the existing government, the Tokugawa Bakufu, and the celebrated *shishi* or "men of high purpose" whom the academy cadets subsequently studied and admired had in fact been rebels against the state. Yoshida Shōin, whose teaching and work inspired so many of the major figures of the Restoration, and whose writings were featured in the *JMA Bulletin* even as late as October 1944, had been an anti-Bakufu dissident who was imprisoned several times and eventually executed for his activities. Indeed, had the Restoration failed, most if not all of the leaders of the Restoration, including the so-called three greats, Ōkubo, Kido, and Saigō, likely would have suffered the same fate as Yoshida.[3]

Herein lay a great and fundamental irony. Once in power the Meiji leaders expected and demanded loyalty to the new system they had established, but the event that had produced that new system, the epochal moment that had given birth to the modern Japanese state, had been an internal revolt against the government by dissatisfied young military men. Like the Park Chung Hee regime in South Korea a century later, the very means by which the Meiji leaders had come to power tended to provide an inherent rationale for future military rebellion. Thus the "Great Saigō," whose virtues generations of cadets through 1945 would continue to extol in classes and songs, would himself lead an abortive countercoup against the new Meiji government in 1877, and Imperial Guard troops at the Takebashi barracks in Tokyo who had helped suppress Saigō's forces would attempt yet another unsuccessful coup d'état the following year.[4]

The Meiji leaders were of course not unaware of the contradiction they faced with respect to the military, and a precursor of the 1882 Rescript to Soldiers and Sailors with its injunction against political activity was in fact issued in response to the Satsuma and Takebashi revolts.[5] But the past could not be undone, and the model of the Restoration as rebellion was there for all who chose to see it. Moreover, the new state was subsequently compelled to glorify the Restoration as the founding event of modern Japanese history, and, as we have seen, academy cadets were urged to respect and emulate the *shishi*. When in the 1930s there was widespread discontent with the government and society among many younger officers, the model to which they harkened was the very one they had been taught to revere most, the Meiji Restoration of 1868, which, they believed, had since been corrupted and needed to be set right through a second or Shōwa Restoration. In the notes

and testaments left behind by the young officers who were tried and executed for their role in the mutiny of February 26, 1936, one finds countless
references to the Meiji Restoration and its *shishi*. First Lieutenant Nakahashi
Motoaki, for example, wrote of being deeply moved on reading the biographies of the *shishi* and his certainty that the spirit of the mutiny was something he and his fellow rebels had "received" from them. He writes also that
he and his fellow rebels were "filled with emotion" at the thought that they
were about to repeat in the same place and in the same kind of snowy
weather the act of a group of samurai from Mito who had assassinated a
high figure in the Tokugawa shogunate in the Sakuradamon Incident of
1860.[6] Second Lieutenant Nakajima Kanji, in prison like Nakahashi and
facing a death sentence, also found strength and solace in the writings of
Yoshida Shōin that had been composed under similar circumstances.[7] And
another second lieutenant, Yasuda Yutaka, echoing a common sentiment
among the rebels, justified the "direct action" of February 26 by arguing
that the Meiji Restoration had been "perverted" (*waikyoku*) by a national
polity that required fundamental "reform" (*kakushin*).[8]

The Weak Constitutional Structure

Even if it was impossible to put the genie of Meiji precedent back into the
bottle, the notion of rebellion as restoration might have been contained by a
strong constitutional structure that kept the military firmly under the control of civilian authority. As is well known, however, the Meiji constitution
had precisely the opposite effect. Under its provisions, the executive branch
had virtually no formal control over the military. In accordance with the
Prussian system that had served as a model, the right of supreme command
was independently vested in the emperor, and the chiefs of staff of the army
and navy reported directly and exclusively to him, not to the prime minister
or even to the army and navy ministers. Indeed, the organization of the
modern IJA had taken place before the Meiji constitution had been promulgated, and the 1882 Rescript to Soldiers and Sailors, which also antedated the
constitution, defined military loyalty or *chūsetsu* in terms of a personal
obligation to the emperor, not in terms of a legal commitment to the Meiji
government. "The emperor was the state [*kokka*]," Yu Yangsu, a 1961 coup
participant who had served as an IJA platoon commander in China and
Korea in the last years of the war, told me in 1997. "You never heard, 'Long
live the Japanese Empire!' [*Nippon Teikoku banzai!*] in the army, only 'Long

live the emperor!' [*Tennō Heika banzai!*]."[9] As the director of the Yasukuni Kaikō Archive put it: "For Japanese imperial officers the Rescript was more important than the constitution."[10] What this meant in practical terms is that dissident officers in the 1930s could justify rebellion against the government by viewing it as an act of higher loyalty to the emperor, exactly as Saigō Takamori had done sixty years earlier.[11]

Cabinet ministers were responsible only to the emperor, not to the Diet, and although it was not written directly into the constitution, it was a stipulation of the army and navy ministries (later combined into a single Ministry of War) that only active-duty officers could serve as ministers of those departments. Not only did this further dilute an already extremely weak civilian authority, but it also had the effect of giving the military veto power in the process of cabinet selection and hence the ability to shape parliamentary governments. One of the best-known examples of this was the army's refusal to name a war minister in 1937, which forced the government's nominee for prime minister, Ugaki Kazushige, to withdraw his name from consideration.[12]

Such a system tended to foster a culture of superiority and even insubordination toward civilian authority within the officer corps. Indeed, by the standard of the times, the army's rejection of Ugaki was only the tip of the proverbial iceberg. By 1937 many other, far more egregious examples of military challenges to the constituted political order had already taken place, including the Manchurian Incident of 1931. The incident was celebrated by the MMA cadets as a great and glorious foundational event in the history of Manchukuo—a Manchurian equivalent of the Meiji Restoration, as it were (see Chapter 4). But within army circles even at the time it was well known that it had involved no small degree of deliberate deception and manipulation of the Japanese government by Kwantung Army staff officers Ishiwara Kanji (JMA 21) and Itagaki Seishirō (JMA 16).[13] Although not quite rising to the level of overt mutiny, the Manchurian Incident also highlighted the extraordinary sense of self-importance and independence that younger officers in the army exhibited at this time, not only toward civilian cabinets but even toward their superiors in the chain of command. Field staff officers such as Ishiwara and Itagaki in particular were prone to such attitudes, for it was they who often drew up the operational plans at central headquarters and were then sent out to serve on the staffs of the very armies for which the plans had been designed. Such officers tended to regard themselves as better-placed and better-equipped to understand and carry out the plans than their immediate (and lower-ranking) successors in Tokyo who had assumed the role of advising central command.[14] The IJA *Field Service Regulations* (in Japanese *Sakusen yōmurei*), the second "bible" of the Japanese officer after the 1882 rescript, also gave extraordinary discretion to commanding officers in the field under the principle of "field initiative" (*dokudan senkō*), whereby orders from superiors could be changed or ignored if in the commander's judgment the situation called for it.[15] The line between boldness of command and insubordination was thus wafer-thin in the IJA, determined in many cases only by the ultimate success or failure of the operation. There was in fact a famous saying in the army dating back at least to Saigō Takamori's time: "If you win, you're the loyal army; if you lose, you're a rebel army."[16] And since the commanders in turn often tended to rely on their operations staff for advice, the role and power of field officers such as Ishiwara and Itagaki were all the more enhanced.

If the Manchurian Incident, in large part because of its "success," fell slightly short of being regarded as actual mutiny, there was no mistaking the mutinous character of the other "incidents" (*jiken*) that followed in its wake between 1932 and 1936, most notably the May 15 (Go-Ichigo) Incident of 1932, in which a group of naval officers and army cadets assassinated the prime minister, Inukai Tsuyoshi, in his residence, and the February 26 (Ni-Niroku) Incident of 1936, a full-blown mutiny in which rebel officers and troops launched assassination attacks on a number of high officials, killing several, and occupied central Tokyo for four days before being dispersed. These were complicated movements that included a range of protagonists and motivations, reflecting and occasionally even overlapping in various ways with the aims of the Kōdōha or Imperial Way Faction in the army's central headquarters and the War Ministry, which included influential generals such as Araki Sadao and Mazaki Jinzaburō. Chapter 6 will devote more attention to this group and its nemesis, the so-called Tōseiha or Control Faction, examining the nationalist visions of state and society that were embedded in the army culture of the academies. For the moment, however, what is important to note is that the above incidents for the most part were led by junior officers who embraced the idea of violent revolution against the government as a means of purging and reforming the nation. In the minds of these officers the Meiji constitution was irrelevant. Loyalty to the emperor and the goal of the Shōwa Restoration were all that mattered, justifying mutiny, mayhem, and even murder by assassination. In the words of Captain Nonaka Shirō, another February 26 officer, the restoration was a "stupendous and sacred task."[17] It was not a *hanran* (rebellion), as it was commonly called in the newspapers, but a *kekki* (*kwŏlgi* in Korean), an "uprising,"

connoting an act of righteous anger, a term employed by the officers themselves in their public manifesto.[18] That was also the term Park Chung Hee
would later use to describe the May 16 coup in 1961.[19]

Army and Public Attitudes and Reactions

Meiji legacies and a weak constitution notwithstanding, such mutinies
might yet have been forestalled by an army command or public that displayed a clear and unequivocal lack of tolerance for such actions. Such was
not the case, however. Indeed, the attitudes and reactions of both the army
and the public often went beyond tolerance to something bordering on sympathy or empathy. The Manchurian Incident was a case in point here, as
well as a harbinger of attitudes toward the later events. "All the main actors
in the Manchurian drama received recognition for their accomplishments,"
Mark Peattie has written.[20] Both Ishiwara and Itagaki were in fact subsequently honored and eventually promoted to general rank, and Itagaki even
went on to serve as war minister. Although Ishiwara later had a personal
and professional falling-out with Prime Minister Tōjō Hideki that forced
him out of active duty, he remained, as we saw in Chapter 4, an inspiring
figure for younger officers and cadets. The almost mythic aura that surrounded Ishiwara within the military was buttressed and complemented
by a "war fever" ignited in the news media by the incident, which, as Louise
Young has shown, helped militarize popular culture in the Shōwa period.[21]

Such militarist sympathies were increasingly evident in the unfolding
and aftermath of the later incidents. The key figures in the so-called November Incident of 1934, another coup d'état plot, were arrested before they
could put any plans into action, and the affair did not become public until
after the war, but both the earlier May 15 Incident and the subsequent February 26 Incident were of course major events and news stories in the 1930s.
Despite their violence and subversion of the democratic order, both received
a remarkable degree of support, especially from the Imperial Way faction
within the army, but also, and especially in the case of May 15, from the general public. As Ben-Ami Shillony notes, after the May 15 Incident the war
minister at the time, General Araki Sadao, a prominent Kōdōha figure, publicly called for leniency in the treatment of the rebels, citing their purity of
motive—a defense of political violence that had deep roots in the modern
Japanese military going back to Saigō and before, and one that had been
publicly endorsed in his day by no less a figure than General Nogi.[22] Moreover,

Araki's friend General Hata Shinji, chief of the Military Police, even visited the rebels at the police station where they were being held, telling them they should have coordinated their activities with his organization, while also instructing the Tokyo police to treat the rebels as "patriots."[23] The public trials that followed, which stretched on over the next two years and were widely and sensationally covered by an increasingly militaristic press, allowed further emotional testimonies by high military figures as to the unblemished patriotism of the defendants. The War Ministry reported receiving more than 10,000 petitions for clemency, as well as a package of little fingers from petitioners in Niigata prefecture as a grim demonstration of their sincerity. In the end, the courts complied with army and public opinion, handing down only light prison sentences, thus allowing the defendants to look forward to release in the near future.[24]

The February 26 Incident in 1936 was of course a full-scale mutiny involving not only assassination but also seizure of government buildings and occupation of the capital city, and the military had no choice in the end but to oppose it, especially after the emperor himself personally ordered its suppression. Unlike the defendants in the May 15 Incident, moreover, the February 26 rebels were subjected to swift and secret special courts-martial without benefit of counsel and out of view of the public. As already noted, their punishments were severe, especially for the officers involved, all of whom were sentenced to either death or life imprisonment. Clearly even the army could not tolerate such an extraordinary breach of discipline within its officer corps and troops. Still, it is astonishing how many high-ranking military officials at the time, especially those with connections to the Kōdōha, seemed to provide encouragement and even varying degrees of support for the rebels before and during the course of the incident. Major General Yamashita Tomoyuki, for example, a close friend of Arikawa Shuichi, Park Chung Hee's military drill instructor at Taegu Normal School, actually met with the rebels beforehand, praising their manifesto and encouraging them to act sooner rather than later, even though he was working in the War Ministry at the time as chief of the Military Research Bureau.[25] Once the mutiny was under way, neither the Tokyo Metropolitan Police nor the Tokyo Military Police did anything to quash it, and General Kashii Kōhei, the commander of the Tokyo garrison, who was in charge of all the army forces in the capital area, not only took no action against the mutiny but actually met with rebel leaders to congratulate them, thus signaling other officers throughout the garrison to act accordingly.[26] Even the war minister himself, General Kawashima Yoshiyuki, was sympathetic, inviting the rebels into his house and later recommending to an irate emperor that he take the rebels' demands seriously.[27] Although Ishiwara was not associated with the Kōdōha and took a leading role in the suppression of the rebels, he too shared some of their critiques of state policy. He also appears, like Yamashita, to have met with some of them prior to the mutiny and was regarded by the rebels, at least until he moved against them on the emperor's orders, as one of their sympathizers.[28] In the end the mutiny was finally put down only on the insistence and ultimately express formal command of the emperor himself, perhaps the most telling sign of the extent of support the rebels enjoyed from well-placed military officers at the time.

Late Chosŏn Resonances

"Loyal rebels" in the Saigō mold were not tolerated, let alone celebrated, in premodern Korea, with its strong affinity for civilian rule. But before we dismiss the idea of any traditional Korean resonances in the realm of military politics, we should remind ourselves that the Chosŏn dynasty was founded in a coup d'état by a disaffected military officer, who used his power of command to establish himself as king. And despite the unquestioned dominance of civilian rule, over the course of the next five centuries the dynasty was frequently beset by internal political convulsions that required military power for resolution and stability.

Political intrigues and conflicts were in fact a virtually continuous feature of life at the Chosŏn court. In the early part of the dynasty, as the foundations of the new state were being laid out and tested, they tended to revolve around issues of royal succession and the respective limits of aristocratic and monarchical power.[29] Although these and other issues continued to recur in various forms throughout the dynasty, beginning in the sixteenth century the political landscape was transformed by the emergence of powerful political factions within the aristocratic bureaucracy. Factions tended to beget factions, and following the usual Korean pattern, these tended to become hereditary over time. Unresolved feuds were often piled one on the other and carried over from generation to generation, with each new generation seeking to defend or avenge the honor of its fathers and ancestors by eliminating its hereditary rivals and exercising control over key bureaucratic posts and the throne. The stronger and more able kings fought back against or manipulated the leading factions to protect royal prerogatives, but the weaker kings were often pawns in the hands of the ruling faction. In the nineteenth century, successive monarchical weakness added yet another element to this seething political cauldron. All four kings of the century came to the throne as minors, opening the door to domination of the political system by the young kings' consort families. The machinations of these royal in-law lineages often overlapped with and exacerbated existing factional interests.

The incessant court struggles of the dynasty were not always limited to wars of words. Not infrequently they led to banishments or executions, or even to coups, countercoups, and rebellions. Control of the military forces, particularly in the capital, was frequently a critical element of success or failure in these life-and-death confrontations, as it was in simply maintaining political hegemony. Factions sought to acquire such control through concurrent civil and military appointments, through the forging of symbiotic relationships with prominent military lineages, and through various pressures on the king. The kings, in turn, were acutely aware that hostile aristocratic factions possessed of such military power would not hesitate to use it to place more amenable candidates on the throne, and they strove to ensure that the military forces in the capital were loyal to them personally. Occasionally they were even forced to set up entirely new military units expressly for that purpose. Indeed, of the five military camps in the capital, only one, the Military Training Agency, established during the Hideyoshi invasions, had been created solely and specifically to enhance the country's defense by incorporating new military technology and tactics. The origins of the others were all connected in one way or another with contemporary court politics.[30]

Military politics under Yŏngjo, arguably the strongest of the late Chosŏn kings, who reigned for more than fifty years (1724–1776) and even managed for a time to tame the political factions, offers a case in point.[31] Unlike many Chosŏn kings, he was able to carry out an ambitious, if only partially and temporarily successful, military strengthening effort. But as Yi T'aejin has suggested, Yŏngjo's interest in the military was stimulated and circumscribed by anxieties stemming from a large-scale factional insurrection in 1728 that attempted to overthrow the government by armed force. His successor, Chŏngjo, also a strong king who ruled for more than two decades (1777–1800), had similar political preoccupations, and his military projects, which included the formation of a new praetorian military unit, the Robust and Brave Guards (Changyongwi), were predicated more on royal protection than on national defense per se. After 1800, with a succession of minority kingships, power tended to devolve into the hands of the royal consort families, and private political interests reigned supreme in the military, as elsewhere in the system.[32]

While the typical Chosŏn coup d'état pattern was thus one of civilian leadership with strategic military backing, the last decades of the dynasty, after the country had been forcibly opened to modern international trade and diplomacy by Japan, began to see a more prominent involvement of military officers in such political movements, including the famous and abortive Kapsin Coup of 1884, in which a group of young Chosŏn reformers briefly seized the government with the support of troops from Japanese embassy and attempted to compel the king to change state policies. Such movements also tended to be more violent than what one saw in the typical Chosŏn pattern, where political coups were more often accompanied by arrests and exile than by assassination or execution. In the case of the Kapsin Coup, for example, six high-ranking ministers of state were murdered and many others were injured.[33]

Not surprisingly, perhaps, most of these late Chosŏn conspirators, including military officers such as Sŏ Chaep'il, a key figure in the Kapsin Coup who had been trained at the Toyama Military School, had studied in Japan and were inspired in their actions by the Meiji Restoration and Japan's subsequent national development. As historian Tabohashi Kiyoshi wrote: "The leaders of the *kapsin* coup were all new faces [in Korean politics] and were influenced by the Japanese civilization. What they learned first from the new Japan was how to take direct action by killing evil men. It is correct to say that the political history of Japan from the end of the Tokugawa to the middle of the Meiji was stained with blood of assassinations. The young *shishi* of that period extolled assassination as a righteous act and never regarded it as a vulgar political measure or a serious crime against morality."[34] Following in this same tradition, a little more than a decade later another group of Koreans, all state-sponsored graduates of the still relatively new JMA, formed a secret club, the Revolution United Society (Hyŏngmyŏng Ilsimhoe), dedicated to overthrowing the Chosŏn government, which they saw as having turned away from Meiji-style reform in favor of Russian patronage. Although the plot never materialized and a number of the group's members were subsequently hanged by the Chosŏn state, the Revolution United Society was significant in that it represented perhaps for the first time since General Yi Sŏnggye had seized power and founded the Chosŏn state in the fourteenth century an instance of Korean military officers directly taking the lead in a planned coup d'état.[35]

Chosŏn Legacies in the 1930s

In the late 1930s and 1940s, when Korean cadets began to enter the MMA, the political upheavals of the late Chosŏn period were still a living memory for their parents, grandparents, and teachers, and a number of the chief protagonists from that earlier time were still alive. Beginning in the late 1920s and early 1930s, moreover, memoirs and commentaries about the period began to appear in newspapers, magazines, and books. Just before his death in 1929, for example, Kim Hyŏngsŏp, one of the officers in the nineteenth-century Revolution United Society who had escaped execution, wrote a memoir that was published in 1930.[36] Since he wrote it in Japanese and its distribution was limited, it is likely that that only a relatively small number of Koreans actually read it. However, around the same time, in a long-running memoir of his life and experiences serialized in the popular Korean-language magazine *Samch'ŏlli*, the prominent journalist Ch'oe Rin, who had been born in 1878 in South Hamgyŏng province, recounted his move to Seoul for study at the age of sixteen and the tumultuous politics of that era, describing the Revolution United Society, in which he had personally been involved, in a way that was not so different from the way journalists a few years later would report on the February 26 mutiny in 1936:

> The Revolution United Society was a secret association to reform the [Chosŏn] government organized by a group of Korean cadets studying at the military academy in Tokyo. They thought that through a "coup d'état" leading a mass of several thousand people to the palace and killing several high officials, the government would fall naturally into their hands. The key to carrying out this movement was military power. As most of the instructors at the Great Han Empire Military Academy [Mugwan Hakkyo] at the time were graduates of the Japanese Military Academy, the Koreans studying in Tokyo at the JMA thought that in the near future when they returned to Korea and began teaching there, they would each come to have control over several hundred troops, all cadets, and this would be constitute their actual [military] force.[37]

The fiftieth anniversary of the Kapsin Coup in 1934 also provided the occasion for a number of serialized reflections and retrospective media reports. Korean intellectuals and writers associated in one way or another

with what Michael Robinson has called the "cultural nationalist" movement, centered on the *Tonga ilbo* publishing group and supported by the
extensive financial resources of the newspaper and its owners, took particular interest in this commemoration.[38] The movement's roots could be
traced back to the Enlightenment Party of the nineteenth century, whose
leaders had led the coup; indeed, Park Yŏnghyo, one of those leaders, had
been selected as the first president of *Tonga ilbo* at the time of its establishment in 1920.[39]

In 1935 the newspaper published a series of front-page recollections about
the coup by its chief military figure, Sŏ Chaep'il, along with three consecutive lengthy editorials that pondered its historical meaning in light of Sŏ's
memoir. Together they provide a fascinating glimpse of the perspectives of
some of the most influential molders of public opinion in Korea at the
time—not only their view of the Kapsin Coup itself but also their assessment of the legitimacy and efficacy of such a military seizure of power in
general.

In his memoir Sŏ elevated the Kapsin Coup, despite its ultimate failure, to
one of the great revolutionary events of both Korean and world history, comparing it not only to the founding of the Chosŏn dynasty in 1392 but also to
the English nobility's appropriation of power from King John at Runnymede
through the Magna Carta and to the Meiji Restoration, both of which,
he wrote, "were without question inspirational examples to the Kapsin reformers."[40] *Tonga ilbo* more or less concurred in this high assessment of the
rebels' intentions, calling them "unlucky men of high purpose" and using the
same term, *chisa* (*shishi* in Japanese), that was commonly applied to the Meiji
patriots.[41] The editorial also agreed that the coup was motivated by "the
highest form of patriotism," with the men participating in it "prepared to die,
giving no thought to their own lives or property."[42] And because it was regarded as a morally pure, patriotic act, just as the May 15 and February 26
incidents would later be described by the Kōdōha and the Japanese press,
neither Sŏ nor the newspaper ever criticized the Kapsin Coup for its violence
or use of military force to usurp power from a legitimately constituted government. What they both did criticize, however, was the failure of the rebels
to secure in advance the understanding and support of the general populace, and their reliance on foreign troops from the Japanese embassy.[43] In
other words, a military coup d'état of patriotic purpose carried out by Korean troops and supported by Korean public opinion not only would have
had a greater chance of success but clearly would have been a legitimate undertaking. Within Korea's own recent past, therefore, or at least a

popular interpretation of it, Korean cadets at Lalatun and Zama could find an inspiring model for "direct action" by patriotic military men—an indigenous Korean counterpart, as it were, to the Meiji Restoration that they were taught to revere so deeply.[44]

Of course, by the late 1930s and early 1940s young Koreans, like their Japanese peers, had been exposed to many other, and even more recent, examples of military intervention in politics and attempted coups by ardent young officers acting in the name of patriotism. For all practical purposes, parliamentary politics in Japan had come to an end in 1932 with the May 15 Incident, as the army subsequently used its cabinet veto power to assert its will upon a government and public that were becoming more amenable to militaristic policies. Manchukuo, the home of the MMA, was of course the political creation of the Kwantung Army, and after 1932 it was more firmly under military rule than ever, despite the army's public obeisance to the emperor and central bureaucracy. And it should never be forgotten that Koreans of Park Chung Hee's generation had all been born after Japan's occupation of the peninsula and had never known anything but military government in their own country, where one high-ranking active or retired military figure had succeeded another as governor-general.[45]

Because of the flourishing Korean-language commercial publishing industry, which had been allowed to grow and blossom in the 1920s and 1930s, before wartime controls later largely closed it down, literate Koreans of those decades were also attuned through newspapers and magazines to all the major news events of the world, including, as noted in Chapter 3, the rise of Hitler and Mussolini and their paramilitary political organizations. Not surprisingly, a great deal of front-page attention in the Korean press was devoted to political developments in Japan, and Koreans were able to follow the increasing trend toward militarism there in almost as much detail as the reading public in Japan itself. The assassinations and attempted coups of the 1930s were of course sensational news at the time, difficult if not impossible to ignore in Japan and its colonies. The logic of print capitalism, in colony as in metropole, also kept the press focused on what were, after all, the kinds of dramatic, even shocking stories that sold newspapers. Thus at the time of the May 15 Incident, which the Korean press called the "Momentous Tokyo Incident" (*Tonggyŏng chungdae sagŏn*), *Tonga ilbo* issued four "extra" flyers in the first two days and followed the story in detail for the next two weeks.[46] There Korean readers read War Minister Araki's interviews, in which he spoke positively of the patriotism of the May 15 young officers and their (and his) demands to "purify the political world" (*chŏnggye rŭl chŏnghwa*), another phrase that would later reemerge in South Korea after the May 16 Coup, when Park Chung Hee proclaimed a law restricting political activity.[47]

The "Tokyo Incident," as *Tonga ilbo* headlined the February 26 rebellion, was also given extensive coverage in the Korean media. As the newspapers had already gone to press when the rebellion began, around midnight, the morning edition of *Tonga ilbo* on February 26 carried a large flyer with the banner "Army Acts under the Command of Young Officers," which tersely provided what information was known about the rebels' occupation of the government buildings and assassinations, as well as excerpts from their manifesto. As the mutiny wound its course, and even long after it came to an end on February 29, the newspaper followed the story and aftermath step by step, using a variety of approaches. There were of course additional flyers for the most dramatic events, such as the declaration of martial law and the suicides of two of the rebel leaders when faced with defeat. But there was also broad regular reportage on a daily basis, including profiles of the young officers, and numerous photographs of the unfolding scene in Tokyo, often spreading over entire pages.[48] Throughout the crisis *Tonga ilbo* frequently published extracts of articles and editorials from the Japanese press, which tended to be sympathetic toward the rebels' motives while condemning their actions. On March 4, for example, *Tonga ilbo* translated and reprinted in full on its front page an editorial by Takaishi Shingorō of the *Ōsaka mainichi shinbun* that laid the blame for the incident not only on high officials in the army but also and primarily on a sufficient "lack" of reflection by the Japanese public on the need for social reform. Because of this lack of social consciousness, Takaishi argued, the "pure young officers" felt compelled to "take direct action to the death" on their own initiative, out of a "sense of patriotism" (*aeguk ŭi ttŭt*).[49]

Tonga ilbo followed suit on March 8 with one of its own editorials. To be sure, it did not go so far as Takaishi and other Japanese journalists and praise the motives of the young officers, in part perhaps because Ikeda Kiyoshi, the director of the colonial government's Police Bureau, fully aware of the attention and press coverage the incident was receiving, had warned the Korean public only days earlier to "exercise self-restraint [*kŭnsin*] in their speech and behavior," lest they be subjected to "severe discipline" (*ŏmjunghan ch'wich'e*).[50] But like Takaishi, the paper identified the core of the problem not as the young officers, who were not even mentioned, but as the inattention of the Japanese polity to pressing social problems.[51]

Lingering Influence of the Young Officers at the Academies

By the time Korean cadets began entering the MMA in 1939, the volatile and violent military politics of the 1930s were to a considerable extent a thing of the past. The February 26 Incident had broken the back of whatever resistance remained to army-dominated government, as civilian politicians came to the conclusion that only the army could control its own zealots. The army, for its part, especially high-level officers associated with the dominant Control Faction, kept its half of this Faustian bargain and took advantage of the moment to carry out what Maruyama Masao has called a "thorough purge" of the Kōdōha from its ranks.[52] General Araki, for example, was forced to retire to the reserves, and General Mazaki, whom the February 26 officers had demanded be appointed prime minister, was prosecuted for his connections with the rebels. Officers such as General Umezu Yoshijirō and General Tōjō Hideki, who had strongly opposed the 1936 rebellion and played a key role in the subsequent Kōdōha purge, were elevated to new positions of power and influence. The outbreak of the war in China in July 1937 further consolidated the army's and the Control Faction's grip on power in Tokyo, and Tōjō of course eventually rose to particular prominence, becoming prime minister in 1941, a post he held for three years while concurrently serving as minister of munitions and also, for a time, as war minister.

Given these circumstances, one might be inclined to conclude that influence of the mutinous young officers of the 1930s had reached its zenith in 1936 and was thereafter contained or suppressed. However, Maruyama's "thorough purge," still by and large the conventional view, was not as thorough as he had suggested. It was in fact confined primarily to higher-level Kōdōha officers, and even here the number was limited. As Shillony points out, only three officers above captain rank were prosecuted in connection with February 26, and the one with perhaps the closest relationship with the rebels, General Mazaki, was eventually acquitted.[53] Major General Yamashita Tomoyuki, who had championed and encouraged the rebels to act, escaped censure entirely, going on to ever more important commands and eventually a full generalship after his capture of Singapore in early 1942.[54] To be sure, other higher-level officers associated with the rebels or the Kōdōha resigned or retired, but, as we shall see, their impact on the military was by no means eclipsed. The elimination of these senior officers did little to diminish a residual admiration for the "pure" and "patriotic" young officers; this sentiment crossed ranks and was widespread within the IJA, especially among officers of the same generation and younger. Although to some degree it was forced underground after 1936, the influence of the rebellious young officers of the early and middle 1930s continued in various ways and through various personnel to percolate beneath the surface in army units, including the military academies themselves, not least of all the MMA. In no small part this influence was directly tied to the legacy of the Manchurian Incident, the unique position of Manchukuo in the empire as a magnet and refuge for dissident officers, and the role of the MMA as the Manchukuo Army's main officer training school.

The Legacy of the Manchurian Incident

To understand how this submerged influence was sustained and came to affect the political orientation of the MMA, one must first grasp the larger world of which the academy was a part. And this, in turn, means thinking of the Manchurian Incident not as a single event but rather as a continuing legacy of a "field initiative" that infused and shaped the new state of Manchukuo and its army officers. As Alvin Coox notes, after the Manchurian Incident the term "Kwantung Army" came to be applied positively as a nickname in IJA circles "to any expeditionary force that ignored or disrespected the High Command's dictates."[55] Although Tokyo was quick to embrace the opportunities of empire afforded by the Manchurian Incident and sought accordingly to rein in the Kwantung Army through key personnel changes from time to time, the penchant for military independence and political intrigue that had defined the Kwantung Army from the beginning and given birth to Manchukuo remained a powerful legacy in Manchuria even after the incident and was passed on to the officer corps of the new state's army.

This legacy was buttressed, first of all, by an institutional structure that was initially set up by Ishiwara, Itagaki, and their fellow conspirators. At its heart was an octopus-like network of Japanese advisors, generally serving in posts secondary to nominal Chinese superiors. Within the nascent Manchukuo Army, this took the form of a military advisory system, whereby Japanese officers associated with the Kwantung Army were assigned to key army units, as well as to all bureaucratic agencies in the government that oversaw the military administration. Although the Japanese advisors were said to be acting only in an unofficial and consultative capacity, in practice they were the true decision makers and policy implementers in each case. At the top of this hierarchy was the supreme advisor (saikō komon) to the Manchukuo army minister (hereafter SA). Invariably an officer of major general or lieutenant general rank, the SA wielded enormous power in the ministry, surpassing that of the minister himself. As Sasaki Tōichi, one of the generals who served in the post later wrote, the SA acted "as a liaison between the commander of the Kwantung Army and the Manchukuo prime minister." "Without the assent of the supreme advisor," Sasaki boasted, "no army or ministerial order or instruction of any kind had any effectiveness."[56]

The power of the SA in the Army Ministry was paralleled by the power of other Japanese officials, both civilian and military, who served as advisors or vice ministers in an overall system of control, characterized as "internal guidance" (naimen shidō), that extended through all parts of the bureaucracy and encompassed the imperial office itself.[57] And since all such appointments had to be approved by the commander of the Kwantung Army in accordance with a letter Puyi had signed in March 1932, it was the Kwantung Army that effectively ran the government as well as the army.[58] This was only too apparent physically and symbolically when one compared the massive Kwantung Army headquarters complex in the center of Xinjing with the emperor's small and shabby residence east of the railway station in an area that was home to small factories, warehouses, and a slaughterhouse, as well as to the Xinjing Prison and the city's prostitution district.[59] So thoroughly was the new government in the hands of the Kwantung Army after 1932, in fact, that even Ishiwara, whose views on Manchukuo tended to be more idealistic than those of his colleagues and successors, later protested, though without effect, that the army's system of "internal guidance" had subverted the original aim of establishing an ethnically diverse and harmonious state where the native inhabitants would largely make their own decisions, albeit with Japanese advice and support.[60] The non-Japanese Manchukuo officials who had to operate within this system were even blunter, calling it simply "legal banditry."[61]

The army as the locus of political as well as military power was widely reflected in the new state ideology, where, as we have seen, soldiers were immortalized not simply as heroes but as "nation-founding heroes" at the Chūreibyō in Xinjing, regularly visited by the MMA cadets during their time at Lalatun. Indeed, "nation-founding" (kenkoku) was a formal subject of study in the MMA's regular curriculum.[62] It was also celebrated by the cadets in song as an "ideal" (risō) to guide them in their training, and the first classes of MMA cadets, MMA 1 in particular, were encouraged to think of themselves as spirited "pioneers" on a long "founding road" (sōgyōdō).[63] Such thinking made perfect sense at the time. Not only were the army and state inextricably conflated in the Manchurian milieu, but everything was new: the army, the academy, and the state itself were all literally still in the process of being constructed, like the capital city itself.[64] In the words of former Korean cadet Kim Tonghun (MMA 6), "The streets were wide, and everything seemed new and clean, much better than Seoul."[65] And the cadets were not merely observers. They themselves were an important part of the *kenkoku* process, creating MMA traditions by doing everything for the first time, even composing the first songs about the academy and helping to design its uniforms.[66] At the same time, the cadets participated in the state's own new and developing rituals of power and commemoration together with the highest officials, and often in the presence of the emperor himself (see Chapter 4). In such a context *kenkoku* was not an empty word. It was, rather, a concept filled with the actual experience and knowledge of Manchukuo military life as lived and understood by the cadets and their instructors.

A third pillar of the Manchurian Incident legacy, in addition to structure and ideology, was a certain continuity in military appointments. Ishiwara and Itagaki had of course been serving together on the Kwantung Army staff since 1928, and even though by the spring of 1932 Ishiwara had begun to turn against the emerging system of hegemonic Kwantung Army control and was reassigned to Geneva later that year, Itagaki stayed on, becoming a central figure in the formation of the new state structure.[67] Except for a brief hiatus in 1933, he remained in Manchuria until 1937, holding key positions with respect to the development of the Manchukuo government, as well as its army and officer corps. During that period and later, as he moved up the ladder of the general staff to the position of war minister, he continued out of friendship to do what he could to shield Ishiwara, who was becoming further estranged from the central command, even though there is no indication that he shared Ishiwara's increasingly critical view of the Manchukuo "internal guidance" system. At the same time he sought to build on what he and Ishiwara had accomplished in 1931 through strategic personnel appointments of like-minded officers who admired both men and shared the Kwantung Army's dedication to "field initiative" and *kenkoku*. The appointment of the supreme advisor was especially important, for it was the SA, more than anyone else, who was directly responsible for the development and training of the officers of the new Manchukuo Army who were to share the burden of *kenkoku* with their Kwantung peers. Ishiwara and Itagaki were of course present at the creation of this crucial position, the apex of the military advisory system they had established, and Itagaki himself even held the post for a brief time in 1934, just prior to his becoming Kwantung Army vice chief of staff. In fact, all ten of the officers who served as supreme advisor between 1932 and 1945 were in one way or another part of the broad personal nexus of Ishiwara and Itagaki, and in some cases had also been directly involved in the Manchurian Incident or the events leading up to it.[68]

Manchuria as Political Refuge

The combination of structure, ideology, and personnel described above, together with the new state's geographical distance from the metropolitan government and army high command, made Manchukuo an attractive and welcoming haven for officers who shared the rebellious inclinations of the young officers of the period, including many who themselves had been involved in one or more of the various incidents. We might begin here with the fates of some of the main conspirators in the 1928 assassination of Chinese warlord Zhang Zuolin, who had been regarded by the Kwantung Army as an obstacle to Japanese expansionist goals in Manchuria.[69] In addition to Colonel Kōmoto Daisaku (JMA 15), the Kwantung Army senior staff officer, these included two younger officers, Captain Tōmiya Kaneo (JMA 27) and First Lieutenant Kanda Yasunosuke (JMA 32), who were serving in the Independent Garrison Corps that was guarding the railway in Mukden at the time and who actually planted the bomb that killed Zhang. A third younger officer, Captain Shimonaga Kenji (JMA 23), based in Beijing, had cabled detailed vital information about the arrangement of the railroad cars, allowing the others to identify Zhang's location. Another key figure had been the commander of the garrison force, Major General Mizumachi Takezō (JMA 10).[70]

As a result of the bombing, Kōmoto was transferred and then retired, but not before he had succeeded in bringing Ishiwara Kanji, whom he correctly judged to be sympathetic to his goals, onto the Kwantung Army staff later that same year.[71] Even in retirement, he continued to maintain and develop his Manchurian ties as a director of the South Manchurian Railway and businessman. In the early 1930s he even acted as an important liaison between the army in Manchuria and right-wing officers in Japan associated with the Kōdōha and Shōwa Restoration advocates, including members of the Cherry Society (Sakurakai), which in October 1931 was stopped only at the last minute from carrying out the kind of large-scale coup d'état against the Japanese government that the February 26 Incident would reprise several years later.[72]

The three younger officers, Tōmiya, Kanda, and Shimonaga, all gradually rose to field rank in the years following the bombing, and all three subsequently had a role in the formation and development of the new Manchukuo Army as instructors or advisors. Tōmiya, along with Kanda, was directly appointed to his first advisory position with the Jilin Province Defense Army in 1932 on Ishiwara's recommendation.[73] He later served as an army advisor in Sanjiang province and was actively involved in promoting Japanese colonization in northeastern Manchuria. He died in combat in China in 1937 and was posthumously promoted to full colonel. In 1940 his life and career were commemorated in a massive official biography with lengthy testimonials not only from his fellow conspirators, Kōmoto and Kanda, but also from Itagaki and Ishiwara, as well as from retired senior generals Honjō Shigeru, Kwantung Army commander at the time of the Manchurian Incident, and Koiso Kuniaki. Sasaki Tōichi, who as senior military advisor and later SA had actively promoted Tōmiya's career, joined in the chorus of tributes, calling him the "guardian spirit of Manchuria, whose honored name will be passed down through the generations."[74]

Though not as celebrated as Tōmiya, Kanda and Shimonaga were also founding figures in the history of the Manchukuo Army. Kanda, who had worked most closely with Tōmiya in 1928 and later praised his departed friend for having the character of an "ancient samurai" (kobushi), was promoted to captain in 1930 and served as a company commander during the Manchurian Incident, afterward joining Tōmiya as an advisor in Jilin. He eventually rose to lieutenant colonel and served as commander of an independent infantry battalion in north China.[75] Shimonaga had a central role as military advisor in the founding of the Xing'an Military Academy, established by the Kwantung Army in 1934 to train native officers for a future Mongolian army. Later he parlayed the spying skills that had made him so valuable at the time of the Zhang bombing into the directorship of a Kwantung Army "special service" or intelligence agency (tokumu kikan) in Inner Mongolia and also a full colonelcy.[76]

Of all the 1928 conspirators, Major General Mizumachi probably came to have the deepest impact on the nascent Manchukuo Army. Like Kōmoto, he retired into the reserves after the bombing, but he was recruited into the Manchukuo Army following the Manchurian Incident by Supreme Advisor Tada Hayao and tapped to implement Tada's plan to establish a first-rate military academy for the new state. Mizumachi thus became the first vice superintendent (kanji) of the Central Training School (CTS), the precursor to the MMA. In a world where the Chinese often held the highest titles but the Japanese actually ruled, Mizumachi's position as vice superintendent made him in effect the head of the new institution, a post he held until the end of 1940.[77]

As it turned out, favorable treatment for officers of questionable background, such as those involved in the 1928 Mukden bombing, was to become a common pattern in Manchuria. In 2000 former MMA 7 cadet Nishikawa Nobuyoshi wrote in an issue of the Japanese army veterans' magazine *Kaikō* that "a number of the officers associated with the May 15 and February 26 Incidents later became central military figures in the Manchukuo Army." This was not an exaggeration. The appointments of Tōmiya, Kanda, Shimonaga, and Mizumachi were only the beginning of a long history of such postings that continued well into the 1930s and encompassed both major mutinies and other incidents as well. Let us consider them in chronological order.

The May 15 Incident in 1932 was carried out by two groups of cadets, one from the naval academy and another from the JMA. Among the eleven JMA cadets, ten were from the forty-fourth class and one from the forty-fifth, all of whom were subsequently expelled and eventually imprisoned for several years.[78] When they were released, four of them, all JMA 44 classmates, entered the Manchukuo Army. There they were enthusiastically embraced by Supreme Advisor Sasaki Tōichi, who in a secret understanding with the Kwantung Army planned to use them as "advance troops" in Southeast Asia to foment nationalist independence movements by native populations against the European colonial powers.[79] Although Sasaki's plans never materialized, they all went on to army careers in Manchuria. One of them, Nakajima Tadaaki, was assigned to the Military Police Training School in Jilin and after that to the Xing'an Military Academy, which Shimonaga had helped establish. He later served in the Rehe (Jehol) Detached Force and eventually died in battle in north China. The others all went into intelligence activities. Ishizeki Sakae and Nomura Saburō, both adept at the Russian language, were taken into the Kwantung Army's shadowy and far-flung "special service" network, while Yagi Haruo came to play a central role in the development of the intelligence section at the Manchukuo Army Ministry in Xinjing under a succession of supreme advisors, rising by 1945 to the rank of lieutenant colonel.[80]

Several of the JMA cadets involved in the 1934 November Incident also found a home in Manchuria. Of the five who were court-martialed and expelled from the academy, two from the JMA 48 class, Satō Katsurō and Mutō Yoichi, seem to have left little trace. The others, Arakawa Yoshiaki, Sasaki Sadao, and Tsugiki Hajime, all JMA 47 classmates, went on to pursue military careers in the new state of Manchukuo. All were given special appointments, exempting them from the regular army training programs in Manchuria at the CTS or other schools. Sasaki went into intelligence activities and was sent to a "special service" agency in Dongning, a city on the railway line east of Mudanjiang, close to the Soviet border. Arakawa and Tsugiki were eventually posted to the Army Ministry in Xinjing, where they were both assigned to the Military Purification Section (Seigunka), a relatively new department established in 1938 to strengthen army ideological or "spiritual" training in the wake of the expanding war in China.[81]

Kanno Hiroshi, another JMA 47 classmate with a possible connection to the November Incident, also withdrew from the academy and went to Manchuria. There he entered the CTS and graduated in the fifth class, together with another JMA 47 classmate, Watanabe Akinori, who also seems to have left the JMA without graduating. After being commissioned in the Manchukuo Army, Kanno and Watanabe were eventually both posted to the Army Ministry, Kanno in the Military Affairs Section (Gunmuka) and Watanabe in the Military Training Section (Kunrenka). Later Kanno was transferred to the MMA, where he spent almost two years as a cadet company commander and developed a particularly close relationship with Korean cadets in the MMA 1 and MMA 2 classes before rejoining Watanabe at the Army Ministry in September 1941.[82]

Rebels from the 1932 and 1934 incidents who found their niche in Manchuria were later joined by refugees from the February 26 Incident of 1936. To be sure, with the exception of one officer who was given a four-year sentence, the twenty-one young officers who had actually led the mutiny, including five from the JMA 47 class, were all either dead by suicide or execution or in prison for life before the end of the year.[83] And the subsequent elimination in Tokyo of the Kōdōha and officers sympathetic to the mutiny by the army high command, as well as a simultaneous sweep in Manchuria carried out by Tōjō Hideki, then head of the Kwantung Army military police, also reduced to some extent the potential scope of the rebellion's influence. But, as noted above, this should not be overstated, especially with respect to Manchuria. The purge there, even more than in Japan itself, was limited and temporary, as Yamashita's subsequent posting as a divisional commander in Mudanjiang in 1939 suggests.[84] And it did not fundamentally alter the military advisory structure and "nation-founding" army culture that had been extending its tentacles in the region for nearly a decade.

Executions, imprisonments, and forced retirements notwithstanding, at least two higher-ranking military figures directly associated with the rebellion, Colonel Shibuya Saburō and Colonel Manai Tsurukichi, managed to carve out subsequent careers in Manchuria and to have a significant influence on the development of the Manchukuo Army and the MMA. Both were contemporaries of Ishiwara Kanji's. Manai was a JMA 21 classmate. Shibuya was Ishiwara's senior by one year at both the JMA and the Army Staff College, and in 1928, when Ishiwara visited the Army Infantry School in Chiba and invited four officers to lunch, including future SA Hirabayashi Morito, to share his excitement and sense of mission about his Kwantung Army appointment, Shibuya was one of the four, and the only one in the group who was not from Ishiwara's own JMA cohort.[85]

In 1936 Shibuya was the commander of the 3rd Infantry Regiment, which together with the 1st Infantry Regiment and 7th Artillery Regiment (all components of the Tokyo-based 1st Infantry Division) and a detachment from the 3rd Imperial Guards provided the bulk of the approximately 1,400 officers and troops who carried out the mutiny on February 26.[86] Since at least the early 1930s, when Yamashita Tomoyuki had been its commander, the 3rd Regiment had served as a gathering place for the reformist-minded young officers, and of the units participating in the rebellion, it was arguably the key.[87] Although Shibuya does not seem to have played a direct role in the planning and execution of the mutiny, he was the 3rd's regimental commander and was certainly in a position to set a tone in the unit that would have discouraged such behavior or to have taken action against it once it commenced. He did neither. What he did do once the rebel troops had occupied the city was to check to make sure that they were sufficiently provisioned with food.[88] Perhaps in gratitude, but certainly with a sense of shared respect, the leader of that regiment's 1st Company, First Lieutenant Sakai Naoshi, wrote his former commander a farewell poem (*jisei*) on July 5, 1936, the day his court-martial handed down a sentence of death; the poem said that his dying would be a "full expression of [my] loyalty."[89]

By the time Sakai wrote his poem Shibuya was more than likely already well on his way to Manchuria. As a result of February 26, he had been removed from his regimental post and forced into retirement, but even in the midst of Tōjō's campaign to eradicate the Kōdōha, he was able to secure a new place in the Manchukuo bureaucracy under the Sasaki-Itagaki regime. By August 1936 he was ensconced in Harbin as the head of the Binjiang provincial police force. This was the beginning of a nearly decade-long Manchurian career that would end with the collapse of Manchukuo: he died in a triple suicide (with his wife and second son) while he was serving as the director of the Harbin Academy (Harubin/Harupin Gakuin), a Russian-language training school for Japanese army and civilian intelligence officers. In between those two appointments he also served as the governor of Mudanjiang province and held important positions in the Manchukuo Army

Ministry, including the position of vice minister, the pivotal post in the ministry in the Japanese-centered system of "internal guidance." He assumed the post at the end of 1939 and remained in it for more than three years, at which point he left to become director of the Harbin Academy in April 1943. His years in the Army Ministry were of course the period in which the MMA first opened its gates and began to take shape as an institution, and as the primary Japanese bureaucrat in the Army Ministry, Shibuya worked closely with successive supreme advisors and other important military figures in Manchuria to move that process along.[90]

One of those military figures was Manai Tsurukichi. Like Shibuya, Manai had moved more or less effortlessly from a regimental command in the February 26 Incident to a new position in Manchuria. At the time of the mutiny he had been the commander of the 1st Division's 7th Artillery Regiment, which had supplied the transportation needs of the rebels. Afterward he retired into the reserves but was quickly recruited into the Manchukuo Army, most likely by Supreme Advisor Sasaki, who was eager to hire experienced Japanese officers, especially of field or general rank, to build up the new state's military power and to train new officers locally. Within a month after the February mutiny he had signed up for his new assignment with the promise of a promotion to major general, the first of what would be two promotions at the general rank and, as in the case of Shibuya, the beginning of a long career that would end only with the end of Manchukuo itself, when he was captured by the Soviets and sent off to a northwestern Siberian prison camp.

Even more than Shibuya, Manai came to play a crucial role in the development of the two major military schools, the CTS and its successor, the MMA. In fact, apart from the early supreme advisors, such as Tada and Sasaki, there was probably no other single figure more central in that regard. And even though Tada and Sasaki's long-term aspirations for the new state army certainly made possible the establishment of the schools, it was really Manai who translated these plans into reality on the ground and in the schools themselves, especially in the case of the MMA.

Manai began his new career in 1936 at the CTS under Major General Mizumachi, the former 1928 conspirator, working as head of the education department (Kyōiku Buchō), where he managed the overall classroom learning and supervised the instructors. He was also in charge of the officer candidate program and its corps of students (kōhosha gakuseitai), senior noncommissioned officers who had been selected for training at the CTS and eventual promotion upon graduation to second lieutenant. For the next seven years he continued to serve at the CTS, eventually succeeding

Mizumachi as vice superintendent in 1940 and presiding over the transformation of the school into two separate institutions, one, at the original Mukden location, specializing exclusively in the training of officer candidates, and the other, newly built in Xinjing, concentrating in the training of staff officers, along the lines of the Army Staff College in Japan. At the same time that he was helping to build up the CTS, he was also being drafted by supreme advisors Sasaki Tōichi and Hirabayashi Morito to lay the foundations for the new four-year military academy based on the JMA that was to replace the CTS's abbreviated officer training program. It was in fact Manai who became the head of the MMA Establishment Committee, set up by the Manchukuo Army Ministry under directives from the supreme advisors and Kwantung Army. In that capacity he was responsible for supervising all aspects of the academy's initial development. This included such things as working out the budget and finances with the Army Ministry, the planning and construction of all the physical facilities and infrastructure, and, not least of all, the recruitment of the first cadets and the hiring of all academy personnel, including military officers, civilian instructors, and even office and service employees. Moving between Mukden and Xinjing, Manai acted as the chief liaison and coordinator among the parties most involved with the project: the Kwantung Army, the Manchukuo Army Ministry and supreme advisor, and finally the CTS, which Manai drew upon heavily for committee staff support and advice and eventually MMA personnel. It is no exaggeration to say that when the MMA welcomed its first class in April 1939, it was Manai above all who had both literally and figuratively paved the way for them.

And his involvement with the MMA did not end there. The first superintendent of the new academy was Guo Enlin, a Chinese general in the Manchukuo Army, but in keeping with the Kwantung Army's policy of "internal guidance," this was only a nominal appointment, and it was also meant to be temporary until a qualified Japanese officer could be hired. Thus until Major General Nagumo Shin'ichirō had been selected and was ready to take up the superintendency, Manai served as MMA vice superintendent concurrently with his various roles at the CTS, holding the MMA post until the end of October 1940 (see Chapter 3). He then returned full-time to the CTS as vice superintendent, remaining there until April 1943, when he moved into the Army Ministry as vice minister, succeeding Shibuya. Manai's appointment as vice minister coincided with a major restructuring of the ministry, which in the wake of the expansion of the Pacific War was separating out its former internal policing activities in order to concentrate solely on army affairs and development. There were few if any officers who were more familiar with the Manchukuo Army and its training programs than the man who had for all practical purposes founded the MMA.[91]

The MMA in Manchurian Context

This, then, was the Manchurian context in which the MMA was established and developed. When the first classes of MMA cadets were training there in the early 1940s, they were being molded into officers by an environment and teaching staff that had been significantly shaped by two refugees from the February 26 Incident who were deeply engaged in the oversight of the new school and of the Manchukuo Army more generally. And the presence of Shibuya and Manai, important as it was, represented only the most visible part of a brave new world at the heart of which the MMA was located both physically and institutionally, a world of politically oriented young officers who conceptualized and practiced the commandment of "loyalty" in radical ways that often challenged the existing military and political hierarchies. That world, as we have seen, was supported by a military advisory system that was set up in the early 1930s after the Manchurian Incident and which consistently gave what Yagi Haruo described as an "enthusiastic welcome" (*seidai na kangei*) into the fold to him and his three classmates, fresh out of prison for their role in the May 15 Incident, and to other radical young officers who followed in their wake.[92] The advisory system, in turn, worked to reinforce and reproduce the culture of "field initiative" and "nation-founding" in the new state's army officer schools and military units. For example, MMA cadets, especially from the early classes, were trained largely by young section and company commanders who, even if Japanese, were in most cases pure products of the Manchukuo system, coming into the army and eventually to the academy out of the officer training course at the CTS. In most cases these CTS officers had been recruited from the margins and byways of the Japanese army system, often from the ranks of the noncommissioned officers, making them more open and amenable to the less conventional practices of the Kwantung and Manchukuo armies. And their CTS instructors, of course, had been drawn from the pool of early military advisors, which included not only the Kwantung officers who had been active in the seizure of Manchuria but also officers associated with one or more of the various army incidents of the early 1930s in Japan who had found a place in the Manchukuo system.[93]

The army units stationed in Manchuria during this period also had a profound impact on shaping the perspectives of the cadets being trained at the MMA. Although the commanding officers of such units may have changed over time, the units themselves, as well as many of their noncommissioned officers and soldiers, often remained in Manchuria for much longer periods of time, in some cases even into the 1940s and as late as 1945. These units were the practical training grounds for the MMA (and often JMA) cadets during their months of regimental attachment duty (*taizuki kinmu*) between the *yoka* and *honka* courses and the final probationary period (*minarai*) after graduation before commissioning (see Chapter 3). In addition to receiving the on-site military training that only active-duty army camps could provide, the cadets were naturally exposed to the particular history and traditions of the units in which they served. In many cases, of course, this included a history of participation in the Manchurian Incident, as in the case of the 30th Infantry Regiment in Harbin, where Park Chung Hee spent his *taizuki*. This regiment had once been commanded by Kanda Yasunosuke, one of the officers involved in the Zhang Zuolin assassination in 1928.[94]

Other units at the time had connections through their personnel, past and present, to the mutinies and rebellions of the 1930s, especially the February 26 Incident. To appreciate the full extent of the February 26 reach in Manchurian military circles, for example, one has to remember that unlike earlier such events, including even May 15, February 26 involved a considerable mobilization of actual troops, largely from the 1st Infantry Division. Most of the approximately 1,400 soldiers who had participated in the rebellion, including troops and noncommissioned officers, were allowed to return to the 1st after interrogations, and the division was then sent to Manchuria in May. Apart from a brief, temporary deployment in China after the Marco Polo Bridge Incident in 1937, the division—including both the 1st and 3rd Infantry Regiments, which had played so central a role in the mutiny—remained in Manchuria until the 1940s, with its headquarters near the Heilongjiang (Amur) River in Heihe province.[95]

There were many other IJA army units in Japan, Korea, and of course Manchuria that displayed a marked sympathy for the February 26 rebels. Although never formally charged, officers in at least seven Kwantung Army infantry regiments, the 4th, 7th, 9th, 38th, and 42nd, as well as other Kwantung military units, were listed by the War Ministry in March 1936 as February 26 "suspects."[96] And at least in some cases such sympathy seems to have continued or been regenerated over time in the same units. Even as late as 1943, seven years after the incident, when Korean cadet Chŏng Naehyŏk

(JMA 58) was assigned to the 7th Infantry Regiment in Mudanjiang for his *taizuki*, his immediate superior in the unit was a young lieutenant, Yamamoto Kenjirō, who had wholeheartedly approved of the mutiny. As Chŏng later wrote in his autobiography, "Second Lieutenant Yamamoto had been greatly influenced by seniors who were part of the Kōdōha, and there was a lot of right-wing talk from him; he held the view that incidents such as February 26 and May 15 were legitimate."[97]

Residual Shōwa Restorationist Sympathies at the JMA

One might surmise that MMA graduates such as Park Chung Hee who went on to complete their officer training at the JMA *honka* were leaving the politicized military world of Manchuria behind. To be sure, the atmosphere at Zama and within the IJA in Japan by the 1940s was far less overtly political than on the continent. In part this was the result of a reaction by the high command to the central role that JMA graduates had played in the major incidents of the first half of the 1930s, not least of all the February 26 mutiny in 1936. Of the nineteen officers who had taken an active part in the rebellion and were subsequently tried and either executed or imprisoned, only one had *not* graduated in a regular JMA class; two other key figures, both JMA graduates, had committed suicide before they could be put on trial.[98] Four years earlier, no fewer than eleven JMA cadets had been enthusiastic participants in the May 15 conspiracy, and two years after that JMA cadets had been active in the incident of November 1934—so prominently, in fact, that the conspiracy came to be known in IJA circles as the "JMA Incident."[99] Precisely because of this history, the JMA began in the mid-1930s to impose a draconian version of the army's long-standing, if often ignored, injunction to stay away from politics. Instructors were not even permitted to discuss the incidents of the past with the cadets, and the cadets were more carefully monitored than ever. By the late 1930s the policy seemed to be working. No JMA cadets, for example, were directly involved in the February 26 Incident. Moreover, the war that broke out in China in 1937 had the effect of rechanneling some of the energies of later classes of JMA cadets away from domestic political concerns.[100]

Nevertheless, it would be a mistake to conclude from this that the spirit of the rebellious 1930s had entirely faded away at the JMA by the time the first MMA classes began to matriculate there.[101] Even if it was no longer a proper subject for discussion, the memory of this past lingered almost palpably in the air, ready to burst forth at a moment's notice. During MMA 1 field exercises in the Bandaisan/Okinajima area in October 1942, for example, a company of cadets who were advancing in attack formation were suddenly halted by their commanders when it was discovered that they were moving directly toward an imperial villa. Fearful of a major misunderstanding, the commanders rushed forward to explain and apologize to the villa's startled guard. Relieved, the guard confessed his fear that something indeed had been afoot with an unknown mass of spirited young men heading toward the villa, although he tried to assure the JMA commanders that he had not really thought it was "a mutiny of the Imperial Army."[102]

The MMA cadets themselves, in no small part because of their Manchurian education, came to the JMA with what their company commander at the time, Major Enami Shigeru (JMA 38), described as an "intense interest" (*fukai kanshin*) in Japanese national policy, the educational system of the army, and their own role and mission. Enami recounted how eager the MMA cadets had been to talk about the various incidents of the 1930s, everything from the Manchurian Incident itself to all the others that followed, but since to do so would have violated academy policy, he felt that he was never able to satisfy their desires.[103] Others at the JMA, however, did try to do so, which was possible so long as it was done more or less surreptitiously. This is what Colonel Kihara Yoshio, the commandant of the International Cadet Corps and Enami's superior, had in mind when he arranged for the MMA 1 cadets to meet as if by accident with Ishiwara Kanji on Kugenuma Beach in the summer of 1942 to hear Ishiwara's typically outspoken critiques of the IJA, Japanese wartime policy, and current conditions in Manchukuo (see Chapter 4). But in the new post–February 26 and post–Pearl Harbor era, Ishiwara's willful insubordination, a stance that had won him so many adherents in the past, including Kihara, was not to be tolerated by the Tōjō government, especially as Ishiwara was also publicly contemptuous of Tōjō himself. In the following year, when Kihara openly tried to extend a formal invitation to Ishiwara to speak to the MMA 2 cadets at the academy, he was quickly transferred out of the JMA to a minor post at another school.[104]

Residual sympathies at the JMA in the 1940s for the defiant actions of the past were not necessarily limited to Kihara. Yamamoto Kenjirō, the officer so admiring of February 26 whom Chŏng Naehyŏk had encountered in Mudanjiang during his *taizuki*, was not a Manchukuo CTS graduate like most of the section commanders at the MMA, but a graduate of the JMA 56 class. That made him an exact contemporary of the MMA 1 cadets, who were officially listed as part of the JMA 56 class with which they eventually graduated.[105] The "seniors" with Kōdōha leanings who had influenced Yamamoto were the same generation of seniors that the MMA 1 and overlapping MMA 2 cadets might claim as their own, officers for whom the rebellions of the 1930s were still relatively fresh. In the 1940s this was precisely the generation that was serving as section and company commanders at the JMA when Yamamoto and the first two classes of MMA cadets were together at Zama. All except one of the eleven section commanders working with the MMA 2 class, for example, had been either *yoka* or *honka* cadets themselves just before, during, or immediately after the February 26 Incident, when both the preparatory and regular courses were still together in Tokyo at Ichigayadai, including both of the officers who served consecutively as Park Chung Hee's *kutaichō*. Seven of them, moreover, had also been cadets at the time of the November/JMA Incident in 1934, including Nishigaki Makoto, Park's first section commander, two of whose classmates in the JMA 48 class had joined three seniors in the JMA 47 class to plan the incident.[106] And Park's second section commander, Tahara Kōzō (JMA 52), had been an active target of recruitment by the February 26 officers, most likely because of his perceived empathy with their cause.[107] That the JMA could still, as late as the 1940s, and despite all the new restrictions on political speech and behavior, produce so zealous an enthusiast for February 26 as Yamamoto speaks volumes about an enduring interest in a Shōwa Restoration at the academy in this period, and the presence of such seniors undoubtedly helped keep such interest alive.

Indeed, we may look no further than the JMA 57 class with which the MMA 2 was affiliated for further evidence of this interest. We already noted the strong attachment of the JMA 57 class to the "ideal" of the "restoration," as reflected in the songs, pledges, and mottos of the class. To be sure, the term "restoration" immediately recalled the Meiji Restoration of 1868, but from the 1930s on, for many cadets the term came to have a second meaning, connoting a future Shōwa Restoration that in the minds of the radical young officers of the time and their sympathizers represented the fulfillment of the original restoration, which over time had gone awry. The conflation of these two events, one historical, one aspirational, was fostered (no doubt deliberately) in class songs and mottos by the deletion of any qualifying adjective, so cadets could openly sing about and pledge themselves simply to the "restoration," interpreting the term as they chose.

And for a number of the cadets in the JMA 57 class, "restoration" indeed meant a Shōwa Restoration. In 1943 the JMA authorities, working with the military police, uncovered a secret organization of cadets within the JMA 57 class that was closely affiliated with the private, right-wing Great Eastern Academy (Daitōjuku), founded by Kageyama Masaharu. An advocate of radical "restoration," Kageyama had been arrested in 1941 for his part in publishing an extreme political tract that had attacked the Tōjō government and, indeed, the leadership of virtually all of the institutional linchpins of imperial Japanese society, including the army itself. The article had gone on to demand that the government clear the reputations of all those who had been associated with the May 15 Incident, including members of the League of Blood (Ketsumeidan), who had assassinated a former minister of finance and the managing director of the Mitsui conglomerate in early 1932.[108]

The academy had discovered that a group of seven cadets in the JMA 57 class with ties to Kageyama had been bringing various publications of the Daitōjuku into the school in violation of school regulations and disseminating them among their peers. At the same time, the group had taken the lead in privately convening members of the JMA 57 class in the academy's Great Lecture Hall and in front of the Otakebi Shrine, where those attending had inaugurated a JMA 57 Class Association and crafted the class pledge to "lead the imperial army in the vanguard of the Restoration" (see Chapter 4). On one such occasion, one of the cadets heading the movement, Satō Tetsuo, pulled out a short sword (tantō), a family heirloom, and laid it on the table, telling his assembled classmates that if what he was about to say to them was in any way false, they should take the dagger and "kill me on the spot." For the next forty-five minutes he proceeded to denounce the current military leadership and to advocate a "restoration in the imperial army," a call to action that his seniors in the February 26 Movement, had they still been alive, would have heartily approved. On another occasion, Satō and his six classmates participated in a Daitōjuku gathering in Roka Park, on the outskirts of Tokyo, where they joined Kageyama and other members of the organization in a conference whose themes were "The Anti-Tōjō Movement" and "Down with the Tōjō Cabinet." Other secret meetings followed, but the conference at Roka Park seems to have been the final straw for the police, who, after months of tracking the seven cadets' movements in connection with the Daitōjuku, finally arrested them at the end of August 1943, bringing the movement within the JMA to an abrupt end.[109]

The "JMA Incident" of 1943, as the affair is known in Daitōjuku history, is revealing and indicative on a number of levels. First, even though the movement was led by the seven cadets most closely linked to Kageyama's organization, it is clear that there was considerable interest in the movement within the JMA 57 class as a whole—enough, in fact, to allow the seven cadets to bring their class together on at least two occasions and to commit it to a restorationist pledge that became an integral part of both the JMA class album and the class song. The group of seven also reached out beyond the JMA 57 class to their contemporaries in the International Corps of Cadets, including Park Chung Hee's MMA 2 class, barracked in the southern section of the academy grounds.[110] Former MMA 2 cadet Origuchi Ryūzō remembers being contacted at the time by his former middle school classmate Ogiwara Ken'ichi, a "hot-blooded" (nekketsukan) member of the JMA 57 class who was also the group of seven's chief contact with the Daitōjuku. Ogiwara asked his old school friend to introduce some foreign students to him, and Origuchi obliged, putting him into contact with two of his MMA 2 classmates, Chinese cadets Wang Chengmei and Zhang Wenshan, who he thought might be interested. When the affair broke, Ogiwara was arrested but kept his silence about his request to Origuchi, and no MMA 2 cadets were implicated in the incident. One can see from this, however, how the movement had spread throughout the academy.[111]

The Daitōjuku affair did not only involve cadets. It also had support from instructors. The JMA 57 class, with about 1,300 members, had a total of ten companies, each with a company commander and several section commanders, and the seven ringleaders came from five different companies of cadets.[112] Even though the ringleaders, individually or as a group, might have been able to take advantage of the free time that Sundays and holidays afforded and make secret visits to the Daitōjuku in Tokyo, there is no way they could have organized meetings within the academy itself without the knowledge and assistance of at least some of their section and company commanders; indeed, this is precisely what the academy's subsequent investigation discovered.

Perhaps because they felt they had such strong support among their peers and instructors, the attitude of the seven cadets appears to have been openly defiant even after they were exposed. After their arrest, they were brought before the head of the Higher Military Police, Lieutenant Colonel Fujino Ranjō, who was in charge of investigating "thought crimes" within the military. When Fujino sternly began to quote the injunction from the Gunjin Chokuyu against army involvement in politics, they immediately retorted by telling him that what he was saying was "nonsense." One would have supposed, given the character of their movement and their recalcitrant stance, especially at the height of the Pacific War, that the seven cadets would have been subjected to severe penalties, at the very least by the academy. But such was not the case, and this is the final point of interest to be noted about this incident. The War Ministry and Inspectorate General of Military Training, at Tōjō's direction, demanded the cadets' dismissal from the school and even proposed bringing criminal charges against them for ideological subversion, but the academy refused to allow the case out of its jurisdiction. In the end, Colonel Watanabe Fujio, the commandant of cadets, allowed them all to remain at the JMA, imposing only a thirty-day penalty of confinement to quarters. The many other cadets who were implicated in the affair as a result of the subsequent investigation were given even lighter sentences of just seven days' confinement. And only the two instructors who were most deeply involved in the affair were actually punished: Captain Nanba Shōroku, a section commander in the 2nd Cadet Company, and Lieutenant Colonel Uchiyama Kazuya, commander of the 5th Cadet Company, to which Ogiwara and two other of the seven leaders had belonged. Both Naniwa and Uchiyama received thirty days' confinement, along with a temporary suspension and a penalty of 50 percent of their pay, but like the cadets whose activities they had facilitated, they retained their positions at the academy, and the spirit of the Daitōjuku cadets, their classmates, and their instructors lives on even today in the JMA 57 class album, where, as noted earlier, Uchiyama's personal calligraphy, "To die for the Restoration," is the centerpiece of the pages devoted to the 5th Cadet Company.[113]

On a bright spring afternoon in 1941, nine years to the day since the May 15 Incident of 1932, Dōtokudai section commander Yano Yutaka led Hosokawa Minoru and other cadets in the Nikkei 5th Section of the MMA 2 class to a secluded, quiet place in the woods in the southeastern part of the academy, where he proceeded to lecture the cadets at length about a "Showa Restoration."[114] Such discussions were not unusual at the MMA, nor were they confined only to the Nikkei sections. Interviewing former MMA Chinese cadets in Changchun in 1992, I was told that a number of the Japanese officers who had instructed and trained them at Lalatun in the 1940s were, like Second Lieutenant Yamamoto, filled with admiration for February 26, and that they had openly exhorted their charges, whatever their nationality, to learn from the young officers who had bravely seized the initiative when the Japanese government had been too timid and ineffectual.[115] Given the military world in which the MMA existed, this is not surprising. Nor is it surprising that under such circumstances political interventions such as February 26 might come to be seen by many of the cadets in largely positive terms, whether they remained in Manchuria or went on to the regular course at the JMA. Even after the purge of the Kōdōha and the attempt, especially at the JMA, to impose more stringent controls over the cadets' political thoughts and activities, the idea of a Shōwa Restoration continued to intrigue, beguile, and inspire.

The academies were powerless to contain such sentiments, which were embedded in the very language of the schools and the officer corps, with its unchanging emphasis on "special favor" and "singular duty," its celebration of the Meiji Restoration and its heroes, and the repeated calls for a new "restoration." Even after February 26, entering cadets at Lalatun and Zama could still find the anthems of May 15 and the Shōwa Restoration in their academy songbooks; indeed, both songs continued to be sung openly at the schools through the entire wartime period, as late as August 1945.[116] And Yoshida Shōin and other late Tokugawa rebels remained a constant source of patriotic inspiration for MMA and JMA cadets such as Hosokawa Minoru (MMA 2), who wrote in his diary that becoming a *shishi* of a Shōwa Restoration meant inheriting the spirit of Yoshida.[117] Whether in Manchuria or Japan, moreover, seniors passed on these sentiments to juniors, and classmates talked to classmates in army units and even within the academies themselves. Not infrequently it was the top-ranking or model cadets such as Yamamoto and Uchiyama, like Park Chung Hee the *gomin* of their classes, who took the lead here and served as examples to others.[118] No MMA or JMA cadet in this period, Japanese, Chinese, or Korean, could easily escape this pervasive influence.

Thus at Kugenuma Beach in July 1942, when Ishiwara Kanji bluntly laid out his criticisms of the current Manchukuo regime for the MMA 1 cadets, their immediate response was to think in terms of radical action, conditioned and captivated as they were by Ishiwara's legendary example of bold "field initiative" and the examples of their rebellious seniors in the 1930s. Sudō Tsukasa, a former MMA 1 cadet who was there, wrote that after listening to Ishiwara, he and his classmates were inspired to think that once they came to know the situation better, they "might even rise up in a Manchurian version of the February 26 Incident."[119] Coincidentally, only a month earlier at the MMA itself, a concerned weekly duty officer had addressed the full company of MMA 2 cadets after roll call, including Park Chung Hee, noting their enthusiasm for singing the Shōwa Restoration song and cautioning them against letting their "great admiration for the spirit of the young men of May 15 and February 26" develop to the point of "thinking about destroying the established order" (*genjō hakai no shisō*).[120] As the duty officer that day reminded them, the young officers of the 1930s had paid for their actions with their lives, sentenced to death by an imperial edict.[121] When he spoke, mutiny was of course still a violation of the military code and punishable by death, but the tenor of the times was such that it was also possible for an impressionable young cadet at the MMA and JMA in the 1940s to imagine being both mutinous and *majime* at the same time.

SIX

STATE AND SOCIETY
Revolution, Reform, Control

Be factious for redress of all these griefs.
—William Shakespeare, *Julius Caesar*

With no thought for the country
Zaibatsu flaunt their wealth.
—"Song of the Showa Restoration"

I reaffirm the resolve of May 16 to sweep out the old evils quickly and
completely . . . and to improve the social and economic life of the people.
—General Park Chung Hee, July 3, 1961

A *majime* devotion to duty in the radical military mode of the 1930s
and 1940s meant more than being "loyal" and bold enough to rebel against
the state; it also meant being rebellious with a cause, rebelling for the sake
of a certain vision of state and society. Park Chung Hee, in his note to Chief of
Staff Chang Toyŏng on the morning of the May 16 coup, wrote not only of
the army's unique obligation and right to seize power in the midst of a national crisis but also of its "unshakeable sense of national mission." That
mission, as it took shape and was worked out over the next eighteen years,
came to have many parts, but from the beginning its core was a fundamental concern with economic and social development focused on national
prosperity and power. "Let me repeat," Park wrote bluntly in 1963, "the revolution arose from my sense of this economic mission."[1]

And although the Park era is today known as the period that saw the
growth of many of the large South Korean business conglomerates or
chaebŏl, underlying that concern and sense of economic mission was a critical orientation toward unfettered capitalism and its practitioners, a view
that was particularly strong at the time of the coup and, despite the regime's
subsequent support for selective *chaebŏl*, never entirely abandoned. In
a book published in early 1962 under Park's name, the new military government set forth its economic philosophy in blistering language and no
uncertain terms, openly warning against the concentration of economic

and political influence among "entrenched cartels and trusts" and denouncing business figures who pretended to act in the national interest while "exercising a monstrous [*musi musi han*] power with bloodshot eyes fixed solely on individual profits." To keep the country and society from falling prey to the "private interests and greed of certain powerful individual economic groups," the book argued, capitalism had to be "regulated and directed" (*chojŏng kwa chido kamdok*) from above.[2]

The strong critique of capitalism that underlay this argument for governmental leadership of the economy and led to the formation of the South Korean modernization state grew in no small part out of the country's painful and debilitating economic experience of the 1950s following the Korean War. Thus Park in his 1962 book also pointedly noted the example of the recent past, when "national administration and policy had been under the sway of business leaders."[3] In a more personal book published the following year, *The Country, the Revolution and I,* he denounced the "privileged stratum" that had dominated the state and economy of this period and allowed foreign capitalist interests to turn the country into a free market for their own goods.

> Conspiring with the monster of politics, they fashioned a postwar upper class that occupied a space between politics and society and became a demon that not only drove the whole country into ruin but also destroyed the nation's sense of self-worth. Fostering a mean and base attitude of frivolity and consumption, they created an economy of unearned income, extreme egoism, and money-worship. . . . Extremes of luxury and vanity then invited a flood of all kinds of foreign commodities into the country, so that by the time of the [May 16] Revolution the South Korean market had become monopolized by outside interests.[4]

While the 1950s provided the most immediate touchstone for Park's critique of capitalism in 1961, that critique actually had even deeper roots, stretching back to a number of revolutionary and statist orientations toward capitalism that were rife in Japanese imperial society of the 1930s and 1940s and particularly ingrained in IJA culture. Here we will examine some of those attitudes, especially as they were embedded and manifested in the academy life of the MMA and JMA cadets of that period.

Premodern Legacies

Neither the formal samurai culture of premodern Japan nor the *yangban* culture of premodern Korea celebrated private commercial enterprise or the individual pursuit of profit. Chosŏn Korea, whose landed ruling elite adhered to a rigid Neo-Confucian orthodoxy in matters of statecraft, was openly and self-righteously hostile to such activity, viewing it not only as a violation of sound physiocratic principles and economic order but also as something leading to immorality and social disintegration in its fixation on material desires and goods "that tempt people's minds and corrupt customs."[5] Even as capitalism developed in Korea after the opening of the country in 1876 and throughout much of the twentieth century, that taint of immorality persisted, and Korean businessmen found it virtually impossible to justify what they did except by publicly abjuring any interest in personal profit and claiming to be acting unselfishly for the sake of the nation.[6]

Post-Restoration Japanese businessmen were often forced to defend their choice of occupation in a similar way, but despite a shared aristocratic disdain for commerce and merchants in premodern Korea and Japan, Japan's actual economic history had been very different from Korea's. Extensive urbanization and commercialization in the Tokugawa period had given rise to a widespread and flourishing merchant culture that came to exist alongside the official ruling ideology and pulled many samurai, now removed from the land and chronically impoverished, into its web. Perhaps in part because of this earlier history, which saw, for example, the formation and rise of the great merchant house of Mitsui, Japanese capitalists in the Meiji period gradually came to feel more confident and were emboldened to act more openly and aggressively in their self-interest. Even so, there were limits to public approval of such behavior. By the late Taishō and early Shōwa periods, especially as economic conditions worsened, Japanese capitalists were incurring sharp public criticism, not least of all from army circles.[7]

The modern Japanese army that grew out of the Restoration, and especially its officer corps, had in fact appropriated many of the older conventionalized anticommercial attitudes of the samurai. In such a world the attitude of the *majime* officer toward money was exemplified by General Nogi Marusuke, who regarded it as "dirty" and unnecessary to the soldierly life.[8] This perspective was enshrined in the fifth precept of the Meiji emperor's 1882 Rescript to Soldiers and Sailors (Gunjin Chokuyu), which commanded military men to aim at "simplicity" (*shisso*) in all things. According to a 1944 official IJA explanatory guide to the rescript, used at the academies and throughout the army at the time, *shisso* was a "virtue" that should "regulate directly and concretely our everyday existence, beginning with dress, food, and residence, and extending to all the various events, economies, interests, and recreational activities of public and private life." At one level it meant adherence to a code of material asceticism and frugality, an avoidance of "extravagance" and "luxury." But it also implied a general detachment from or restraint on personal, selfish desires and pursuits, including an "insatiable greed for money and other valuables."

For soldiers the concept had an undeniable practical dimension. In the unforgiving life of the battlefield, where seriousness of purpose and adequate material supplies were crucial to survival and victory, there was little room for frivolousness or waste, and selfish concerns or actions could undermine the solidarity and effectiveness of the military unit as a whole. But *shisso* as taught in the academies carried a powerful moral dimension as well. Cadets were taught that ignoring it led to a slippery slope of physical and spiritual degeneration. The deterioration began with an inclination toward comfort and idleness that "softened" the body and drew the soldier ever more deeply into a liking for luxuries and vain indulgences. Eventually he became consumed by a lust for material things that destroyed his "will" or "spirit" (*kokorozashi*) and reduced him finally to a state of utter "baseness" (*iyashiku nari*) from which there was no hope of rescue.[9]

At the MMA and JMA in the 1940s the virtue of *shisso* not only was chanted by the cadets in their daily recitations of the Gunjin Chokuyu but also was an integral part of their everyday life and training. Money and commercialism were not allowed to intrude in that life in any significant way. Academy regulations, for example, forbade cadets to possess more than the roughly 10-yen-per-month stipend that was provided by the school and handed out by section commanders. Any amount that came into their possession beyond that they had to report and turn over to their section commander for safekeeping, including, as Kim Muk (MMA 2) later recalled, any money they might receive in letters from family.[10] Their meals, especially at the MMA a prime example of Spartan simplicity, were of course provided for them, and although it was common practice for cadets to try to sneak in extra food from the outside when returning from a leave, they were officially forbidden to do so.[11] Only at the academy canteens (*shuho*), set up and controlled by the schools, were they permitted to use their 10 yen to purchase a small number of limited items beyond the common food and articles supplied to all. To ravenous young men after a day of arduous physical training, the canteen was a constant temptation. But even there the cadets were monitored in their purchases and reprimanded for extravagance. In his diary Hosokawa Minoru (MMA 2), ever conscious of the rigorous standards of *shisso,* recorded an ongoing and often unsuccessful personal struggle to control his "gluttonous" (*bōin bōshoku*) appetite for canteen treats.[12]

Any manifestation of a "selfish" desire for personal comfort or display was severely condemned as well. Thus, as noted in Chapter 4, cadets had to surrender all private possessions, including clothes, upon entering the academy, except for a single photograph of their family, which they were allowed to keep at their self-study desk. At the JMA in January 1943, when the academy authorities discovered that a cadet in the JMA 57 class had replaced what he regarded as the "beautiful" training boots of one of his peers in another section (*kutai*) with the "ugly" boots with which his own section had been provisioned, they convened the entire corps of cadets and commanders for a stern lecture from the corps commandant on the evils of self-interest (*riko*).[13]

Shisso at the academies and in the army generally was closely connected with the concept of "inventory" (*inzū*). In regular and surprise barracks inspections the section and company commanders required that the cadets account for every item of personal or military use that had been supplied by the academy or army. A finding of "inventory short" (*inzū ga awanai*) brought shame and disciplinary action on the entire section, reinforcing the injunctions against extravagance and waste while also emphasizing the communal nature of army property and responsibility.[14] Losing or damaging one's gun, the most basic and personally valuable military item, supplied by the army was an especially grievous offense for a cadet. While on a JMA infantry training exercise in Toyohashi, for example, Park Chung Hee once rushed forward to extinguish a spreading fire from an exploded grenade, unthinkingly laying his gun down on the ground in the literal heat of the moment. When it was discovered afterward that the gun had been singed by the fire, he was sent to the academy stockade as punishment.[15]

The same strict lessons of *inzū* applied to other military items as well. Hiruma Hiroshi (JMA 57) noted that one of the aspects of field training that was long remembered by all who passed through the academy gates was the experience of the cadets of each section searching for fired blank cartridges and for any screws (*neji*) that had fallen off their light machine guns during practice. The screws were a particular challenge, as they were tiny, no bigger than the tip of a little finger, and the training exercises often concluded at the end of the day, when the sun was already setting. But no matter how long it took, even the entire night, the cadets were forced to continue scouring the field until every casing and every screw used in the exercise had been recovered.[16]

Critiques of Capitalism

Frugality and strategic self-denial, as Weber and others have long argued, are not necessarily antithetical to capitalist endeavor and may indeed contribute to it, especially at the level of the individual entrepreneur.[17] For soldiers steeped in an ideal of *shisso,* however, a life dedicated ultimately to the pursuit of personal profit, however deftly managed, would always be suspect, lived precariously as it was on the edge of a fathomless abyss of potential moral disintegration. Nevertheless, such suspicions appropriated from the samurai past were not the only building blocks of IJA anticapitalist sentiment in the first several decades of the twentieth century. More immediate and important were the negative reconsiderations of capitalism as a system that spread throughout the world after World War I, and in the midst and aftermath of global depression in the 1930s. These included criticisms that would find their own voices and forms, openly or covertly, in the Japanese and Manchurian armies, and by extension in the MMA and JMA of the 1940s. Three of these critiques were particularly influential in various forms and to varying degrees at the academies. The first, the earliest and most revolutionary, was Marxism and its various socialist and communist offshoots, coming from the left. The second, coming from the right, was a somewhat disparate collection of reformist ideas loosely cohering around the goal of a "Showa Restoration" (see Chapter 5). The third, which came directly out of the army's own strategic planning channels, was integrally linked to the concept of "total war" and its accompanying apparatus of national mobilization and control.

Revolution: Marxism and the Left

One might not have expected an ideology of revolution based on class conflict and modeled on the Soviet Union to have had much support at the pre-1945 JMA, where national unity under the imperial banner and anti-Soviet military strategy were the norm, but the general popularity and influence of leftist thought among Japanese students and intellectuals, especially in the 1920s and 1930s, were such that even the JMA and the IJA officer corps were not entirely immune.[18] In his prison notes, written while awaiting trial, Isobe Asaichi (JMA 38), one of the February 26 ringleaders, who had also been deeply involved in earlier conspiracies, including the JMA (November) Incident of 1934, wrote of the deep concern he and other young officers had felt at the growing influx of leftist ideas into the army:

> The idea that the army was not contaminated by the evils of leftist thought is absolutely false. I know even from my own experience that to a frightening degree the army was disrupted by such thinking. At the Army Cadet School [Yōnen Gakkō] and the JMA there were many cadets who were infected by leftist thought and expelled. Even among the officers there were many with leftist tendencies. These included noncommissioned officers to be sure, but the level [of infection] reached such a degree that that even a division commander during his first round of inspection might give a moral lecture on the good points of communism.[19]

Emiko Ohnuki-Tierney's fascinating recent work reveals a strong interest and in some cases a serious commitment to Marxist ideology even among the student soldiers who volunteered as pilots for the suicidal "special attack units" (tokkōtai) in the 1940s, better known as the kamikaze.[20] Although the soldiers Ohnuki-Tierney studied were university students, not JMA graduates, they were nevertheless products of the same public educational system upon which the JMA was increasingly relying to fulfill its expanding admissions quotas. Between 1933 and 1945 (JMA 45–JMA 61), for example, the number of JMA entrants from the public middle schools rose dramatically relative to the number of entrants from the lower-level military schools that had traditionally acted as feeder institutions to the academy, only on two occasions dropping below 50 percent and at one point even exceeding 90 percent.[21]

Apart from Marxism's intellectual cachet among teachers and educators, what led such seemingly diverse groups as leftist students and tokkōtai pilots to embrace Marxist ideas in this period was above all was a profound generational revulsion at the exploitative aspects of the existing capitalist system. This feeling was shared by many cadets at the JMA. Indeed, so deep and widespread was this disgust that it touched even the most apolitical cadets, including, for example, Sejima Ryūzō, the top infantry graduate in the JMA 44 class of 1932, who after the war would return from eleven years of imprisonment in a Soviet labor camp and go on to head Itochū, one of Japan's largest international trading companies. In his autobiography, Se jima, who had come from a humble though not destitute rural background, recalled how his "social perspective" had been changed in the early 1930s when, after graduation from the JMA, he was put in charge of the education of newly enlisted soldiers in the 35th Infantry Regiment, based in the Toyama/Gifu area, and came face-to-face with the impoverished lives of his young recruits. It was an experience that was commonplace at the time for officers of Sejima's generation, and it is worth quoting at some length:

> About half of the newly enrolled soldiers under my charge were poor peasants and fisherman. In some cases their families were so pressed by debt that their younger sisters had gone into prostitution. Meanwhile, as I read in the newspapers about our country's severe internal and external problems, including such things as *zaibatsu* profiteering through foreign currency speculation or the corruption of politics, my own social perspective also changed. I'm not talking about Marxism or the national reform ideas of Kita Ikki.[22] It's just that my responsibility for recruit education led me to feel that somehow things in the world were not right, that something was off, whether it was the enormous disparity between rich and poor, or the absence of morality in politics, and I gradually developed a sense that social reform was needed. I avoided saying or doing anything openly, but these thoughts sometimes came out and were somehow even conveyed to the recruits, and I once had a letter sent to me censored by the military police. Thinking of the conditions of those times, I was able to understand why a number of my JMA classmates participated in the subsequent February 26 Incident.[23]

As Sejima suggests, despite a common repugnance toward the existing socioeconomic system, those JMA cadets who did become political in the end tended to move more toward the right than the left. There were many reasons for this, including the state's severe repression of leftist activities of any kind in the late 1920s and early 1930s, and especially during the war years, when, as an official history of the academy notes, there was virtually "no space" for leftist thought to penetrate the JMA.[24] In addition to state repression and censorship, this space was further and perhaps fatally constricted by the failure of leftist thought, as a class-based, international ideology, to resonate or connect deeply with the intensifying Japanese nationalism of those years.[25] At the MMA, however, where at least half or more of the cadets were non-Japanese, including both Chinese and Koreans, it was precisely a connection with these ethnic nationalist sentiments, largely anti-Japanese, that opened up and sustained a space for leftist thought.

Marxism and Ethnic Nationalism in the Empire

In both Korea and China, Marxism and later Marxism-Leninism came to be seen by many students in the post–World War I generation as an ideology of national liberation, in which the overthrow of the international capitalist system, structurally entwined with imperialist aggression in Leninist thought, was also the key to ending Japanese colonialism and semi-colonialism. Marxist study societies on the peninsula and continent, which burgeoned at roughly the same time as those in Japan, were thus simultaneously anticapitalist and nationalist, with each perspective reinforcing and strengthening the other like the proverbial two sides of the same coin. In Korea the local newspapers of the late 1920s and early 1930s, as in Japan a period of economic depression characterized by rural immiseration, factory wage cuts, and widespread unrest, reported countless instances of Korean students and faculty being arrested and in many cases expelled or imprisoned for their participation in such study or "reading" societies. These incidents, by no means confined to Seoul, could be found throughout the peninsula, from Pusan to Hamhŭng, from Kwangju to Ch'unch'ŏn.[26] In Taegu, for example, where Park Chung Hee attended teachers college between 1932 and 1937, a group of Korean students at Taegu Commercial School, along with several of their Japanese classmates, secretly formed a branch of a proletarian study society based in Tokyo and engaged in numerous activities in the early 1930s. In January 1931, on the anniversary of Lenin's death, they spread handbills throughout the city urging its residents to "topple the capitalists" and, in an echo of *Les Misérables*, Victor Hugo's famous nineteenth-century novel of rebellion and redemption that was so admired among students at the time, to "struggle for bread!" Inside the school they exhorted fellow students to expose the capitalist "essence of the imperialist educational system," while outside they formed covert factory and village "circles," including a Taegu cooperative society with the goal of establishing a labor union.[27]

At Taegu Normal School (TNS), Park's own institution, immediately next door to the commercial school, a similar situation prevailed. Only two months before Park matriculated in April 1932, Korean newspapers announced the arrest of a group of TNS students who had formed a Marxist study society under the guidance of Hyŏn Chunhyŏk, a graduate of colonial Korea's Keijō Imperial University and one of the most revered teachers at TNS. Hyŏn, a native of South P'yŏngan province who after Japan's surrender would serve briefly as P'yŏngyang's key communist leader until his assassination in September 1945, was a classic example of a Korean nationalist who saw the salvation of his nation in terms of Marxist-Leninist ideology. At TNS he taught English to the first-, second-, and third-year students, using portions of his class time to talk about a wide range of subjects unrelated to the actual class: Korean history, the March First Movement, Japanese imperialism, and of course the ever popular *Les Misérables.* As at Taegu Commercial, Hugo's masterpiece was so much a part of the discourse of the times among students at TNS that they secretly nicknamed the Japanese teacher at the school who patrolled their dormitories at night "Javert," the name of the fanatical policeman who relentlessly pursues the novel's hero. For that very reason the book served as an ideal intellectual bridge to the 400 "red" books the Taegu police later discovered in Hyŏn's possession—in effect the library for the study society he had organized.[28]

Even after Hyŏn's arrest and dismissal from the school and a subsequently much stricter supervision of "subversive thought" by the school authorities, TNS students continued to form study societies on their own well into the 1940s and avidly read potentially subversive classics such as *Les Misérables,* Tolstoy's *Resurrection,* and Dostoyevsky's *Crime and Punishment,* none of which were officially forbidden. Invariably they moved on to proscribed books such as *Mother,* Gorky's famous novel of socialist conversion and revolutionary struggle, as well as explicitly Marxist texts on capitalism in Japanese, including *Dai-ni binbō monogatari* (The second tale of poverty), by the well-known Japanese Marxist economist and communist Kawakami Hajime—a work that, according to former TNS 3 student Chin Tuhyŏn, was particularly influential and produced a "great shock."[29] In a reminiscence for the school's sixtieth anniversary, Chin described in detail how reading groups at the school in the early 1930s continued to thrive even after Hyŏn had left, driven by a passionate desire to master socialist thought that was fueled by nationalist aspirations:

We met often, expressing our views on current events, and read books that we had purchased cheaply and passed around. In those days as a way of mastering socialist thought, we bought a Japanese book called *Lectures on Marxism,* which we cut up to fit into our pockets and read in small snatches. If we had been found out, we would have been expelled, so we were always very careful, even in the dormitories. There was no reason for us to have to know about such basic Marxist ideas in *Capital* as surplus value or dialectical materialism, but we felt somehow that the intellectual current of the times was flowing from nationalism to socialism, and we wanted to know what socialism was all about. Our seniors who were being expelled and the people who were being arrested with the breakup of underground movements were for us only shining examples of firm and spirited comrades, people who were correct in their thinking. As soon as we managed to scrape through our exams without failing, we spent all our free time reading social science books, along with novels and magazines. We even read in the dormitories with flashlights after the lights were turned out. We really made an effort to hide those books, because after the lights were turned out "Javert" and his ilk would come in and always ransack our bookcases and sometimes even our wardrobes.[30]

In Manchuria too, one could find the same heady and empowering blend of nationalism and Marxist thought among student groups, not least of all among the Han Chinese, who made up almost 90 percent of the population of the country.[31] There, as in China more generally, the interest in Marxism-Leninism among students was strengthened by the presence of an active and armed Communist Party that was fighting the Japanese and could not be controlled or suppressed to the extent it was in Korea and Japan. As in Korea, the study societies were not limited to one school or one locality, though they were more numerous in the larger cities of Mukden, Harbin, and Xinjing, where the greatest numbers of students were concentrated. Xinjing was also home to Kenkoku University (Kendai), which had opened in 1938. Originally set up with the support of the Kwantung Army to educate a multiethnic, though largely Han Chinese, civilian elite to aid in the administration of the new Manchurian state, the school had actually sanctioned the reading and teaching of Marxist-Leninist and communist books that were forbidden in Japan itself or at other Manchurian schools as a way to train its students to counter growing communist influence in the region.[32] This of course turned out to be a mistake, as Chinese students, disgruntled with the arrogant and inherently discriminatory policy of "internal guidance" through which the Kwantung Army and civilian Japanese bureaucrats operated in the country, often responded positively to the double message of revolution and nationalism that had captivated so many of their peers in

Korea, and in some cases even wound up joining the Communist Party. At the MMA, on the outskirts of the capital city and easily connected by train to Mukden in the south and to Harbin in the north, Chinese cadets, especially in the first five MMA classes, felt the sting of Japanese superiority and discrimination on a daily basis, as noted in Chapter 3. There too, despite a much more restrictive academic atmosphere, secret societies combining nationalism and Marxism in a potent mix found fertile ground. Indeed, the extent of such revolutionary activity at the MMA was nothing short of remarkable.[33]

Revolutionary Activity at the MMA

The activity began with the very first class of Dōtokudai Mankei cadets, the non-Japanese component of the MMA 1 class, which entered the school in April 1939. Within a month of matriculation, seven MMA 1 Chinese cadets, led by Cui Lifu and Lü Dianyuan, met secretly to form a group called the Recovery Society (Huifuhui). By the fall of 1941, it had grown to encompass more than 20 percent of the 160-member MMA 1 Mankei class. Through Cui Lifu, moreover, it established contacts with a study society in Xinjing composed of university students.[34]

At the same time as the Recovery Society was taking shape, another secret group at the academy called the True Bravery Society (Zhenyongshe) was also recruiting MMA 1 Mankei cadets. In both cases the MMA 1 cadets went on to enlist juniors from the MMA 2 and MMA 3 classes, who in turn brought in new members from the classes below them. By 1945 the two societies had links to all seven MMA Mankei classes. And through the first three classes, which by then had already been commissioned and deployed, the links extended even further, going well beyond the academy to a considerable number of Manchukuo army units throughout the country, where the MMA officers continued to recruit members even after graduation and eventually went on to lead anti-Japanese insurrections at the end of the war.[35]

In addition to the relatively large-scale Huifuhui and Zhenyongshe, which had their roots in the MMA 1 and MMA 2 Mankei cadets and gradually spread to other classes, smaller secret societies with or without formal names burgeoned independently in later classes. In the case of the MMA 3 Mankei, which matriculated in April 1941 and overlapped with both MMA 1 and MMA 2, some cadets joined the Huifuhui and Zhenyongshe, while others formed their own associations such as the Xianzhou Society. Inspired by their seniors, cadets from the MMA 4 Mankei, which entered a year later, founded a group called Ten Brothers (Shixiongdi) and actively recruited their juniors in the MMA 5 and MMA 6 classes. Both MMA 5 and MMA 6 had their own secret organizations as well, including the MMA 6 Blood and Iron Society (Tiexueshe), whose members pledged their allegiance by slicing their fingers and letting their blood drip into a bowl of water from which they all drank. If the cadets in the MMA 7 class, only eight months in residence when the war came to an end in August 1945, had not yet developed their own secret societies, it was only because they had first to explore so many already established groups, all eager to recruit additional members from the first-year class.[36]

Despite their numbers, the basic character of the groups seeking to enroll the first-year cadets in any given year was very similar. All were born of an intense aversion to the Japanese occupation and a desire to "recover" Manchuria for China. Like most of the student groups there or in Korea, they were essentially reading or study societies. Some were more ideologically neutral than others, fueled by a simple patriotism or the nationalism of Sun Yatsen, but all, to a greater or lesser degree, found inspiration in the subversive literature of the times. As in Korea, translations of Dostoyevsky and Gogol often provided the first steps toward a revolutionary consciousness. More often than not these books, along with works by Chinese authors such as Ba Jin, Lu Xun, and Mao Dun, eventually led to the study of Marxist theoretical writings and communist literature obtained secretly from former middle school classmates attending college or university in Xinjing, from obliging bookstores, and even in some cases directly from the Chinese Communist Party (CCP).[37]

Some of the MMA groups in fact actively sought support or formal recognition from the CCP. The True Bravery Society, for example, although independently founded, appears to have received covert encouragement and assistance from the CCP from the beginning. The two leaders of the Recovery Society, MMA 1 cadets Cui Lifu and Lü Dianyuan, were also eager to establish a CCP connection. Lü, wary of exposure, was the more cautious, and worked quietly through a female relative, whose brother was a CCP county secretary in Hebei province, to make contact with the party. When it proved impossible to break through the security cordon the Japanese military had established around the CCP, Lü turned his attention to building up the Huifuhui within the MMA itself, recruiting from the first three classes. Cui, however, was determined to link the group to the party at all costs, and as a result in December 1941 he found himself drawn into a trap set up by the Manchukuo police, leading to his arrest and a nine-year prison sentence.[38]

Despite Cui Lifu's arrest, Mankei interest in communism continued un-abated. Cadets in the MMA 3 class, some of whose members had been deeply involved with Cui Lifu, secretly formed an explicitly pro-communist reading society, centered on Marx's *Das Kapital,* that was formally recognized by the Xinjing CCP.[39] And some of their juniors in the MMA 4 class managed to make contact with nearby CCP forces while on training exercises in Rehe (Jehol) province and smuggle communist literature back into the academy.[40] One of the liveliest pro-communist groups was in the MMA 5 class, which supplemented its theoretical readings on Marxist historical materialism and proletarian revolution with practical lessons from the history of the Soviet revolution and the CCP.[41]

Resilience of the Marxist Societies at the Academies

One might well ask how such groups managed not just to survive but to flourish and reproduce themselves so effectively and consistently at the MMA year after year. One of the most important reasons lay in the way the Mankei and Nikkei classes were constituted for most of the MMA's history. Until the MMA 6 class, when the Mankei and Nikkei were combined into mixed companies, the Japanese and non-Japanese cadets were sectioned and barracked separately. Thus, though their studies and training were identical, even overlapping, and they came together daily in the dining hall and regularly at all-school ceremonies and events, their interaction on a personal and private level was more limited (see Chapter 3).

Of course the Mankei were under the watch of their section and company commanders, many of whom were Japanese, and Japanese was the official language of the academy, but the Mankei cadets in the societies made good use of all unsupervised time allowed by the school. Sunday and holiday day leaves and summer and winter vacations were particularly important. If the former provided opportunities for the cadets to meet among themselves at a restaurant in downtown Xinjing, at a relative's house in the suburb of Erdaohezi, or at a designated place such as the old Shibeiling fort just outside the MMA, the latter offered the chance for cadets such as Cui Lifu to connect with like-minded students at other schools, including former middle school classmates at Kendai, who would often pass on the books and articles they were reading in their own study groups.[42]

The cadets made brilliant use of their more structured and supervised time at the academy to promote their causes. Although after Cui Lifu's arrest in 1941 the cadets in the societies tended to hide their forbidden books outside the school grounds, some, including those in the Xianzhou Society, followed a practice similar to the Korean TSA students in Taegu, cutting up their books to disguise them as lecture notes, which they read during self-study periods before taps and in the barracks latrines at night. As noted above, periodic field exercises in Rehe province, often lasting two weeks or longer, offered opportunities for establishing contacts with the Chinese communist Eighth Route Army and acquiring communist literature. Cadets sent to Rehe for their three-month regimental attachment duty (*taizuki kinmu*) after graduation from the *yoka* had even more time to develop such connections, which is precisely what happened to the MMA 5 Mankei cadets, who spent their *taizuki* there in the summer of 1944.[43]

One of the most ingenious methods of self-propagation by the various secret societies was to take advantage of the opportunities presented when one of their members was chosen to serve as a counselor cadet (*shidō seito*). As noted earlier, the counselor cadet was an upperclassman selected by the school to billet in one of the first-year *yoka* sections and serve as a model and advisor to the new cadets. In most cases he was the first upperclassman the younger cadets came to know, and his senior rank and status as *shidō seito* gave him immense influence and power over those in his section, second only to the section commander (*kutaichō*) himself. He was thus in an ideal position to recruit new members for his study group, and indeed, this is precisely how many of the societies spread their influence to junior classes. The Ten Brothers group in MMA 4 was particularly successful here, relying almost exclusively on this method to expand its membership into the MMA 5 and MMA 6 classes.[44]

And then, of course, there were the songs. Many of the secret societies had their own group songs, which were sung at private meetings outside the academy, but Mankei cadets in the societies also used the communal singing sessions that were an integral part of their daily regimen to subvert the system and foster morale for their own cause. When the Manchukuo and Japanese national anthems were being played, or when they sang Chinese songs, such as Yue Fei's "Manjianghong," that were popular among both the Mankei and Nikkei, cadets in the societies silently mouthed or focused on alternative lyrics they had memorized denouncing discrimination at the academy or Japanese imperialist political and economic exploitation of Manchuria. They also designated certain words in seemingly innocuous class songs as code terms to subvert or transpose meanings. In one of the MMA 1 Mankei songs that railed against Western imperialism, for example,

"English and American devils" became code for "Japanese invaders," so cadets could sing the former loudly and boldly while actually thinking the latter. Two MMA 2 songs were composed with similar double meanings, where common phrases such as "fighting for righteousness" were understood as covert expressions of anti-Japanese patriotism.[45]

To no small degree the Mankei secret societies owed their survival to the patronage and protection they received from a network of Chinese officers or instructors working at Dōtokudai itself. The network was extensive. It included section commanders such as Zhang Lianzhi, who composed the two MMA 2 class songs mentioned above, one with the help of MMA 2 cadet Wu Zongfang, who was sent to Zama with Park Chung Hee and other top-ranked Mankei only to defect to the Chinese communists soon after graduation.[46] It also included company commanders with strong communist sympathies, such as Yu Qinghuai and Deng Chang. Yu was famous for regaling the MMA 3 cadets with stories about the CCP's Eighth Route Army, and a number of them had hoped to approach him for assistance in obtaining CCP sponsorship of their organization, but he was transferred before they could act.[47] Deng had had a long secret history as a CCP member even before arriving at the MMA. He was a Manchurian native who had joined the party in Shanxi in 1931, where he had been successful in organizing a pro-CCP peripheral group of about seventy members called the Great Anti-Imperialist Alliance. After returning to Manchuria in 1933, he was arrested twice in the late 1930s but released for lack of evidence. Eventually finding his way into the Manchukuo Army, he was sent to Japan for training and returned to become a military instructor and company commander at the Harbin Military Medical Academy, where he actively recruited cadets for the party, a practice he continued after being posted to the MMA in 1945. Focusing on the MMA 5 cadets, he used the time allotted for spiritual or moral lectures (seishin kunwa) to talk about historical materialism, the Soviet revolution, and the CCP.[48]

Support for the secret societies came not just from various commanders in the corps of cadets but from a number of instructors in the school's division of academic affairs as well. Park Chung Hee's classmate Wu Zongfang, for example, began his intellectual journey toward communism not only with the help of his Mankei senior Cui Lifu, one of the founders of the Recovery Society, but also under the guidance of Yang Rizhe, a professor of Chinese literature at the school. Yang lent him numerous forbidden books, including Gorky's *Mother*, which, Wu later wrote, led him "for the first time to feel the spirit of revolution."[49]

The MMA's military tactics instructors, who often served as section commanders in the cadet corps, were another pillar of support in the academic
division for the secret societies. The key figure in the propagation and protection of the True Bravery Society was Liu Qimin, a tactics instructor for
the MMA 1 class who in addition served as a section commander for the
MMA 2 and eventually as a staff officer for Manchukuo Army vice minister
Manai Tsurukichi. The first MMA 1 cadets to be initiated into the True
Bravery Society were actually recruited by Liu, and they took their pledges
to the society in Liu's home, just outside the Dōtokudai gates.[50] Successive
tactics instructors followed in Liu's subversive footsteps. When company
commander Yu Qinghuai was transferred before the MMA 3 cadets could
seek his help in securing formal CCP acknowledgment of their society, they
turned to Tong Zhishan, their tactics instructor at the time. Tong was well
known for spending a good portion of his class time lecturing on *Das Kapital,* social history, and the anti-Japanese struggle. In fact, his furtive lectures were so popular that the cadets asked him to dispense with the tactics
lessons altogether, which they promised to learn on their own, and he agreed.
One of the reasons Tong agreed was that he was a member of the Xinjing
branch of the CCP, and he became an important liaison for the MMA 3
cadets in achieving formal recognition from the party.[51]

That the academic division of the MMA was able to function so effectively as a support for the secret societies could be traced directly to the
Manchukuo army officer Wang Jiashan, who was the division's dean in the
early 1940s. By the time he came to Dōtokudai Wang had already attained
general rank, having studied at the IJA Army Staff College in the 1930s and
served in a number of important positions related to the development of the
Manchukuo Army, and in September 1942 he was chosen to act as chief of
staff of the military review for Prince Takamatsu's visit to Manchukuo on
the tenth anniversary of the founding of the state. At the end of the war he
was serving as a combat brigade commander in the country's Seventh District Army in Sanjiang province.

More to the point, and unbeknownst to his Japanese superiors at the
time, Wang was also the original leader of the True Bravery Society, which
he had founded when he was at the Japanese Army Staff College and which
he continued to monitor and guide for the next decade, including during
his deployment at the MMA, when Liu Qimin was effectively his chief subordinate and recruiter for the society. As noted above, the True Bravery Society had a strong communist bent from its beginning, but like many patriotic
Chinese during this period, Wang looked to both the nationalists and the
communists for assistance in his activities, and following Japan's defeat he

initially organized his troops in Manchuria as a provisional division under the Guomindang. But when the Chinese civil war spread to the northeast, he led his entire division over to the communists at the crucial Battle of Yingkou in 1947, thus helping to ensure the CCP's ultimate victory in that region. Notably, many of the officers under his command at Yingkou were men who had been recruited into the True Bravery Society when they had been cadets at the MMA.[52]

Exactly how vital the patronage of Wang and his colleagues was to the continued existence of the MMA secret societies can be seen in the aftermath of the arrest of Cui Lifu and other members of the Recovery Society in December 1941. As soon as the society's cofounder Lü Dianyuan heard of Cui's arrest and realized that the society risked full exposure, he contacted several sympathetic MMA instructors and section commanders, including Liu Qimin, asking them to spread the word to authorities within the MMA and in wider army circles downplaying any communist influence or connections in the society and suggesting instead that the Manchukuo police, posing as communists, had deliberately tried to compromise the innocent cadets in order to arrest them. The story proved to be effective, in no small part because of long-standing antagonistic relations between the police and the military, who believed that the former had concocted a scheme to corrupt the education of the national army and tarnish its reputation. Although several cadets, including Cui, who had openly admitted their interest in establishing relations with the CCP during the police sting operation could not escape official punishment, and despite the MMA subsequently intensifying its surveillance of the Mankei cadets, the Recovery Society and other secret groups continued to thrive at the academy over the next four years.[53]

Korean Cadets within the Mankei

While there is no explicit evidence linking any of the Korean cadets at Dōtokudai between 1939 and 1945 to the Mankei secret societies, we do know that a significant number of them, including Park Chung Hee and nearly half of his MMA 2 Korean classmates, became involved in various activities associated with the communist South Korean Workers Party after 1945.[54] To be sure, such interest in communism could have either antedated or postdated the MMA experience, but it is important to remember that all Koreans in the first five MMA classes were assigned to the Mankei group (see Chapter 3). Some who had attended middle school in Manchuria, like many in the MMA 1 class, already spoke fluent Chinese; all were required to learn it if they did not know it already. Indeed, language classes were held every day, five days a week, with about four times as much class time devoted to language training as to any other subject in the *yoka* course.[55] Even more important, until the MMA 5 class, when they were officially incorporated into the Nikkei, the Korean cadets barracked, studied, and trained with the Chinese cadets, sharing commanders at all levels (section, company, corps), as well as instructors in the academic division.

Park Chung Hee's experience here is a case in point. Although there is no indication he knew any spoken Chinese when he entered the academy, he seems to have developed a reasonable level of conversational fluency, enough at least to impress his Japanese classmates at Zama, who described him as a "great Chinese-speaker."[56] His Chinese Mankei classmate Gao Qingyin, who later served with him in the same Manchukuo Army unit in Rehe province, told me that they communicated in Chinese as well as Japanese.[57] When Park was at Lalatun, both the Recovery Society and the True Bravery Society were especially active, enjoying the support of academic affairs dean Wang Jiashan and tactics instructor Liu Qimin, His Chinese literature teacher was Yang Rizhe, who at the time was introducing revolutionary books to Wu Zongfang and other cadets.[58] And his section commander (2nd Section of 3rd Company) was none other than Zhang Lianzhi, the composer of the dissident version of MMA 2 class song.[59]

Park's 3rd Company, comprising four sections, appears to have been a hotbed of Marxist secret society activity. In the fall of 1941, as the MMA authorities began to suspect the existence of subversive activity at the academy, they zeroed in on 3rd Company, which included not only Wu Zongfang (2nd Section) but many other Chinese cadets who were reading and passing around proscribed books, including original works by Marx. One of the cadets in the 4th Section, Bai Guohua, remembered how close they had come to being caught. Fortunately, Bai noted, they had managed to hide the most seditious books before the authorities struck, and no one was arrested. But the school had conducted a thorough examination of 3rd Company's quarters. One morning when the cadets returned to their barracks after class, they discovered that every part of the building had been systematically and meticulously searched, including the toilets and ceilings as well as the sleeping quarters. All reading materials had been checked page by page; bags and boxes containing materials for cleaning weapons and boots had been opened; the contents of briefcases had been taken out and strewn across the beds; and in some cases even the tatami floor mats had been sliced open. The entire 3rd Company had its weekly leaves rescinded for six months, and the cadets were ordered to "reexamine" themselves in their daily journals of self-reflection.[60]

Clearly the cadets in the secret societies had to be careful. For that reason they were hesitant about recruiting fellow Mankei cadets they did not know, and particular caution was often exercised toward the Korean cadets, who were regarded as subjects of Japan, and toward Chinese cadets from Dalian, who were suspected of being spies of the Kwantung Army.[61] On the other hand, there were some Chinese cadets who felt a special bond with their Korean classmates because, as Li Tiancheng put it, "we were both oppressed nationalities, and we sympathized with one another."[62] Moreover, even if the Koreans were never directly approached by the secret societies, within the Mankei they were living in perhaps the only part of the MMA community where a certain tolerance of socialist and communist ideas and activities was both possible and to some degree practiced. And even if Mankei cadets were not themselves members of secret societies and did not know of the societies' existence, many knew and simply accepted the fact that certain cadets and instructors were sympathetic to Marxist ideas and were possibly even communists. One sees this in the treatment of Gao's and Park's MMA 2 classmate Lu Wenkong, who was from Gao's hometown. According to Gao, Lu was one of a number of "strong communists" at the MMA, and it was well known within the class that he kept a cache of communist books. But Lu was never reported to the authorities by any of his fellow cadets, and Gao, who, like most of the Mankei, resented the Japanese occupation but remained outside the secret societies, was content to let Lu do as he wished. As Gao put it, "I just didn't care."[63]

This laissez-faire attitude toward leftist views within the Mankei group at both the cadet and officer levels not only buttressed the growth of secret societies but also empowered cadets to express revolutionary views privately among themselves. Such was the case with Kim Chaep'ung, one of the three MMA 2 Koreans who went to Zama with Park Chung Hee for the *honka* course and after 1945 was active in the South Korean Labor Party before defecting to the north.[64] Bai Guohua, who was in Kim's section at Lalatun, remembered him boasting in Chinese that the communists under Kim Il Sung would save Korea. When Bai replied that Kim Il Sung was actually fighting under the leadership of the Chinese communists, Kim at first took umbrage, but a third cadet from Taiwan, also in the 4th Section, who had overheard the conversation reminded his two classmates that they should all focus on the struggle that bound Koreans and Chinese together, and the three thereafter became friends.[65]

Shortly before his death, Chŏng Ilgwŏn, with whom Park Chung Hee often spent his MMA Sunday leaves in Xinjing, told Lee-Jay Cho that Park, even as a cadet, "liked to talk about socialism," and that he occasionally even attended "secret meetings."[66] And in his memoir, Yi Hallim, another MMA 2 Korean classmate who joined Park and Kim Chaep'ung at Zama, recounted numerous occasions of ideologically tinged private conversations at Lalatun with Park and Yi Pyŏngju, another MMA 2 Korean cadet with whom Park was particularly close. As a practicing Catholic, Yi Hallim was offended by Yi Pyŏngju's agnosticism, but he was even more repelled by his praise of communism, and by Park Chung Hee's apparent agreement with Yi Pyŏngju's position:

> He [Yi Pyŏngju] was steeped in communism to the core. Since childhood, I had regarded communism as something frightening and bad, so I did not think well of him. And sometimes, when Park Chung Hee came with him, I thought it strange that Park expressed no objections to what he was saying. But that was not yet a time when I had to worry seriously about ideological problems, so I just considered their ideas strange and let it go.[67]

Chong Ilgwŏn's comments to Cho are of course thirdhand, and Yi Hallim's remarks are anecdotal and retrospective, written in the full knowledge of Park's and Yi Pyŏngju's post-1945 involvement in communist activity, as well as from the perspective of one who was for a time punished and ostracized by Park for opposing the May 16 coup in 1961. What gives some credence to both Chŏng's statement and Yi's story, however, is Park's own background. While the precise origins of his interest in leftist ideas are impossible to determine, it seems safe to say that by the time he entered the MMA, Park was certainly no stranger to such thought and may well have been sympathetic. As we have seen, to a certain extent such interest was simply generational, not at all uncommon among his peers at TNS. There may also have been familial influences. Park's admired older brother, Pak Sanghŭi, who was a well-known journalist in the Sŏnsan area of North Kyŏngsang province, where the family lived, was an outspoken critic of the colonial economic and social system, arguing that it was increasingly penetrated by Chinese and Japanese goods and creating a destitute and dependent rural class of "propertyless" (*musan*) families and children, and according to Kim Chongp'il, Pak Sanghŭi's son-in-law (as well as Park Chung Hee's co-conspirator in the 1961 coup), Pak Sanghŭi was definitely leftist or "progressive" (*chinbojŏk*) in his political orientation. Pak Sanggil, a former Blue House spokesman when Park Chung Hee was president, also told me that Park, as a child of that impoverished rural class his brother had written about, had also developed a strong "hatred of landlords."[68]

Whatever the genesis of Park's interest in leftist thought, what can be said with certainty is that the MMA was in no sense an effective foil against socialism and communism. Within the Mankei at Lalatun Koreans were in fact living in an environment that was permeated in various ways and at various levels with communist influence. At its most porous, it facilitated an astonishing proliferation of secret societies that involved highly committed Chinese cadets. But such porousness in the Mankei also provided a certain amount of space and even encouragement for quiet and covert consideration and discussion of the merits of socialism and communism among any cadets so interested or inclined.

Reform: Shōwa Restorationism

Far more deeply entrenched in IJA culture and institutions was a second, fundamentally reactionary critique of capitalism that had its roots in the Shōwa Restorationism advocated by the radical young officers of the 1930s and their admirers. After the army's suppression of the February 26 Incident, enthusiasm for a Shōwa Restoration, as for socialism and communism, had to be covert, but as noted earlier, it remained widespread within the Japanese officer corps in the 1940s, not least of all in Manchuria. "Covert" is perhaps not quite the right word here, for expressions of such enthusiasm, though officially not condoned, were scarcely hidden. As we have seen, many Japanese officers in fact took pride in voicing to colleagues and juniors their respect for the rebellious young officers of the 1930s, seeing both the rebels and their supporters as the most *majime* of officers. It was a telling sign of this high regard that the Shōwa Restoration song, as well as the song of the May 15 Incident, continued to be sung at the MMA and JMA right down to the end of the war in 1945 (see Chapter 5).

Mutiny as patriotic duty was at the core of the young officers' understanding of a Shōwa Restoration in the 1930s, but beyond that, what did a Shōwa Restoration represent? In particular, what did it signify with respect to the capitalist system in place at the time? The ideas of the February 26 rebels were often vague and differed somewhat from officer to officer, but it is possible on the basis of the prison testimonies left behind by the key figures to get a sense of their general social concerns and visions. On the day before his execution, Yasuda Yutaka, the February 26 officer who had shot and killed the Lord Keeper of the Privy Seal, Saitō Makoto, and the Inspector General of Military Training, General Watanabe Jōtarō, wrote that Japan was confronting the "terrible destructiveness of capitalism," which only the "heavenly sword" of the young officers could "relieve."[69] Yasuda's view was commonplace among the mutinous young officers of the 1930s. Their hatred of capitalism as a system was certainly no less intense than their socialist or communist peers' feelings about capitalism, and one might have expected them to join hands with the leftist groups and work together. But while the two perspectives were overlapping or similar in some respects, in others they were significantly different. The young officers were indeed repulsed by the capitalist system in which they lived, but as the excerpt from Isobe Asaichi's prison notes quoted earlier indicates, they were not communists in any conventional sense, and in fact regarded Marxism and other leftist movements as enemies. To understand their motivations and goals more clearly, we might therefore begin by looking at some of the ways in which they both resembled and differed from their Marxist counterparts.

The "Terrible Destructiveness" of Capitalism

In terms of their understanding of the primary perpetrators and victims of capitalism's "terrible destructiveness," the young officers had much in common with the socialist and communist left.[70] Although they tended not to use the Marxist term "bourgeoisie," they were unequivocal in their denunciation of the huge business conglomerates or *zaibatsu* that were dominating the economy at the time. "*Zaibatsu* vaunt their wealth," ran the second verse of "Song of the Shōwa Restoration," "with no thought for the country."[71] And Yasuda, still seething with moral indignation literally hours before his death, wrote that "the wealth of the *zaibatsu* surpasses that of the imperial household; with it they manipulate the robber politicians and monopolize national policy."[72] As Yasuda's words suggest, the young officers saw the *zaibatsu* and their wealth as part of a larger ruling stratum they tended to call the "privileged class" (*tokken kaikyū*).[73] Here, although they did employ the usual Marxist word for "class" (*kaikyū*), their understanding of the term was both broader and vaguer, referring to a self-serving and corrupt elite that encompassed, in addition to the *zaibatsu*, the parliamentary political parties, government bureaucrats and advisors, the intelligentsia, and even the senior echelons of the army itself. Within this group, however, the *zaibatsu* were key, for it was their ability to subvert and manipulate the system that had brought the country economically and morally to its present state of crisis, with, in Yasuda's vivid phrase, the emperor's key civil and military advisors "conspiring with the bureaucrats by day and knocking on the gates of the zaibatsu henchmen by night."[74]

In speaking of the victims of Japanese capitalism's "terrible destructive-ness," the young officers used a variety of terms, including "common people" (shomin), "poor people" (kyūmin), and "impoverished families" (hinkon katei). Sometimes they spoke broadly of "the people" (tami) or simply "the Japanese people" (Nihon kokumin).[75] But their deepest sympathies were clearly reserved for the peasantry (nōmin, hyakushō), especially the rural poor, mainly poor tenants, who had been hit hardest by the Depression years of the late 1920s and early 1930s.[76] The rebellious young officers them-selves had not for the most part been born into this rural social stratum; in fact, a number had come from very wealthy or distinguished families. But as Sejima Ryūzō noted, the young officers of this period were forced to con-front the wretched socioeconomic conditions of the countryside in the faces and lives of the soldiers in the units they commanded, and they were moved and often outraged by what they saw and learned. These feelings later burst forth time and again in their trial testimonies and prison writings. At his public trial in 1933, for example, May 15 leader Yagi Haruo, who, as we saw, went on to an important career in the Manchukuo Army Ministry, was asked to explain what specifically troubled him about the social conditions of the time. "The root of the present evil," Yagi replied, "lies in the corrup-tion and depravity of the privileged class, the political parties and zaibatsu who constitute the ruling elite. . . . The present government cries about rural policy and saving the villages, but the money they put into this only rescues the insolvent banks, which is to say a few capitalists, nothing more. It does not reach the general peasantry."[77]

One sees this same focus on the plight of the peasants and the responsi-bility of the zaibatsu and their political allies in the writings of the con-demned February 26 officers, epitomized once again by Yasuda, who spent the last full day of his life writing about these subjects. None of this was conventional Marxism, to be sure, where the issue of exploitation was cen-tered on the industrial working class. But here too, although they would have been loath to admit it, the young officers were not so different in their thinking from their leftist peers in Japan and Korea, who had expanded the class focus of revolution to a more generalized category of the propertyless poor to ac-count for the fact that the majority of the populations in those two countries were still engaged in agriculture.[78] As both Sejima's and Yagi's comments suggest, the question of relieving peasant distress was an issue that crossed political and ideological lines and was discussed widely in the public media not only in Japan but in Korea as well, where conditions were even worse. A little more than a week after the May 15 Incident, for example, Korea's *Tonga ilbo* newspaper editorialized that the question of "peasant relief," which had been at the core of the rebellion, was an issue for reflection not only in Japan but also in Korea, where the problem was a "life-and-death" issue for all Koreans.[79]

Reform, Not Revolution

While Shōwa Restorationism thus had much in common with the Japanese and Korean left in the 1930s, it was significantly different in several respects. Although they sometimes employed the word "revolution" (*kakumei*) in their writings, for the most part the February 26 officers spoke of their aspirations in terms of "reform" (*kakushin*) or "reorganization" (*kaizō*). During their trials the prosecuting authorities tried to link the actions of the young officers with both the social revolutionary left and also the work of Kita Ikki, a right-wing ideologue who in 1919 had written a famous subversive tract called *Nihon kaizō hōan taikō* [Fundamental principles for the reorganization of Japan].[80] But as Isobe stated in his extensive defense against these charges, the young officers had vehemently opposed a class-based leftist revolution, which would have divided the national body (*kokutai*).[81] Or as another rebel officer, Nakahashi Motoaki, succinctly put it, "In no way did we seek to carry out a social democratic revolution."[82] Nor had they, the rebel officers insisted, acted in concert with Kita Ikki and his followers. To be sure, as Isobe acknowledged, the rebels had been sympathetic to many of the ideas expressed in Kita's *Taikō*, but Kita and his followers had not been directly involved in the February 26 Incident, and the officers had not risen up expressly to implement Kita's ideas. Moreover, as Isobe went on to point out, quoting relevant passages from Kita's work, the *Taikō* itself was not revolutionary in the leftist sense. It explicitly recognized the right of private property, although it set limits on how much an individual or organization might own, beyond which private wealth would be confiscated by the state without compensation. Thus, Isobe insisted, the *Taikō* did not advocate Marxist socialism, which "had no respect for private property," let alone a fully communal system of "primitive communism" or even an "egalitarian communism" of equalized ownership. Capitalism, not the existence of private ownership per se, was the problem, because in its glorification of the pursuit of individual profit the capitalist system allowed the bulk of the nation's wealth to be concentrated in the hands of a small group of businessmen who used it to further their own private interests, rather than for the benefit of the society and nation as a whole.[83]

Despite their distaste for the term "socialism," the economic system the young officers envisioned on the basis of Kita's work did in fact have a strong socialist tinge to it, and Kita himself had claimed that his ideas represented a true form of socialism, as opposed to what he, as well as the young officers echoing him in their prison writings, called the "foreign" or "doctrinaire" socialism of the left.[84] Their economic reformism is perhaps best understood as a socialism of the right, similar though far from identical to the national socialist and fascist economies that were developing in Germany and Italy at the time. Kita's work had of course been produced before the rise of Hitler and Mussolini, and the Shōwa Restoration officers themselves explicitly rejected any such comparisons.[85] But all three ideologies had emerged in no small part in response to the perceived failures—economic, social, political, and moral—of capitalism, and all sought national salvation and unity through a largely command economy that restrained but did not entirely eliminate private enterprise. Indeed, the system articulated by Kita and taken up by the young officers was even more radical in its economic dirigisme and restrictions on private property than were the systems of Germany and Italy in the late 1930s. It was, as Isobe wrote, "an ideology of high statism and high nationalism" (*takai kokkashugi, kokuminshugi no shisō*).[86]

Capitalism as a National Toxin

Isobe's idea of "high nationalism" reflects yet another way in which capitalism was perceived by army Shōwa Restorationists in the 1930s and how that perspective differed from orthodox Marxism as well as democratic liberalism at the time. While capitalism was regarded negatively by Marxists and more positively by liberal democrats, both saw it as the basis of a historical and universalistic world order in which all countries were inevitably embedded. Thus liberation in the communist sense, notwithstanding Stalin's promotion of "socialism in one country," was for Japanese and Korean leftists of this period closely linked to the idea of world revolution, as in the case of Chang Chirak, whose activities in the Chinese Communist Party in the 1920s and 1930s were captured in a well-known 1941 work by Helen Foster Snow.[87]

For the young officers of this period, on the other hand, capitalism was seen primarily as a noxious foreign intrusion into an organically conceived Japanese national body (*kokutai*), a deadly toxin that not only had wrought economic destruction but since the Meiji Restoration had brought in its wake a host of other debilitating and potentially fatal "spiritual" evils, including individualism, utilitarianism, liberalism, democracy, parliamentarianism, constitutionalism, and even socialism and communism themselves. In that sense it had effected a betrayal of the goals and promises of the Meiji Restoration. It was "antithetical," as Muranaka Takaji wrote, "to the *kokutai* ideology reestablished by the Great Meiji Emperor."[88] Thus, despite widely shared concerns about what they saw as Japan's diminishing status in the world and its unfair treatment by foreign powers, the focus of the February 26 rebels was essentially more domestic than international. A Shōwa Restoration and "high nationalism" for them signified above all an internal national reform, a cleansing of the capitalist evils that had begun to infect the national body, particularly since the more open and liberal Taishō era, and through that cleansing, a return, as it were, to the original spirit of the Meiji Restoration.

Coup as Catalyst, Not Control

But how was all this to be brought about? How could "high statism" and "high nationalism" be achieved? For the Shōwa Restoration officers of this period, the road to reforming the evils of capitalism lay not through class conflict or social revolution from below, for these methods were themselves nothing more than aspects of the toxic environment they despised. The solution lay instead through a coup d'état. In his *Taikō*, Kita had made the argument for a coup followed by a period of martial law, but he had not specifically called upon the army to lead it, only citing the examples of Napoleon and Lenin as historical figures who had successfully led such revolutionary seizures of state power.[89] As noted earlier, however, for the February 26 officers there was only one group that could save the nation. As First Lieutenant Nakahashi wrote: "Kita and [his disciple] Nishida did not lead us; only soldiers could act to reform the evils of the present day."[90] "Only we could shoulder this burden," Muranaka went on, "and our duty as soldiers demanded it."[91]

Nevertheless, the goal of the coup was not to establish any form of military rule or hegemony. About this the young officers were explicit. They did not even like the term "coup d'état," because it seemed to imply political ambitions they insisted they did not have. "We did not plan a coup d'état," Muranaka wrote. "We did not act out of a selfish scheme to seize political power through military force."[92] Those were the ambitions of the "Control Faction" (Tōseiha) now running the army, the young officers argued. The Tōseiha was part of the "privileged class" and sought to establish military control of the state and implement a "Hitlerian modernization" of the army that would increase army budgets at the expense of the peasantry. The young officers, by contrast, vehemently opposed such plans. Indeed, Isobe insisted, they had no "concrete plan, no blueprint for construction, and no intention to implement any plan or blueprint."[93] As already noted, this included even Kita's *Taikō,* despite how compelling the officers had found his ideas.

What, then, was their goal in rising up in rebellion? Over and over again in their prison writings, the young officers insisted that their main purpose had simply been to "restore" (*kaifuku*) full power to the emperor, whose prerogatives since the Meiji Restoration had been trampled upon by the "privileged class" that surrounded him.[94] This, they believed (however naively in retrospect), would "pave the way" for a new restoration in which the Shōwa emperor himself would lead the country in carrying out reform, presumably along the lines the young officers desired.[95] Their role, as the young officers saw it, was not to rule but simply to free the emperor himself to rule by suppressing the people around him who were "violating his supreme authority and corrupting the *kokutai.*"[96] Muranaka evoked the image of General Nogi taking Hill 203 at the Battle of Port Arthur. Just as the seizure of the hill had led to the fall of the city, so was their action to be the beginning or starting point (*shuppatsuten*) of the Shōwa Restoration.[97] It was, Yasuda wrote, to be no more and no less than a "single blow of the heaven-endowed sword against the privileged class."[98] At the same time they sought through the shock of mutiny and assassination to "awaken" (*kakusei*) the Japanese people, who they hoped would then spontaneously follow a newly empowered emperor in his quest for reform.[99] Indeed, the trope of "awakening" is pervasive in Shōwa Restoration discourse, not only in the prison writings of the rebels but in the Shōwa Restoration song as well, where the people are described as blind, dancing their lives away, following a path of delusion, as "the individual prospers and the nation falls," and "as order and chaos rise and fall as in a dream." "Awake from your eternal sleep," the song cried out to the people, "to greet the dawn of Japan."[100]

Shōwa Restorationism at the Academies in the 1940s

At Lalatun and Zama in the 1940s army cadets were still singing the Shōwa Restoration song, but the meaning of "restoration" had shifted somewhat since the great mutiny of 1936. With the outbreak of war in China and later in the Pacific, the idea of "restoration" had expanded both domestically and internationally. As an internal reform, it had become even more radical, comprehensive, and anti-Western, as we can see in the writings of Kageyama Masaharu, the founder of the Great Eastern Academy (Daitōjuku), who had developed close ties with a number of cadets in the JMA 57 class (see Chapter 5). Kageyama and his followers had argued that to prosecute the "holy" war effectively, Japan had first to transform itself into a truly "holy country" (*shinkoku*) by carrying out a "pure" Shōwa Restoration. According to Kageyama, the first step here, as for the army rebels of 1936, was to purge the privileged class that was paralyzing the imperial office, just as the Meiji Restorationists had crushed the shogunate in the nineteenth century and restored power to the emperor. But the Daitōjuku took the idea of "restoration" to a new xenophobic extreme, seeing the war against the United States and England as a chance to eradicate once and for all the foreign toxins that they believed were polluting and destroying every aspect of Japanese society. To carry out this "thoroughgoing restoration purge," as Kageyama called it, the Daitōjuku and its followers advocated the establishment of a "special restoration court" with breathtaking scope and powers that would expose, try, and punish all those who were considered impediments to the restoration and, by extension, hindrances to the successful execution of the war.[101]

First on the list to be purged were the *zaibatsu*: Mitsui, Mitsubishi, Yasuda, Sumitomo, and others, a veritable "shogunate of financial power," as Kageyama had written, whose disestablishment would usher in an "economic restoration." Close behind, however, were their accomplices in the imperial court, bureaucracy, legal profession, and political arena—high-ranking notables whose pro-Western inclinations had helped foster capitalism and its attendant evils, and whose removal would lead to a "reformed parliament" and a "restoration in politics." Sweeping reforms in culture and religion were to be undertaken as well. Major newspapers and magazines that were deemed to reek of "liberalism," such as *Asahi, Nich-nichi, Yomiuri, Kaizō, Chūō kōron,* and *Bungei shunjū,* were to be suspended; literary figures, critics, and scholars of a "socialist" bent were to be forbidden to write. Indeed, throughout the cultural world a "cultural restoration" was to be imposed that would obliterate (*tachi-horoboshi*) all aspects of Western "civilization and enlightenment," not least of all any forms of pro-Anglo-American or pro-Soviet spiritual contamination. A "religious restoration," moreover, would be proclaimed to elevate state Shintōism even further as Japan's national religion with its own government ministry, and concurrently to disband all "anti-*kokutai* sects," such as Catholicism, the Salvation Army, and even various forms of Buddhism, including the Tenri and Pure Land schools.[102] And an "ideological restoration" would exonerate and glorify as national heroes all the young officers and participants in the May 15, February 26, and other incidents who had acted patriotically for the sake of "the great cause."[103]

During the Pacific War the idea of "restoration" began to take on a much more pronounced international character. This shift in meaning could already be seen before the attack on Pearl Harbor and the outbreak of war with the United States, especially in Manchuria, where officers at the academies frequently reminded the cadets of an internationally expanding imperial mission in which the establishment of Manchukuo was to be both a symbol and a model. In May 1941, for example, when section commander Yano Yutaka took his MMA 2 *kutai* into the Dōtokudai woods to talk about the meaning of a Shōwa Restoration, he defined it in terms of a fifty-year, three-stage process of construction, from base to main pillar to roof, in which the tasks of Japan (the "Cherry Nation") and Manchukuo (the "Orchid Nation") were integrally linked.[104] And as we have seen, the wartime class songs of cadets in the early 1940s at both major academies reflected the idea of "restoration" as a "vast and far-reaching great ideal," advancing not only "in the endless ten thousand leagues beneath the North Star" of Manchuria but also throughout "the eight corners of the world."

Although their main interest was in domestic reform, Kageyama and his disciples in the Daitōjuku also envisioned the Shōwa Restoration ultimately as an anti-Western "world restoration" (*sekai ishin*).[105] When Park Chung Hee and his classmates arrived at Zama in October 1942, they found in the current issue of the *JMA Bulletin* a "moral lecture" on that subject by JMA 57 company commander Uchiyama Kazuya, who would later be disciplined with other academy officers for his complicity in the Daitōjuku's infiltration of the school. Addressing his "disciples" (*deshi*) at the school, Uchiyama wrote that he wanted to reflect on the "relationship between history and the present basic direction of what is commonly known as the 'Shōwa Restoration.'" He then denounced the past century and more of "capitalist invasion" by the West in Asia and Africa and noted the Japanese people's slow "awakening from dark night" that began with the "lone gunshots" of the Manchurian Incident, the calls for national reform, and the February 26 mutiny, leading finally to a "return to being true Japanese" with the "Great Asia War." "In other words," Uchiyama wrote, "the Shōwa Restoration is a reform directed outward," not only to "all the people of Asia" but to "all the people of the world." Its goal was nothing less than to summon the "higher spiritual ideology" of the Japanese "holy nation" (*shinminzoku*) to oppose "everything and anything from the West," which was hopelessly "mired in liberalism, capitalism, and materialism." Speaking as a senior and teacher, Uchiyama then concluded his lecture with an exhortation to the cadets to prepare for this international struggle against the forces of individualism, selfishness, and consumerism by suppressing such tendencies "concretely in your own daily lives" at the JMA, and by developing instead a sense of "organic connection" with fellow classmates.[106] Thus by the 1940s Shōwa Restorationism at the wartime academies had become, in a sense, *shisso* writ large, an outward extension of the Gunjin Chokuyu from the individual to the nation and now finally to the world, and a comprehensive denunciation of Western capitalism with all its perceived accompanying social, political, and intellectual evils.

Control: Total War Ideology

Uchiyama's focus on the international aspects of a Shōwa Restoration allowed him to escape the censorship and reprimand that a focus on domestic national reform likely would have incurred. Nevertheless, that it was even possible for him to deliver a lecture on that potentially subversive subject to his JMA charges, and then to have it selected for inclusion in the *JMA Bulletin*—especially a lecture that mentioned in a positive light, albeit obliquely and in passing, the reformist upheavals of the late 1930s—was telling testimony to the widespread if tacit Shōwa Restorationist thinking both at the academy and in the officer corps more generally. In the case of what we might call "total war ideology," however, where we can find a third critique of capitalism prominent in IJA circles in this period, we leave behind the secret or quiet realms of illicit Marxists and covert Restorationists and enter the open and forthright public instructive spaces of the academies. For there and throughout the IJA in the 1940s, total war was army doctrine.

Total War as Army Doctrine

The theory of "total war" in the Japanese army had grown out of the IJA's close study of World War I in the 1920s and had been emphasized at the academies even before Park Chung Hee and his fellow MMA 2 cadets picked up their textbooks at Zama in 1942. But since the ever expanding China Incident five years earlier, and all the more since the launching of the Pacific War only ten months before, the theory had assumed a central importance and become practiced doctrine in Japan and its greater imperial domain, including Korea and Manchukuo. Its essential premises were both simple and breathtaking in their scope, as well as compelling, given the historical experience of 1914–1918. And they were laid out plainly in a new edition of the JMA's military history text approved by Superintendent Ushijima, issued the very month that Park's MMA 2/JMA 57 class arrived. There the cadets found a sixty-page chapter on the "Great World War," covering all the major European engagements, and concluding with a section on the war's "special character."[107] The war "provided us with many lessons," the text stated, especially about the "shape of future wars." Not least of these was the new importance of scientific and aerial warfare. But the war's greatest lesson, what made it the first "modern war," a war "unprecedented in history," was the "total mobilization of knowledge and ability" by the participating countries. The Great War, in other words, had been a war of competing "national power" in the widest sense. Victory then and in the future belonged to those who could "not only destroy the enemy in a military war, but also in an economic war, a diplomatic war, and an ideological war." "Therein lay the reason," the text declared, "that each country began devising a national total mobilization plan [kokka sōdōin keikaku] in the aftermath of the war."[108]

In postwar Japanese army circles the need for such a plan was widely recognized, but its actual formulation was largely the work of Nagata Tetsuzan, a brilliant academy (JMA 16) and Army Staff College graduate and linguist who had served as a military attaché in Europe before and during World War I and was influenced by the ideas of German general Erich Ludendorff, who first coined the term "total war" in 1918. As early as 1920 Nagata had drafted Japan's first attempt at a systematic plan for general mobilization, a proposal that he and other officers who came to be associated with the Tōseiha in the army would continue to develop and refine in the 1930s, when Nagata served as head of the powerful Military Affairs Section of the War Ministry.[109]

Officers who were associated with the opposing Kōdōha or Imperial Way Faction proffered little objection to the idea and necessity of general mobilization in any future war, usually assumed to be a conflict with the Soviet

Union. One of the brightest and most active of these, Obata Toshishirō, had joined Nagata in an informal study group on army reform and total war planning that began in 1921 when both were military attachés in Europe and continued after they both returned to Japan.[110] Bitter disagreements subsequently ensued between the factions, however, on when and how the mobilization was to be carried out. The Tōsei Faction, including key figures such as Ugaki Kazushige, Minami Jirō, and Tōjō Hideki, in addition to Nagata, envisioned a protracted total war in the somewhat distant future and advocated gradual army modernization and the economic development of continental resources to support a long war, even at the expense of alienating China. Army modernization in turn meant reducing the number of divisions and focusing instead on supplying a smaller, more efficient, and mechanized army with the most up-to-date equipment, including tanks and airplanes. For leading Kōdōha officers such as Obata, as well as the outspoken and vociferous Araki Sadao and Mazaki Jinzaburō, whom we encountered in Chapter 5, such a focus on matériel over men was anathema. The next war, in their view, was imminent; there was no time for that kind of long-range strategic economic exploitation of imperial resources. More to the point, there was no need for such a strategy. The next war would be short in duration, won by a quick and decisive victory based on a concentration of overwhelming manpower imbued with an intangible spiritual power that would outweigh any deficiencies in firepower.[111]

At neither the personal nor doctrinal level were the divisions between the two main army factions quite as distinct or clear-cut as they might appear from a distance today.[112] As in the case of Nagata and Obata, meetings and study groups in the 1920s and 1930s often brought together men who leaned in one direction or the other, or were simply curious or uncertain. And, notwithstanding their advocacy of a more modern, mechanized army, the Tōsei group also believed strongly, as we shall see, in the power of "spirit" (*seishin*). Ludendorff himself had stressed the centrality of the psychological aspects of national mobilization, and Nagata had made this same point in his 1920 report and in later analyses of total war, including a seminal War Ministry pamphlet produced under his direction in 1934 entitled *Kokubō no hongi to sono kyōka no teishō* [The essentials of national defense and a proposal for their strengthening].[113]

Nevertheless, the differences and divisions between the two groups were real, widespread within the army, and deeply felt. They reached a climax in August 1935 with the assassination of Nagata by a young lieutenant colonel, Aizawa Saburō (JMA 22), whose ensuing public trial provided one of the catalysts for the February 26 mutiny the following year. With the purge of the Kōdōha that followed the mutiny, however, Tōsei officers reasserted and consolidated their leading position within the army, a hegemony that was strengthened even further by the outbreak of war in 1937 and its expansion in 1941, and Tōsei ideas on total war gradually became not only state policy but also part and parcel of formal cadet instruction at the academies.[114] Before we turn to the academies, however, let us consider some of the economic implications of these ideas.

Total War and Capitalism

As the JMA's military history textbook indicated, total war mobilization was to be as much an economic undertaking as a military one, and as such, it embodied a number of distinctive attitudes toward capitalism. These were all clearly articulated in the writings of Nagata and his staff and widely disseminated in a voluminous assortment of books, magazines, articles, and government reports during the actual war years.

Perhaps the first thing to note is that Tōsei total war thinking was oriented around the idea of national defense—an obvious point, one might think, but on the other hand, Tōsei national defense was not just national defense in the conventional sense. In the words of Nagata's 1935 War Ministry pamphlet, which was front-page news throughout the empire, including in Seoul's Korean-language newspapers, to the extent that "war was the father of creation and the mother of culture," the goal of national defense was to "activate the fundamental energies of national growth and development."[115] In other words, defense and economic development were inseparably linked, with the former acting as a spur to the latter, and the latter complementing and buttressing the former, a strategy that Park Chung Hee would also later embrace and make one of the hallmarks of his Yusin regime in the 1970s.[116]

To pursue such development, at least two things were deemed essential. The first was "reform and regulation" (kaizen seichō), which would introduce state planning and coordination over the entire range of the economy—exploitation of natural resources, industrial growth, trade, and not least of all the national budget—to ensure that the "full capacity" of the nation in all areas could be "mobilized and uniformly exercised" in accord with the "absolute requirements of national defense." Such a national defense, moreover, was to be completely "independent" of external pressures or constraints (kokubō no jishu), another goal and slogan that Park Chung Hee would

later adopt and popularize as president of South Korea. The second requirement for developing a total war defense and economy, closely related to the
first, was psychological mobilization, as emphasized by both Ludendorff
and Nagata, the aim being to create a national public that was ideologically
cohesive, working toward national defense goals with a unity of purpose
and responsibility in tandem with the state. Above all, this meant an abjuring
of self-interest and individualism for a spirit of self-sacrifice and public or
national service. The implications here were far-reaching. In a total war
economy businessmen were to be expected to serve state interests and not
vice versa, and potential conflicts such as those arising from uneven capitalist
growth and distribution of wealth between city and countryside, employers
and laborers, and landlords and tenants were somehow to be managed in
such a way as to foster a unitary sense of "mutual dependency" and "national co-existence and co-prosperity."[117]

On a scale of anticapitalist economics, total war thinking lay somewhere
between a socialist/communist revolution and the radical reform of the
Shōwa Restorationists. The Tōsei officers did not call for an overthrow of the
capitalist system, as did the Marxist-Leninists, or even for the elimination of
the *zaibatsu,* a point on which the young officers of May 15 and February 26
were willing to brook no compromise. The Tōseiha were also opposed to the
idea of a military coup and willing to work within a reformed version of the
existing institutional structure. But as the radical young officers who despised them for this well knew, there was no need for the Tōsei officers to
stage a coup, since the system of economic guidance and control they proposed, centered as it was on national defense development, gave the military, and by extension themselves, a place of extraordinary precedence and
power in the state. Thus for the young officers and later Shōwa Restorationists such as the Daitōjuku, the Tosei officers were just another self-serving,
aggrandizing clique within the "privileged class" (*tokken kaikyū*) they loathed
and sought to eradicate.[118]

Despite these significant differences, which were highly emotional issues
at the time, when we look back today we can see that Tōseiha ideas tended
to overlap in various ways with Marxist-Leninist and Shōwa Restorationist
perspectives. State economic planning was, after all, a central feature of socialist thought and practice, and the Soviet Union provided a highly visible
and seemingly successful economic model for both right and left in the
prewar period, one carefully studied and tracked by Nagata and other Tōseiha officers.[119] Indeed, as Pang Kijung points out, the idea of a statist
economy that would hold capitalism in check led many socialists in Korea

in the late 1930s to embrace the implementation of a total war mobilization system with great expectations and enthusiasm.[120]

And it was certainly true that total war officers shared with both Marxist-Leninists and Restorationists a profound aversion toward capitalism's focus on personal and corporate profits and its tendency to concentrate wealth in the few while impoverishing the many, especially the peasantry on which Japan's conscript army depended. Not only did they tend to regard such a system as immoral, a gross departure from *shisso* that debased all who actively engaged in it, but they also saw it as dangerous to the well-being of the nation, fostering class conflict and other social divisions that threatened national unity—views that the young officers of February 26 would have found entirely congenial. For the Tōseiha, however, the solution to these and other perceived capitalist ills lay not in socialist revolution or in radical Restorationist reform but rather in the restructuring and reorienting of the state and economy toward total war economic development. Such development, they believed, would help protect and defend the nation from external enemies while simultaneously bringing justice and resolution to the nation's internal social problems, including the problem of the peasantry, whose poverty and disaffection directly affected the strength of both the army and the nation as a whole.[121]

Of course, by 1939, when the MMA cadets first began to matriculate at Dōtokudai, total war was no longer simply an abstract theory emanating from the War Ministry. Since March 1938, with the promulgation of Japan's National Mobilization Law, it was official state and indeed imperial policy. Whether the cadets came from Japan, Korea, Manchukuo, or other parts of the empire, they were already acquainted with the concept and had experienced in one way or another and to varying degrees its implementation in their own local areas. Controls on the prewar capitalist system were now a reality in all parts of the empire, though they differed somewhat from place to place and were never as complete as the most anticapitalist Tōsei officers, let alone socialists and Shōwa Restorationists, might have hoped.[122] In Japan, just as the young officers had warned, total war had allowed the military elite, exemplified perhaps above all by Tōjō Hideki, to rise within the institutional structure to unprecedented heights of political power. In fact, as the new system was being put into place in the late 1930s, when the great mutiny of February 26 was still a palpable memory, there appears even to have been some official concern that the most radical total war officers might follow the February 26 example and actually attempt a coup d'état. Thus the IJA's handbook on the Gunjin Chokuyu, issued by the Inspectorate General of Military

Training in 1939, revised its explanation of the long-standing injunction against political activity for the times by specifically warning soldiers not to "mix war strategy with political strategy" or to imagine that the "entirety of national policy can be understood from a total war perspective."[123]

Of course, a coup proved quite unnecessary in a state structure where a general such as Tōjō could serve concurrently as prime minister, minister of war, and army chief of staff.[124] That having been said, in the end it was in Japan where the envisioned Tōsei management of capitalism turned out to be least effective. The *zaibatsu* were too powerful for even the army to tame, and they benefited enormously from the rationalization and cartelization of industry during the war, actually enhancing their position within the overall economy.[125] The blunt truth was that the army simply could not carry out its total war development without the cooperation of the *zaibatsu*.

As one moved further away from the metropole, however, into areas such as Korea and Manchuria, where the army exercised more or less direct political control, the army's managerial role in the economy grew accordingly, even though it continued to depend on private capital to finance its ambitious wartime plans for the development of heavy industry. One sees this in Korea most dramatically in the semi-wartime and wartime expansion of a vast nitrogenous fertilizer and hydroelectric power complex in the northern part of the peninsula.[126] But it was in Manchuria where what might be called state capitalism reached its imperial apogee. There, in the new state of Manchukuo, where the Kwantung Army reigned supreme and where a potent combination of Tōseiha total war thinking and lingering Kōdōha and Shōwa Restorationist sympathies flourished within the army, anticapitalist sentiment was particularly naked and virulent. Although in pursuit of funding for its industrial projects the army found itself honoring its early slogan of "No *zaibatsu* in Manchuria" largely in the breach, in Manchukuo the government did indeed retain control of the major enterprises, and the army, with the help of an accommodating government led by reformist bureaucrats from Japan, set developmental goals and priorities and exercised general supervision over the economy.[127] The *zaibatsu*, whether older groups such as Mitsui and Mitsubishi or newer groups such as Nissan, were for their part generally content to provide the money for projects the army desired under remarkably favorable conditions that not only absolved them of risk but also provided them with government-guaranteed profits and numerous special privileges and protections. Given the army's dislike of the *zaibatsu*, it was an "uneasy partnership," as Louise Young aptly notes, "more of a nonaggression pact than a working alliance," but the industrial results of the thirteen years that constituted Manchukuo's brief history were undeniably stunning. For the army elite in Manchuria, plants such as the Shōwa Steel Works at Anshan and the Fushun Coal Mines were a vindication of total war state-led economic development and a spectacle with which to dazzle doubters and to teach and inspire younger generations of officers, including their impressionable young charges at the MMA.[128]

Total War Synergies at the Academies

Teaching total war was one of the distinctive aspects of academy education in the 1940s, whether at Lalatun or Zama. Whatever experience the cadets may have had of total war in their own lives before entering the schools, it was quite another thing for them to be taught and trained as military officers who would be responsible not only for practicing it but also for implementing it within their particular commands and territorial jurisdictions. Before we turn to the some of the more explicit forms of total war instruction, however, it is worth noting certain striking synergies between the standard instruction and regimen of the academies and what is noted above as two of the most crucial elements of total war strategy: planning and social mobilization. The first of these can be found in the importance the academy placed on determining the *gen'an* or "basic plan" for any form of military engagement; the second lay in the school's unrelenting emphasis on *danketsu* or "unity" in military units.

Gen'an: The Basic Plan

Planning came naturally to army officers, for whom the choice of tactical plan or grand strategy could mean the difference between victory and defeat in combat and war, and the Japanese, with their long military tradition, were quick to perceive the benefits of European-style war planning and a general staff organization when they first set about forming a modern army shortly after the Meiji Restoration, modeling themselves first on French and later contemporary German practice.[129] Of course, there was no guarantee that plans devised by army officers in the War Ministry, where Nagata and other Tōsei officers developed their ideas for total war mobilization, or by staff officers attached to central headquarters or one of the units throughout the army's chain of command would be effective or even implemented. As the war years between 1937 and 1945 demonstrated only too well, many factors in Japan's state and military structure militated against the formation and execution of clear and coordinated battle plans, let alone a precisely articulated and overarching strategic war plan and set of objectives. These included such things as the constitutional independence of the central command from the civilian government, the virtual autonomy of various military units such as the Kwantung Army from the central command, conflicting perspectives and factionalism among staff at both the central and field levels, and differing priorities and rivalries among the different branches, especially between the army and the navy.[130] Nevertheless, to command as an officer fundamentally meant to work within a plan. When Park Chung Hee and other MMA cadets turned to the opening pages of the 1938 IJA *Field Service Regulations*, or *Sakuyō*, as they commonly called it, the essential combat manual for every Japanese officer and the doctrinal basis for the MMA/JMA cadets training in the 1940s, they were told that the "key to command" (*shiki no yōketsu*) lay in "issuing timely and appropriate orders under a clear plan" (*meikaku naru kito no moto ni*).[131] It was an injunction frequently repeated by instructors, as one can see in the diary of Park's MMA 2 classmate Hosokawa Minoru, who often reminded himself of the importance of "acting quickly within a plan" or "acting in accordance with a considered plan" (*keikaku*).[132]

Of course, the cadets at the academies, unlike their seniors at the Army War College, were not learning to plot extensive military campaign strategies so much as trying to master the tactics of specific combat engagements, but the principle was the same: command based on a well-conceived plan. In 1940, moreover, just as the first MMA classes were donning their cadet uniforms, the army modified its tactical doctrine to counter Soviet-style defenses, giving junior officers at the second lieutenant (platoon) and first lieutenant (company) levels even greater responsibility than before, and making it all the more imperative that the cadets, who would be commanding these platoons and companies soon after graduation, master the new tactical concepts during their training.[133]

Tactical training was centered on the concept of the "original" or "basic" plan, known in Japanese military parlance as the *gen'an*. Every tactical challenge had its corresponding *gen'an*, the preferred solution to the problem at hand. In most cases it was based on the *Sakuyō* or the appropriate line branch manual, but it could vary to some extent on the particular instructor's interpretation of the regulations or his own personal combat experience. There was a certain rigidity in the way it was taught and applied, especially at the academies, but it was meant more as a kind of ideal default response to certain given conditions rather than an absolute correct answer that could encompass all similar situations—a professional first choice, in other words, which might be modified or even abandoned altogether for a second or third plan if actual circumstances called for it, especially in the event an officer felt that adhering to the *gen'an* would not allow him to accomplish his military objective within the allotted time.[134] On the other hand, an officer did not abandon the *gen'an* lightly, and mastering the *gen'an* of a wide variety of tactical maneuvers lay at the core of academy combat teaching and training.

Cadets were introduced to basic tactical issues and corresponding field service at the preparatory (*yoka*) level, but for the most part, intensive tactical instruction took place in the regular (*honka*) course, after the cadets had been assigned to a particular army line branch or service and experienced *taizuki* deployment in an actual military unit for several months following graduation from the *yoka*.[135] Thus non-Japanese cadets in the early MMA classes who were selected to join the Japanese Nikkei cadets for the *honka* at the JMA (as Park Chung Hee was) received their advanced branch and tactical training at Zama, while others who remained at the MMA (such as Kim Muk) received their *honka* tactical training at Lalatun. In either case tactics were taught in various ways and settings, each meant to complement and reinforce the others.

Fundamental to all were the *honka* academic tactics courses. As noted above, the basic text here was the 1938 edition of the *Sakuyō,* which incorporated wholly or partially several earlier tactical manuals and outlined in detail both the general principles of battle in the Imperial Japanese Army as well as the combat doctrines and duties of each army branch. The cadets also spent many hours poring over military history, especially the history of the Russo-Japanese War, which instructors used to discuss and highlight certain tactical ideas as they had actually been applied and tested in actual combat.

Activities outside the classroom were designed to drive home the tactical principles taught in the academic curriculum. MMA cadets of course had easy access to the Manchurian battlefields of the Russo-Japanese War, which allowed them to visualize the physical and topographical aspects of the combat in ways that simply reading about the battles in a textbook could not. Lessons learned in class were tested at the *honka* level through designated "drill units" (*kyōrenhan*), which brought together cadets in the same army branch, regardless of their barracks/sectional (*kutai*) affiliation, for specialized training in infantry or other branch tactics.

Tactics were also taught through three sets of periodic field exercises, each roughly six months apart, depending on the total length of the *honka,* which varied somewhat during the war years. Each set consisted of two types of advanced, high-level situational training that distinguished the post-*yoka* regimen. One was an on-site tactical exercise (*genchi senjutsu*), in which the instructors took the cadets into the field for a week or more, training and challenging them in hypothetical combat situations based on the particular location. This was either preceded or followed by field maneuvers (*yaei enshū*) near the academy or in different parts of the country, also usually a week or more in length. Here various exercises took place, including mock battles with live ammunition, in which the cadets were divided up into opposing forces and deployed in units according to their branch of service, with cadets being assigned the key roles of platoon and company commander on a ro-tating basis. In addition, once a year, usually in the fall, all the cadets from the three most prestigious army officer training schools in Japan, the JMA at Zama, the JMA Preparatory Academy (*yoka*) at Asaka (JMAP), and the Army Air Force Academy at Toyooka, participated in a three-school combined exercise, where the senior cadets in each school commanded their juniors. In November 1942, for example, the MMA 1 cadets led Park Chung Hee and other newly matriculated MMA 2 cadets in three days of maneuvers in the environs of the Sagamihara Plain near Tachikawa, Hachiōji, and Hashimoto.[136]

Whether in the classroom or in the field, a primary concern of instruc-tors was to test the ability of the cadets to rapidly assess hypothetical combat conditions (*sōtei*) and to determine and justify the best plan of action (*gen'an*) to be implemented without hesitation on the basis of their studies and training—skills they would need as unit commanders. Planning was key, the essential first step from which all else followed. In an article for the April 1944 *JMA Bulletin*, Park Chung Hee's section commander, Captain Tahara Kōzō, who was also his infantry tactical drill instructor, wrote that the first principle he followed in training was to give the cadets the *sōtei* a day in advance so that they could come to the exercise with a well-researched and considered plan in their minds. While in field maneuvers the focus was on platoons and companies, in the classroom, drill units, and on-site tac-tical exercises, instructors such as Tahara pushed the cadets to decide the *gen'an* from the point of view of a senior staff officer or even a battalion or division commander.[137]

Blistering criticism and humiliation in front of one's classmates was the norm for cadets who were individually called upon to produce the *gen'an* but failed to do so adequately, or for those who dared to challenge an instructor's idea of what the *gen'an* should be. One MMA 1 Chinese cadet named Zhang Yousong suffered such a fate at Zama when he tried in class to explain his idiosyncratic choice of a battle plan. The furious instructor, Fuji Takeshi (JMA 36), suddenly shouted Zhang's name out several times, forcing him to rise embarrassedly from his seat. Freezing Zhang with an icy glare, Fuji warned him, "When a commander with no ability acts as if he knows what he's doing when he doesn't, he winds up killing his precious soldiers."[138]

Outside the classroom a similar atmosphere prevailed. Instructors mercilessly quizzed cadets one by one until an appropriate *gen'an* for the stipulated *sōtei* was produced, and some section commanders were known to force entire cadet platoons to repeat combat scenarios step by step over and over again until they executed a satisfactory *gen'an* or understood why their plans were falling short. Those infrequent occasions when a cadet's response elicited the approbatory shout of "Gen'an da!" from the officer in charge tended to remain long in memory. In 2011, when I interviewed Kaneko Tomio, one of the MMA 2 cadets, he still took pride in describing a field exercise when only he among the group of classmates being questioned that day had managed to produce a *gen'an* that pleased the instructor.[139] Kiyoizumi Nobuo, another MMA 2 graduate, clearly remembered his class's on-site tactical exercises at Toyohashi in April 1943, in which all the cadets in the class were taken out into the field for their first experience with tactical problem solving. Only months after their matriculation at Zama, facing what was then a still unknown exercise, the cadets were naturally feeling a certain nervousness, mitigated only partially by the fact that the tactics instructor that day was Lieutenant Colonel Fukaya Tadashi, an officer from the Tōhoku region, whose distinctive accent (at least to Kiyoizumi, a Tokyo native) sounded more amusing than intimidating. After Fukaya laid out a hypothetical problem, he called on one of the cadets to come forward and present a plan. It was Park Chung Hee, not Kiyoizumi, whom Fukaya selected, but perhaps in part because he had felt such a sense of relief in not being singled out himself, seventy years after the event Kiyoizumi could still vividly recall Park standing in front of all the other cadets, articulating and justifying the *gen'an* with "ease and proficiency" (*ryūchō de*) while everyone else listened.[140]

A final point to note here on the importance and ubiquity of *gen'an* thinking at the academies is that classroom lessons and field experience in tactics were reinforced in the schools' official publications and periodic examinations, where the problem/plan format was again the norm. The monthly *JMA Bulletin* for cadets and officers regularly featured articles on applied tactics based on historical or hypothetical situations, where initially the *sōtei* and associated tactical problems (*mondai*) were laid out for readers and then the preferred *gen'an* was described and explained in detail, sometimes together in the same issue, sometimes serially in consecutive issues, both generally with elaborate corresponding maps and diagrams. In a monthly section of the *Bulletin* called "JMA News" (*Sōbudai dayori*), cadets could find examples of actual questions from recent exams. Thus Ch'oe Chujong, a cadet in the MMA 3 class, and Korean cadets in later classes as well, would have been able to look back to the March 1944 *Bulletin* and discover that their seniors in the MMA 2 class, including Park Chung Hee, had been given an hour and a half on the morning of February 9 of that year to write a tactics final exam essay discussing the *Sakuyō's* "key to command" and, additionally, the points to which a commander faced with certain "unfavorable combat conditions" should pay particular attention as he formulated his *gen'an* for battle.[141]

Danketsu: Unity

One of the most frequently encountered terms in the documents of the academies both before and after the outbreak of war with China in 1937 is *danketsu*, meaning "unity" or "solidarity." Here we find another important synergy between the long-established regimen of the schools and the total war ideology of the 1940s, which emphasized not only a planned economy but also social and psychological cohesion and mobilization. An emphasis on *danketsu* (K: *tan'gyŏl*) was nothing new to the Korean cadets at Lalatun or Zama in this period. Like most of their classmates, regardless of ethnicity, they had already been inundated for years, especially in their primary and secondary school systems, with total war exhortations to "unity" of various kinds, not least of all "Japanese-Korean unity" (*Nai-Sen ittai*).[142] For Koreans, moreover, *tan'gyŏl* had a special significance, resonating as it did with a large body of Korean nationalist writing going back to the late nineteenth and early twentieth centuries, when patriotic authors such as Yu Kilchun and Sin Ch'aeho had urged Koreans to think of themselves as sharing a common "Korean" identity, and to eschew the "small I" of self (*so-a*) for the "big I" (*tae-a*) of the ethnic Korean nation.[143] Later, after Korea came under Japanese occupation and rule, the idea of *tan'gyŏl* continued to be a nationalist cry, traversing otherwise impenetrable ideological boundaries between right and left. "Unity" in such writing, girded by a strong sense of group membership and goals, represented a virtue to which Koreans were to aspire in order to save or recover the Korean nation; it was an antonym to the evil of traditional Korean "factionalism," which had led to the loss of nation in 1910. No one said all this more clearly or forcefully than Yi Kwangsu in his famous 1922 *Minjok kaejoron,* where Yi denounced the Chosŏn dynasty political factions for their failure to rise above selfish individual or party interests and attributed the collapse of the late nineteenth-century Independence Club to its "inability to forge a firm unity" (*tan'gyŏl ŭi gonggoch'i motham*).[144]

While "unity" was thus already fixed in the minds of the Korean cadets and their classmates as a positive, necessary, and even noble idea before they matriculated as cadets, nothing they had read or experienced fully prepared them for the rigor of training in *danketsu* that they would encounter at the academies. There "unity" was promoted on a number of levels. Class unity (*ki*) was basic, and for the rest of their lives the cadets would be identified, and would identify themselves, by number as members of a particular *ki.* Hence Korean cadets such as Park Chung Hee who did their *yoka* at Lalatun and their *honka* at Zama would refer to each other as MMA 2/JMA 57 (a convention used in this book as well). In addition, as we have seen, each class was divided during its residence at the academies into companies (*ren* at the MMA, or *lian* in Chinese; *chūtai* at the JMA) and sections (*kutai*), with approximately thirty cadets to a section and usually three or four sections constituting a company. In Park Chung Hee's time at Lalatun, for example, there were three MMA companies, two Mankei and one Nikkei, each company housed in a separate building, while later MMA 2 cadets such as Park who went on to Zama for the *honka* were grouped together in a single MMA company in the academy's International Corps of Cadets and further subdivided into five sections. As a result, each cadet had class, company, and section identities while at the academies. Park and others in his *kutai* at Lalatun were thus not only Mankei MMA 2 but also 3/3 or *san no san,* 3rd Section in 3rd Company, and at Zama the *dai-go* or 5th Section of the Manchukuo Company.[145]

The section or *kutai* functioned as the core of academy *danketsu.* As the smallest and most intimate focus of loyalty and solidarity, the *kutai* was meant to provide a critical training ground and template in an ascending hierarchy of *danketsu* that led internally at the academies from the section to the company to the class, then outward to the army units to which the cadets would be deployed, to the army as a whole, to the nation, and ultimately to the emperor.

Kutai unity was fostered in two fundamental ways. The first was structural. The *kutai* was not merely a convenient bureaucratic category, a paper

concept for organizing and tracking the cadets. It was also and most impor-
tantly the key social unit around which their everyday life revolved. Quite
literally the cadets woke and slept, reported for roll call, studied, trained,
exercised, shouted commands during voice modulation, sang, and even
washed and bathed together as a *kutai*. Within the academy grounds, as
they moved from one activity to another, they moved as a *kutai*; so too
when they left the school for study and field exercises. In fact, there were
only three occasions in the academy regimen when the cadets did not function as a *kutai*. One was during their *kyōrenhan* exercises at the JMA, when
they trained with other cadets in the same army branch; another was during
a daily hour of free time at both Lalatun and Zama following afternoon
training and before the evening meal; and the third was during Sunday leaves.
By the time they graduated, the cadets, as a result of their *kutai* experience,
had become thoroughly accustomed to living and acting as a group.

But *thinking* as a group was important as well. The academies not only
sought to turn communal living into a natural organizational mode of existence but through the *kutai* also attempted to inscribe the idea of unity or
danketsu in the minds of the cadets as a positive moral virtue. *Danketsu* was
linked in the Gunjin Chokuyu to the fifth cardinal precept, "simplicity"
(*shisso*), with its injunction against self-interest; to the second precept, "propriety" (*reigi*), focusing on relationships with superiors and inferiors; and
to the fourth precept, "faithfulness" (*shingi*) in relationships.[146] It was a
ubiquitous theme in academy textbooks, moral lectures, speeches by officials and visiting dignitaries, and practical training exercises, and it also
figured prominently in the grade each cadet received for his "moral" or
cadet corps training (*kun'iku*), the nonacademic part of the curriculum that
was centered on the *kutai* and *ren/chūtai* and supervised by the section and
company commanders.

It is therefore not surprising that a considerable portion of a 1942 practical
manual on *kun'iku* for newly appointed *yoka* section commanders was devoted to the subject of group psychological or "spiritual" training to "solidify
unity" (*danketsu o kyōko ni shi*).[147] Such training was considered especially
important in the first two years of general academy officer education that
constituted the *yoka* course, preparatory to the *honka* branch training that
followed, whether at the MMA or JMA, for it was in the *yoka* that the cadets
were first introduced to the goals, customs, and practices of the army officer's
life and profession, where *danketsu* reigned supreme.

As the manual makes clear, drawing on the actual experiences of both
former cadets and section commanders, one of the first steps in the process

of building section *danketsu* was to heighten awareness of the evil of egoism (*riko*) and to encourage each cadet to work to overcome it in everything he did.[148] The standards were high. Overcoming the ego meant not only "abandoning self-interest" (*shishin o sutete*) in even the most trivial matters, as, for example, in the case of JMA 57 cadet Hiruma Hiroshi's desire for beautiful boots, noted earlier in this chapter.[149] It also meant subduing "personal emotions" (*shijō*) that might interfere with the bonding process, including any negative feelings that one cadet might have for another.[150] One former cadet reminiscing about his own section in the *kun'iku* manual wrote, "Showing a smiling face to someone one likes and a scowling face to someone one does not is the attitude of a middle school student. For the sake of our 4th Section, I even cheerfully accepted the comments of someone I disliked."[151]

In place of egoistic interests, the cadet was expected to embrace and cherish the interests of the *kutai* as his own, while in return the *kutai* would embrace and cherish him as one of its members. All effort in the *kutai* was to be "uniformly collaborative" (*kyōdō itchi*), a case of one for all and all for one.[152] One for all meant that when a cadet competed in an academy sports event, which generally matched section against section or company against company, he competed above all for his group, when he prepared for examinations, he was urged to study hard and do well for the glory of his section. To diminish the potential for jealousy or friction within the *kutai* or class as a whole, a cadet was not told even at graduation of his final ranking in his class, so apart from a few top graduates who were singled out for special awards, every cadet could claim that he had ranked "just after the honor graduates" in the class, a practice that Park Chung Hee followed throughout his life in discussing his *honka* record at the JMA.[153]

On the other side of the collaboration, all for one meant that the cadets were enjoined to help each other (*tasukeai*) in every aspect of their daily regimen, and to care especially for their "bunkmates" (literally "bunk-classmates," *shindai gakuyū*, or "bunk-brothers-in-arms," *shindai sen'yū*), who slept at their side in the barracks, as if they were part of the "same single body" (*isshin dōtai*), making sure that they were not sick, in trouble, or late for roll call or other appointments, and that they were meeting all the other demands of the day.[154] And if any cadet did fall sick or was disciplined for some reason, his fellow *kutai* or *chūtai* members were to rally around him. Indeed, decades after the fact, former members of a section or company could still relate numerous stories of such mutual aid and support. In the case of the MMA 2 at Zama, for example, Kiyoizumi Nobuo recalled how his Korean bunkmate Yi Sŏpchun, later a regular drinking companion of Park Chung Hee during his presidency, took care of him when he got frostbite in one of his fingers and ran a high fever. And Kiyoizumi sadly recollected accompanying one of his Chinese classmates, Liu Yushan, also in the same *kutai,* to the hospital when he became very sick, and donating blood in what turned out to be a futile attempt to save Liu's life.[155] Park Chung Hee's own section mate and fellow infantryman Kaneko Tomio remembered how he and others in the MMA 2 5th Section had all visited Park in turn, bringing him things to eat, when Park had been put in confinement for allowing his gun to be burned in a field exercise.[156] And Park himself at Lalatun had taken special care of one of his MMA 2 classmates from an adjacent section, Cai Chongliang (Tsai Chung Liang), a Taiwanese who had found it especially difficult to adjust to the bitter winter temperatures of Manchuria and was often sick or even in the infirmary.[157]

Joint effort implied joint responsibility, and this too was a crucial part of *danketsu* thinking and training. Although in certain circumstances, such as Park Chung Hee's neglect of his gun in the field, cadets might be held individually accountable, in general it was the section or company as a whole that was disciplined for an offense, as in the case, noted above, where JMA 57 Hiruma Hiroshi's entire *kutai* was forced to spend the night looking for the little screws that fell off some of his section members' light machine guns during field training. As we shall see later when we focus in detail on academy disciplinary practices, this was in fact a decisively mild group punishment, but the point here is that, gentle or harsh, discipline by *kutai* was a way of driving home to each cadet the idea that he was responsible for the actions of every other member in his group. Another way this lesson was drilled into the cadets was through the *torishimari seito* system, whereby each week a cadet in the section was appointed on a rotating basis to serve as the duty cadet for that week, regardless of grades or class rank. In addition to giving every cadet an opportunity to exercise leadership in the group, it served to reinforce in each cadet's mind the sense that he was responsible for the group as a whole, for when he was duty cadet it was his role to see that the *kutai* met all its daily obligations on time and in accordance with the section commander's orders. In fact, the *torishimari seito* literally led the *kutai* from one activity to another in the course of the day, reporting in each case to the section commander or to the particular officer or instructor in charge.[158]

So intense and pervasive was the emphasis on communal responsibility that it could on occasion get out of hand, with tragic results. Such was the case at Zama shortly before the MMA 2/JMA 57 graduation in April 1944, when one of the JMA 57 cadets who had seen a classmate cheating on an exam, instead of reporting it to the section commander as required, had asked him to meet that night at the Otakebi Shrine. There in the wooded bowing area (*yōhaijo*) near the shrine, he had brought out a sword and pressed his classmate to commit ritual suicide. When the classmate refused, saying he knew he had done wrong but did not feel it merited suicide, his accuser cut him with the sword. Although wounded, the classmate survived, but the other cadet, thinking he had killed him, fled the school and later committed suicide by throwing himself under a train. The next day, when Park and the other cadets routinely headed to the *yōhaijo* for their morning oblations and chanting of the Gunjin Chokuyu, they were stopped at the second gate of the shine. The *yōhaijo* was still covered in blood from the previous night and being cleaned, a grim testimony to the ideal of *danketsu* at its most extreme.[159]

In Hosokawa Minoru's *yoka* diary we can trace on a daily basis the various forms of *danketsu* that inflected the cadets' lives at Lalatun in the period when Park Chung Hee and the MMA 2 class were resident there. Hosokawa's *kutai,* the fifth in the Nikkei company, began and ended its existence in April 1941 and March 1942, respectively, with exhortations to *danketsu,* while the year in between was richly punctuated with cautions about egoism and the challenges and celebrations of "our entire *kutai* pushing ahead with one mind" (*hitotsu-kokoro ni maishin*).[160] Hosokawa dutifully noted all the lectures and reprimands from his superiors, including, for example, inaugural remarks in September 1941 from a new company commander, Hōshu Ikkō, that ironically took up same trope of "small I" versus "big I" that Sin Ch'aeho had expounded for a Korean nationalist audience decades earlier, and that Park Chung Hee would use in speeches once in power after 1961.[161] Often he drew charts in the diary that covered half a page or more to highlight in large, bold letters the main points of the weekly duty officer's comments or other key maxims of the moment, together with his reflections on them and his plans for actualizing them. Not surprisingly, they were frequently centered on some aspect of *danketsu,* such as a chart drawn only days after he entered the MMA on which he reminded himself to "crush [*daha*] egoistic behavior," or another from a few months later, where he emphasized the importance of "actively practicing the way of brothers-in-arms" (*sen'yūdō*), which required "forsaking egoistic feelings and working instead for his comrades" in the *kutai,* for their health and well-being in all things.[162]

As always, however, it is Hosokawa's own personal thoughts and his ongoing struggles to live up to the ideals that he was being continually pressed

to put into practice that bring the *danketsu* regimen of that time most vividly to life in the diary. Thus he noted with pleasure and pride a swelling
sense of *danketsu* in the *kutai* during group singing sessions and on those
occasions when he and others were working in close solidarity with the
weekly duty cadet, even in the absence of the section commander.[163] He was
also exhilarated by the bonding that he felt with the other cadets in the *kutai*
when they spent three hours searching "with all their might" (*issho kenmei
ni*) for a muzzle cap that had fallen off one of their members' guns during a
late-summer exercise, refusing to give up until they had found it.[164]

But maintaining *danketsu* was no simple task. It required continuous
effort and humility. A naturally conscientious and competitive student,
Hosokawa could not help exulting in his diary on April 26, 1941, that he had
received an almost perfect score on an early Chinese-language examination,
the highest score in both the 5th and 6th Sections, and his section commander, Yano Yutaka, even scribbled a note next to the diary entry, thanking
him on behalf of the *kutai* and urging him to "work even harder." However,
Yano's message carried a double meaning, not only praising Hosokawa for
his diligence but also implicitly reminding him that his performance was
part of a group effort and that he should be exerting himself as much for the
sake of the *kutai* as for himself.[165] Throughout the rest of his time at Lalatun
Hosokawa clearly wrestled with himself to transform his personal ambitions
into *kutai* ambitions. During the end-of-term examination period five
months later, for example, he wrote that "one must strongly resist a tendency
toward egoism at exam time, to be swept away by it in studying for the
exams," and he drew one of his big charts in bold characters to encourage
himself "to abandon egoistic feelings and strive to do one's duty for the honor
of the *kutai*."[166] It was a common refrain in his diary, repeated again during
the examination period just before graduation and again at other times such
as school athletic meets, as on September 27, 1941, when, exhausted after a day
of discus throwing, high-vaulting, and endurance contests, he wrote that he
"had really made an effort on behalf of the fifth *kutai*," which had come in
second in the overall competition.[167]

Hosokawa also recorded numerous episodes when his section fell short,
when members failed to do what was required of them, or when they did
not watch over each other as they should have, and the *kutai* as a whole was
penalized as a result. Most egregious in Hosokawa's mind were his own
shortcomings and failures, not least of all once on Sunday leave in December
1941, when he was serving as the *torishimari seito* and was mortified to be
late for a section rendezvous that he himself had arranged in front of the

Xinjing Chūreitō. Such unpunctuality, he wrote, had diminished his authority as duty cadet and "disgraced" his *kutai*. It was "an eternal shame" for which he must "try with all his heart to make amends."[168]

At the last meeting of Hosokawa's *kutai* a little more than three months later, it appears that the shame of the previous December had been forgotten, as Hosokawa and his fellow 5th-section cadets listened "with deep emotion" to Commander Yano's final lecture. But one could never be lax about unit cohesion. He and the other cadets vowed that even after the section's dissolution they would strive "all the more to strengthen the feeling of unity" they had developed over the past year.[169] And indeed, when his section with Yano still in command was reconstituted the following day as the 3rd *kutai* in combination with another section, there too the first order of section business was once again the imperative of "building anew a great unity."[170]

Teaching Total War

Standard academy immersion in *gen'an* and *danketsu* resonated well with the army's prevailing total war ideology of the 1940s, but total war as concept and strategy was also taught directly to the cadets of Lalatun and Zama. At both *yoka* and *honka* levels, it was a subject of classroom study, but it figured most prominently in courses on "military organization" (*gunseigaku*) that were taught as part of the *honka* curriculum. *Gunseigaku*, together with military history and tactics, constituted the largest segment of the academic program, about 40 percent of the total number of class hours.[171] Its focus was army development, maintenance, supervision, and operation, based on the premise that victory or defeat depended in no small part on the skill with which an army was managed. As the China Incident had metastasized into full-scale war on the Asian continent and after December 1941 into a second world war in the Pacific, total war ideas were fully integrated into the academy instruction on military organization and regularly updated and expanded. Four months after Park Chung Hee and the other MMA 2 cadets entered the JMA for their *honka* training, a revised version of the basic *gunseigaku* textbook was issued by Superintendent Ushijima, the second part of which was devoted entirely to the idea and practical implementation of total war.

The total war section began with a discussion of the concept itself, the idea and "necessity" in "modern warfare" of supporting the nation's military campaign with an all-embracing "systematic control" (*soshiki tōsei*) of politics, economics, thought, and culture.[172] It then traced the general history of the concept from its origins in World War I through its specific development and eventual implementation in Japan itself in the 1920s and 1930s, emphasizing that the nation now found itself at the beginning of 1943 not merely in the midst of total war but in a "stage of long-term total war" (chōki sōryokusen no dankai) with the United States and England that could require a "hundred years" of military engagement.[173] The next chapter focused on the various key components of total war planning and coordination, followed by additional chapters on the organizational structure thus required, and on Japan's 1938 National Mobilization Law itself. The final three chapters dealt with certain general features of total war planning policies and execution.[174]

Though never fully or harmoniously actualized in practice during the war, a total war planning and coordination "framework" centered around the objective of national defense and corresponding military requirements was indeed one of the main themes of this section of the textbook. Japan's total war organizational structure, including a unit of central control, an advisory body of government officials and citizens, a research institute, and various organs of implementation, all under the supervision of the prime minister and cabinet, was laid out there in detail. The desirability of a centralized, synchronized management of the war effort that would encompass the whole empire, not least Manchukuo with its abundant natural resources and developing industrial economy, was also expressed, even though by 1943 there were already clear signs that this would prove to be a daunting challenge.[175]

Much attention was given in the textbook to control and coordination of the economic and financial system, including the expansion of industrial production and the development of "key industries" (jūten sangyō) related to the war effort, such as steel, coal, oil, light metals, and the precision machine industry.[176] Total war was envisioned in a very real sense as a war of populations (jin'insen), requiring improvement in the physical and mental capacities of the people, especially a rapid expansion of technical and scientific education.[177] But the psychological or "spiritual" aspect of total war (seishinsen) was not neglected either. Successful prosecution of the war, the text declared, depended on the "combined strength of matter and mind," but ultimately it depended on internal "spiritual power," which in turn rested on the eradication of enemy thought, the elimination of the threat from air attacks and other machinations, and the stabilization of the people's livelihood.[178]

Classroom study of total war at the academies was complemented by appropriate lectures from section and company commanders as well as from the superintendent and visiting government and military dignitaries. In addition, the academies maintained a close relationship with the Total War Research Institute (Sōryokusen Kenkyūjo), which had been established under the Japanese cabinet in September 1940 as part of the government's organizational framework, mentioned above. Its purpose was to study all aspects of total war—military, political, economic, and ideological—separately as well as synthetically, and to provide education and training in total war strategies to government officials and other public servants. Given its comprehensive mandate, the institute's members came from a broad cross-section of society. In addition to many active duty military officers, they included men from the major ministries and other Japanese government offices, as well as businessmen, bankers, journalists, and various representatives from Manchuria, Taiwan, and other parts of the empire.[179] As part of its mission, the institute conducted on-site inspection visits to the JMA, as it did on May 8, 1942, when the MMA 1 class was in residence, to observe the daily life and education of the cadets. On that particular day virtually the entire institute participated, including the director, Vice Admiral Endō Yoshikazu, and assistant director, Major General Fujimuro Ryōsuke, along with fifty-five staff members and research aides.[180] The institute also dispatched its members to Zama to give special total war lectures. Thus in October 1942 and again in May 1943, when Park Chung Hee's MMA 2 class was at the JMA, the institute sent Nishiuchi Masashi there for five lectures, all of which were later printed in full in the *JMA Bulletin*. Nishiuchi, listed as an "army professor" on the institute's roster, had been working there since early 1941, specializing in the ideological aspects of total war, and his lengthy talks centered on the themes of "The Pervasive Japanese Spirit in National History" and "The Way of the Imperial Nation," reflecting his particular research interests.[181]

Undoubtedly more effective and engaging than Nishiuchi's abstruse and repetitive discourses were school excursions to key industrial sites that gave tangible meaning and visuality to the total war template of state planning and control for national defense and development that the cadets had been studying. Here Manchuria was the ideal location: despite having had to make some inevitable accommodations with Japanese capitalists, the Kwantung Army had for the most part been able to construct its own version of a brave new world of state-controlled enterprises turning out steel, coal and coal derivatives, paper, hydroelectric power, and other products on the basis of five-year plans, and at capacities and levels of sophistication that in some cases rivaled or surpassed anything to be found in Japan itself, or even in other parts of the industrialized world. By the early 1940s, for example, the Shōwa Steel Works at Anshan, just southwest of Liaoyang, was already one of the world's great steel production centers.[182] Only 70 miles away to the northeast, the immense colliery of Fushun, boasting 25 square miles of deposits and at the time the largest known open-cut coal mine in the world, was fueling the Anshan steel furnaces and supplying coal to Japan as well as Manchuria.[183] And the Yalu River Dam and hydroelectric complex at Shuifeng (J: Suihō; K: Sup'ung), completed in August 1941, was a more massive undertaking than the Boulder (Hoover) Dam, built in the United States on the Colorado River only five years earlier.[184]

A twenty-day excursion to Manchuria had been a part of every JMA *yoka* cadet's education since the JMA 49 class in the late 1920s, but following the outbreak of war in China in 1937, wartime conditions determined whether such trips to the continent were curtailed or canceled. In the early years of the excursions, moreover, the focus was almost exclusively on former battlegrounds and memorials, especially those relating to the Russo-Japanese War and, after 1931, to the Manchurian Incident. Later, as the Manchurian economy grew, stops at the great state enterprises were added to the itinerary.[185]

For the MMA cadets at Lalatun, of course, these industrial showcases were not only relatively short distances away but also approaching the zenith of their wartime development in the 1940s, and visits to them were incorporated into the academy's overall program. The MMA 1 cadets who were scheduled to go on to Zama for the *honka* were taken on such a trip in early May 1941, as part of a week-long combined military history and economic study tour of southern Manchuria, stopping at the Shōwa Steel Works, the Benxihu (Penhsihu) Coal and Iron Company, the Yalu River Paper Mill, and other sites. This group of course included the MMA 1 Korean cadets who were going on to the JMA (eight of the thirteen Koreans in the class). After visiting the paper mill at Dandong, the tour crossed over the Yalu to the Korean town of Ŭiju, where Korean cadet Pak Imhang was asked to serve as the class representative and interpreter.[186] A year later, in July 1942, the MMA 2 class, including Park Chung Hee and the other Koreans who had been tapped for *honka* training at Zama and transferred into the Nikkei, made a similar week-long trip that included the Fushun colliery.[187] Not surprisingly, the sight of these new and enormous industrial complexes tended to leave a lasting impression on the cadets who visited them. Forty-five years after their 1941 excursion, former cadets who were compiling and editing an MMA 1 history for their classmates recalled the awe they had felt at the time. "As we looked on at the magnificent [*yūsō na*] scene of new steel being produced," they wrote, "we knew that the peace and security of the country lay in the strength of its heavy industry."[188]

The MMA cadets' recollections of their visit to the Shōwa Steel Works in 1941 immediately brings to mind Park Chung Hee's own well-known view of "steel as national power," a vision he pursued persistently and uncompromisingly during his South Korean presidency.[189] But when the MMA sent its cadets to the industrial sites of southern Manchuria in the 1940s, the lesson the school sought to teach was not simply that heavy industry was crucial to national development. An equally important lesson was that the Kwantung Army's great experiment in economic state planning and control was working—and working, as the MMA cadets were to remember, "magnificently."

Within the Kwantung Army and within the IJA more generally, there was little love for capitalism, and the academies had reflected that dislike, disdain, and distrust throughout their existence. What had been a profound moralistic contempt for selfishness expressed in the 1882 Imperial Rescript had been greatly magnified in the wake of the growth and behavior of the *zaibatsu* in the 1920s and by the economic depression and political turmoil of the 1930s. By the 1940s, strange as it might sound, one could more easily imagine a cadet who was inclined toward Marxism than one who touted the virtues of unrestrained capitalism. Indeed, depending on the particular cadet, capitalism could be seen as imperialistic, either in a Marxist sense, or in the sense of a foreign toxin threatening the stability and values of the nation; it could be seen as wreaking a "terrible destructiveness" on the social fabric, especially on the poorest and most vulnerable of the citizenry; and it could be seen as dangerous and subversive to the security of the nation, which demanded that personal or corporate interests be subordinated to the needs of a coordinated national defense and development. Capitalism could not, however, be seen as an unqualified force for good. Whether through revolution, reform, or control—or perhaps some combination of the three—it was an evil that needed somehow to be overcome or tamed. While a cadet might be mutinous and *majime*, or possibly even Marxist and *majime*, he could never be capitalist and *majime*. At Lalatun and Zama, and especially the former, such a juxtaposition would have been inconceivable, an oxymoron that defied both common sense and morality.

SEVEN

TACTICS AND SPIRIT
Certain Victory

Caesar shall forth. The things that threatened me
Ne'er looked but on my back. When they shall see
The face of Caesar, they are vanished.
—William Shakespeare, *Julius Caesar*

Dash forward bravely, and with joy.
—*Hagakure*

As if camped on a battlefield with the river behind us, our backs are to
the wall, and there is now no retreat. Our future lies only in advance.
—Park Chung Hee, July 3, 1961

Whether one tends toward praise or criticism of the eighteen-year rule of
Park Chung Hee, few would deny that Park and his associates brought to
the South Korean modernization project of the 1960s and 1970s an affirma-
tive "can-do" spirit that the new government then sought to infuse into the
populace as a whole. Indeed, the phrase *ha'myŏn toe nŭn kŏsida* (literally
"We can do [anything] if we try") eventually became as well known a motto
of the period as the term *kŭndaehwa* (modernization) itself. It was used by
Park publicly at least as early as 1963 in the final chapter of his book *Kukka
wa hyŏngmyŏng kwa na,* where he summed up his views on "what we should
do and how we should to do it" if the nation, not least of all the national
economy, was to be rebuilt. "We say 'it's too difficult,' we say '[it's impos-
sible] given our situation,'" Park wrote.

> But we have to put aside these useless thoughts. Has the time not
> come for us to throw out this legacy of negativity, doubt, and
> despair? Let us say, "We can do [anything] if we try." Let us say,
> "However high a great mountain, it is still under the sky [and
> can be climbed]." We must begin by arming ourselves with these
> unshakeable convictions.[1]

To be sure, the Park state's promotion of this "can-do" spirit could be as ruthless as it was relentless, intolerant of any sign of "negativity" that might dampen the spirit and the pursuit of *kŭndaehwa*. The poet-singer Kim Min'gi, whose early 1970s songs, and especially "Morning Dew" (Ach'im isŭl), were officially banned at the time, only to become unofficial anthems of resistance by the opposition, once remarked to me how puzzled he had been that his songs had been read so politically, even leading at one point to his arrest and beating by government henchmen in 1971. The songs, according to Kim, were not explicitly anti-government, either in intent or in subject matter. Rather, like "Morning Dew," they tended to be reflections of Kim's philosophical attempts to deal with loss in his own life, and with the loss and sadness he observed in the world around him. But this sadness, he came to believe, was precisely the offense. From the government's point of view, the songs were simply too dark, out of sync with the official drumbeat of optimism and progress, and therefore potentially subversive.[2]

At the same time, however, the Park government's "can-do" spirit could also serve as a powerful force for national transformation, an antidote to the negative sense of personal and national self-worth and defeatism that was all too common in South Korea in the 1950s after the Korean War and eloquently captured in Yi Pŏmsŏn's famous 1959 short story "Stray Bullet" (Obalt'an).[3] Even the late former president, Kim Dae Jung, the Park government's most celebrated opponent, who was kidnapped and nearly murdered by Park's brutal Korean CIA in 1973, conceded the power of that spirit. In an autobiography published shortly after his death, Kim wrote that although he saw no justification for the military coup that had brought Park to power and did not subscribe to the view that dictatorship had been necessary for economic development, he did "acknowledge to some degree the Park regime's economic accomplishment," adding, "It is also a fact that the regime planted in the people a sense that 'we too can do [anything] if we try.'"[4]

It is notoriously difficult for a historian to trace over time something so intangible as a feeling or sensibility, but as such comments by both friends and foes of the regime suggest, a "can-do" spirit was so central a feature of the Park Chung Hee modernization state that the attempt must be made. What, then, were the wellsprings of this orientation? To argue for a single lineage would of course be simplistic. Certainly premodern Korean influences, for example, played a role here. Indeed, when Park wrote in 1963 that "however high a great mountain, it is still under the sky [and can be climbed]," he was borrowing a line from a sixteenth-century Korean *sijo* poem that he and his fellow students at Taegu Normal School had clandes-tinely learned in the 1930s.[5]

Such influences notwithstanding, one of the most direct and robust lin-eages of the "can-do" attitude of the Park era lay within the army culture that Park and other MMA/JMA cadets imbibed in the 1940s. That culture contained not only political and social elements but also tactical and mental perspectives on how to achieve desired goals. Although these perspectives were fundamentally related to the conduct of war, especially the goal of winning on the battlefield, once they had been thoroughly absorbed through repetitive study and training, they could easily become part of the ingrained psychical framework through which the cadets subsequently came to view the world and to approach problems or crises even outside the scope of actual combat itself. In such a transposition, the world, in effect, could be envisioned as a battlefield, where the general principles underlying the tac-tics of warfare could also be applied to achieve personal, professional, po-litical, or national goals, as one sees, for example, in the speech by Park Chung Hee quoted at the beginning of this chapter. The key elements here were the IJA's tactical doctrine of the offensive and the emphases on "will" and "certain victory" that followed from it.

The Doctrine of the Offensive

While common sense might suggest that modern military organizations would inherently prefer offensive doctrines, this has not in fact been the case historically. Even after what might be described as an "ideology of the offensive" took deep root in international military circles as a result of Na-poleon's emphasis on "decisive battle" and the subsequent influence of Clausewitz and his great disciple, Helmuth von Moltke, chief of the Prus-sian general staff, European armies did not thereafter uniformly adopt of-fensive doctrines. They chose rather to emphasize either offense or defense depending on a variety of factors, including, as Elizabeth Kier has argued, the culture of the particular military organization itself. "If we are to cate-gorize a military's interests in a way that leads to accurate explanations of its doctrinal choices," Kier has written, "we must recognize that different militaries view the world differently."[6]

The Imperial Japanese Army's embrace of the offensive represented a combination of two streams of thinking that both overlapped and rein-forced each other. One was the reappropriation of the *bushidō* or warrior code from the Tokugawa period that was itself an invented tradition at the time for a samurai class that had long since ceased to engage in actual warfare.[7] Elements of this code—exemplified perhaps above all by Yamamoto Tsunetomo's eighteenth-century classic *Hagakure,* which was filled with injunctions to samurai to "dash forward bravely and with joy" even in the most difficult combat circumstances, and which at one point even defined the core of *bushidō* as "rushing headlong" (*muni-musan*) into battle heedless of danger—were incorporated into the 1882 Gunjin Chokuyu by army founder Yamagata Aritomo and the philosopher Nishi Amane and, as we have already seen, remained an integral part of the army's moral education and training until 1945.[8] Especially important in this regard was the rescript's third cardinal precept, focused on military valor (*buyū*), a pledge that IJA soldiers facing an enemy on the battlefield were enjoined never "even for an instant" to forget, and which came to be defined, particularly in the 1940s, as "decisive action to the death" (*kesshi dankō*).[9]

A second and probably even more important stream of influence that led to the IJA's adoption of an offensive doctrine came from outside Japan. In accordance with the Meiji emperor's Charter Oath of 1868, which had declared that "knowledge shall be sought throughout the world so as to strengthen the foundations of imperial rule," the new Japanese leaders carefully and systematically combed and studied the West in search of appropriate models for a new army.[10] While they were initially attracted to the French example, in the end it was the Prussian system that trumped France, not only on the battlefield in 1871 but also in the minds of the Meiji military planners, including Yamagata Aritomo. Yamagata introduced many elements of the contemporary German army into Japan's new imperial military organization, such as the Prussian system of reserves as a complement to universal male conscription, and the Prussian concept of an autonomous general staff, responsible only to the emperor. Prussian influence, moreover, extended to army education and training, especially with the appointment to the Japanese general staff in 1885 of Major Klemens Wilhelm Jakob Meckel, an infantry officer who had been awarded the Iron Cross for bravery in the recent Franco-Prussian War and who was a scholar of infantry tactics. His work, published before and after his appointment in Japan, was widely read in European army circles.

For Meckel and his fellow Prussian officers, who believed that the offensive, centered on the infantry, was crucial for winning battles and wars, the great tactical question of the late nineteenth century was how to preserve a viable offensive in the face of new long-range, fast, and accurate firepower.

Earlier in the century, as in the time of Napoleon, massed infantry formations that were able to hold tight and fire accurately on command had swept all before them, providing shock value against the other side and enhancing the individual confidence and courage of the men as they moved toward enemy positions, even in the crucial last fifty yards, when they came within range of their opponents' guns. New weapons, however, like the Minié rifle, with an accuracy of 650 yards and a range of 1,200 yards, to say nothing of the inventions that would come later, such as the light machine gun, greatly expanded the danger zone for the attacking soldiers. As a result, long before they ever reached the enemy, the advancing battalions and regiments tended to dissolve under fire into thin, extended lines of frightened, confused, and uncontrolled swarms of men that made fighting in depth and effective frontal attacks impossible, while encouraging nervous commanding officers to call in reserves too early, even before they were needed. Worse still, to avoid the terrible wave of bullets, individual soldiers or even whole units broke off from the formation, running away or taking refuge in wooded areas or wherever else they could find it.

Most military tacticians at the time realized that the inevitable technological advance of firepower would render the conventional massed infantry attack increasingly dangerous and costly in terms of manpower, and they advocated replacing it with a dispersed line of skirmishers, albeit one that would continue to advance in unison under the direction of junior officers while taking full advantage when necessary of the particular battle terrain for protection. A minority, however, continued to insist that the infantry simply "close ranks and move forward regardless of the cost." The leading proponent of this extreme position was none other than Meckel himself, and it was a view that he worked tirelessly to inculcate in the new Meiji army during the three years he spent in Japan, with great success. The IJA's high respect for Prussian military prowess, Meckel's own personal appeal and skills as a teacher, and the *bushidō* predispositions of the new Japanese army all worked to enhance Meckel's influence and impact, and when he left the country in 1888 with the Order of the Rising Sun and a personal message of appreciation from the Meiji emperor, his tactical perspectives had become thoroughly embedded in Japanese army doctrine, even as they were being questioned and reworked in Germany itself.[11]

The human cost of the Meiji army's embrace of Meckel's tactics proved predictably horrific in its subsequent wars with China and Russia, epitomized by General Nogi Maresuke's unrelenting attacks on the Russian position at Port Arthur despite tens of thousands of Japanese casualties. Gradually, even before Port Arthur, officers at the ground level, appalled at the havoc being wreaked on their units in the wars, started to modify the tactics, and by the time the IJA encountered the Russian forces at Mukden in late February 1905, the infantry had adopted somewhat looser and more extended formations in its approach to the enemy. These more flexible tactics would be further adjusted to the weapons and terrain of the battles with China and the Allied powers in World War II.[12]

Nevertheless, the IJA never departed from Meckel's fundamental belief in the centrality of the infantry offensive. Nor did it ever fully turn away from his insistence on the importance of massed infantry attacks. As a French captain studying the Japanese army after the Russo-Japanese War aptly put it, Meckel's peculiar mix of Prussian infantry doctrine and *bushidō* "combined to bring combat to one single act—the shock."[13] Thus even while the army came to accept the idea of greater tactical dispersion in the approach toward the enemy, the ultimate tactical ideal of the IJA remained unchanged from Mukden in 1905 to Okinawa in 1945: to close ranks in a final and decisive bayonet charge of hand-to-hand combat regardless of the strength of the firepower arrayed against it. So deeply ingrained was this perspective, reinforced by the victory over Russia in 1905, that the tactical successes of that war became models for all future IJA conflicts, despite the increasingly crucial role that tanks, artillery, and airpower were coming to assume in modern warfare. Even Japan's overwhelming defeat at Nomonhan by the Russians in 1939, which clearly demonstrated the ineffectiveness of Meckel's infantry tactics against an enemy with vastly superior firepower, was not enough to dislodge these outdated templates from their place of honor in the army—and in the textbooks and training grounds of the academies at Lalatun and Zama.[14]

The Offensive at the Academies

When Park Chung Hee and other members of the International Cadet Corps marched past the emperor in the JMA 57 commencement ceremonies in April 1944, it was the infantry, to which Park himself belonged, that led the imperial review parade. Within the IJA the infantry was regarded as the "core branch," the leader of the offensive and the key to victory in the army's battle tactics described above.[15] The other line branches—cavalry, artillery, engineers, transport, and even the air force, which was part of the army both in Japan and in the United States before 1945—were all regarded in IJA tactical doctrine as secondary and supplementary, their common purpose being to support the infantry's advance and attacks against the enemy. Thus, even though they did not specialize in a particular branch until their *honka* years, all cadets, regardless of the branch to which they were eventually assigned, were broadly trained in infantry tactics and the doctrine of the offensive.

Academic Instruction in the Offensive

The concept and importance of the offensive were deeply integrated into all aspects of a cadet's life. At the academic level, these ideas permeated the two main tactical handbooks used by the cadets, the IJA's *Field Service Regulations* (*Sakusen yōmurei/Sakuyō*) and the *Infantry Manual* (*Hohei sōten*). The opening paragraph of the *Sakuyō's* second part, which was focused on the principles of combat, could not have been clearer in this regard: "Whether to adopt offense or defense must be decided primarily on the basis of the mission, but an attack is the only way to smash the enemy forces and achieve definitive annihilation." For that reason, the *Sakuyō* continued, "except when circumstances make it truly impossible, an attack must always be executed." As to what constituted "truly impossible circumstances," the *Sakuyō* set a very high bar: "Even if the enemy forces were overwhelmingly superior, or they temporarily had the advantage, one should all the more make every effort to carry out a decisive attack and turn the battle situation around."[16]

To be sure, defensive tactics were carefully studied as well, but they constituted a much thinner part of the handbooks. Unauthorized withdrawal was absolutely forbidden, and even defense was conceived largely as an interim tactic to be followed as quickly as possible by a decisive attack at the first good opportunity.[17] In the end, what really mattered was the offensive. As Meckel had taught, it was the infantry assault (*totsugeki*) that would "ultimately determine victory or defeat."[18] In a section that might have been written by General Nogi himself, the *Sakuyō* even enjoined "repeated assaults" in the face of severe setbacks.[19] The *Hohei sōten* echoed this injunction. The "Main Principles" (*kōryō*) section at the front of the manual stated that the role of the infantry was to "annihilate the enemy through a combat assault irrespective of topography and timing" and, as the "core branch" of the army, "to carry out combat on its own as best it could even in the absence of any support from other army branches."[20] As offensive operations were to be executed even without regard to the nature of the terrain or the enemy's superior numbers or firepower, IJA doctrine also stressed the importance of good reconnaissance, speed, and stealth, all culminating in a surprise "night attack" (*yakan kōgeki*) that gave the advantage to an infantry assault, even when it was weakly supported by artillery or other combined arms.[21] Indeed, the IJA's partiality for the rapid, aggressive night attack, which had been widely employed during the Russo-Japanese War, later came to be seen by American military tacticians during World War II as a distinguishing characteristic of the Japanese army.[22]

Classroom study in the academic division was correlated with *sōtei/gen'an* articles on applied tactics in the *JMA Bulletin* that cited relevant sections in the handbooks (see Chapter 6). Invariably the articles drove home to the cadets the importance of the offensive in all kinds of operations. Issues of the *Bulletin* from 1943 and 1944, for example, commonly asked readers to consider the specific orders for attack or follow-up pursuit to be issued by commanding officers given certain combat conditions, often drawing from actual battles of the Russo-Japanese War, such as Port Arthur, Liaoyang, Nanshan, and Mukden. Situations in which an officer felt compelled to adopt defensive maneuvers were discussed as well, but there too the ulti-mate focus generally reverted to the offensive. In one typical example from January 1944, the *Bulletin* concentrated on the optimal defensive tactics re-quired for a division commander to withstand an enemy assault and move his army safely to a more level area, where he could then launch an attack against the enemy under more favorable conditions.[23]

As one might expect, examinations in military tactics at the end of each term highlighted the lessons of the classrooms, often posing questions re-lated to the offensive. In their second-term tactics exams at Zama in Sep-tember 1943, for example, Park Chung Hee's MMA 2 class was given four general questions, only the last of which dealt with defense. The other three questions all dealt with offensive operations in one way or another. The first asked the cadets to explain how to seize the initiative in an "encounter battle" (*sōgūsen*), when two armies came upon each other unexpectedly in the field; the second asked for a diagram and explanation of the essentials of the "pursuit attack" (*tsuigeki*) of a retreating enemy; and the third re-quired the cadets to write about "night marches" (*yakan kōgun*). The cadets were also given separate tactical exams related to their branch specialty, and Park and the other infantry cadets that term were queried both in general and in detail about the position and role of an infantry company com-mander in an attack.[24]

Practical Training in the Offensive

As we have seen, textbook mastery of military tactics in the classroom and in examinations was a prelude to corresponding practical training on the ground, either within the school perimeter or beyond. There too the offensive reigned, whether in the drill units (*kyōrenhan*) at the JMA, organized by branch; the on-site tactical exercises (*genchi senjutsu*) and "field camp" exercises (*yaei enshū*), which followed quickly upon each of the three periods of examinations at the schools and took the cadets into the field for extended periods of time; or in the autumnal three-school joint exercises that brought together all the classes of cadets of the JMA (*honka*) at Zama, the JMAP (*yoka*) at Asaka, and the Army Air Force Academy at Toyooka.[25] Cadets were also exposed to the tradition and practice of the offensive in the actual army units to which they were assigned during *taizuki* service between their *yoka* graduation and entry into the JMA at Zama.

The branch drill units at the JMA, which were closely correlated both with the classes and with the field exercises, were particularly important in inculcating the ideology of the offensive. The units met virtually every day, and the specific drill or lesson they sought to teach, especially in the case of the infantry units, was often related in one way or another to an offensive operation. In a record of one such drill from 1944 left behind by Tahara Kōzō, Park Chung Hee's infantry drill instructor, we can see an example of this. The problem posed for the cadets that day was how successfully to infiltrate an enemy camp at night and gather information for their battalion. While the drill was centered on the secret penetration of the enemy lines and reporting of intelligence, ultimately it was understood as a preparatory step in the course of the battalion's offensive that would help identify precisely where the attack against the enemy should most effectively be concentrated. As Tahara himself described it, it was a drill in the techniques of "night officer patrol," but the lesson or "virtue" (*tokumoku*) it was meant to teach was "prudent preparation followed by bold and fearless execution."[26]

Such thinking was at the heart of the most intense and demanding of the academies' practical training regimens, the field camp exercises held at the close of each term. For the MMA cadets the *yaei enshū* began in their Lalatun years and continued at levels of increasing difficulty throughout the course of their *honka* years at Zama. Bivouacked in a designated location for as long as three weeks, the cadets were subjected to simulated combat situations, including the use of live ammunition, that tested their ability in the "command of actual troops" (*jippei shiki*). Cadets were divided into platoons and companies, and certain cadets in each case were selected without advance notice as commanders of the units and asked to apply their accumulated tactical skills toward the attainment of specific combat objectives, as, for example, was Park Chung Hee in the infantry exercises at Ōjōjihara in October 1943 following his second-term JMA exams.[27]

In general, *yaei enshū* followed the usual *sōtei/gen'an* model of problem/ solution, but rather than testing the cadets through oral or written responses, the camp exercise focus was above all on their actual performance as commanders in the field, where weather, terrain, physical discomforts, lack of sufficient sleep, accidents and failure of equipment, inattention and mistakes, or other unknown and unexpected conditions could all affect a unit leader's actions and the final outcome of the exercise. In October 1942, for example, at the third and final *honka* field exercise for the MMA 1 class, held in Fukushima Prefecture, one of four large field guns malfunctioned, causing its projectile to explode almost directly in front of the gun. What could have been not only a major setback in the exercise for the cadet serving as company commander, Tsubokura Tadashi, but also a lethal accident for the cadets handling the weapon was resolved by the quick response of Yi Chuil, who would years later join Park in the May 16 coup, but who that day, fortunately for Tsubokura, was acting as the gun platoon commander.[28]

Needless to say, the *yaei enshū,* as in the above example, were invariably offensive maneuvers, and a high premium was placed by the supervising officers on the personal audacity and aggressiveness of the cadets acting as commanders in the exercises. Especially with an increased emphasis after 1940 on the role of junior and even noncommissioned officers in the tactics of attack and assault, "bold and fearless execution" by company and platoon commanders was especially prized.[29] Exactly what this meant in practice is clear from the tactical exam on company commandership mentioned above that Park Chung Hee and his fellow MMA 2 infantry cadets took in the fall of 1943. The cadets were asked to formulate their answers based on five specific sections of the *Hohei sōten.* The sections in question placed great weight on the company commander positioning himself personally as much as possible in the vanguard of the attack, as "such valiant behavior," the manual noted, "rallies his subordinates and in itself constitutes the first step toward victory." The exam also referenced a section on antitank warfare, which, in accordance with the modified IJA tactical directives of 1940, and despite the terrible losses incurred by Japanese infantry assaults against Soviet armored units at Nomonhan four years earlier, called for company commanders to deploy and maintain "direct control" of platoon or squad-level antitank, hand-to-hand combat teams led by lieutenants and sergeants.[30]

While the offensive pervaded virtually all aspects of study and practice at the academies, particular experiences and instructors could be especially influential in imparting the doctrine. Regimental duty (*taizuki*) for several months between the *yoka* and *honka* programs was a case in point. Such service provided each cadet, newly assigned to a particular army branch, with his first direct experience of actual army life, and the intensity of the *taizuki* could of course vary depending on the character of the particular unit to which the cadets were sent.

For the Zama-bound MMA cadets in the early 1940s, who were posted for regimental service to various Kwantung Army units in Manchuria, the *taizuki* was an especially intense and memorable experience. To begin with, most of these units had long and distinguished Manchurian genealogies of fierce offensive operations and victories going back to the Russo-Japanese War or earlier (see Chapter 5). When Park Chung Hee, for example, was sent in the summer of 1942 to the Kwantung Army's 30th Infantry Regiment, one of thirty-six MMA 2 cadets assigned there, he was joining a military unit that was famed for its night attacks in the Russo-Japanese War, as well as for offensive operations related to the Manchurian Incident of 1931 and the China Incident of 1937.[31] Only three years before Park entered the unit, moreover, the 30th had been part of Task Force Katayama at Nomonhan, where hundreds of IJA officers and men without artillery support had given their lives and limbs in the kind of close-quarters "human bullet" charges against tanks on which Park would later be tested at the JMA.[32]

Timing and location deeply colored the *taizuki* experience for all the MMA 1 and MMA 2 cadets. First, it took place at a moment when there were still recent memories of Nomonhan and the anxieties about Soviet intentions that the campaign had stirred. Second, it coincided with the outbreak of war between Germany and Russia following Hitler's invasion in June 1941, an unforeseen event that had further exacerbated those anxieties. Only the previous year Japan had formally allied itself with Germany, and now, fearing that the war might spread east and somehow spill over into Manchuria, the Kwantung Army had responded by launching the largest-scale maneuvers in its history. These exercises, known in official coded documents by the acronym "Kantokuen," were designed to bring all army units in the country up to a state of full alert and readiness as quickly as possible.[33] They were long remembered by the MMA cadets for their scope and intensity, not least by those who served in regiments such as the 30th Infantry, which was based in the Harbin area, far to the north and closer to the Soviet border than many other units. Indeed, Ibayashi Kiyonaga, one of the Japanese cadets who served with Park Chung Hee in the 30th, later wrote that the MMA 2 *taizuki* was a time when "the Kwantung Army was pushing the 1941 Kantokuen ahead with full momentum, and morale was truly as high as the sky."[34]

Instructors of the Offensive

Certain officers at the academies, even more than others, seemed to embody the doctrine of the offensive in their personalities and actions, leaving a lasting impression on the cadets whose lives they touched. Major Enami Shigeru, for example, whose tenure as company commander of the Manchukuo cadets in the JMA International Corps encompassed both the MMA 1 and MMA 2 classes, made a strong impact on the MMA 1 class during the JMA Fukushima exercises mentioned above. Enami had been convalescing for months from a severe cut to his Achilles tendon suffered during a practice *kendō* match, and the cadets had not expected him to participate actively in the exercises, which were that day centered on an infantry night attack mock-up. As twilight fell, however, and the exercise was just about to commence, to their great astonishment Enami suddenly and dramatically came forward wrapped in a military cape and announced that he would personally lead the cadets in the attack as company commander. Then, as if stepping directly out of a page of the *Hohei sōten,* he assumed a position at the front of the company, raised the company's handheld signal flag above his head, and led the company's platoons in the charge. Enami's unexpected appearance that day, the MMA 1 cadets would later write in their class history, was a moment of "universal unspoken wonder and emotion," and his skillful handling of the troops in the attack was "still remembered, fixed in the mind's eye."[35]

Company commanders at the academies such as Enami, however, tended to have only occasional and formal contact with the cadets; indeed, one of the reasons his assumption of command in Fukushima was so unexpected, apart from the fact that he was still recovering from a serious *kendō* injury, was that the cadets actually saw relatively little of him, especially in comparison with their *kutaichō* or section commanders. These younger and junior officers, who were often not much older than the cadets themselves, saw and worked with their charges on a daily basis, both as military instructors on the training grounds and as monitors and counselors in the barracks, and they were thus in a position to exert a far more powerful and lasting influence on the cadets than any other single officer or group of officers. It is precisely in that sense that Hosokawa in his diary describes his section commander as similar to "a father and a god."[36] Like Hosokawa, cadets naturally had the closest relationship with their own section commanders, but in the course of their training, they came to know the entire group of officers, as each *kutaichō* served on a rotating basis as the weekly duty officer (*shūban shikan*) for the whole company, working closely with the other commanders and their sections in a variety of daily activities.

Although all section commanders emphasized the offensive, which was at the core of IJA tactical doctrine, some were more zealous about it than others. The most zealous, according to Park Chung Hee's MMA 2 classmate Kaneko Tomio, were those whom Kaneko called the "*samurai-kutaichō*," the very "serious" (*majime*) officers, who were "hard, tough, sharp, formal, difficult to approach," and sometimes even "scary." Kaneko knew of what he spoke, since his *kutaichō* at the MMA had been Oka Chōji, "a real samurai," according to Kaneko, and "very tough; he didn't care about small things, but once he got angry, he was really scary."[37] Of all the MMA 2 Nikkei section commanders, however, none was more of a *samurai-kutaichō* than Yano Yutaka, who figures so prominently in Hosokawa Minoru's diary. Kiyoizumi Nobuo, who was also in Hosokawa's section, described Yano, who had fought at Nomonhan, as "the strictest of the six section commanders" in his company, "a very aggressive person," who would "continue training exercises even after the other sections had finished for the day."[38]

When Kiyoizumi arrived at Zama for his *honka* course, however, his understanding of what constituted a "very aggressive person" was to take on a whole new meaning when he and his classmates, like the MMA 1 cadets before them, were introduced to Section Commander Sakai Masao. Sakai, whose tenure, like Enami's, coincided with the first two MMA classes at Zama, left an indelible impression on both classes, but especially perhaps on the MMA 1 cadets, whose time at the JMA overlapped more closely with his. As in his unforgiving treatment of a sick MMA cadet whom he excoriated for spending too much time in the infirmary (see Chapter 4), Sakai's strictness as a section commander tended toward the extreme, so much so that, as one MMA 1 cadet put it, "all of us in his section harbored a deep-seated fear of him," a fear that was only compounded by his physical strength and a dark, scowling face that had led the cadets to nickname him "Carbon."[39]

Not surprisingly, Sakai's embrace of the offensive bordered on the excessive. Even though he taught that an officer had to be able to adjust tactics learned in the manuals on the basis of actual battle conditions, his focus was ultimately always on the offensive, even in the most impossible of situations. Although he did not fight at Nomonhan like Yano, Sakai had served in Manchuria at the time of the battle, and he knew well the high costs of the infantry attacks that had characterized the fighting. Still he remained inextricably wedded to the classic high-risk IJA tactics. Former cadets remembered him talking about how the army would not have become encircled by the Russians at Nomonhan if the Japanese commanding officers had surveyed the situation better, including topography, and adequately prepared their subordinates. In the end, however, what Sakai had wanted to drive home to the cadets was the importance of returning to the offensive *regardless* of battle conditions: "Even if you become encircled," he had thundered at them, "charge forward into the enemy without thinking!"[40] Pak Imhang, one of the MMA 1 Korean cadets who later joined Park Chung Hee in the 1961 coup, liked to tell the story of how once when commanding troops in combat during the Korean War, he had had a profound existential moment of doubt about how to proceed. Suddenly "Carbon" Sakai's face had risen before him, and Pak's doubts vanished as he shouted out to his men, "Don't think—just attack!"[41] Park Chung Hee himself also seems to have had a high regard for the former JMA *kutaichō*, even though Sakai had not been his own section commander. In November 1961, when Park left South Korea for a visit to the United States and stopped over in Tokyo for his first meeting with Japanese government leaders since seizing power, he scheduled a private meeting with Sakai, then an officer in Japan's Self-Defense Forces, at the state guest house in Mejiro where he was staying.[42]

What of Park Chung Hee's own *kutaichō*? Altogether Park was assigned to three different officers at Lalatun and Zama. About his MMA section commander, a Chinese officer in the Manchukuo Army named Zhang Lianzhi, mentioned briefly in Chapters 3 and 6, little is known apart from the fact that he regarded Park as a model for other cadets to emulate and seems to have been actively involved in subversive political activities carried out by the Chinese Mankei cadets. Of the two Japanese officers who served consecutively as Park's *kutai* commander at the JMA, Nishigaki Makoto and Tahara Kōzō, it was Tahara who arguably exerted the greater influence. Nishigaki worked with the MMA 2 class only a short time (about six months) before he was succeeded by Tahara, who acted as Park's *kutaichō* until the MMA 2 cadets graduated more than a year later.[43] Moreover, as noted earlier, in addition to serving as Park's section commander, he was also Park's infantry drill instructor, which meant that most of Park's day—morning, afternoon, and evening—fell under Tahara's supervision, and it was of course Tahara who actually trained Park in the practical application of IJA tactics.

Tahara Kōzō

In Kaneko Tomio's taxonomy of section commanders, both Nishigaki and Tahara were *samurai-kutaichō*. Nishigaki was in fact Sakai's former classmate at the JMA (JMA 48), along with another MMA 2 *kutaichō*, Imamura Hirozumi, all three of whom were "tough guys," with Sakai and Imamura characterized as particularly "scary." According to Kaneko, however, even though Tahara was a "tough guy" in the *samurai* mode, he was also "quiet and meticulous," more "correct and serious" (*majime*) than "rough or frightening"; he was, Kaneko added, "much like Park Chung Hee himself," who was well known in the class for his taciturnity and "very *majime*" demeanor.[44] Despite his natural reserve, Tahara could be explosive and intimidating at times, as when once in front of his peers at the JMA he publicly embarrassed Takayama Toshitake, another *samurai-kutaichō* and a senior by one year to Tahara in the JMA class lists (JMA 51 as opposed to Tahara's JMA 52), by loudly and critically commenting on the "poor mental attitude" of one of Takayama's cadets without consulting privately with Takayama first.[45] And on the infantry drill grounds, that seriousness and attention to detail made Tahara, in Kiyoizumi Nobuo's words, "the most spirited" of all the MMA 2 section commanders, the clear successor in that regard to Sakai, who had been routinely transferred to another post only a month after Tahara arrived.[46] Reminiscences from Tahara's own JMA 52 classmates echo the MMA 2 cadets' appraisal. According to Tanaka Ken'ichi, for example, Tahara was "of average height, muscled . . . with nothing in particular that made him stand out," but "his personal appearance concealed a strong will," and "those who knew him knew that he had a spirit that would charge into danger without saying a word."[47]

Tahara seems to have lived up to the image his classmates and JMA charges had of him. Takayama noted that his fellow *kutaichō* had been impatient for a combat assignment while he was serving Zama and had "welcomed with great enthusiasm" his new posting to the Philippines as a battalion commander in October 1944, six months after the MMA 2 graduation.[48] In private letters to his wife, Yoshiko, and other family members, made available to me by his son, this enthusiasm is palpable. Writing to Yoshiko in Manila in early November of that year, shortly after learning that he would be sent to the Philippines front, he told his wife of the "deep emotion" he felt on hearing the news of his deployment: "When I think that I will be joining the battle that will decide the life or death of my country, I cannot help but be excited." And in the next sentence he asked Yoshiko, who was pregnant at the time, to name their child Naotake if it was a boy, the two Chinese characters of which could also be read as *shōbu,* the Japanese word for "militarism."[49]

As it turned out, the Philippines front at the time was on the island of Leyte, where General MacArthur had recently made his dramatic landing after a colossal sea battle that had destroyed the Japanese fleet, and the Americans, together with friendly Filipino guerilla forces, were in the process of mopping up all remaining Japanese troops on the island. Common sense should have dictated at this point that the IJA generals in Manila accept the inevitable and turn their attention to the defense of the capital. As Edward Drea has written, "The Japanese had no air cover, no surface fleet, and no reason to waste reinforcements on Leyte." But a combination of misinformation about their alleged successes against the Americans in the naval battle, together with their ingrained disdain for retreat, led the Japanese commanders to see Leyte as the decisive land battle of the Philippines, and they began to move reinforcements onto the island as fast as possible.[50]

Tahara could easily have avoided being sent to Leyte, as his home unit, the 31st Infantry Regiment of the 8th Division, was not part of the deployment.[51] His messages to his family indicate that he was fully aware of the rapidly deteriorating conditions at the front. In his early November letter to his wife he had written that "the war situation has become increasingly severe," and at the end of a postcard sent just before his departure, his last communication with Yoshiko, he had hastily scribbled that "the war front on Leyte is not good."[52] All this notwithstanding, he appears to have volunteered to transfer from his home regiment to another "brother" regiment in the 8th Division (the 5th Infantry) in order to serve on the command staff of a special three-battalion unit that was being detached from the 5th and sent to the island.[53] This detached unit was in fact the very last of the desperate and futile Leyte reinforcement efforts carried out by the Japanese army, and Tahara's great eagerness to join it, captured in his November letter to his wife, would seal his fate.

On December 9 Tahara left Manila with about 3,000 men in a convoy of three ships, one battalion per ship, but two of the ships were sunk by American planes near the island's port of Palompon, forcing Tahara and many of the men to swim ashore and leaving them virtually bereft of clothing, weapons, and supplies. The third battalion did manage to land and disembark, but its combat capacity was quickly destroyed by the overwhelmingly superior firepower of American artillery. Thereafter Tahara and his men, defending themselves from pursuing American and Filipino forces largely with bamboo spears, took refuge in the nearby Canquipot Mountains in the northwest corner of Leyte, where, refusing to surrender, they all eventually perished, mainly from starvation.[54] This grim ending, which became the basis of a celebrated postwar Japanese novel, *Fires on the Plain* (*Nobi*) by Ōoka Shōhei, was eloquent if sober testimony to the power of the offensive in Japanese military thinking and in the minds of the IJA's most dedicated young officers serving on the front lines or at the academies.[55]

The "Attack Spirit" and Will

When his JMA 52 classmates noted that Tahara had had "a spirit that would charge into danger without saying a word," they were bestowing on their friend one of the highest compliments one IJA officer could tender another. In IJA thinking, the offensive in combat was above all a matter of spirit and had little to do with manpower, firepower, or any other material advantage. And the "attack spirit" (kōgeki seishin), as it was called, like the offensive itself, was unrelentingly promoted at the academies, not only in the manuals, military dictionaries, songs, classrooms, and training grounds of the academies but also in the everyday life of the sections and companies to which each cadet belonged. Martial arts, gymnastics, and other section-based athletic activities, for example, constituted about 17 percent of the academy regimen, all of which provided natural opportunities for the cadets to develop and display their commitment to the doctrine.[56] The periodic school athletic meets were particularly important. Held under the supervision of the academy's officers, as well as in the full gaze of classmates, seniors, and juniors, they were designed to boost physical prowess and group unity, of course, but another goal was to encourage cadets to be as aggressive as possible in all their competitions. As Hosokawa wrote in his diary on the eve of one such meet at Lalatun in October 1941, "Everything, from beginning to end, depends on giving full rein to the 'attack spirit.'"[57]

Apart from the athletic activities and events, the "attack spirit" was deeply incorporated into the "moral education" (kun'iku) that was at the core of quotidian barracks life in the kutai. Week after week, day and night, soon after rising and just before sleeping, the cadets in each kutai were subjected to a systematic barrage of lectures, instructions, criticisms, and exhortations by their section and company commanders. Brief excerpts from these sermon-like talks and other corresponding quotations were often posted in the cadets' sleeping and self-study rooms, and each cadet was required to reflect on their meaning and application in his daily diary, often highlighting the key words and phrases in special boldface charts. Much of this moral education, needless to say, was related in one way or another to the doctrine of the offensive and the "attack spirit," like Hosokawa's entry cited above. Only a month later, in fact, Hosokawa's section commander, Yano Yutaka, reflecting on the German advance into Poland two years earlier and the Wehrmacht's recent strike into Russia, urged him and his fellow cadets to note and emulate the "spirit and power" of Hitler's Blitzkrieg or "lightning attacks" (dengeki).[58]

To be sure, Hosokawa, who, like Park Chung Hee, aspired to become an infantry officer, was particularly conscious while at Lalatun of his need not only to "study with special care" the *Sōten* (i.e., *Hohei sōten*) and the *Sakuyō* but to "execute with vigor" the principles they taught, the most important of which was "always, without end, to attack" (*doko made mo kōgeki*).[59] But the "attack spirit" was pervasive at both the *yoka* and *honka* institutions and in all branches of the military. It was even incorporated into the inter-*kutai* rivalry and hazing that was so much a part of officially unrecorded barracks life, such as the post-taps "night assaults" (*yashū*) that one or more *kutai* launched against other *kutai* in their company, generally with the permission and under the direction of the respective section commanders. Not infrequently the assaults coincided with the anniversary of a decisive offensive in the Russo-Japanese War, as in late August 1940, when the MMA 1 Japanese cadets from the 3rd and 4th *kutai* raided the sleeping quarters of the 1st and 2nd *kutai,* in commemoration of the Japanese victory against the Russians at Liaoyang almost precisely thirty-five years earlier to the day.[60]

But how did one ensure that the "attack spirit" would always be there when it was needed, not simply in mock battles at Shibeiling or on the Sagami plain or in "night assaults" on unsuspecting fellow cadets in the barracks, but in the most adverse and extreme conditions of war, when body and mind both cried out for surcease or, worse, for the unthinkable, shameful, forbidden safety of retreat? For the IJA the answer to this dilemma lay in a rigorous cultivation of the human will (*ishi*). Indeed, so central and fundamental was the concept of will to IJA thinking that it would not be an exaggeration to say that it informed every aspect of academy education and training and defined, in a very real sense, what it meant to be a commanding officer. Cadets were told in the opening pages of the *Field Service Regulations,* for example, that the bedrock of military leadership lay in the strength of an officer's "resolution" (*kesshin*), and that strength, in turn, always depended on a "firm will" (*kyōko naru ishi*).[61] And the introduction to the 1942 modern Japanese military history text used by Park Chung Hee and other MMA 2 cadets at the JMA stressed that "firmness of will" was the "supreme martial virtue" of any military commander.[62]

In its obsessive attention to willpower, the IJA was of course not acting in an educational vacuum. Here again the IJA freely reappropriated elements of a now commonly accepted samurai tradition, including the *Hagakure,* which told the cadets that if they would "concentrate the mind" (*ichinen okoru to*), they could do anything, even "move heaven and earth."[63] Korean (and Chinese) cadets could find a similar resonance with the past in the deeply rooted Neo-Confucian idea of "setting the mind" (*ipchi*)—not for warfare, but for study and self-cultivation.[64] Most important, however, was an emphasis on the power of will that had come to infuse modern ideas of psychology and pedagogy since the nineteenth century.[65] Indeed, it was precisely this modern "cult of the will," in Michael Cowan's phrase, that underlay the meaning of the Meiji neologism for "will" that eventually became the common vocabulary of East Asia (C: *yizhi*; J: *ishi*; K: *ŭiji*), a two-character Sinitic compound combining "intention" and "purpose," whose second character, *shi* (*chi*), was also used in the compound *shishi*, the term for the Meiji Restoration patriots or "men of high purpose" (see Chapter 4).[66] Will as *ishi* or *ŭiji* became a textbook category in Meiji and late Chosŏn moral primers for primary and secondary school children, as in the following passage from a 1906 secondary-level text for the Hwimun School in Seoul, a private institution established and supported by Koreans as part of the "patriotic enlightenment movement" in the Japanese protectorate period before the annexation.[67] "The activity of the will," the section on *ŭiji* opened, "is the most important factor for us in our consideration of morality." The reason for this, it continued, was self-evident: "If a human being knows well what is good but cannot effectively act on it, what on earth is the use of extensive knowledge and burning passion? When it comes to directing that knowledge and acting upon it, the power of the will is everything."[68]

An emphasis on willpower continued to be an integral feature of imperial school education throughout the pre-1945 period. And by the late 1930s and early 1940s, of course, when the first MMA cadets were matriculating, will as the instrumental key to action had taken on new meanings of revolutionary and national empowerment with the rise of Marxism-Leninism and fascism. Kawakami Hajime, for example, whose work had transfixed so many of Park Chung Hee's fellow students at TNS (see Chapter 6), was deeply interested in the role of "revolutionary will" in the process of class struggle and social transformation.[69] And Chang Chirak (alias "Kim San"), in his well-known memoir of life as a Korean communist in China in the 1930s, had defined the essence of humanity, as distinct from that of animals, in terms of an ability to control desires through an exercise of will: "Man can control his desires and render them unnecessary, I decided. Man existed as such only when he had intellectual will and idea."[70]

Similarly, the adulation of Hitler and Mussolini by many Japanese and Koreans in this period, including Park Chung Hee (see Chapter 3), arose not only from media depictions of these figures as national saviors but also from the charismatic quality of their published writings and speeches, which glorified personal and national struggle and privileged the will in attaining desired ends. Mussolini's autobiography, which had enthralled Yun Ch'iho with its "energy" when he first read it in 1929, was filled with paeans to the power of a "clear and decisive will, both personal and also corporate in the form of the fascist state."[71] Hitler of course apotheosized the idea of will, and under propaganda minister Joseph Goebbels's direction the Third Reich transformed it into national spectacle, epitomized by the massive Nazi Party rally captured in Leni Riefenstahl's 1934 cinematic masterwork, *Triumph des Willens,* which was well received in Japan.[72] Among the many excerpts from Hitler's autobiography and speeches that found their way into the Korean and Japanese press during this period was his assertion from *Mein Kampf* that Germany's problem was a "lack of will, and not the lack of arms."[73] This was a view that struck a deep chord with Shōwa Restorationists such as JMA 57 company commander Uchiyama Kazuya, who quoted the phrase in an article for the October 1942 *JMA Bulletin* that appeared just as Park Chung Hee and his MMA classmates arrived at Zama.[74]

But Shōwa Restorationists were hardly exceptional here. As noted above, will as the ultimate wellspring of action was a view common to all groups in the IJA and at the academies as well. On the day Chŏng Naehyŏk (JMA 58) entered the JMAP in April 1942, for example, the very first lecture he heard was about the power of will.[75] Indeed, a considerable part of his and every other cadet's moral education (kun'iku) grade, the most heavily weighed component of the overall academy record (see Chapter 3), was based on the section commander's assessment of the quality and strength of a cadet's will. Assessment of will at the *yoka* level was a central factor in determining to which branch of the army a cadet would be assigned. The infantry was the most prestigious and popular choice among cadets, but as the linchpin of the revered tactical offensive, it was in many ways the most physically and mentally demanding of the branches, and academy instructors took pains to satisfy themselves that the will of the cadets assigned there was such that they could meet those demands. The idea of "guiding" and "disciplining" the will (ishi no tanren) permeated the parlance and practices of academy life, and it would not at all be an exaggeration to describe academy education in general as a form of "will training."[76]

Will Training at the Academies: In the Classroom

Like so much else that was taught at the academies, will training began in the classroom in the mornings, moved to the exercise grounds in the afternoons, and ended with lectures, self-study, and reflection in the barracks in the evenings. In all cases it was about mastering the will to carry out soldierly tasks and state goals, a mastery that was regarded, like the "attack spirit" (seen as an application of will), both in gendered terms, as an expression of masculinity, and in moral terms, as a demonstration of patriotism.

Classes on psychology and pedagogy, with textbooks specifically written for the academies to enlighten the cadets about their own mental processes as well as to teach them how most effectively to instruct and train the men who would come under their command, placed great emphasis on the function of the will, which, according to one textbook, "determined objectives and motives, bringing both to completion." The exercise of will by the officer was to be "firm," "strong," and "quick." It was also to be "self-regulating," that is, so deeply internalized that it would be virtually instinctive, arising "autonomously and spontaneously" in any given situation, oblivious to the approval or opprobrium of others. Such autonomy and spontaneity, however, did not imply a license for indiscriminate behavior; quite the opposite. Willful activity was to be "virtuous" (zenryō), "healthy" (kenzen), and "just" (seitō). That is, it was to be directed not toward "individualistic" or "selfish" ends but toward national goals, defined by the state and army, which for the IJA soldier meant ultimately and literally a willingness to die for the country.[77] And there was more. The *majime* officer was expected to exercise his virtuous will in a manner that was "lively or vigorous" (ōsei), "energetic" (genki), and "bright and cheerful" (meirō), terms that infuse the academy documents of this period and recall the *Hagakure*'s exhortation to samurai that they "dash forward" in battle not only bravely but "with joy."[78]

Molding the ideal will was of course not easily accomplished, and academy textbooks took note of the manifold ways in which will could be weakened or perverted. Foremost among them was the bane of "fatigue" (hirō), the effect of continuous physical or mental activity that could be measured quantitatively or qualitatively in terms of a soldier's diminished performance in his assigned duty. Fatigue could be alleviated through physical means by providing the soldier with rest, nutrition, or a change of task. Ultimately, however, it was regarded by the IJA as a "mental condition" that arose from a sense of boredom, unhappiness, or other personal or psychological reasons, as in the case of case of an infantry branch cadet who was actually more suited for artillery or the engineers.[79]

Academy instructors, section commanders in particular, were acutely sensitive to any signs of tapering enthusiasm among their charges. Once such a sign had been detected, the commander would summon the cadet to his office to confront the problem, with the goal of reinvigorating the cadet's will and reinstilling his "energy" and "cheerfulness." To that end the 1942 practical manual on moral education (kun'iku) for section commanders laid out in detail a number of "special" types of personal and family issues and character traits that might sap a cadet's will and suggested how to deal with them. In addition to private meetings with the cadet, the commander might, for example, work in tandem with the cadet's family, especially if they were able to visit. Or, instead of singling out a particular cadet for a failing or lack of enthusiasm, the commander might use the section meetings in the evening to raise the problem in general terms and exhort all the cadets in the *kutai* to improve themselves.[80]

While the section or company commander was thus enjoined to do everything within his power—discuss, advise, console, encourage, or admonish—to identify and resolve the underlying cause of a cadet's poor attitude and performance, in the end it was up to the cadet himself somehow to find his way back to a state of *ōsei* or *meirō-genki*. An example from the manual clearly makes this point. It tells of a cadet who was called in by one of the JMA's senior supervising officers for a talk after the officer had reviewed the cadet's "weak-willed" (*hakujaku*) performance. In the course of the meeting, the cadet "confessed" that from the moment he had entered the academy he had taken such a personal dislike to his section commander that he had been unable to think positively about anything the commander had said or to establish a close relationship with him. The cadet admitted to an "lack of earnest will," and the senior officer agreed, counseling him that the section commander, whatever his faults, was only a vehicle for the cadet to learn his duty: "Just as the subject remains a subject when the king falls short of being a king, so the cadet officer remains a cadet officer when the section commander falls short of being a section commander." In other words, it was up to the cadet to find the will, as it were, to reassert his will. And so as to leave no doubt as to the point of the example, the manual added in a coda: "At present, the thankful [cadet], having given thought to his earlier error, is pushing ahead in his training with cheerfulness and joy."[81]

Will Training at the Academies: Outside the Classroom

If the above unnamed cadet was indeed trying to work with a spirit of "cheerfulness and joy," as the 1942 manual asserts, he would have faced a particular challenge in the training exercises outside the classroom. These exercises, whether on academy grounds or elsewhere, were designed not only to provide the cadets with opportunities to test their practical application of military knowledge, particularly in the areas of tactics and leadership, but also to be strenuous tests of will.

At their most basic the tests were trials of endurance, such as the lengthy, uphill double-time (*kakeashi*) marches long remembered by the MMA cadets. Often these marches were emergency musters to nearby Shibeiling Hill and back (see Chapter 4). But regular and lengthy field maneuvers of two weeks or more took the cadets to even more rugged Manchurian terrain, where each day was filled with arduous exercises and long treks back to camp on which the exhausted cadets learned the knack of catching some sleep even while marching. Manchuria's temperature extremes, ranging from nearly tropical heat in the summer to almost Arctic cold in the winter, provided numerous occasions for heat-endurance (*tainetsu*) and cold-endurance (*taikan*) marches lasting as long as two nights and three days, again in full gear and often at an accelerated pace.[82]

Learning to endure was only a first step in field training of the will. Cadets were expected to confront and overcome any obstacle, natural, physiological, and mental, that they might encounter in their advance. Indeed, in planning an attack, the cadets were taught always to assume the worst possible conditions of weather and topography. In a training exercise at the Atsugi Bridge on the Sagami River, for example, a platoon-level (*shōtai*) infantry drill section of MMA 1 cadets was ordered to secure the steel bridge for the Japanese army as a hypothetical enemy on the other side of the river was preparing to blow it up. The platoon launched its mock attack, running across the bridge, theoretically subduing the enemy, and capturing the bridge. Sugiyama Masayuki, one of the cadets in the platoon, said he and the other cadets had been triumphant afterward; they felt it had been a perfect operation, "like something out of a great fight scene in a war movie." But there had been no shout of "Correct!" (*Gen'an da!*) from the drill instructor. Instead, he had yelled "Assault unsuccessful!" (*Totsugeki fuseikō!*). He had in fact wanted the cadets to assume the worst, that the bridge had already been blown up, and to move directly across the river to attack the enemy.

The cadets then prepared to repeat the attack, this time stripping off all their gear except for their underwear (*fundoshi*) and bayonets because the river at this point was deep and fast-moving. Again the instructor stopped them. "What is the point," he asked them, "of crossing the river in *fundoshi*? Put on your gear and cross!" Only after they had charged across the river in full gear, a dangerous maneuver given the hazardous waters, did the instructor give his approval, telling them that they must deal decisively with whatever impediment might hinder or block their path: "If there is a river, advance by crossing it; if a mountain, by going over it—no hesitation even for a moment is allowed on the battlefield."[83]

Bad weather, mountains, rivers—these were of course challenges posed by the natural environment. Unfamiliar or contaminated food and drink, poor sanitation, and pests, common threats to a healthy solider on the march, were also concerns at the academies, especially at the MMA (see Chapter 4). In their first year especially, the MMA cadets were cautioned almost daily by their section commanders to observe hygienic practices in everything they did. But in the event they did become ill, they were enjoined as a matter of course to assert their martial "*budō* spirit" to combat the offending sickness, just as they were to exercise their will against the elements of nature.[84] And, as noted in Chapter 4, the most fanatic section commanders, such as "Carbon" Sakai, evinced little sympathy for cadets who required extended stays in the infirmary, even for a serious infection such as malaria. Even if a strong will by itself could not cure malaria, it could, or so officers such as Sakai believed, at least quicken the recovery, and a cadet who did not apply it was falling short of expectations.

Fear, with its power to paralyze or panic troops on the battlefield, was something that concerned the academy instructors. Many of the training exercises, especially those using live ammunition, were in fact dangerous and could quickly go wrong, like the grenade fire that damaged Park Chung Hee's gun (see Chapter 6), and cadets facing these conditions were often unnerved or even terrified. But fear, like cold or sickness, was regarded as a mental state to be willed into submission, and the academies forced the cadets to confront their fear by deliberately placing them in training situations where to advance was consciously to put themselves in physical jeopardy, as when they had to inch forward on their bellies under repeated volleys of live machine-gun fire.[85] The same held true for the cadets' first basic instructions in swimming, horseback riding, and other skills. In the case of swimming, for example, as one former MMA 5 Chinese cadet, Li Tiancheng, remembered, he and his classmates were initially taken out in a boat and simply pushed into deep water, where they had to struggle on their own until the instructor felt they could no longer stay afloat. At that point they would be picked up and allowed to rest briefly in the boat while the instructor gave them some pointers before being pushed back into the water. "In this way," according to Li, "everyone would become a good swimmer within a week."[86]

Occasionally some instructors took such will training to an extreme. One weekly duty officer, according to Hiruma Hiroshi (JMA 57), who overlapped at the JMA with Park and the other MMA 2 cadets, called an emergency muster in the middle of the night and turned his company of 160 cadets into "an utterly crazed group," forcing them to run totally naked at double-time around the academy grounds and then out through the school gates into the town of Zama. It was also the middle of winter, and when they reached the destination the officer had chosen, a river-shore training area, the cadets were chilled to the bone; the water itself was frozen. But there was worse to come. The officer then ordered the cadets to dive into the river. When they all held back, frightened to plunge headfirst into what looked like solid ice, the officer kept barking his order until the unlucky head duty cadet for that week (*torishimari seito*), whose role was to lead the other cadets in the company, resigned himself to his fate and dived in. As feared, the ice was more than a centimeter thick, cutting into the cadet's forehead and drawing blood. Only then did the officer call a halt to the exercise. In this case the officer had gone too far, but such nighttime water musters, known in JMA jargon as "purifications" (*misogi*), were not uncommon. They were intended to instill in cadets the idea of "absolute obedience" to orders from a superior (see Chapter 8), but they were also designed to teach the cadets to conquer their fears through force of will.[87]

Ultimately, of course, will training was about the will to advance regardless of circumstances, enduring whatever had to be endured, confronting whatever had to be confronted, overcoming whatever had to be overcome, so as to push the offensive forward toward a decisive attack. Rapidity of advance was normally a desideratum and often a point of pride among eager, newly commissioned young officers. Occasionally, however, as Park Chung Hee's MMA 2 classmate Kaneko Tomio pointed out, the *gen'an* could be a "step-by-step" approach. "Once," Kaneko remembered, "I was praised in an exercise for suggesting that troops first occupy a hill before going over it. The other students all said just go over the hill, but I thought it was better to occupy the hill first. This was the right answer." It was the right answer in part because, as Kaneko noted, this was yet another lesson drawn from the Russo-Japanese War, when Japanese units relied on capturing points one at a time and moving forward, "so they needed to occupy the top of a hill first, so that they could use their artillery to move forward. Young officers were eager to advance quickly, but their equipment did not allow them to do it." But it was also the correct answer for the 1940s, when the Japanese were still relying on artillery-backed infantry instead of heavily armed tanks that could have moved up a hill with ease and confidence. In any case, whether one moved in the usual mode of full speed ahead or more deliberately step by step, the aim was the same. As Kaneko put it, "The Russo-Japanese War tactics were just like the tactics of the Warring States period . . . just go forward. So many casualties."[88]

Will Training at the Academies: No Slacking

Precisely because the academies placed such an emphasis on the power of will regardless of conditions and casualties, instructors had little patience with any form of "slacking," or *zuberu* in the argot of the schools.[89] The war's demand for officers had led the academies to recruit beyond their usual pre-academy military feeder schools and draw heavily from the regular civilian school system (see Chapter 6), and academy instructors often contemptuously denounced slacking as a legacy of middle school "liberalism," unworthy of an officer.[90] Cadets were continuously exhorted to recognize and eradicate such weak-willed attitudes in themselves, and any cadets found exhibiting such thinking or behavior were immediately taken to task—more often than not, in the spirit of *danketsu,* together with their entire section or company (see Chapter 8). Machine-gun drills with blank cartridges, for example, often led to *zuberu* behavior, as the cadets tried to avoid shooting as much as possible because residue from the blanks fouled up the gun and had to be laboriously cleaned afterward. A watchful officer, however, would notice this, and as one of the MMA 1 cadets remembered, his instructor forced the cadets to fire all their remaining blanks in the air, while berating them for their laziness and lack of resolve.[91]

Officers were on the alert for cadets who seemed too concerned with physical comfort, especially in the face of difficult weather conditions. Kaneko Tomio remembered one wintry occasion at Zama when one of the MMA 2 section leaders, Miyamoto Masami (JMA 50), who was serving as the weekly duty officer, discovered some of the cadets in the company warming themselves around the barracks stove. He immediately led them outside, where he ordered them to undress except for *fundoshi* and to run around the academy grounds barefoot in double-time. To shame the cadets even further and drive the point home, Miyamoto, "a real samurai," according to Kaneko, stripped down to *fundoshi* and ran with them.[92]

Section commanders tended to keep an eye out for slacking particularly on rainy days. According to Sugiyama Masayuki (MMA 1), all the cadets hated training in the rain. On rare occasions, as in the summer monsoon downpours at Zama, exercises might be canceled, and one of the cadets' frustrations was waiting around to see if they would actually have to go out or not, always hoping they would not, but never knowing until the last minute what the final order would be. Training in the rain, which invariably meant training in mud, posed other problems apart from sheer physical strain and discomfort, as the cadets had to their spend free time removing any traces of dirt or mud from their gear when they returned. As Sugiyama's *kutaichō* was

"Carbon" Sakai, he had many stories to relate about his section commander's finely tuned ability to spot the slightest hint of disinclination in the *kutai* for exercises in the rain. If he sensed such an attitude, Sakai would use the moment as an opportunity for will training and force the cadets in his section to go out when the rain was heaviest and spend an extended time in the inescapable mud holes created by the storm.[93] One of the reasons Park Chung Hee was regarded as a model cadet by his academy instructors and resented by some of his less ardent classmates was that he rarely exhibited any signs of *zuberu,* whether in the rain or in other training situations. Once at the MMA his section commander abruptly canceled a drill and dismissed the cadets because the rain was coming down too hard to continue. All the cadets immediately ran back to the barracks as quickly as possible, except for Park, who marched back stiffly, as if still in formation, ignoring the rain. According to his MMA 2 Chinese classmate, Xu Shudong, who watched the scene from the barracks with a combination of astonishment and revulsion, this was yet another example of Park's "crazy-*majime*" conduct as a cadet.[94]

Will Training at the Academies: In the Barracks

As it turned out, rain-soaked drill grounds, or whatever the training sites of the day had been, were only a prelude to an evening of will training in the barracks, where the cadets were lectured by their section commanders and required to note and reflect in their diaries on the activities of the day and their performance in them. In the end willpower was not only to be taught in the classroom and exercised in the fields but also to be inscribed in the mind through a nightly regimen of self-criticism and self-exhortation. In his MMA 2 cadet diary, for example, Hosokawa Minoru hardly let a day go by without making a reference to some aspect of will training, whether in recalling an event or lecture or in evaluating his own shortcomings and aspirations. There one finds, first of all, the recurrent theme of affirmation and optimism, the importance, as Hosokawa wrote, of always being "positive" (*sekkyokuteki*), however dire the situation, and of always acting "brightly and energetically," whether at the academy as his section's weekly duty cadet or later on the battlefield in the service of the emperor.[95] There too one finds the repeated call to swift and decisive action, whether one was rising in the morning, lining up for roll call, or charging forward on the mock battlefields of the academy.[96] "Action not debate!" Hosokawa wrote, underscoring the theme of a lecture by Commandant Akiyama.[97] "Action not words!" he wrote again two weeks later after a visit from Superintendent Nagumo.[98]

Finally, one finds in the diary constant self-reminders of the power of the will, whatever the circumstances. After a day of battling debilitating temperatures in the field, Hosokawa would go on to battle them again in his mind at night, vowing in his diary, for example, in the face of frostbite from the "most extreme cold" of the 1941 winter at Lalatun, to conquer the elements through a proper "mental attitude" (*kokorogamae*), which he equated with the "way of the warrior" (*budō*).[99] So too with illness. Especially in his early months at the school, as he struggled to acclimate himself to Manchurian food and water, Hosokawa recorded numerous instances of sickness in his section, so many that in July 1941 his section commander, Yano Yutaka, lectured on the benefits of "early diagnosis," suggesting that the cadets watch themselves and each other closely for any signs of illness and, if necessary, go to the infirmary. But Yano's caution was not meant as an encouragement to go to the infirmary as early as possible; his point was that going to the infirmary should be a last resort, something to be done only after the cadets had made every effort (*ganbari*) to resist and overcome the illness through their own will. Thus Hosokawa attributed the stomach flu so prevalent in his section not merely to bad water but "in the final analysis to a slackening of spirit." Such "minor illnesses," he wrote, "must be conquered through spirit."[100] And on one occasion, when the cadets were finally granted a Sunday leave after a long hiatus and Hosokawa found himself feeling "extremely sick," he nevertheless forced himself to walk the two and a half hours to Xinjing Station to join the duty officer and other cadets who were going to a movie.[101]

The point, as Hosokawa wrote time and again, was never to give up, to persevere (*ganbari*) "down to the last five minutes," "to the point of collapse," "to the end"—indeed, "to the very end of the very end" (*saigo no saigo made ganbari*), like the iconic bugler Kiguchi Kohei at the Battle of Sŏnghwan (see Chapter 4).[102] Developing such willpower, Hosokawa frequently noted, was at the core of his masculine identity: "I am a man; I will persevere" (*otoko da; ganbaruzo*).[103] But even more it was at the core of his military identity as a "man among men" (*otoko no naka no otoko*) and the robust, energetic "continental man" (*tairiku otoko*) associated with the Japanese forces in Manchuria.[104]

The Belief in Certain Victory
In April 1944, as Hosokowa, together with Park Chung Hee and other members of the graduating MMA 2/JMA 57 class listened to a commencement address by Yamada Otozō, Inspector General of Military Training, over and

over again they heard Yamada extol the power of "belief in certain victory" (*hisshō no shinnen*).[105] It was a phrase all the cadets knew well. Only a month after they had entered the JMA for the regular course eighteen months earlier, Yamada had used it no fewer than eight times in a lecture following the November 1942 three-school joint exercises.[106] Prime Minister Tōjō Hideki, who addressed the graduating cadets in 1944, invoked it as well.[107] This phrase, which peppered the cadets' diaries, was considered so important by the IJA that it was given its own special section in both the *Field Service Regulations* and the *Infantry Manual,* as well as in the *Field Service Code* (*Senjinkun*) that had been issued under Tōjō's name in 1941 and thereafter distributed to all soldiers called up for active service.[108]

The phrase had first entered the army handbooks in 1928 at a time when Mazaki Jinzaburō, superintendent of the JMA in the late 1920s, and other officers associated with the Imperial Way faction in the army had opposed what they saw as a growing materialism in both military and civilian life.[109] As an antidote to everything from capitalist consumerism to Marxism to a post–World War I emphasis on military technology and firepower, they had championed "spiritual education" (*seishin kyōiku*) not only as a virtue in itself but also as a key to success on the battlefield. Thereafter the "belief in certain victory" became a fixed element of IJA thinking, the final and perhaps most fundamental component in the tactical ideology of the offensive, a belief to sustain the will to advance and attack whatever the battlefield conditions, even against an enemy with overwhelmingly superior weapons. By the 1940s it was not only a topic in all the handbooks but also the subject of educational studies by the army's Inspectorate General and the academic divisions of the military schools.

One such study commissioned as a pedagogical aid for company commanders at the JMAP in 1944 provides a window on how the IJA understood the term. A "belief in certain victory" was essential on the battlefield, the report argued. Only if it was armed with such a conviction would an army in chaotic and desperate circumstances be able to muster the will to concentrate all its knowledge and skill to overpower the enemy. Without it, despairing of any chance of victory, the army would find its will to fight shaken and its strength dissipated.[110]

But how did one inculcate or sustain such a belief, especially in the face of what was a worsening wartime situation, as in the spring of 1944, when the report was being written and the MMA 2/JMA 57 class was preparing to graduate? The answer, according to the authors of the report, depended largely on three things, also laid out in the field manuals, which instructors at the academy were enjoined to emphasize to the cadets under their charge. One was to hold in mind the "glorious history of the army" with its unblemished record of victories, whether over the Mongols in the thirteenth century or more recently over the Russians four decades earlier—what Yamada in his commencement speech had called "the army's tradition of certain victory in a hundred wars."[111] The report also stressed, as did Yamada, that regular IJA training properly carried out and absorbed, not least of all the rushing bayonet charge, would give cadets the skills and confidence to go into battle calmly (*jijaku*) and instinctively (*shinshu kisezu*), heedless of consequences even under the most dire conditions.[112]

The third and most important pillar of the belief in certain victory, however, according to the report, was the attitude and behavior of the commanding officer. Ultimately it was he who had to muster the will to go on in that moment when the situation was at its most extreme, when victory could go either way. It was he, as the axis of command and core of unity, whose belief in certain victory had to be strongest, and it was he who had to demonstrate a firm conviction and will to his adjutants and men both by showing composure in the face of adversity and by setting an example with his own actions by taking the lead in an attack. If he did so, he could rouse his men to victory; if he showed pessimism, hesitation, or indecision, he could destroy the morale of his unit and any chance of victory. Before, after, and between bouts of combat, his role was no less crucial, taking the initiative, preparing for the next battle, grasping the defects of each unit and taking countermeasures, giving praise where praise was due, making sure his subordinates were fully committed, and promoting trust between junior and senior officers and close cooperation based on a clear and common understanding of the group's purpose and goals.[113] Above all, the report concluded, he had "unceasingly to inspire" a belief in certain victory in all under his command, in the tradition of the great samurai warriors such as Uesugi Kenshin and more recently Admiral Tōgō Heihachirō, the naval hero of the Russo-Japanese War, who in response to a question from an Army War College student about his state of mind during battle replied that for him the belief in certain victory had meant not only that "we would inevitably win" but also, for that very reason, "we must never give up."[114]

Kendō as the Embodiment of Tactics and Spirit

While in a sense all education and training at the academies revolved in one way or another around the ideology of the offensive, with its focus on the attack spirit, the power of will, and ultimately a belief in certain victory, there was one activity in particular that epitomized all those ideas and by the 1940s had become virtually synonymous with the much vaunted "spirit" of the Imperial Japanese Army. This was the practice of Japanese swordsmanship or *kendō*.

The traditional aim of the Japanese swordsman had been to disable or kill his opponent with a single, concentrated blow, delivered as quickly and precisely as possible—a goal that had meshed well with Meckel's Prussian tactics of "shock" in the Meiji period, and one that academy section commanders such as Yano Yutaka later identified with Hitler's "lightning strikes" into Poland and Russia. Indeed, the idea of a "single flash of the sword" (*guntō issen*), cleanly and surgically struck deep into the heart of the enemy camp, came to encapsulate for the army the essence not only of *kendō* but of IJA tactics more generally, symbolized historically by Japan's sudden attack on the naval base of Port Arthur in the Russo-Japanese War and later by its surprise attack on the U.S. fleet at Pearl Harbor.[115] Not surprisingly, on December 8, 1941, when Park Chung Hee and the other MMA 2 cadets at Lalatun were informed of Japan's declaration of war against the United States and England, Hosokawa Minoru wrote in his diary that evening not only that the "secret to winning the war" lay in "holding fast to the belief in certain victory" but also that Japan had "finally seized the sword of justice."[116] And Park himself would later describe his May 16 coup d'état as a "sharp sword" (*k'waedo*) to "gouge out" (*ch'ŏkkyŏl*) the evils of society.[117]

To be sure, as combat swordsmanship had evolved into the sport of *kendō* in the Tokugawa and Meiji periods, actual swords had been replaced with bamboo foils (*shinai*) and contestants were clothed in protective head and body gear.[118] But offense and attack continued to define the practice; no points were ever awarded in a *kendō* match for defense. This was true of European fencing as well, but unlike the latter, where strikes were sometimes counted wherever they touched the body, points in *kendō* were given only for strikes in specifically targeted parts of the body—head, chest, forearm, and throat—whose impact in actual battle would have been debilitating or lethal. Also unlike its European counterpart, scoring in *kendō* took into account the practitioner's state of mind. It was not enough simply to strike in the right place. The strike had to be carried out with what referees judged to be a sufficiently robust attack spirit (*seme*) and exclamation (*kiai*) that signified the attacker's total concentration of will and energy. After the strike, moreover, the attacker had to exhibit an attitude and posture of calm but heightened alertness (*zanshin*) that indicated his readiness for a possible counterattack from his stricken opponent. A strike, however well executed physically, would not be counted if the proper spirit was deemed to be lacking.[119]

Koreans as well as Japanese entering the academies in the 1940s were already well acquainted with the basics of *kendō*. It had been introduced to Korea from Japan as early as the last decade of the nineteenth century, and as war loomed ever more threateningly after 1931, it had become a fixture in both countries' secondary school systems and sports competitions. It was, moreover, the only activity in the physical education curriculum that was taught in combination with an accompanying academic course, reflecting the view, particularly prevalent in the military, that *kendō* was more a mental and philosophical practice than a purely physical sport—the heart and soul, as it were, of traditional warrior culture. *Kendō* was certainly not to all Koreans' liking, especially during the war years, when it tended to become an icon of Japanese militarism and a required component of Japan's project to promote the "imperialization" of its Korean subjects.[120] Nevertheless, it continued to find adherents among Korean students, not least of all Park Chung Hee, who, as we saw in Chapter 3, was known among his classmates at Taegu Normal School for his passion for the sport. However, neither Park nor any of the other cadets coming into the academies in the 1940s, regardless of nationality, would have been fully prepared for the dedication with which the IJA embraced and practiced *kendō* at the schools.

First there was the frequency of the practice. *Kendō* figured prominently in academy athletic meets, such as those held at the MMA on September 18, the anniversary of the Japanese invasion of Manchuria, and it was also an integral feature of the commencement exercises at Lalatun.[121] But behind such events lay a regular regimen of instruction and practice. Every day after classes and before the evening meal at both the MMA and the JMA an hour was set aside for athletics.[122] Although other sports, including gymnastics and *jūdō*, were a standard part of the program, *kendō* tended to dominate the hour, and, as was the case in imperial secondary schools, *kendō* at the preparatory (*yoka*) level was also taught in the classroom as part of the regular academic curriculum.[123] In addition to the daily athletics, cadets at both schools were allotted an hour of "free time," where they could theoretically pursue "voluntary" activities, in the evening following dinner at the MMA and immediately after the athletics period at the JMA. But as Park Chung Hee's less than zealous MMA 2 Chinese classmate Gao Qingyin told me, the free time was not really free. It was actually supervised by other cadets under instructions from the section commanders, and almost invariably it meant another hour of *kendō:* in Gao's words, "Every day *kendō,* every day!"[124] Indeed, one of the axioms by which the MMA 2 cadets were expected to live, reproduced in bold letters by Hosokawa in his diary, was "to seize the sword in moments of leisure."[125]

Apart from the tactical and psychic significance the IJA attached to the sword and bayonet, the stress on *kendō* in the daily regimen was a product of section commanders' own enthusiasm for the sport, which they made every attempt to pass on to their subordinates and charges. At the JMA, where most of the commanders were only a few years out of the academy themselves, they often enjoyed challenging and competing against the cadets during practice and athletic meets. Takayama Toshitake, the commander of the 3rd Section of MMA 2 at the JMA, for example, had been on his *kendō* team in middle school and gone on in his JMA years to attain the second rank *(dan).* Back at the JMA five years later as a section commander, he managed to achieve the fourth rank, and he later wrote how much he had relished the *kendō* periods as an instructor at the school and taken pride in the fact that none of the MMA 2 cadets had ever been able to defeat him in a match.[126]

The frequency of *kendō* practice at the schools was exceeded only by its intensity. As one MMA graduate noted, the nature of the *kendō* training at the academies was entirely different from what Japanese and Koreans had experienced in middle school. *Kendō* practice at the academies had reverted to its original purpose. As in bayonet instruction, with which it was often paired in training, the purpose was once again to teach cadets how to kill, and proper form was considered less important than the sheer strength and ferocity a cadet brought to a match.[127] "Confidence in swordsmanship meant strength on the battlefield," Hosokawa noted in his diary, quoting his section commander.[128] One of Park Chung Hee's MMA 2 classmates, Origuchi Ryūzō, was even blunter: "Even in the first two years we had to practice so much in order to learn how to kill someone. We had to do it every morning and night. Everybody got to the first rank whether they liked it or not."[129] And while actually killing an opposing classmate was of course not a viable option, the cadets were encouraged, indeed pressured, to attack and strike as fiercely as possible short of permanently disabling their opponents. Section commanders saw their role in no small part as eradicating any signs of what they considered effete "middle school" student *kendō* techniques, even to the point of encouraging the cadets to make "cutting attacks" *(zangeki).*[130] The *kendō* instructors themselves were no less severe. Gao Qingyin retained a vivid memory of Kuwahara Ryōichi, with whom he and Park Chung Hee trained at the MMA. Kuwahara, a native of Fukui, was a graduate of the Mukden CTS and already a sixth-rank master by the time he was posted to MMA as a *kendō* instructor. His eyes, Gao remembered, would "bulge wildly like an ox" and he would often beat the cadets mercilessly on the head with his bamboo sword.[131]

With their mentors and teachers setting so brutal a tone, the cadets themselves took to brandishing their *shinai* against each other with equal vehemence. According to Gao, the cadets who supervised the daily *kendō* practice, not only the upperclassmen counselor cadets (*shidō seito*) but also the rotating weekly duty cadets (*torishimari seito*), who were themselves members of the MMA 2 class, would regularly beat poorly performing fellow cadets on the head as if they were "herding sheep."[132] For Chinese cadets like Gao, most of whom had had no previous *kendō* training, practice with their Japanese and Korean peers at the academy was an especially harsh and humiliating ordeal. Gao had tended to accept it all with resignation and a sense of humor, but many of his Chinese classmates had not.[133] Fifty years after the fact, Bai Guohua still smoldered as he recalled the continuous "vicious" stabs to his arm and abdomen he had received from an MMA 2 Korean classmate, Kim Chaep'ung, one of which had finally cut through his chest protector and knocked him down, battered and humbled, to the ground.[134] Another MMA 2 Chinese cadet, Wu Zongfang, had been so mortified in *kendō* practice and angry at the "arrogant" attitude of the more experienced Japanese cadets that he had inserted a strip of iron in his four-ply bamboo sword and exercised with it daily to increase his arm strength, finally gaining satisfaction when he was able to strike a Japanese cadet so forcefully directly in his face helmet that he nearly passed out.[135]

For the Japanese and Korean cadets, including Park Chung Hee, who, though small of stature, was known among his classmates for his defiant "big mountain" stance and "thunderous" *kendō* shout when he attacked an opponent, the transition to combat *kendō* may have been less of a challenge, but it was still no less violent.[136] In addition to the daily rounds of savage practice, the weekly duty officer might suddenly announce an "emergency muster" in the middle of the night, in which one designated section on a rotating basis would be pitted hopelessly against all the others in an aggressive free-for-all *kendō* match that left few unbruised. In one such match at the MMA in the fall of 1941, for example, when Iwai Masatoshi (MMA 2) in defense lay down on his face after having his *shinai* knocked out of his hand and his mask ripped off in the attack, his classmates from the other sections continued to beat him on the back with their own *shinai* until the match

ended and he was completely covered in welts.[137] Such punishing strikes in
kendō often split the joined foils at the tip of the *shinai*, giving it the appearance of an outsized *sasara*, the bamboo tea whisk used in Japanese tea ceremonies, and it is one indication of the fierceness with which the sport was
practiced at the academies that in the common parlance of the cadets *kendō*
was known as *sasara-odori,* or the "dance of the *sasara.*"[138]

Intensity in the Final Years of War

It is important to point out that the intensity of *kendō* practice at the academies in the 1940s, and indeed of all military training during that period,
was enormously heightened by the sense of urgency and desperation that
characterized the last years of World War II in Japan and its empire. The
MMA of course had been founded in the aftermath of Japan's Manchurian
invasion and the Kwantung Army's violent "pacification" of the country,
and also with an eye to assisting the latter in keeping the Soviet Union in
check (see Chapter 3). By the time the MMA 1 class entered in 1939, internal
rebellion was less serious a threat, but Chinese (and to a lesser degree
Korean) communist guerrillas continued to be a source of concern for
Japanese forces (see Chapter 6), and the decisive defeat of Kwantung Army
units by the Soviets at Nomonhan that same year had stirred new anxieties
about Soviet intentions and Japan's military preparedness. Two years later,
when the Germans invaded the Soviet Union in June 1941, a crisis atmosphere took hold within the Kwantung Army that colored the training at
the MMA as well, especially for Park Chung Hee's MMA 2 class, which at
that time was in the middle of its preparatory (*yoka*) course at Lalatun.[139]
And at both the MMA and the JMA, the continuing war in China since
1937 had led not only to a dramatic increase in the number of cadets and a
shortening of the term times by two to three months but also to an even
greater emphasis on the physical and spiritual conditioning of the cadets,
the nonacademic or *kun'iku* component of training that even in peacetime
had always been given a somewhat heavier weight in the cadet's final class
ranking.[140]

All these changes paled, however, in comparison to the intensification of
academy education that occurred after the outbreak of war with the United
States in December 1941. According to one MMA 1 graduate, the attack on
Pearl Harbor changed everything, "taking the intensity of daily training to
another level."[141] In their combined preparatory and regular courses at

Lalatun and Zama, moreover, the MMA 1 and MMA 2 classes in particular felt the brunt of their schools' increasing anxiety, as the victories of December 1941 gave way to successive military defeats. As Major Enami Shigeru, company commander of the Manchukuo cadets at Zama, later wrote, when the MMA 2 class entered the JMA in October 1942, Japan was advancing all over Asia, but soon thereafter came the loss of Guadalcanal (February 1943), the death of Admiral Yamamoto Isoroku (April 1943), the destruction of Japanese forces on the Aleutian island of Attu (May 1943), and the first fire-bombings of Tokyo (November 1944). All of these events except the last had taken place while Park Chung Hee's MMA 2 class was in training at the JMA.[142]

As Japan's position in the war worsened and its fundamental weaknesses in material resources and firepower became ever more apparent and worrying, the IJA turned more and more to the ideas of "will," "attack spirit," and the "belief in certain victory" as the army's unique and ultimate assets to overcome all obstacles. Hence Inspector General Yamada's repeated iterations of these ideas in his MMA 2/JMA 57 commencement address at Zama at the end of April 1944, at the very moment when, in struggling to counter the Allied forces' Burma Campaign in India, the IJA was about to experience its largest defeat to date. It is not surprising, then, that a year later, when concern about troop morale reached a new peak in the wake of Hitler's death and Germany's unconditional surrender, the inspector general's office produced for academy pedagogical use a paper entitled "The German Defeat and the Belief in Certain Victory." In addition to restating now familiar shibboleths about the inevitable end of Western capitalism and communism and a historic shift to Asia with Japan at its center, the authors of the paper blamed Germany's defeat not only on its two-front war but above all on its reliance on science and material strength, as seen in the hope it had placed in its V1 and V2 rockets. In contrast to the German case, the "secret weapon" of the IJA was its "spiritual power," passed down from time immemorial. Therefore Germany's defeat, the paper concluded, was an opportunity to "renew resolve" and to "firm up the belief in certain victory."[143]

As victory became ever less certain, however, the IJA and academy instructors pushed the cadets to ever more fervent applications of will and spirit, exemplified, as seen above, by the weekly duty officer who ordered a company of JMA 57 cadets to dive headfirst into the frozen Sagami River. Eventually, when it became only too clear that the Japanese empire had little left with which to continue fighting except the bodies of its young soldiers, cadets were told to think of the will to advance and fight essentially as a will to die, an ultimate form of will training that focused on overcoming the fear of death.[144] The idea of sacrifice *pro patria* was of course not unique to IJA culture. One thinks of the line from Horace declaring that "it is sweet and fitting to die for your country," or the mural by John Singer Sargent in Harvard's Widener Library celebrating the university's students who, "happy . . . with that glowing faith/in one embrace clasped death and victory" in World War I.[145] Within the IJA as well such sentiments had always been present throughout its history, assuming special prominence after hostilities broke out between Japan and China in 1937. When Park Chung Hee had written to the MMA in 1939 asking for special consideration in admission, for example, he was only following what had then already become a wartime linguistic convention by pledging "to die for the greater good" (*isshi gohōkō*). Still, the early 1940s, and especially the final years of the war, were different and more intense than the earlier years, as the jubilation of Pearl Harbor gradually changed to the despondency and desperation of Guadalcanal. By the time Park graduated from the JMA a year after Guadalcanal, the will to die had become embedded and aestheticized in IJA culture far more deeply than ever before. It was also buttressed in the larger society by a thoroughly militarized educational system and an equally militarized popular culture, where what Peter High denotes as "spiritist" films such as *Navy* (*Kaigun*) and *Army* (*Rikugun*), sponsored by the military, featured extreme close-ups of fictional cadets listening intently to their instructors' exhortations of self-sacrifice with "eyes of fanatical determination."[146]

While such films greatly idealized and romanticized military life at the academies and in actual service, "spiritist" instruction at the schools was in fact both pervasive and insistent. Of all the *Hagakure*'s famous dictums that cadets studied in the 1940s, from those expressing contempt for commerce and profit calculation to those celebrating resolution, attack, and joy in battle, the one they encountered most frequently was from the first page of the book's opening chapter, enjoining them to remember that "the way of the warrior [*bushidō*] is to be found in death."[147] General Nogi Maresuke, a perennial hero at the schools for his refusal during the Russo-Japanese War to abandon his assault on Port Arthur whatever the costs, was now, in these last years of Japan's "Greater East Asia" war, celebrated as much or more for his "pure and selfless" suicidal "martyrdom" on the death of the Meiji emperor as for his unyielding tactics of attack.[148] And instructors at the wartime academies were now advised to explain the "belief in certain victory" to their cadets as a "belief in certain death." Not that they would necessarily die, the cadets were to be told, but if they wished in the end to secure victory, and possibly their lives as well, the only way was to transcend their anxieties about death and to go into battle fearlessly, without any expectation of personal survival. "Resolve to die, and you will live; resolve to live, and you will die," a traditional saying attributed in Japan to the sixteenth-century warrior Uesugi Kenshin, was to be their guiding principle on the battlefield; it was later frequently quoted and calligraphed by Park Chung Hee,.[149]

Such "spiritist" maxims were the cadets' daily fare in the 1940s, literally from the moment they entered the academies to the day they left. One MMA 7 Japanese cadet recalled his "shock" (dokittoshite) soon after arriving at Lalatun when the weekly duty officer walked into the self-study room one evening and ordered him and his classmates to make out their wills and to place them, together with clippings of their hair and fingernails, in an envelope for safekeeping in their desk drawers.[150] Another cadet in the JMA 57 class was startled soon after matriculation at Zama when his section commander told him and his classmates to forget any aspirations they might have had of becoming a general: they should aim instead, he told them, to die in battle as a second lieutenant.[151] At the height of the Guadalcanal fighting at the end of 1942, shortly after the MMA 2 class had arrived at Zama and the MMA 1 class was preparing to graduate, section commander "Carbon" Sakai, never one to mince words, bluntly told the MMA cadets that their duty was nothing more or less than "to become a corpse."[152] And when Park Chung Hee and other members of the MMA2/JMA57 graduating class listened to Inspector General Yamada urge them toward a "belief in certain victory," they also heard him add that it would be a victory "soaked in blood" (chimidoro no). Victory would require, Yamada continued, that they emulate the example of Colonel Yamasaki Yasuyo, the Japanese commander at the Battle of Attu, who less than a year before had led his men on an all-but-hopeless final banzai charge against an astonished contingent of American troops, penetrating the enemy lines by his boldness, but in the end leaving virtually all of the Japanese men and officers, including Yamasaki himself, dead on the field.[153]

Removed in time and space and prone to the greater cynicism of our own age, we may find it easy and tempting to regard such will-to-die injunctions as little more than overblown, hackneyed rhetoric of questionable sincerity and little impact. But that would be a mistake. The moment was dire, and the officers, however misguided one may judge them to have been, were, perhaps more often than we can imagine, deadly serious. Colonel Yamasaki, a graduate of the JMA 25th class, had indeed led a suicidal banzai charge on Attu. Only eight months after the MMA 2 commencement, Park Chung Hee's section commander, Tahara Kōzō, as we have seen, would volunteer for what he surely knew or suspected was a one-way posting to Leyte. And five months after that, the JMA superintendent himself, Ushijima Mitsuru, who had shared the MMA 2 commencement dais with Tōjō and Yamada and had bid the graduates a "grand farewell," entreating them literally "to smash bone and body" (*funkotsu-saishin*) to honor the Sōbudai name, would, like Park Chung Hee's former TNS drill instructor, Arikawa Shuichi, commit ritual suicide rather than surrender to American forces on Okinawa.[154]

Given the atmosphere that enveloped them, it is not surprising that many cadets took their instructors' words to heart. On the night of the MMA 2 (*yoka*) graduation at Lalatun, Hosokawa Minoru, reflecting back on his months of preparatory training and contemplating his future in the infantry branch into which he would soon be formally inducted, wrote that "there was nothing more ennobling for a soldier than to die for the emperor" and, echoing the *Hagakure,* that he must now "go forward in the way of the warrior, the way of death" (*bujin no michi, shi no michi*). He would, Hosokawa vowed, renew his effort, with the fixed purpose of turning himself into a "human bullet."[155] In the end Hosokawa would survive the war, but almost a quarter of the combined MMA 2/JMA 57 class of Zama would not, including two of the seven Korean cadets.[156]

It is impossible to know for sure to what extent, if at all, the former MMA 2/JMA 57 cadets who perished during the war, or even their peers who survived, had embraced the will-to-die dogma of the academies. For the Chinese and Koreans especially, with their sense of ethnic difference or even separate nationalist sensibility, the emperor was certainly less of a potent symbol for self-sacrifice than he was for their Japanese classmates such as Hosokawa (see Chapter 3). But even Yi Hyŏnggŭn (JMA 56), a Korean who remembered the confusion he had felt on his first day of cadet life when the superintendent of the JMAP had told him and his classmates that the school was a place "to teach the young men of the Japanese empire how to die for the emperor," would also describe his years at the academy as "a thorough-going education in the life-and-death philosophy of the Japanese army."[157] Whatever their national backgrounds, whatever their feelings about dying for the emperor, all of the cadets had undergone one of the most sustained, intense, and arguably effective experiences in will training that any twentieth-century institution had to offer. At the conclusion of my interviews with former MMA/JMA cadets, I invariably asked each what had been the most impressive and enduring lesson or legacy of his academy experience. In Tokyo, Seoul, Changchun, or elsewhere, the answer was always more or less the same: "The will to endure, no matter how severe the situation"; "The confidence to face any difficulty."[158] Even Xu Shudong (MMA 2), who had hated the MMA and had found Park Chung Hee's displays of will training there excessive, admitted that one good thing he had gained from the experience was the capacity "to keep on doing whatever I had to do, never to give up, and always to complete the task before me."[159]

In the case of Park Chung Hee, the will training regimen at the academies seems to have touched something deep in his psyche; he would later write that his "conviction and will" to lead the 1961 coup had been nurtured in the "environment of the army."[160] Those who knew him would not have disagreed. Time and again his former classmates, regardless of nationality, would recall instances of what Yi Hallim (MMA 2) called his "willpower and tenacity," his "dislike of giving in to anyone else."[161] Among those who knew this best were the MMA 1 Korean cadets, who constantly monitored and tested their MMA 2 juniors at the academy (see Chapter 3) and who would later provide the core military backing for the coup. When I once asked one of them, Pang Wŏnch'ŏl, why he and other Korean MMA 1 classmates in the ROKA had decided to follow Park's leadership in 1961, he replied without hesitation that they not only had agreed with his criticism of the existing South Korean government but, equally important, knew that Park had "the will [ŭiji] and ambition [yasim] to carry it off."[162] After the May 16 coup, that same will and ambition, tempered to no small degree in the tactical crucibles of the IJA at Lalatun and Zama, would become an essential part of the South Korean state's tactics of "modernization."

EIGHT

ORDER AND DISCIPLINE

Joyful Submission

When Caesar says "Do this," it is performed.
—William Shakespeare, *Julius Caesar*

For cadets there was only one way: to say "Yes! Yes!" and obey the order.
—Matsui Shigeru, MMA 1/JMA 56

Binta education is the best way to strengthen an army.
—Park Chung Hee, November 12, 1961

If it was an aggressive and confident "can-do" will that drove the Park Chung Hee state, it was the state's disciplinary regime that in the end implemented and enforced that will. As noted earlier, the Park government had a visceral, historically rooted distaste for unfettered capitalism, and this orientation ensured, in the words of economist Alice Amsden, that "discipline by the state over private enterprise was part and parcel of the vision that drove the state to industrialize."[1] But the disciplinary reach of the state would eventually range far beyond private enterprise, an aspiration toward which Park himself had hinted on his first official day as chairman of the military junta's Supreme Council for National Reconstruction in July 1961, only two months after seizing power. "While citizens are free and natural persons," Park had said, "they are simultaneously members of the state and society, and there are times when their fundamental rights must naturally be restricted by the demands of state and society."[2] Ultimately those restrictions would extend deeply into politics, society, culture, and everyday life, especially during the state's final, most authoritarian incarnation, the Yusin (Yushin) structure that Park adopted in 1972 to carry out his national goals within "a total security posture as impregnable as a steel drum."[3]

Park's images of "total security" and an "impregnable steel drum" capture well the "garrison state" atmosphere of 1970s South Korea, which fused the discipline of economic development with the discipline of national security.[4] But the state's discipline of development was never envisioned merely, or even primarily, as negative or punitive. Ideally the aim was to achieve a form of what Foucault has termed "governmentality" and "bio-power," in which the subject population has absorbed or been so deeply conditioned mentally and physically in the ends and means of the regime as to embrace them as "truth"—what Antonio Gramsci might have called "common sense."[5] Thus conditioned, the populace could potentially serve as a kind of "coproducer" in the achievement of the government's goals, eager and willing, as it were, to "work toward the Führer," in Ian Kershaw's memorable description of policy implementation in Hitler's Third Reich.[6] Of course, if despite everything one failed to internalize and embrace the state's objectives and methods as one's own, or worse, demonstrated any form of active opposition to them, the consequences could be punishing in mind and body, whether in Nazi Germany or in Park's Korea. Coproduction was always the hope and expectation of developmental discipline, but violence was always a possibility, a last resort in the wake of noncompliance, or of waning enthusiasm or efficiency.

In these combined disciplinary ideas of coproduction and punishment one finds yet another military template linking the South Korean state of the Park Chung Hee era to the education and training that Park and other MMA/JMA graduates received in the 1940s. Like the tactical perspectives previously discussed, the disciplinary practices to which the cadets were subjected at Lalatun and Zama were an integral part of their everyday lives. Psychologists today would generally agree that people who undergo such experiences in their formative years often tend later to reprise those behaviors, even unconsciously. Because the disciplinary regimen discussed here also involved both physical and also psychic violence and pain, often on a daily basis over the course of several years, it became arguably one of the most deeply ingrained and enduring aspects of the military culture that infused the South Korean modernization project. "Pain," as Nietzsche once observed, "is the most powerful aid to mnemonics."[7]

The Order and Regulation of Everyday Life

Discipline at the academies began with the order and regulation of everyday life. This was of course something that Koreans entering Lalatun and Zama in the late 1930s and 1940s, as well as their Japanese counterparts, already knew well. All had experienced a strictly ordered institutional life since their primary school days, an experience that had only intensified once the war had broken out and the imperial education system, like everything else in

society, had become increasingly militarized. And among the most militarized of the schools in Korea in this period, as noted earlier, were the teacher-
training colleges, such as the one in Taegu from which Park Chung Hee had
graduated. But as in the case of Park's favorite sport of *kendō,* which he first
learned at Taegu Normal School, the order and arrangement of everyday life
at the academies was at an "entirely different" level from that of the civilian
schools. As the cadets learned on their first day and were continually reminded thereafter, their daily lives were to be rigorously governed by the
Regulations (*Kokoroe*), the uncompromising handbook for cadets, which
prescribed in succinct but minute detail how every aspect of life at the academies was to be lived from reveille to taps. Regarded at the schools as the
"guidebook for the cultivation of army officers," the *Kokoroe* was the fount of
discipline from which everything else flowed, and the "degree of perfection"
attained by each cadet in meeting its stringent demands was seen as a testimony to that cadet's *majime* attitude, as well as to his moral strength as an
aspiring officer.[8]

Basic to the *Kokoroe* regimen of daily life at the academies was the discipline of time. At both the MMA (*yoka*) and JMA (*honka*) the cadets followed
a meticulous daily schedule divided into units of hours and minutes, with
even short periods of rest and optional activities specifically written into the
timetable, and with all the main activities of the day punctuated by the blare
of a bugle. At the MMA the days began at 0500 and ended with the lights
extinguished at 2130. Mornings were taken up with roll call, personal hygiene, care of weapons and other items, barracks cleanup, breakfast, and self-
study in the study hall attached to the barracks, followed by inspections of
dress, equipment, and sleeping quarters, the first classes of the day, and
lunch. Classes resumed in the afternoons, followed by sports activities, free
time, and supper. Evenings were devoted largely to another round of self-
study, after which came the night roll call and sleep.[9] At the JMA, there was a
greater emphasis on military science and specific branch training, but the
schedule there was otherwise much the same as at the MMA, and equally
demanding.[10] As Isobe Kei (MMA 1) put it: "Between rising and sleeping, the
daily schedule at the JMA was organized with virtually no breaks; there was
almost no time for oneself, or for taking care of one's bodily needs."[11]

So exact and relentless a daily schedule was designed to accustom the
cadets to the routines of army life and to keep them focused on their commitment to becoming an officer without undue distractions. But one of the
main disciplinary challenges of the schedule for the cadets was simply to
keep to the appointed times. Many things could go wrong, and often did, as

they rushed from one scheduled activity to another, sometimes at considerable distance and usually with only minutes to spare. Being present and seated at one's desk on time for the morning and evening self-study sessions could be especially taxing, as the cadets were hard-pressed in the morning to get themselves, their equipment, and their barracks all in order in the allotted time before self-study, and equally hard-pressed in the evening to get back to their barracks on time from an activity in some other part of the school. And sudden changes of schedule announced by the weekly duty officer or unannounced emergency musters, frequently in the middle of the night, presented the cadets with additional tests of making the roll call or reaching the designated venue on time. Invariably, to keep the cadets alert and quick, orders for such activities were deliberately issued only minutes before they were required to assemble (*shūgō*) in front of the barracks in appropriate dress and gear.[12]

Keeping to the schedule, however, was only the first and most fundamental of the cadets' disciplinary challenges. As Isobe (MMA 1) suggested, there was little time in a day for the cadets to take care of their bodily needs, yet they were required to keep their hair clipped razor-close to the head and their bodies clean, even though the bath, for example, was open only for limited periods of time in the evening. It was really only during the hour of "free time" (*zuii jikan*) at the end of each day when the cadets could conceivably have a bath, but even that hour was often circumscribed or devoted to additional training (see Chapter 7). At Lalatun the cadets were fortunate, according to Yoshida Katsusuke (MMA 7), if they could manage to visit the bath at least two times a week.[13] And as Hosokawa Minoru (MMA 2) indicated in his diary, the weekly duty commanders could even impose restrictions on when the cadets could go to the toilet: Hosokawa's section was forbidden to do so, for example, during the gymnastic exercises that usually followed roll call in the morning.[14]

Certain bodily movements and activities were also regulated. Kim Muk (MMA 2) and other former cadets interviewed complained decades later about always having to move in double-time, essentially a measured run, from one place to another during the day, and about restrictions on sitting, apart from study and mess.[15] In the barracks especially, cadets could never sit or lie down except when sleeping, and even then, each had to place his body on his sleeping mat in such a way that the direction of his head and feet was always opposite to that of the cadet lying to his right or left in the same row.[16] In class, cadets were required to sit attentively, spine straight, always maintaining a "solemn" demeanor, with clenched fists resting on their knees, a posture that was deemed manly and martial, as well as respectful to the instructor.[17] They could take notes only when specifically told to do so, and they signaled if they had questions by raising a fist.[18] When queried by an instructor, they had to rise immediately from their seat and answer loudly and clearly, standing rigidly erect, arms at their sides.[19]

Eating and singing, both everyday activities at the schools, were highly ritualistic. At the MMA mess hall, for example, the cadets filed in by company (*ren*) and took up their chopsticks only after the appointed company duty cadet had read aloud a black-ink maxim posted on the wall to the left of the entrance that gave thanks for the food being received and acknowledged the officers and men on the front lines who might not be so fortunate.[20] And the rules of singing stipulated not only that the cadets sing as loudly and forcefully as possible in what was deemed the proper masculine and soldierly way, but also that they adopt a certain posture: legs apart, with the right hand resting on hip and the left hand holding the songbook at eye level. If they sang without songbooks, they were to rest both hands on their hips.[21] There was, in fact, a proper way of doing everything at the academies, as the cadets quickly learned upon entering, even in such mundane activities as washing, brushing one's teeth, flushing the toilet, and cleaning boots. As Hiruma Hiroshi (JMA 57) noted, even in case of the simple and natural act of gargling, the cadets in his section were given precise instructions and demonstrations by the section commander himself.[22] In the morning and evening self-study halls, which, as another cadet (MMA 7) remembered, provided one of the few opportunities for the "occasional daydream," the cadets when reading were expected to sit rigidly straight in traditional samurai mode, and for that purpose were provided with a book rest (*kendai*) to keep their reading material at eye level.[23]

In the daily tyranny of rules and regulations at the academies probably nothing was more demanding than what might be called the discipline of things. The key word here was *seiton,* a common term in Japanese meaning "order" or "arrangement," but one that signified for the cadets an all-encompassing system and mentality, with respect to which they were instructed, monitored, occasionally praised, and usually berated nearly every day. Suffice it to say that almost every entry in Hosokawa's MMA 2 diary contained some kind of *seiton* admonition from the section commander or weekly duty officer, if not always the actual word itself.

Seiton was of course essential to military life. The correct care and placement of things ensured that whatever the conditions in which an officer might find himself, including total blackness, he would be able to locate and make use of what he needed, whether it was a gun, a flashlight, a pen, or something else.[24] At the academies, however, a cadet's regard for and attention to *seiton* was also seen as a sign of his general attitude and commitment toward duty and discipline and of his future professional life as an officer, and the *seiton* regimen was for that reason particularly strict and onerous. Indeed, it would not be an exaggeration to say that it bordered on the obsessive.

At the core of the *seiton* regimen was the care and cleaning of military arms. Cadets were roundly scolded and punished, for example, for not taking proper care of their "honorable Type 38 infantry rifle" (*san-pachi shiki hoheijū dono*).[25] Weapons were the "soul of a soldier" (*gunjin no tamashii*), as Hosokawa's company commander, Kanno Hiroshi, had told the MMA 2 Japanese cadets at a conferral-of-ordnance ceremony (*heiki ju-yoshiki*) during their first week at Lalatun, and Hosokawa had dutifully vowed in his diary that night that he would always make a "commendable" effort, for "rust on our guns is the same as rust on our souls."[26] But the daily task of keeping the guns polished and in good working order was painstaking and arduous work, especially after practice in foul weather. And as Park Chung Hee later discovered when he was temporarily put under arrest at the JMA for allowing his gun to be damaged in a field exercise, failure to take proper care of one's "soul" was regarded as a serious lapse of discipline, even when, as in Park's case, there were mitigating circumstances (see Chapter 6).

Guns, however, were only one of the many things that claimed the cadets' attention in the daily routine of *seiton*. Morning was a special challenge. If they had not been able to use some of their limited free time the day before to clean their guns and other weapons, they had to do it the following day in the half hour or so allotted for "interior administration" (*naimu*) between morning roll call and self-study. But time was short and interior administration was long, involving much more than the care of weapons. Everything in the barracks had to be cleaned, including tables and floors.[27] And in what was the most exacting of task of all, each cadet's bedding, dress, gear, and numerous other accoutrements of academy life had to be precisely folded (with measured lengths, widths, and creases) or otherwise arranged before being shelved or arranged in a designated place within his sleeping area—all as set forth and graphically illustrated in the *Kokoroe,* with no fewer than nineteen specific rules for cadets at the preparatory (*yoka*) level and eighteen for those at the higher or regular (*honka*) level.[28] Whether it was sheets, blankets, and pillows on the bed or slippers underneath, whether it was clothes on the shelves, boots in the box, or belts and other objects on hooks, everything had to be unerringly ordered and positioned according to the regulations.[29] A slightly wrinkled blanket on the bed or a loose string dangling from a pair of underpants (*fundoshi*) on the shelf was totally unacceptable, as Hosokawa (MMA 2) and Hiruma (JMA 57) learned early on in their academy years.[30]

Everything in the sleeping area had to be intact, fully functional, and spotless. Included in the *Kokoroe,* in fact, was a chart detailing for the cadets how frequently they had to launder each article of their bedding or clothing at different times of the year. These ranged from regular fatigues (once every two months) and blanket slips (once every six months) to pillowcases and collars (both twice a month from May through October, once a month from November through April). Additional items mentioned were bedsheets (twice a month), athletic clothes (twice a month), winter fatigues (once every two months), extra fatigues (once every three months), summer dress (once a month), and, not least of all, underwear, which the *Kokoroe* specified should be washed three times a month from November through April but otherwise four times a month—except for the hot and humid months of July, August, and September, when the washing times should be doubled to eight.[31] Needless to say, dirty clothes were not to be stored with clean clothes on the shelves, another rule driven home to Hiruma (JMA 57) by a reprimand when he was still a new cadet.[32]

Seiton was by no means limited to the section (*kutai*) sleeping quarters. The cadets were also responsible every morning for cleaning any areas assigned to the company (*ren/chūtai*) to which their sections were attached, as well as their classrooms and self-study halls.[33] And the study halls, like the sleeping quarters, presented yet another *seiton* trial for the cadets. As with the latter, the *Kokoroe* provided detailed descriptions and sketches of the placement of every object that was to be found on a cadet's self-study desk: large books and documents on the flat surface of the elevated front shelf; dictionaries, notebooks, and textbooks in the alcove immediately below—and in a fixed order from left to right; a movable book rest for reading in the center of a large, thick desk pad; a paperweight, a bottle of Athena (J: Atena) fountain-pen ink and a container for India ink in the upper right-hand corner of the desk pad, flush to the edge of the pad—again in a fixed order from left to right; an ink stone, also flush to the right edge of the desk pad and centered just in front of the inks and paperweight; and, finally, the cadet's hat and portable briefcase on a hook below the left side of the desk top.[34] Desks used in the classrooms were simpler in design, basically a flat surface having no shelves or slots for books and other materials, but they too required a proper arrangement of objects when the cadets were present. This varied somewhat, depending on whether the desk was single- or double-seated, but in any case the placement of name plates, the elliptical writing cases (*hittō*), ink, briefcases, and hats was always something to which the cadets had to be attentive.[35] A famous story passed down from class to class at the JMA told of a cadet who had been taken to task in self-study hall by an inspecting officer for placing a bottle of Athena ink with the head of the goddess, the ink's logo, facing in the wrong direction—left rather than right, as stipulated in the *Kokoroe*, according to the officer. In fact, there was no such stipulation in the *Kokoroe*, and it would have been impossible in any case to correct the error, since the logo was designed with the goddess facing left. But for the cadets, as Hiruma Hiroshi (JMA 57) observed, this well-known story was a reminder and a caution about the unchallengeable *seiton* regimen and its excessive focus on "minute detail," even in the somewhat less formal setting of the study hall.[36]

Obedience and Hierarchy

The *seiton* regime of the academies was designed to incorporate disciplinary practices into the most mundane aspects of everyday life, making them in effect natural and routine. It was not surprising, then, as Hosokawa (MMA 2) noted in his diary, that his weekly duty officer's first "notice" (*chūi*) to the entering cadets at Lalatun was an injunction to "maintain *seiton* in both the sleeping quarters and self-study rooms."[37] But *seiton* had another disciplinary purpose as well: to teach "the virtue of obedience" (*fukujū no bitoku*), a phrase that Hosokawa, and indeed all the assembled cadets of the MMA, had heard that same morning in the welcoming remarks of MMA officials.[38]

Obedience lies at the core of any modern military organization, but, as in the case of its tactical preference for the offensive, the Imperial Japanese Army had historically adopted what was an extreme form of the idea in Europe and turned it into a canonical imperative. Once again the roots of this phenomenon can be traced back to Yamagata Aritomo's veneration for the Prussian army, and the influence of Major Klemens Wilhelm Jakob Meckel, the Prussian officer who had been brought over to Japan to help train the new Meiji army in the late nineteenth century. As noted in Chapter 7, even in an age of increasingly deadly long-range rifles, Meckel had remained an ardent advocate of decisive battle based on aggressive, close-order infantry tactics, and it was these tactics, more reminiscent of the armies of Frederick the Great than of his own changing contemporary German army, that he taught to his Japanese students. To sustain such suicidal infantry assaults, he stressed to an almost fanatical degree the importance of maintaining "the strictest discipline grounded in absolute obedience" (*strengsten Mannszucht, gegründet auf unbedingten Gehorsam*), even suggesting that the combination of an offensive spirit and tactics rooted in the discipline of "blind obedience" (*der Gehorsam blind*) could in the end triumph over the new firepower.[39]

Meckel's emphasis on "absolute obedience" (*unbedingten Gehorsam*) became a fundamental tenet of Japanese army training and barracks life. It was enshrined in the second cardinal precept of the 1882 Imperial Rescript to Soldiers and Sailors (Gunjin Chokuyu) that focused on the proper relationship (*reigi*) between military superiors and inferiors and was incorporated into all the major army protocols, including the IJA *Field Service Regulations*, the *Infantry Manual*, and the *Interior Administration Handbook* (*Naimusho*). The phraseology varied slightly from text to text, but in the popular lexicon of the IJA, the most commonly used term was simply *zettai fukujū*, literally "absolute obedience." As to what exactly the IJA meant by "absolute," the *Interior Administration Handbook*, the key manual for the organization and management of army barracks life and the reference on which the academies' *Kokoroe* itself was based, provided a clear and unequivocal explanation. First, obedience was to be "rigorous [*genjū*], whatever the situation." Second, orders were to be "received with reverence and carried out immediately and decisively, without discussion as to their appropriateness, or any questioning of their source or rationale." And third, once a superior officer had made his decision, a soldier was "to concentrate wholeheartedly on fulfilling his commander's intention without thought of self."[40] Whenever the MMA officials and instructors praised the "virtue of obedience," it was precisely these "absolute" guidelines that they were enjoining the cadets to follow. So intense and continuous was the instruction in obedience from matriculation to commencement that nearly a half century later in Changchun, when I separately asked several former Chinese MMA cadets, including one from the MMA 2 class who had been in Park Chung Hee's section, to write down in Japanese any terms or phrases from their academy education that immediately came to mind, they all independently put *zettai fukujū* at the top of their lists.[41]

As one might expect, obedience and hierarchy went together, at the academies as well as in the army itself. At the academies hierarchy followed the

rank order of the officials and instructors, beginning with the superintendents, who were general officers, down to the section commanders, who
were company officers, and finally down to the noncommissioned officers
who assisted them. But a clear sense of hierarchy also existed among the
classes and the cadets themselves. Cadets were given official army rank only
once they began their regimental attached service (*taizuki*) following graduation from the preparatory program (*yoka*), so it was only at Zama that
the classes were formally distinguished by official military rank, with the
first-years as corporals (*gochō*) and the second-years as sergeants (*gunsō*).
But even in the preparatory programs, such as the one Park Chung Hee attended at Lalatun, it was customary for the junior classes to defer to their
seniors. And in the first year of academy life every section was assigned a
counselor cadet (*shidō seito*) from one of the upper classes, who barracked
with the new cadets in their section and whose word was law, second only
to that of the section commander himself (see Chapter 3). Even among cadets of the same class, those in each section rotating as weekly duty cadets
(*torishimari seito*) and charged with seeing that the section commander's
orders were carried out held sway over their peers during their terms of
service (see Chapter 6).

Obedience was expressed in various ways at the academy, most commonly through everyday rituals of language and saluting. The superintendent, like other high-ranking officers in the army, was referred to with the
honorific *kakka* (excellency) attached to his title—a two-character Sinitic
compound, with roughly similar pronunciation in Korean, that would later
find its way into the South Korean army and government, and eventually
become a term of deference for Park Chung Hee during his presidency.[42]
Company and section commanders were addressed by the cadets with the
respectful suffix -*dono* added to their title, and even upperclassmen got their
due as seniors, regardless of their actual age.[43] As Kim Muk (MMA 2) told
me, "We didn't know how old anyone was, but we always called the upperclassmen 'honorable gods' (*kami sama*), even if they were only one year
ahead of us."[44] And of course counselor cadets, the gods among the gods,
were ordinarily addressed with the -*dono* honorific.[45]

Proper saluting was strictly required, and in fact much of the cardinal
precept on *reigi* was devoted to this very point, with an emphasis on both
rank and seniority. In the *Kokoroe*, moreover, the cadets found four pages
of regulations laying out a precise system of salutes for various occasions
and people.[46] And of course the reminders did not stop there. Among other
things, Hosokawa Minoru's (MMA 2) diary was a record of frequent

admonitions from his commanding officers to be scrupulous about saluting etiquette.[47] But even something so fundamental to army and academy life was not always easy. While bugles proclaimed the comings and goings of the superintendent through the academy gates, cadets in the barracks had to be on the alert for the often unannounced appearance of their section commander, or weekly duty officer, whose entry called for the first cadet to see him to shout "Senior officer!" (*Jōkan!*) followed by a general salute from all the cadets in the section.[48]

Visiting the section commander's officer was even more of a choreographed exercise in deference and saluting. According to Yoshida Katsusuke (MMA 7), a cadet began by standing in front of his commander's office door, politely requesting permission to enter. When permission was granted, he entered, closing the door with his back turned to the commander (closing the door with hands behind the back was not allowed). He then executed a right about-face. Now facing the commander, he delivered a precise 15-degree salute, announcing his section number and his name in a loud voice. After receiving the commander's acknowledgment, he proceeded to state his business. Business completed, he announced his intention to withdraw, saluted once again at an exact 15-degree angle, turned around in a right about-face, opened the door, stepped out, made another right about-face, closed the door, and proceeded into the corridor.[49]

It was especially important for the cadets to be properly respectful when they were crossing paths or in mixed company with officers or upperclassmen, as at morning visits to the JMA *yōhaijo*, a circular area for bowing centered by a large inscribed rock, where cadets performed obeisance to the emperor and their parents.[50] Such visits were strongly encouraged but not absolutely required by the school authorities, especially given the cadets' constricted morning schedule and the considerable distance between the barracks and the shrine. Cadets could also be excused from the ritual in the case of rain.[51] But, as Kaneko Tomio (MMA 2) told me, limited time and bad weather were not the only reasons for skipping the visit in the morning. Equally important was avoiding upperclassmen also on their way to and from the area, as meeting them, as Kaneko put it, was always a "painful experience."[52]

Other areas were cautionary zones as well. One was the academy baths. If an officer happened to enter the bathing area when the cadets were there, they were required to get out of the water and stand waiting in formation, naked and shivering.[53] Meeting upperclassmen there could be even more of a trial, but it could not always be avoided, as when Hosokawa's company found itself on a Saturday bathing schedule in April 1941 that overlapped with a company of senior cadets.[54] The canteen, open to any and all cadets to visit for a snack when they were able to manage a bit of rare free time, was yet another place where juniors might happen to encounter seniors, and where they not only had to execute the obligatory salutes but to wait, as Kim Muk (MMA 2) pointed out, until the seniors had taken everything they wanted, often leaving little or nothing for the juniors.[55] One of the first "notices" issued by Hosokawa's counselor cadet, Ishikawa Seijirō (MMA 1), shortly after matriculation was in fact a warning to the section to show proper deference (enryo) to upperclassmen, "especially in the canteen."[56] And the mess hall, where everyone ate together, was always a potential land mine in the regimen of saluting. As noted in Chapter 3, at Lalatun in early December 1941 it was the MMA mess hall that was the scene of a conflict between a Chinese and a Japanese cadet over the question of who exactly owed a salute to whom.

Beyond showing proper deference, what mattered most in the exercise of obedience was of course following orders. And absolute obedience required the absolute following of orders, an obligation that was not limited to daily tactical drills and exercises but encompassed the entirety of a cadet's academy life, including the seiton regimen and every other aspect of his moral training (kun'iku) in the barracks. Precisely to drive home the point that orders were orders and that the cadets had an absolute duty, whatever, whenever, and wherever, to carry them out, the academy instructors often deliberately issued commands that were frivolous, absurd, or seemingly impossible to execute, such as the officer who had rebuked Hiruma Hiroshi (JMA 57) for his incorrectly facing Athena ink bottle. Upperclassmen, with a year or more of acculturation in such practice, and encouraged by academy traditions, were naturally quick to imitate their instructors. One of the reasons that Kaneko and the other MMA 2 cadets found morning visits to the yōhaijo so "painful" was that the seniors they had to confront, in addition to exacting a salute, also invariably dressed them down and ordered them about for no real purpose except to assert their authority and inculcate obedience before letting them go.[57] Under the code in which they lived, as Matsui Shigeru (MMA 1) recalled, there was only one possible response to any order given, however ridiculous or bizarre, and that was the simple word "Yes" (Hai).[58] For example, if it was raining when the cadets asked to be excused from visiting the yōhaijō, but their section commander told them, contrary to fact, that it was not raining at all, that it was only foggy, they had no choice but to agree that yes, it was only foggy, and then to go to the shrine.

And later in their diaries they would also record the weather that day as "foggy," not "rainy."[59] Perception, like the orders that followed from it, was in the mind of the commander, absolute, not to be questioned.

If for the academies there was method in such madness, there were also occasions when the madness got out of hand. In their zeal to inculcate the idea of absolute obedience, some instructors went too far, as in the case cited in Chapter 7 of the JMA 57 weekly duty officer who ordered his cadets to dive into a body of solid ice. Another episode, even more extreme, was recounted to me by Kim Kwangsik (Kim Kwangsic), a former Korean cadet from the last MMA class (MMA 7). As part of a mock night exercise in June 1945, Kim was heading a three-member scout team mission with two Japanese classmates, all in their first year, when they uncovered an "enemy" squad (*buntai*) of other cadets; following a skirmish, they forcibly seized one of the squad members' rifles as evidence of their discovery. On return to the school they learned that in confiscating the opposing side's gun, they had committed one of the gravest violations of the IJA code regulating training exercises, and their section commander, beside himself with anger, ordered Kim, as leader of the team, to commit ritual suicide by disembowelment (*seppuku*). That order, Kim was certain, had been given to him in complete seriousness (*chinji hage*), but because it too would have constituted a violation of the IJA code, the section commander was forced to relent, and his order only hung in the air as an expression of his frustrated fury and "strong will."[60]

Reciprocity between Ranks

Aside from its illegality, ordering a soldier to disembowel himself also ran counter to one of the fundamental values in IJA culture, which honored and celebrated the ideal of a harmonious, reciprocal relationship between commanders and subordinates. If commanders were to demand and receive absolute obedience, in return they were to tender to those who so faithfully followed them respect, consideration, and affection, both in the line of duty and beyond. In explaining the Gunjin Chokuyu's cardinal precept of *reigi*, the army's 1939 official handbook on the rescript was explicit on this point, stating that although in the direct performance of duty it was necessary for senior officers to maintain the "gravity" of command, they must eschew a contemptuous or arrogant attitude toward their men. In all other situations, however, the handbook continued, apart from those "special times" on the battlefield, they should make every effort to treat their men with kindness and to "love them with undivided affection."[61] This view was also inscribed in the opening pages of the IJA *Field Service Regulations,* which charged commanders to "share their joys and sorrows" with their subordinates.[62] It found its way into many of the wartime films of the 1940s as well. One of these was a *kamikaze* recruitment film called *Believe That Others Will Follow* (*Ato ni tsuzuku o shinzu*), which told the story of a JMA 52 graduate, Captain Wakabayashi Tōichi, who had died in the 1943 battle of Guadalcanal.[63] In July 1945, several months after the film had come out, the MMA 7 class was taken to see it at the Manchukuo Film Association in Xinjing, and even decades later, what one former cadet remembered most about the film was the depiction of Wakabayashi's deep affection for his subordinate (*buka*), expressed most poignantly in a song that he had composed about him, "Gazing Reverently on the Pale Sleeping Face of a Soldier Exhausted from Battle."[64]

Such handbooks and films, of course, offered exemplary models rather than descriptions of reality. On the other hand, Captain Wakabayashi was indeed a real officer, a JMA classmate, in fact, of Park Chung Hee's Zama section commander Tahara Kōzō, and he had a reputation for taking care of his men.[65] Yu Yangsu (Yoo Yangsoo), who, as a young Korean IJA officer, had commanded a platoon in north China in the 1940s, told me that it was a well-established custom in the Japanese army for officers to "treasure" their subordinates, and even to check in on them at night while they were sleeping to make sure they were well.[66] And Kim Kwangsik was quick to point out that the officer who had ordered him to kill himself had not been his regular section commander. His regular section commander had been one of Park Chung Hee's fellow MMA 2 graduates, Ogasawara Harutsugu, temporarily in Dalian on R&R at the time of the incident.[67] Kim also mentioned that another MMA 2 graduate who was serving as a section commander for the MMA 7 class, Hosokawa Minoru, whose diary has been frequently cited in this book, had been particularly "kind and loving" to the cadets, who in turn "greatly respected and followed him."[68] Finally, it might also be noted here that according to Kim Muk and other Korean graduates of the MMA/JMA, cultivation of subordinates was a lesson that Park Chung Hee himself seemed to have taken to heart from his academy years, one that later stood him in good stead when he sought supporters in his bid for power in 1961 and afterward.[69]

Exceptions Prove the Rule

Whether a section commander was "loving" or not, to obey or not to obey was generally not a question at the academies, and Kim Kwangsik's good fortune in being able to evade a fatal direct order from a senior officer was

clearly an exceptional case. There were other, far less consequential exceptions as well, deliberately condoned by the academies as part of accepted
school tradition. Together these minor violations acted as a kind of safety
valve relieving some of the stress of the cadets' excessively regulated life,
while also serving as a bonding mechanism to promote that sense of "unity"
(*danketsu*) among cadet sections and companies so highly prized by the
academies (see Chapter 6). Some violations, such as the unauthorized
washing of clothes, were almost inevitable, given the insistence on cleanli-
ness and the extremely tight schedule on which the cadets operated. While
certain articles, with permission, could be sent out to the academy laundry,
many other items, especially the smaller ones in daily use, such as collars,
underwear, socks, and gloves, had to be washed by the cadets themselves. To
conserve time, it was thus common practice at both the MMA and the JMA
for the cadets to wash such things clandestinely in the academy baths, thereby
killing the proverbial two birds with one stone.[70]

Always hungry from their grueling daily routines, the cadets also
sneaked in forbidden snacks from the outside to share with their section
mates, either by secretly bringing them in themselves from a Sunday leave
or by making use of willing accomplices among the local non-military
working staff and errand boys. Known in academy jargon as *janku,* a reference to the traditional Chinese junk that ferried small loads of goods and
people, these illicit treats were a fixed part of academy lore and long remembered by the cadets who enjoyed them.[71] "Arabian Nights" (*Arabian naito*),
the whispered telling of stories to each other after lights-out, was another
breach of the rules permitted up to a point, although, as Hiruma Hiroshi
(JMA 57) noted, his section took no chances in that regard by posting two
of their fellow cadets as sentries on watch for a sudden appearance of the
weekly duty officer.[72]

The key, as with "Arabian Nights," was to avoid being caught *in flagrante
delicto,* in which case an officer would have no choice but to enforce regulations. Although conditions could vary from section to section, depending
on the strictness of the commander, such was generally the case even with
smoking and drinking, both of which were proscribed for the cadets inside
and outside the academies. Sharing cigarettes and alcohol, however, was as
much a part of IJA, and indeed Japanese and Korean, culture as singing,
which often went hand in hand with the former, and so long as they were
not caught, cadets were usually able to steal a few drags in the barracks latrine or another relatively secluded place, or to enjoy a few drinks together
(though in the case of drinking, never on academy grounds). Of course

Sunday leaves literally opened the gates to such guilty pleasures, and if they could stay clear of the authorities who often tried to monitor their outside activities, it was not impossible for the cadets to return to their barracks in the evening reeking of tobacco and spirits and still escape censure.[73] Many of the Korean MMA 1 and MMA 2 cadets, for example, not least of all Park Chung Hee, with his fondness for drinking, took advantage of their Sunday leaves from the MMA to visit Chŏng Ilgwŏn (CTS 5/JMA 55) in Xinjing, where Chŏng, then a young Korean company-level officer at Manchukuo army headquarters, fulfilled the preceptive role of a generous senior officer by obligingly providing his fellow Koreans and protégés with ample amounts of difficult-to-obtain high-quality *sake*.[74]

Such exceptions, relished as they were by the cadets, and useful from the viewpoint of the academy authorities, only served to prove the rules in the end, however. Discipline at both the MMA and JMA was otherwise thoroughly checked and administered, not least so at the MMA, where, as noted in Chapter 3, the first superintendent, Nagumo Shin'ichirō (JMA 19) had set a strict and demanding tone for the first three MMA classes who fell under his tenure. But regardless of the personality of the superintendent at any given time, the schools themselves were organized and operated systematically as institutions of discipline, and surveillance was comprehensive and constant.

Surveillance from Above

While MMA Superintendent Nagumo may have been a strict disciplinarian, neither he nor others in the upper echelon of governance at the academies, including even the commandant of cadets, had much contact with the cadets apart from periodic reviews and other largely ceremonial occasions.[75] As we have seen, on an everyday level it was the company commanders, and above all the section commanders, simultaneously serving on a rotating basis as weekly duty officers, who for the most part supervised and monitored the cadets' lives. Outside the classrooms or the branch drill units (at Zama), where the cadets were under the control of their academic instructors and branch trainers, respectively, it was the company and section commanders, with their offices in the barracks, who were in charge. And it was they, especially the section commanders, who came to know the cadets in their sections as individuals and who—step by step, day by day, explaining, encouraging, scolding, and working together with the other company and section commanders and instructors—imparted, modeled, and inculcated the disciplines of academy life. In doing so, they were able to make use of a compendium of information in the 1942 manual for section commanders, including examples of actual section schedules and meeting agendas and records from past sections, organized by term, week, and day, as well as detailed practical advice, again with specific historical examples, from former section commanders and cadets about the kinds of questions and problems that they had confronted or experienced in their own time at the academies.

Authority and resources combined to make the commanders a continuous and entrenched presence in the cadets' lives. Hosokawa Minoru's MMA 2 diary shows the level of mundane detail with which these young officers concerned themselves, even on ordinary days of no special significance, and quite apart from their almost daily moral lectures on army, duty, emperor, and nation. Theirs were the first voices of news, admonition, and command heard in the morning and the last at night. They presided over roll calls and barracks *seiton* inspections. They corrected carriage and posture, voice modulation, saluting, dress, attitudes toward superiors, and the many other proprieties of academy life. They cautioned about eating, drinking unboiled water, and specific health and hygienic practices (which varied with the weather and season), as well as the wasteful use of water and electricity. They examined the cadets' mail and diaries, and even checked any graffiti in the section's privy. It would not be an exaggeration to say that they scrutinized and recorded every discernible aspect of a cadet's evolving physical and mental condition and development in the course of his academy years. With regard to the latter in particular, they were advised by the section commander's manual to pay close attention to their cadets' facial expressions and behavior for anything worrisome they might reveal or suggest. They were to be especially vigilant about "special types of cadets," such as those who were judged for one reason or another to be "weak-willed" or who exhibited other "character" (*seikaku*) faults: sloppiness or negligence, lack of seriousness (stemming, for example, from the baneful effects of a commercial school education), profligacy with money, general negativity, egoism, and ideological or philosophical anxiety. Another category of special concern was cadets whose unusual or difficult family circumstances or problems in some way affected their performance at the academy. There was even a section in the manual on "guiding Korean cadets," written by a former section commander who had been deployed in southwestern Korea and claimed to have expert knowledge of the "weak points" (*ketten*) of the Korean people.[76]

Married or single, the company and section commanders went home in the evenings to lodgings in Xinjing or Zama or to officer quarters attached to the schools, but their reach was long, stretching into the nights as well. The upperclassmen who were dispatched to each section as counselor cadets (*shidō seito*) during the first year of academy life not only worked with the section commanders throughout the day to guide and monitor the cadets in the course of their activities but also served as surrogates for the commanders in their absence, including at night in the barracks, where they stayed with their first-year charges. Chosen for their diligence and *majime* attitude and held responsible for everything that happened in the section, the counselor cadets (*gomin* in academy slang) could at times be extraordinarily kind and helpful to their new juniors, but they were also often keener on surveillance than the section commanders themselves. Kim Muk (MMA 2) described the counselor cadet's role as akin to that a military policeman (MP) who "lived with them, slept with them, pointed out the rules, and watched them." Some, like Cho Yŏngwŏn (MMA 1/JMA 56), who served in Kim Muk's own section, or Ch'oe Ch'angŏn, another MMA 1/JMA 56 Korean who was Park Chung Hee's *gomin* in Park's first year at Lalatun, were particularly strict, and some were even frightening.[77] Borrowing a phrase from a Russo-Japanese War song, Hiruma Hiroshi (JMA 57) and his section mates at Zama, for example, nicknamed their intimidating beak-nosed *shidō seito* "ugly eagle" (*shiko washi*) and were nervously on alert for him throughout the day.[78]

Surveillance from Within

In addition to the counselor cadet program, the academies had in place a complex, multitiered system of guidance and surveillance, buttressed by tradition, which extended beyond the first year and functioned both at an individual and sectional level within the classes themselves. To grasp how this worked, one first must understand one of the most pervasive and important aspects of the moral education (*kun'iku*) taught and practiced in the barracks culture, the concept of *sessa-takuma*. A four-character term drawn from the Confucian *Analects* with the literal meaning of "cut and file, carve and polish," over time it came to be associated in Japanese education circles and institutions with the idea of the acquisition, development, and refinement of knowledge or skills.[79]

At the academies it also came to be closely allied with the idea of "unity" (*danketsu*), a theme continually stressed by section commanders as a moral principle that should govern the thoughts and actions of all the cadets in a particular section and the behavior of the section as a whole. It was a key consideration in the determination of every cadet's final *kun'iku* grade (see Chapter 6). In that sense, *sessa-takuma* carried the meaning of "leaning on and helping each other."[80] It served, first of all, as an ethical imperative for the transformation of each section or *kutai* into a powerful unit of male bonding and mutual aid, part of a general mystique of strength and masculinity that pervaded academy life from beginning to end. Women, to the extent that they figured at all in the life of the academies, were an antipodal symbol of unmanly weakness, everything a cadet was not supposed to be. Indeed, the word "woman" (*onna*) itself, as Park Chung Hee's Chinese classmate Gao Qingyin recalled, was more often than not a humiliating verbal expletive at the academies, flung, for example, at Gao and other cadets by the MMA *kendō* instructor Kuwahara Ryōichi while he beat them over the head with his bamboo sword for a poor showing in a match.[81] Men, and especially army officers, who were "men among men," had to be fierce, even "barbaric" in their duty. If at Lalatun Hosokawa Minoru (MMA 2) found emblazoned above the door to his section's self-study a banner warning him and other cadets against the "soft-heartedness" that could emasculate a strong soldier, at Zama he could hear Captain "Carbon" Sakai shouting at his charges in the MMA 1 and MMA 2 classes: "Only when you become the basest savage as well as the most accomplished man of letters will you be worthy of the name of 'officer.'"[82] Not surprisingly, contact with women outside one's immediate family was strongly discouraged by the academies. Women were considered dangerous, literally embodying the potential for weakening a cadet emotionally or physically. If a cadet received a letter from a woman, he had to "explain in detail the nature of the relationship" to his section commander, and cadets going on leave or vacation were warned in vague but unmistakable language by the *Kokoroe* to eschew any "recreation" that might "enfeeble" (*nanjaku*) them.[83]

In contrast, the promotion of close relationships among men, especially within the same section, was one of the main goals of *sessa-takuma* at the academies, at times even seeming to border on the homoerotic, as in the example of Captain Wakabayashi's much heralded love for his subordinates. Such connotations aside, the group bonding encouraged by *sessa-takuma* was intense, as each cadet was made to feel responsible, and indeed *held* responsible, for the actions of every other cadet in his section, whether simply making sure everyone made roll call, caring for a sick classmate, or taking food to another classmate when he was in confinement, as Park Chung

Hee's MMA 2 classmates did for him at Zama (see Chapter 6). Literally among the first words that Hosokawa Minoru (MMA 2) and his classmates heard from his section commander at Lalatun, Yano Yutaka, was the imperative of "mutual *sessa-takuma*."[84]

But *sessa-takuma* at the academies was not only about the kind of male bonding that the cadets would later, as young officers, be expected to foster in their army squads, platoons, and companies. It was also about joint surveillance and discipline. Indeed, the ethic of "leaning on and helping each other," whether making sure a classmate's blanket was folded properly or he was staying clean and healthy, went hand in hand with keeping a close eye on him for any signs of concern or infractions of the rules—precisely what the section commanders and counselor cadets themselves were doing from their own perspectives as disciplinary superiors. The 1942 manual for section commanders explicitly recommended that the *kutaichō* rely on and work in tandem with selected cadets in their section who could serve as models for other cadets with problems of one kind of another, rather than simply dealing directly with those cadets themselves. It was in this sense, of course, that Park Chung Hee's section commander at Lalatun had also often relied on Park to serve as such a model, especially for his Chinese classmates (see Chapter 3). The manual went on to cite the case of a Korean cadet who was seen as typically "narrow-minded" and "self-centered" and for those reasons "did not make an effort to fit in" with his section when he first entered the academy. The problem was "rectified," according to the manual, when his section commander asked another cadet in the section, a Japanese graduate of the Sendai Military School who had been in military life since he was thirteen, to take the Korean cadet under his wing and to guide him. In the words of the section commander, "the indirect influence was exceedingly powerful," and soon the Korean cadet was "progressing in harmony not only with the Japanese cadet who had befriended him but also with the entire *kutai*."[85]

To be sure, not all such indirect approaches ended so satisfactorily. Like superiors, peers could also be overzealous, as in the case of the JMA 57 cadet who privately confronted a classmate in his section with cheating on an exam and then cut him with a sword when he refused to commit suicide as atonement (see Chapter 6). But in general the tenet of *sessa-takuma* seems to have worked effectively as an ethic of informal mutual surveillance among the cadets in a given section, a fact that is supported by the extraordinary number of pages devoted to its principles and practice in the section commander's manual. Such informal surveillance was enhanced, moreover, by regulations forbidding cadets to go anywhere or do anything completely on their own. As Kim Muk (MMA 2) told me, "You always had to go with someone."[86]

Sessa-takuma went far beyond informal mutual surveillance, providing the rationale for a more formal, elaborate structure of communal responsibility and peer surveillance within the sections and companies at the academies. At the heart of this structure was the weekly duty cadet (*torishimari seito*) system, by which one cadet in the section each week was appointed by the section commander on a rotating basis to serve as the leader and spokesman of the group as a whole. Given the cadets' precise and demanding daily schedule, together with the fact that the cadets generally operated as a group, the tasks of the sectional weekly duty cadet or *kutori*, as he was informally called, were considerable. Not without reason did Hosokawa Minoru (MMA 2) write in his diary on his first day in that role that he "could not help but reflect on the burden and importance of the responsibility" thrust upon him as the "nucleus" (*chūkaku*) of his section.[87] It was the watchful *kutori* above all who made sure the cadets in his section were up in the morning and ready for roll call and barracks inspection; who led the salutes and roll call, calling out each cadet's number; who received and transmitted orders from the section commander and reported any problems or incidents; and who led the cadets through their daily round of classes and other activities. On those occasions when the cadets in different sections came together as a company, the *kutori* whose section commander was acting as the weekly duty commander also assumed the role of a "head duty cadet" (*sōtori*), who took precedence over his fellow appointees and led the cadets as a company.

It was also the *kutori* who approved and monitored any individual or personal actions that took a cadet out of his section, however briefly. In the evenings, for example, the *kutori* supervised the self-study room, keeping a black wooden pyramid on the top shelf of his desk with his title inscribed in white. Cadets needing to leave the room to use the bathroom or for some other purpose had to report to him first and leave an identifying wooden tag next to the pyramid so that he always knew where everyone was at any given time. Day leaves on Sundays and holidays also always had to be requested first through the *kutori*, who would then obtain approval from the section commanders. And except in emergencies, even sick cadets seeking to be excused from one or more of the day's activities had to report first to the *kutori* after morning roll call.[88]

Toward the end of the war, as class sizes increased and surveillance intensified, the *kutori* was joined by an assistant weekly duty cadet (*shintori*), who worked under him, mainly helping to manage the sleeping quarters and self-study room. Weekly "night sentry duty" cadets (*fushinban*), two to a section, were also deployed at this time in each of the company barracks by the weekly duty officer, to whom they reported. In addition to patrolling the company barracks at night, they concerned themselves with fire, burglary, hygiene, and counterespionage issues, as well as light control during air raids.[89] By the time Park Chung Hee and other cadets in the MMA 2 class had graduated from Zama in 1944, they had become quite accustomed to having no fewer than four peers from their own class watching and shepherding them throughout the day and night.

Self-Surveillance

The gaze of the academy did not work only through superiors and peers. By design it also made use of what Michel Foucault has called "technologies of the self," a set of practices by which an individual might monitor and transform his subjectivity to "constitute, positively, a new self."[90] Indeed, that the new self be "actively or autonomously positive" (*jishu sekkyoku*), productively attuned and oriented toward the goals of the academies, was for the schools a crucial element in the process of molding cadets into officers, and the phrase itself was a recurring term in the 1942 manual for section commanders.[91] As frequently noted throughout this book, what the academies sought in every aspect of officer training was to instill in the cadets a zeal that went beyond dutiful acceptance or passivity and harkened back to the *Hagakure's* idealized image of the samurai "dashing forward bravely and with joy" in battle. They wanted, in a word, a commitment of the soul as well as the body. The regimen of drills, exercises, and maneuvers and the constant emphasis on will training might equip a soldier to advance bravely and with confidence, but it did not guarantee that in the end he would move with an enthusiasm that would drive him to the ultimate sacrifice. Only some kind of inner affect could do that, a profoundly positive, energizing passion that could be articulated and modeled to some extent by instructors and seniors but which in the end, the academy authorities believed, could only be fully inscribed in the hearts and minds of the cadets by the cadets themselves.

But as the schools also tirelessly preached, achieving such a state of positive passion required a cadet to reconstitute his pre-academy, pre-IJA person, not least of all the part that derived from his earlier civilian middle school education, with its psychically debilitating "liberalism" (see Chapter 7). Nothing short of a total alteration was required, as Hosokawa (MMA 2), echoing this view, wrote in his diary in November 1941 in the form of an imperative to himself: "Beginning today, work toward effecting a complete change [*ippen*] to the point of feeling like a fundamentally transformed human being."[92]

To aid Hosokawa and other cadets in this effort, the academies had instituted two time-honored practices that Foucault would immediately have recognized. One was a ritual of confession, known in academy language as the "report" (*hōkoku*). Cadets were encouraged to inform their section commanders of any violations of the *Kokoroe* or of other "incidents" (*jiko*) that came to their attention. The nature of the offense, as Hiruma Hiroshi (JMA 57) noted, was irrelevant with respect to the injunction to report. It might be as trivial as losing a button or the bristles on a brush, or as serious as failing to salute a superior properly, or worse. The point was to report it, voluntarily and regularly. Even more to the point, cadets were asked to report their own violations as well as any incidents involving other cadets. The whole process, according to Hiruma, was much like the sacrament of confession in the Catholic Church, except that it was performed in a more public manner, with cadets lining up before classes in front of their section commander's office door in full view of their peers and, once inside, being forced to admit their shortcomings in a stentorian voice in the presence of all the section commanders in the company barracks.[93] Cadets were also told not to offer any qualifying explanation unless specifically asked, as it was considered unbecoming for officers to make excuses for bad behavior to their superiors. Section and company commanders, in turn, were advised by the 1942 manual to encourage "autonomous and positive" reporting from their cadets by "intentionally eschewing solemnity for a more lighthearted attitude" when receiving confessions. Avoid "tedious" lecturing, the manual cautioned; if the reporting cadet was judged to be satisfactorily penitent, he should be heard sympathetically and dismissed with a simple "Be careful!"[94]

Complementing the ritual of individual reporting, moreover, was a collective confession, which was held periodically in each section in what was known as a "sessa meeting" (*sessa-takuma kai/sessakai*), usually on a Saturday night when the section's commander was rotating on as weekly duty officer. The meeting would generally take place during evening self-study time or even later, after lights-out, commencing with an order from the section commander to assemble in his office. There, under the leadership of the *kutori*, the cadets would be encouraged to express their feelings and opinions to each other on subjects related to their life in the section and at the academies.

The *sessakai,* like the reports, were of course useful as a form of surveillance both from above and from peers, allowing the section commanders a glimpse into the developing minds and emotions of their cadets as they proceeded toward commencement and commissioning, while also permitting section mates to express grievances or problems and thus monitor and correct each other. To that end, section commanders were instructed mainly to listen, letting the *kutori* run the meetings, and intervening only to defuse personal clashes or to rectify "incorrect" views. But above all the *sessakai* were meant to serve as venues for self-improvement and self-transformation, especially with respect to "eradicating selfishness" (*shishin o saru*) and developing a new sense of self as part of a larger unit of communal sharing and responsibility (see Chapter 6).[95]

The act of writing, as Foucault observed, was also another effective way of reconstituting the self.[96] Hosokawa Minoru's MMA 2 cadet diary (*nikki*), where he recorded his vow to "change completely," is testimony to the significance that the academies attached to the cadets' keeping a daily record of their lives. Indeed, the 1942 manual for section commanders devoted more than forty pages, a full, separate chapter, to the "uses" (*riyō*) of the cadet diary.[97] Again, one of the main purposes of requiring the cadets to maintain such a journal was surveillance from above, providing an opportunity, as the 1942 manual stated, for the section commander to "peer into a cadet's tendencies and thinking."[98] With that aim in mind, the diaries were often checked once a week, and sometimes daily, by the section commander, who, like Yano Yutaka, Hosokawa's *kutaichō* at Lalatun, wrote terse comments in red ink at the top of the pages and often underlined particular passages that he deemed especially important, or substantively or grammatically inaccurate. On the final page reviewed in any given period, the section commander would also affix his personal stamp (also in red) certifying that he had read and approved the cadet's entries. If a commander did not like what a cadet had written, he might well summon him to his office for a reprimand. At *sessa* meetings a commander might ask cadets to read excerpts from their diaries aloud to their section mates as a way of initiating discussion while also bringing peers into the surveillance process.[99]

Academy officials were of course alert to the possibility that cadets, knowing the diary would be checked, might deliberately fashion or shade their writing to please their commanders or even to conceal their "real, naked, innermost feelings." Nevertheless, from the diary it was possible, the

1942 manual argued, "to understand in a general sense the content and direction of a cadet's thought."[100] When I asked Park Chung Hee's MMA 2 Chinese classmate Gao Qingyin about this, noting that cadets were unlikely to write anything they thought would be objectionable to the authorities, he acknowledged the problem but still said he believed that section commanders could learn a lot about their cadets from the diaries.[101] And even Hiruma Hiroshi (JMA 57), who upon rereading his own diary decades later was struck by its "excessive earnestness" and desire to please, also tended to agree that when read over time by the same section commander, who came to know the cadets personally through other means as well, the diaries could be very revealing of their real thinking.[102]

But facilitating surveillance from above was only one of two main uses of the diaries mentioned in the 1942 manual for section commanders. Equally important from the academy viewpoint, and in fact listed first, was "helping the cadet achieve his objectives"—or as Hosokawa Minoru (MMA 2) wrote as a concise reminder at the top of the first page of his Lalatun diary, "The purpose of this diary is to train the self" (jiko shūyō).[103] In other words, the diary was to serve as a self-disciplining tool for internalizing the culture and practices of IJA army life and combat and, as we saw, for cultivating that crucial fillip of passion in the exercise of "making the will manifest."[104]

Taking Hosokawa's diary as an example, we can appreciate how the academy nikki was structured to achieve those goals. The diary covered every day from April 3, 1941, when the Japanese MMA 2 cadets (Nikkei) entered Lalatun, to May 31, 1942, shortly before they left, together with Park Chung Hee and other top-ranking Korean and Chinese MMA 2 cadets (Mankei), for their three-month regimental attachment duty (taizuki kinmu) in the Kwantung Army. The number of pages Hosokawa filled each day varied from one to several, depending in part on the nature of the activities that day, but the total was substantial. Comprising seven notebooks in all, each 10 inches long and 8 inches wide, the diary ran to about 620 pages. And with seventeen columns per page and approximately 15–25 characters per column, the word count, in effect, reached roughly between 160,000 and 200,000, about the size of this book.[105]

Each entry followed a similar format, beginning with a simple summary of that day's program of study (kagyō no taiyō), divided into academic subjects (classical Chinese, Mandarin, psychology, chemistry, math, etc.), and moral (kun'iku) training (e.g., precepts from the Gunjin Chokuyu, passages from the Infantry Manual). This was followed by a listing of the advisements or "notices" (chūi) orally issued that day by both the weekly duty officer and section commander. Invariably these included admonitions calling attention to one or more shortcomings of the section with respect to *seiton* discipline or other aspects of barracks life, but they also ranged over the complete spectrum of academy culture and education, depending on the circumstances of the moment and the performance of the section in any given activity.[106]

The first two parts of each entry thus recalled the significant lessons and events of the day and briefly noted them for the record. While this daily act of memory inscription was itself an element in the self-cultivation process, from the academies' perspective the more important pedagogical aspects of the diary came in the two sections that followed and were more expansive. The first of these was a section Hosokawa always labeled "Impressions" (*shokan*) and the second a section he called "Reflections" (*hansei*). As the words themselves suggest, these were the portions of the entry where cadets expressed their personal feelings about the day's regimen of study and training and about the notices delivered by the commanders to their section and company. It was here above all, as the many quotations from Hosokawa's diary cited throughout this book demonstrate, that cadets were called upon to examine their attitudes toward their course of study, to review and evaluate their performance critically, and to begin through an act of confessional and redemptive writing to "fundamentally transform" themselves into men worthy of being commissioned as IJA officers.[107] Unlike the other forms of academy surveillance, moreover, which would come to an end with commencement, self-surveillance and self-correction through recording and writing were meant to continue throughout an officer's career. Indeed, the academies regarded this practice as so important that, apart from the personal effects they had brought with them at matriculation, one of few things cadets were allowed to take with them when they left the schools was their diaries.[108]

In view of the underground networks of ideological subversion described in Chapter 6, one cannot conclude that the tiered system of surveillance at the academies, including the use of proctored, self-regulating diaries, was entirely foolproof. Even leaving aside such political fissures, the effectiveness of the system, as already noted, varied to some extent depending on the strictness with which individual instructors and senior cadets were inclined to enforce it. Even within the sections themselves, the level and seriousness of peer surveillance could vary considerably depending on who was serving at any given time as the group's duty cadet. Park Chung Hee's MMA Chinese classmate Gao Qingyin, for example, by his own admission was "very lax" when he served as *kutori*, whereas Park in the same position, according to

Gao, was "too *majime,* too strict—go-go-go all the time . . . always making the cadets move from one place to another in double-time."[109] Such imperfections notwithstanding, by the time they graduated, the MMA/JMA cadets of the 1940s—not least of all those of a *majime* predisposition, like Park—had generally become acclimated to a multilevel structure of surveillance as a routinized feature of their daily existence. Such surveillance would serve as part of a larger template of order and control that they would forever after associate with the discipline of military life.

Punishment

Looming even larger in that template of discipline, however, was the praxis of punishment. In academy thinking, the ideal cadet response to any given order or situation was "joyful submission" (*eppuku*), but cadets of course differed in their abilities and levels of enthusiasm, and some tasks, as already noted, were in effect too difficult or dangerous, and sometimes even impossible, to carry out.[110] Nevertheless, if instructors, particularly the section commanders and weekly duty officers, detected anything less than perfection executed in a spirit of *eppuku,* the result was generally a torrent of verbal abuse and various disciplinary measures, everything from standing at attention in a present-arms position (*sasage-tsutsu*) all day long outside the section commander's office or copying out the entire Gunjin Chokuyu to one or more forms of corporal punishment.[111]

Corporal punishment, despite varying legal restrictions from place to place, was widely practiced in educational institutions throughout the world in the 1940s, and it is safe to say that most cadets entering the MMA and JMA at that time, Koreans as well as Japanese and Chinese, had already had some experience with it in their earlier years.[112] It is difficult to state definitively whether or not such corporal punishment had its roots in Korean tradition or sprang more from subsequent Western or Japanese influences, or a combination of the two. Certainly there is no denying that the Chosŏn dynasty like most of its contemporaries, had a ghastly array of torture and punishment mechanisms reserved for criminal and other offenses.[113] There was also a more sophisticated and calibrated set of penalties, including strokes with bamboo, intended to maintain the Neo-Confucian social order.[114]

Corporal punishment seems to have been a normative educational discipline during the dynasty, as suggested by a law enacted in 1895 by the reformist Kabo government forbidding the use of violence (*kangp'o*) in the teaching of children, apparently a common practice at the time.[115] Anecdotal evidence of such violence is also abundant. In a record of his grandson's upbringing, for example, Yi Mun'gŏn, a sixteenth-century *yangban* scholar, wrote of frequently losing his temper at his charge's inattention to his studies and furiously beating the boy on his buttocks with the rod and in other ways, including "countless times" (*pulsu*) with his cane.[116] Palais notes that the famous seventeenth-century "practical learning" (*sirhak*) scholar Yu Hyŏngwŏn administered fifteen strokes of the whip to his students if they failed to pass exams.[117] And Kim Hongdo's famous genre painting of a eighteenth-century village school (*sŏdang*) gives us a graphic image of a young boy about to be caned on his calves and buttocks with a bamboo or horsehair rod (*hoech'ori*).[118] Sin Yongha also tells us that before Sin Ch'aeho became an iconic nationalist writer in the early twentieth century, he had been severely thrashed as a boy by his grandfather when he could not immediately recite a lesson from memory.[119]

On the other hand, Yi Mun'gŏn, after describing his harsh caning of his grandson, also wrote of his regret at such violent anger and admonished himself to guard against it and to show more "affection," suggesting that he did not regard the beatings as a particularly positive measure.[120] Similarly, in an account of his shipwreck and thirteen-year sojourn on the peninsula in the seventeenth century, a rare if not unique early Western perspective on Chosŏn society, the Dutch seaman Hendrik Hamel wrote that the education of children at the elite level in Chosŏn Korea was on the whole carried out "gently and with good manners."[121] And while he spared no detail in recounting the violence of his late nineteenth-century peasant childhood in rural Hwanghae Province, where drunkenness and beating seem to have been everyday aspects of family and village life, the famous nationalist Kim Ku in his autobiography had only kind words for his "dignified and erudite" local *sŏdang* teacher.[122]

"Gentleness and good manners" are of course to some extent a matter of perception, and, as the weeping *sŏdang* boy about to be punished in Kim Hongdo's painting suggests, the bamboo rod from a student's perspective was undoubtedly always an unwelcome and unpleasant experience. What seems clear, however, is that somewhere between the turn of the century and the 1920s, when the first Korean-language commercial newspapers began to report and record the news of the day, corporal punishment in colonial Korean schools, despite its official illegality, seems to have become less restrained than in the past, whether the supervising teachers were Korean or Japanese, men or women. From the 1920s on, horrific stories abound in the Korean newspapers of elementary school teachers "wildly kicking" their young pupils, or beating them with their palms, fists, sticks, and even steel hammers, leading in many instances to loss of consciousness, bone fractures, severe abdominal injuries, or even death. In nearly all cases, the precipitating cause was a minor mistake or offense on the part of the student, such as not responding immediately to a teacher's question or summons, or failing to pay proper attention in class.[123] By the late 1930s so many such stories had appeared, along with stories of grieving, outraged parents, that both *Chosŏn ilbo* and *Tonga ilbo* were publishing editorials condemning the illegal but widespread practice of corporal punishment, while also arguing its ineffectiveness as a teaching methodology.[124]

Even if they had not been beaten themselves as students, the prevalence of corporal punishment in the colonial school system suggests that Korean cadets entering the MMA and JMA in the 1940s would have had little reason to be surprised by its existence at the academies. Indeed, corporal punishment, including what the army called "private discipline" (*shiteki seisai*), had long been acknowledged to be a rampant feature of Japanese military life, and, as in civilian society, it continued to persist despite official IJA condemnation since at least the early 1930s.[125] What might have surprised the cadets, however, was the extent to which corporal punishment was practiced at the academies and—notwithstanding the mounting critiques against it in civilian society and official injunctions against it within the military itself—its enshrinement as a virtuous pedagogy and, as Hosokawa (MMA 2) would write in his Lalatun diary soon after matriculation, "a noble tradition of the school."[126]

Beating as Academy Pedagogy and Tradition

Extant MMA or JMA documents from the time, including Hosokawa Minoru's diary, contain few specific or detailed references to corporal punishment. Indeed, both the Japanese term *taibatsu*, with its negative connotations, and the military's own term, "private discipline," are completely absent from Hosokawa's diary. Officially nonexistent, the practice was shrouded in euphemisms. Nevertheless, such expressions, once decoded, together with the evidence of memoirs and personal interviews, leave no doubt that corporal punishment was carried out at the academies by numerous people, in different places, for multiple reasons, and in different forms.

Most routine, perhaps, was the discipline meted out by the officers who worked with the cadets on a daily basis as section commanders and weekly duty officers. But upperclassmen, counselor cadets, and even classmates serving as rotating *kutori* in each section were also free to administer corporal punishment as they saw fit. Underlying ethnic frictions notwithstanding, rank and position ruled in punishment as in obedience. Japanese beat Koreans and Chinese; Koreans and Chinese beat Japanese; Chinese beat Koreans; Koreans beat Chinese; and Japanese, Koreans, and Chinese all beat members of their own groups. In Park Chung Hee's MMA 2 Mankei company at Lalatun beatings occurred "every day," according to former Taiwanese cadet Cai Chongliang.[127] A Chinese member of the company in the same section as Cai wrote that he had been beaten by officers 420 times in the first year.[128] And when I asked yet another member of the company, Gao Qingyin (MMA 2), if he or Park Chung Hee had ever beaten anyone while at the school, he replied simply, "Everybody did it."[129]

Given the unrelenting daily schedule of the schools and the exacting regulations of the *Kokoroe*, almost any situation or venue could be an occasion for beating, especially in the first year of the preparatory course (*yoka*) at Lalatun, when the cadets were still learning and adjusting to the academy regimen. Some of the specific behaviors recalled by former MMA cadets that had led to corporal punishment by their section commanders included such things as being late for regular activities like roll call, self-study, or lights-out; failing to pass dress or barracks inspection; falling asleep or committing mistakes in tactical exercises; losing a part of a gun or other piece of equipment; performing poorly in any task or role assigned; or even something as seemingly inconsequential as failing to remove a piece of straw from the socket of a bayonet.[130] Because the officers held them responsible for the overall conduct of their groups, counselor cadets and *kutori* could often be even stricter disciplinarians than the section commanders themselves when a cadet fell short in his duty (e.g., folding the blankets on the bed incorrectly) or performance in an activity (e.g., *kendō* practice).[131]

Perhaps the most demanding and punishing figures of all for the cadets were their seniors in the classes above, who resorted to corporal punishment at the slightest sign of perceived disrespect or even insufficient "cheerfulness" from their juniors. Pang Wŏnch'ŏl (MMA 1) told me that he used to beat Park Chung Hee and Kim Chaep'ung "frequently" in their first year as MMA 2 cadets, simply because both, and especially Park, lacked a "bright and sunny" (*myŏngnang*) disposition and were so "stiff" (*kutta*) in their behavior.[132] Indeed, as noted in Chapter 3, according to Kim Muk (MMA 2), the Korean senior cadets were in general "very severe" with their Korean juniors, regularly beating them as a punishment or as an incitement to work harder and to surpass all the other non-Korean cadets, especially the Japanese.

Not infrequently, disciplinary action by seniors resembled covert hazing rituals historically associated with American college fraternities and military schools, including West Point.[133] At Lalatun and Zama, however, such activities were far from hidden. Officers on duty simply looked the other way, or even tacitly or expressly encouraged such behavior. In fact, a well-established tradition of "bed-assaults" (shindai-shūgeki) at the schools sanctioned sudden "invasions" by seniors, who swept into the junior barracks in the middle of the night, turning everything upside down and beating the junior cadets.[134] Park Chung Hee's Taiwanese classmate, Cai Chongliang, remembered such a "bed-assault" on his first night at Lalatun, when MMA 1 Mankei cadets woke him, Park, and the other MMA 2 Mankei at night and forced them to run around outside in their underwear in the still-freezing Manchurian air, while pouring cold water on them.[135] And the first night was far from the last. According to Gao Qingyin (MMA 2), in the course of the first year the MMA 1 Mankei cadets often came into the MMA 2 barracks on Saturday nights "and did anything they wanted."[136] According to Zhu Huan and Wang Jingyue, both former MMA 6 cadets interviewed in Changchun, basically "seniors had the right to beat juniors at any time."[137]

The type and severity of corporal punishment varied depending on the situation and on the person who was administering it. Facial slapping with an open palm, known as binta, was perhaps the most common form of physical discipline at the academies, and when Liu Qian (above) mentioned his 420 beatings during his first year at Lalatun, he was talking about binta.[138] But head cuffs, kicks, and facial clouts were also employed.[139] Reprimands with bamboo kendō swords or shinai were common as well, and not only during kendō practice. Once at Lalatun, when Kim Muk (MMA 2) was using the latrine and got into his bed late, after the bugle for lights-out had already sounded, he was beaten with one of the shinai, which, unfortunately for him, were stored and readily at hand in the barracks.[140]

The MMA 1 and MMA 2 cadets particularly remembered the full-fisted punches of section commander Sakai Masao at the JMA. Called "Carbon punches" by the cadets after the commander's nickname, these were "death-blows," in the words of Sugiyama Masayuki (MMA 1) that "flew through the air without mercy"—so powerful, according to Kiyoizumi Nobuo (MMA 2), that "we were just knocked over."[141] Again, counselor cadets and other upperclassmen could also wield memorable blows. The "bed-assaults" at Dōtokudai could be "very bloody," according to one former MMA 7 cadet.[142] And many decades after the fact, Xu Shudong, an MMA 2 cadet in Park Chung Hee's section at Lalatun, still vividly recalled nearly passing out in his first year from a *binta* slap from the Korean counselor cadet Ch'oe Ch'angŏn (MMA 1) when Ch'oe discovered that Xu had placed his gloves (*shutō*) on his barracks shelf (*seitondana*) incorrectly according to *Kokoroe* regulations.[143] Indeed, the no-holds-barred, stinging *binta* slaps, according to Kaneko Tomio (MMA 2), were often "decidedly more painful" than the fist punches, depending on how tightly the fist was clenched and on how forcefully the blow delivered, with the "Carbon punch" representing the extreme end of the scale.[144]

Whatever form a beating took, it was often carried out as a group punishment for the entire section, even if the offense had been committed by only one of its members. This practice, also known as the "whip of love" (*ai no muchi*), was in keeping with the academies' encouragement of group unity and solidarity (*danketsu*), and was the other, more physical and violent side of *sessa-takuma*, with its vaunted spiritual ideal of "leaning on each other."[145] It was in that sense, for example, that Hosokawa, who never used the word "beating" or anything similar in his MMA 2 diary, frequently employed the term *sessa-takuma*, or just *sessa*, as a verb or part of a verbal compound.[146] Thus he and the cadets of his 5th Section were "favored [*mei kudasareta*] with an order from the section commander to *sessa-takuma*."[147] They were warned that being late for self-study would lead to the section "doing [*su*] *sessa-takuma*."[148] They were exhorted "to carry out [*seyo*] *sessa-takuma* with sincerity."[149] And they were compelled "to perform [*okonau*] *sessa*" because of a poor barracks inspection during which the cadets had also failed to remember the name of the commander of the adjoining 6th Section.[150] Not surprisingly, whenever I asked former MMA cadets, irrespective of ethnic background and class year, exactly what *sessa-takuma* had meant to them, they invariably answered, like Kim Kwangsik (MMA 7), with a single word: "beating."[151]

The *sessa* beatings might be either fist punches or *binta* slaps, again depending on the person who was ordering them. From the perspective of the school authorities, what mattered in a *sessa* punishment was less the mode of beating than the full, active and "positive" (*sekkyokuteki*) participation of every member of the group, a word Hosokawa frequently used in his diary to encourage himself in the practice.[152] Ideally, an order to perform what Hosokawa had called the "noble tradition" was to be welcomed as an opportunity to use the communal pain of physical punishment to reflect on the shortcomings and joint responsibility of the group as a whole, to "master the self" (*jiko o osame*) in favor of the group, and together (*tagai ni*) to "spur each other on" (*hakusha o kakete*) as constituents of a single unit.[153]

In a 1997 interview, Gao Qingyin (MMA 2) described and demonstrated for me what he said had been a typical *sessa* for him and his classmates, including Park Chung Hee, who had been in the same Mankei company and had barracked with Gao in an adjoining section of the same building at Lalatun, thus sharing the same weekly duty officers and many of the same experiences in their first two years of academy life. *Binta* slapping was the norm, and could take place either inside or outside the barracks, with the latter being more common because of the need for space. In general *sessa* was carried out as a section (*kutai*), but it could also be done as a company (*ren/chūtai*) if the weekly duty officer directed it. At the sectional level, *sessa* usually occurred on the orders of the section commander, but it could also be imposed separately by the counselor cadets as well as the *kutori*, as on May 11, 1941, when the counselor cadet in Hosokawa's section forced the whole group to do *sessa* at 1930 because of rumpled bedding discovered in that morning's inspection.[154]

According to Gao, cadets were first ordered to form two horizontal lines, with about fifteen cadets in each. The line in front was then directed to perform an about-face so that each cadet was facing another in the second line. The front-line cadets were then ordered to begin slapping (*nagure*) their counterparts in *binta* fashion on each cheek, after which the cadets in the second line who had received the first slaps then proceeded to return the slaps to the cadets in the front line, until the entire section was engaged in continuous, rapid-fire, back-and-forth volleys of reciprocal slapping. Indeed, the *sessa* was to be carried out in high spirits, with the officers, upperclassmen, and even the cadets themselves all "spurring each other on," in Hosokawa's phrase. If a cadet did not beat his counterpart effectively or hard enough, according to Gao, an officer or counselor cadet would immediately step in and show him how to do it by slapping the negligent cadet himself.[155] Xu Shudong, another Chinese MMA 2 cadet in the same company and also one of Park Chung Hee's section mates, said that such "spurring on" often involved shouting "*Uchite shi yaman!*," a ubiquitous wartime slogan seen and heard throughout the empire in the 1940s meaning "Never stop shooting" or "Shoot to kill."[156] Since the verb *utsu* could mean to "hit" or "beat" as well as to "shoot," the slogan was a perfect, ready-made pun for use in the execution of *sessa* punishment.[157]

To be sure, although the academy authorities wanted the pain of *sessa* to be memorable, they did not intend for it to go on indefinitely, let alone result in a cadet's death. Still, testimony suggests it could go on for some time. Kim Muk, another MMA 2 classmate, though in a different company from Gao and Park, told me that it usually continued for at least ten minutes.[158] A Chinese cadet from a later class, Sun Jingda (MMA 3), thought that the duration was about two minutes.[159] In his diary Hosokawa (MMA 2) never mentioned a particular length of time for any given *sessa* punishment. He did, however, sometimes write down the number "30" on such occasions, as on the last day of June in 1941, when he recorded: "On the order of the section commander: *sessa-takuma* 30"—by which he meant that each cadet in the line that day had delivered and received thirty blows to and from his counterpart in the facing line.[160] The length and severity of *sessa* thus clearly varied. The only fixed rule, as Gao suggested, was that it basically went on until the person in charge ordered it to be stopped.[161]

Some former MMA 2/JMA 57 cadets have suggested that *sessa* and other punishments tended to taper off somewhat as the cadets became more accustomed to the academy regimen, and especially after they moved to Zama for their branch training, a view that is supported to some extent by Hosokawa's diary.[162] On the other hand, even as late as mid-February 1942, only slightly more than a month before the MMA 2 *yoka* graduation at Lalatun, Hosokawa had filled a whole page in his diary with a large chart to emphasize graphically that week's instructions from the weekly duty officer, including the injunction "to execute *sessa-takuma* rigorously [*reikō*]."[163] And it was of course at Zama that the "Carbon punches" had flown through the air, and where the MMA 2 cadets in Park Chung Hee's class had tried to minimize the "painful experience" of accidentally running into upperclassmen on the way to the Otakebi Shrine.

The fact was that corporal punishment was deeply ingrained in academy culture, though it may have waxed or waned somewhat depending on particular individuals and circumstances. Kaneko Tomio (MMA 2), for example, felt that there was always a special "intensity" that prevailed at Lalatun, which stemmed from Manchuria's location on the very front line of Japan's imperial defense perimeter, a perspective shared by other former cadets in interviews and memoirs.[164] It is worth reiterating, moreover, that the final years of the war also brought a new intensity to all aspects of army life. For anxious academy instructors, already burdened by larger class cohorts and shortened training periods, an enhanced dedication to unforgiving IJA discipline may well have seemed the one and only hope of Japan's salvation against overwhelming material superiority on the other side. Top-secret War Ministry reports from 1942–1943 in fact provide clear evidence that "private discipline" by IJA army officers was becoming progressively more "brutal" (*kakoku*) in China, Manchuria, and Japan (in that order) as the war-time situation deteriorated.[165]

Despite such concerns by the War Ministry, and a renewed rhetorical commitment to the "eradication" (*konzetsu*) of "private discipline" within the army at the end of 1943, there is no question that the practice continued both in the ranks and at the academies through 1945.[166] For the MMA 7 cadets, who were in the middle of their first year at Lalatun when the war ended, *sessa-takuma* meant much the same thing it had meant to their seniors in the MMA 1 and MMA 2 classes, and in all the other classes that had come before them: *binta* slaps and other forms of beating. The "noble tradition," passed down from commander to cadet, from senior to junior, and from class to class, was in the end always stronger than any critique raised against it or resolution to see it eliminated. And like the will training they had experienced, the corporal punishments they had suffered were deeply inscribed in the memory of the cadets, even when, much later, and much to my chagrin as an interviewer, many other details of life at Lalatun and Zama had faded in their minds to shadow or nothingness. Here, pain and remembrance do indeed seem intimately intertwined, as Nietzsche had suggested.

This is not to say, of course, that every cadet experienced the same degree of pain or responded to or remembered it in the same way. At the time some cadets, such as Kim Chaep'ung (MMA 2), just surrendered to the rain of blows from upperclassmen and fell to the ground, while others, such as Park Chung Hee, who was a "real tough ass" (*tokchong*), according to Pang Wŏnch'ŏl (MMA 1), "just kept coming back for more."[167] And many cadets were deeply resentful of being beaten, a resentment that especially at the MMA had not infrequently been charged with ethnic tensions. Ironically, however, such anger often served only to fuel and to perpetuate the custom, as juniors or classmates became seniors or duty cadets, newly empowered to take revenge on lowerclassmen or on peers under their command. As Gao Qingyin (MMA 2) noted, "We Chinese cadets could always beat up the Japanese cadets in the classes below us!"[168] But such assertive behavior by Chinese cadets could in turn provoke a strong reaction on the part of the Japanese cadets, who were always told by their commanders that, as Japanese, they had a special place as models and teachers to the other cadets within the "harmony of races" that Manchukuo and the Manchukuo Army were said to embody (see Chapter 3). Thus on December 1, 1941, for example, when an MMA 1 Chinese cadet slapped one of Hosokawa's MMA 2 section members for failing to properly salute, the duty officer and the entire section treated the incident as a "humiliation" (*kutsujoku*), even though the Chinese cadet clearly had higher standing as an upperclassman and was acting perfectly within the tradition of the school.[169]

A similar cycle of anger and retribution could also be found within the classes and sections themselves. After Xu Shudong, Park Chung Hee's MMA 2 section mate at Lalatun, was knocked nearly unconscious by his Korean first-year counselor cadet, Ch'oe Ch'angŏn (MMA 1), he developed, in his own words, a particular "hatred" of Koreans. A year later, when he was serving as *kutori* for the section on a topographical exercise on Longshou Mountain, he ordered Park and another classmate to carry all the required poles and other equipment up to the top of the mountain for the scheduled surveying. It was heavy work, disliked by all, and when the surveying was completed at the end of the day, the equipment had then to be carried back down again to the base camp at the foot of the mountain. Given the onerousness of the task, it was customary for the *kutori* to assign one group of cadets to bring the equipment up and another to bring it down. Contrary to convention, however, Xu again appointed Park as one of the cadets to shoulder the load, and when a disgruntled Park grumbled under his breath about the assignment, Xu struck him on the face in *binta* fashion, finally giving vent, as he put it, to his long-held grievance against Koreans.[170]

In telling this story to me some forty-five years after the fact, it was clear that Xu was still angry, both at Park Chung Hee and (especially) at Ch'oe Ch'angŏn to some degree, but even more so at what he regarded as the "abnormal psychology" that had prevailed at the academies and led him to beat his fellow cadets.[171] Equally interesting, and perhaps even more important, is the extent to which many other cadets, pain and resentment notwithstanding, came to regard "private punishment" simply as a matter-of-fact component of their overall academy experience. According to the MMA 7 class history, many cadets were at first indignant and resistant toward the *sessa-takuma* "whip of love" and felt bitter toward classmates who were beating them. As time went on, however, they came to accept the "essential purpose" of the practice as a masculine group-strengthening and bonding exercise, and sometimes even "cried together" while performing it. Many cadets who initially had had difficulty striking their classmates later "hit them with force," having come to see such beating as entirely "natural" (*tōzen*).[172] Even Park Chung Hee's always less than enthusiastic Chinese MMA 2 classmate Gao Qingyin said he just came to accept beating as "part of the teaching."[173] And perhaps Takezawa Rikio (MMA 2), Park Chung Hee's bunkmate at Zama, put it best: "We just took it for granted."[174]

For the more enthusiastic, *majime* cadets, such as Park himself, it is possible that *sessa* and other forms of corporal punishment at the academies may, then or later, have come to be seen as entirely positive, something approaching what Stanley Payne, in his study of European fascism, has called a "moralistic concept of therapeutic violence."[175] At a private lunch with Japanese leaders on his first trip to Japan six months after the May 1961 coup, Park Chung Hee discussed possible "good plans" (*meian*) for dealing with South Korea's pressing problems, economic and otherwise. According to former prime minister Kishi Nobusuke, who had hosted the lunch and was interviewed afterward by *Asahi* reporters, Park stressed in his accented but fluent Japanese that his experience as a cadet at the JMA had taught him the efficacy of the "Japanese spirit" and "*binta* education" (*binta kyōiku*). In a new Japan where such terms harkened back to a militarist past that many Japanese at the time were trying to forget or distance themselves from, even Kishi, who had played a key role in the industrial development of Manchukuo and Japan's own wartime economy and was later often called the "monster of the Shōwa era" (*Shōwa no yōkai*), admitted to feeling a bit "embarrassed" (*omohayui*) by Park's remarks.[176] But for Park, who had not been back to Japan since 1944, this was the discourse of strength and discipline that he knew and admired from his years at Lalatun and Zama, and it would continue to guide him in the years to come.

Japanese Military Academy main gate (1944). Courtesy of Hosokawa Akio.

Japanese Military Academy (Sōbudai) stone slab and Great Lecture Hall (1944). Courtesy of Hosokawa Akio.

Japanese Military Academy Otakebi Shrine entrance (1944). Courtesy of Hosokawa Akio.

Lieutenant General Ushijima Mitsuru (Japanese Military Academy superintendent 1942–1944). Courtesy of Yi T'aeyŏng.

Major Enami Shigeru (Japanese Military Academy International Corps company commander for MMA 2 Class 1944). Courtesy of Yi T'aeyŏng.

Japanese Military Academy International Corps section commanders for Manchurian Military Academy 2 Class (1944). From left to right: First Lieutenant Wada Yoshihide; Captain Tahara Kōzō; Captain Miyamoto Masami; Company Commander Major Enami; Captain Takayama Toshitake; Captain Ōura Ryōzō. Courtesy of Yi T'aeyŏng.

Other Japanese Military Academy International Corps section commanders for Manchurian Military Academy 2 Class who were transferred before the class graduation in 1944. From left to right: Captain Nishigaki Makoto; Captain Shiki Hiroteru; Captain Sakai Masao, aka "Carbon." Courtesy of Yi T'aeyŏng.

Japanese Military Academy infantry exercises at Sagamihara Exercise Field (1943). Courtesy of Yi T'aeyŏng.

Japanese Military Academy cadets performing morning bows to emperor and parents, and reverential reading (*hōdoku*) of the Imperial Rescript to Soldiers and Sailors (1944). Courtesy of Yi T'aeyŏng.

Superintendent Ushijima welcoming Park Chung Hee and other members of the Manchurian Military Academy 2 Class (and Japanese Military Academy 57 Class) to the Japanese Military Academy (October 1, 1942). From *Kiji* 56 (December 1942).

Park Chung Hee with section commander Captain Tahara Kōzō and other members of the 5th Section at the Japanese Military Academy (1944). Park is seated in the front row, third from left. Takezawa Rikio is standing two rows up from Park, first on the left. Captain Tahara (with sword) is seated in the center of the front row. Courtesy of Yi T'aeyŏng.

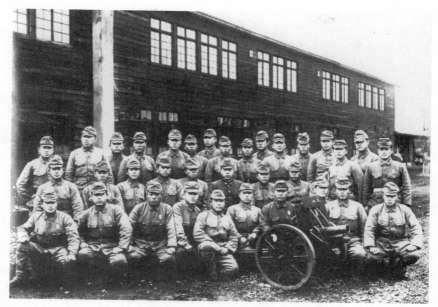

Park Chung Hee in his infantry drill unit at the Japanese Military Academy (1944). Park is in the front row, first from the right. Kaneko Tomio is in the same row, first from the left. Captain Tahara Kōzō is seated in the center of the row above, sixth from the left. Courtesy of Yi T'aeyŏng.

Park Chung Hee and Manchurian Military Academy 2 classmates during Japanese Military Academy swimming exercises at Koshigoe (August 1943). Park is in the front row (sitting), fourth from the right. Courtesy of Yi T'aeyŏng.

Japanese Military Academy graduation photo of Manchurian Military Academy 2
Class (April 1944). Courtesy of Yi T'aeyŏng.

Hosokawa Minoru (July 1942) and his Manchurian Military Academy 2 diary. Courtesy of Hosokawa Minoru and Hosokawa Akio.

Park Chung Hee and family with Manchurian Military Academy 1 graduates and families at Hwagyesa Temple in Seoul (1958). Park, wearing sunglasses, is seated in the front row, far right, holding daughter Kŭnhye (Park Geun-hye). His wife, Yuk Yŏngsu, is in the top row, far left. Courtesy of Pang Wŏnch'ŏl.

Park Chung Hee meeting with Chinese Manchurian Military Academy graduates in Taiwan (1966). Park is shaking MMA 2 classmate Gao Qingyin's hand. Another MMA 2 classmate, Cai Chongliang, wearing glasses, is standing next to Gao. Courtesy of Gao Qingyin.

Alumni gathering of former Korean Manchurian Military Academy cadets (Seoul 1968). Park Chung Hee was not present. Seated figures include Yi Hallim (first from the right); Yi Chuil (second from the right); Ch'oe Ch'angŏn (fourth from the right). Standing figures include Kim Yun'gŭn (third from the right); Kim Yŏngt'aek (fourth from the right); Kim Kwangsik (fifth from the right); Pang Wŏnch'ŏl (eighth from the right); Yi Sŏpchun (ninth from the right); Kim Min'gyu (tenth from the right); Kim Muk (twelfth from the right). Courtesy of Kim Kwangsik.

CONCLUSION

In the early morning of August 6, 1945, oblivious to the atomic bombing that was occurring at that very moment in Hiroshima and would soon end the war, the MMA 7 Nikkei class, including all the MMA 7 Korean cadets, was setting out from Lalatun in high spirits on one of the academy's grueling seasonal endurance marches.[1] On the evening of August 8 they trudged back to the school exhausted from three days of fiery, "steel-melting" summer heat and continuous heavy rains. Soon after the 2130 lights-out they were deep asleep in their sections. About five hours later, in the pre-dawn dark of August 9, they suddenly woke to urgent bugling and shouts of the sentry duty cadets yelling "Emergency muster!" and then "Air raid alert!" Scrambling into their uniforms and grabbing their guns and swords, they rushed outside, lining up next to the antiaircraft shelters in front of their barracks. Outside they could hear, and literally feel under their feet, the earth-shaking crash of bombs reverberating from all four corners of the Manchukuo capital, Xinjing. In the distance they could also see bluish white flashes of light where the bombs were striking the city, all the more visible in the wartime blackout that was in effect at the school. Eventually the bombing subsided and then stopped, and the cadets returned uneasily to their barracks.[2] MMA officials thought at first that the bombing was an American incursion from north China, but later that morning they learned that it was in fact the opening foray of a massive, three-pronged invasion of Manchuria by the Soviet Union—from the Trans-Baikal region in the west, across the Amur River in the north, and across the Ussuri River in the east. The invasion had commenced about ten minutes after midnight with a full frontal assault in the north and aerial bombings by small Soviet planes in all parts of the country. As the cadets and their commanders stood looking in surprise and disbelief at the pyrotechnics over Xinjing, a Soviet force of forty-seven divisions, 1.6 million troops, 6,500 aircraft, and 4,500 armored vehicles was converging upon them, with the tanks moving as fast as 30 miles per hour.[3] Although few if any of the officers or cadets could have imagined it at the time, the end of the Imperial Japanese Army and its academies was at hand.

The End of the MMA

Despite incredulity at the MMA, a full-scale Soviet invasion had been long in the planning. It had even been regarded as imminent for some time by Kwantung Army intelligence, if only to be downplayed by a more sanguine Kwantung Army headquarters that had envisioned an attack coming months later at the earliest.[4] Since at least October 1944, as Germany's defeat became ever more palpable, the Soviets had in fact been moving men and matériel from the western front into Siberia in preparation for a final offensive against the Japanese. By the spring of 1945, as Alvin Coox notes, a Soviet division was being diverted east every three days, an astonishing rate of about ten divisions per month.[5] In contrast, during this same period the Kwantung Army, which had peaked in numbers and strength during the Kantokuen buildup and maneuvers following Hitler's invasion of Russia in June 1941, was seeing its finest divisions being redeployed to more urgent combat theaters as the war in China expanded throughout Asia after Pearl Harbor. By the summer of 1945 it was desperately filling its ranks with not only inexperienced but also unqualified conscripts, including men who ordinarily would have been rejected for service on account of their age or physical condition.[6]

Fully aware of its deficiencies, the Kwantung Army had fallen back on the IJA's bedrock ideology of "spirit" and "belief in certain victory," which, as we have seen, had reached new levels of intensity at the MMA and JMA during the war.[7] While exhorting its soldiers to suicidal attacks against anticipated superior forces and firepower, however, the army had also made more practical contingency plans to pull back and concentrate its depleted forces for a final stand in a redoubt area centered on the city of Tonghua, near the Manchurian-Korean border, about 175 miles from Xinjing.[8] On August 11, two days after the Soviet bombings, the Kwantung Army headquarters moved to Tonghua, followed by the Manchukuo emperor and his entourage and most of the state's central bureaucracy. Left behind to defend the capital from the approaching Russians was an assortment of small units from the Manchukuo Army, supported by one newly conscripted division, one equally untested independent mixed brigade of the Kwantung Thirtieth Army, both at only 15 percent capacity, and the MMA's corps of cadets at Lalatun.[9] Lieutenant General Yamada Tetsujirō (JMA 20), who had succeeded Nagumo Shin'ichirō as MMA superintendent in 1943, was placed in charge of the Manchukuo Army units under the overall command of the Thirtieth Army and appointed head of the Xinjing Defense Garrison.[10]

Yamada moved quickly to integrate the MMA cadets into the overall defense plan.[11] Altogether in August 1945 there were 1,737 cadets enrolled at the academy in four classes (MMA 4-MMA 7) in various stages of progress.[12] There were also about thirty Japanese and Korean medical and veterinary service cadets in the MMA 6 class who were doing their *taizuki* in Kwantung Army units on the Soviet-Manchukuo border, more than half of whom were killed in the first thrust of the Soviet invasion.[13] Of the cadets resident at the academy, most were Chinese; the Japanese and Koreans were concentrated in the MMA 7 class.[14] Having entered only about eight months earlier, the MMA 7 cadets had just completed their first-term exams, and few even knew how to handle some of the weapons they were now being asked to field in defense of the city.[15] On Yamada's orders, a small contingent of about 20 Nikkei, along with assorted Mankei cadets, civilian instructors, clerks, subordinate officials, and officers, was organized as a home defense unit to guard the MMA.[16] The rest of the cadets were organized into a combat unit of seven infantry companies (five Mankei infantry companies from different classes plus two Nikkei companies from the MMA 7 class).[17] After burning academy documents, including even the school's textbooks, the combat unit held a "going to war" ceremony (*shutsujin no shiki*) on August 13 at the MMA shrine, sang both the Japanese and Manchukuo anthems, shouted three *banzai* cheers, and left for Xinjing.[18] Once there the Nikkei companies were ordered to take the lead in the construction of an 11,000-meter (about 36,000-foot) north-south defense line stretching across Jilin Avenue west of the Yitong River bridge in the southeastern part of the city. Perhaps less than fully confident of Chinese loyalties, a concern that would later prove prescient, Yamada deployed the Mankei cadet companies on the far side of the river to the east. The Nikkei companies were given grenades and sent into the newly dug trenches with orders to attack and disable the Soviet tanks that were expected early the next morning.[19]

As it turned out, the battle with the Soviets never ensued. August 14 came and went with the Nikkei cadets continuing to build up the defense fortifications and hunkered down in the Jilin Avenue trenches nervously holding their grenades. At noon on August 15 Superintendent Yamada joined the commander of the Thirtieth Army, Lieutenant General Iida Shōjirō, and his staff at their headquarters to listen to the Japanese emperor's radio broadcast. Yamada later recollected that the speech was difficult to understand in its entirety, but the main point was clear: the war was over and Japan had accepted defeat. He returned to the Jilin Avenue defense line to report the surrender to the combat units. Shock and depression spread out among the

Japanese cadets and officers.[20] According to Nishikawa Nobuyoshi (MMA 7), "We just felt drained and collapsed on the ground."[21]

But worse was yet to come. General pandemonium swept the capital and country after news of the Japanese defeat, with masses of terrified Japanese civilians fleeing in fear of Chinese reprisals, and widespread looting and violence.[22] The Kwantung Army also had to deal with revolts within the Manchukuo Army, often led by Chinese graduates of the MMA who had been active in the secret anti-Japanese nationalist and communist organizations that had proliferated at the academy throughout its existence.[23] One of the largest incidents occurred on the Sungari (Songhua) River where Chinese troops who were part of the Manchukuo Army's river force (*kōjōgun*) mutinied after encountering a Soviet vessel moving upstream, killing all the Japanese officers in their unit, including three of Park Chung Hee's former Zama classmates.[24] Kim Tonghun (MMA 6), who had graduated from the MMA preparatory course in July 1945 and was doing a medical service *taizuki* with a Manchukuo Army regiment when the war ended, recalled that "many people died in the mutinies" and that he and other Korean (and Japanese) cadets in the regiment owed their lives to the Japanese commander, who protected them with a guard and saw that they were taken safely to a Kwantung Army unit.[25]

At the same time Superintendent Yamada was trying to cope with wholesale rebellions of Manchukuo Army units in Xinjing itself. Even as early as August 13, rumors of an impending Japanese surrender had led to a defection from Yamada's defense command of a unit of the imperial guards, whose Chinese commander had shot and killed the Japanese officer who had tried to dissuade him, and took his troops east in the direction of Jilin.[26] On August 15, immediately after the emperor's speech, the five MMA Mankei companies who had formed the bulk of the academy's combat defense unit also mutinied against their Japanese section and company commanders, wounding two in the process, and left the city to join Chiang Kai-shek's Chinese nationalist forces.[27] Simultaneously at Lalatun itself, Chinese officers and cadets were turning against the small group of Japanese who had remained behind to lead the academy's defense and were firing shots at the MMA headquarters building. Eventually an agreement was reached between the two sides, transferring control of the academy to the Mankei and allowing the Japanese officers and cadets to leave the school and join the two Nikkei companies already in Xinjing.[28]

While the Manchukuo Army was disintegrating, pockets of the Kwantung Army throughout the country were continuing to hold out and fight despite a cease-fire order from the headquarters in Tonghua. Not until the end of August, two weeks after the Japanese emperor's speech, did resistance completely come to an end.[29] In other units, numbers of high-ranking IJA officers and their staff, despondent at the news of Japan's surrender, were committing suicide.[30] Even the cadets were not immune to such despair: in Xinjing on August 15, two of Park Chung Hee's MMA 2 classmates, both of whom, like Park, had just been promoted to first lieutenant on August 1, took their own lives. One of them, Toda Tokuji, who had been attached to the imperial guards infantry unit, felt responsible for the unit's defection on August 13 and the resulting murder of his senior officer.[31] The other, Noda Hiroshi, who in his years at Zama had been one of Park Chung Hee's MMA 2 section mates and infantry drill partners, was serving at the academy in August 1945 as a section commander for the MMA 7 class when he was tapped by Superintendent Yamada to act as the general's personal liaison to the Thirtieth Army as part of the overall capital defense plan.[32] On what would be his final dispatch to the Thirtieth following the surrender, he made a detour to Kodama Park, where he killed himself in front of the chūkonhi, the park's monument to Japan's "loyal spirits" who had perished during the Russo-Japanese War.[33]

Resistance and self-sacrifice did little to stem the inevitable Soviet advance. After the emperor's speech and Mankei mutinies, the Japanese units of the Xinjing Defense Garrison, including the MMA 7 Nikkei combat companies, withdrew from Jilin Avenue to the Manchukuo Army Staff College in the southern part of the city, where they huddled in a single building, waiting for the Russians to arrive, while Superintendent Yamada negotiated a truce line between the Nikkei and Mankei forces to maintain order and prevent bloodshed. On August 18 a Soviet advance army unit arrived in Xinjing by plane, and the next day the Kwantung and Manchukuo Army units in the capital were disarmed and disbanded.[34]

Through the Kwantung Army command, which was handling all the surrender negotiations, Yamada tried to secure the release of the MMA 7 Japanese cadets on grounds of their youth, but there was no immediate response from the Russians. Nearly two anxious weeks passed as the cadets waited to hear some word about their fate. On the night of September 1, the Japanese officers, sensing negotiations were not going well, secretly told the cadets that if they had any relatives or contacts in the area and wanted to leave, they would be erased from the roll call list and allowed to escape. Of the 375 MMA 7 Japanese cadets, only about 50 left, including 20 who were sick. In the spirit of danketsu in which they had been trained, more than 300 chose to remain with the group. At 0600 the next morning all those still on the list were officially designated prisoners of war of the Soviet army. Eventually they were shipped off to labor camps in Siberia, together with Superintendent Yamada and his officers and about 600,000 officers and soldiers of the Kwantung Army. Like Yamada and many other regular army prisoners, many of the MMA 7 cadets would not be repatriated for another five years, and eighty-three would never return at all.[35]

The end of the MMA thus came suddenly and swiftly, like the proverbial thief in the night. Only six days after they had watched the Soviet bombs falling on Xinjing, the last small unit of MMA 7 Nikkei cadets and their officers who had remained at the school assembled at the MMA shine for a final late afternoon "bowing from afar" (yōhai). Then, under the command of Captain Moriwaki Tameo (CTS 7), who had helped to negotiate the group's safe withdrawal from the school, the cadets set the shrine on fire and watched it burn to the ground before marching out the Lalatun gates one final time on their way to the capital.[36] Later, as they and their classmates were being packed into freight cars for the long and hard trip north, the Soviet army was busily turning the academy into a base for its occupying forces in the area.[37] As the Manchurian fall of 1945 was settling in, it was only too clear that the MMA, together with the army and country that had created and built it, had ceased to exist.

The End of the JMA

The end of the JMA was less sudden but no less final.[38] Enrolled at the academy in August 1945 were two classes that had taken their yoka at the JMA Preparatory Academy (JMAP) in Asaka, the JMA 59 and the JMA 60, together with associated classes from other parts of the empire in the International Corps of Cadets, including the MMA 4 and MMA 6 classes from Lalatun.[39] All of these classes had been dramatically expanded in size as a result of the war, while their training time had been radically shortened. There were Korean cadets in all of the classes: three in the JMA 59, six in the JMA 60, five in the MMA 4, and seven in the MMA 6.[40] A number of these would later play important roles in the 1961 South Korean coup and its aftermath.[41] The JMA 58 class, with six Koreans, and its associated MMA 3 class, with two Koreans, had only just graduated on June 17, 1945, in what would turn out to be the academy's last commencement. A sign perhaps of the dangerous times and an omen of worse to come, no member of the Japanese imperial family had attended the ceremony; the emperor, as was customary, had gone to Zama the previous year when Park Chung Hee and the MMA 2/JMA 57 class had graduated, but in June 1945 he had sent his military aide-de-camp in his place.

By the summer of 1945 the JMA was in a high state of emergency. Unlike Manchuria, which until the Soviet attack had been largely free of aerial bombings, Japan had been experiencing devastating air strikes by the United States since late 1944, and the JMA was well within the targeted areas. The academy itself was bombed and suffered damage on various occasions during that period, and in May 1945 retaliating cadets had succeeded in shooting down a U.S. Grumman Avenger attack plane that had flown into Zama airspace. A full-scale invasion by enemy forces was expected at any moment, and because of its location near Sagami Bay, where a major U.S. landing was anticipated, officers and cadets were certain that the JMA would play a crucial role in the decisive battle for the homeland. By April 1945, the Fifty-third Army had moved its headquarters into the south barracks of the academy, where the International Corps of Cadets was also housed, and a unit of the 1st Anti-Aircraft Division was also being bivouacked on school grounds to defend the Kyōto-Yokohama area.

Even as air strikes continued, anxieties increased, and a restrictive food regimen was put into place, the JMA authorities continued throughout the late spring and early summer of 1945 to heed as closely as possible to the regular school schedule. In the end, however, they decided to make plans for evacuation to the Mochizuki area of Nagano Prefecture northwest of Zama, appropriating local elementary schools and other facilities in the region for JMA use. The JMA 59 class left first, in early June, even before the JMA 58 commencement. At the beginning of July they were followed by the JMA administrative headquarters and other key units of the school, including the academic and equestrian divisions and material stores. Typically, the move was officially described in positive, aggressive terms as a "long-term exercise" (chōki enshū), but the fact that the shinrei or "divine spirit" of the academy's Otakebi Shrine was also evacuated and reenshrined with another spirit (gōshi) in a shrine in the Mochizuki area indicated the seriousness of the move and the uncertainty about the future that it entailed.[42] At the end of the month, immediately upon matriculation, the entering JMA 60 and its associated international classes, including the MMA 6, were evacuated to Mochizuki and another evacuation camp in Gunma Prefecture.

By the beginning of August, then, the JMA was largely deserted, except for about 300 JMA 60 cadets in "special branches."[43] The JMA 59 class, which had been the first to evacuate, was dispersed in various locations for its scheduled second set of field exercises, with the academy superintendent, Lieutenant General Kitano Kenzō (JMA 22), and the commandant of cadets, Colonel Yanoi Hiroshi (JMA 35), making inspection rounds at each encampment, while the bulk of the JMA 60 class was training at two sites in the Nagano-Gunma evacuation area under the supervision of the vice superintendent, Major General Matsumura Hiroshi (JMA 33). Shortly before noon on August 15 all of the scattered units were ordered to line up at their respective training sites to hear the emperor's broadcast. Afterward the stunned cadets were ordered by their commanders to remain in place until further instructions, and warned against any rash behavior. The warning was by no means routine, given the cadet suicides at the MMA and those that were to follow at Zama, but in the immediate aftermath of the surrender, it was one of JMA 59 section commanders himself whose reaction was extreme and tragic. Crazed by the news of the defeat, he called his section together and, accusing one of the JMA 59 Korean cadets, Kim Chaegon, of being a dangerous collaborator with the enemy because of Kim's connections with a Christian organization in Yokohama, he proceeded to kill Kim on the spot, subsequently taking his own life the next day. Horrified, the JMA authorities moved all Koreans in the JMA 59 and JMA 60 classes, including those in the MMA classes from Lalatun, to separate quarters to maintain order and avoid any further possible bloodshed.[44] Eventually the order came for all the cadets to return to the JMA, and one by one each unit began to make its way back to Zama.

By August 18 most of the units had returned to the academy, rejoining the 300 special branch cadets who had remained there, and the atmosphere quickly shifted from despair to defiance, fueled by rumors that the reports of Japan's defeat were not genuine and that the emperor's broadcast had been faked. Some cadets printed a manifesto vowing resistance to any surrender, and on the evening of August 20, as the movement was reaching its peak, all interested parties met with Commandant Yanoi to decide what to do. A division of opinion ensued between those who advocated continuing to fight and those who called for collective suicide. In the absence of the superintendent, who was still in Nagano, the final decision was left to the commandant.

In the meantime, orders had been sent out from Imperial General Headquarters in Tokyo to cease resistance and demobilize, and the next day, August 22, Superintendent Kitano returned to the academy. Assembling the cadets, he explained the decision to end the war and told them they had no choice but to accept it. Commandant Yanoi repeated this injunction on August 23 in a speech to the cadets in the Great Lecture Hall, adding that the orders had also come down for an emergency evacuation back to Nagano Prefecture, which would commence the following day. After addresses by both the superintendent and commandant, the resistance movement within the school gradually dissipated. For the most part the cadets began their preparations for the move, putting their personal things in order and randomly burning textbooks, notebooks, and in some cases even diaries in front of the anti-aircraft barracks, where tables and chairs had been piled up like small mountains, tinder for a great burning of academy documents. Two cadets in the JMA 59 class, however, Suzuki Teruyuki and Sajima Hiroyuki, refused to accept the surrender. Together around 2300 that evening they attempted suicide by ritual disembowelment in the bowing area of the Otakebi Shrine. Sajima survived; Suzuki did not.

Early in the morning of August 23, as Suzuki lay dying in the nearby Sagamihara Army Hospital, each cadet unit, still reeling from the news of the night before, successively departed through the JMA gates. Major Ikegami Kunio (JMA 53) and other officers attached to the academy remained behind to make certain that all important items had been destroyed or properly disposed of. When finished, they pulled down and buried the great stone slab on which the imperial name of the school, Sōbudai, had been carved. They also buried the two large stone lions on either side of the entrance to the Great Lecture Hall that had been seized as trophies from China during the war (see Chapter 2). Finally, they burned down the Otakebi Shrine. Having completed their assigned tasks, they boarded a truck and followed after the cadet units, "looking back at the smoke from the documents burned the day before rising into the summer evening sky between the now empty barracks."[45]

A week later, on August 30, all of the cadet units were officially demobilized at their evacuation sites and left the next day for their homes in Japan, Korea, and other parts of the former empire. On September 5 a battalion of the U.S. 1st Cavalry Division entered and took possession of the JMA, turning it into an American army base and bringing to a decisive end the school's long history as the cradle of the Imperial Japanese Army's officer corps.[46]

New Beginnings

Imperialism, war, and two successive waves of militarization had significantly changed Korea since the late nineteenth century, adding new martial dimensions to Korean life that had had little or no prominence before. A first wave beginning in the 1860s and ending with the dissolution of the

Great Han Empire army in 1907 had shattered more than two centuries of Chosŏn peace and transformed Korean thinking about the military. Modernity and military had appeared simultaneously on Korean shores, most dramatically in the form of Western and Japanese gunboats, and it was not surprising that the two would be deeply linked in the minds of Chosŏn reformers seeking to establish a viable modern nation-state. For them and many of their intellectual successors in the twentieth century, the very loss of nationhood to Japan in 1910 served only to prove the point: military strength was as essential to the viability of the modern nation-state as martial virtues were essential to the development of its citizenry, most particularly its men.

A second wave of militarization, beginning with Japan's invasion of Manchuria in September 1931, further shaped and deepened these martial orientations. It drew more of the population than ever before into its net; it also introduced Koreans to a new form of nationalism embodied in the Imperial Japanese Army, a military nationalism that, while resonating with many aspects of martial thinking in Korea since the late nineteenth century, also reshaped and combined them in unique ways. Above all, it placed military officers at the center of the nation-building effort and exalted a military ethos with distinct conceptions of status, leadership, economic and social organization, tactics, spirit, and discipline, all of which could be applied to the tasks of nation building as well as to war.[47] Most important, the second wave also gave birth to a Korean officer corps that had been rigorously trained and molded by the IJA precisely in this ethos at Lalatun and Zama and especially at Lalatun, where IJA ideology had assumed a radical character under Kwantung Army influence and nation building was seen as an integral part of the army's role and mission. And among the MMA Korean graduates, no one had imbibed and embraced this ethos more thoroughly and enthusiastically than Park Chung Hee, who had left a secure and respected teaching position, as well as a wife and daughter, to pursue his dream of becoming an officer, and who, according to his MMA 2 classmate Yi Hallim, had also always had a strong "political" bent, even as a cadet.[48] By the autumn of 1945, however, the season of war was over, the wave of militarization that had begun in the 1930s had peaked and crashed, and the principal apparatuses of IJA military culture and practice were being dismantled and transformed under foreign occupation. All that had once seemed so solid, so inexorable, had vanished or collapsed in the wake of Japan's defeat. And Korea's martial lineages seemed finally to have run their course.

In fact, the course was only just beginning. Though severed from their original temporal and institutional contexts, the lineages of military culture and practice continued to exist in various ways and to varying degrees in the memory and psyche of an entire generation of Koreans, but most markedly in the orientations, dispositions, and habits of the former cadets of Lalatun and Zama, most notably Park Chung Hee. And after August 15, 1945, individually and in groups, the Korean alumni of the schools were gradually making their way back to the peninsula. Those deployed in Manchuria faced particular dangers and challenges. Some, like the Korean cadets of the MMA 7 class, managed to slip away soon after the surrender and before the Soviet arrival.[49] Others were taken prisoner by the Russians but allowed to leave after identifying themselves as Korean.[50] Some, like Kim Yŏngt'aek (MMA 1), who spoke fluent Mandarin, simply changed into Chinese clothes and blended into the population, heading south by whatever means available: train, horse-drawn wagon, or foot.[51]

Many stopped for a time in Xinjing, where a considerable number of Korean CTS and MMA graduates had congregated, forming an ad hoc military security unit in the Korean section of the now defunct capital to protect themselves and Korean residents of the city in the ensuing anarchy following Japan's surrender.[52] Others, such as Park Chung Hee, deployed in more distant parts of the country at the end of the war, took different, more circuitous routes back to their homes. Park, together with his MMA 2 Chinese classmate Gao Qingyin and three other Korean officers, including two MMA 1 graduates who would later participate in the 1961 coup, was serving near the Mongolian and north China borders more than 500 miles southwest of Xinjing in the 8th Infantry Regiment of the Manchukuo Fifth District Army, headquartered at Banbishan in Rehe province. Typical of the Fifth District Army, whose primary mission was to suppress the communist guerilla forces from the Chinese Eighth Route Army that were constantly infiltrating the region, Park's regiment was organized into "flying columns" (yūgekitai), small, independent land units capable of rapid mobility. Park first commanded a combat platoon in the regiment's 6th Company before being appointed as adjutant to the Chinese regimental commander, Colonel Tang Jirong, in Banbishan, where Gao was also serving as the regiment's financial officer. After the Soviets invaded on August 9, the various components of the regiment were ordered to regroup in Xinglong, southeast of Banbishan, before proceeding to Mongolia to block the attack, but by the time the headquarters and other units arrived in the town on August 17, delayed by torrential rains and flooding, the war had already been over for two days. Unlike the situation in many other parts of the country, the surrender and demobilization in Xinglong proceeded peacefully. The thirteen Japanese officers in the 8th Regiment were turned over to a Kwantung Army battalion, while Park and the other Korean officers were allowed to leave without incident.[53]

As they straggled back to Korea from various directions in the months after the surrender, the Korean graduates of the MMA and JMA discovered a country very different from the one they had left. Unlike Park Chung Hee, most of the former cadets had family roots in the northern half of a now divided peninsula, and the occupying Soviet forces, together with their Korean communist allies, were quick to arrest and imprison Korean officers who had served the Japanese Imperial Army either in Manchuria or elsewhere, regardless of their personal motivations or intentions.[54]

In the southern half of the peninsula, however, in an irony only history can muster, these men would find a welcoming presence in the American occupation forces, who were more concerned with building up a native force for maintaining order and, later, for containing a potent communist political threat than with arresting or punishing men who had served a now utterly defeated enemy that was also rapidly turning into a key Cold War ally. In what would eventually become the Republic of Korea Army, many of the former graduates of the MMA and JMA thus found a home, and Korea's martial lineages, honed at Lalatun and Zama, gained a new lease on life, one that would be sustained and reconfigured in a new international order and a third wave of war and militarization on the peninsula that would dwarf anything previously seen.

As Park Chung Hee was returning to Korea from China in 1946, the contours of this new world were only just beginning to emerge, but there were already some telling signs. When Park disembarked at Pusan on May 8 of that year, already eight regiments of a nascent South Korean army had been created under American tutelage, and only seven days earlier a military academy had been established at T'aenŭng in the northeastern part of Seoul on the site of a former Japanese army camp.[55] The Japanese soldiers were of course gone, but within the gates of the new academy and the still untested military units, aspects of IJA culture and practice continued to flourish, and in the after-hours drinking houses patronized by recommissioned Korean officers, one could still hear robust renditions of "Song of the Shōwa Restoration."[56]

Notes

Korean MMA Cadets by Class

Glossary of Names and Terms

Bibliography

Sources and Acknowledgments

Index

NOTES

Introduction

1. By "modernization," I do not mean to imply any kind of normative or linear process. Rather, I employ the term "modernization" here historically, as a catchall expression or slogan that was used frequently at the time by Park Chung Hee and others to describe the state's overall development goals, which were largely concentrated in one way or another on economic growth. On *kaebal tokchae*, see, for example, Yi Pyŏngch'ŏn, ed., *Kaebal tokchae wa Pak Chŏnghŭi sidae: uri sidae ŭi chŏngch'i-kyŏngjejŏk kiwŏn* [The era of developmental dictatorship and Park Chung Hee: the political-economic origins of our time] (Seoul: Ch'angbi, 2003).

2. The terms "militarism" and "militarist" as used in this book are best understood empirically in the context of Korean history. Indeed, explaining these terms and exploring their implications and reach are central to this study. Here I simply use the terms in a general, eclectic sense as relating to a form of nationalism that privileges the military, especially in politics, and seeks to organize the nation on the basis of military ideals and models. Although the terms "fascist" (*p'asisŭt'ŭ*) and "fascism" (*p'asijŭm*) are more commonly applied in South Korean historiography to Japanese colonial rule, from time to time (as seen in Yi Pyŏngch'ŏn above, note 1) one also encounters the terms in reference to Park and his regime, and indeed, the *p'asijŭm* of the former is not infrequently linked in such work to the latter. As I point out in this book, Park, like many Koreans of his generation, was fascinated by both Hitler and Mussolini and found much to admire in both. Depending on how one defines the term, moreover, I think it is possible to make an argument that the Park Chung Hee regime had certain "fascist" characteristics. In my own work, however, I choose to avoid the term, preferring instead to use "militarist" or "militarism." I do this for several reasons. First, even more than "militarism," which also requires definition but unequivocally places the military at the center of any definition, it is very difficult for scholars to agree on a general definition of "fascism," one, for example, that might at once encompass Mussolini's Italy, Hitlerian Germany, 1940s Japan, and Park Chung Hee's Korea. Even some South Korean writers who use the term struggle with its meaning, finding it "unreasonable" to apply the term in a blanket sense to the whole of Park's rule. See, for example, Chin Chunggwŏn, "Chugŭn tokchaeja ŭi sahoe" [Society of the dead dictator], in Yi Pyŏngch'ŏn, *Kaebal tokchae wa Pak Chŏnghŭi sidae*, 349–350. Second, precisely because a clear meaning is so elusive, the term when used tends to serve largely as a pejorative or denunciatory political epithet, which does nothing tangible to expand our knowledge of the subject in question, and even confuses the issue by implying correspondences with other "fascist" regimes, especially Italy or Germany, that may not in fact stand up to empirical scrutiny. In that sense the use of the term in Korean scholarship might be said to resemble the use of another term, "feudal" (*ponggŏn*), which has often been applied without precision to the Chosŏn dynasty and earlier Korean states as a kind of general negative signifier of pre-modernity. Third, and most important, I prefer the term "militarism" because, quite simply, my focus in this work is on the history of the South Korean military, the army especially, and the ways in which that institution, its culture and practice, helped to create and shape the country's development. Using "militarism" in that grounded sense seems entirely appropriate and instructive; indeed, it underscores the core thesis of this book.

3. On democratic politics, see, for example, David Chamberlin Cole and Princeton N. Lyman, *Korean Development: The Interplay of Politics and Economics* (Cambridge, MA: Harvard University Press, 1971). On corporatist labor policies, see Hwasook Nam, *Building Ships, Building a Nation: Korea's Democratic Unionism under Park Chung Hee*

(Seattle: University of Washington Press, 2009); on a more inclusive approach to business, see, for example, Eun Mee Kim, *Big Business, Strong State: Collusion and Conflict in South Korean Development,* 1960–1990 (Albany: State University of New York Press, 1997). And for an excellent new study of the last seven years of Park's rule, see Paul Y. Chang, *Protest Dialectics: State Repression and South Korea's Democracy Movement, 1970–1979* (Stanford, CA: Stanford University Press, 2015).

4. Chŏng Chaegyŏng, ed., *Pak Chŏnghŭi silgi: haengjŏk ch'orok* [The true record of Park Chung Hee: selected excerpts] (Seoul: Chimmundang, 1994), 629.

5. Both Kim and O have written important and detailed memoirs indispensable to any study of the Park regime. See Kim Chŏngnyŏm, *Han'guk kyŏngje ch'ŏngch'aek 30-nyŏnsa: Kim Chŏngnyŏm hoegorok* [A thirty-year history of Korean economic policy: the memoirs of Kim Chŏngnyŏm] (Seoul: Chungang Ilbosa, 1995), and *A, Pak Chŏnghŭi* [Ah, Park Chung Hee] (Seoul: Chungang M&B, 1997). See also O Wŏnch'ol, *Han'guk kyŏngje kŏnsŏl: enjiniŏring ŏp'ŭroch'i* [The economic construction of Korea: an engineering approach], 7 vols. (Seoul: Kia Kyŏngje Yŏn'guso, 1995), and *Pak Chŏnghŭi nŭn ŏttŏk'e kangguk mandŭrŏnna: pulgul ŭi tojŏn Hangang ŭi kijŏk* [How Park Chung Hee made a strong country: never bending to challenge: the miracle on the Han River] (Seoul: Tongsŏ Munhwasa, 2006).

6. Japanese who knew Park tended to echo this view. In 1977, for example, when Kishi Yonesaku, one of Park's former teachers at Taegu Normal School in the 1930s, visited Park at the South Korean presidential Blue House, he was struck not only by Park's precise Japanese but also by what he described as a "temperament . . . forged at the Japanese Military Academy." Kishi Yonesaku, *Ruten kyōiku rokujūnen* [Constant motion: my 60 years in education] (privately published, 1982), 241.

7. The phrase is from Jo Guldi and David Armitage, *The History Manifesto* (Cambridge: Cambridge University Press, 2014), 121.

8. This is not of course meant in any sense as a reductionist statement. Though I would argue that the IJA templates were fundamental and pervasive in the construction and character of the Park Chung Hee state, I certainly would not deny that other forces, influences, and models also played a part in the state's formation and South Korea's development. In an earlier work I myself explored this question in terms of the rise of a Korean capitalist class during the colonial period and the colonial government-business relationship. See Carter J. Eckert, *Offspring of Empire: The Colonial Origins of Korean Capitalism, 1876–1945* (Seattle: University of Washington Press, 1991). Also, with respect to the immediate post-1945 decades, including the Park years, it need hardly be said that the influence of the United States in South Korea in this period was at its peak. One should also note that Park himself was intrigued by a variety of economically successful contemporary state models, including West Germany, Israel, and, not least of all, postwar Japan. See, for example, Pak Chŏnghŭi, *Kukka wa hyŏngmyŏng kwa na* [The country, the revolution, and I] (Seoul: Hyangmunsa, 1963), 158–220. See also Nishino Junya, "Ilbon model essŏ Han'gukchŏk hyŏksin ŭro: 1970 nyŏndae chunghwahak kongŏphwa rŭl tullŏssan chŏngch'aek kwajŏng" [Korean innovation on the Japanese model: policy formation surrounding the 1970s heavy and chemical industrialization], in *Tet'angt'ŭ wa Pak Chŏnghŭi* [Détente and Park Chung Hee], ed. Sin Ukhŭi (Seoul: Nonhyŏng, 2011), 167–206.

9. Foucault, "Nietzsche, Genealogy, History," in *The Foucault Reader,* ed. Paul Rabinow (New York: Pantheon, 1984), 80. See also Roger Chartier, "Chimera of the Origin: Archeology, Cultural History, and the French Revolution," in *Foucault and the Writing of History,* ed. Jan Goldstein (Oxford: Blackwell, 1994), 167–186.

10. Carol Gluck, *Japan's Modern Myths: Ideology in the Late Meiji Period* (Princeton, NJ: Princeton University Press, 1985), 6.

11. William H. Sewell Jr., *Logics of History: Social Theory and Social Transformation* (Chicago: University of Chicago Press, 2005), 102.

12. The quote is from ibid., 172.

13. Keith Michael Baker, "A Foucauldian French Revolution?" in Goldstein, *Foucault and the Writing of History*, 192.

14. For an empirical explanation of "militarization" in the Korean historical context, see Chapters 1 and 2. Here I simply employ the term in a commonly understood general sense as a multifaceted process by which a society equips and prepares itself for war. See, for example, Alagappa Muthiah, ed., *Coercion and Governance: The Declining Political Role of the Military in Asia* (Stanford, CA: Stanford University Press, 2001), 502.

15. Max Weber, *Economy and Society*, ed. Guenther Roth and Claus Wittich (Berkeley: University of California Press, 1968), 2:1155–1156.

16. Michel Foucault, *Discipline and Punish: The Birth of the Prison,* trans. Alan Sheridan (New York: Vintage Books, 1979), 138.

17. Samuel P. Huntington, *Political Order in Changing Societies* (New Haven, CT: Yale University Press, 1968), 197. Although still generally less historical than theoretical, the subfield of military sociology within this literature, pioneered by Morris Janowitz, has offered an important alternative to Huntington's perspective, putting greater emphasis on the particular characteristics of a given military establishment and its officers. See Morris Janowitz, *Military in the Development of New Nations: An Essay in Comparative Analysis* (Chicago: University of Chicago Press, 1964). See also Michel Louis Martin and Ellen Stern McCrate, eds., *Military, Militarism, and the Polity: Essays in Honor of Morris Janowitz* (New York: The Free Press, 1984); also Morris Janowitz and Jacques Van Doorn, eds., *On Military Ideology* (Rotterdam: Rotterdam University Press, 1971). This view can also be found in some of the related social science work specifically on Korea. See, for example, Se-Jin Kim, *Politics of Military Revolution in Korea* (Chapel Hill: University of North Carolina Press, 1971; see also Jon Huer, *Marching Orders: The Role of the Military in South Korea's "Economic Miracle," 1961–1971* (New York: Greenwood Press, 1989), based on English-language sources, including Se-Jin Kim. One of Janowitz's former students, Hong Tusŭng, has been a key figure in the development of military sociology in Korea, and although his work does not deal directly with IJA legacies and influences, it provides an insightful social analysis of the post-1945 South Korean military elite, civil-military relations, and other related subjects. See Hong Tusŭng, *Han'guk kundae ŭi sahoehak* [Sociology of the Korean military] (Seoul: Nanam, 1993). For a study of the changing political role of the military in Asia in more recent years, see Alagappa, *Coercion and Governance.*

18. For an excellent introduction to this literature as a whole, see Meredith Woo-Cumings, ed., *The Developmental State* (Ithaca, NY: Cornell University Press, 1999). On Korea specifically, see, for example, Chalmers Johnson, *MITI and the Japanese Miracle: The Growth of Industrial Policy, 1925–1975* (Stanford, CT: Stanford University Press, 1982), 317; Alice H. Amsden, *Asia's Next Giant: South Korea and Late Industrialization* (New York: Oxford University Press, 1989); Stephan Haggard, *Pathways from the Periphery: The Politics of Growth in the Newly Industrializing Countries* (Ithaca, NY: Cornell University Press, 1990); Jung-en Woo, *Race to the Swift: State and Finance in Korean Industrialization* (New York: Columbia University Press, 1991). The applicability of the "developmental state" model to Korea has been a subject of debate in Korea as well: see, for example, Kim Ilyŏng, "Han'guk essŏ palchŏn kukka ŭi kiwŏn, hyŏngsŏng kwa palchŏn kŭrigo chŏnmang" [Origins, formation and development, and future of the developmental state in South Korea], *Han'guk chŏngch'i oegyo saron ch'ŏng* 23, no. 1 (August 2001): 87–126; Pak T'aegyun, "Pak Chŏnghŭi sigi rŭl t'onghae pon palchŏn kukka e taehan pip'anjŏk siron" [A critical view of developmental state theory by

looking at the Park Chung Hee era], *Yŏksa wa hyŏnsil* 74 (December 2009): 15–43. See also Byung-Kook Kim and Ezra F. Vogel, eds., *The Park Chung Hee Era: The Transformation of South Korea* (Cambridge, MA: Harvard University Press, 2011), especially the introduction by Byung-Kook Kim, as well as chapters 3 (by Hyung-A Kim) and 7 (by Byong-Kook Kim).

19. A number of scholars here deserve particular mention. See Yi Chunsik, "Pak Chŏnghŭi sidae chibae ideollogi ŭi hyŏngsŏng" [Formation of the ruling ideology of the Park Chung Hee period], in Hong Sŏngnyul, Pak Taegyun, Yi Wanbŏm, Yi Chunsik,and Mun Hyŏna, eds., *Pak Chŏnghŭi sidae yŏn'gu* [The Park Chung Hee period] (Seoul: Paeksan Sŏdang, 2002), 173–208; Sin Chubaek, "Manjugukkun sok ŭi Chosŏn'in changgyo wa Hangukkun" [Manchukuo army Korean officers and the South Korean army], *Yŏksa munje yŏn'gu* 9 (December 2002): 77–132; Chung-in Moon and Byung-joon Jun, "Modernization Strategy: Ideas and Influences," in Byung-Kook Kim and Ezra F. Vogel, eds., *The Park Chung Hee Era: The Transformation of South Korea* (Cambridge, MA: Harvard University Press, 2011), 115–139. Suk-Jung Han points to Manchukuo "as an important laboratory for post-liberation South Korea in such realms as state-making, the disciplining of its subjects and the developmental state," and wonders why it has "remained so long hidden or contained in Korean historiography"; Suk-Jung Han, "From Pusan to Fengtian: The Borderline between Korea and Manchukuo in the 1930s," *East Asian History* 30 (December 2005): 106. See also Han's more extensive development of this theme in a new work that came out just as this book was going to press: Han Sŏkchŏng, *Manju modŏn: 60-nyŏndae Han'guk kaebal ch'eje ŭi kiwŏn* [Manchuria modern: the origins of South Korea's developmental system in the 1960s] (Seoul: Munhak kwa Chisŏng Sa, 2016). Choong Soon Kim and Roger Janelli have also noted military influences in South Korea's corporate culture; see Janelli (with Dawnhee Yim), *Making Capitalism: The Social and Cultural Construction of a South Korean Conglomerate* (Stanford, CA: Stanford University Press, 1993), esp. 48–49; Choong Soon Kim, *Culture of Korean Industry: An Ethnography of Poongsan Corporation* (Tucson: University of Arizona Press, 1992); Kang Chŏngin, *Han'guk hyŏndae chŏngch'i sasang kwa Pak Chŏnghŭi* [Contemporary Korean political thought and Park Chung Hee] (Seoul: Ak'anet, 2014), 277–280. Other scholars have focused on ways in which the country's "militarized" history has structured gender in South Korea; see Seungsook Moon, *Militarized Modernity and Gendered Citizenship in South Korea* (Durham, NC: Duke University Press, 2005); Sheila Miyoshi Jager, *Narratives of Nation Building in Korea: A Genealogy of Patriotism* (Armonk, NY: M. E. Sharpe, 2003). Outside the Korean studies field, the scholarship on historical militaries and military cultures and their impact on politics and society is considerably more developed. I found the following particularly helpful: Mary P. Callahan, *Making Enemies: War and State Building in Burma* (Ithaca, NY: Cornell University Press, 2003); Isabel V. Hull, *Absolute Destruction: Military Culture and the Practices of War in Imperial Germany* (Ithaca, NY: Cornell University Press, 2005); Geoffrey Jensen, *Irrational Triumph: Cultural Despair, Military Nationalism, and the Ideological Origins of Franco's Spain* (Reno: University of Nevada Press, 2002); and M. Naim Turfan, *Rise of the Young Turks: Politics, the Military and Ottoman Collapse* (London: I. B. Tauris, 2000). See also Joel Gordon, *Nasser's Blessed Movement: Egypt's Free Officers and the July Revolution* (Cairo: American University in Cairo Press, 1992); Edna Lomsky-Feder and Eyal Ben-Ari, *Military and Militarism in Israeli Society* (Albany: State University of New York Press, 1999); Katharine E. McGregor, *History in Uniform: Military Ideology and the Construction of Indonesia's Past* (Honolulu: University of Hawaii Press, 2007); S. Victor Papacosma, *Military in Greek Politics: The 1909 Coup d'État* (Kent, OH: Kent State University Press, 1977); Andrew Selth, *Burma's Armed Forces: Power without Glory* (Norwalk, CT: East-

bridge, 2002); Peter Stanley, *White Mutiny: British Military Culture in India* (New York: New York University Press, 1998).

20. Cho Kapche, *Pak Chŏnghŭi: han kŭndaehwa hyŏngmyŏngga ŭi pijanghan saengae* [Park Chung Hee: the resolute life of a modernizing revolutionary], 13 vols. (Seoul: Cho Kapche Datk'om, 2006). While Cho's work is the most extensive and detailed study of Park Chung Hee, the past two decades have seen an enormous outpouring of popular writing on Park in South Korea, led in no small part by Cho's own effort, which was originally serialized in various forms, especially in the monthly magazine *Wŏlgan Chosŏn*, before being published in book form. Critics acknowledge Cho's impressive investigative journalism, which unearthed many hitherto unknown facts about Park, but criticize him for what they regard as a flattering, even heroic portrait that unduly elevated Park's public image and contributed to a pathological nostalgia for the man and his era that became known as the "Park Chung Hee syndrome" (*Pak Chŏnghŭi sindŭrom*). See, for example, Chin Chunggwŏn, "Chugŭn tokchaeja ŭi sahoe," 340. One popular version of Cho's work, *Nae mudŏm e ch'im ŭl paet'ŏra* [Spit on my grave], whose title was taken from a response Park had once publicly made to criticism of his regime, in fact spawned a three-volume parody by Chin Chunggwŏn called *Ne mudŏm e ch'im ŭl paet'ŭma* [I will spit on your grave], 3 vols. (Seoul: Kaemagowŏn, 1998), in which Chin made use of much of Cho's new factual material to attack Park as a "fascist." Within the scholarly community there has also been a growing general interest in Park and his era, especially in South Korea. For an excellent introduction to some of the more recent work in Korean, see Hong Sŏngnyul et al., *Pak Chŏnghŭi sidae yŏn'gu;* Chŏng Sŏnghwa, ed., *Pak Chŏnghŭi sidae yŏn'gu ŭi chaengjŏm kwa kwaje* [Debates and issues in the study of the Park Chung Hee period] (Seoul: Sŏnin, 2005). English-language scholarship in this area is also growing. Chong-Sik Lee, a doyen of political science in the Korean studies field in North America, recently published a biography of Park incorporating material from Cho Kapche and other sources. See Lee, *Park Chung-Hee: From Poverty to Power* (Palos Verdes, CA: KHU Press, 2012). In 2011 Harvard University Press also published a voluminous collection of essays on the Park regime by many of South Korea's preeminent social scientists and other scholars, who examined many diverse aspects of Park's leadership and policies. See Kim and Vogel, *The Park Chung Hee Era*. See also Hyung-A Kim and Clark Sorensen, eds., *Reassessing the Park Chung Hee Era 1961–1979: Development, Political Thought, Democracy, and Cultural Influence* (Seattle: University of Washington Press, 2011). Somewhat belatedly, historians are now also actively turning their attention to the Park period. See Kim Hyung-A, *Korea's Development under Park Chung Hee: Rapid Industrialization, 1961–1979* (London: Routledge, 2004); Hwasook Nam, *Building Ships, Building a Nation: Korea's Democratic Unionism under Park Chung Hee* (Seattle: University of Washington Press, 2009).

21. Byung-Kook Kim also makes this point in his "Introduction: The Case for Political History," in Kim and Vogel, *The Park Chung Hee Era*, 5.

22. This political divide was reinforced and heightened as a result of Park's daughter Park Geun-hye's entry into the political area and her presidential campaigns and successful election in 2012.

23. Ian Kershaw, *Hitler: 1889–1936: Hubris* (New York: W. W. Norton, 1998), xxiv.

24. Robert C. Tucker, ed., *The Marx-Engels Reader* (New York: W. W. Norton, 1972), 437.

25. Nak-Chung Paik, "How to Think about the Park Chung Hee Era," 85–91. Paik was a prominent professor of English literature at Seoul National University when he was dismissed from his professorship in 1974 for demanding a democratic constitution. He returned to his post after Park's death and is now a professor emeritus at the university.

26. Recently South Korean historian Im Chihyŏn has argued, for example, that the Park Chung Hee regime drew considerable strength from a historically based "fascist" mentality imbedded in the psyche of the Korean masses, and that one should think of the period as one of "mass dictatorship." His argument has provoked considerable criticism in academic circles for its emphasis on society rather than the state in explaining South Korea's history of authoritarianism. Although I would avoid the term "fascism" here for the reasons stated above, I do find Im's thesis compelling in many ways, resonating as it does with my own argument that the historical impact of military culture and practice has been widespread and deep, affecting not only Park himself and the ROK military but several generations of Koreans, including those like Park who lived through the colonial wartime mobilization and later the Korean War, as well as those who were raised and educated under the aegis of Park's developmental regime itself. See Im Chihyŏn, *Uri an ŭi p'asijŭm* [The fascism within us] (Seoul: Samin, 2000). Feminist scholar Kwon Insook, a former anti-government student activist in South Korea, has also written a fascinating study of this kind of internalized militarism, which, she argues, profoundly affected her consciousness both as a dissident and as a woman. See Kwon Insook, "Militarism in My Heart: Militarization of Women's Consciousness and Culture in South Korea," Ph.D. dissertation, Program in Women's Studies, Clark University, 2000.

27. See Chapters 7 and 8.

28. F. Scott Fitzgerald, *The Great Gatsby* (New York: Scribner's, 2004), 180.

1. Militarizing Time

1. Pang Wŏnch'ŏl, interview, Seoul, June 2, 1997. See also Pang Wŏnch'ŏl, *Kim Chongp'il ege koham* [Speaking truth to Kim Chongp'il] (Seoul: Sach'o, 1987), photograph on unnumbered last page. Ch'oe Ch'angŏn, another MMA 1 graduate who was also in the picture, was commander of the ROKA 3rd Corps, headquartered in Kangwŏn Province, at the time of the coup. Although he did not play a direct role in the coup and it is not clear whether or not he knew of it in advance, in the end he was clearly supportive, as indicated by his promotion to lieutenant general in August 1961. On Ch'oe, see Ch'in-Il Inmyŏng Sajŏn P'yŏnch'an Wiwŏnhoe, *Ch'in-Il inmyŏng sajŏn* [Pro-Japanese biographical dictionary], 3 vols. (Seoul: Minjok Munje Yŏn'guso, 2009) (henceforth CIS), 3:794. The best work in English on the coup remains Kim Se-Jin, *Politics of Military Revolution in Korea* (Chapel Hill: University of North Carolina Press, 1971); for a Korean-language account, see Cho Kapche, *Pak Chŏnghŭi: han kŭndaehwa hyŏngmyŏngga ŭi pijanghan saengae* [Park Chung Hee: the resolute life of a modernizing revolutionary], vol. 4 (Seoul: Cho Kapche Datk'om, 2006); for the Park regime's official history of the coup, see Kunsa Hyŏngmyŏngsa P'yŏnch'an Wiwŏnhoe, *Oillyuk kunsa hyŏngmyŏng ŭi chŏnmo* [The complete account of the 5.16 military revolution] (Seoul: Mun'gwangsa, 1964). For separate biographical accounts of the key figures in the MMA 1 class, see CIS 2:171–172 (Pang Wŏnch'ŏl); CIS 2:96 (Pak Imhang); CIS 3:150–151 (Yi Chuil); CIS 2:705–706 (Yun T'aeil). Kim Chongp'il's memoirs were recently serialized in the South Korean newspaper *Chungang ilbo* (March–December 2015).

2. The official name of the school used on official documents such as diplomas was the Manchukuo Imperial Military Academy (Dai Manshū Teikoku Rikugun Gunkan Gakkō). For an example of a 1939 diploma, see georgcl, post 125, "Axis History Forum: Manchukuo Empire," October 23, 2004, accessed October 16, 2014, http://forum .axishistory.com/viewtopic.php?f=65&t=30285&start=120.

3. *Manshū nichi-nichi shinbun,* March 21, 1941. Unfortunately, the quality of these newspaper photos is too poor to be included in this book.

4. Yun Ch'iho, *Yun Ch'iho ilgi* [Diary of Yun Ch'iho] (Seoul: Kuksa P'yŏnch'an Wiwŏnhoe, 1973–1989), vol. 10, entry for December 1, 1934.

5. Most of the works on the second wave are referenced in this book. Some of the most recent works in English include Mark Caprio, *Japanese Assimilation Policies in Colonial Korea, 1910–1945* (Seattle: University of Washington Press, 2009); T. Fujitani, *Race for Empire: Koreans as Japanese and Japanese as Americans during World War II* (Berkeley: University of California Press, 2011); Brandon Palmer, *Fighting for the Enemy: Koreans in Japan's War, 1937–1945* (Seattle: University of Washington Press, 2013); and Jun Uchida, *Brokers of Empire: Japanese Settler Colonialism in Korea, 1876–1945* (Cambridge, MA: Harvard University Asia Center, 2011).

6. Bruce Porter, *War and the Rise of the State: The Military Foundations of Modern Politics* (New York: Free Press, 1994), 63.

7. On the global militarization process discussed above, see ibid. See also Trevor N. Dupuy, *Evolution of Weapons and Warfare* (New York: Da Capo, 1984), 10–26, 47, 91–98, 113–115, 130–131, 136–140, 144–152, 154–165, 190–196, 198–202, 202–206, 316–333; John Keegan, *A History of Warfare* (New York: Vintage, 1993), esp. 301–392; William H. McNeil, *The Pursuit of Power: Technology, Armed Force, and Society since A.D. 1000* (Chicago: University of Chicago Press, 1982), esp. 117–306; Geoffrey Parker, *The Military Revolution: Military Innovation and the Rise of the West, 1500–1800*, 2nd ed. (Cambridge: Cambridge University Press, 1996); Geoffrey Best, "The Militarization of European Society, 1870–1914," in John R. Gillis, ed., *The Militarization of the Western World* (New Brunswick, NJ: Rutgers University Press, 1989), 13–29; Charles Tilly, *Coercion, Capital, and European States, AD 990–1992*, rev. ed. (Malden, MA: Blackwell, 1992), 67–95; E. J. Hobsbawm, *The Age of Empire 1875–1914* (New York: Pantheon, 1987), 34–83. For a general history of the Meiji Restoration, see Andrew Gordon, *A Modern History of Japan: From Tokugawa Times to the Present* (New York: Oxford University Press, 2003), 61–137. For a general history of the late Chosŏn period, see Carter J. Eckert, Ki-baik Lee, Young Ick Lew, Michael Robinson, and Edward W. Wagner, *Korea Old and New: A History* (Cambridge, MA: Korea Institute, Harvard University, 1995), 178–253. See also Bruce Cumings, *Korea's Place in the Sun: A Modern History* (New York: W.W. Norton, 1997), 76–138; Kyung Moon Hwang, *A History of Korea* (New York: Palgrave Macmillan, 2010), 118–160; Michael E. Robinson, *Korea's Twentieth-Century Odyssey: A Short History* (Honolulu: University of Hawaii Press, 2007), 8–35.

8. The quotation is from William Henry Wilkinson, *The Corean Government: Constitutional Changes, July 1894 to October 1895* (Shanghai: Statistical Department of the Inspectorate General of Customs, 1897), 16. On the French invasion, see Choe, *The Rule of the Taewŏn'gun: Restoration in Yi Korea* (Cambridge, MA: East Asian Research Center, Harvard University, 1972), 91–108.

9. On the decline and transformation of the Chosŏn military discussed above, see Eugene Y. Park, *Between Dreams and Reality: The Military Examination in Late Chosŏn Korea, 1600–1894* (Cambridge, MA: Harvard University Asia Center, 2007); Kyung Moon Hwang, *Beyond Birth: Social Status in the Emergence of Modern Korea* (Cambridge, MA: Harvard University Asia Center, 2004), 290–328; James Palais, *Confucian Statecraft and Korean Institutions: Yu Hyŏngwŏn and the Late Chosŏn Dynasty* (Seattle: University of Washington Press, 1996), 391–577; Lee Kibaik, "Korea: The Military Tradition," in *The Traditional Culture and Society of Korea: Thought and Institutions*, ed. H. W. Kang (Honolulu: Center for Korean Studies, University of Hawaii, 1975), 1–42; Yukkun Sagwan Hakkyo Han'guk Kunsa Yŏn'gusil, *Han'guk kunjesa* [History of the military system in Korea] (Seoul: Yukkun Ponbu, 1977), 2:3–262; Yi Taejin, *Chosŏn hugi ŭi chŏngch'i wa kunyŏngje pyŏnch'ŏn* [Late Chosŏn politics and changes in the system of central military garrisons] (Seoul: Han'guk Yŏn'guwŏn, 1959).

10. Park, *Between Dreams and Reality*, 182–183.

11. JaHyun Haboush, ed., *Epistolary Korea: Letters in the Communicative Space of the Chosŏn, 1392–1910* (New York: Columbia University Press, 2009), 292.

12. See Wilkinson, *Corean Government,* 4.

13. The terms refer to archery and artillery exam candidates, respectively. See Pak Ŭnsik's 1907 blistering critique of the Chosŏn dynasty's neglect and disdain of the military: Pak Ŭnsik, "Munyak p'yehae nŭn nara rŭl mangch'inda" [The evil of effeteness is destroying the country], in Pak Ŭnsik, *Pak Ŭnsik chŏ* [The Works of Pak Ŭnsik], ed. Yi Manyŏl (Seoul: Han'gilsa, 1980), 91. For more on the idea of "effeteness" (*munyak*), see Chapter 2.

14. Charles Dallet, *Traditional Korea* (New Haven, CT: Human Relations Area Files, 1954), 36. Dallet's work was originally published in French in 1874, based on letters from French missionaries working in Chosŏn Korea.

15. See Palais, *Confucian Statecraft and Korean Institutions,* 436–437, 537–577. On the fall in social status of the military and *muban* discussed above, see Park, *Between Dreams and Reality,* 143–186; Hwang, *Beyond Birth,* 290–328. It should be acknowledged, however, that as one moved away from the capital, the center of prestige and power, the status distinctions between civil and military officials may have weakened or blurred to some extent, and the composition of the local elites may have been somewhat more diversi-fied, as in the case of the leadership of the great Hong Kyŏngnae Rebellion of 1812 in the north. See Sun Joo Kim, *Marginality and Subversion in Korea: The Hong Kyŏngnae Re-bellion of 1812* (Seattle: University of Washington Press, 2007), esp. 107–126.

16. See Park, *Between Dreams and Reality,* and Hwang, *Beyond Birth,* respectively.

17. Chŏng Yagyong, *Pyŏngjŏn* [On the military], trans. Chang Sunbŏm (Seoul: Minjok Munhwa Ch'ujinhoe, 1981), 112–113.

18. Ibid., 112.

19. Hwang, *Beyond Birth,* 298.

20. Frank A. Kierman Jr. and John K. Fairbank, eds., *Chinese Ways in Warfare* (Cambridge, MA: Harvard University Press, 1974), 25.

21. Quoted in Yong-ho Ch'oe, "Private Academies and the State in Late Chosŏn Korea," in *Culture and the State in Late Chosŏn Korea,* ed. JaHyun Kim Haboush and Martina Deuchler (Cambridge, MA: Harvard University Asia Center, 1999), 19.

22. Chŏng Yagyong, *Pyŏngjŏn,* 110.

23. Cho Usŏk, a prominent military official in the 19th century, and author of a well-known military text, is a good example of this kind of officer. See Hwang, *Beyond Birth,* 305–306.

24. Edward Sylvester Morse, *Korean Interviews* (New York: D. Appleton, 1897), 1. Morse (1838–1925) was a pioneering American zoologist and later director of the Peabody Mu-seum at Harvard. He introduced Darwinian evolutionary thought to Japan, and while there took also an interest in Korea through Korean students studying in Tokyo. Back in the United States, he became a mentor to Yu Kilchun (1856–1914), one of Korea's most prominent late Chosŏn reformists, and the first Korean student to study in the United States. For an introduction to Morse and his relationship with Yu, see Yi Kwangnin, *Han'guk kaehwasa yŏn'gu* [Studies in Korean enlightenment history] (Seoul: Ilchogak, 1969), 258–274. For more on Yu, see Chapter 2.

25. *Chŏngjŏng yŏnp'yo* [Diary of government service]: *Ŭmch'ŏngsa* [History cloudy and clear]: *chon* [complete] (Seoul: Kuksa P'yŏnch'an Wiwŏnhoe, 1958), 122. See also Yukkun Sagwan Hakkyo Han'guk Kunsa Yŏn'gusil, *Han'guk kunjesa* 2:308. Pak Yŏng-ghyo also used it in his memorial to the king in 1888; see Chapter 2.

26. Yukkun Sagwan Hakkyo Han'guk Kunsa Yŏn'gusil, *Han'guk kunjesa* 2:267.

27. Choe, *Rule of the Taewŏn'gun,* 49.

28. James Palais, *Politics and Policy in Traditional Korea* (Cambridge, MA: Harvard Uni-versity Press, 1975), 86–109.

29. H. H. Gosnell, "The Navy in Korea, 1871," *American Neptune* 7 (April 1947): 111.

30. On the rule and military policies of the Taewŏn'gun, discussed above, including his response to the French and American intrusions, see Yukkun Sagwan Hakkyo Han'guk Kunsa Yŏn'gusil, *Han'guk kunjesa* 2:262–292; Choe, *Rule of the Taewŏn'gun*, 8–12, 42–51, 91–133; Palais, *Politics and Policy in Traditional Korea*, 23–42, 86–109. Palais also notes that "the one area where the Taewŏn'gun tended to place greater weight on performance than on ascriptive criteria was military training and recruitment" (52).

31. Kim's and Hong's full reports (in classical Chinese, with an introduction in Korean) can be found in Kuksa P'yŏnch'an Wiwŏnhoe, ed., *Susinsa kirok: chŏn* [The complete record of the Japanese missions] (Seoul: T'amgudang, 1971). For a Korean translation of Kim's report, see Kim Kisu, *Iltong kiyu* [Record of a trip to Japan], trans. Yi Chaeho (Pusan: Pusan Taehakkyo Han-Il Munhwa Yŏn'guso, 1962). See also Yukkun Sagwan Hakkyo Han'guk Kunsa Yŏn'gusil, *Han'guk kunjesa* 2:303–304.

32. See, for example, Hyŏn Kwangho, "Taehan Chegukki chingbyŏngje nonŭi wa kŭ sŏnggyŏk" [On the discussions and character of the conscription system of the Great Han Empire], *Han'guksa yŏn'gu* 105 (June 1999): 156–158. All the original reports of the Courtiers Observation Mission, including those discussed above, have been published in Hŏ Tonghyŏn, ed., *Chosa sich'altan kwan'gye ch'aryojip* [Collected documents relating to the Courtiers Observation Mission], 14 vols. (Seoul: Kukhak Charyowŏn, 2000). For the details and consequences of the mission itself, see Hŏ Tonghyŏn, "1881 Chosŏn chosa Ilbon sich'altan e kwanhan il yŏn'gu" [A study of the Chosŏn Courtiers Observation Mission], *Han'guksa yŏn'gu* 53 (March 1986): 97–151, and Hŏ Tonghyŏn, *Kŭndae Han-Il kwan'gyesa yŏn'gu: Chosa Sich'altan ŭi Ilbon'gwan kwa kukka kusang* [The Courtiers Observation Mission's attitude toward Japan and conception of the state] (Seoul: Kukhak Charyowŏn, 2000). See also Yukkun Sagwan Hakkyo Han'guk Kunsa Yŏn'gusil, *Han'guk kunjesa* 2:306–308. For a brief description of the mission in English, see Martina Deuchler, *Confucian Gentlemen and Barbarian Envoys: The Opening of Korea, 1875–1885* (Seattle: University of Washington Press, 1977), 101–102.

33. Kim Kisu, *Iltong kiyu*, 280.

34. See Palais, *Politics and Policy*, 252–271; Deuchler, *Confucian Gentlemen and Barbarian Envoys*, 48.

35. Yukkun Sakwan Hakkyo Han'guk Kunsa Yŏn'gusil, *Han'guk kunjesa* 2:303, 311.

36. On the T'ongni Kimu Amun and other military innovations in the 1870s and 1880s discussed above, see Yukkun Sakwan Hakkyo Han'guk Kunsa Yŏn'gusil, *Han'guk kunjesa* 2:293–320; Deuchler, *Confucian Gentlemen and Barbarian Envoys*, 92–98; Kirk W. Larsen, *Tradition, Treaties, and Trade: Qing Imperialism and Chosŏn Korea, 1850–1910* (Cambridge, MA: Harvard University Asia Center, 2008), 70–82; Kyung Moon Hwang, *Rationalizing Korea: The Rise of the Modern State, 1894–1945* (Oakland: University of California Press, 2016), 26–29.

37. A week after the signing of the Shimonoseki Treaty concluding the Sino-Japanese War in 1895, Russia, France, and Germany, in what became known as the "Triple Intervention," delivered an ultimatum forcing Japan to return the Liaodong Peninsula that China had ceded to Japan in the treaty.

38. Yu Yŏngik, *Kabo Kyŏngjang yŏn'gu* [Studies on the Kabo reforms] (Seoul: Ilchogak, 1990), esp. 178–222. On Pak Yŏnghyo, see Yu Yŏngik, *Kabo Kyŏngjang yŏn'gu*; Young I. Lew, "The Reform Efforts and Ideas of Pak Yŏng-hyŏ, 1894–1895," *Korean Studies* 1 (1977): 21–61; see also Chapter 2. On the queen's murder, see Eckert et al., *Korea Old and New*, 229. Pak Yŏnghyo and the queen had been bitter enemies, and the Japanese minister Miura Gorō, who was supporting the Kabo reform group, hatched a plot to have her killed in 1895.

39. C. I. Eugene Kim and Han-Kyo Kim, *Korea and the Politics of Imperialism, 1876-1910* (Berkeley: University of California Press, 1967), 89.
40. Yukkun Sagwan Hakkyo Han'guk Kunsa Yŏn'gusil, *Han'guk kunjesa* 2:364-382. See also Sŏ Inhan, *Taehan Cheguk ŭi kunsa chedo* [The military system of the Great Han Empire] (Seoul: Hyean, 2000), 29-99.
41. The rebellion had also exposed the profound weakness of the government army.
42. Yukkun Sagwan Hakkyo Han'guk Kunsa Yŏn'gusil, *Han'guk kunjesa* 2:367-369; Sŏ Inhan, *Taehan Cheguk ŭi kunsa chedo*, 206-207; Hyŏn Kwangho, "Taehan Chegukki chingbyŏngje nonŭi wa kŭ sŏnggyŏk," 168-169.
43. See the *Korean Repository* 4, no. 10 (October 1897): 390. The Meiji emperor's charter oath can be found in Wm. Theodore de Bary, Carol Gluck, and Arthur E. Tiedemann, eds., *Sources of Japanese Tradition*, vol. 2, *1600-2000*, 2nd ed. (New York: Columbia University Press, 2005), 671-672.
44. See the *Independent*, August 17, 1897.
45. On the king's elevation to imperial status discussed above, see: the *Independent*, October 14, 1897; *Korean Repository* 4, no. 10 (October 1897): 385-387.
46. See Yukkun Sagwan Hakkyo Han'guk Kunsa Yŏn'gusil, *Han'guk kunjesa* 2:398. On the Independence Club, see Vipan Chandra, *Imperialism, Resistance, and Reform in Late Nineteenth-Century Korea: Enlightenment and the Independence Club* (Berkeley: Institute of East Asian Studies, University of California, 1988).
47. On the Wŏnsubu discussed above, see Sŏ Inhan, *Taehan Cheguk ŭi kunsa chedo*, 101-167; Yukkun Sagwan Hakkyo Han'guk Kunsa Yŏn'gusil, *Han'guk kunjesa* 2:391-409; Hwang, *Rationalizing Korea*, 30-32. On the Great Han Empire's military uniforms, including those worn by the emperor and crown prince, see Yi Mi'na, "Taehan Cheguk sidae yukkun changbyŏng pokche chesik kwa taewŏnsu ye-sangbok e taehayŏ" [Military dress codes in the Great Han Empire and formal and informal dress of the marshal commander in chief], *Hagyeji* 4 (1993): 241-277; Yukkun Pokchesa P'yŏnjip Wiwŏnhoe, ed. *Yukkun pokchesa* [History of army uniforms] (Seoul: Yukkun Ponbu, 1980), 75-97.
48. Yukkun Sagwan Hakkyo Han'guk Kunsa Yŏn'gusil, *Han'guk kunjesa* 2:318-319, 321-323; Deuchler, *Confucian Gentlemen and Barbarian Envoys*, 103, 129-131.
49. Ralph L. Powell, *Rise of Chinese Military Power, 1805-1912* (Princeton, NJ: Princeton University Press, 1955), 39. See also S. C. M. Paine, *The Sino-Japanese War of 1894-1895: Perceptions, Power, and Primacy* (Cambridge: Cambridge University Press, 2003), 147-149. On Yuan Shikai in Korea, see Young Ick Lew, "Yüan Shih-k'ai's Residency and the Korean Enlightenment Movement," *Journal of Korean Studies* 5 (1984): esp. 100-104; see also Larsen, *Tradition, Treaties, and Trade*, esp. 128-163, where Larsen argues for a more nuanced assessment of Yuan's residency.
50. See Yukkun Sagwan Hakkyo Han'guk Kunsa Yŏn'gusil, *Han'guk kunjesa* 2:337-339.
51. On military changes during the Kabo Reform era discussed above, see ibid., 337-358; Sŏ Inhan, *Taehan Cheguk ŭi kunsa chejo*, 29-99; Russia, Ministerstvo Finansov, *Opisanie Korei* [Description of Korea] (St. Petersburg: Tip. Lu. N. Erlikh, 1900), 2:408-430 (Chapter 13).
52. *Independent*, January 8, 1898.
53. On such differences and inconsistencies, for example, see Lee Kwang-rin, "Role of Foreign Military Instructors in the Later Period of the Yi Dynasty," in *International Conference on the Problems of Modernization in Asia* (Seoul: Asiatic Research Center, Korea University, 1965), esp. 247.
54. On the military changes between 1895 and 1904 discussed above, see Yukkun Sagwan Hakkyo Han'guk Kunsa Yŏn'gusil, *Han'guk kunjesa* 2:364-409; Sŏ Inhan, *Taehan Cheguk ŭi kunsa chedo*, 101-222; Ch'a Munsŏp, *Chosŏn sidae kunsa kwan'gye yŏn'gu* [Studies on the Chosŏn period military] (Seoul: Tan'guk Taehakkyo Ch'ulp'anbu,

1996), 40–44, 287–343. Two Russian sources from this period are especially useful given Russia's involvement at that time in Korean affairs, including in the training of Korean troops. One is a detailed survey of the Great Han military published in 1903 by a Russian officer, Staff Captain Afanas'ev, who served as a military advisor in Korea: see Afanas'ev, *Sovremennoe sostoianie vooruzhhennykh sil Korei* [Current state of Korean armed forces] (Vladivostok: Tip. T-va Sushchinskii I KO, 1903). The other, cited earlier, is a study of the Korean military by the Russian finance ministry published in 1900: Russia, Ministerstvo Finansov, *Opisanie Korei* 2:408–430 (Chapter 13). The first volume of the Russian finance ministry report has been translated into Korean: see Rŏsia Taejangsŏng, *Ku Hanmal ŭi sahoe wa kyŏngje: yŏlgang kwa ŭi choyak* [Late Chosŏn society and economy: treaties with the great powers], trans. Kim Pyŏngnin (Seoul: Yurye Ch'ulp'ansa, 1983). I am grateful to Avram Agov, who brought these sources to my attention and translated both of them for me into English. See also Avram Asenov Agov, "Origins of the Annexation of Korea by Japan in 1910: Military and Financial Systems of the Late Choson Dynasty, International Relations, 1895–1905," master's thesis, Regional Studies East Asia (RSEA) Program, Harvard University, 1995.

55. Why a national conscription system was never implemented remains something of a puzzle, especially given Korean concerns as early as the 1880s about a new "Warring States" period, and early Korean recognition of the central role conscription played in modern nation building in Meiji Japan and elsewhere. Certainly budgetary restraints played a role here, but other factors may have been important as well, including Kojong's tendency to see the army primarily as a domestic police force and to rely on foreign alliances for external threats, and traditional *yangban* reluctance to embrace universal military service regardless of status. Belatedly in 1903, however, Kojong seemed to actively promote the idea, and a conscription law was finally promulgated. It was never implemented, in part because of a lack of funding, and after 1905 the Japanese protectorate government refused to move ahead on it, despite Kojong's objections. See Hyŏn Kwangho, "Taehan Chegukki chingbyŏngje nonŭi wa kŭ sŏnggyŏk," 151–187; Cho Chaegon, "Taehan Chegukki kunsa chŏngch'aek kwa kunsa kigu ŭi unyŏng" [Military policy and the functioning of the military structure in the Great Han Empire period], *Yŏksa wa hyŏnsil* 19 (1996): 115–117; Yumi Moon, *Populist Collaborators: The Ilchinhoe and the Japanese Colonization of Korea, 1896–1910* (Ithaca, NY: Cornell University Press, 2013), 267–268; Peter Duus, *The Abacus and the Sword: The Japanese Penetration of Korea, 1895–1910* (Berkeley: University of California Press, 1995), 178.

56. Kojong is a figure of some controversy in the historiography of this period. He is generally praised for his embrace of the enlightenment movement in the late 1870s and early 1880s, but the enlightenment group's attempted coup in 1884 seems to have made him wary and suspicious of the leaders of that movement, if not many of the ideas associated with the movement itself. See Palais, *Politics and Policy,* 252–253; Deuchler, *Confucian Gentlemen and Barbarian Envoys,* 48–49, 99–107; Yong-ho Ch'oe, "The Kapsin Coup of 1884: A Reassessment," *Korean Studies* 6 (1982): 105–124. Other scholars have tended to see Kojong negatively as a traditional monarch, more concerned, for example, with putting down internal threats to the dynasty and protecting and enhancing his own royal prerogatives and power than with building a modern nation state along Meiji Japanese lines. See, for example, Yi Tonghŭi, *Han'guk kunsa chedo ron* [On the Korean military system] (Seoul: Ilchogak, 1982), 212–213; Cho Chaegon, "Taehan Chegukki kunsa chŏngch'aek kwa kunsa kigu ŭi unyŏng," 101, 134; Sŏ Yŏnghŭi, *Taehan cheguk chŏngch'isa yŏn'gu* [Studies on the political thought of the Great Han Empire] (Seoul: Sŏul Taehakkyo, 2005), esp. 390–403. More recently some scholars have attempted to burnish Kojong's view as a "nationalist" figure, focusing largely on his antagonism to Japan, especially between 1904–1907. See Yi T'aejin, *Kojong sidae ŭi chae*

chomyŏng [Reilluminating the Kojong era] (Seoul: T'aehaksa, 2000); Yi T'aejin, Kim Chaeho, et al., *Kojong Hwangje yŏksa ch'ŏngmunhoe* [Inquiry on the history of Emperor Kojong] (Seoul: P'urŭn Yŏksa, 2005); Yi T'aejin, Kim Kisŏk, Paek Ch'unghyŏn, Yi Kŭngwan, Sin Hyosuk, and Yi Yonggwŏn, *Han'guk pyŏnghap ŭi pulbŏpsŏng yŏn'gu* [Studies on the illegality of the annexation of Korea] (Seoul: Sŏul Taehakkyo Han'guk Munhwa Yŏn'guso, 2003). JaHyun Haboush notes that Chosŏn Korea "maintained a military establishment more to keep order within the country than to expel foreign incursions." See Haboush, "Constructing the Center: The Ritual Controvery and the Search for a New Identity," in *Culture and the State in Late Chosŏn Korea*, ed. JaHyun Kim Haboush and Martina Deuchler (Cambridge, MA: Harvard University Asia Center, 1999), 68.

57. F. A. McKenzie, *The Tragedy of Korea* (Seoul: Yonsei University Press, 1969 [1908]), 107.

2. Militarizing Minds

1. Cho Ilmun and Sin Pongnyong, eds., *Kapsin chŏngbyŏn hoegorok* [Memoirs of the Kapsin coup] (Seoul: Kŏn'guk Taehakkyo Ch'ulp'anbu, 2006), 234.
2. On Yu Kilchun, see Yu Yŏngik, *Kabo kyŏngjang yŏn'gu* [Studies on the Kabo reforms] (Seoul: Ilchogak, 1990), 88–133. See also Chŏng Yonghwa, *Munmyŏng ŭi chŏngch'i sasang: Yu Kilchun kwa kŭndae Han'guk* [Civilization and political thought: Yu Kilchun and modern Korea] (Seoul: Munhak kwa Chisŏngsa, 2004), 60–110. On Fukuzawa, see Albert M. Craig, *Civilization and Enlightenment: The Early Thought of Fukuzawa Yukichi* (Cambridge, MA: Harvard University Press, 2009). On Morse and his relationship with Yu, see also Chapter 1. For a brief sketch in English of Yu's life and work, see Peter H. Lee, ed., *Sourcebook of Korean Civilization*, vol. 2, *From the Sixteenth to the Twentieth Centuries* (New York: Columbia University Press, 1996), 241.
3. *Sŏyu kyŏnmun: chŏnmun* [Observations on the West: the complete text], comp. and ed. Yi Hansŏp, Ch'oe Kyŏngok, Chŏng Yŏngsuk, and Kang Sŏnga (Seoul: Pagijŏng, 2000), 357–358.
4. Ibid., 262.
5. Ibid., 263–264.
6. Ibid., 264.
7. Ibid., 266.
8. Ibid., 270–271.
9. Ibid., 270.
10. Ibid., 272.
11. See Young Ick Lew, "The Reform Efforts and Ideas of Pak Yŏng-hyo, 1894–1895," *Korean Studies* 1 (1977): 22–24; 37–44; Yong-Ha Shin, "The Coup d'Etat of 1884 and the Pukch'ŏng Army of the Progressive Party," *Korea Journal* 33, no. 2 (Summer 1993): 6–8. Pak's memorial can be found in *Nihon gaikō bunsho* [Documents on Japanese foreign relations] (Tokyo: Nihon Kokusai Rengō Kyōkai, 1949), 21:292–311.
12. *Nihon gaikō bunsho* 21:296, 303.
13. Ibid., 295, 303. Pak also stressed to the king that Korea was perfectly capable of duplicating Japan's success; in his view the only real difference between the two countries in that regard was that Japan had begun the process earlier.
14. Ibid., 304–305. Both Pak and Yu Kilchun were advocates of a strong navy, especially after seeing Japan, but financing a national navy was an enormously expensive prospect, well beyond the means of the late Chosŏn state. Kojong also seemed to take relatively little interest in naval development and actually abolished the state's fledgling navy department in 1898, saying he was "too busy" with other things. In 1903 the Great Han Empire purchased its first and only modern battleship not as part of a strategic military policy but as a celebratory showpiece in honor of Kojong's fortieth year of rule.

The purchase, which consumed about 18 percent of the entire military budget for that year, was widely criticized in the public media as a wasteful extravagance. See Chang Hakkŭn, *Haeyang cheguk ŭi ch'imnyak kwa kŭndae Chosŏn ŭi haeyang chŏngch'aek: haeyang chŏngch'aeksa ŭi kyohun* [Imperial naval invasions and Chosŏn naval policy: the lessons of naval policy history] (Seoul: Han'guk Haeyang Chŏllyak Yŏn'guso, 2000), 263–297; Yi Yunsang, "1894–1910 chaejŏng chedo wa unyŏng ŭi pyŏnhwa [Management and changes in the financial system 1894–1910]" (Ph.D. dissertation, History Department, Sŏul Taehakkyo Taehagwŏn, 1996), 340.

15. *Nihon gaikō bunsho* 21:304.
16. Stuart Creighton Miller, *Benevolent Assimilation: The American Conquest of the Philippines, 1899–1903* (New Haven, CT: Yale University Press, 1982), 75.
17. Ibid., 74.
18. Ragnar Redbeard, *Might Is Right or the Survival of the Fittest* (New York: Revisionist Press, 1972), 90.
19. Ibid., 130.
20. Ibid., 14, unnumbered last page.
21. Ibid., unnumbered pages at end of book.
22. Friedrich Nietzsche, *Twilight of the Idols: Or, How to Philosophize with the Hammer,* trans. Richard Polt (Indianapolis: Hackett, 1997), 27.
23. *Eagle and the Serpent* 1, no. 1 (February 15, 1898): 4, 3, 5.
24. *Eagle and the Serpent* 2, no. 1 (January–March 1901): 26.
25. See Gerhard Ritter, *The Sword and the Scepter: The Problem of Militarism in Germany,* vol. 1, *The Prussian Tradition 1740–1890,* trans. Heinz Norden (Coral Gables, FL: University of Miami Press, 1969), 51, 209.
26. Helmuth Moltke, *Moltke on the Art of War: Selected Writings,* ed. Daniel J. Hughes, trans. Daniel J. Hughes and Harry Bell (Novato, CA: Presidio, 1993), 22.
27. Friedrich von Bernhardi, *Germany and the Next War,* trans. Allen H. Powles (New York: J. S. Ogilvie, n.d.), 18–21.
28. See Berunherudi, *Doitsu kōkoku ka metsubōka* [Germany: world power or downfall], trans. Nishimura Jirō (Tokyo: Dōbunkan, 1916), which combined a translated excerpt of Bernhardi's book with an introduction to his ideas and writings. See also Charles Townshend, ed., *The Oxford History of Modern War* (Oxford: Oxford University Press, 2000), 83, 90.
29. William Graham Sumner, *War and Other Essays,* ed. Albert Galloway Keller (New Haven, CT: Yale University Press, 1919), 9.
30. Herbert Spencer, *The Study of Sociology* (New York: D. Appleton, 1875), 193.
31. Benjamin Kidd, *Principles of Western Civilization* (New York: Macmillan, 1902), 146, 150.
32. Sumner, *War and Other Essays,* 30.
33. William James, *Pragmatism and Other Essays* (New York: Washington Square Press, 1963), 289, 291, 297–298.
34. Thomas Hughes, *Tom Brown's School Days* (Boston: Houghton, Mifflin, 1895), 272. On Hughes and his book, see Clifford Putney, *Muscular Christianity: Manhood and Sports in Protestant America, 1880–1920* (Cambridge, MA: Harvard University Press, 2001), 11–19. As Putney notes (20), Roosevelt regarded the book as one of two that every boy should read. On the effect of the book in Japan, see Ikuo Abe, "Muscular Christianity in Japan: The Growth of a Hybrid," in *Muscular Christianity and the Colonial and Post-Colonial World,* ed. John J. Macaloon (New York: Routledge, 2008), 14–38. On "muscular Christianity" more generally, see also Donald E. Hall, ed., *Muscular Christianity: Embodying the Victorian Age* (Cambridge: Cambridge University Press, 1994).
35. Putney, *Muscular Christianity,* 26.

36. Ibid. On military drill in the schools, see Alan Penn, *Targeting Schools: Drill, Militarism and Imperialism* (London: Woburn Press, 1999); Mark Moss, *Manliness and Militarism: Educating Young Boys in Ontario for War* (Don Mills, ON: Oxford University Press, 2001), 26, 59, 90, 97, 97–103, 108, 144. On the YMCA and the Boy Scouts, see Putney, *Muscular Christianity*, 61–72, 113–116; Moss, *Manliness and Militarism*, 115–117. On militarism more generally in the United States in the early twentieth century, see Roger Possner, *The Rise of Militarism in the Progressive Era, 1900–1914* (Jefferson, NC: McFarland, 2009).

37. Hŏ Tonghyŏn, ed., *Chosa sich'altan kwan'gye ch'aryojip* [Collected documents relating to the Courtiers Observation Mission] (Seoul: Kukhak Charyowŏn, 2000), 13:54. See also Hŏ Tonghyŏn, "1881 Chosŏn chosa Ilbon sich'altan e kwanhan il yon'gu" [A study of the Chosŏn Courtiers Observation Mission], *Han'guksa y'ongu* 53 (March 1986): 139–140.

38. See Yu Yŏngik, *Kabo kyŏngjang yŏn'gu* [Studies on the Kabo reforms] (Seoul: Ilchogak, 1990), 229.

39. Tanjae Sin Ch'aeho Sŏnsaeng Ki'nyŏm Saŏphoe, *Tanjae Sin Ch'aeho chŏnjip 4 (pyŏl)* [The complete works of Tanjae Sin Ch'aeho] (Seoul: Hyŏngsŏl, 1998), 219.

40. Pak Ŭnsik, *Pak Ŭnsik chŏ* [The works of Pak Ŭnsik], ed. Yi Manyŏl (Seoul: Han'gilsa, 1980), 288.

41. Tanjae Sin Ch'aeho Sŏnsaeng Ki'nyŏm Saŏphoe, *Tanjae Sin Ch'aeho chŏnjip*, 4:200–201, 12.

42. Pak Ŭnsik, *Pak Ŭnsik chŏ*, 89.

43. Ibid., 90, 288.

44. Ibid., 91.

45. Ibid., 94.

46. Ibid., 288.

47. Tanjae Sin Ch'aeho Sŏnsaeng Ki'nyŏm Saŏphoe, *Tanjae Sin Ch'aeho chŏnjip* 3:72–80.

48. Pak Ŭnsik, *Pak Ŭnsik chŏ*, 90.

49. Tanjae Sin Ch'aeho Sŏnsaeng Ki'nyŏm Saŏphoe, *Tanjae Sin Ch'aeho chŏnjip* 2:413–414. On Sin Ch'aeho, see Sin Yongha, *Sin Ch'aeho ŭi sahoe sasang yŏn'gu* [Studies on the social thought of Sin Ch'aeho] (Seoul: Han'gilsa, 1984). See also Michael Robinson, "National Identity and the Thought of Sin Ch'aeho: *Sadaejuŭi* and *Chuch'e* in History and Politics," *Journal of Korean Studies* 5 (1984): 121–142; Henry H. Em, *The Great Enterprise: Sovereignty and Historiography in Modern Korea* (Durham, NC: Duke University Press, 2013), esp. chaps. 3–4. On Sin and the *mun/mu* discourse specifically, see Sin Yongha, *Sin Ch'aeho ŭi sahoe sasang yŏn'gu*, 126–129; Sheila Miyoshi Jager, *Narratives of Nation Building in Korea: A Genealogy of Patriotism* (Armonk, NY: M. E. Sharpe, 2003), 1–19, esp. 9–11.

50. Pak Ŭnsik, *Pak Ŭnsik chŏ*, 92–94.

51. On IJA curtailments and changes in the 1920s, see Leonard A. Humphreys, *The Way of the Heavenly Sword: The Japanese Army in the 1920s* (Stanford, CA: Stanford University Press, 1995), 43–99, esp. 89–99. On the deployment of active-duty military officers in the school system, see Nihon Kindai Kyōiku Shi Kankōkai, ed., *Nihon kindai kyōiku shi* [History of Japanese modern education] (Tokyo: Kōdansha, 1973), 298–304.

52. On the Korean uprising in 1919 (March 1), see Frank Prentiss Baldwin Jr., "The March First Movement: Korean Challenge and Japanese Response" (Ph.D. diss., Columbia University, 1969). On the GGK's attitude toward Koreans as soldiers in the 1920s, see *Tonga ilbo*, July 7, 1923, and July 21, 1923.

53. On elementary school textbooks, see, for example, a compilation of elementary school morals textbooks (J: *shūshinsho*; K: *susinsŏ*) from the first twenty years of colonial rule: Kim Sunjŏn et al., eds., *Chosŏn Ch'ongdokpu ch'odŭng hakkyo susinsŏ: wŏnmun* [Ele-

mentary school morals textbooks of the Government General of Korea] (Seoul: Chei-aenssi, 2006), 1:15–302. On the morals textbooks more generally, see Robert King Hall, *Shūshin: The Ethics of a Defeated Nation* (New York: Bureau of Publications, Teachers College, Columbia University, 1949). On earlier Korean civics textbooks, see, for example, An Chonghwa, ed. and trans., *Ch'odŭng yullihak kyogwasŏ* [Elementary school textbook on morals] (Hwangsŏng [Seoul]: Kwanghak Sŏp'ŏ, 1907), 48. This was a Korean translation of a Chinese textbook, apparently published in 1907 for the Hwimun School (Hwimun Ŭisuk), one of the private schools founded by Korean nationalists in the last years of the Chosŏn dynasty.

54. On the Korean YMCA, see Taehan YMCA Yŏnmaeng, *Han'guk YMCA undongsa, 1895–1985* [History of the activities of the Korean YMCA, 1885–1985] (Seoul: No Ch'ulp'an, 1986), 3–148; Chŏn T'aekpu, *Han'guk Kidokkyo ch'ŏngnyŏn hoe undongsa (1899–1945)* [Activities of the Korean YMCA 1899–1945] (Seoul: Chŏngŭmsa, 1978), 128–129, 374–377; Koen De Cuester, "Wholesome Education and Sound Leisure: The YMCA Sports Programme in Colonial Korea," *European Journal of East Asian Studies* 2, no. 1 (2003): 53–88, esp. 62–69. For a description of a 1920s YMCA martial arts event featuring *jūdō* and *kendō* matches, see *Tonga ilbo*, July 28, 1926. On the Korean Boy Scouts, see Hŏ Chaeuk, "Han'guk poisŭk'autt'ŭ undong: ch'ŏngsonnyŏn kyoyuk e mich'in yŏnghyang" [The activities of the Korean Boy Scouts: influence on the education of youth] (master's thesis, Koryŏ Taehakkyo Kyoyuk Taehagwŏn, 1971); Chŏn T'aekpu, *Han'guk Kidokkyo ch'ŏngnyŏn hoe undongsa*, 310–311; Chŏng Sŏngch'ae, *Sonyŏn ch'ŏkhudan kyobŏm* [Boy Scout handbook] (Kyŏngsŏng [Seoul]: Sonyŏn Chŏkhudan Chosŏn Yŏn-maeng, 1931), esp. 29.

55. On the cultural nationalist movement, see Michael Edson Robinson, *Cultural Nationalism in Colonial Korea, 1920–1925* (Seattle: University of Washington Press, 1988). An Ch'angho, a figure revered within the cultural nationalist movement, argued that "if the war of independence is not to be a mere fantasy but a reality, every man and woman of the twenty million Koreans must become a soldier. . . . Let us all undergo military training, even if only for an hour a day." See Lee, *Sourcebook of Korean Civilization*, 2:443.

56. Chang Tobin, "Chosŏn kŭndaesa sang ŭi muyongjŏn" [Valorous lives of the late Chosŏn], *Samch'ŏlli* 5, no. 1 (1933): 76.

57. See, for example, the series of articles by Hyŏn Sangyun in *Tonga ilbo*, January 1–15, 1932.

58. On the policy of "cultural rule," see Carter J. Eckert, Ki-baik Lee, Young Ick Lew, Michael Robinson, and Edward W. Wagner, *Korea Old and New: A History* (Cambridge, MA: Korea Institute, Harvard University, 1995), 283–285.

59. *Tonga ilbo*, July 8, 1923.

60. Ibid., July 21, 1923. Ariyoshi's clarification came after a number of Korean middle schools had applied to the GGK for guns to be used in military drill.

61. See, for example, ibid., August 16 and September 6, 1925.

62. Ibid., April 12, 1928. On Yi Chinho, see Ch'in-Il Inmyŏng Sajŏn P'yŏnch'an Wiwŏnhoe, *Ch'in-Il inmyŏng sajŏn* [Pro-Japanese biographical dictionary], 3 vols. (Seoul: Minjok Munje Yŏn'guso, 2009) (henceforth *CIS*), 2:162–165.

63. *Tonga ilbo*, June 16, 1934.

64. Ibid., July 18, 1934.

65. Ibid.

66. Ibid., June 15, 1935.

67. Ibid., August 4, 1935.

68. See, for example, the advertisement for Kuroba (Clover) lipstick in the popular Korean-language magazine *Chogwang* 10, no. 4 (1944): 69. Many such ads can be found in

Chogwang during the war years, as well as photographs of Korean urban life. See also Nanba Kōji, *Uchiteshi yaman: Taiheiyō Sensō to kōkoku no gijutsushatachi* [Never stop fighting: the Pacific War and the engineers of advertising] (Tokyo: Kōdansha, 1998). Recently recovered Korean colonial films produced during the 1940s also provide a fascinating glimpse of wartime Seoul. See, for example, the 1941 film *Chiwŏnbyŏng* (Volunteer Soldier), directed by An Sŏgyŏng.

69. See, for example, Carter J. Eckert, *Offspring of Empire: The Colonial Origins of Korean Capitalism, 1876–1945* (Seattle: University of Washington Press, 1991), 246.

70. T. Fujitani, *Race for Empire: Koreans as Japanese and Japanese as Americans during World War II* (Berkeley: University of California Press, 2011), 245–271. By the time a conscription system for Koreans was formally enacted in 1943, to be implemented in December 1944, the expansion of the war into the Pacific and mounting numbers of deaths and casualties had diminished enthusiasm for the military among Koreans, and there was considerable draft evasion. See Brandon Palmer, *Fighting for the Enemy: Koreans in Japan's War, 1937–1945* (Seattle: University of Washington Press, 2013), 92–138. Nevertheless, as Fujitani notes, at the peak of the volunteer soldiers program in 1943, before conscription, more than 300,000 Korean men volunteered for a quota of only about 6,000 slots, a 10,000 percent increase over 1938 (245). On Korean participation in the IJA, see also Miyata Setsuko, *Chōsen minshū to 'kōminka' seisaku* [The Korean people and the imperialization policy] (Tokyo: Miraisha, 1985); Utsumi Aiko, *Chōsenjin 'Kōgun' heishitachi no sensō* [The Korean "Imperial Army" soldiers' war] (Tokyo: Iwanami Shoten, 1991).

71. See Carter J. Eckert, "Total War, Industrialization, and Social Change in Late Colonial Korea," in *The Japanese Wartime Empire, 1931–1945*, ed. Peter Duus, Ramon H. Myers, and Mark R. Peattie (Princeton, NJ: Princeton University Press, 1996), 14–39; Fujitani, *Race for Empire*, 64–77; Jun Uchida, *Brokers of Empire: Japanese Settler Colonialism in Korea, 1876–1945* (Cambridge, MA: Harvard University Asia Center, 2011), 363–393; Mark Caprio, *Japanese Assimilation Policies in Colonial Korea, 1910–1945* (Seattle: University of Washington Press, 2009), 153–170.

72. Kenneth J. Ruoff, *Imperial Japan at Its Zenith: The Wartime Celebration of the Empire's 2,600th Anniversary* (Ithaca, NY: Cornell University Press, 2010).

73. To be sure, not all Korean young men were so inclined. Todd Henry's recent book demonstrates how even at the height of the war in colonial Korea, significant numbers of Koreans found ways to exercise their autonomy from wartime rhetoric and pressures, often in subtle ways. See Todd Henry, *Assimilating Seoul: Japanese Rule and the Politics of Public Space in Colonial Korea, 1910–1945* (Berkeley: University of California Press, 2014), esp. 168–203. And many of Park Chung Hee's middle-school classmates were far less enthusiastic about the military than he; see Chapter 3. As noted above, the general conscription implemented in the final two years of the war was also generally unpopular, and there were many draft dodgers. Still, the wartime rhetoric and pressures were intense. According to Yu Yangsu, an ideology of militarism *(kun'gukchuŭi)* and praise of army activities "colored everything in this period," including movies, essays, novels, tales of heroism, biographies of great men displayed in bookstore windows, and even comic books. Yu Yangsu, letter to author, May 6, 2004. Yu, originally from Kwangju, South Chŏlla province, had been recruited as an IJA officer and served in north China and Korea (near Hŭngnam), leading a platoon of about fifty-five men. After Korea's liberation from Japan, he joined the ROKA, graduating from the Korean Military Academy (KMA) in the KMA Special 7 class, and there first met Park Chung Hee, who was his cadet company commander *(chungdaejang)*. After Park was arrested, court-martialed, and discharged from the army for communist activity in 1948–1949, Yu, who was then head of the ROKA headquarters combat intelligence section, allowed

Park to work in his office as a civilian. Yu continued to distinguish himself in the military, including during the Korean War, and eventually rose to the rank of lieutenant general. Although he was not directly involved in the planning of the 1961 coup, as soon as he had ascertained that it was Park who was leading it, he joined the new military government and went on to serve in numerous key posts, including as ambassador to the Philippines, Austria, South Vietnam, and Saudi Arabia. Yu Yangsu, interview, Cambridge, MA, September 17, 1990, and November 7, 1999. See also the online obituary of Yu by Cho Kapche at http://www.chogabje.com/board/view.asp?C_IDX=16225 &C_CC=AZ. On Yu's diplomatic career, see his memoir, *Taesa ŭi ilgijang* [Diary of an ambassador] (Seoul: Samsŏng Ch'ulp'ansa: Konggŭpch'ŏ Samsŏng Idea, 1989). On the pervasiveness of militarism in colonial wartime media and discourse, see also Michael Kim, "The Aesthetics of Total Mobilisation in the Visual Culture of Late Colonial Korea," *Totalitarian Movements and Political Religions* 8, no. 3–4 (2007): 483–502.

3. Militarizing Places and Persons

1. The official name of the JMA was the Greater Japan Imperial Army School (Dai Nihon Teikoku Rikugun Shikan Gakkō), and the official name of the MMA was the Greater Manchuria Imperial Officer School (Dai Manshū Teikoku Gunkan Gakkō).

2. Carter J. Eckert, *Offspring of Empire: The Colonial Origins of Korean Capitalism, 1876–1945* (Seattle: University of Washington Press, 1991), 114.

3. *Jinjō shōgaku shūshinsho* 1: *jidōyō* [Elementary school morals text, vol. 1: for children's use] (Tokyo: Monbushō, 1936), 30–31. Earlier textbooks had identified the bugler as Shirakami Genjirō. On Kiguchi, as well as Shirakami, see Nishikawa Hiroshi, *Rappashu no saigo: sensō no naka no minshū* [The bugler's last moment: commoners during the war] (Tokyo: Aoki Shoten, 1984), 99–119; Donald Keene, *Landscapes and Portraits* (Tokyo: Kodansha International, 1971), 274–281. See also Robert King Hall, *Shūshin: The Ethics of a Defeated Nation* (New York: Bureau of Publications, Teachers College, Columbia University, 1949), 180.

4. See Kim Sunjŏn et al., eds. *Chosŏn Ch'ongdokpu ch'odŭng hakkyo susinsŏ wŏnmun* [The elementary school morals textbooks of the Government General of Korea: original texts] (Seoul: Cheiaenssi, 2006), 2:55.

5. Hwangbo Kyun and Yun Ch'idu, interview, Taegu, August 3, 1990; Yi Sŏngjo, interview, Seoul, December 15, 2008. See also Cho Kapche, *Pak Chŏnghŭi: han kŭndaehwa hyŏngmyŏngga ŭi pijanghan saengae* [Park Chung Hee: the resolute life of a modernizing revolutionary] (Seoul: Cho Kapche Datk'om, 2006), 1:127, 184.

6. See Richard J. Smethurst, *A Social Basis for Prewar Japanese Militarism: The Army and the Rural Community* (Berkeley: University of California Press, 1974), 10–11; *Taegu Sabŏm simsanggwaji* [History of the elementary school department of Taegu Normal School], ed. Han Sŏktong (Taegu: Taegu Sabŏm Simsanggwa Tongmunhoe, 1991; courtesy of Cho Kapche), 96.

7. *Taegu Sabŏm simsanggwaji*, 98–99. Normal schools were also established in Chŏnju (1936) and Kwangju (1938) in South Chŏlla province: see *Han'guk minjok munhwa taebaekkwa sajŏn* at encykorea.aks.ac.kr/Contents/Contents?contents_id=E0049664 and encykorea.aks.ac.kr/Contents/Contents?contents_id=E0005258, respectively.

8. *Taegu Sabŏm simsanggwaji*, 99–104.

9. Torikai Ikoma, "Kyōgaku Kenkyūjo no rensei jōkyō" [Training at the Educational Research Institute], *Chōsen* (December 1942): 50; on the purpose of the institute, see ibid., 47. For Torikai's background, see *Chōsen jinji kōshinroku* [Chōsen Biographical Directory] (Keijō: Chōsen Shinbunsha: Chōsen Jinji Kōshinroku Hensabu, 1935), 327–328; Chōsen Sōtokufu, *Chōsen Sōtokufu oyobi shozoku kanshō shokuinroku* [Directory of the Chōsen Government-General and affiliated government offices] (Keijō: Hatsubaijō

Chōsen Gyōsei Gakkai, 1940); *Chōsen toyū taikan* [Survey of Chōsen cities and towns] (Keijō: Minshū Jironsha, 1937), 276–277. See also *Taegu Sabŏm simsanggwaji*, 230–231.
10. Sŏ Pyŏngbuk, interview, Taegu, August 4, 1990.
11. See *Tonga ilbo*, February 26, 1926. See also Chapter 2.
12. *Taegu Sabŏm simsanggwaji*, 133.
13. Ibid., 134.
14. Yi Sŏngjo, interview, Seoul, December 15, 2008.
15. Sŏ Pyŏngbuk, interview, Taegu, August 4, 1990. See also *Taegu Sabŏm simsanggwaji*, 189, 234, 247. On the 80th Regiment, see *Hohei Dai-Hachijū Rentai shi* [History of the 80th Infantry Regiment], ed. Hohachijūkai (n.p.: Hohachijūkai, 1982); see also Tsuji Sutezō, *Keihoku taikan* [Encyclopedia of North Kyŏngsŏng] (Taegu: Tsuji Sutezō, 1936), 344–347; *Kyŏngsang Puktosa* [History of North Kyŏngsang province] (Taegu: Kyŏngsang Puktosa P'yŏnjip Wiwŏnhoe, 1983), 73–74.
16. Torikai Ikoma, "Kyōgaku Kenkyūjo no rensei jōkyō," 50; *Taegu Sabŏm simsanggwaji*, 230. For more on military training in Korean colonial schools, especially after 1942, see Sin Chubaek, "Ilche malgi Chosŏn'in kunsa kyoyuk, 1942.12–1945" [Korean military education at the end of the Japanese imperial period, 12.1942–1945], *Han-Il minjok munje yŏn'gu* 9 (2005): 161–166.
17. For the first generation of reformers, such as Yu Kilchun and Pak Yŏnghyo, the professionalism of Korea's new army had been linked above all to the cultivation of a corps of modern military officers trained according to Western methods and standards—men who would serve, as it were, as the leaders of the military arm of the enlightenment effort. In arguing their case to a Chosŏn officialdom steeped in an exclusionary world of hereditary status distinctions, they had also stressed the importance of a completely open process of recruitment and promotion based on merit. Briefly in power in 1894–1895, they acted quickly to put their ideas into practice through the Kabo-Ŭlmi reform government. The old army's officer ranks, for example, were abolished, and a new system was implemented that would have been familiar to any Western or Japanese officer at the time and quite recognizable even today: three levels of general officers or *changgwan* (major general, lieutenant general, and general); three levels of field officers or *yŏnggwan* (major, lieutenant colonel, and colonel); three levels of company officers or *wigwan* (second lieutenant, lieutenant, and captain); and several levels of noncommissioned officers or *hasagwan* (including lance corporal, corporal, and sergeant). Salaries and allowances for all officers, commissioned and noncommissioned, were fixed according to rank, and clear rules were established regarding the term of service, following the Prussian and Japanese precedent of dividing army service into three tiers: active duty (*hyŏnyŏk*), reserves (*yebi*), and second reserves or territorial army (*hubi*). Regular rules of promotion based on seniority and merit were also announced, but seniority was to be given equal weight only up to the rank of captain; after that promotion was to be strictly on the basis of ability and record. Merit was also to be the chief consideration in any exceptional promotions outside the usual pattern of advancement. Such unusual elevation might be granted in the case of "signal bravery before the enemy," or where "an officer's industry, conduct, and attainments are so remarkable as to justify, with the King's assent, special promotion." At the center of all the various enlightenment plans for the training of an officer corps was of course the idea of establishing an official Korean military academy. The first step in that direction had been made in the early 1880s at King Kojong's initiative, when the king, hoping to counteract Yuan Shikai's overweening influence, had importuned the United States, as a neutral third party, to send military instructors for the Korean army. After years of delay, the result of Washington's general indifference to the question and governmental red tape, a retired officer and West Point graduate, William McEntyre Dye, was finally sent to

Korea in 1888 by the U.S. War Department to head an American military advisory mission. Dye was given the rank of general by the king, and together with three junior American officers selected by Dye, he began to train Koreans in a new facility established by the king in 1888 expressly for that purpose, the Military Training Institute (Yŏnmu Kongwŏn). Although historically the institute may be regarded as Korea's earliest military academy, in reality it was still a far cry from contemporary counterparts in Europe or Japan, as well as Dye's own alma mater in the United States. Before 1894 the old military examination system (*mukwa*), through which military officers were traditionally selected, was still in place, and the institute's students were selected by recommendation from a pool of people that was limited to the young relatives of current and former high-ranking military officials. Apart from the personal training offered by Dye and his associates, there also appears to have been little in the way of a formal curriculum of courses and programs, and in fact only one recruitment seems to have actually taken place during the six years that the institute was in operation. The institute was also beset with numerous problems, including strained relations between the American instructors and the Korean government over issues of compensation and other matters, a lack of support if not obstruction from elements of the Korean bureaucracy who saw their interests more closely aligned to Yuan Shikai and Qing China than to the United States, incompetence and offensive behavior on the part of some of the Americans under Dye, and, finally, a lack of enthusiasm for any kind of rigorous training on the part of the students themselves, who for the most part seem to have been looking for a shortcut to a bureaucratic appointment. A Russian military observer in 1889 described the atmosphere at the institute as follows: "Training was supposed to begin at five or six in the morning. The American instructors would come out on the parade ground and find no Koreans present. They would try to assemble the soldiers, dealing through Korean officials. Two hours would pass in useless arguments. Then, when everyone had finally fallen in, the Koreans would announce that it was too hot . . . everyone would go back to the barracks." In 1894–1895 under the Kabo-Ŭlmi reform government, the effort to create a modern military academy took a major leap forward. The traditional examination system was abolished, along with the Military Training Institute, and a new officer school was established, called the Drilled Troops Officer Training Center (Hullyŏndae Sagwan Yangsŏngso). As its name suggested, the center was set up to provide officers for the battalions of the Drilled Troops, the new battalions under Japanese guidance that were to serve as a nucleus for the development of a new army. The course of study was initially only three months, but it was quickly extended to eighteen. The new school also had at least the rudiments of a real curriculum, and admission was legally open to all regardless of social background. With the old examination system no longer operative, the new school also assumed a unique importance as the only Korean route to a military commission, and following the practice in Japan and other countries, cadets were to be given appointments in the Korean army as second lieutenants following their successful completion of the course of study. Like the Hullyŏndae itself, however, the new school failed to survive the decline of Japanese influence in Korea following the assassination of the queen and the Triple Intervention, and in early 1896 it was closed. Nevertheless, just as the battalions of the defunct Hullyŏndae provided the raw material for the new Korean army of the Great Han Empire, the Hullyŏndae Training Center laid the foundation for the establishment of the Great Han Empire Military Academy (Mugwan Hakkyo), discussed here. For Yu Kilchun's and Pak Yŏnghyo's views on officer training, see Chapter 1. On the 1894–1895 Kabo-Ŭlmi military reforms, see Yukkun Sagwan Hakkyo Han'guk Kunsa Yŏn'gusil, *Han'guk kunjesa* [History of the military system in Korea] (Seoul: Yukkun Ponbu, 1968–1977), 1:337–363; William Henry Wilkinson, *The Corean Government: Constitutional Changes, July 1894 to October 1895* (Shanghai: Statistical Department of the Inspectorate General of Customs, 1897), 92–98. On the military training directed by American officers in the 1880s and 1890s, see Young Ick Lew, "Yüan Shih-k'ai's Residency and the Korean Enlightenment Movement," *Journal of Korean Studies* 5 (1984): 100–104; Donald M. Bishop, "Shared Failure: American Military Advisors in Korea, 1888–1896," *Transactions of the Royal Asiatic Society, Korea Branch* 58 (1983): 53–76.

18. On the Mugwan Hakkyo, see Im Chaech'an, "Ku Hanmal Yukkun Mugwan Hakkyo yŏn'gu" [Study of the Late Chosŏn Army Military Academy] (Ph.D. dissertation, History Department, Tonga Taehakkyo, 1989), 3–95. Im's work also contains an extensive appendix of teaching materials from the school, largely Korean translations of Japanese counterparts.

19. Bishop, "Shared Failure," 75 n. 74.

20. See Eckert, *Offspring of Empire*, 32.

21. On these schools, see Chapter 1. On the students, see Yi Kidong, *Pigŭk ŭi kun'indŭl: Ilbon Yuksa ch'ulsin ŭi yŏksa* [Soldiers of tragedy: a history of the graduates of the JMA] (Seoul: Ilchogak, 1982), 3–5.

22. In 1920 the Cadet School became the Japanese Military Academy Preparatory Academy (Rikugun Yoka Shikan Gakkō), abbreviated here as JMAP. See Theodor Failor Cook Jr., "The Japanese Officer Corps: The Making of a Military Elite, 1872–1945" (Ph.D. dissertation, History Department, Princeton University, 1987), 127.

23. Yi Kidong, *Pigŭk ŭi kun'indŭl*, 5–6; Harold F. Cook, *Korea's 1884 Incident: Its Background and Kim Ok-kyun's Elusive Dream* (Seoul: Royal Asiatic Society, Korea Branch, 1972), 85.

24. Yi Kidong, *Pigŭk ŭi kun'indŭl*, 7–17.

25. Ibid., 14.

26. Kin Kyōshō (Kim Hyŏngsŏp), "Kin Kyōshō Taisa kaikoroku" [Memoir of Colonel Kim Hyŏngsŏp], in *Nikkan gaikō shiryŏ*, ed. Ichikawa Masaaki (Tokyo: Hara Shobō, 1981), 10:203.

27. Yi Kidong, *Pigŭk ŭi kun'indŭl*, 17. See also Ŏ Tam's memoir: Gyo Tan (Ŏ Tam), "Gyo Tan Shōshō kaikoroku" [Memoir of Major General Ŏ Tam], in *Nikkan gaikō shiryŏ* 10:3–186.

28. Im Chaech'an, "Ku Hanmal Yukkun Mugwan Hakkyo yŏn'gu," 24.

29. Yi Kidong, *Pigŭk ŭi kunindŭl*, 280–285.

30. Ibid., 43.

31. *Samch'ŏlli* 12, no. 9 (1940): 48.

32. *Tonga ilbo*, March 2, 1940.

33. Yi Kidong, *Pigŭk ŭi kun'indŭl*, 283–288.

34. Prasenjit Duara, *Sovereignty and Authenticity: Manchukuo and the East Asian Modern* (Lanham, MD: Rowman & Littlefield, 2003), esp. 1–6.

35. Kiyoizumi Nobuo, interview, Tokyo, January 12, 2011. Kiyoizumi was trained in the *jidōsha* branch.

36. On the development of the Manchukuo Army, see Nishikawa Nobuyoshi, "Manshūkokugun tenbyō" [An outline of the Manchukuo Army], series of twelve monthly articles in *Kaikō*, January–December 2000, esp. articles 1–7. See also Makinami Yasuko, *Gosennichi no guntai: Manshūkoku Gun no gunkan tachi* [The army of 5,000 days: officers of the Manchukuo Army] (Tokyo: Sōrinsha, 2004), esp. 11–66; *Manshūkokugun* [The Manchukuo Army], ed. Manshūkokugun Kankō Iinkai (Tokyo: Ranseikai, 1970) (henceforth *MG*), esp. chaps. 1–5; *Manjugukkunji* [Record of the Manchukuo Army], ed. Kim Sŏkpŏm (CTS 5) (n.p., 1987), courtesy of Kim Yun'gŭn (henceforth *MKJ*), esp. 4–2. On the Jiandao Special Force, see *MG*, 193–194; Makinama Yasuko, *Gosennichi no guntai*, 90–95. On Koreans in the Force, see *MKJ*, 32–39.

37. On the ethnic harmony ideal, see Yamamuro Shin'ichi, *Manchuria under Japanese Dominion*, trans. Joshua A. Fogel (Philadelphia: University of Pennsylvania Press, 2006), 88–93. On the recruitment of Japanese officers, see Nishikawa Nobuyoshi, "Manshūkokugun tenbyō," esp. article 5; *Changchun wenshi ziliao* 2 [Changchun cultural history materials, vol. 2], ed. Changchun Shi Zhengxie Wenshi Ziliao Weiyuanhui (Changchun: Changchun Shi Zhengxie Wenshi Bangongshi Faxingzu, 1991) (henceforth *CWZ*), 28–30; *MG*, 65–82; Makinami Yasuko, *Gosennichi no guntai*, 3, 21–30.

38. On the various army schools in Manchuria, see *MG*, 615–672. For information on Koreans in many of these schools, see *MKJ*, 31–63.

39. On Mizumachi, see Chapter 5.

40. Hong was the only Korean of commoner status to reach general rank in the IJA. Yi Ŭn (JMA 29), Emperor Kojong's son and Chosŏn crown prince, was also given lieutenant general rank. As of 1943, there were approximately 291 Korean officers in the IJA. See *Chōsen hantō shusshin no gen Nihongun shōkō meibo* [List of Koreans in the former Japanese Army officer corps] (Tokyo: Kōseishō, Hikiage Engo Fukuin Chōsaka, n.d.), 1–3; Yi Kidong, *Pigŭk ŭi kun'indŭl*, 282. Using different sources, Utsumi gives a somewhat different figure of 228, including two lieutenant generals and one major general. See Utsumi Aiko, *Chōsenjin 'Kogun' heishitachi no sensō* [The Korean "Imperial Army" soldiers' war] (Tokyo: Iwanami Shoten, 1991), 44. Neither figure, however, includes Korean officers in the Manchukuo Army. Hong was executed as a war criminal in Manila in 1946 for atrocities committed by his subordinates at a Japanese prisoner-of-war camp in the Philippines. On Hong, including his time at the CTS, see Yi Kidong, *Pigŭk ŭi kun'indŭl*, 35–37, 189–221. For a full biography of Hong, including his trial and execution, see Yamamoto Shichihei, *Kō Shiyoku Chūjō no shokei* [The execution of Lieutenant General Kō Shiyoku] (Tokyo: Bungei Shunjū, 1986); Yamamoto's work has also been translated into Korean. See Yamamoto Shichihei, *Hong Saik Chungjang ŭi ch'ŏhyŏng* [The execution of Lieutenant General Hong Saik], trans. Yi Myŏngsŏng (Seoul: Tonam Sŏsa, 1986).

41. See Chapter 5.

42. Chŏng Ilgwŏn, *Chŏng Ilgwŏn hoegorok* [Memoir of Chŏng Ilgwŏn] (Seoul: Koryŏ Sŏjŏk, 1996), 73. According to Sin Hyŏnjun, who was also in Chŏng's CTS 5 class, the course lasted eleven months: Sin Hyŏnjun, *No haebyŏng ŭi hoegorok* [Memoir of an old marine] (Seoul: Katollik Ch'ulp'ansa, 1989), 36. Among other positions, Chŏng served seven years as prime minister and later seven years as head of the National Assembly under Park Chung Hee. For a brief sketch of Chŏng's life and career, see Ch'in-Il Inmyŏng Sajŏn P'yŏnch'an Wiwŏnhoe, *Ch'in-Il inmyŏng sajŏn* [Pro-Japanese biographical dictionary], 3 vols. (Seoul: Minjok Munje Yŏn'guso, 2009) (henceforth *CIS*), 3:494–495. For Sin, see *CIS* 2:368–370, 407.

43. On the founding and development of the CTS, see Nishikawa Nobuyoshi, "Manshūkokugun tenbyō," esp. article 3; *MG*, 75–82, 582; Makinami Yasuko, *Gosennichi no guntai*, 28–29. On Korean graduates of the CTS, see *MKJ*, 41–44. Comparing the CTS and the MMA, Yi Hallim (MMA 2) described the MMA as a full-scale military university "like West Point," while the CTS was a "short-term army training center." Yi Hallim, interview, Seoul, July 12, 1990. On Yi Hallim, see *CIS* 3:212. See also Yi's autobiography: Yi Hallim, *Segi ŭi kyŏngnang: hoesangnok* [The raging waves of the century: a memoir] (Seoul: P'albogwŏn, 1994).

44. Nishikawa Nobuyoshi, "Manshūkokugun tenbyō," article 7.

45. See Mark R. Peattie, *Ishiwara Kanji and Japan's Confrontation with the West* (Princeton, NJ: Princeton University Press, 1975), 158–159.

46. *Ren* was the Japanese pronunciation of the character *lian*, the Chinese term for the "company" unit used at the MMA. The corresponding term at the JMA was *chūtai*.

Both the MMA and JMA used the same term for "section," pronounced *kutai* in Japanese.

47. Relevant sources on the MMA here include: *MG*, 615–621; Nishikawa Nobuyoshi, "Manshūkokugun tenbyō," esp. article 9; *Rikugun Shikan Gakkō* [The Japanese Military Academy], ed. Yamazaki Masao, with the collaboration of the Kaikōsha, 4th ed. (Tokyo: Akimoto Shobō, 1984) (henceforth *RSG*), 68; *CWZ*, 1–27; *MKJ*, 54–63. On the JMA, see *RSG*, 8, 15–20. See also Cook, "The Japanese Officer Corps," esp. 50–66.

48. *Manshū nichi-nichi shinbun*, March 14, 1941. On Nagumo's selection, see also *Dōtokudai dai-shichikisei shi* [History of the MMA 7 class], ed. Dōtokudai Dai-Shichikiseikai (Tokyo: Dōtokudai Dai-Shichikiseikai, 1990) (henceforth *Dōtokudai*), 805–806. On Nagumo's life and military career, see *SJS (Rikugun)*, 247; Nagumo Katsurō, letter to author, August 31, 1990.

49. *Dōtokudai*, 802–805; Nishikawa Nobuyoshi, "Manshūkokugun tenbyō," article 8; *CWZ*, 28–30.

50. On the various Nikkei and Mankei classes, see Kiyoizumi Nobuo, "Manshūkoku Rikugun Gunkan Gakkō" [The MMA] (n.d.; personal compilation, courtesy of Kiyoizumi Nobuo), 2–3, 5. See also Manshū Teikoku Chianbu, *Manshūkoku shōkō seito shigansha no tame ni* [On Manchukuo officer and cadet volunteers], document marked "Secret: Internal Use Only," 1939. There was no separate MMA 5 (Nikkei) class, which was incorporated into the MMA 6 (Nikkei) class: Nishikawa Nobuyoshi, interview, Yokohama, January 10, 2011. On the interaction and integration of the Nikkei and Mankei units, see *Dōtokudai*, 35; *CWZ*, 105; Kiyoizumi Nobuo, interview, Tokyo, January 12, 2011. The MMA 7 Mankei cadets would have been integrated into the Nikkei companies in their second semester, but the war ended before the second semester had begun: Nishikawa Nobuyoshi, interview, Yokohama, January 10, 2011. See also the Conclusion. On the Mongolian army, see Nishikawa Nobuyoshi, "Manshūkokugun tenbyō," article 7. On the selection of outstanding Mankei for the JMA *honka* course, see *CWZ*, 6. Mankei cadets selected for the JMA *honka* course joined the Nikkei group at the MMA after their branch (*heika*) assignments were announced; Takezawa Rikio, interview, Tokyo, January 12, 2011.

51. All the MMA 5 Korean cadets were sent on to the JMA with their Nikkei counterparts. In the last two MMA classes Koreans were incorporated from the beginning into the Nikkei group. Relevant sources on the Korean cadets here include: Kiyoizumi Nobuo, "Manshūkoku Rikugun Gunkan Gakkō," 5; Nishikawa Nobuyoshi, interview, Yokohama, January 10, 2011; *MKJ*, 62–63; 79–81. See also the Conclusion.

52. Nishikawa Nobuyoshi, interview, Yokohama, January 10, 2011. Nishikawa was particularly inspired by the story of nine midget submarine crewmen who died in the attack, and who were glorified in both the Japanese and Korean media. See Peggy Warner and Sadao Seno, *Coffin Boats: Japanese Midget Submarine Operations in the Second World War* (London: Leo Cooper, 1986); see also *Maeil sinbo*, March 7, 1942.

53. Kaneko Tomio, interview, Tokyo, January 12, 2011.

54. Nishikawa Nobuyoshi, interview, Yokohama, January 10, 2011; Kaneko Tomio, interview, Tokyo, January 12, 2011; *CWZ*, 28–30.

55. On Kenkoku University (Kenkoku Daigaku/Kendai), see also Chapter 6.

56. Nearly every Chinese former cadet mentioned the prestige attached to the MMA. See, for example, *CWZ*, 3; Gao Qingyin, interview, Las Vegas, March 11, 1997.

57. Wang Jingyue and Zhu Huan, interview, Changchun, August 28, 1992.

58. Gao Qingyin, interview, Las Vegas, March 11, 1997. A national conscription law was promulgated in Manchukuo in 1940 and went into effect the following year; see Nishikawa Nobuyoshi, "Manshūkokugun tenbyō," article 6.

59. On the opening of the MMA, see *Tonga ilbo*, April 26, 1938. The popular Korean magazine *Samch'ŏlli* also carried numerous stories about Koreans serving in the Chōsen

Army and attending the various military schools. See, for example, *Samch'ŏlli* 6, no. 9 (1934): 36–40; *Samch'ŏlli* 12, no. 4 (1940): 22; *Samch'ŏlli* 13, no. 4 (1941): 186–187. In the 1941 article the author mistakenly situates the MMA in Mukden rather than Xinjing.

60. On Chŏng Naehyŏk, see his autobiography: *Kyŏkpyŏn ŭi saengae rŭl torabomyŏ: kijŏk ŭi kamyŏ, yŏksa nŭn namŭmyŏ: Chŏng Naehyŏk hoegorok* [Looking back on a tumultuous life: the miracle passes, history remains: the memoir of Chŏng Naehyŏk] (Seoul: Han'guk Sanŏp Yŏn'guwŏn, 2001), 11–30. Chŏng also wrote a Japanese version of his autobiography, which is useful for comparative purposes and contains additional information. See Tei Raikaku (Chŏng Naehyŏk), *Watashi no ayunde kita michi: eijoku no nanajūnen* [The path I took: seventy years of honor and shame] (Tokyo: Tendensha, 2003). See also *CIS* 3:438.

61. Chŏng Naehyŏk, *Kyŏkpyŏn ŭi saengae rŭl torabomyŏ*, 38–39. According to Kim Chaehak, who had grown up with Park Chung Hee in the same village, Park had been very impressed by the deference he had seen being shown to Japanese soldiers even by the "frightening" local Japanese police. See Cho Kapche, *Pak Chŏnghŭi* 1:92.

62. Chŏng Naehyŏk, *Kyŏkpyŏn ŭi saengae rŭl torabomyŏ*, 16, 25–26.

63. A typical example here was Major Kim Sŏgwŏn (JMA 27), who, as a battalion commander in the IJA, served on the China front and returned to Korea in 1939 to give lectures on the war situation and his personal experience to audiences throughout the country, including in Seoul's Citizens Hall, the city's main auditorium for public events. In his diary Yun Ch'iho writes of attending one of these events in Citizens Hall, with "the big Hall jammed with people of every description." Yun, *Yun Ch'iho ilgi* [Diary of Yun Ch'iho] (Seoul: Kuksa P'yŏnch'an Wiwŏnhoe, 1973–1989), vol. 11, entry for April 13, 1939. See also *Tonga ilbo*, April 8, 1939; June 13, 1939; June 17, 1939; August 6, 1939; August 18, 1939. On Kim Sŏgwŏn, see *CIS* 1:412–414; Kim Sŏgwŏn, *Nobyŏng ŭi han: chasŏjŏn* [Lament of an old soldier: autobiography] (Seoul: Yukpŏpsa, 1977), esp. 146–200. In August 1944 Kim was promoted to full colonel in the IJA, and after the war he became an officer in the ROKA, retiring in 1956 as a major general.

64. Pang Wŏnch'ol, interview, Seoul, July 2, 1997. Kim Yŏngt'aek, another former MMA 1 cadet and Kwangmyŏng student, also cites Chŏng Ilgwŏn's influence here as crucial: Kim Yŏngt'aek, interview, Seoul, May 31, 1997. On Kim Yŏngt'aek, see *CIS* 1:496. In his memoir Chŏng mentions a visit to Kwangmyŏng, but this is apparently another, later visit, after he had graduated from the JMA. Chŏng graduated from the JMA (JMA 55) in 1941, when Pang and Kim were already finishing up their second year at the MMA. Chŏng also incorrectly gives 1940 as the date of his JMA graduation. See Chŏng Ilgwŏn, *Chŏng Ilgwŏn hoegorok*, 71–77. The visit to which Pang and Kim referred probably took place sometime in late 1937 or early 1938, after Chŏng had graduated from the CTS but before he was sent on to Zama. Chŏng's CTS class (CTS 5) was commissioned in the Manchukuo Army in December 1937, but Chŏng did not enter the JMA until April 1940, so it appears he spent more than two years as an officer in the Manchukuo Army before being sent to the JMA for additional training, and his visit to Kwangmyŏng, where he met Pang, Kim, and other members of what would become the MMA 1 class undoubtedly took place sometime during this period. Chŏng's memoir is confusing here, and his dates are unreliable. See *MKJ*, 43; Sin Hyŏnjun, *No haebyŏng ŭi hoegorok*, 38–39; *RSG*, 225–226. A Japanese roster of Korean graduates of the JMA and MMA drawn up for alumni in 1975 also clearly states that Chŏng was admitted to the JMA through the Manchukuo Army officer corps: see *Kankoku shusshin: Nihon Rikushi-Manshū Gunkō dōsōsei meibo* [List of the Korean graduates of the JMA and MMA] (n.p., August 1975), 17–18. On Kwangmyŏng school, see Pang Wŏnch'ol, "Kwangmyŏng Kodŭng Hakkyo yŏnhyŏk" [History of Kwangmyŏng High School], Seoul, 1991, courtesy of Pang Wŏnch'ol.

65. Chŏng Naehyŏk, *Kyŏkpyŏn ŭi saengae rŭl torabomyŏ*, 26.
66. Yi Hallim, *Segi ŭi kyŏngnang*, 18–21. Yi told me his decision to apply to the MMA was very simple: "I wanted to be a soldier, no other reason." He took the MMA 2 entrance examination in Mukden. Yi Hallim, interview, Seoul, July 12, 1990.
67. See, for example, *CIS,* frequently cited in this book, a scholarly biographical dictionary of Koreans designated as "pro-Japanese" during the late Chosŏn and colonial periods, which includes as a matter of course all Korean officers of company rank and higher who served in the IJA or MMA.
68. Yun Haedong, "Singminji insik ŭi 'hoesaek chidae': Ilcheha gongongsŏng kwa kyuyul kwŏllyŏk" [The gray areas of "colonial perception": blank spaces and disciplinary power in Japanese imperialism], in *Kŭndae rŭl tasi ingnŭnda: Han'guk kŭndae insik ŭi saeroun p'aerodaim ŭi wihayŏ* [Rereading the modern era: toward a new paradigm of understanding Korea's modern age], ed. Yun Haedong, Ch'ŏn Chŏnghwan, Hŏ Su, Hwang Pyŏngju, Yi Yonggi, and Yun Taesŏk (Seoul: Yŏksa Pip'yŏngsa, 2006), 1:37–61. See also Gi-Wook Shin and Michael Robinson, "Rethinking Colonial Korea," in *Colonial Modernity in Korea,* ed. Gi-Wook Shin and Michael Robinson (Cambridge, MA: Harvard University Asia Center, 1999), 1–18; Carter J. Eckert, "Exorcising Hegel's Ghosts: Toward a Postnationalist Historiography of Korea," in Shin and Robinson, *Colonial Modernity in Korea,* 363–378; Carter J. Eckert, "Preface," in special issue of *Journal of International and Area Studies* 11, no. 3 (2004): 1–4.
69. Kim Tonghun, interview, Seoul, July 11, 1990.
70. See also Chapters 5 and 6.
71. See, for example, Hosokawa Minoru Nikki [Hosokawa Minoru diary], April 10, 1941 (Nagumo); May 15, 1941; June 13, 1941 (Nagumo); September 3, 1941; December 9, 1941; February 6, 1942.
72. Ibid., December 9, 1941.
73. See, for example, ibid., September 3, 1941; September 14, 1941.
74. Ibid., February 6, 1942, and December 21, 1941.
75. Nishikawa Nobuyoshi, interview, Yokohama, January 10, 2011.
76. Hosokawa Minoru Nikki, January 17, 1942.
77. Ibid., November 6, 1941.
78. Ibid., December 10, 1941.
79. Ibid., October 14, 1941; November 20, 1941.
80. *Gojūshichikiseikai tsūshin* [The 57th class news] 36 (December 25, 1991): 11–12.
81. Hosokawa Minoru Nikki, November 30, 1941.
82. Ibid., June 4, 1941.
83. See *Dōtokudai*, 35. Kaneko Tomio (MMA 2) told me that sorghum was a "normal staple" in Manchuria at the time and did in fact make the Japanese cadets sick, at least at first. But he also conceded that since the cadets all ate together in the same dining hall, the Mankei undoubtedly felt a sense of discrimination. Kaneko Tomio, interview, Tokyo, January 12, 2011. For the reaction of the Mankei cadets to the food policy, see *CWZ,* 36, 105. Such official discrimination in food was a common practice in the Manchukuo government and education system. See Yamamuro Shin'ichi, *Manchuria under Japanese Dominion,* 199–201.
84. There were a total of forty-eight Koreans in the MMA 1-MMA 7 classes, as follows: MMA 1 (13); MMA 2 (11); MMA 3 (2); MMA 4 (2); MMA 5 (5); MMA 6 (11); MMA 7 (4). See *MKJ,* 62–63; *Kankoku shusshin,* 18–25; Kiyoizumi, "Manshūkoku Rikugun Gunkan Gakkō," 5 (Kiyoizumi gives forty-nine here as the total number of Korean cadets, but he has incorrectly added his own numbers, which total forty-eight).
85. Park Chung Hee, for example, was in the 3rd Mankei Company, 3rd Section, or 3/3 *(san no san),* according to the way the cadets at both the MMA and JMA identified their

company and section groupings. In Park's MMA 2 class there were two companies of Mankei (with about 120 cadets in each company), each subdivided into four sections (with about 30 cadets in each section). Gao Qingyin, interview, Las Vegas, March 11, 1997. Koreans continued to be lodged in the Mankei group until the MMA 6 class, when they were fully integrated in the Nikkei from the beginning. Even before this, however, the great majority of Koreans in the Mankei, like Park, were being sent on to the JMA with a respective Nikkei group for their *honka* training. All the MMA 3 and MMA 5 Koreans were thus sent to Zama. The MMA 5 Koreans were actually incorporated into the Nikkei MMA 4/JMA 59 group. Koreans in the early classes who were not sent on to Zama, together with most of the Chinese cadets, remained at the MMA for the completion of their *honka* training. For some reason not entirely clear, Koreans in the MMA 4 class also remained in Manchuria, perhaps because of their particular branch assignment. MMA medical and veterinary service cadets, for example, such as Kim Tonghun (MMA 6), stayed on in Manchuria after completing their *yoka*, as they went on to attend specialized professional schools in their fields. Relevant sources here include Kiyoizumi Nobuo, "Manshūkoku Rikugun Gunkan Gakkō," 2–3, 5; Nishikawa Nobuyoshi, interview, Yokohama, January 10, 2011; *MKJ*, 62–63; Kim Tonghun, interview, Seoul, July 11, 1990. On the MMA 4 Nikkei class, which absorbed the MMA 5 Koreans, see *Byōbō senri: sanju kinen gō* [The boundless thousand miles: on the anniversary of our 80th year of age], ed. Dōtokudai Yonkiseikai (n.p.: Dōtokudai Yonkiseikai, 2004), 3:98, 2:137.

86. Gao Qingjin, interview, Las Vegas, March 11, 1997. Park Chung Hee's Japanese name, used in JMA and IJA documents, was Takagi Masao. See, for example, Rikugun Shikan Gakkō, *Manshūkoku Gunkan Gakkō dai-nikkisei: Shōwa 19-nen 4-gatsu 20-nichi sotsugyō* [The MMA 2 class: graduated April 20, 1944], personal property of Sekine Tomiji, copy in Yasukuni Kaikō Bunkoshitsu, Tokyo. According to Park's MMA 2 classmate Kim Muk, Korean cadets who had not taken Japanese names were called into the section commander's office in the evenings and "disciplined" (*kihap*). Kim said that one of the MMA 2 cadets, Kang Ch'angsŏn, nevertheless refused to change his name. Kim Muk, interview, Seoul, May 28, 1997. On Kang, see *CIS* 1:123. On Korean name changes in this period more generally, see Miyata Setsuko, Kimu Yondaru, and Yan Teho, *Sōshi kaimei* [The name change] (Tokyo: Akashi Shoten, 1992); a Korean translation of Miyata et al.'s book is *Ch'angssi kaemyŏng*, ed. and trans. Chŏng Ŭnhyŏn (Seoul: Hangminsa, 1994).

87. Kim Tonghun, interview, Seoul, July 11, 1990.

88. Hosokawa Minoru Nikki, January 12, 1942.

89. Origuchi Ryūzō et al., interview, Tokyo, September 1, 1990.

90. Kaneko Tomio, interview, Tokyo, January 12, 2011.

91. *Senku: kaikoroku* [Vanguard: memoirs], ed. Dōtokudai Ikkiseikai (Tokyo: Dōtokudai Ikkiseikai, 1986–1987), 1:318–319; see also Chapter 7. On Yi Chuil, see *CIS* 3:150–151. See also Se-Jin Kim, *Politics of Military Revolution in Korea* (Chapel Hill: University of North Carolina Press, 1971), 99.

92. Chŏng Naehyŏk, *Kyŏkpyŏn ŭi saengae rŭl torabomyŏ*, 50.

93. Kim Muk, interview, Seoul, May 28, 1997; Pang Wŏnch'ŏl, interview, Seoul, May 30, 1997. On Kim Muk (Kim Myŏngch'ŏl), see *CIS* 1:354, 349–350.

94. According to former IJA officer Yu Yangsu, "As Koreans, we could not help but be conscious of the historical and personal irony of wearing a Japanese military uniform, and always felt deep within us a sense of being Korean in our relations with Japanese.... For that reason we were determined to be outstanding officers, not inferior to the Japanese." Yu Yangsu, letter to author, May 6, 2004.

95. See *CWZ*, 4–5, 117, 143, 157.

96. Kim Muk, interview, Seoul, May 28, 1997.
97. Gao Qingyin, interview, Las Vegas, March 11, 1997.
98. Ibid. See also *RSG,* 28; Hiruma Hiroshi, *Rikugun Shikan Gakkō yomoyama monogatori* [Sundry stories of the JMA] (Tokyo: Kōjinsha, 1983) (henceforth *Yomoyama*), 152–154.
99. Gao Qingyin, interview, Las Vegas, March 11, 1997.
100. *Pak Chŏnghŭi Changgun tamhwa munjip* [Collected statements of General Park Chung Hee] (Seoul: Taet'ongnyŏng Pisŏsil, 1965), 494.
101. On Park's family and early childhood, see Pak Chŏnghŭi, "Na ŭi sonyŏn sijŏl" [My childhood], *Wŏlgan Chosŏn,* May 1984, 84–94. See also Cho Kapche, *Pak Chŏnghŭi* 1:1–56.
102. Yu Yangsu, interview, Seoul, May 28, 1997. On Yu, see Chapter 2.
103. Pak Chŏnghŭi, "Na ŭi sonyŏn sijŏl," 95.
104. See Cho Kapche, *Pak Chŏnghŭi* 1:122–123; *Taegu Sabŏm simsanggwaji,* 99.
105. Hwangbo Kyun and Yun Ch'idu, interview, Taegu, August 3, 1990.
106. Ibid.; Yi Sŏngjo, interview, Seoul, June 22–23, 1998.
107. Sŏ Pyŏngguk, interview, Taegu, August 4, 1990.
108. Hwangbo Kyun and Yun Ch'idu, interview, Taegu, August 3, 1990; Yi Sŏngjo, interview, Seoul, June 22–23, 1998; *Sotsugyō kinen shashin: jinjōka dai-4 kai: Kanritsu Taikyū Shihan Gakkō* [Graduation commemorative photos: the 4th class of the elementary school department of the Government Normal School of Taegu], ed. Taikyū Shihan Gakkō Arubamu Iin (Taegu: Eimei Shashinkan, 1937). Yi Sŏngjo, one of the original editors, kindly provided me with a copy of this album, one he had in fact intended to give to President Park Chung Hee, who for some reason did not have one, but Park was assassinated before he could do so.
109. *Taegu Sabŏm simsanggwaji,* 230; Hwangbo Kyun and Yun Ch'idu, interview, Taegu, August 3, 1990. Arikawa served at TNS from August 1935 to March 1939, thus supervising Park's military training for about two years. Makiyama Nozomu, *Rikugun chūjō Arikawa Shuichi shōden* [Brief biography of army lieutenant general Arikawa Shuichi] (Akashi [Hyōgo Ken]: Makiyama Nozomu, 1980), 11–12.
110. Makiyama Nozomu, *Rikugun chūjō Arikawa Shuichi ryakuden: Okinawa sen, Arikawa ryodan no sentō gaiyō* [Short biography of army lieutenant general Arikawa Shuichi: a summary of the combat of the Arikawa brigade in the battle of Okinawa] (Kagoshima: Kagoshima Ken Okinawa Sen'ekisha Ireikai, 1981), 9–11. Arikawa ranked 87th out of 473 graduates in the JMA 25 infantry class. Rikugun Shikan Gakkō, *Rikugun Shikan Gakkō sotsugyō jinmeibo: Meiji 30-Shōwa 16 (Dai-ikki–Dai-gojūgoki)* [Roster of graduates of the JMA: 1897–1941 (JMA 1–JMA 55)] (n.p.: n.d.), Dai-nijūgoki (hoheika).
111. *Taegu Sabŏm simsanggwaji,* 230. Arikawa had had ample opportunity to observe the capabilities of Koreans as soldiers while he was a cadet at the JMA. Although there were no Koreans in his own JMA 25 class, there were thirteen in the class immediately below (JMA 26), which, as an upperclassman, he would routinely have helped monitor and supervise. Koreans in the JMA 26 class included Hong Saik, who would also achieve lieutenant general rank in the IJA, and several others who went on to become generals in the ROKA after 1945. See Yi Kidong, *Pigŭk ŭi kun'indŭl,* 280–281.
112. Makiyama Nozomu, *Rikugun chūjō Arikawa Shuichi ryakuden,* 72–74.
113. Hwangbo Kyun and Yun Ch'idu, interview, Taegu, August 3, 1990.
114. Sŏ Pyŏngguk, interview, Taegu, August 4, 1990.
115. Park was married to Kim Honam, a local girl from a different township in the same North Kyŏngsang county of Sŏnsan where Park grew up. A daughter, Pak Chaeok, was born to the couple in November 1937. See Cho Kapche, *Pak Chŏnghŭi* 1:145, 171, 178–179.

116. Yu Chŭngsŏn, interview, Seoul, August 13, 1990. Park's focus on a military career did not apparently negatively affect his teaching. By all accounts he was popular among his students. See Cho Kapche, *Pak Chŏnghŭi* 1:180–184.

117. Ibid.; *Manshū shinbun*, March 31, 1939. Such "blood pledges" from young men aspiring to be soldiers were not at all uncommon in this period and were frequently reported in Korean and Japanese newspapers. A search on Neibŏ Nyusŭ Raibŭrŏri, the Korean on-line news library, using the keyword *hyŏlsa*, reveals that 1939–1940 was in fact a peak year for such reported pledges in colonial Korea's most popular Korean-language newspaper, *Tonga ilbo*. See also Brandon Palmer, *Fighting for the Enemy: Koreans in Japan's War, 1937–1945* (Seattle: University of Washington Press, 2013), 80, 82, 94, 100, 115. To be eligible for the MMA, a young man had to be between sixteen and twenty years of age. See *Zheng fu gong bao*, September 7, 1938, 195. In 1939 Park Chung Hee was almost twenty-two. Being unmarried was another eligibility requirement, but the documents Park sent the Manchukuo authorities apparently did not disclose his marital status.

118. Yu Chŭngsŏn, interview, Seoul, August 13, 1990. See also Pak Chŏnghŭi Biographical Notes, Yi Naksŏn Papers. Yi was Park's chief secretary (*pisŏ silchang*) in the period following the 1961 coup, and collected a considerable body of information on Park's life from a variety of sources, including from Park himself. This is a particularly valuable source on Park's early life, since much of the most personal information, could only have come from Park himself, and has since been confirmed by others, including this author. I am grateful to Cho Kapche, who acquired Yi's papers after his death in 1989, for providing me with copies of this document and others in the collection. Park Chung Hee received a high score on the MMA 2 entrance examination, ranking 15th in the overall list of 236 successful Mankei applicants. The list can be found in *Zheng fu gong bao*, January 1, 1939, 61–64. For samples of MMA entrance examination questions, see Fukushi Tadashi, *Manshūkoku daigaku-senmon gakkō ryūgaku shiken mondai: zenka kaisetsu* [Manchukuo university and college entrance examination questions: explanations for all subjects] (Mukden: Manshū Tosho Monku Kabushiki Kaisha, 1943), 1–5, 12–14, 61–64.

119. Yi Hallim, *Segi ŭi kyŏngnang*, 385.

120. See *Manshū nichi-nichi shinbun*, March 24, 1942; Kiyoizumi Nobuo, *Manshūkoku Rikugun Gunkan Gakkō*, 5. The *Manshū nichi-nichi shinbun* features a picture of Park saluting during the award ceremony. The term *onshi shōkin* literally means "imperial prize money." In 1962 a South Korean newspaper serial (*Han'guk ilbo*) about Park's MMA experience stated that Park had received a "gold watch" from the emperor as one of the top-ranked students in the MMA 2 class, a story that has since seen wide circulation in the South Korean media. As noted above, Puyi himself was not present at the MMA 2 *yoka* graduation ceremony, and neither newspaper accounts from the time or later memoirs by former MMA 1 or MMA 2 cadets mention anything about the bestowal of imperial watches (as opposed to money), but the story nevertheless has a certain degree of credibility. In both Japan and Manchukuo it was common practice for the emperor to meet privately with the top-ranked cadets before the public *yoka* or *honka* ceremonies. During such audiences the cadets were asked a particular question about military tactics and allowed to address the emperor briefly, after which the emperor presented them with a silver watch (for *yoka* graduates) and a gold watch (for *honka* graduates). It is quite possible, therefore, that Park also received a watch from the emperor's aide in such a private ceremony, and two of Park's MMA 2 Chinese classmates, Gao Qingyin and Cai Chongliang, told me that this in fact was their understanding at the time. *Han'guk ilbo*, September 12, 1962; CWZ, 25; Daitō Shinsuke, interview, Tokyo, January 16, 2007; Gao Qinguin, interview, Las Vegas, March 11, 1997; Cai Chongliang, interview, Elyria, OH, May 17, 1997.

121. *RSG,* 126–127. See also Chapter 8.

122. *RSG,* 28.

123. Xu Shudong, interview, Changchun, August 29, 1992.

124. *Yomoyama,* 143.

125. Kaneko Tomio, interview, Tokyo, January 12, 2011; Kiyoizumi Nobuo, interview, Tokyo, January 12, 2011; Takezawa Rikio, interview, Tokyo, January 12, 2011.

126. Gao Qingyin, interview, Las Vegas, March 11, 1997.

127. Origuchi Ryūzō et al., interview, Tokyo, September 1, 1990.

128. Rikugun Shikan Gakkō, *Rikugun Shikan Gakkō sotsugyō jinmeibo.*

129. Nagumo Katsurō, letter to author, August 31, 1990.

130. *Dōtokudai,* 805–806.

131. Nagumo Katsurō, letter to author, August 31, 1990.

132. "In'gan Pak Chŏnghŭi ŭi samuraisik chŏngsin kujo: In'gan Pak Chŏnghŭi chae p'yŏngga: Pak Chŏnghŭi chŏn'gi chakka chŏn Ch'ŏngwadae pisŏgwan Kim Chongsin hoego" [The samurai mentality of Park Chung Hee the person: a reconsideration of the person Park Chung Hee: reflections of former Blue House secretary Kim Chongsin on Park Chung Hee's autobiographical work], *Wŏlgan ŏpsŏbŏ,* October 1991, 190. On Kim Chongsin and his seven years in the Blue House with Park Chung Hee, see Kim Chongsin, *Yŏngsi ŭi hwaetpul: Pak Chŏnghŭi Taet'ongnyŏng ttara ch'illyŏn* [Torch in the midnight hour: seven years with President Park Chung Hee] (Seoul: Hallim Ch'ulp'ansa, 1966).

133. Yu Chŭngsŏn, interview, Seoul, August 13, 1990.

134. The Japanese media was more effusive than the Korean here, but in both the term "newly risen" (*shinkō/sinhŭng*) preceding the name of each country (or of the two combined) became a common epithet. See, for example, *Tonga ilbo,* July 16, 1936. And it was not uncommon for both Hitler and Mussolini to be put in the category of historic "heroes." See, for example, Chu Unsŏng, "Yŏngung kwa hogŏl ron" [On heroes and great men], *Samch'ŏlli,* July 1935, 111–113.

135. Yun would also write of Hitler later that "he has shown himself to be the greatest warrior since Napoleon." *Yun Ch'iho ilgi,* vol. 11, entry for June 1, 1940.

136. The first full Japanese translation of *Mein Kampf* was published in December 1937, several months after Park had graduated from TNS. See Hittora Adorufu, *Waga tōsō* [My struggle], trans. Ōkubo Yasuo (Tokyo: Mikasa Shobō, 1937). But a partial translation of the work had apparently been circulating earlier under the title *Yo no tōsō,* and this was most likely the version that Park had acquired. See Hitora Ādorufu, *Waga tōsō* [My struggle], trans. Manabe Ryōichi (Tokyo: Kōfūkan, 1942), 12. Hitler's writings and speeches were also frequently quoted in Korean newspapers and magazines in the 1930s, even before he actually took power in 1933. See, for example, the April 1932 issue of the well-known Korean-language monthly newsmagazine *Sindonga.*

137. Sŏ Pyŏngguk, interview, Taegu, August 4, 1990.

138. Xu Shudong, interview, Changchun, August 29, 1992.

139. Kim Muk, interview, May 28, 1997. Kim also noted in this interview that Kang Chaeho, who had arranged for Park to take the MMA examination, had also introduced Park to Chŏng Ilgwŏn. On Wŏn Yongdŏk, see *CIS* 2:563–564. Pak was of course several years older than most of his classmates and may also have preferred the company of men closer to his own age. He was in fact one month older than Chŏng Ilgwŏn.

140. Xu Shudong, interview, Changchun, August 29, 1992.

4. Politics and Status

1. Pak Chŏnghŭi (Park Chung Hee), handwritten letter to Chang Toyŏng, May 16, 1961. I received a copy of the original letter from Kim Chaech'un (KMA 5), president of the

May 16 National Award Foundation (Chaedan Pŏbin 5.16 Minjoksang). A printed version of the letter can also be found in Chŏng Chaegyŏng, ed., *Pak Chŏnghŭi silgi: haengjŏk ch'orok* [The true record of Park Chung Hee: selected excerpts] (Seoul: Chimmundang, 1994), 33–34.

2. *Rikugun Shikan Gakkō seito oyobi gakusei kokoroe* [JMA regulations for cadets and students], Rikugun Shikan Gakkō, March 1937 (henceforth *Kokoroe*), 2. Cadets often heard the same thing from their section commanders. Captain Sakai Masao, who served in that capacity at the JMA for the MMA 1 and MMA 2 classes, told the cadets that "through the grace of the emperor," they were a "superior race," and as officers they received the "admiration of society." *Senku: kaikoroku* [Vanguard: memoirs], ed. Dōtokudai Ikkiseikai (Tokyo: Dōtokudai Ikkiseikai, 1986–1987), 1:284.

3. *Kiji* 56 (December 1942): frontispiece. On Ushijima, see *Riku-kaigun shōkan jinji sōran* [Biographical dictionary of army-navy officers], ed. Toyama Misao (Tokyo: Fuyō Shōbō, 1981), 255.

4. *Rikugun Shikan Gakkō* [The Japanese Military Academy], ed. Yamazaki Masao, with the collaboration of the Kaikōsha, 4th ed. (Tokyo: Akimoto Shobō, 1984) (henceforth *RSG*), 140.

5. *Dōtokudai dai-shichikisei shi* [History of the MMA 7 class], ed. Dōtokudai Dai-Shichikiseikai (Tokyo: Dōtokudai Dai-Shichikiseikai, 1990) (henceforth *Dōtokudai*), 165.

6. *RSG*, 54–63; Makino Kikuo, ed., *Rikushi-Rikuyō: bessatsu ichiokunin no Shōwashi* [Officer and cadet schools: supplement to the Shōwa history of 100 million people] (Tokyo: Maininchi Shinbunsa, 1981), 108, 142–143.

7. *RSG*, 56. See also *Tōkei Kanagawa kenshi: sengo 20-nen no ayumi* [Statistics of the history of Kanagawa Prefecture: through 20 years after the war] (Yokohama: Kanagawa Prefecture, 1966), 1:70. *Sōbu*, meaning "looking to the military or military matters," was an archaic term from the ancient Japanese chronicles (*Kojiki* and *Nihon shoki*), associated with the fourth-century crown prince Yamato Takeru, who was said to have conquered this area and also declared it an excellent military training ground. Morimatsu Toshio, "Fūsetsu hachinen: Sōbudai no wakazakura: hajime no gojūki kara kuriage shutsujin" [Eight years of wind and snow: the young cherry blossoms of Sōbudai: early dispatch to war beginning with the JMA 50 class]," in *Rikushi-Rikuyō: bessatsu ichiokunin no Shōwashi* [Officer and cadet schools: supplement to the Shōwa history of 100 million people], ed. Makino Kikuo (Tokyo: Maininchi Shinbunsa, 1981), 190; Community Relations Office, U.S. Army Garrison, Japan, "Camp Zama Historical Monument Walking Tour," March 21, 2005, 7; "History of Camp Zama," http://zahsalumni.com/misc/history_of_camp_zama.htm, accessed September 8, 2009; Ivan Morris, *Nobility of Failure: Tragic Heroes in the History of Japan* (New York: Holt, Rinehart, and Winston, 1975), 1–3.

8. *Dōtokudai*, 806–807.

9. *Changchun wenshi ziliao* 2 [Changchun cultural history materials, vol. 2], ed. Changchun Shi Zhengxie Wenshi Ziliao Weiyuanhui (Changchun: Changchun Shi Zhengxie Wenshi Bangongshi Faxingzu, 1991) (henceforth *CWZ*), 3; *Senku* 1:94.

10. Ibid.

11. *Senku* 1:94. The population of the area in the early 1930s was about 150,000; today (2016) Changchun's population is around 4 million. See Tucker, "Building 'Our Manchukuo': Japanese City Planning, Architecture, and Nation-Building in Occupied Northeast China, 1931–1945" (Ph.D. dissertation, Department of History, University of Iowa, 1999), 260.

12. *Senku* 1:93–94.

13. See, for example, Hiruma Hiroshi, *Rikugun Shikan Gakkō yomoyama monogatori* [Sundry stories of the JMA] (Tokyo: Kōjinsha, 1983) (henceforth *Yomoyama*), illustrated

cover, and 44; *Dōtokudai*, 128. For images of the "modern boy" and "modern girl," a popular style with colonial Korean youth as well, see Jackie Menzies, ed., *Modern Boy Modern Girl: Modernity in Japanese Art 1910–1935* (Sydney: Art Galley of New South Wales, 1998).

14. *RSG*, 150; *Dōtokudai*, 150.

15. For descriptions, sketches, and photos of dress regulations of the Manchukuo Army and cadets of the MMA, see Chianbu Kanbō, ed., *Manshūkokugun reiki ruishū* [Regulations by category of the Manchuko Army] (Shinkyō: Manshū Gyōsei Gakkai, 1942), ("Fukusei"), 2:27–183, esp. 83–84; *Dōtokudai*, 963–970; Philip S. Jowett, *Rays of the Rising Sun: Armed Forces of Japan's Asian Allies 1931–45*, vol. 1, *China and Manchukuo* (Solihull: Helion, 2004), 22, 25, 105, 11–117.

16. *RSG*, 158.

17. *Yomoyama*, 164–165.

18. *RSG*, 146.

19. *Sakufū banri: Manshūkoku Gunkan Gakkō nikisei no kiroku* [The north wind of ten thousand leagues: the record of the MMA 2 class] (Hadano: Dōtokudai Nikiseikai, 1981), 72.

20. *Dōtokudai*, 188. On *sōrōbun*, see also Donald Keene, *Dawn to the West: Japanese Literature in the Modern Era: Fiction* (New York: Holt, Rinehart, and Winston, 1984), 371.

21. *Yomoyama*, 16–17.

22. See *RSG*, 27–28, 60, 124. See also Terada Chikao, *Nihon guntai yōgoshū* [Japanese military terms], 2 vols. (Tokyo: Rippū Shobō, 1992), which provides an even more extensive listing and explanation of IJA terms and expressions.

23. Ibid.

24. *Yomoyama*, 10.

25. *RSG*, 27; *Sakufū banri*, 72.

26. For the above terms, see *RSG*, 27–28, 60, 124. On *gen'an*, see also Chapter 6.

27. *Dōtokudai*, 191, 194.

28. *Yomoyama*, 153.

29. *Senku* 1:284.

30. *Yomoyama*, 78.

31. *Senku* 1:281–282.

32. *Dōtokudai*, 160.

33. Wang Jingyue and Zhu Huan, interviews, Changchun, August 28, 1992.

34. *Senku* 1:390; *Sakufū banri*, 14; *Dōtokudai*, 165.

35. Rikushikō Honbu, "Rikugun Shikan Gakkō rekishi" [History of the JMA] (handwritten official history of the JMA through 1945), Bōei Kenkyūjo, Tokyo, December 30, 1943. For a picture of the monument, see *RSG*, 74.

36. Yi Hallim, *Segi ŭi kyŏngnang* [The raging waves of the century: a memoir] (Seoul: P'albogwŏn, 1994), 19; Hosokawa Minoru Nikki [Hosokawa Minoru Diary] (courtesy of Hosokawa Minoru, via Suzuki Michihiko), entries for April 3, 1941–May 31, 1942, November 27, 1941, and May 10, 1941. The term "continental man" in pre-1945 Japanese parlance referred to men who had involved themselves deeply in continental affairs, including military figures such as Itagaki Seishirō and Ishiwara Kanji, who had planned and executed the Manchurian Incident, as well as civilians such as Matsuoka Yōsuke, who had served as director of the South Manchurian Railway before becoming foreign minister. See, for example, "Toki no hito: sassō/tairiku otoko Itagaki Seishirō" [People of the times: the gallant continental man Itagaki Seishirō], *Keizai magajin*, July (no year), 2; Otani Tsuyoshi, "Tairiku otoko Matsuoka Gaisō" [Continental man foreign minister Matsuoka], *Kyōwa: Mantetsu shainkai kikanshi*, August 1940, 2. On Matsuoka, see Janet Hunter, *Concise Dictionary of Modern Japanese History* (Berkeley: University

of California Press, 1984), 124. From the diary entries, it is clear that Hosokawa also associates the "continental man" idea with Japan's imperial mission on the continent, as well as with the Restoration figure Saigō Takamori, who forcefully argued for continental expansion (into Korea) in 1873.

37. *Senku* 1:137–139.
38. *Dōtokudai,* 194.
39. Ibid., 128.
40. Hosokawa Minoru Nikki, July 14, 1941.
41. *Dōtokudai,* 170–172; *Senku* 1:389.
42. Gao Qingyin, letter (in Chinese) to Yi Naksŏn, May 15, 1962. Translated (Korean) excerpts from Gao's letter also appeared in a special serialized feature on Gao's relationship with Park in *Han'guk ilbo,* September 11–15, 1962.
43. *Senku* 1:389.
44. *Sakufū banri,* 11; *CWZ,* 40; Hosokawa Minoru Nikki, March 3, 1942. On the Manchurian cold, see also *Byōbō senri: sanju kinen gō* [The boundless thousand miles: on the anniversary of our 80th year of age], ed. Dōtokudai Yonkiseikai (n.p.: Dōtokudai Yonkiseikai, 2004), 3:34–35.
45. Hosokawa Minoru Nikki, November 13, 1941.
46. *Dōtokudai,* 124.
47. Ibid., 128, 162.
48. Ibid., 125.
49. Kim Muk, interview, Seoul, May 28, 1997.
50. *Dōtokudai,* 194–195.
51. Ibid., 150.
52. *RSG,* 146; *Sakufū banri,* 75.
53. Kim Muk, interview, Seoul, May 28, 1997. After 1945 An became an officer in the South Korean constabulary (KMA 1) but was arrested and court-martialed on suspicion of connections with the South Korean Labor Party between July 1947 and November 1948. According to *CIS* 2 and other secondary sources, he was executed for his activity, but the court record indicates only that he was found guilty and given a seven-year prison sentence, which was subsequently reduced to three years. Ch'in-Il Inmyŏng Sajŏn P'yŏnch'an Wiwŏnhoe, *Ch'in-Il inmyŏng sajŏn* [Pro-Japanese biographical dictionary], 3 vols. (Seoul: Minjok Munje Yŏn'guso, 2009) (henceforth *CIS*), 2:441; *Kankoku shusshin: Nihon Rikushi-Manshū Gunkō dōsōsei meibo* [List of the Korean graduates of the JMA and MMA] (n.p., August 1975), 25; Yukkun Kodŭng Hoeŭi, Yukkun Kodŭng Hoeŭi myŏngnyŏng, Ministry of Defense special order 5 and order 6, December 20, 1948.
54. *Dōtokudai,* 188.
55. *RSG,* 149.
56. *Dōtokudai,* 189. For more examples of movies shown to cadets during this period, see the complete calendar of events for the JMAP / JMA 58 class compiled by Nakajima Satoshi, "Shuyō gyōji ichiranhyō: Rikugun Yoka Shikan Gakkō: dai-gojūhachikisei: Shōwa 19.5–20.6" [Calendar of important activities: JMA 58: May 1944–June 1945], February 1994 (copy provided to author by Chŏng Naehyŏk). Amakasu Masahiko was a notorious right-wing figure in pre-1945 Japan. As a captain in the IJA military police, he was involved in the murders of many leftist labor leaders and dissidents, including the famous anarchist Ōsugi Sakai, along with his common-law wife and six-year-old nephew. Public opinion forced the army to court-martial Amakasu for Ōsugi and his family's murder, and he was eventually sentenced to ten years' imprisonment, but he was released after only three years and moved to Manchuria, where he went on to participate in the Manchurian Incident and eventually to control the film industry in the

new state of Manchukuo. See Michael Baskett, *The Attractive Empire: Transnational Film Culture in Imperial Japan* (Honolulu: University of Hawaii Press, 2008), 28–33; Elise K. Tipton, *The Japanese Police State: The Tokkō in Interwar Japan* (Honolulu: University of Hawaii Press, 1990), 21. On *Rikugun,* see also Peter B. High, *Imperial Screen: Japanese Film Culture in the Fifteen Years' War, 1931–1945* (Madison: University of Wisconsin Press, 2003), 386–388, 402, 411.

57. Plato, *The Republic of Plato: The Wisdom of Socrates Recounted by His Pupil Plato,* trans. A. D. Lindsay (New York: E. P. Dutton, 1957), 105.

58. Ibid., 101.

59. See *Hokushin: gunka: Rikugun Gunkan Gakkō* [North Star: army songs: MMA], ed. Hokushin Henshū Iinkai (Tokyo: Dōtokudai Dōsōkai, 1968), 1–12; *Otakebi* [War cry], ed. *Otakebi* Henshū Iinkai (Tokyo: Zaidan Hōjin Kaikōsha Jimukyoku, 1960), 1–12. See also *Dōtokudai,* 147.

60. *Dōtokudai,* 147–148; *RSG,* 139; *Sakufū banri,* 73.

61. *Dōtokudai,* 147.

62. *Hokushin,* unpaginated preface.

63. Kim Kwangsik, interview, Seoul, May 28, 1997. In my many meetings with Kim Kwangsik over the years, he frequently made this comment to me about the significance of the songs, and it was also not uncommon for other former MA or IJA cadets or officers to answer my queries by referring to one of the songs in the academy songbooks. See also Sakuramoto Tomio, *Uta to sensō: minna ga gunka o utatte ita* [Songs and war: everyone was singing military songs], 2nd ed. (Tokyo: Atene Shobō, 2005). For a useful introduction in English to many of these songs, see Satoshi Sugita, "Cherry Blossoms and Rising Sun: A Systematic and Objective Analysis of *Gunka* (Japanese War Songs) in Five Historical Periods (1868–1945)" (B.A. thesis, Ohio State University, 1972).

64. *Dōtokudai,* 188. *RSG,* 148.

65. *RSG,* 154.

66. See Kyōiku Sōkanbu, "Kyōiku Sōkan shodo junshi yōzu [Sketch for the Inspector General's first tour of inspection], revised July 1939. This was a map of the JMA from the Department of Military Training, marked "Secret: Internal Use Only." Even official JMA wartime photo albums were stamped with similar restrictions, such as the album of the JMA 57 class. See Rikugun Shikan Gakkō, *Sotsugyō shashinchō: Rikugun Shikan Gakkō dai-gojūshichikisei* [Graduation photo album: JMA 57 class], 1944, which is marked "restricted" on the cover.

67. *RSG,* 153.

68. *Sakufū banri,* 73.

69. *Dōtokudai,* 195–196; *Yomoyama,* 61; Kim Muk, interview, Seoul, May 28, 1997.

70. *Senku* 1:53; *Dōtokudai,* 195–198; *CWZ,* 27, 41.

71. *Yomoyama,* 61; *Dōtokudai,* 195.

72. *RSG,* 150–151.

73. *Dōtokudai,* 195–196.

74. *Sakufū banri,* 7; Hosokawa Minoru Nikki, July 23, 1941. On the Kwantung Army special maneuvers (Kantokuen), see Chapter 7.

75. *Sakufū banri,* 10.

76. *Senku* 1:389–391; *Sakufū banri,* 13–18.

77. *Kiji* 74 (June 1944): 1–2.

78. Makino Kikuo, *Rikushi-Rikuyō,* 190–191; Haraguchi Kenzō, ed. *Rikugun gahō: rinji zōkan* [Army pictorial: special edition] (Tokyo: Rikugun Gahōsha, 1938), 99.

79. In the early years of the MMA, when there were as yet no MMA graduates to fill these positions, the section commanders were largely CTS graduates. In time, however, most positions came to be filled by MMA graduates.

80. *RSG,* 129–131.
81. Yasukuni Kaikō Bunkoshitsu, Kōjin jōhō, Nishigaki Makoto (ID 23196). See also Chapters 5 and 7.
82. Yasukuni Kaikō Bunkoshitsu, Kōjin jōhō, Tahara Kōzō (ID 25086). See also Chapters 5, 6, and 7.
83. Yasukuni Kaikō Bunkoshitsu, Kōjin jōhō, Enami Shigeru (ID 20204); *Sakufū banri,* 148–150, 169. See also Chapters 5 and 7.
84. In official JMA records the MMA 2 class from Lalatun was designated as the Manchukuo 11 class in the International Corps of Cadets, reflecting the fact that Manchukuo had been sending groups of selected graduates of the CTS for advanced training at the JMA even before the MMA had been founded. Chŏng Ilgwŏn, for example, was one of those graduates. The Manchukuo 11 class of MMA 2 cadets was constituted as a single company with five sections, headed by Major Enami as company commander. See Rikushikō Honbu, "Rikugun Shikan Gakkō rekishi"; *Sakufū banri,* 182–185. On Chŏng Ilgwŏn, see Chapter 3.
85. Yasukuni Kaikō Bunkoshitsu, Kōjin jōhō, Kihara Toshio (ID 15081); *Sakufū banri,* 169. See also Chapter 5.
86. Nagumo Katsurō, letter to author, August 31, 1990; *SJS* (Rikugun), 247, 255; see also Chapter 3.
87. See, for example, *RSG,* 72.
88. See Mary Elizabeth Berry, *Hideyoshi* (Cambridge, MA: Council on East Asian Studies, 1982), 93–96.
89. Rikushikō Honbu, "Rikugun Shikan Gakkō rekishi," January 3, 1943–January 11, 1943.
90. *Senku* 1:392; *Sakufū banri,* 17. An extant JMA album of the MMA 2 class contains several photographs taken of the class (including Park Chung Hee) at Koshigoe Beach, near Enoshima, in the summer of 1943. See Rikugun Shikan Gakkō, *Manshūkoku Gunkan Gakkō dai-nikisei: Shōwa 19-nen 4-gatsu 20-nichi sotsugyō* [The MMA 2 class: graduated April 20, 1944] (personal property of Sekine Tomiji; copy in Yasukuni Kaikō Bunkoshitsu, Tokyo). According to Kiyoizumi Nobuo, all members of the class received such an album, but the only one extant is that given to Sekine Tomiji. Kiyoizumi Nobuo, interview, Tokyo, January 12, 2011.
91. *Senku* 1:391. On Takeda Shingen and his rival Uesugi Kenshin, see Hiroaki Sato, *Legends of the Samurai* (Woodstock, NY: Overlook Press, 1995), 204–231.
92. Chōsen Sōtokufu, *Futsū gakkō kokugo tokuhon* 10 [Elementary school national language reader, vol. 10] (Keijō: Chōsen Sōtokufu, 1934), 63–67.
93. Translation from Haruo Shirane, ed., *Early Modern Japanese Literature: An Anthology 1600–1900* (New York: Columbia University Press, 2002), 919.
94. High, *Imperial Screen,* 423. See also "Kawanakajima kassen (1941)," www.imdb.com /title/tt0033800, accessed February 2, 2010.
95. *Otakebi,* 308.
96. Yun Ch'idu, interview, Taegu, August 3, 1990.
97. See *Asahi shinbun,* November 13, 1961; *Nihon keizai shinbun,* November 13, 1961. On the *shishi* and the Meiji Restoration, see Albert M. Craig, *Chōshū in the Meiji Restoration* (Cambridge, MA: Harvard University Press, 1961); see also Fraleigh, "Songs of the Righteous Spirit: 'Men of High Purpose' and Their Chinese Poetry in Modern Japan," *Harvard Journal of Asiatic Studies* 69, no. 1 (June 2009): 109–116. See also Chapter 5.
98. Nagumo Katsurō, letter to author, August 31, 1990.
99. See Kim Sunjŏn et al., eds., *Chosŏn Ch'ongdokpu ch'odŭng hakkyo susinsŏ: wŏnmun* [The elementary school morals textbooks of the Government General of Korea: original texts] (Seoul: Cheiaenssi, 2006), 1:86, 389.

100. Kim Sunjŏn et al., eds., *Cheguk ŭi singminji susin: Chosŏn Ch'ongdokpu p'yŏnch'an "susinsŏ" yŏn'gu* [Morals of the imperial colony: studies of "morals textbooks" compiled by the Government-General of Korea] (Seoul: Cheiaenssi, 2008), 89.

101. See Chōsen Sōtokufu, *Chūtō kyōiku shūshinsho 3* [Morals textbook for secondary education] (Keijō: Chōsen Kyōgaku Tosho, 1940), 19–30. On Saigō, see Mark Ravina, *The Last Samurai: The Life and Battles of Saigō Takamori* (Hoboken, NJ: John Wiley and Sons, 2004).

102. *Tonga ilbo*, January 1–15, 1932.

103. This could vary from about one-fifth to more than one-third depending on the text used. See, for example, the following textbooks: Kyōiku Sōkanbu, ed., *Kokushi kyōtei: Rikugun Yoka Shikan Gakkō yō* [National history textbook: for JMAP use], 2 vols. (n.d.); Rikugun Yoka Shikan Gakkō Kōchō Amakasu Jūtarō, *Honpōshi kyōtei: zen* [Our national history: complete], 1937.

104. *RSG*, 127.

105. *Otakebi*, 164–165, 308.

106. Rikugun Yoka Shikan Gakkō Kōchō Amakasu Jūtarō, *Seito bunshū: 1927–1937* [Collection of cadet writings], writings for 1931, 7.

107. Ibid., 13.

108. *Hokushin*, 36–37, 38–39.

109. *Otakebi*, 91–92.

110. Rikugun Shikan Gakkō, *Sotsugyō shashinchō* (unnumbered).

111. Ibid.

112. *Kiji* 74 (June 1944): 4.

113. Rikugun Shikan Gakkō Kōchō Ushijima Mitsuru, *Senshi kyōtei* 1 [Miliary history textbook, vol. 1], October 1942, 1–3 (preface).

114. Nishikawa Hiroshi, *Rappashū no saigo: sensō no naka no minshū* [The bugler's last moment: commoners during the war] (Tokyo: Aoki Shoten, 1984), 190–191.

115. S. C. M. Paine, *The Sino-Japanese War of 1894–1895: Perceptions, Power, and Primacy* (Cambridge: Cambridge University Press, 2003), 165–168.

116. *Otakebi*, 171–173.

117. Ibid., 173–174.

118. Donald Keene, *Landscapes and Portraits* (Tokyo: Kodansha International, 1971), 274.

119. Rikugun Shikan Gakkō Kōchō Ushijima Mitsuru, *Senshi kyōtei* 1:111–112.

120. Kim Sunjŏn et al., *Cheguk ŭi singminji susin*, 88–99.

121. Yi Sŏngjo, interview, Seoul, June 22–23, 1998.

122. On the siege at Port Arthur, see Edward J. Drea, *Japan's Imperial Army: Its Rise and Fall, 1853–1945* (Lawrence: University Press of Kansas, 2009), 105–108; Denis Warner and Peggy Warner, *The Tide at Sunrise: A History of the Russo-Japanese War, 1904–1905* (London: Angus and Robertson, 1975), 427–440; Richard Connaughton, *Rising Sun and Tumbling Bear: Russia's War with Japan* (London: Cassell, 2003), 205–257; Ernst L. Presseisen, *Before Aggression: Europeans Prepare the Japanese Army* (Tucson: University of Arizona Press, 1965), 146. The "203" of Hill 203 refers to its height: 203 meters (666 feet). The total number of Japanese casualties in the battle for Port Arthur was staggering, reaching upward of 60,000.

123. Rikugun Shikan Gakkō Kōchō Ushijima Mitsuru, *Senshi kyōtei* 1:16–112.

124. See *Kiji* 72 (April 1944): 7.

125. *Otakebi*, 8–9, 187–209.

126. See Naoko Shimazu, *Japanese Society at War: Death, Memory, and the Russo-Japanese War* (New York: Cambridge University Press, 2009), 197–229, esp. 212. See also Drea, *Japan's Imperial Army*, 121.

127. Kim Sunjŏn et al., *Cheguk ŭi singminji susin*, 90, 94–95; for the full text of the morals primers (in Korean), see Kim Sunjŏn et al., trans., *Chosŏn Ch'ongdokpu ch'odŭng*

hakkyo susinsŏ [Elementary school morals textbooks of the Government-General of Korea] (Seoul: Cheiaenssi, 2006), 5:191–192; for the text in Japanese, see Kim Sunjŏn, et al, *Chosŏn Ch'ongdokpu ch'odŭng hakkyo susinsŏ: wŏnmun* 2:415–416.

128. *Otakebi*, 8, 191–196; *Hokushin*, 8, 162–169.
129. Sugita, "Cherry Blossoms and Rising Sun," 32–33.
130. Doris G. Bargen, *Suicidal Honor: General Nogi and the Writings of Mori Ōgai and Natsume Sōseki* (Honolulu: University of Hawaii Press, 2006), 64–81; Shimazu, *Japanese Society at War*, 227.
131. For the material the cadets read, see, for example, Rikugun Yoka Shikan Gakkō Kōchō Amakasu Jūtarō, *Seito bunshū*, writings for 1937, 10–11. For the songs, see *Hokushin*, 173–177; *Otakebi*, 206–209, 308.
132. Wang Jingyue and Zhu Huan, interview, Changchun, August 28, 1992. The poem had been composed by the general on a visit to the Nanshan battlefield near Jinzhou after arriving in Manchuria and learning that his first son had been killed there only a short time before. It was one of Nogi's pieces included in the *Otakebi* collection. Below is a translation of the poem found in Warner and Warner, *Tide at Sunrise*, 302:

> Mountains, rivers, grass, and trees. Utter desolation.
> For ten miles the wind smells of blood from the new battlefield.
> The steed advances not, men speak not.
> I stand outside the town of Jinzhou in the light of the setting sun.

133. Carter J. Eckert, *Offspring of Empire: The Colonial Origins of Korean Capitalism, 1876–1945* (Seattle: University of Washington Press, 1991), 169.
134. See, for example, *Tonga ilbo* beginning September 20, 1931, including the first "extra" on that date entitled "Japanese and Chinese Armies Clash."
135. *Manjugukkunji* [Record of the Manchukuo Army], ed. Kim Sŏkpŏm (CTS 5) (n.p., 1987), courtesy of Kim Yun'gŭn (henceforth *MKJ*), 83–128. See also Han Sŏkchŏng, *Manjuguk kŏnguk ŭi chaehaesŏk: koeroeguk ŭi kukka hyogwa 1932–1936* [A reinterpretation of the founding of Manchukuo: the state effect of the puppet state], rev. ed. (Pusan Kwangyŏksi: Tong Taehakkyo ch'ulp'anbu, 2007), esp. 64–93. Han's book is based on his English-language doctoral dissertation. See Han Suk-Jung, "Puppet Sovereignty: The State Effect of Manchukuo, from 1932 to 1936" (Ph.D. thesis, Sociology Department, University of Chicago, 1995), 50–99. On Nomonhan, see Alvin D. Coox, *Nomonhan: Japan against Russia, 1939* (Stanford, CA: Stanford University Press, 1985).
136. Rikugun Yoka Shikan Gakkō Kōchō Amakasu Jūtarō, *Seito bunshū*, writings for 1932, 47; *Otakebi*, 9, 211–225; *Hokushin*, 137.
137. Mark R. Peattie, *Ishiwara Kanji and Japan's Confrontation with the West* (Princeton, NJ: Princeton University Press, 1975), 139. For a detailed and authoritative account of the Manchurian Incident in English, see also Danny Orbach, *Curse on This Country: Japanese Military Insubordination and the Origins of the Pacific War, 1860–1936* (Ithaca, NY: Cornell University Press, forthcoming).
138. *Senku* 1:300–302.
139. *Dōtokudai*, 167–168; *Hokushin*, 39.
140. Tucker, "Building 'Our Manchukuo,'" 360.
141. Ibid., 357. Originally called Nishi (West) Park, the park's name was changed in 1938. For a photograph of the *chūkonhi* monument, see www.himoji.jp/database/db04 /permalink_img.php?id=191, accessed November 24, 2014.
142. Today the building is the headquarters of the Chinese Communist Party of Jilin province.
143. Tucker, "Building 'Our Manchukuo,'" 360–362.
144. *Senku* 1:390; *Sakufū banri*, 8. On Manchukuo holidays, see Kishi Toshihiko, *Manshūkoku no bijuaru media: posutā, ehagaki, kitte* [Visual media of Manchukuo: posters, illustrated postcards, postage stamps] (Tokyo: Yoshikawa Kōbunkan, 2010), 13–16; also

Senku 1:183. On the Chūreibyō (including photograph), see Manchuria Daily News, *Kagayaku Manshū/Kōki no Manshū/Flourishing Manchoukuo* (n.p.: Manchuria Daily News, n.d).

145. Tucker, "Building 'Our Manchukuo,'" 364; *Senku* 1:389; *Sakufū banri,* 14.

146. *Senku* 1:389. See also Toshioka Chūka, *Shinjin Yokokawa Shōzō den* [Biography of a true man: Yokokawa Shōzō] (Tokyo: Shinjin Yokokawa Shōzō Den Kankōkai, 1935).

147. *Senku* 1:389. *Sakufū banri,* 7.

148. Shi had graduated from the 5th infantry officer-student higher command course (*senkō gakusei*) of the college in 1929. Jōhō Yoshio, ed., *Rikugun Daigakkō* [The Army War College] (Tokyo: Fuyō Shobō, 1973), Appendix (Furuko) 7. On Akiyama, see Yasukuni Kaikō Bunkoshitsu, Kōjin jōhō, Akiyama Hiizu (ID 11200).

149. *Senku* 1:199–211, 390.

150. *Sakufū banri,* 14. For a detailed description of the museum, including its sand table of the battle with miniature buildings and wax soldiers of both forces, see *CWZ,* 108–109.

151. The stone lions had originally stood in front of the headquarters of a Chinese army transport school on the outskirts of Nanjing. Haraguchi Kenzō, ed., *Rikugun gahō: rinji zōkan* [Army pictorial: special edition] (Tokyo: Rikugun Gahōsha, 1938), 97–98.

152. The hall was open from 9:00 a.m. to 4:00 p.m. on holidays specifically for that reason.

153. On the memorial hall, see *RSG,* 154–156.

154. Ibid., 155.

155. Yamamuro Shin'ichi, *Manchuria under Japanese Domination,* trans. Joshua A. Fogel (Philadelphia: University of Pennsylvania Press, 2006), 162–165; Tucker, "Building 'Our Manchukuo,'" 408–409.

156. *Dōtokudai,* 155. When the MMA 1 and MMA 2 cadets, including Park Chung Hee, were in residence at the academy, the shrine had not yet been built; construction did not begin until July 1944.

157. *Senku* 1:389.

158. Ibid., 390.

159. See Ryusaku Tsunoda, Wm. Theodore de Bary, and Donald Keene, eds., *Sources of Japanese Tradition* (New York: Columbia University Press, 1958), 2:705–706. See also Hackett, "Imperial Rescript to Soldiers and Sailors," 279–280.

160. Quoted in Tsunoda, de Bary, and Keene, *Sources of Japanese Tradition* 2:705–706.

161. *Dōtokudai,* 156.

162. Ibid.

163. The Yasukuni Kaikō Archive includes the contents of the libraries and archives of the Kaikōsha, an organization of former IJA officers originally founded before 1945. The Kaikōsha donated these materials to the Yasukuni Shrine in 1999.

164. Daitō Shinsuke, interview, Tokyo, January 16, 2007.

165. *Senku* 1:389.

166. *Sakufū banri,* 17.

167. Rikugun Shikan Gakkō, *Sotsugyō shashinchō.*

168. *Sakufū banri,* 6, 12 (for photographs of the event); *Senku* 1:390. For a detailed description of the event at the time by one of the MMA 2 cadets, see Hosokawa Minoru Nikki, June 20, 1941.

169. *Sakufū banri,* 15.

170. *CWZ,* 2, 25–26, 31–32.

171. *Sakufū banri,* 14.

172. Ibid., 15.

173. Rikushikō Honbu, "Rikugun Shikan Gakkō rekishi," February 10, 1944.

174. The U.S. Army has occupied Zama as a military base since 1945, but in 1978 the former imperial residence was relocated to a JSDF army post at Asaka, formerly the site of the

JMAP, and turned into a JMAP museum or "memorial hall" (*kinenkan*). For a history of the building and guide to the museum, see Asaka Chūtonchi Kōhōhan, *Kinenkan shiori* [Guide to the Memorial Hall] (Asaka: Asaka Chūtonchi Kōhōhan, n.d.). After the annexation of Korea in 1910, it also became customary for male members of the Chosŏn royal house, now incorporated into the Japanese imperial lineage, to attend the JMA. See Chapter 3.

175. *Senku* 1:203–206.

176. Hosokawa Minoru Nikki, June 20, 1941.

177. *Gojūshichikiseikai tsūshin 36* (December 25, 1991): 11–12. "Umezu" was Umezu Yoshijirō (JMA 15); see *Nihon riku-kaigun sōgō jiten* [Comprehensive dictionary of the Japanese army-navy], ed. Hata Ikuhiko (Tokyo: Tokyo Daigaku Shuppankai, 1991) (henceforth *SJ*).

178. *Sakufū banri*, 155.

179. Rikugun Yoka Shikan Gakkō, *Seito kun'iku no jissai* [Practicum of cadet moral education] (n.p.: Rikugun Yoka Shikan Gakkō, March 1942), 134.

180. Yi Hyŏnggŭn, *Kunbŏn 1-bŏn ŭi oegil insaeng: Yi Hyŏnggŭn hoegorok* [The steadfast life of army service number 1: the memoir Yi Hyŏnggŭn] (Seoul: Chungang Ilbosa 1993), 17.

181. Yu Yangsu, letter to author, May 6, 2004.

182. Kim Muk, interview, Seoul, May 28, 1997.

183. *CWZ*, 2, 25–26.

5. Politics and Power

1. See Roger F. Hackett, "Imperial Rescript to Soldiers and Sailors," *Kodansha Encyclopedia of Japan* 3:279–280.

2. See, for example, Andrew Gordon, *A Modern History of Japan: From Tokugawa Times to the Present* (New York: Oxford University Press, 2003), 180–181.

3. On Yoshida and the other Restoration leaders, see also Chapter 4.

4. Danny Orbach has recently completed a major study of the historical roots of Japanese military insubordination, which also points out the importance of late Tokugawa and early Meiji periods in this regard: *Curse on This Country: Japanese Military Insubordination and the Origins of the Pacific War, 1860–1936* (Ithaca, NY: Cornell University Press, forthcoming). On the Takebashi Mutiny, see also Roger F. Hackett, *Yamagata Aritomo in the Rise of Modern Japan, 1838–1922* (Cambridge, MA: Harvard University Press, 1971), 83–85; Janet Hunter, *Concise Dictionary of Modern Japanese History* (Berkeley: University of California Press, 1984), 221.

5. Hunter, *Concise Dictionary of Modern Japanese History*, 221.

6. Kōno Tsukasa, *Ni-niroku jiken: gokuchū shuki isho* [The 2–26 incident: prison notes and testaments] (Tokyo: Kawade Shōbō Shinsha, 1972), 92, 94. See also Ben-Ami Shillony, *Revolt in Japan: The Young Officers and the February 26, 1936 Incident* (Princeton, NJ: Princeton University Press, 1973), 133–134. Shillony also references Kōno and quotes Nakahashi on Sakuradamon, translating *kangai-muryō* as "great joy," but he mistakenly cites the referent page number in Kōno as 255 instead of 94.

7. Kōno Tsukasa, *Ni-niroku jiken*, 125.

8. Ibid., 137–139.

9. Yu Yangsu, interview, Seoul, May 27, 1997.

10. Daitō Shinsuke, interview, Tokyo, January 16, 2007.

11. See the comment of Isobe Asaichi, one of the February 26 leaders, quoted in Shillony, *Revolt in Japan*, 187.

12. See, for example, the account in Mark R. Peattie, *Ishiwara Kanji and Japan's Confrontation with the West* (Princeton, NJ: Princeton University Press, 1975), 259–260; also

Edwin O. Reischauer and Albert M. Craig, *Japan: Tradition and Transformation* (Boston: Houghton Mifflin, 1978), 253.

13. See Peattie, *Ishiwara Kanji*, 118–139; also Alvin D. Coox, *Nomonhan: Japan against Russia, 1939* (Stanford, CA: Stanford University Press, 1985), 55–62.

14. Daitō Shinsuke, interview, Tokyo, January 16, 2007.

15. Rikugunshō, *Sakusen yōmurei* [Field service regulations] (Tokyo: Ikeda Shoten, 1970; reprint of the 1938 edition), Part I, 1; See also Peattie, *Ishiwara Kanji*, 119. On the history of the *Sakusen yōmurei* (commonly abbreviated *Sakuyō*), see Ōe Shinobu, *Tennō no guntai* [Army of the emperor] (Tokyo: Shōgakkan, 1982), 146–147, 216–220; see also Chapters 6, 7, and 8.

16. Coox, *Nomonhan*, 61.

17. Kōno Tsukasa, *Ni-niroku jiken*, 25.

18. For the text of the manifesto, see ibid., 441–442. It was signed by Nonaka, the ranking officer among the rebels.

19. Pak Chŏnghǔi (Park Chung Hee), handwritten letter to Chang Toyŏng, May 16, 1961.

20. Peattie, *Ishiwara Kanji*, 139.

21. Louise Young, *Japan's Total Empire: Manchuria and the Culture of Wartime Imperialism* (Berkeley: University of California Press, 1998), 55–114.

22. Shillony, *Revolt in Japan*, 36, 64. On the May 15 Incident, see also Orbach, *Curse on This Country*.

23. Shillony, *Revolt in Japan*, 36.

24. See Royal Jules Wald, "The Young Officers Movement in Japan, ca. 1925–1937: Ideology and Actions" (Ph.D. dissertation, Department of History, University of California, 1949), 146–148.

25. Shillony, *Revolt in Japan*, 117, 130. On the February 26 Incident, see also Orbach, *Curse on This Country*. On Arikawa, see Makiyama Nozomu, *Rikugun chūjō Arikawa Shuichi ryakuden: Okinawa sen, Arikawa ryodan no sentō gaiyō* [Short biography of army lieutenant general Arikawa Shuichi: a summary of the combat of the Arikawa brigade in the battle of Okinawa] (Kagoshima: Kagoshima Ken Okinawa Sen'ekisha Ireikai, 1981), 14.

26. Shillony, *Revolt in Japan*, 144.

27. Ibid., 146, 149, 167.

28. Ibid., 119, 151.

29. See Edward Willett Wagner's classic work, *The Literati Purges: Political Conflict in Early Yi Korea* (Cambridge, MA: East Asian Research Center, 1974).

30. See James B. Palais, *Confucian Statecraft and Korean Institutions: Yu Hyŏngwŏn and the Late Chosŏn Dynasty* (Seattle: University of Washington Press, 1996), 19, 85–86; Eugene Y. Park, *Between Dreams and Reality: The Military Examination in Late Chosŏn Korea, 1600–1894* (Cambridge, MA: Harvard University Asia Center, 2007), 79. For a detailed study of the military's involvement in court factions and intrigues, see Yi T'aejin, *Chosŏn hugi ŭi chŏngch'i wa kunyŏngje pyŏnch'ŏn* [Late Chosŏn politics and changes in the system of central military garrisons] (Seoul: Han'guk Yŏn'guwŏn, 1959).

31. See JaHyun Haboush, *The Confucian Kingship in Korea: Yŏngjo and the Politics of Sagacity* (New York: Columbia University Press, 2001).

32. Yi T'aejin, *Chosŏn hugi ŭi chŏngch'i wa kunyŏngje pyŏnch'ŏn*, 220–325, esp. 319–325.

33. On the 1884 coup, see Harold F. Cook, *Korea's 1884 Incident: Its Background and Kim Ok-kyun's Elusive Dream* (Seoul: Royal Asiatic Society, Korea Branch, 1972); Sin Yong-Ha, "The Coup d'État of 1884 and the Pukch'ŏng Army of the Progressive Party," *Korea Journal* 33, no. 2 (Summer 1993): 5–16; Yŏng-ho Ch'oe, "The *Kapsin* Coup of 1884." Chu Chin'o, *Kim Okkyun*.

34. Quoted in Yŏng-ho Ch'oe, "The *Kapsin* Coup of 1884: A Reassessment," *Korean Studies* 6 (1982): 120; see also Tabohashi Kiyoshi, *Kindai Nissen kankei no kenkyū* [Study of

Japanese-Korean relations in the modern period] (Tokyo: Bunka Shiryō Chōsakai, 1963–1964), 1:946. Sin Yong-ha, while noting the "immense influence" of Tabohashi's work in both Korea and Japan, also criticizes him for his "Japanese imperialist historical viewpoint." See *Kyŏnghyang sinmun*, February 11, 1976.

35. On the Revolution United Society, see Yi Kidong, *Pigŭk ŭi kun'indŭl: Ilbon Yuksa ch'ulsin ŭi yŏksa* [Soldiers of tragedy: a history of the graduates of the JMA] (Seoul: Ilchogak, 1982), 52–107.

36. Kim Hyŏngsŏp (Kin Kyōshō), "Kin Kyōshō Taisa kaikoroku" [Memoir of Colonel Kim Hyŏngsŏp], in *Nikkan gaikō shiryŏ*, ed. Ichikawa Masaaki (Tokyo: Hara Shobō, 1981), 10:189–255.

37. Ch'oe Rin, "Chahwasang chungch'ŏp osimnyŏn'gan" [Self-portrait: fifty years of turbulence], *Samch'ŏlli*, September 1929, 30. On Ch'oe Rin, see Ch'in-Il Inmyŏng Sajŏn P'yŏnch'an Wiwŏnhoe, *Ch'in-Il inmyŏng sajŏn* [Pro-Japanese biographical dictionary], 3 vols. (Seoul: Minjok Munje Yŏn'guso, 2009), 3:704–709.

38. See Michael Robinson, *Cultural Nationalism in Colonial Korea, 1920–1925* (Seattle: University of Washington Press, 1988).

39. Carter J. Eckert, *Offspring of Empire: The Colonial Origins of Korean Capitalism, 1876–1945* (Seattle: University of Washington Press, 1991), 97–98.

40. *Tonga ilbo*, January 1, 1935.

41. Ibid., January 4, 1935. See also Cho Ilmun and Sin Pongnyong, eds., *Kapsin chŏngbyŏn hoegorok* [Memoirs of the Kapsin coup] (Seoul: Kŏn'guk Taehakkyo Ch'ulp'anbu, 2006), 227–239; Philip Jaisohn, *My Days in Korea and Other Essays*, ed. Sun-pyo Hong (Seoul: Institute for Modern Korean Studies, Yonsei University, 1999), 15–22.

42. *Tonga ilbo*, January 4, 1935.

43. Ibid., January 1, 1935; January 4, 1935.

44. The early nineteenth-century anti-dynastic rebel leader Hong Kyŏngnae was also celebrated in the media of the 1920s and 1930s as a revolutionary hero seeking to overthrow an oppressive and corrupt society. See Sun Joo Kim, *Marginality and Subversion in Korea: The Hong Kyŏngnae Rebellion of 1812* (Seattle: University of Washington Press, 2007), 169–170.

45. For a complete list of colonial Korea's governors-general, see Eckert, *Offspring of Empire*, 260–261.

46. *Tonga ilbo*, May 17, 1932.

47. Ibid., May 20, 1932. On the "Purification of Political Activity Law" (Chŏngch'i Hwaltong Chŏnghwabŏp) passed by the May 16 junta in March 1962, see Kukka Chaegŏn Ch'oego Hoeŭi, *Han'guk kunsa hyŏngmyŏngsa* [The history of the military revolution in South Korea] (Seoul: Kunsa Hyŏngmyŏngsa P'yŏnch'an Wiwŏnhoe, 1963), 2:67–68.

48. See the daily issues and flyers of *Tonga ilbo* from this period beginning February 26, 1936.

49. *Tonga ilbo*, March 4, 1936.

50. Ibid., March 1, 1936.

51. Ibid., March 8, 1936.

52. Masao Maruyama, *Thought and Behavior in Japanese Politics*, expanded ed., ed. Ivan Morris (London: Oxford University Press, 1969), 66.

53. Shillony, *Revolt in Japan*, 201, 211.

54. On Yamashita's career, see Fukuda Kazuya, *Yamashita Tomoyuki: Shōwa no higeki* [Yamashita Tomoyuki: Shōwa tragedy] (Tokyo: Bungei Shunjū, 2004), 200–201.

55. Coox, *Nomonhan*, 62.

56. Sasaki Tōichi, *Aru gunjin no jiden* [Autobiography of a soldier], expanded ed. (Tokyo: Keisō shobō, 1967), 243. See also Yamamuro Shin'ichi, *Manchuria under Japanese Dominion*, trans. Joshua A. Fogel (Philadelphia: University of Pennsylvania Press,

2006), 160–161. It was of course also clear to the MMA cadets where the real power in Manchuria lay. When the MMA 6 Nikkei class was told that an order had come down to the effect that they would have to complete their *honka* training at Lalatun rather than Zama because of the difficulties of wartime travel, a group of Japanese cadets privately protested to the supreme advisor, Lieutenant General Akiyama Yoshitaka. Although the cadets were disciplined for their insubordination, Akiyama subsequently reversed the original order, and in the end the class was allowed to complete its training at Zama. *Dōtokudai dai-shichikisei shi* [History of the MMA 7 class], ed. Dōtokudai Dai-Shichikiseikai (Tokyo: Dōtokudai Dai-Shichikiseikai, 1990), 175–176.

57. Yamamuro Shin'ichi, *Manchuria under Japanese Dominion*, 124–125.

58. Ibid., 112–113.

59. David Vance Tucker, "Building 'Our Manchukuo': Japanese City Planning, Architecture, and Nation-Building in Occupied Northeast China, 1931–1945" (Ph.D. dissertation, Department of History, University of Iowa, 1999), 396.

60. Peattie, *Ishiwara Kanji*, 311–313.

61. Hirabayashi Morito, *Waga kaikoroku: uzumaki no naka no zen'i* [Good intentions in the middle of a maelstrom] (Tokyo: Hirabayashi Morito Waga Kaikoroku Kankōkai, 1967), 14.

62. Chianbu Kanbu, ed., *Manshūkokugun reiki ruishū* [Regulations by category of the Manchukuo Army] (Shinkyō: Manshū Gyōsei Gakkai, 1942) ("Kyoiku"), 2:36.

63. *Hokushin: gunka: Rikugun Gunkan Gakkō* [North Star: army songs: MMA], ed. *Hokushin* Henshū Iinkai (Tokyo: Dōtokudai Dōsōkai, 1968), 37, 50–51.

64. See Tucker, "Building 'Our Manchukuo,'" esp. 235–287.

65. Kim Tonghun, interview, Seoul, July 11, 1990.

66. Nishikawa Nobuyoshi, "Manshūkokugun tenbyō" [An outline of the Manchukuo Army], series of 12 monthly articles in *Kaikō* (January–December 2000), article 10.

67. Peattie, *Ishiwara Kanji*, 154. On Ishiwara's apostasy from the Manchukuo system, see also Yamamuro Shin'ichi, *Manchuria under Japanese Dominion*, 136–145. Ishiwara later returned as vice chief of staff of the Kwantung Army in 1937–1938 but was unable to change anything. Peattie, *Ishiwara Kanji*, 311–337.

68. The first two officers to serve in the post apart from Itagaki himself were Tada Hayao (JMA 15) and Sasaki Tōichi (JMA 16). Both were critical in preserving the original Itagaki legacy and establishing a tone for their successors that would keep the legacy alive. Each of these men was handpicked by Itagaki, and each also served for at least two years, longer than most of their successors, some of whom served only a few months. Together with Itagaki their combined tenure totaled more than five years, running from the inauguration of the new state of Manchukuo through the founding of its army and the development of its first military training schools for officers.

Tada, the first SA, had been only one class behind Itagaki at the JMA, graduating in 1903 just in time for the Russo-Japanese War, where he served on the front lines for nearly a year. By the time he assumed the supreme advisorship, he had become an established China expert within the army, having spent considerable time there, including three stints as an instructor at the War College in Beijing between 1917 and 1931. By then he had also established a relationship with Ishiwara, with whom he had served as an instructor at the Army Staff College in the late 1920s, just before Ishiwara's fateful deployment to the Kwantung Army general staff. Although he had been in China at the time of the Manchurian Incident, he clearly shared, like many of his fellow China officers in the army, the Ishiwara-Itagaki predilection for "field initiative" and *kenkoku*, and it was under his direction as SA that the system of recruiting Japanese military advisors and instructors was "forcefully and actively begun" and a vision laid out for a new officer training institution in Manchuria modeled on the JMA.

Tada's successor, Sasaki Tōichi, who, as we have seen, clearly reveled in his power as SA, had actually been Tada's and later Itakagi's deputy in the Manchukuo Army Ministry, where he had served as senior military advisor from 1932 to 1934 before assuming the SA post himself. His full tenure, in a sense, including the nearly three years he served as SA, thus amounted to about five years, precisely those years in which the new government, army, and military advisory system took shape, and he, more than any other SA, is credited with transforming the Manchukuo military from a purely domestic peacekeeping force into a regular army capable even of foreign expeditions. Even as Tada's subordinate he was an influential presence, enjoying, as he himself noted, the full confidence of his superior. As SA, moreover, he worked very closely with Itagaki, who during that period was serving in Kwantung Army headquarters first as vice chief of staff and later as chief of staff. Indeed, it would not be an exaggeration to think of these foundational years for the Manchukuo Army as the Sasaki-Itagaki era, for as Sasaki himself wrote in his autobiography, he shared with Itagaki a "great common understanding with respect to our tasks" as SA.

This "great common understanding," as it turned out, had a long history. Like Tada and Itagaki, who were his JMA seniors by only a few years, Sasaki had been an army China expert. Stationed in Dalian in 1911, he had joined in the elation of the younger Japanese officers who had welcomed the Chinese revolution at the time. And even before the Manchurian Incident in 1931, as China gradually descended into warlordism and the IJA sought to control and manipulate the contending Chinese military factions for its own ends, Sasaki had already become deeply involved in the politics of the continent. In the 1920s he was assigned to Guo Songling, a divisional commander in Zhang Zuolin's Fengtian Army, when Guo suddenly turned against his leader, only to be defeated by Zhang with the help of Japanese troops. Sasaki was then reassigned to Chiang Kai-Shek (Jiang Jieshi) in 1928. That was of course the year of the Manchurian incident *before* the Manchurian Incident: the bombing murder of Chinese warlord Zhang Zuolin in his private railway car, the first violent attempt by the Kwantung Army at a "final solution" of its Manchurian problems in disregard of any orders from Tokyo. And in his autobiography Sasaki later wrote proudly that it was he who had originally recommended the assassination plot to Colonel Kōmoto Daisaku, the key conspirator in the bombing, whom he had first met in Vladivostok in 1919 during Japan's Siberian Expedition.

Following Sasaki in the SA office was Hirabayashi Morito (JMA 21), who held the position from August 1937 to August 1939, during which he presided over the opening of the MMA and negotiated the admission of the first MMA cadets from Japan. Unlike his predecessors, all seasoned China veterans, Hirabayashi had neither visited the country nor studied Chinese before his appointment, and he himself was "nonplussed" when he was offered a post that had been previously filled by "famous China experts" such as Tada, Itagaki, and Sasaki. He had, however, been a JMA classmate of Ishiwara's, and in his own words had always had the highest regard for his friend, sensing even from the moment they had first met as cadets that Ishiwara was a "great man" (*erabutsu*). In turn, Ishiwara clearly thought of Hirabayashi as someone he could trust. In 1928, when Hirabayashi was teaching at the Infantry School in Chiba and Ishiwara was an instructor at the Army Staff College, Ishiwara invited his old classmate to lunch, along with two other officers from the JMA 21 class and one from the JMA 20 class. This was right after the assassination of Zhang Zuolin and shortly before Ishiwara was to leave for Manchuria, and Hirabayashi remembered that Ishiwara had told them "with a face of tragic heroic resolve" that he wanted to share especially with the four of them the news of his Kwantung Army appointment, saying he was heading to Manchuria "with a firm determination to carry out his final great public service in the army." And eleven years later, when Ishiwara was once again returning to Manchuria as Kwantung Army vice chief of staff, it was Ishiwara, according to Hirabayashi, who facilitated the SA appointment.

In arranging for his old friend to assume the SA post, Ishiwara had undoubtedly hoped to mitigate or even end the "internal guidance" policy that had come to define *kenkoku* in Manchuria, and Hirabayashi indeed appears to have been sympathetic to Ishiwara's critical perspective. But by the end of 1937, when Hirabayashi took office, the unidirectional military advisory system was already firmly in place, and Ishiwara himself was also constrained by the fact that the Kwantung Army's chief of staff at the time, his immediate superior, was Tōjō Hideki, who opposed any relaxation of army control over Manchurian affairs. In less than a year Ishiwara was gone, and when Hirabayashi stepped down in 1939, the system reverted, if it had ever changed at all, to the default Sasaki/Itagaki mold.

Thus Hirabayashi's successor, Matsui Takurō (JMA 22/1939–1940), one year below Ishiwara and Hirabayashi at the JMA, had had considerable experience in China and had worked on the Kwantung Army staff with Ishigaki and Ishiwara in the aftermath of the incident as head of the policy section that was directly engaged in the configuration of the new state and its personnel. In turn, his successor, Nakano Hidemitsu (JMA 24/ 1940–1941), who as SA attended the *yoka* graduation of Park Chung Hee and other members of the MMA 2 class, was an intelligence officer who had served under both Tada and Sasaki. Nakano was followed by Takeshita Yoshiharu (JMA 23/1941–1942), another China expert, as well as one of the "prime movers," along with Itagaki and Ishiwara, of the Manchurian Incident, providing crucial support for the expansion of the incident in the months that followed as head of the Kwantung Army's logistics section. Takeshita was succeeded by yet another China intelligence officer and Sasaki/Itagaki protégé, Kōno Etsujirō (JMA 25/1942–1943). Following Kōnō was Kusumoto Sanetaka (JMA 24/ 1943–1944), who had worked with Tada in Beijing before the latter left for Manchuria. And finally, Akiyama Yoshitaka (JMA 24/1944–1945), the tenth and last of the supreme advisors, like most of his predecessors, had a Manchurian history that went back to the early 1930s. Like Matsui, he had handled political and military affairs as chief of the Kwantung Army's policy section, where he had worked closely with Tada, Sasaki, and even Itagaki himself, vice chief of staff at the time, to whom he had directly reported.

Sources for this note include Sasaki Tōichi, *Aru gunjin no jiden;* Hirabayashi Morito, *Waga kaikoroku;* Nishikawa Nobuyoshi, "Manshūkokugun tenbyō," articles 3 and 4; *SJS* (Rikugun); *SSJ;* Peattie, *Ishiwara Kanji;* Coox, *Nomonhan;* Yamamuro Shin'ichi, *Manchuria under Japanese Dominion.*

69. On Zhang Zuolin (Chang Tso-lin), see Yoshihisa Tak Matsusaka, *The Making of Japanese Manchuria, 1904–1932* (Cambridge, MA: Harvard University Asia Center, 2001), 312–348. See also Orbach, *Curse on this Country.* See also note 68 above.

70. Sasaki Tōichi, *Aru gunjin no jiden,* 192–193; Nishikawa Nobuyoshi, "Manshūkokugun tenbyō," article 5. Orbach notes that Kōmoto in particular had dreams of becoming "the king of Manchuria." Orbach, *Curse on this Country.*

71. Peattie, *Ishiwara Kanji,* 93.

72. Nishikawa Nobuyoshi, "Manshūkokugun tenbyō," articles 1 and 5; Kimura Takeo, *Kōmoto Daisaku* [Kōmoto Daisaku] (Tokyo: Tsuchiya Shoten, 1978), 127–152; Coox, *Nomonhan,* 24–25. For a full discussion of the Sakurakai, see Orbach, *Curse on This Country.*

73. On the defense armies see Chapter 3.

74. Tōmiya Taisa Kinen Jugyō Iinkai, *Tōmiya Kaneo den* [Biography of Tōmiya Kaneo] (1940; reprint, Tokyo: Ōzorasha, 1997); Sasaki's comment is on 705. See also *Manshūkokugun* [The Manchukuo Army], ed. Manshūkokugun Kankō Iinkai (Tokyo: Ranseikai, 1970) (henceforth *MG*), 87, 248. Sasaki's embrace of these men, including

Tōmiya, could be traced in part to his own complicity in the Zhang assassination (see note 68 above). According to Danny Orbach, he had also been deeply involved with the Sakurakai. Orbach, *Curse on This Country*.

75. Tōmiya Taisa Kinen Jugyō Iinkai, *Tōmiya Kaneo den*, 770; *Nihon riku-kaigun sōgō jiten* [Comprehensive dictionary of the Japanese army-navy], ed. Hata Ikuhiko (Tokyo: Tokyo Daigaku Shuppankai, 1991) (henceforth *SJ*), 44.

76. *SJ*, 74; *MG*, 624, 626. The "special service" agencies of the IJA were engaged in much more than intelligence gathering, including drug trafficking and prostitution. See Meirion Harries and Susie Harries, *Soldiers of the Sun: The Rise and Fall of the Imperial Japanese Army* (London: Heinemann, 1991), 244–245.

77. *SJS* (Rikugun), 152; Nishikawa Nobuyoshi, "Manshūkokugun tenbyō," article 5; *MG*, 75–76. See also Chapter 3.

78. *Rikugun Shikan Gakkō* [The Japanese Military Academy], ed. Yamazaki Masao, with the collaboration of the Kaikōsha, 4th ed. (Tokyo: Akimoto Shobō, 1984) (henceforth *RSG*), 52–53.

79. Yagi Haruo, *Go-ichigo jiken to shikan kōhosei* [The May 15 incident and JMA cadets] (Fukuoka: Fukuoka Keimusho Sagyōka, 1988), 289–290; *MG*, 150.

80. Yagi Haruo, *Go-ichigo jiken to shikan kōhosei*, 1–3; *MG*, 150, 153, 545, 674, 629.

81. *RSG*, 53; Matsuzawa Tetsunari and Suzuki Masasetsu, *Ni-niroku to seinen shōko* [February 26 and the young officers] (Tokyo: San'ichi Shobō, 1974), 130–132; *MG*, 929–930; *Tsuioku yonjūshichiki* [Reminiscences of the JMA 47 class], ed. Rikushi Dai-Yonjūshichikiseikai (n.p.: Rikushi Yonjūshichikiseikai, 1976), 436; *Dai-yonjūshichikiseikai shi 7* (April 1940): 85–87, 99; *MG*, 606. On the November Incident, see also Shillony, *Revolt in Japan*, 45–46.

82. For some reason former Korean cadets I interviewed, such as Pang Wǒnch'ǒl (MMA 1), who knew Kanno as a company commander at the MMA believed he had had a connection to February 26. Cho Kapche, relying on this testimony, writes that Kanno was dismissed from the IJA for his involvement in the February 26 Incident. But there is no documentary evidence to that effect in the extensive interrogation and trial records of the February 26 participants. In fact, Kanno never served in the IJA, having left the JMA before his JMA 47 class graduation and commissioning in 1935. At the time of February 26 Incident, it appears that he was already in Manchuria at the CTS, from which he graduated in November of that year. It is not clear why he "left" (*chūtai*) the JMA before graduating, whether through voluntary withdrawal or expulsion (the term *chūtai* can mean either), but it is possible that his leaving might have been connected in some way with radical thought or activities, or even tangentially with the November Incident. That he would have voluntarily relinquished his prestigious JMA status and future career as an IJA officer for the CTS and a career in the Manchurian Army seems unlikely. On the JMA background of Kanno and his classmates, see Rikugun Shikan Gakkō, *Rikugun Shikan Gakkō sotsugyō jinmeibo: Meiji 30–Shōwa 16 (Dai-ikki–Dai-gojūgoki* [Roster of graduates of the JMA: 1897–1941 (JMA 1–JMA 55)] (n.p., n.d.), JMA 47 class; *Rikugun Shikan Gakkō dai-yonjūshichikiseikai kaihō 62* (September 1995): 274–275 (anniversary issue marking the sixtieth year since the commissioning of the JMA 47 class in 1935). Other sources for this note include Cho Kapche, *Pak Chŏnghŭi: han kŭndaehwa hyŏngmyŏngga ŭi pijanghan saengae* [Park Chung Hee: the resolute life of a modernizing revolutionary] (Seoul: Cho Kapche Datk'om, 2006), 1:220; *MG*, 582; *Dai-yonjūshichikiseikai shi 7* (April 1940): 85–87, 99; Pang Wǒnch'ǒl, interview, Seoul, May 30, 1997.

83. Shillony, *Revolt in Japan*, 198. 201.

84. This was the 4th Infantry Division. *SJS* (Rikugun), 225; W. Victor Madej, ed., *Japanese Armed Forces Order of Battle* (Allentown, PA: Game Marketing Company, 1981), 1:30.

85. Hirabayashi Morito, *Waga kaikoroku*, 317–318. See also note 68 above.

86. Hayashi Shigeru, ed., *Ni-niroku jiken hiroku* [Secret record of February 26] (Tokyo: Shōgakkan, 1971–1972), 1:13.

87. *SJ*, 73; Shillony, *Revolt in Japan*, 54, 98, 114–115, 117, 128, 133. See also Matsuzawa and Suzuki, *Ni-niroku to seinen shōko*, 216–231, which identifies the key officers by regiment and company.

88. Shillony, *Revolt in Japan*, 144.

89. Hayashi Shigeru, *Ni-niroku jiken hiroku* 4:65–66. On Sakai, see Kōno Tsukasa, *Ni-niroku jiken: gokuchū shuki isho* [The 2-26 incident: prison notes and testaments] (Tokyo: Kawade Shōbō Shinsha, 1972), 111–114; Shillony, *Revolt in Japan*, 22, 98–99, 101–102, 136, 188, 201, 205. For more on Shibuya during the February 26 Incident, see Hayashi Shigeru, *Ni-niroku jiken hiroku* 1:173, 206, 241, 438, 458, 4:515.

90. *SJ*, 73. See also Hōchi Takayuki, *Harubin Gakuin to Manshūkoku* [Harbin and Manchukuo] (Tokyo: Shinchōsha, 1999), 187.

91. On Manai's life and career see *SJ*, 131; Yasukuni Kaikō Bunkoshitsu, Kōjin jōhō, Manai Tsurukichi (ID 11236); Nishikawa Nobuyoshi, "Manshūkokugun tenbyō," articles 5, 8; *MG*, 76, 616, 635–637; *Sakufū banri: Manshūkoku Gunkan Gakkō nikisei no kiroku* [The north wind of ten thousand leagues: the record of the MMA 2 class] (Hadano: Dōtokudai Nikiseikai, 1981), 29–30; *Rikugun Shikan Gakkō nijūichikiseikai kaihō* 21 (June 1937): 88–89, 125; *Rikugun Shikan Gakkō nijūichikiseikai kaihō* 28 (June 1958): 28–29 (anniversary issue marking the fiftieth year since the JMA 21 class graduation).

92. Yagi Haruo, *Go-ichigo jiken to shikan kōhosei*, 290.

93. Nishikawa Nobuyoshi, "Manshūkokugun tenbyō," article 5. Some of the first MMA section commanders who came out of the CTS were even resentful and defiant toward senior Kwantung Army officers, who, they thought, looked down upon the Manchukuo Army generally, and also upon them personally, because they had not graduated from the JMA. As a result of such attitudes, two of the CTS section commanders were eventually punished by being transferred to the front lines. Kiyoizumi Nobuo, interview, Tokyo, January 12, 2011.

94. *Sakufū banri*, 77–78; Shiino Hattō, ed. *Nihon rikugun rentai sōran: chiiki betsu; hohei hen* [Compendium of Japanese army regiments: classified by region; infantry edition] (Tokyo: Shinjinbutsu Ōraisha, 1990), 134; *SJ*, 44.

95. On the First Infantry Division, see Hatakeyama Seikō, *Tōkyō heidan* [Tokyo division], (Tokyo: Kōfūsha, 1963), 1:67; Madej, ed., *Japanese Armed Forces Order of Battle* 1:25–26. According to Madej, the Third Company remained with the division until 1940 and the First Company at least until 1944. See also Shillony, *Revolt in Japan*, 198.

96. See "Ni-niroku jiken sōran," accessed March 4, 2015, http://homepage1.nifty.com/kitabatake/rikukaigun55.html.

97. Chŏng Naehyŏk, *Kyŏkpyŏn ŭi saengae rŭl torabomyŏ: kijŏk ŭi kamyŏ, yŏksa nŭn namŭmyŏ: Chŏng Naehyŏk hoegorok* [Looking back on a tumultuous life: the miracle passes, history remains: the memoir of Chŏng Naehyŏk] (Seoul: Han'guk Sanŏp Yŏn'guwŏn, 2001), 54; Tei Raikaku (Chŏng Naehyŏk), *Watashi no ayunde kita michi: eijoku no nanajūnen* [The path I took: seventy years of honor and shame] (Tokyo: Tendensha, 2003), 56.

98. Matsuzawa Tetsunari and Suzuki Masasetsu, *Ni-niroku to seinen shōko*, 216–230; Shillony, *Revolt in Japan*, 198.

99. See, for example, *RSG*, 53; Matsuzawa Tetsunari and Suzuki Masasetsu, *Ni-niroku to seinen shōko*, 130.

100. *RSG*, 53–54, 70. Daitō Shinsuke, interview, Tokyo, January 16, 2007.

101. *RSG*, 70.

102. *Senku: kaikoroku* [Vanguard: memoirs], ed. Dōtokudai Ikkiseikai (Tokyo: Dōtokudai Ikkiseikai, 1986–1987), 1:315–316.

103. *Sakufū banri*, 148–150. On Enami, see also Yasukuni Kaikō Bunkoshitsu, Kōjin jōhō, Enami Shigeru (ID 20204), and Chapter 7.
104. *Sakufū banri*, 148, 168; Yasukuni Kaikō Bunkoshitsu, Kōjin jōhō, Kihara Yoshio (ID 15081).
105. Tei Raikaku (Chŏng Naehyŏk), *Watashi no ayunde kita michi*, 56; *RSG*, 250.
106. For a list of the MMA 2 section commanders at Zama, see *Sakufū banri*, 182–185. On Nishigaki, see Yasukuni Kaikō Bunkoshitsu, Kōjin jōhō, Nishigaki Makoto (ID 23196); see also Chapter 7.
107. In the end Tahara declined to participate. Yoshida Shōichi, letter to author (via Matsutani Motokazu), March 13, 2012. Yoshida was Tahara's JMA 52 classmate and also barracked with him in the same section (*kutai*).
108. *Daitōjuku sanjūnenshi* [Thirty-year history of the Daitōjuku], ed. Daitōjuku Sanjūnenshi Hensan Iinkai (Tokyo: Daitōjuku Shuppanbu, 1972), 98–99, 867. On the Ketsumeidan, see Shillony, *Revolt in Japan*, 75–76.
109. *Daitōjuku sanjūnenshi*, 869–873.
110. *Sakufū banri*, 152.
111. Origuchi's account is in *Sakufū banri*, 162–163.
112. *RSG*, 227; see also Rikugun Shikan Gakkō, *Sotsugyō shashinchō: Rikugun Shikan Gakkō dai-gojūshichikisei* [Graduation photo album: JMA 57 class], 1944.
113. *Daitōjuku sanjūnenshi*, 869–873; Rikugun Shikan Gakkō, *Sotsugyō shashinchō*. See also Chapters 4 and 6. A telling sign, perhaps, of his political inclinations, Uchiyama seems to have had a strong affinity for Kunisada Chūji, a legendary Edo-period outlaw with a strong social conscience and the subject of several 1930s films; the cadets in Uchiyama's company even nicknamed him "Chūji." Hiruma Hiroshi, *Rikugun Shikan Gakkō yomoyama monogatori* [Sundry stories of the JMA] (Tokyo: Kōjinsha, 1983), 154. On Kunisada Chūji, see Shimozawa Kan, *Kunisada Chūji* [Kunisada Chūji] (Tokyo: Kaizōsha, 1933); Donald Richie, *A Hundred Years of Japanese Film: A Concise History, with a Selective Guide to DVDs and Videos*, rev. ed. (Tokyo: Kodansha International, 2005), 69–71.
114. Hosokawa Minoru Nikki [Hosokawa Minoru diary] (courtesy of Hosokawa Minoru, via Suzuki Michihiko), entry for May 15, 1941.
115. Wang Jingyue and Zhu Huan, interview, Changchun, August 28, 1992.
116. See *Hokushin*, 93, 226–227; *Otakebi*, 81–82; Kim Kwangsik, interview, Seoul, January 8, 2011.
117. Hosokawa Minoru Nikki, entry for April 24, 1942.
118. Chŏng Naehyŏk describes Yamamoto, under whom he served, as an "honor cadet" (*udŭngsaeng*) of the JMA. Chŏng Naehyŏk, *Kyŏkpyŏn ŭi saengae rŭl torabomyŏ*, 54. Uchiyama was ranked 48th out of 117 infantry cadets in the JMA 42, and his classmates described him as a cadet of "superior" ability, who was affectionately nicknamed "Mr. Model Cadet" (Mr. Gomin, *gomin-san*) by underclassmen. See Rikugun Shikan Gakkō, *Rikugun Shikan Gakkō sotsugyō jinmeibo*, Dai-yonjūnikisei (hoheika); *Heisei kyūnendo "Take no Kai dayori": seikaban* [Heisei Year 9 "Take no Kai news": midsummer edition], ed. Take no Kai Kanjikai (n.p.: Rikushi Dai-Yonjūnikisei, July 31, 1996), 26.
119. *Senku* 1:299–302.
120. Park and the other top-ranked Koreans in the MMA 2 class, who would go on to Zama with the Japanese cadets, had been moved from the Mankei into the Nikkei about two months earlier, in late March, once the branch assignments had been decided. Takezawa Rikio, interview, Tokyo, January 12, 2011.
121. Hosokawa Minoru Nikki, entry for May 12, 1942.

6. State and Society

1. Pak Chŏnghŭi, *Kukka wa hyŏngmyŏng kwa na* [The country, the revolution, and I] (Seoul: Hyangmunsa, 1963), 70.

2. Pak Chŏnghŭi, *Uri minjok ŭi nagal kil* [Our nation's path] (Seoul: Koryŏ Sŏjŏk Chusik Hoesa, 1965), 254–255. Even in the mid-1970s, when the *chaebŏl* were becoming a prominent central feature of the expanding South Korean economy, Park described them in a press conference as "public institutions" (*sahoe ŭi konggi*) and warned that they "should not forget that they are being entrusted with the business of the state." *Pak Chŏnghŭi Taet'ongnyŏng yŏnsŏl munjip* [Collected speeches of President Park Chung Hee] (Seoul: Taet'ongnyŏng Pisŏsil, 1974), 11:61.

3. Pak Chŏnghŭi, *Uri minjok ŭi nagal kil*, 255.

4. Pak Chŏnghŭi, *Kukka wa hyŏngmyŏng kwa na*, 50–51. The book was written by Pak Sanggil, but in close collaboration with Park Chung Hee, who personally checked, revised, and made additions to Pak's original manuscript. Pak Sanggil, interview, Seoul, August 31, 2000.

5. Ch'oe Yŏng-ho, Peter H. Lee, and Wm. Theodore de Bary, eds., *Sources of Korean Tradition*, vol. 2, *From the Sixteenth to the Twentieth Centuries* (New York: Columbia University Press, 2000), 240.

6. Carter J. Eckert, "The South Korean Bourgeoisie: A Class in Search of Hegemony," in *State and Society in Contemporary Korea*, ed. Hagen Koo (Ithaca, NY: Cornell University Press, 2000), 95–130 esp. 110–123.

7. See Byron K. Marshall, *Capitalism and Nationalism in Pre-War Japan: The Ideology of the Business Elite, 1868–1941* (Stanford, CA: Stanford University Press, 1967).

8. Denis Warner and Peggy Warner, *The Tide at Sunrise: A History of the Russo-Japanese War, 1904–1905* (London: Angus and Robertson, 1975), 301.

9. Kyōiku Sōkanbu, *Gunjin chokuyu kinkai* [Respectful understanding of the Imperial Rescript to Soldiers and Sailors] (Tokyo: Gunjin Kaikan Toshobu, 1944), 95–97, 101–105.

10. *Rikugun Shikan Gakkō* [The Japanese Military Academy], ed. Yamazaki Masao, with the collaboration of the Kaikōsha, 4th ed. (Tokyo: Akimoto Shobō, 1984) (henceforth *RSG*), 147; Kim Muk, interview, Seoul, May 28, 1997. Kim also noted that the section commanders always returned such money or other items sent to the cadets, never keeping any of it for themselves.

11. *RSG,* 148. See also Chapter 8.

12. Hosokawa Minoru Nikki [Hosokawa Minoru diary], 7 vols. (courtesy of Hosokawa Minoru, via Suzuki Michihiko), entry for April 12, 1941.

13. Hiruma Hiroshi, *Rikugun Shikan Gakkō yomoyama monogatori* [Sundry stories of the JMA] (Tokyo: Kōjinsha, 1983) (henceforth *Yomoyama*), 151.

14. Terada Chikao, *Nihon guntai yōgoshū* [Japanese military terms] (Tokyo: Rippū Shobō, 1992), 1:229; *Yomoyama,* 72–75.

15. Kaneko Tomio, interview, Tokyo, January 12, 2011. According to Park's section commander, there were three serious incidents of fire that day, and the exercise had to be stopped. Tahara Kōzō, letter to Tahara Yoshiko, February 18, 1944.

16. *Yomoyama,* 77–78.

17. Max Weber, *The Protestant Ethnic and the Spirit of Capitalism,* trans. and updated by Stephen Kalberg (New York: Oxford University Press, 2011).

18. See, for example, Henry Dewitt Smith II, *Japan's First Student Radicals* (Cambridge, MA: Harvard University Press, 1972), 132–139.

19. Kōno Tsukasa, *Ni-niroku jiken: gokuchū shuki isho* [The 2-26 incident: prison notes and testaments] (Tokyo: Kawade Shōbō Shinsha, 1972), 324–325.

20. Emiko Ohnuki-Tierney, *Kamikaze, Cherry Blossoms, and Nationalisms: The Militarization of Aesthetics in Japanese History* (Chicago: University of Chicago Press, 2002), 5, 7, 19, 186–297.

21. See chart in Theodor Failor Cook Jr., "The Japanese Officer Corps: The Making of a Military Elite, 1872–1945" (Ph.D. dissertation, Department of History, Princeton University, 1987), 69.
22. Kita Ikki is discussed later in this chapter.
23. See Sejima Ryūzō, *Ikusanga: Sejima Ryūzō kaisōroku* [Ikusanga: the memoir of Sejima Ryūzō] (Tokyo: Sankei Shinbun Nyūsu Sābisu: Fusōsha, 1995). The quotation is on page 38.
24. *RSG*, 70.
25. See, for example, Robert A. Scalapino, *The Japanese Communist Movement* (Santa Monica, CA: RAND Corporation, 1966), 1–78; George Oakley Totten III, *The Social Democratic Movement in Prewar Japan* (New Haven, CT: Yale University Press, 1966), 63–108, 381–402.
26. See Robert A. Scalapino and Chong-Sik Lee, *Communism in Korea* (Berkeley: University of California Press, 1972), 1:3–232; Dae-Sook Suh, *The Korean Communist Movement, 1918–1948* (Princeton, NJ: Princeton University Press, 1967); see also Chong-Sik Lee, *The Korean Workers' Party: A Short History* (Stanford, CA: Hoover Institution Press, 1978), 1–57. See also Sunyoung Park, *The Proletarian Wave: Literature and Leftist Culture in Colonial Korea 1910–1945* (Cambridge, MA: Harvard University Asia Center, 2015), 103–104.
27. *Taegu Sabŏm simsanggwaji* [History of the elementary school department of Taegu Normal School], ed. Han Sŏktong (Taegu: Taegu Sabŏm Simsanggwa Tongmunhoe, 1991), 180–181.
28. Ibid., 178–179, 194–199, 211–218. On Hyŏn Chunhyŏk, see also Na Iltae, "Hyŏn Chunhyŏk ŭi naeryŏk" [The life of Hyŏn Chunhyŏk], *Sinch'ŏnji* 1, no. 9 (October 1946): 142–143; Sim Chiyŏn, *Song Namhŏn hoegorok: Kim Kyusik kwa hamkke han kil: minjok chaju wa t'ongil ŭi wihayŏ* [Reminiscences of Song Namhŏn: together with Kim Kyusik: for national independence and unification] (Seoul: Hanul, 2000), 19–22; Scalapino and Lee, *Communism in Korea* 1:235, 248–249, 316, 320–323, 380; Charles K. Armstrong, *The North Korean Revolution 1945–1950* (Ithaca, NY: Cornell University Press, 2003), 58 nn. 87, 88. Hyŏn's arrest and the exposure of his reading group at TNS were widely covered in the Korean newspapers in the period following his arrest in February 1932. See, for example, the article in *Tonga ilbo*, February 23, 1932, titled "Ringleader in Taegu Arrests Is Current TNS Instructor: On Suspicion of Propagating Communism," which also featured a photograph of Hyŏn. See also *Tonga ilbo*, April 2, 1932, for pictures and information about some of the students involved.
29. See Kawakami Hajime, *Dai-ni binbō monogatari* [The second tale of poverty] (Kyōto: San'ichi Shobō, 1948 [1930]), esp. 384–418. On Kawakami, see Gail Lee Bernstein, *Japanese Marxist: A Portrait of Kawakami Hajime, 1879–1946* (Cambridge, MA: Harvard University Press, 1976), esp. 87–102.
30. *Taegu Sabŏm simsanggwaji*, 213–218. The quotation is on pages 214–215. According to Park Chung Hee's TNS 4 classmate, Yi Sŏngjo, one student in the class was expelled for reading socialist books, and the school was so concerned about student interest in the subject that it even sent teachers to students' homes when the students were in class to check any reading materials they had there. Yi Sŏngjo, interview, Seoul, June 22–23, 1998.
31. Manchuria Daily News, *Kagayaku Manshū/Kōki no Manshū / Flourishing Manchoukuo* (n.p.: Manchuria Daily News, n.d.), 4.
32. *Changchun wenshi ziliao* 2 [Changchun cultural history materials, vol. 2], ed. Changchun Shi Zhengxie Wenshi Ziliao Weiyuanhui (Changchun: Changchun Shi Zhengxie Wenshi Bangongshi Faxingzu, 1991), 143–144.
33. Rana Mitter's work on the "Manchurian myth" of resistance against the Japanese occupation is an important caution against an uncritical acceptance of post-1949 writing

by Chinese seeking to rewrite their collaborationist Manchurian past. See Rana Mitter, *The Manchurian Myth: Nationalism, Resistance and Collaboration in Modern China* (Berkeley: University of California Press, 2000). In the case of the collection of memoirs by former MMA Chinese cadets used in this book (*CWZ*), such caution is also justified. On the other hand, other sources, including Hosokawa Minoru's MMA 2 diary, information provided by former non-Chinese cadets, and information provided by former Chinese cadets who did not contribute to the *CWZ*, or who, like Gao Qingyin, did not remain in China, tend on the whole to support the descriptions of cadet life in the *CWZ*, including the often antagonistic atmosphere between the Nikkei and the Mankei, and the presence of leftist revolutionary influence and activity. Nishikawa Nobuyoshi (MMA 7), for example, confirmed that secret societies had deeply infiltrated the MMA and that instructors as well as cadets were involved. He said that the secret societies became a serious problem particularly from the time of the MMA 2 class, and that in his own class he knew of two classmates who were members of secret societies and engaged in underground activities. Nishikawa Nobuyoshi, interview, Yokohama, January 10, 2011. My thanks to Vincent Leung for help with *CWZ* translations.

34. *CWZ*, 70–72, 86–89.
35. Ibid., 77–82, 121–123. See also the Conclusion.
36. *CWZ*, 72–75, 80–83.
37. Ibid., 70–71, 144–146.
38. Ibid., 89–97, 101, 125.
39. Ibid., 75–77.
40. Ibid., 81.
41. Ibid., 68–69.
42. Ibid., 70, 73, 80, 88, 90, 144–145.
43. Ibid., 11, 73.
44. Ibid., 80.
45. Ibid., 43, 145–146, 187–188, 198.
46. Ibid., 141–151, 187–188.
47. Ibid., 76.
48. Ibid., 67–69.
49. Ibid., 144.
50. Ibid., 121; *Dōtoku* 40 (September 30, 1988): 20.
51. *CWZ*, 11, 76.
52. Information about Wang Jiashan has been compiled from the following sources: *CWZ*, 20, 77–80, 121–128; Jōhō Yoshio, ed. *Rikugun Daigakkō* [The Army War College] (Tokyo: Fuyō Shobō, 1973), appendix 7, list of foreign officer students; *Manjugukkunji* [Record of the Manchukuo Army], ed. Kim Sŏkpŏm (CTS 5) (n.p., 1987), courtesy of Kim Yun'gŭn (henceforth *MKJ*), 93; *Manshūkokugun* [The Manchukuo Army], ed. Manshūkokugun Kankō Iinkai (Tokyo: Ranseikai, 1970), 142, 163, 602, 801; Harold Miles Tanner, "Guerrilla, Mobile, and Base Warfare in Communist Military Operations in Manchuria, 1945–1947," *Journal of Military History* 67, no. 4 (October 2003): 1199 n. 71; E. R. Hooton, *The Greatest Tumult: The Chinese Civil War: 1936–49* (London: Brassey's, 1991), 96. I am also grateful to Nancy Hearst at Harvard's H. C. Fung Library for information gleaned from the following sources: Sheng Ping, ed., *Zhongguo Gongchangdang renming da cidian* [Biographical dictionary of the Chinese Communist Party] (Beijing: Zhongguo Guoji Guangbo Chubanshe, 1991); Sheng Ping, ed., *Zhonggong renmin lu* [Record of Chinese communist figures], rev. ed. (Taibei: Guoli Zhengzhi Daxue Guoji Guanxi Yanjiu Zhongxin, 1978); Sheng Ping, ed., *Zhongguo renmin da cidian: Dangdai renwu juan* [China biographical dictionary: contemporary volume] (Shanghai: Shanghai Cishu Chubanshe, 1992); "Jilin Liaoning Rehe Guangxi gesheng renmin daibao dahui juxing huiyi," *Renmin ribao*, February 19, 1955; Malcolm L. Lamb,

Directory of Officials and Organizations in China, 3rd ed., vol. 2 (Armonk, NY: M. E. Sharpe, 2003).

53. *CWZ,* 90–92.

54. As many as six of the eleven former MMA 2 Korean cadets, including Park himself, may have been involved in such activities. Besides Park, these were An Yŏnggil, Kang Ch'angsŏn, Kim Chaep'ung, Yi Pyŏngju, and Yi Sangjin. See *CIS* 1:123, 1:574, 2:108, 2:441, 2:888, 2:907.

55. Kim Yŏngt'aek, interview, Seoul, May 31, 1997; *MKJ,* 56; Nishikawa Nobuyoshi, interview, Yokohama, January 10, 2011.

56. Origuchi et al., interview, Tokyo, September 1, 1990.

57. Gao Qingyin, interview, Las Vegas, March 11, 1997.

58. Ibid.

59. Ibid.

60. *CWZ,* 156.

61. Gao Qingyin, interview, Las Vegas, March 11, 1997.

62. *CWZ,* 12.

63. Gao Qingyin, interview, Las Vegas, March 11, 1997.

64. *CIS* 1:574.

65. *CWZ,* 154. Li refers to Kim as Jin Tai Zhi (Kim T'aech'i in Korean), which was apparently another name that Kim used, but his original and official name in the records was Kim Chaep'ung. See *Sakufū banri: Manshūkoku Gunkan Gakkō nikisei no kiroku* [The north wind of ten thousand leagues: the record of the MMA 2 class] (Hadano: Dōtokudai Nikiseikai, 1981), 8, 184.

66. Lee-Jay Cho, interview, Cambridge, MA, April 21–22, 2000. Cho, a prominent developmental economist at the East-West Center in Honolulu, was close to Chŏng Ilgwŏn and spent much time with him, especially in his final years. Chŏng died in Hawaii in 1994. On Park's relationship with Chŏng when he was a cadet, see Chapter 3 and Chapter 8. See also Chŏng Ilgwŏn, *Chŏng Ilgwŏn hoegorok* [Memoir of Chŏng Ilgwŏn] (Seoul: Koryŏ Sŏjŏk, 1996), 79.

67. Yi Hallim, *Segi ŭi kyŏngnang* [The raging waves of the century: a memoir] (Seoul: P'albogwŏn, 1994), 385–386.

68. See Pak Sanghŭi's article "Urging the People of Sŏnsan to Wake Up!" in *Chosŏn ilbo,* March 13, 1932, written when his younger brother was just entering TNS. On Pak Sanghŭi, see also Kim Chinhwa, *Ilcheha Taegu ŭi ŏllon yŏn'gu* [Studies of the Taegu press under Japanese imperialism] (Taegu: Hwada, 1978), 163–168; Cho Kapche, *Pak Chŏnghŭi: han kŭndaehwa hyŏngmyŏngga ŭi pijanghan saengae* [Park Chung Hee: the resolute life of a modernizing revolutionary], vol. 1 (Seoul: Cho Kapche Datk'om, 2006), esp. 106–118. Kim Chongp'il, interview, Seoul, August 21, 2000; Pak Sanggil, interview, August 31, 2000. On Park Chung Hee's involvement with the South Korean Workers Party in the late 1940s, see Cho Kapche, *Pak Chŏnghŭi* 2:33–59. On Yi Hallim's opposition to the coup in 1961 and subsequent arrest, see Yi Hallim, *Segi ŭi kyŏngnang,* 355–381.

69. Kōno Tsukasa. *Ni-niroku jiken,* 140.

70. See, for example, Christopher W. A. Szpilman, "Fascist and Quasi-Fascist Ideas in Interwar Japan, 1918–1941," in *Japan in the Fascist Era,* ed. Bruce Reynolds (New York: Palgrave Macmillan), 87.

71. *Otakebi,* 81.

72. Kōno Tsukasa, *Ni-niroku jiken,* 140.

73. Ibid., 139.

74. Ibid., 140.

75. Ibid., 188, 190, 191.

76. Ibid., 98, 190.

77. Rikugunshō, *Chōsa ihō gōgai: 5.15 jiken rikugun gunpō kaigi kōhan kiji* [Investigative report extra issue: proceedings of the public trial of army court martial in connection with the 5.15 incident] (Tokyo: Rikugunshō, 1933), 109.

78. In Korean: *musanja;* in Japanese: *musansha*. See, for example, Michael Robinson, *Cultural Nationalism in Colonial Korea, 1920–1925* (Seattle: University of Washington Press, 1988), 121; Kōno, *Ni-niroku jiken,* 320. This was of course the same term that Park Chung Hee's brother used in his *Chosŏn ilbo* article "Urging the People of Sŏnsan to Wake Up!" See note 68, above.

79. *Tonga ilbo,* May 25, 1932.

80. On Kita Ikki, see Brij Tankha, *Kita Ikki and the Making of Modern Japan: A Vision of Empire* (Folkestone, UK: Global Oriental, 2006); Christopher W. A. Szpilman, "Kita Ikki and the Politics of Coercion," *Modern Asian Studies* 36, no. 2 (2002): 467–490.

81. Kōno Tsukasa, *Ni-niroku jiken,* 320.

82. Ibid., 89.

83. Ibid., 318–330; see also 183.

84. Ibid., 319; Tankha, *Kita Ikki and the Making of Modern Japan,* 228.

85. Kōno Tsukasa, *Ni-niroku jiken,* 319.

86. Ibid., 323.

87. See Nym Wales [Helen Foster Snow] and Kim San, *Song of Arian: A Korean Communist in the Chinese Revolution* (San Francisco: Ramparts Press, 1941), esp. 139–160.

88. Kōno Tsukasa, *Ni-niroku jiken,* 184. Muranaka (JMA 37), a leader in the February 26 mutiny, had, like Isobe, earlier been a central figure in the November or JMA Incident of 1934, which had led to his discharge from the army and reserves. See ibid., 182; Ben-Ami Shillony, *Revolt in Japan: The Young Officers and the February 26, 1936 Incident* (Princeton, NJ: Princeton University Press, 1973), 45–47.

89. Tankha, *Kita Ikki and the Making of Modern Japan,* 169.

90. Kōno Tsukasa, *Ni-niroku jiken,* 89. Nishida was Nishida Mitsugi (JMA 34), who was a key figure in the original formation of the Young Officers Movement in the 1920s. Nishida had met Kita Ikki as a JMA cadet in the early 1920s and became a close friend and lifelong disciple, introducing him and his work to other JMA cadets, including some who went on to lead the February 26 Incident. See Shillony, *Revolt in Japan,* 15–17.

91. Kono Tsukasa, *Ni-niroku jiken,* 192.

92. Ibid., 183.

93. Ibid., 319, 330. On the same grounds, the young officers did not approve of army rule in Manchukuo. See ibid., 186.

94. Ibid., 193, 329.

95. Ibid., 183.

96. Ibid., 329.

97. Ibid., 195.

98. Ibid., 142.

99. Ibid., 185, 191.

100. *Otakebi,* 81–82. For a clear and succinct parsing of the often confused and confusing discourse of the young officers who led the February 26 Incident, see also Danny Orbach, *Curse on This Country: Japanese Military Insubordination and the Origins of the Pacific War, 1860–1936* (Ithaca, NY: Cornell University Press, forthcoming).

101. *Daitōjuku sanjūnenshi* [Thirty-year history of the Daitōjuku], ed. Daitōjuku Sanjūnenshi Hensan Iinkai (Tokyo: Daitōjuku Shuppanbu, 1972), 867–868.

102. Interestingly, Nichiren Buddhism was not included here among the various "anti-state" religions to be abolished. In the pre-1945 period Nichiren Buddhism was closely associated with Japanese nationalism, even spawning a movement that fused the two called Nichirenism, which attracted Kita Ikki and many of the rebellious young officers of the

1930s. See Ōtani Eichi, *Kindai Nihon no Nichirenshugi undō* [The Nichrenism movement in modern Japan] (Kyoto: Hōzōkan, 2001); Tankha, *Kita Ikki and the Making of Modern Japan,* 142–150; Shillony, *Revolt in Japan,* 72–78. When JMA cadets went for regular summer swimming exercises on the beaches of Enoshima, they stayed at a nearby Nichiren temple called Ryūkōji. For a photograph of the temple taken at the time, as well as a photograph of Park Chung Hee and fellow cadets in the MMA 2 class taken at nearby Koshigoe Beach in the summer of 1943, see Rikugun Shikan Gakkō, *Manshūkoku Gunkan Gakkō dai-nikisei: Shōwa 19-nen 4-gatsu 20-nichi sotsugyō* [The MMA 2 class: graduated April 20, 1944], personal property of Sekine Tomiji, copy in Yasukuni Kaikō Bunkoshitsu, Tokyo.

103. *Daitōjuku sanjūnenshi,* 866–867.
104. Hosokawa Minoru Nikki, May 15, 1941. See also Chapter 5.
105. *Daitōjuku sanjūnenshi,* 867.
106. For Uchiyama's lecture, see *Kiji* 54 (October 1942): 1–14.
107. Rikugun Shikan Gakkō Kōchō Ushijima Mitsuru, *Senshi kyōtei* 1 [Miliary history textbook, vol. 1], October 1942, 132–191.
108. Ibid., 191.
109. On Nagata, see Nagata Tetsuzan Kankokai, *Hiroku: Nagata Tetsuzan* [Secret record: Nagata Tetsuzan] (Tokyo: Fūyō Shobō, 1980), esp. 275–362. See also James B. Crowley, "Japanese Army Factionalism in the Early 1930's," *Journal of Asian Studies* 21, no. 3 (May 1962): 309–326; Michael A. Barnhart, *Japan Prepares for Total War: The Search for Economic Security, 1919–1941* (Ithaca, NY: Cornell University Press, 1987), 22–49; Leonard A. Humphreys, *The Way of the Heavenly Sword: The Japanese Army in the 1920s* (Stanford, CA: Stanford University Press, 1995), 34, 36, 94, 115; Mark R. Peattie, *Ishiwara Kanji and Japan's Confrontation with the West* (Princeton, NJ: Princeton University Press, 1975), 20, 111–112, 186–189, 197; Shillony, *Revolt in Japan,* 38, 44. On Ludendorff, see Charles Townshend, ed., *The Oxford History of Modern War* (Oxford: Oxford University Press, 2000), 139.
110. See Humphreys, *Way of the Heavenly Sword,* 34.
111. See Edward J. Drea, *Japan's Imperial Army: Its Rise and Fall, 1853–1945* (Lawrence: University Press of Kansas, 2009), 146–162. Crowley's analysis of army factionalism in this period, cited above, is still one of the best. See also Szpilman, "Fascist and Quasi-Fascist Ideas in Interwar Japan."
112. See Crowley, "Japanese Army Factionalism in the Early 1930s." Crowley also points to many other factional differences, including personnel appointments, in the officer corps in this period, that overlapped or transcended doctrinal differences and complicate the basic Tōsei/Kōdō split.
113. See Rikugunshō, *Kokubō no hongi to sono kyōka no teishō,* accessed April 4, 2015, http:// teikoku.xxxxxxxx.jp/1934_kokubo.htm. The first section of the Kokubō can also be found in Jōhō Yoshio, *Rikugunshō Gunmukyoku* [War Ministry Military Affairs Section] (Tokyo: Fuyō Shobō, 1979), 398–406. See also Crowley, "Japanese Army Factionalism in the Early 1930s," 318; Peattie, *Ishiwara Kanji,* 189.
114. On Nagata's assassination and aftermath, see Nagata Tetsuzan Kankokai, *Hiroku,* 113–271; see also Takahashi Masae, *Shōwa no gunbatsu* [Army cliques in the Shōwa era] (Tokyo: Chūō Kōronsha, 1969), 179–225; Crowley, "Japanese Army Factionalism in the Early 1930s," 321–325.
115. See, for example, *Tonga ilbo,* October 3, 1934.
116. Rikugunshō, *Kokubō no hongi to sono kyōka no teishō.* On the defense industry during Park's Yusin period, see Peter Banseok Kwon, "The Anatomy of *Chaju Kukpang:* Military-Civilian Convergence in the Development of the South Korean Defense Industry under Park Chung Hee, 1968–1979" (Ph.D. dissertation, History and East Asian Languages, Harvard University, 2016).

117. Ibid. See also Jōhō Yoshio, ed., *Rikugun Daigakkō,* 341–344, and Kwon, "Anatomy of *Chaju Kukpang.*"

118. See, for example, Kōno Tsukasa, *Ni-niroku jiken,* 140, 319; *Daitōjuku sanjūnenshi,* 865–868.

119. See Peattie, *Ishiwara Kanji,* 187.

120. Pang Kijung, "Chosŏn chisik ŭi kyŏngje t'ongjeron kwa 'sin ch'eje' insik: Chung-Il chŏnjaenggi chŏnch'ejuŭi ŭi kyŏngjeron ŭl chungsim ŭro" [The Korean intelligentsia's perceptions of economic controls and the "new system": the debate on the totalitarian economic system in the period of the Second Sino-Japanese War], in *Ilcheha chisikin ŭi p'asijŭm ch'eje insik kwa taeŭng* [Perceptions and responses of the intelligentsia toward the fascist system under Japanese imperialism], ed. Pang Kijung (Seoul: Hyean, 2005), 87–91.

121. See Rikugunshō, *Kokubō no hongi to sono kyōka no teishō.*

122. On wartime controls in Japan, see T. A. Bisson, *Japan's War Economy* (New York: International Secretariat, Institute of Pacific Relations, 1945); Chalmers Johnson, *MITI and the Japanese Miracle: The Growth of Industrial Policy, 1925–1975* (Stanford, CA: Stanford University Press, 1982), esp. 157–172; on wartime controls in Korea, see Carter J. Eckert, *Offspring of Empire: The Colonial Origins of Korean Capitalism, 1876–1945* (Seattle: University of Washington Press, 1991), 103–126.

123. Kyōiku Sōkanbu, *Gunjin chokuyu kinkai,* 61–62.

124. Prime minister October 18, 1941–July 22, 1944; minister of war July 22, 1940–July 22, 1944; army chief of staff February 21, 1944–July 18, 1944.

125. See Bisson, *Japan's War Economy,* esp. 133–162.

126. Barbara Molony, *Technology and Investment: The Prewar Japanese Chemical Industry* (Cambridge, MA: Council on East Asia Studies, Harvard University, 1990), 216–258.

127. See Johnson, *MITI and the Japanese Miracle,* 116–156. Among the most important of these Manchukuo bureaucrats was Kishi Nobusuke, who later served twice as Japanese prime minister after the war (1957–1958 and again 1958–1960), and personally reached out to Park Chung Hee soon after the 1961 coup to establish a relationship. Kishi Nobusuke Papers, handwritten letter to Park Chung Hee, August (day not specified), 1961. Park welcomed the relationship and continued to correspond with Kishi. See, for example, Kishi Nobusuke Papers, handwritten letter from Park Chung Hee, August 1, 1963. I am grateful to Andrew Levidis for providing me with copies of this correspondence. See also Andrew Levidis, "War, Asianism and National Renovation: Kishi Nobusuke and the Politics of Conservatism, 1918–1944" (Ph.D. dissertation, Faculty of Law, Kyoto University, 2013).

128. On industrial development in Manchuria, see Louise Young, *Japan's Total Empire: Manchuria and the Culture of Wartime Imperialism* (Berkeley: University of California Press, 1998), 183–259. The quotations from Young are on pages 185 and 186.

129. See Roger F. Hackett, *Yamagata Aritomo in the Rise of Modern Japan, 1838–1922* (Cambridge, MA: Harvard University Press, 1971), 81–83.

130. See Alvin D. Coox, *Nomonhan: Japan against Russia, 1939* (Stanford, CA: Stanford University Press, 1985), 1087–1088; Ryuzo Sejima, *Reminiscences: History of Japan from the 1930s to the Outbreak of the Greater East Asia War* (n.p.: Ryuzo Sejima, 1972), 11–18; Tobe Ryōichi et al., *Shippai no honshitsu: Nihongun no soshikironteki ken'kyū* [The essence of failure: an organizational theory analysis of the Japanese military] (Tokyo: Daiyamondosha, 1984), 217–229.

131. Rikugunshō, *Sakusen yōmurei* [Field service regulations] (Tokyo: Ikeda Shoten, 1970 [1938], Part I, 5. *Sakuyō* is an abbreviation of *Sakusen yōmurei.* See Chapter 5 and, for example, Hosokawa Minoru Nikki, January 21, 1942.

132. See, for example, Hosokawa Minoru Nikki, July 30, 1941; January 20, 1942.

133. Edward J. Drea, "The Japanese Army on the Eve of the War," in *Battle for China: Essays on the Military History of the Sino-Japanese War of 1937–1945,* ed. Mark Peattie, Edward Drea, and Hans Van de Ven (Stanford, CA: Stanford University Press, 2011), 113–115. A detailed explanation of the new tactics can be found in a 1945 publication by the Inspectorate General of Military Training. See Kyōiku Sōkanbu, *Hohei sentō kyōren* [Infantry combat training], January 1945.

134. Kaneko Tomio, interview, Tokyo, January 12, 2011; Suzuki Michihiko, interview, Tokyo, January 12, 2011.

135. In its personnel classifications the IJA distinguished between "line branches," called *heika* in Japanese (infantry, cavalry, artillery, engineers, air, and transport), and "services," called *kakubu* in Japanese (medical, veterinary, intendance, technical, judicial, and military bands). See U.S. War Department, *Handbook on Japanese Military Forces* (Baton Rouge: Louisiana State University Press, 1991), 1, 392.

136. Rikushikō Honbu, "Rikugun Shikan Gakkō rekishi," [History of the JMA], Bōei Kenkyūjo, Tokyo, entry for November 10–12, 1942; *Senku: kaikoroku* [Vanguard: memoirs], ed. Dōtokudai Ikkiseikai (Tokyo: Dōtokudai Ikkiseikai, 1986–1987), 1:330–331. See also *RSG,* 45–50.

137. *Kiji* 72 (April 1944): 17–21.

138. *Senku* 1:262–263.

139. Kaneko Tomio, interview, Tokyo, January 12, 2011.

140. Kiyoizumi Nobuo, interview, Tokyo, January 12, 2011; *RSG,* 28.

141. *Kiji* 71 (March 1944): 86–87. Ch'oe Chujong would later join Park Chung Hee in the 1961 coup. On Ch'oe, see *CIS* 3:782.

142. See Eckert, *Offspring of Empire,* 235–239.

143. *Sŏyu kyŏnmun: chŏnmun* [Observations on the West: the complete text], comp. and ed. Yi Hansŏp, Ch'oe Kyŏngok, Chŏng Yŏnguk, and Kang Sŏnga (Seoul: Pagijŏng, 2000), 323–324; *Tanjae Sin Ch'aeho Sŏnsaeng Ki'nyŏm Saŏphoe, Tanjae Sin Ch'aeho chŏnjip 4 (pyŏl)* [The complete works of Tanjae Sin Ch'aeho] (Seoul: Hyŏngsŏl, 1998), 100–104.

144. Yi Kwangsu, *Yi Kwangsu chŏnjip* [Complete works of Yi Kwangsu], ed. Chu Yohan et al. (Seoul: Samjungdang, 1962–1964), 17:177. For a recent analysis of the *Minjok kaejoron,* see Ellie Choi, "Yi Kwangsu and the Post-World War I Reconstruction Debate," *Journal of Korean Studies* 20, no. 1 (Spring 2015): 33–76. Leftist groups also warned continuously about the dangers of factionalism and the necessity for group unity, arguing, like Yi, that the former had historically weakened Korea and only the latter could save it. Dae-Sook Suh, *Documents of Korean Communism, 1918–1948* (Princeton, NJ: Princeton University Press, 1970), esp. 149–167.

145. *Sakufū banri,* 181–185; Gao Qingyin, interview, Las Vegas, March 11, 1997. See also Chapter 3.

146. Kyōiku Sōkanbu, *Gunjin chokuyu kinkai,* 64–75, 86–95.

147. Rikugun Yoka Shikan Gakkō Seitotai, *Seito kun'iku no jissai* [Practicum of cadet moral education], March 1942, 108.

148. Ibid., 109.

149. Ibid., 58.

150. Ibid., 111.

151. Ibid., 115.

152. Ibid., 108.

153. *Senku* 1:339–340. Cho Kapche, for example, writes that Park graduated "third" in his Manchukuo class at Zama. See Cho Kapche, *Pak Chŏnghŭi* 1:230. Here Cho is probably following Yi Naksŏn's notes based in part on Yi's conversations with Park. See Pak Chŏnghŭi Biographical Notes, Yi Naksŏn Papers. In fact we do not know Park's actual record or ranking at Zama, although we do know from internal JMA documents that

Park was not one of the class's four honor graduates. Three of the four honor graduates were Japanese: Kanbe Hajime, Ogasawara Harutsugu, and Noda Hiroshi. The fourth was Mongolian: Xu Dianxiang. See Rikushikō Honbu, "Rikugun Shikan Gakkō rekishi," entry for April 20, 1944.

154. Rikugun Yoka Shikan Gakkō Seitotai, *Seito kun'iku no jissai*, 109; see also *RSG*, 60.

155. Kiyoizumi Nobuo, interview, Tokyo, January 12, 2011. On Yi Sŏpchun, see *CIS* 2:928–929. According to Yi T'aeyŏng (son of Yi Sŏpchun), Park Chung Hee, when president, liked to get away from the Blue House and go drinking with his father in Changch'ungdong. His father, in Yi T'aeyŏng's words, was "a great hail-fellow-well-met type" person with male friends, very different in that sense from Park Chung Hee, who, based on his father's descriptions, was "lonely, introspective, silent, and kept people at bay." Yi T'aeyŏng, interview, Seoul, May 27, 1997.

156. Kaneko Tomio, interview, Tokyo, January 12, 2011.

157. Cai Chongliang, interview, May 17, 1997. Cai had become particularly close to Park and other Korean cadets in the MMA 2 class because they took Chinese (Mandarin) together at Lalatun. Like Park, Cai was in the MMA's 3rd Company, all sections of which were barracked within the same building. Park was in the 3rd Section, and Cai was in the 4th. Cai's native language was Taiwanese.

158. On the *torishimari seito* system, see *RSG*, 131–132; *Yomoyama*, 35–37; *Dōtokudai daishichikisei shi* [History of the MMA 7 class], ed. Dōtokudai Dai-Shichikiseikai (Tokyo: Dōtokudai Dai-Shichikiseikai, 1990), 132. See also Chapter 8.

159. *Yomoyama*, 160–162.

160. Hosokawa Minoru Nikki, April 3, 1941; March 29, 1942; April 11, 1941.

161. Ibid., September 29, 1941; *Pak Chŏnghŭi Changgun tamhwa munjip* [Collected statements of General Park Chung Hee] (Seoul: Taet'ongnyŏng Pisŏsil, 1965), 494.

162. Hosokawa Minoru Nikki, April 15, 1941; June 28, 1941.

163. Ibid., October 6, 1941; October 10, 1941.

164. Ibid., August 21, 1941.

165. Ibid., April 26, 1941.

166. Ibid., September 21, 1941.

167. Ibid., February 23, 1942; September 27, 1941.

168. Ibid., December 14, 1941.

169. Ibid., March 29, 1942.

170. Ibid., March 30, 1942.

171. *Senku* 1:258.

172. Rikugun Shikan Gakkō Kōchō Ushijima Mitsuru, *Gunseigaku kyōtei* [Military organization textbook], rev. ed., 1943–1944, 1:39.

173. Ibid., 40, 44.

174. Ibid., 41–55.

175. Ibid., 41–49.

176. Ibid., 44–46.

177. Ibid., 43.

178. Ibid., 42.

179. On the Total War Research Institute, see *Nihon riku-kaigun sōgō jiten* [Comprehensive dictionary of the Japanese army-navy], ed. Hata Ikuhiko (Tokyo: Tokyo Daigaku Shuppankai, 1991), 661–663. For a detailed study of the organization, see Morimatsu Toshio, *Sōryokusen Kenkyūjo* [The Total War Research Institute] (Tokyo: Hakuteisha, 1983).

180. Rikushikō Honbu, "Rikugun Shikan Gakkō rekishi," May 8, 1942. Endō's name is incorrectly written as Itō here; see Morimatsu Toshio, *Sōryokusen Kenkyūjo*, 224.

181. *Kiji* 58 (February 1943): 1–18; *Kiji* 59 (March 1943): 15–29; *Kiji* 60 (April 1943): 1–19; *Kiji* 65 (September 1943): 13–25; *Kiji* 66 (October 1943): 11–23. On Nishiuchi, see Morimatsu Toshio, *Sōryokusen Kenkyūjo*, 61, 225.

182. See Young, *Japan's Total Empire*, 255; F. C. Jones, *Manchuria since 1931* (London: Royal Institute of International Affairs, 1949), 160.
183. Young, *Japan's Total Empire*, 255; Jones, *Manchuria since 1931*, 154–156. See also Victor Kian Giap Seow, "Carbon Technocracy: East Asian Energy Regimes and the Industrial Modern" (Ph.D. dissertation, Harvard University, 2014).
184. Jones, *Manchuria since 1931*, 156–158; Molony, *Technology and Investment*, 236–243.
185. *RSG*, 50.
186. *Senku* 1:196–209, 390. See also Chapter 4. Pak Imhang played an important role in the 1961 coup as well; see Chapter 1.
187. *Sakufū banri*, 14.
188. *Senku* 1:202.
189. See Sang-young Rhyu and Seok-jin Lew, "Pohang Iron and Steel Company," in *The Park Chung Hee Era: The Transformation of South Korea*, ed. Byung-Kook Kim and Ezra F. Vogel (Cambridge, MA: Harvard University Press, 2011), 322–344.

7. Tactics and Spirit

1. Pak Chŏnghŭi, *Kukka wa hyŏngmyŏng kwa na* [The country, the revolution, and I] (Seoul: Hyangmunsa, 1963), 268.
2. See Carter J. Eckert, "A Gentle Voice in the Darkness: The Musical Genius of Kim Min'gi," in *Kim Min'gi* (Seoul: YMB Sŏul Ŭmban, 1994). See also Kim Ch'angnam, ed., *Kim Min'gi* (Seoul: Tosŏch'ulp'an Han'ul, 2004).
3. For the story in both Korean and English, see Yi Pŏmsŏn, *Obalt'an* [A stray bullet], bilingual ed., trans. Mashal P'il [Marshall Pihl] (Seoul: Asia, 2015). The story was turned into a film of the same name, directed by Yu Hyŏnmok and released in 1961. See Hyangjin Lee, *Contemporary Korean Cinema: Identity, Culture, Politics* (Manchester: Manchester University Press, 2000), 58, 118–125.
4. Kim Taejung [Kim Dae Jung], *Kim Taejung chasajŏn* [Autobiography of Kim Dae Jung] (Seoul: Tosŏch'ulp'an Sam'in, 2010), 1:382.
5. This poem and twenty-six others were given out secretly one by one to Park and other classmates at TNS by their Korean teacher Kim Yŏnggi, and compiled by the students into a handwritten booklet simply called "Sijo." Yi Sŏngjo, Park's TNS classmate and editor of the 1937 class yearbook, said he believed he had the only remaining booklet in existence and kindly provided me with a copy. Yi Sŏngjo, interview, Seoul, June 22–23, 1998. The poem quoted by Park is attributed in the booklet to Yi I (Yulgok), but Peter Lee identifies the author as Yang Saŏn, one of Yi I's contemporaries. See "Sijo," unnumbered; Peter H. Lee, comp. and trans., *Poems from Korea: A Historical Anthology* (Honolulu: University of Hawaii Press, 1974), 82. See also *Taegu Sabŏm simsanggwaji* [History of the elementary school department of Taegu Normal School], ed. Han Sŏktong (Taegu: Taegu Sabŏm Simsanggwa Tongmunhoe, 1991), 232. Kim Yŏnggi was the father of entrepreneur Kim Ujung, the founder of the Daewoo *chaebŏl*, which played an important role in the 1970s in Park Chung Hee's state-led economic development. Daewoo collapsed following the 1997 Asian financial crisis. A brief memoir by Kim Yŏnggi about his time at TNS can be found in *Taegu Sabŏm simsanggwaji*, 529–541.
6. Elizabeth Kier, *Imagining War: French and British Military Doctrine between the Wars* (Princeton, NJ: Princeton University Press, 1997), 20. See also Jack L. Snyder, *Ideology of the Offensive: Military Decision Making and the Disasters of 1914* (Ithaca, NY: Cornell University Press, 1984); Robert M. Citino, *Quest for Decisive Victory: From Stalemate to Blitzkrieg in Europe, 1899–1940* (Lawrence: University Press of Kansas, 2002), 1–30; Helmuth Moltke, *Moltke on the Art of War: Selected Writings*, ed. Daniel J. Hughes, trans. Daniel J. Hughes and Harry Bell (Novato, CA: Presidio, 1993), 1–19.

7. See Harold Bolitho, "The Myth of the Samurai," in *Japan's Impact on the World*, ed. Alan Rix and Ross Mauer (Nathan, Australia: Japanese Studies Association of Australia, 1984), 2–9.

8. The original verses in Japanese can be found in Yamamoto Tsunetomo, *Hagakure* (Tokyo: Iwanami Shoten, 1940), 1:116, 190. See also Yamamoto Tsunetomo, *Hagakure: The Book of the Samurai*, trans. William Scott Wilson (Tokyo: Kodansha International, 1979), 51, 66.

9. Kyōiku Sōkanbu, *Gunjin chokuyu kinkai* [Respectful understanding of the Imperial Rescript to Soldiers and Sailors] (Tokyo: Gunjin Kaikan Toshobu, 1944), 76.

10. Wm. De Bary, Carol Gluck, and Arthur E. Tiedemann, eds., *Sources of Japanese Tradition*, vol. 2, *1600-2000*, 2nd ed. (New York: Columbia University Press, 2005), 671–672.

11. On Meckel and his extraordinary influence in Japan, see Ernst L. Presseisen, *Before Aggression: Europeans Prepare the Japanese Army* (Tucson: University of Arizona Press, 1965), esp. 69–88. On nineteenth-century developments in warfare more generally, see Trevor N. Dupuy, *Evolution of Weapons and Warfare* (New York: Da Capo, 1984), 169–202.

12. Presseisen, *Before Aggression*, 145–146.

13. Ibid., 147. See also Alvin D. Coox, *Nomonhan: Japan against Russia, 1939* (Stanford, CA: Stanford University Press, 1985), 445.

14. Coox, *Nomonhan*, 991–1032. See also Edward J. Drea, *Japan's Imperial Army: Its Rise and Fall, 1853-1945* (Lawrence: University Press of Kansas, 2009), 132–133.

15. See Terada Chikao, *Nihon guntai yōgoshū* [Japanese military terms] (Tokyo: Rippū Shobō, 1992), 1:58. See also *Senku: kaikoroku* [Vanguard: memoirs], ed. Dōtokudai Ikkiseikai (Tokyo: Dōtokudai Ikkiseikai, 1986–1987), 1:180; Coox, *Nomonhan*, 374.

16. Rikugunshō, *Sakusen yōmurei* [Field service regulations] (Tokyo: Ikeda Shoten, 1970 [1938]), Part II, 1.

17. Ibid., 15. See also Coox, *Nomonhan*, 239, 314, 523.

18. Rikugunshō, *Sakusen yōmurei*, Part II, 96.

19. Ibid., 144.

20. Kyōiku Sōkanbu, *Hohei sōten chūkai* [Infantry manual commentary], Tokyo, Seibutō, June 20, 1940, 11. On the history of the *Hohei sōten*, see Ōe Shinobu, *Tennō no guntai* [Army of the emperor] (Tokyo: Shōgakkan, 1982), 145–147, 214–215.

21. Rikugunshō, *Sakusen yōmurei*, Part I, 111; Part II, 146–157.

22. U.S. War Department, *Handbook on Japanese Military Forces* (Baton Rouge: Louisiana State University Press, 1991), 97–99.

23. *Kiji* 69 (January 1944): 53–57.

24. *Kiji* 66 (October 1943): 75–77.

25. Park Chung Hee's class participated in one of these exercises in November 1942. See Rikushikō Honbu, "Rikugun Shikan Gakkō rekishi" [History of the JMA], Bōei Kenkyūjo, Tokyo, entry for November 10–12, 1942. See also *Senku* 1:330.

26. *Kiji* 72 (April 1944): 16–21.

27. Rikushikō Honbu, "Rikugun Shikan Gakkō rekishi," entry for September 25–October 16, 1943. See also *Sakufū banri: Manshūkoku Gunkan Gakkō nikisei no kiroku* [The north wind of ten thousand leagues: the record of the MMA 2 class] (Hadano: Dōtokudai Nikiseikai, 1981), 149.

28. *Senku* 1:318–319. On Yi Chuil's role in the 1961 coup, see Chapter 1.

29. On these new tactics, see Chapter 6.

30. *Kiji* 66 (October 1943); Rikugun Shikan Gakkō Kōchō Ushijima Mitsuru, *Senjutsugaku kyōtei* 1 [Military tactics textbook, vol. 1], November 1943, 88–89, 102, 126, 145–146. See also Coox, *Nomonhan*, 757–762.

31. Shiino Hattō, ed., *Nihon rikugun rentai sōran: chiiki betsu; hohei hen* [Compendium of Japanese army regiments: classified by region; infantry edition] (Tokyo: Shinjinbutsu Ōraisha, 1990), 134.

32. Coox, *Nomonhan*, 842–847.
33. See ibid., 1041; Drea, *Japan's Imperial Army*, 217. See also Terada, *Nihon guntai yōgoshū* 2:48–49.
34. *Sakufū banri*, 78–79.
35. *Senku* 1:312–313.
36. Hosokawa Minoru Nikki [Hosokawa Minoru diary] (courtesy of Hosokawa Minoru, via Suzuki Michihiko), entry for June 30, 1941.
37. Kaneko Tomio, interview, Tokyo, January 12, 2011. Kaneko contrasted *samurai-kutaichō* with *oyabun-kutaichō*. The latter were also "tough, but more informal, easier to approach."
38. Kiyoizumi Nobuo, interview, Tokyo, January 12, 2011.
39. *Senku* 1:251; Kiyoizumi Nobuo, interview, Tokyo, January 12, 2011.
40. *Senku* 1:285.
41. Ibid.
42. Because of heavy security and traffic congestion, however, the meeting was canceled. *Sakufū banri*, 159–160.
43. Yasukuni Kaikō Bunkoshitsu, Kōjin jōhō, Nishigaki Makoto (ID 23196); Tahara Kōzō (ID 25104). Tahara's appointment at the JMA began March 26, 1943. See Rikushikō Honbu, "Rikugun Shikan Gakkō rekishi," *tennyūsha meibō*, 1943.
44. Kaneko Tomio, interview, Tokyo, January 12, 2011.
45. *Sakufū banri*, 151–156, esp. 153. For more on Takayama, see his autobiography: Takayama Toshitake, *Yomoyamakatari* [Speaking of this and that] (n.p.: Takayama Toshiyake, 1994).
46. Kiyoizumi Nobuo, interview, Tokyo, January 12, 2011.
47. *Sakimori no fu: ninkan 40-shūnen kinen gojūniki* [Genealogy of soldiers: on the 40th anniversary of the commissioning of the JMA 52 class], ed. Rikushi-Kōshi Dai-Gojūnikisei, 1979, 563.
48. *Sakufū banri*, 155.
49. Tahara Kōzō, letter to Tahara Yoshiko, early November 1944.
50. Edward J. Drea, *In the Service of the Emperor: Essays on the Imperial Japanese Army* (Lincoln: University of Nebraska Press, 1998), 135–137.
51. Yasukuni Kaikō Bunkoshitsu, Kōjin jōhō, Tahara Kōzō (ID 25104); *Sakimori no fu*, 563.
52. Tahara Kōzō, letter to Tahara Yoshiko, early November 1944; Tahara Kōzō, postcard to Tahara Yoshiko, late November 1944.
53. *Sakimori no fu*, 563–564.
54. Ibid., 564.
55. The novel was also turned into a popular Japanese film of the same name by director Ichikawa Kon in 1959. For help with the Tahara letters, my thanks to Yori Oda.
56. *Senku* 1:258.
57. Hosokawa Minoru Nikki, October 3, 1941.
58. Ibid., November 18, 1941.
59. Ibid., January 21, 1942.
60. *Senku* 1:134–137. See also Chapter 8.
61. Rikugunshō, *Sakusen yōmurei*, Part I, 6.
62. Rikugun Shikan Gakkō Kōchō Ushijima Mitsuru, *Senshi kyōtei* 1:3.
63. Yamamoto Tsunetomo, *Hagakure* 1:144.
64. See Sun Joo Kim, "Fathers' Letters Concerning Their Children's Education," in *Epistolary Korea: Letters in the Communicative Space of the Chosŏn, 1392–1910*, ed. JaHyun Haboush (New York: Columbia University Press, 2009), 277–286.
65. Michael Cowan traces these ideas in detail, focusing on sites of psychology, body culture, and educational reform, especially in early twentieth-century Germany. See Cowan, *Cult of the Will: Nervousness and German Modernity* (University Park: Pennsylvania State University Press, 2008).

66. Ibid.
67. See Ki-baik Lee, *A New History of Korea*, 327–338. Eckert et al., *Korea Old and New*, 244–253. See also Chapter 3.
68. Hwimun Ŭisuk P'yŏnjippu, ed. *Chungdŭng susin kyogwasŏ* [Secondary level morals textbook] (Hansŏng [Seoul]: Hwimun Ŭisuk Inswaebu, 1906), 20–22.
69. Gail Lee Bernstein, *Japanese Marxist: A Portrait of Kawakami Hajime, 1879–1946* (Cambridge, MA: Harvard University Press, 1976), 117–128.
70. Nym Wales [Helen Foster Snow] and Kim San, *Song of Arian: A Korean Communist in the Chinese Revolution* (San Francisco: Ramparts Press, 1941), 135.
71. Benito Mussolini, *My Rise and Fall*, 257.
72. Michael Baskett, "All Beautiful Fascists? Axis Film Culture in Imperial Japan," in *Culture of Japanese Fascism*, ed. Alan Tansman (Durham, NC: Duke Universitiy Press, 2008), 220; Peter B. High, *The Imperial Screen: Japanese Film Culture in the Fifteen Years' War, 1931–1945* (Madison: University of Wisconsin Press, 2003), 135.
73. Adolf Hitler, *Mein Kampf* (New York: Reynal and Hitchcock, 1939), 624. The full quotation is: "It is this lack of will, and not the lack of arms, that today makes us incapable of all serious resistance. It is ingrained in our entire people, it prevents every decision which involves a risk, as though the greatness of an act did not lie in the very risk."
74. *Kiji* 54 (October 1942): 11.
75. Nakajima Toshiyuki, "Shūyō gyōji ichiranhyō: Rikugun Yoka Shikan Gakkō: daigojūhachikisei: dai- 32 chūtai: dai-6 kutai: Shōwa 17.4–18.11" [Calendar of important activities: JMAP 58: 32nd company: 6th section: April 1942–November 1943] (copy provided to author by Chŏng Naehyŏk), entry for April 1, 1942.
76. See Rikugun Yoka Shikan Gakkō Seitotai, *Seito kun'iku no jissai* [Practicum of cadet moral education], March 1942, esp. 27–29, 33, 66, 156.
77. Rikugun Shikan Gakkō Kōchō Yamamuro Munetake, *Kyōikugaku: zen* [Pedagogy: complete], March 1939, 73–77.
78. Rikugun Yoka Shikan Gakkō Seitotai, *Seito kun'iku no jissai*, 156. Hosokawa's diary is filled with these expressions. For example, see Hosokawa Minoru Nikki, June 7, 1941; November 24, 1941; November 26, 1941, November 29, 1941. Hosokawa often uses the combined expression "energetic and cheerful" (*meirō-genki*).
79. Rikugun Yoka Shikan Gakkō Kōchō Amakasu Jūtarō, *Shinrigaku kari kyōtei (ippan shinri)* [Provisional psychology textbook: general psychology], 1937, 16–24.
80. Rikugun Yoka Shikan Gakkō Seitotai, *Seito kun'iku no jissai*, 41–106, 132–170.
81. Ibid., 156.
82. *Senku* 1:389–390; *Sakufū banri*, 11; *Dōtokudai dai-shichikisei shi* [History of the MMA 7 class], ed. Dōtokudai Dai-Shichikiseikai (Tokyo: Dōtokudai Dai-Shichikiseikai, 1990) (henceforth *Dōtokudai*), 173–175; Hosokawa Minoru Nikki, March 3, 1942. See also Chapter 4.
83. *Senku* 1:270–272.
84. See Hosokawa Minoru Nikki, July 5–8, 1941; November 15, 1941; April 12, 1942.
85. *Dōtokudai*, 159–160.
86. *Changchun wenshi ziliao* 2 [Changchun cultural history materials, vol. 2], ed. Changchun Shi Zhengxie Wenshi Ziliao Weiyuanhui (Changchun: Changchun Shi Zhengxie Wenshi Bangongshi Faxingzu, 1991) (henceforth *CWZ*), 4–5.
87. Hiruma Hiroshi, *Rikugun Shikan Gakkō yomoyama monogatori* [Sundry stories of the JMA] (Tokyo: Kōjinsha, 1983) (henceforth *Yomoyama*), 181–183.
88. Kaneko Tomio, interview, Tokyo, January 12, 2011.
89. *Rikugun Shikan Gakkō* [The Japanese Military Academy], ed. Yamazaki Masao, with the collaboration of the Kaikōsha, 4th ed. (Tokyo: Akimoto Shobō, 1984) (henceforth *RSG*), 60.

90. Hosokawa Minoru Nikki, November 11–12, 1941. See also Rikugun Yoka Shikan Gakkō Seitotai, *Seito kun'iku no jissai,* 155.

91. *Senku* 1:270. After the firing, all the blank cartridge cases also had to be strictly accounted for, as cadets who could not endure the academy training would sometimes commit suicide using blanks. *Yomoyama,* 78–79.

92. Kaneko Tomio, interview, Tokyo, January 12, 2011.

93. *Senku* 1:268–269, 284.

94. Xu Shudong, interview, Changchun, August 29, 1992.

95. See, for example, Hosokawa Minoru Nikki, June 7, 1941; November 24, 1941; November 29, 1941.

96. Ibid., November 12, 1941; November 25, 1941.

97. Ibid., October 28, 1941.

98. Ibid., November 9, 1941.

99. Ibid., November 14–19, 1941. Hosokawa also drew a large chart that filled the page before his regular entry for November 23, 1941. The chart contains a reminder to "overcome the cold weather through mental attitude" and a vow to "develop though the *bushidō* spirit a vigorous [*ōsei*] mental and physical strength to endure the cold weather."

100. Ibid., July 6–July 8, 1941.

101. Ibid., April 12, 1942.

102. Ibid., February 14, 1942; March 3, 1942; January 21, 1942; March 6, 1942.

103. Ibid., November 29, 1941.

104. Ibid., November 25, 1941; May 10, 1941. See also Chapter 4.

105. *Kiji* 74 (June 1944): 3–6.

106. *Kōchō kunjishū (Yoka/Honka/Hohei Gakkō): dai-gojūrokukisei kunren shiryō* [Collected lectures of the Superintendent (JMAP, JMA, Infantry School): training materials for the JMA 56 class], Rikugun Shikan Gakkō, n.d., lecture by Yamada Otozō, November 12, 1942.

107. *Kiji* 74 (June 1944): 1–2.

108. On the *Senjinkun,* see Awaya Kentarō, "Senjinkun," *Kodansha Encyclopedia of Japan* 7:65. Drea translates it as "Code of Battlefield Conduct": Drea, *Japan's Imperial Army,* 212.

109. Rikugun Yoka Shikan Gakkō Kyōjūbu, *Kōgun hisshō no shinnen* [Belief in certain victory of the Imperial Army], September 8, 1944, 1. See also Mark R. Peattie, *Ishiwara Kanji and Japan's Confrontation with the West* (Princeton, NJ: Princeton University Press, 1975), 15 n. 19; Chapter 6.

110. Rikugun Yoka Shikan Gakkō Kyōjūbu, *Kōgun hisshō no shinnen,* 1.

111. Ibid., 5; *Kiji* 74 (June 1944): 3–6. See also Chapter 4.

112. Rikugun Yoka Shikan Gakkō Kyōjūbu, *Kōgun hisshō no shinnen,* 5–6.

113. Ibid., 6–7.

114. Ibid., 7, 2, 4. See also Chapter 4.

115. *Senku* 1:244.

116. Hosokawa Minoru Nikki, December 8, 1941.

117. Chŏng Chaegyŏng, ed., *Pak Chŏnghŭi silgi: haengjŏk ch'orok* [The true record of Park Chung Hee: selected excerpts] (Seoul: Chimmundang, 1994), 629.

118. G. Cameron Hurst III, *Armed Martial Arts of Japan: Swordsmanship and Archery* (New Haven, CT: Yale University Press, 1998), 82–100, 153–161; Andrew Bennett, *Kendo: Culture of the Sword* (Oakland: University of California Press, 2015), 57–86.

119. Jinichi Tokeshi, *Kendo: Elements, Rules, and Philosophy* (Honolulu: University of Hawaii Press, 2003), 85–90, 119–144, 175–179. For a bilingual explanation of *kendō* terms (Japanese and English), see *Kendō Wa-Ei jiten* [Japanese-English dictionary of *kendō*] (Tokyo: Zen Nihon Kendō Renmei, 2000).

120. Chōsen Sōtokufu Gakumukyoku, *Chōsen ni okeru kyōiku kakushin no zenbō* [Full picture of the education reforms in Chōsen] (Keijō: Chōsen Sōtokufu Gakumukyoku Gakumuka, 1938), 149. See also Kim Yŏnghak, "Han'guk ch'eyuksa yŏngyŏk e ttarŭn kŏmsul mit kŏmdo ŭi paltal kwajŏng e kwanhan yŏn'gu" [The development of the art of the sword and *kendō* in the history of Korean physical education] (Ph.D. dissertation, Myŏngji University, 1999), 102.

121. Hosokawa Minoru Nikki, September 18, 1941; *Senku* 1:183; *Manshū nichi-nichi shinbun*, March 24, 1942.

122. *Dōtokudai*, 114; *CWZ*, 27; *RSG* 144.

123. Hosokawa Minoru Nikki, August 16, 1941.

124. Gao Qingyin, interview, Las Vegas, March 11, 1997.

125. Hosokawa Minoru Nikki, November 23, 1941.

126. *Sakufū banri*, 153-154. Perhaps because of his own passion for the sport, Park Chung Hee seems to have had fond memories of Takayama, and made a point of sending his regards to the former section commander in a letter to an MMA 2 classmate after visiting Japan in 1961. Pak Chŏnghŭi, letter to Origuchi Ryūzō, December 2, 1961.

127. *Dōtokudai*, 167. On wartime *kendō* instruction, see Bennett, *Kendo*, 148-149, 151, 161.

128. Hosokawa Minoru Nikki, August 15, 1941.

129. Origuchi Ryūzō et al., interview, Tokyo, September 1, 1990.

130. *Dōtokudai*, 162.

131. Gao Qingyin, interview, Las Vegas, March 11, 1997; Gao Qingyin, letter (in Chinese) to Yi Naksŏn, May 15, 1962, reproduced in part in Korean in *Han'guk ilbo*, September 11–15, 1962 (Kuwahara mentioned in September 11 issue). On Kuwahara, see also *Tairiku no kōbō: Manshūkokugun Nikkei gunkan yonkiseishi* [Light of the continent: history of the CTS 4 Nikkei officers of the Manchukuo Army], ed. Manshūkokugun Nikkei Gunkan Yonkiseikai (Osaka: Manshūkokugun Nikkei Gunkan Yonkiseikai, 1983), 2:168–169; Shōji Munemitsu, *Kendō gojūnen* [Fifty years of *kendō*] (Tokyo: Jiji Tsushinsha, 1956), 112, 208. Kuwahara had achieved the sixth rank in *kendō* by 1940.

132. Gao Qingyin, interview, Las Vegas, March 11, 1997.

133. *CWZ*, 143.

134. Ibid., 154. On Kim Chaep'ung, see Chapter 6.

135. *CWZ*, 143.

136. Kim Muk, interview, Seoul, May 28, 1997; Gao Qingyin, letter (in Chinese) to Yi Naksŏn, May 15, 1962, reproduced in part in Korean in *Han'guk ilbo*, September 11–15, 1962 (Park's characteristic *kendō* attack described in September 11 issue).

137. *Sakufū banri*, 73.

138. *RSG*, 28.

139. *Yomoyama*, 137–138.

140. *RSG*, 68, 126–127.

141. *Senku* 1:292.

142. *Sakufū banri*, 148-149. At Zama the entire school turned out in formation for a silent tribute to Yamamoto on the day of his state funeral, June 5, 1943. See the entry for that date in Rikushikō Honbu, "Rikugun Shikan Gakkō rekishi." Yamamoto, who had studied at Harvard in the 1920s, had been the architect of Japanese naval policy in the Pacific, overseeing the attack on Pearl Harbor. He was deliberately targeted and shot down by the United States over the Solomon Islands in April 1943. For a brief biography, see Janet Hunter, *Concise Dictionary of Modern Japanese History* (Berkeley: University of California Press, 1984), 247.

143. Kyōiku Sōkanbu, Dai-Nika, *Doitsu haisen to hisshō no shinnen* [The defeat of Germany and the belief in certain victory], reproduced for the JMAP, May, 7, 1945, introduction (unnumbered); 1–8.

144. For a brilliant description and analysis of this will-to-death culture fostered within the *kamikaze* or "special attack forces" (*tokkōtai*) in this period, see Emiko Ohnuki-Tierney, *Kamikaze, Cherry Blossoms, and Nationalisms: The Militarization of Aesthetics in Japanese History* (Chicago: University of Chicago Press, 2002). This culture in fact was by no means confined to the *kamikaze*; it permeated the IJA at all levels and was especially prevalent in the academies in the last years of the war. Drea notes in fact that "the concept of literally fighting to the death did not gain popular acceptance until the late 1930s and was not institutionalized until 1941." Drea, *Japan's Imperial Army*, 257.

145. Horace, *Odes and Epodes*, ed. and trans. Niall Rudd (Cambridge, MA: Harvard University Press, 2004), 144–145. On the Singer mural, see John T. Bethell, *Harvard Observed: An Illustrated History of the University in the Twentieth Century* (Cambridge, MA: Harvard University Press, 1998), 86–87; Jane Dini, "The Art of Selling War: Sargent's World War I Murals for Harvard University," *Harvard University Art Museums Bulletin* 7, no. 1 (Autumn 1999–Winter 2000): 67–84. The mural is called "Death and Victory," and the lines quoted above, written by Sargent and Abbot Lawrence Lowell, Harvard's president at the time, are inscribed below the mural.

146. High, *Imperial Screen*, 389.

147. *RSG*, 72; Yamamoto, *Hagakure*, 1:2.

148. See, for example, *Kiji* 65 (September 1943). See also Naoko Shimazu, *Japanese Society at War: Death, Memory, and the Russo-Japanese War* (New York: Cambridge University Press, 2009), 254. On the twenty-ninth anniversary of Nogi's death in 1941, Hosokawa wrote in his diary that the thought of General Nogi's "martyrdom" (*junshi*) and its "pure and selfless" (*seiren*) character was "particularly significant [*toku ni taisetsu*] for officers of our national army." Hosokawa Minoru Nikki, September 13, 1941; Cai Chongliang, interview, Elyria, OH, May 17, 1997.

149. Rikugun Yoka Shikan Gakkō Kyōjūbu, *Kōgun hisshō no shinnen*, 2; Chŏng Chaegyŏng, ed., *Pak Chŏnghŭi silgi*, 475, 480, 509. Koreans of course associate this phrase with Admiral Yi Sunsin, who used it in his diary, written during the war years of 1592–1598, when Yi was defending Chosŏn Korea against the Japanese invasions led by Toyotomi Hideyoshi. Park was probably acquainted with the phrase even before he joined the Manchukuo Army from reading Yi Kwangsu's famous novel about the admiral. See Yi Kwangsu, *Sosŏl Yi Sunsin* [Novel of Yi Sunsin] (Seoul: Usinsa, 1991), 352. The phrase was likely one of ancient Chinese origin, familiar to both Japanese and Koreans in the sixteenth century and before, and Yi Sunsin in fact introduces the phrase in his diary as a maxim of classical military tactics (*pyŏngbŏp*). See Yi Sunsin, *Nanjung ilgi: Yi Ch'ungmu kong chinjung kirok* [War diary: the battle record of Yi Ch'ungmu kong], trans. Yi Yongho (Seoul: Tonggwang Munhwasa, 2005), 349, 568. See also *The Art of the Warrior*, trans. and ed. Ralph D. Sawyer with Mei-chun Lee Sawyer (Boston: Shambhala, 1996), 175. On Yi Sunsin, see also Chapter 2. On Park and Yi Kwangsu's novel, see Chapter 3.

150. *Dōtokudai*, 130–131.

151. *Yomoyama*, 13.

152. *Senku* 1:248–249.

153. *Kiji* 74 (June 1944): 3–6. On Yamasaki, see *Nihon riku-kaigun sōgō jiten* [Comprehensive dictionary of the Japanese army-navy], ed. Hata Ikuhiko (Tokyo: Tokyo Daigaku Shuppankai, 1991), 151; see also Brian Garfield, *The Thousand-Mile War: World War II in Alaska and the Aleutians* (Garden City, NY: Doubleday, 1969).

154. *Kiji* 74 (June 1944): 7. The character for *fun* in *funkotsu* is incorrect in the original text. On Arikawa Shuichi, see Chapter 3. On Ushijima, see Okuda Kōichirō, *Okinawa Gunshireikan Ushijima Mitsuru* [Okinawa Commanding Officer Ushijima Mitsuru] (Tokyo: Fuyō Shobō, 1985), 97–106, 191–248. It is important also to distinguish such

attitudes in the professional officer corps from the perspective of the common conscript soldier, who more often than not found himself thrust into life-or-death combat
on the battlefield through no choice of his own. See, for example, Shimazu, *Japanese
Society at War*, 107.

155. Hosokawa Minoru Nikki, March 23, 1942. The term "human bullets" (*nikudan*) was associated with General Nogi's suicidal assaults on Hill 203 at Port Arthur and was the title of
a famous novel of the Russo-Japanese War by Sakurai Tadayoshi. See Sakurai Tadayoshi,
Human Bullets: A Soldier's Story of Port Arthur, trans. Masujiro Honda (Boston:
Houghton, Mifflin, 1907). See also Terada Chikao, *Nihon guntai yōgoshū* 1:85–87.

156. *Chiru sakura: Rikushi dai-57-ki senbotsusha kiroku* [Fallen cherry blossoms: the record
of the fallen soldiers of the JMA 57 class], ed. Rikushi 57-ki Kaikō Bunko Taisaku Iinkai
Senbotsusha Kiroku Sakuseihan (Tokyo: Rikushi 57-ki Dōkiseikai, 1999), 15, 339, 780,
889. The two Koreans were Kim Yŏngsu, who died in combat in the Philippines, and
Chŏng Sangsu, who died in the Okinawa aerial fighting. See Yi Kidong, *Pigŭk ŭi
kun'indŭl: Ilbon Yuksa ch'ulsin ŭi yŏksa* [Soldiers of tragedy: a history of the graduates
of the JMA] (Seoul: Ilchogak, 1982), 49, 286.

157. Yi Hyŏnggŭn, *Kunbŏn 1-bŏn ŭi oegil insaeng: Yi Hyŏnggŭn hoegorok* [The steadfast life
of army service number 1: memoir of Yi Hyŏnggŭn] (Seoul: Chungang Ilbosa, 1993), 17.

158. Takezawa Rikio, interview, Tokyo, January 12, 2011; Wang Jingyue and Zhu Huan, interview, Changchun, August 28, 1992.

159. Xu Shudong, interview, Changchun, August 29, 1992.

160. Pak, *Kukka wa hyŏngmyŏng kwa na*, 84.

161. Yi Hallim, *Segi ŭi kyŏngnang: hoesangnok* [The raging waves of the century: a memoir]
(Seoul: P'albogwŏn, 1994), 385.

162. Pang Wŏnch'ŏl, interview, Seoul, June 2, 1997.

8. Order and Discipline

1. Alice H. Amsden, *Asia's Next Giant: South Korea and Late Industrialization* (New
York: Oxford University Press, 1989), 14.

2. *Pak Chŏnghŭi Changgun tamhwa munjip* [Collected statements of General Park Chung
Hee] (Seoul: Taet'ongnyŏng Pisŏsil, 1965), 18.

3. Chŏng Chaegyŏng, ed., *Pak Chŏnghŭi silgi: haengjŏk ch'orok* [The true record of Park
Chung Hee: selected excerpts] (Seoul: Chimmundang, 1994), 481.

4. The term is from Harold D. Lasswell's prophetic 1941 essay, included in Lasswell, *The
Analysis of Political Behavior: An Empirical Approach* (London: Kegan, Paul, Trench,
Trubner, 1947), 146–157.

5. Antonio Gramsci, *Selections from the Prison Notebooks*, ed. and trans. Quintin Hoare
and Geoffrey Nowell Smith (New York: International, 1971), 323–343. On "governmentality," see Michel Foucault, "Governmentality," in *The Foucault Effect: Studies in
Governmentality*, ed. Graham Burchell, Colin Gordon, and Peter Miller (Chicago:
University of Chicago Press, 1991), 87–104. On "biopower," see Michel Foucault, *History of Sexuality*, vol. 1 (New York: Vintage, 1990), 135–159.

6. Ian Kershaw, *Hitler: 1889–1936: Hubris* (New York: W. W. Norton, 1998), 532. I am
borrowing the idea of "coproduction" here from a study by Michael Gibbons and his
associates, who define it as a new method of producing knowledge or "truth" in a dy-
namic interaction between science and society, or, one might say, between state and
society. Of course, interaction in the case of both Nazi Germany and Park's Korea was
deliberately hierarchical, with the state assuming the dominant role in the coproduction
process. One could be active and creative, but generally only within certain par-
ameters determined by the state. Still, it is important to note that the disciplining process of governmentality in both cases was one in which the state sought the active

participation of the population. See Michael Gibbons et al., *The New Production of Knowledge: The Dynamics of Science and Research in Contemporary Societies* (London: Sage, 1994).

7. Friedrich Nietzsche, *On the Genealogy of Morals, Ecco Homo,* trans. and ed. Walter Kaufman (New York: Vintage Books, 1967), 61.

8. *Senku: kaikoroku* [Vanguard: memoirs], ed. Dōtokudai Ikkiseikai (Tokyo: Dōtokudai Ikkiseikai, 1986–1987), 1:53

9. *Changchun wenshi ziliao* 2 [Changchun cultural history materials, vol. 2], ed. Changchun Shi Zhengxie Wenshi Ziliao Weiyuanhui (Changchun: Changchun Shi Zhengxie Wenshi Bangongshi Faxingzu, 1991) (henceforth *CWZ*), 27.

10. *Senku* 1:258; *Rikugun Shikan Gakkō* [The Japanese Military Academy], ed. Yamazaki Masao, with the collaboration of the Kaikōsha, 4th ed. (Tokyo: Akimoto Shobō, 1984) (henceforth *RSG*), 144.

11. *Senku* 1:249.

12. *Dōtokudai dai-shichikisei shi* [History of the MMA 7 class], ed. Dōtokudai Dai-Shichikiseikai (Tokyo: Dōtokudai Dai-Shichikiseikai, 1990) (henceforth *Dōtokudai*), 114.

13. Ibid., 128.

14. Hosokawa Minoru Nikki [Hosokawa Minoru Diary], 7 vols. (courtesy of Hosokawa Minoru, via Suzuki Michihiko), entry for November 18, 1941.

15. Kim Muk, interview, Seoul, May 28, 1997; Cai Chongliang, interview, Elyria, OH, May 17, 1997; Hiruma Hiroshi, *Rikugun Shikan Gakkō yomoyama monogatori* [Sundry stories of the JMA] (Tokyo: Kōjinsha, 1983) (henceforth *Yomoyama*), 150.

16. See *Yomoyama,* 171, 194; *RSG,* 149 (photo). The alternating sleep positions may have been for health reasons, to minimize chances of contagion from colds, etc., or to discourage talking after lights-out.

17. Hosokawa Minoru Nikki, December 7, 1941.

18. *Dōtokudai,* 124–125; *Yomoyama,* 41; Hosokawa Minoru Nikki, April 7, 1941.

19. *Senku* 1:262–263.

20. *Dōtokudai,* 115.

21. Ibid., 147–148.

22. *Yomoyama,* 14–16.

23. *Dōtokudai,* 129; *Yomoyama,* 31.

24. Chŏng Naehyŏk, *Kyŏkpyŏn ŭi saengae rŭl torabomyŏ: kijŏk ŭi kamyŏ, yŏksa nŭn namŭmyŏ: Chŏng Naehyŏk hoegorok* [Looking back on a tumultuous life: the miracle passes, history remains: the memoir of Chŏng Naehyŏk] (Seoul: Han'guk Sanŏp Yŏn'guwŏn, 2001), 40.

25. *Senku* 1:66–67.

26. Hosokawa Minoru Nikki, April 9, 1941.

27. Ibid., April 10, 1941; *RSG,* 145; *Senku* 1:54–59.

28. *Rikugun Shikan Gakkō seito oyobi gakusei kokoroe* [JMA regulations for cadets and students], Rikugun Shikan Gakkō, March 1937 (henceforth *Kokoroe*), graphs (*fuzu*) 1.1, 1.2.

29. Ibid., 1.1–1.3. See also *Dōtokudai,* 149.

30. Hosokawa Minoru Nikki, May 11, 1941; *Yomoyama,* 30.

31. *Kokoroe,* chart (*fuhyō*) 3.

32. *Yomoyama,* 30.

33. Hosokawa Minoru Nikki, April 10, 1941; *RSG,* 145; *Senku* 1:54–59.

34. *Kokoroe,* graphs (*fuzu*) 2.1, 2.2. The hook could also be on the right side.

35. Ibid., graph (*fuzu*) 3.

36. *Yomoyama,* 31.

37. Hosokawa Minoru Nikki, April 3, 1941.

38. Ibid.

39. [Jacob Meckel], *Befehlsführung und Selbstständigkeit, von einem alten Truppenoffizier* [Command leadership and independence, by an old troop officer] (Berlin: Mittler und Sohn, 1885), 62, 64.

40. Ōhama Tetsuya and Ozawa Ikurō, eds., *Teikoku Riku-Kaigun jiten* [Dictionary of the imperial army and navy] (Tokyo: Dōseisha, 1984), 122. See also Yamazaki Keiichirō, *Guntai naimu kyōiku* [Instruction in army interior administration] (Tokyo: Takumasha, 1943), 16. On "interior administration" and the history of the handbook, see Ōhama and Ozawa, *Teikoku Riku-Kaigun jiten*, 118–119; Ōe Shinobu, *Tennō no guntai* [Army of the emperor] (Tokyo: Shōgakkan, 1982), 85–90.

41. Zhu Huan and Wang Jinhyue, interview, Changchun, August 28, 1992; Xu Shudong, interview, Changchun, August 29, 1992.

42. See, for example, Hosokawa Minoru Nikki, April 3, 1941. The term is not used today.

43. Ibid.

44. Kim Muk, interview, Seoul, May 28, 1997.

45. See, for example, Hosokawa Minoru Nikki, April 12, 1941.

46. *Kokoroe*, 4–7. See also *RSG*, 137–139.

47. Especially in the first months after matriculation. See Hosokawa Minoru Nikki, April 13, 1941; April 24, 1941; May 11, 1941.

48. *Dōtokudai*, 124; *Yomoyama*, 35; Hosokawa Minoru Nikki, April 13, 1941.

49. *Dōtokudai*, 135.

50. See picture in Rikugun Shikan Gakkō, *Manshūkoku Gunkan Gakkō dai-nikisei: Shōwa 19-nen 4-gatsu 20-nichi sotsugyō* [The MMA 2 class: graduated April 20, 1944], personal property of Sekine Tomiji, copy in Yasukuni Kaikō Bunkoshitsu, Tokyo.

51. Kiyoizumi Nobuo, interview, Tokyo, January 12, 2011.

52. Kaneko Tomio, interview, Tokyo, January 12, 2011.

53. Cai Chongliang, interview, Elyria, OH, May 17, 1997. See also Hosokawa Minoru Nikki, April 23, 1941.

54. Hosokawa Minoru Nikki, April 12, 1941.

55. Kim Muk, interview, Seoul, May 28, 1997; Kiyoizumi Nobuo, interview, Tokyo, January 12, 2011.

56. Hosokawa Minoru Nikki, April 12, 1941; *Sakufū banri*, 181.

57. Kaneko Tomio, interview, Tokyo, January 12, 2011.

58. *Senku* 1:65.

59. *Yomoyama*, 160.

60. Letters from Kim Kwangsik to author, July 23, 2011; July 26, 2011. The episode is also briefly mentioned in the MMA 7 class history. See *Dōtokudai*, 160.

61. Kyōiku Sōkanbu, *Gunjin chokuyu kinkai* [Respectful understanding of the Imperial Rescript to Soldiers and Sailors] (Tokyo: Gunjin Kaikan Toshobu, 1944), 70–71.

62. Rikugunshō, *Sakusen yōmurei* [Field service regulations], Part I: Kōryō (Tokyo: Ikeda Shoten, 1970 [1938]), 10.

63. Peter B. High, *The Imperial Screen: Japanese Film Culture in the Fifteen Years' War, 1931–1945* (Madison: University of Wisconsin Press, 2003), 387, 488, 503. The film was lost or deliberately destroyed at the end of the war.

64. *Dōtokudai*, 189.

65. See Jūzenkai, ed., *Ato ni tsuzuku mono o shinzu: Gunshin Wakabayashi chūtaichō tsuitōroku* [Believe that others will follow: Memorial record of the war-god company commander Wakabayashi] (Sakai: Jūnzenkai, 1993); Mainichi Shinbunsha, ed., *Wakabayashi Tōichi chūtaichō* [Company commander Wakabayashi Tōichi] (Tokyo: Mainichi Shinbunsha, 1944). On Tahara Kōzō, see Chapter 7.

66. Yu Yangsu, interview, Seoul, May 27, 1997.

67. Kim Kwangsik, letter to author, July 26, 2011.
68. Ibid.
69. According to Kim Muk: "Park loved the younger officers with whom he associated. If they came to his home, he would feed them, take them drinking. So the younger officers followed him." Kim Muk, interview, Seoul, May 28, 1997. Kim Chongp'il told me almost exactly the same thing: "Park loved his subordinates. He used his small salary to buy drinks for them, invited them to his house. That's how I met my wife." Kim Chongp'il, interview, Seoul, August 22, 2000. Kim married Park's niece, the daughter of Park's older brother, Pak Sanghŭi. On Pak Sanghŭi, see Chapter 6. Both men were speaking of Park's relationship with subordinates in the ROKA in the years between 1946 and 1961.
70. *Dōtokudai,* 137. See also *RSG,* 146–147.
71. *RSG,* 60, 148; *Dōtokudai,* 196; *Yomoyama,* 59–60.
72. *Yomoyama,* 169–172.
73. *RSG,* 147–148.
74. Chŏng Ilgwŏn, *Chŏng Ilgwŏn hoegorok* [Memoir of Chŏng Ilgwŏn] (Seoul: Koryŏ Sŏjŏk, 1996), 79; Kim Muk, interview, Seoul, May 28, 1997.
75. Park Chung Hee had been an exceptional case in this regard. See Chapter 3.
76. Rikugun Yoka Shikan Gakkō Seitotai, *Seito kun'iku no jissai* [Practicum of cadet moral education], March 1942, 132–134.
77. Kim Muk, interview, Seoul, May 28, 1997; *CWZ,* 157–158.
78. *Yomoyama,* 152–153. Hiruma's "ugly eagle" died in combat after graduating from the JMA. Hiruma says he could imagine him "charging gloriously to death" in battle. See Chapter 3.
79. See entry for *sessa-takuma* in Morohashi Tetsuji, *Dai Kan-Wa jiten* [Japanese dictionary of Chinese characters], 13 vols. (Tokyo: Taishūkan Shoten, 1989–1990). See also *Dōtokudai,* 158.
80. *Kokoroe,* 3.
81. Gao Qingyin, interview, Las Vegas, March 11, 1997.
82. Hosokawa Minoru Nikki, May 29, 1942; *Senku* 1:284.
83. *Dōtokudai,* 188; Origuchi Ryūzō et al., interview, Tokyo, September 1, 1990; *Kokoroe,* 32–33. Needless to say, Park Chung Hee did not reveal his marital status during his academy years. Gao Qingyin, interview, Las Vegas, March 11, 1997.
84. Hosokawa Minoru Nikki, April 3, 1941. See also *Yomoyama,* 160–162.
85. Rikugun Yoka Shikan Gakkō Seitotai, *Seito kun'iku no jissai,* 132–134. It seems clear from the manual that what the officer was describing in personal terms as "narrow-mindedness" and "self-centeredness" was actually more a result of the Korean cadet's natural sense of ethnic difference and loneliness in a new and unfamiliar environment. See also Chapter 3.
86. Kim Muk, interview, Seoul, May 28, 1997.
87. Hosokawa Minoru Nikki, June 7, 1941.
88. On the various duties of the *torishimari seito,* see *RSG,* 131–132, 140–141; *Yomoyama,* 35–37; *Dōtokudai,* 132–135.
89. *RSG,* 141–142; *Dōtokudai,* 131–132.
90. Michel Foucault, "Technologies of the Self," in *Technologies of the Self: A Seminar with Michel Foucault,* ed. Luther H. Martin, Huck Gutman, and Patrick H. Hutton (Amherst: University of Massachusetts Press, 1988), 49.
91. Rikugun Yoka Shikan Gakkō Seitotai, *Seito kun'iku no jissai,* beginning with the first page of the first chapter.
92. Hosokawa Minoru Nikki, November 24, 1941.
93. *Yomoyama,* 20–23; *Dōtokudai,* 136. See also Hosokawa Minoru Nikki, April 16, 1941.
94. Rikugun Yoka Shikan Gakkō Seitotai, *Seito kun'iku no jissai,* 9.

95. Ibid., 46–132, esp. 46–49.
96. Foucault, "Technology of the Self," 27.
97. Rikugun Yoka Shikan Gakkō Seitotai, *Seito kun'iku no jissai,* 25–69.
98. Ibid., 26.
99. *Yomoyama,* 27–28; Rikugun Yoka Shikan Gakkō Seitotai, *Seito kun'iku no jissai,* 46. Yano's red-inked comments begin on the third page of the first entry in Hosokawa's diary. See Hosokawa Minoru Nikki, April 3, 1941.
100. Rikugun Yoka Shikan Gakkō Seitotai, *Seito kun'iku no jissai,* 27.
101. Gao Qingyin, interview, Las Vegas, March 11, 1997.
102. *Yomoyama,* 27–28. In his recent book on diary writing during World War II, where he examined two hundred diaries by Chinese, Japanese, and American servicemen, Aaron Moore also argues strongly that such diaries were effective tools of self-discipline, "employed by individuals to become more efficient and effective as a person," even if they did not represent the "whole truth" of the person. He also emphasizes, rightly in my view, how critical such diaries were for securing active support for the war effort. The soldier's act of developing a coherent voice in the diary, he writes, had "profound implications for social discipline in times of total war: strange as it may sound for the wartime period, ultimately the state did not command, it had to suggest, and even then its success, was dependent on the willingness of individuals to accept (and their ability to understand) its message." Moore, *Writing War: Soldiers Record the Japanese Empire* (Cambridge, MA: Harvard University Press, 2013), esp. 2–17, 299–303.
103. Rikugun Yoka Shikan Gakkō Seitotai, *Seito kun'iku no jissai,* 26; Hosokawa Minoru Nikki, April 3, 1941.
104. Rikugun Yoka Shikan Gakkō Seitotai, *Seito kun'iku no jissai,* 26.
105. See Hosokawa Minoru Nikki.
106. Ibid.
107. Ibid.
108. Nishikawa Nobuyoshi, interview, January 10, 2011. Unfortunately, to the best of my knowledge, there are no extant diaries of Korean MMA cadets, including Park Chung Hee, and according to Kaneko Tomio, Hosokawa's diary may be the only surviving diary of the MMA 2 class as a whole. Kaneko Tomio, interview, Tokyo, January 12, 2011.
109. Gao Qingyin, interview, Las Vegas, March 11, 1997.
110. Hosokawa Minoru Nikki, August 3, 1941.
111. *Dōtokudai,* 160–161.
112. For a fascinating if sobering history of corporal punishment in the United States, see Philip J. Greven, *Spare the Child: The Religious Roots of Punishment and the Psychological Impact of Physical Abuse* (New York: Knopf, 1990).
113. See, for example, Sun Joo Kim and Jungwon Kim, eds., *Wrongful Deaths: Selected Inquest Records from Nineteenth-Century Korea* (Seattle: University of Washington Press, 2014), 130–132. See also Charles Dallet, *Traditional Korea* (New Haven, CT: Human Relations Area Files, 1954), 67–72. On punishments in Tokugawa Japan, see Daniel V. Botsman, *Punishment and Power in the Making of Modern Japan* (Princeton, NJ: Princeton University Press, 2005), 14–40. Botsman also notes: "As anyone who has read Foucault's account of the 1757 execution of Damiens the regicide is aware, Europe's absolute monarchs were just as capable of devising horrifying methods of execution as the fiercest of Japanese warlords, and in general it is fair to say that penal practices in early modern Europe and Japan differed from each other not so much in kind, as in degree" (131). See also Michel Foucault, *Discipline and Punish: The Birth of the Prison,* trans. Alan Sheridan (New York: Vintage Books, 1979), 3–6.
114. Martina Deuchler, "The Practice of Confucianism: Ritual and Order in Chosŏn Dynasty Korea," in *Rethinking Confucianism: Past and Present in China, Japan, Korea, and*

Vietnam, ed. Benjamin A. Elman, John B. Duncan, and Herman Ooms (Los Angeles: UCLA Asian Pacific Monograph Series, 2002), 292–334, esp. 312–334.

115. See Yu Yŏngik, *Kabo Kyŏngjang yŏn'gu* [Studies on the Kabo reforms] (Seoul: Ilchogak, 1990), 244. On the Kabo reforms, see Chapter 1.

116. Yi Mun'gŏn, *Yangarok* [Record of child-rearing], trans. Yi Sangju (Seoul: T'aehaksa, 1997), 151–152. I am grateful to Professor Sun Joo Kim for bringing this book to my attention.

117. James B. Palais, *Confucian Statecraft and Korean Institutions: Yu Hyŏngwŏn and the Late Chosŏn Dynasty* (Seattle: University of Washington Press, 1996), 179.

118. An Taehoe, *Tanwŏn p'ungsokto ch'ŏp* [Genre paintings of Kim Hongdo] (Seoul: Miŭmsa, 2005), 8–9. For an actual photograph of a similar scene in late nineteenth- or early twentieth-century Chosŏn Korea, see *Sajin ŭro ponŭn Chosŏn sidae* [The Chosŏn period through photographs: everyday life and customs], text by Cho P'ungyŏn (Seoul: Sŏmundang, 1986), 14.

119. Sin Yongha, *Sin Ch'aeho ŭi sahoe sasang yŏn'gu* [Studies on the social thought of Sin Ch'aeho] (Seoul: Han'gilsa, 1984), 13.

120. Yi Mun'gŏn, *Yangarok*, 152.

121. Boudewijn Walraven, "Reader's Etiquette, and Other Aspects of Book Culture in Chosŏn Korea," in *Books in Numbers: Seventy-Fifth Anniversary of the Harvard Yenching Library: Conference Papers,* ed. Wilt Idema (Cambridge, MA: Harvard Yenching Library, 2007), 243.

122. *Paekpŏm Ilchi: The Autobiography of Kim Ku,* trans. Jongsoo Lee (Lanham, MD: University Press of America, 2000), 23.

123. See, for example, *Chosŏn ilbo,* March 23, 1926 (fist-beating), *Chosŏn ilbo,* June 30, 1926 (kicking to death), *Tonga ilbo,* May 23, 1927 (beating with baseball bat/broken arm), *Tonga ilbo,* August 4, 1927 (wild beating with stick), *Tonga ilbo,* November 26, 1929 (beating until student passes out), *Tonga ilbo,* April 25, 1936 (beating to death with hammer), *Tonga ilbo,* May 19, 1938 (beating/bone fracture), *Tonga ilbo,* July 28, 1938 (beating to death). This is only a small sampling of countless such cases and stories in the 1920s and 1930s that were reported in the newspapers. The pupils included both boys and girls. It is probably fair to say that many more cases, perhaps the majority, went unreported. See also Satō Hideo's remembrance of wartime beatings and slappings "half for pleasure" at his elementary school in Japan (Ibaragi) in Haruko Taya Cook and Theodore F. Cook, *Japan at War: An Oral History* (New York: The New Press, 1992), 234.

124. See *Tonga ilbo,* April 21, 1935, August 19, 1935, April 13, 1940; *Chosŏn ilbo,* August 15, 1936.

125. See Edward J. Drea, *Japan's Imperial Army: Its Rise and Fall, 1853–1945* (Lawrence: University Press of Kansas, 2009), 68, 134–135, 259; Ōe Shinobu, *Tennō no guntai,* 86–87.

126. Hosokawa Minoru Nikki, April 27, 1941.

127. Cai Chongliang, interview, Elyria, OH, May 17, 1997.

128. *CWZ*, 105.

129. Gao Qingyin, interview, Las Vegas, March 11, 1997.

130. Ibid.; Hosokawa Minoru Nikki, May 15, 1941, and May 2, 1941; *Dōtokudai*, 158, 160; *CWZ,* 4; *Yomoyama,* 157.

131. Hosokawa Minoru Nikki, May 11, 1941; Gao Qingyin, interview, Las Vegas, March 11, 1997.

132. Pang Wŏnch'ŏl, interview, Seoul, May 30, 1997.

133. On West Point, see, for example, Philip W. Leon, *Bullies and Cowards: The West Point Hazing Scandal, 1898–1901* (Westport, CT: Greenwood Press, 2000), which details the notorious hazing scandal at the American military academy between 1898–1901, which in the end led to congressional legislation in March 1901 officially prohibiting all forms

of hazing. See also Theodore J. Crackel, *West Point: A Bicentennial History* (Lawrence: University Press of Kansas, 2002), 141–145.

134. *Dōtokudai*, 176–177. Chŏng Naehyŏk notes that such "bed assaults," as well as emergency musters at night, were considered part of the essential training for officers, who had to be prepared at all times for unexpected attacks. See Chŏng Naehyŏk, *Kyŏkpyŏn ŭi saengae rŭl torabomyŏ*, 40.

135. Cai Chongliang, interview, Elyria, OH, May 17, 1997.

136. Gao Qingyin, interview, Las Vegas, March 11, 1997.

137. Zhu Huan and Wang Jinhyue, interview, Changchun, August 28, 1992.

138. Ōhama Tetsuya and Ozawa Ikurō, *Teikoku Riku-Kaigun jiten*, 402; Terada Chikao, *Nihon guntai yōgoshū*, 1:234–236; *Senku* 1:66. See also Meirion Harries and Susie Harries, *Soldiers of the Sun: The Rise and Fall of the Imperial Japanese Army* (London: Heinemann, 1991), 482.

139. *CWZ*, 39; *Senku* 1:285.

140. Kim Muk, interview, Seoul, May 28, 1997.

141. *Senku* 1:285, 1:341; Kiyoizumi Nobuo, interview, Tokyo, January 12, 2011.

142. *Dōtokudai*, 177.

143. *CWZ*, 157.

144. Kaneko Tomio, email to author via Suzuki Michihiko, April 14, 2013.

145. *Dōtokudai*, 158.

146. On usage of the term, see *Dōtokudai*, 157–158.

147. Hosokawa Minoru Nikki, April 27, 1941.

148. Ibid., May 15, 1941.

149. Ibid., July 5, 1941.

150. Ibid., September 20, 1941.

151. Kim Kwangsik, interview, Seoul, January 8, 2011.

152. Hosokawa Minoru Nikki, July 5, 1941.

153. Ibid., April 27, 1941; April 3, 1941; September 20, 1941.

154. Gao Qingyin, interview, Las Vegas, March 11, 1997; Hosokawa Minoru Nikki, May 11, 1941.

155. Gao Qingyin, interview, Las Vegas, March 11, 1997.

156. See Nanba Kōji, *Uchiteshi yaman: Taiheiyō Sensō to kōkoku no gijutsushatachi* [Never stop fighting: the Pacific War and the engineers of advertising] (Tokyo: Kōdansha, 1998).

157. Xu Shudong, interview, Changchun, August 29, 1992.

158. Kim Muk, interview, Seoul, May 28, 1997.

159. *CWZ*, 39.

160. Hosokawa Minoru Nikki, June 30, 1941. My thanks to Hosokawa's classmates Kaneko Tomio and Kiyoizumi Nobuyoshi, who confirmed this interpretation of the diary entry in an e-mail to the author via Suzuki Michihiko, April 13, 2013.

161. Gao Qingyin, interview, Las Vegas, March 11, 1997.

162. Kaneko Tomio, e-mail to author via Suzuki Michihiko, April 14, 2013. However, the Zama portion of Hosokawa's diary has been lost; Hosokawa Minoru, e-mail to author via Suzuki Michihiko, March 6, 2011.

163. Hosokawa Minoru Nikki, February 10, 1942.

164. Kaneko Tomio, e-mail to author via Suzuki Michihiko, April 14, 2013. See also Chapter 4.

165. Rikugunshō, "Rikugun Jikan kōen yōshi," 1–5; "Gunki fūki ni kansuru shiryō." See also Chapter 7.

166. Yamazaki Keiichirō, *Guntai naimu kyōiku*, 58–70.

167. Pang Wŏnchol, interview, Seoul, May 30, 1997.

168. Gao Qingyin, interview, Las Vegas, March 11, 1997.

169. Hosokawa Minoru Nikki, December 1, 1941; December 3, 1941.
170. *CWZ*, 157–158. Xu Shudong, interview, Changchun, August 29, 1992.
171. *CWZ*, 158.
172. *Dōtokudai*, 158.
173. Gao Qingyin, interview, Las Vegas, March 11, 1997.
174. Takezawa Rikio, interview, Tokyo, January 12, 2011.
175. Stanley G. Payne, *A History of Fascism 1914–45* (Madison: University of Wisconsin Press, 1995), 488. Payne sees the roots of this aspect of European fascism in Sorel's idea of the moral character of violence (28). This same idealized conception of violence was also very much at the core of the academies' understanding of *sessa-takuma*, which in turn was seen as central to the cadets' moral training (*kun'iku*). The *Interior Administration Handbook*, for example, the key manual for barracks life and *kun'iku*, made a sharp distinction between the positive, educative idea of *kun'iku* or *sessa-takuma*, and the purely negative idea of "punishment" (*shobatsu*). See Yamazaki Keiichirō, *Guntai naimu kyōiku*, 61–63.
176. On the "monster" epithet, see, for example, Tariji Ikuzō, *Shōwa no yōkai: Kishi Nobusuke* [The monster of Shōwa: Kishi Nobusuke] (Tokyo: Gakuyō Shobō, 1979). On Kishi's "embarrassment," see *Asahi shinbun*, November 13, 1961. On Park's 1961 visit to Japan, see also Chapter 4.

Conclusion

1. The new policy since MMA 6 had been to integrate the classes. Koreans in the MMA 7 were fully integrated with the Japanese from matriculation. Chinese were scheduled to be integrated from the second term, which had not yet begun in early August 1945. Nishikawa Nobuyoshi, interview, Yokohama, January 10, 2011. See also Chapter 3.
2. *Dōtokudai dai-shichikisei shi* [History of the MMA 7 class], ed. Dōtokudai Dai-Shichikiseikai (Tokyo: Dōtokudai Dai-Shichikiseikai, 1990) (henceforth *Dōtokudai*), 231.
3. *Dōtokudai*, 809–810; David M. Glantz, *The Soviet Strategic Offensive in Manchuria, 1945: "August Storm"* (London: Frank Cass, 2003), 139–181; Alvin D. Coox, *Nomonhan: Japan against Russia, 1939* (Stanford, CA: Stanford University Press, 1985), 1061, 1067; Nishikawa Nobuyoshi, interview, Yokohama, January 10, 2011.
4. Coox, *Nomonhan*, 1066–1067. Coox says that even as late as August 1945 the higher echelons of the Kwantung Army were living in a "fool's paradise."
5. Ibid., 1061.
6. Ibid., 1058–1064. See also Edward J. Drea, *Japan's Imperial Army: Its Rise and Fall, 1853–1945* (Lawrence: University Press of Kansas, 2009), 250.
7. Coox, *Nomonhan*, 1064.
8. Ibid, 1064–1065.
9. Ibid., 1066; *Dōtokudai*, 236; Glantz, *The Soviet Strategic Offensive in Manchuria*, 358.
10. *Dōtokudai*, 36–37. On Yamada, see *SJS* (Rikugun), 255.
11. *Dōtokudai*, 36.
12. Kiyoizumi Nobuo, "Manshūkoku Rikugun Gunkan Gakkō" [The MMA] (n.d., personal compilation, courtesy of Kiyoizumi Nobuo), 5.
13. Nishikawa Nobuyoshi, "Manshūkokugun tenbyō" [An outline of the Manchukuo Army], series of twelve monthly articles in *Kaikō* (January–December 2000), article 12; *Rikugun Shikan Gakkō* [The Japanese Military Academy], ed. Yamazaki Masao, with the collaboration of the Kaikōsha, 4th ed. (Tokyo: Akimoto Shobō, 1984) (henceforth *RSG*), 119.
14. There were two Koreans in the MMA 4 class, who were completing their *honka* at the MMA; and there were four Koreans in the MMA 7 class. See "Korean MMA Cadets by Class" in the appendix.

15. Nishikawa Nobuyoshi, interview, Yokohama, January 10, 2011; see also *Dōtokudai*, 236.

16. *Dōtokudai*, 809–810.

17. Ibid., 36.

18. Nishikawa Nobuyoshi, interview, Yokohama, January 10, 2011. Between the emperor's announcement and the cease-fire on August 15 and the formal surrender on September 2, the cabinet ordered all ministries to destroy their records, including those of the War Ministry and General Staff, and similar orders were also sent out to all army units. See Drea, *Japan's Imperial Army*, 260. On the departure: *RSG*, 119; *Manshūkokugun* [The Manchukuo Army], ed. Manshūkokugun Kankō Iinkai (Tokyo: Ranseikai, 1970) (henceforth *MG*), 776; *Dōtokudai*, 237–238.

19. Nishikawa Nobuyoshi, interview, Yokohama, January 10, 2011. *Dōtokudai*, 37.

20. *Dōtokudai*, 38.

21. Nishikawa Nobuyoshi, interview, Yokohama, January 10, 2011.

22. *Dōtokudai*, 38–39; *RSG*, 119.

23. *Dōtokudai*, 38–39. Nishikawa Nobuyoshi, interview, Yokohama, January 10, 2011.

24. Nishikawa Nobuyoshi, interview, Yokohama, January 10, 2011; *Chiru sakura: Rikushi dai-57-ki senbotsusha kiroku* [Fallen cherry blossoms: the record of the fallen soldiers of the JMA 57 class], ed. Rikushi 57-ki Kaikō Bunko Taisaku Iinkai Senbotsusha Kiroku Sakuseihan (Tokyo, Rikushi 57-ki Dōkiseikai, 1999), 832–834. The classmates were Asano Hideo, Inari Teizō, and Tsukai Yaichi.

25. Kim Tonghun, interview, Seoul, July 11, 1990.

26. *Dōtokudai*, 37–38.

27. Ibid., 38.

28. Ibid., 810.

29. Coox, *Nomonhan*, 1073.

30. Ibid., 1072.

31. See *Chiru sakura*, 836.

32. *Sakufū banri: Manshūkoku Gunkan Gakkō nikisei no kiroku* [The north wind of ten thousand leagues: the record of the MMA 2 class] (Hadano: Dōtokudai Nikiseikai, 1981), 185.

33. *Dōtokudai*, 38; *Chiru sakura*, 839. Drea notes that "for all the bluster about one's responsibility to emulate samurai values, only about 600 officers committed suicide to atone for their roles in bringing Japan to defeat and disaster . . . just 22 of the army's 1,501 generals." Drea, *Japan's Imperial Army*, 261. What is interesting for our purposes, however, is that those officers who arguably exercised the most influence on Park Chung Hee in terms of his IJA training, especially Arikawa Shuichi at TNS and Tahara Kōzō at the JMA, to say nothing of Superintendent Ushijima and the classmates mentioned here, belonged to that zealous minority.

34. *Dōtokudai*, 38–39.

35. Ibid., 39. Nishikawa Nobuyoshi, interview, Yokohama, January 10, 2011; Nishikawa Nobuyoshi, "Manshūkokugun tenbyō," article 12; Coox, *Nomonhan*, 1074. Of those who left the group, Nishikawa notes that ten died or went missing in Manchuria or Korea. See also *RSG*, 120, which cites the total number of MMA 7 cadets who never returned to Japan as 94. On the Japanese POW experience in Siberia, see Andrew E. Barshay, *The Gods Left First: The Captivity and Repatriation of Japanese POWs in Northeast Asia, 1945–1956* (Berkeley: University of California Press, 2013).

36. *Dōtokudai*, 810–811. Ironically, the cadets had "worked hard" to build the shrine, completed only weeks earlier. Kim Kwangsik, interview, Seoul, June 17, 2014. See also Chapter 3.

37. Nishikawa Nobuyoshi, interview, Yokohama, January 10, 2011. According to Nishikawa, who remained in Changchun throughout the Soviet occupation, the Russians

used the MMA as a barracks for their troops, because it could accommodate up to 2,000 troops. In 1992, however, when I visited the former MMA, which was then being used as an elite armored vehicle school for the People's Liberation Army (PLA), my guide, who was a full colonel in the PLA, told me that the school had not been occupied by the Soviets or Chinese until 1952, when it was taken over by the PLA.

38. The main sources for this section include RSG, 86–97; Rikugun Shikan Gakkō dai-rokujūkisei shi [History of the JMA 60 class], ed. Rokujūkiseikai (Tokyo: Rokujūkiseikai, 1978), esp. 411–419; Kiyoizumi Nobuo, "Manshūkoku Rikugun Gunkan Gakkō." Direct quotations and information from other sources are explicitly noted.

39. There was no MMA 5 Nikkei. The MMA 5 Nikkei had been incorporated into the MMA 6 Nikkei. Kiyoizumi Nobuo, "Manshūkoku Rikugun Gunkan Gakkō," 5.

40. All Koreans originally in the MMA 5 Mankei at Lalatun were moved into the MMA 4 Nikkei and went on to Zama. Kiyoizumi, "Manshūkoku Rikugun Gunkan Gakkō," 5. See also Byōbō senri: sanju kinen gō [The boundless thousand miles: on the anniversary of our 80th year of age], ed. Dōtokudai Yonkiseikai (n.p.: Dōtokudai Yonkiseikai, 2004), 2:137. MKJ (63) incorrectly lists the MMA 5 Koreans as being "probationary officers" (minarai shikan) in August 1945, but in fact they had not yet graduated from the JMA.

41. See Yi Kidong, Pigŭk ŭi kun'indŭl: Ilbon Yuksa ch'ulsin ŭi yŏksa [Soldiers of tragedy: a history of the graduates of the JMA] (Seoul: Ilchogak, 1982), 287–288. One of the MMA 6 Koreans, Kim Yun'gŭn, commander of the First Marine Brigade in 1961, would lead the coup forces across the Han River into Seoul on May 16. See Se-Jin Kim, The Politics of Military Revolution in Korea (Chapel Hill: University of North Carolina Press, 1971), 93. See also Kim Yun'gŭn, Haebyŏngdae wa 5.16 [The Marine Corps and May 16] (Seoul: Pŏmjosa, 1987), 36–50; Kim Yun'gŭn, interview, Seoul, July 20, 1990.

42. RSG, 92.

43. The exact meaning of this term is not clear, except that it refers to branches separate from the infantry, artillery, engineers, signal, and transport, all of which had been evacuated. RSG, 92.

44. Kim Yun'gŭn, Haebyŏngdae wa 5.16, 165; Kim Kwangsik, e-mail to author, January 28, 2016.

45. RSG, 97.

46. Today known as Camp Zama, it serves as the headquarters of the United States Army Japan. See Community Relations Office, U.S. Army Garrison, Japan, "The Camp Zama Historical Monument Walking Tour," March 21, 2005, 4–5.

47. Koreans had been exposed to many other forms of nationalism since the late nineteenth century, but none before with a military class and militarist ethos at its core. See, for example, Pak Ch'ansŭng, Minjok, minjokjuŭi [Nation, nationalism] (Seoul: Sohwa, 2010), 17–202. See also Sin Yongha, Han'guk kŭndae sahoe sasangsa yŏn'gu [Studies of Korean modern social thought] (Seoul: Ilchisa, 1987); Chong-Sik Lee, The Politics of Korean Nationalism (Berkeley: University of California Press, 1963); Michael Robinson, Cultural Nationalism in Colonial Korea, 1920–1925 (Seattle: University of Washington Press, 1988); Kenneth M. Wells, New God, New Nation: Protestants and Self-Reconstruction Nationalism in Korea, 1896–1937 (Honolulu: University of Hawaii Press, 1990); Andre Schmid, Korea between Empires: 1895–1919 (New York: Columbia University Press, 2002); Shin Gi-Wook, Ethnic Nationalism in Korea: Genealogy, Politics, and Legacy (Stanford, CA: Stanford University Press, 2008).

48. Yi Hallim, interview, Seoul, July 12, 1990.

49. Nishikawa Nobuyoshi said that the MMA 7 Koreans who were with him in Changchun in Superintendent Yamada's defensive combat unit "disappeared" on August 15. Nishikawa Nobuyoshi, interview, Yokohama, January 10, 2011. Kim Kwangsik, who was one of the MMA 7 Koreans with Nishikawa, said before the Russians arrived, his Japanese

company commander, Oikawa Shōji, went to one of the Xinjing banks and demanded money at gunpoint, which he subsequently distributed to Kim and the other cadets in his company, telling them to leave the unit if they wished. Eventually Kim found his way back to Seoul, arriving on November 3, 1945. Kim Kwangsik, interview, Seoul, June 17, 2014.

50. Kim Tonghun, interview, Seoul, July 11, 1990.

51. Kim Yŏngt'aek, interview, Seoul, May 31, 1997.

52. Kim Kwangsik, interview, Seoul, June 17, 2014. See also *Manjugukkunji* [Record of the Manchukuo Army], ed. Kim Sŏkpŏm (CTS 5) (n.p., 1987), courtesy of Kim Yun'gŭn (henceforth *MKJ*), 92; *Dōtokudai*, 301–302.

53. Sources on Park Chung Hee's Rehe deployment at the end of the war include *MKJ*, 82–85; Sin Hyŏnjun, *No haebyŏng ŭi hoegorok* [Memoir of an old marine] (Seoul: Katollik Ch'ulp'ansa, 1989), 65–72; Pang Wŏnch'ŏl, interview, Seoul, May 30, 1997; Gao Qingyin, interview, Las Vegas, March 11, 1997.

54. Kim Muk and Kim Min'gyu, interview, Seoul, May 28, 1997. Kim Yun'gŭn (MMA 6) and Kim Kwangsik (MMA 7) were also from the south, although Kim Yun'gŭn was attending middle school in Mukden when he applied to the MMA; Kim Kwangsik was a graduate of the same middle school in Kwangju (South Chŏlla) as Chŏng Naehyŏk and Yu Yangsu. Kim Kwangsik, interview, Seoul, January 8, 2011; Kim Yun'gŭn, *Haebyŏngdae wa 5.16*, 32. On Chŏng and Yu, see Chapter 3.

55. Chŏng Chaegyŏng, ed., *Pak Chŏnghŭi silgi: haengjŏk ch'orok* [The true record of Park Chung Hee: selected excerpts] (Seoul: Chimmundang, 1994), 15; Han Yongwŏn, *Ch'anggun* [Creating an army] (Seoul: Pagyŏngsa, 1984), 95; *Yukkun Sagwan Hakkyo samsimnyŏnsa* [Thirty-year history of the Korean Military Academy], ed. Yuksa Samsimnyŏnsa P'yŏnch'an Wiwŏnhoe (Seoul: Yukkun Sagwan Hakkyo, 1978), 558; Robert K. Sawyer, *Military Advisors in Korea: KMAG in Peace and War*, ed. Walter G. Hermes (Washington, DC: Center of Military History, United States Army, 1988), 14.

56. Yu Yangsu, interview, Seoul, June 11, 1996. Yu mentioned that in the late 1940s, when he worked with Park in South Korean army intelligence, they would often go out drinking together at the end of the day, and Park would frequently sing the Showa Restoration song. According to Yu, "Park loved the song." Yu, who later joined Park in the 1961 coup, also told me that the song "captured the spirit of May 16."

KOREAN MMA CADETS BY CLASS (期)

MMA 1
13 KOREANS
(ENTERED APRIL 1939)

Preparatory Course 豫科 and Main Course 本科 at MMA
(Graduated from Main Course December 16, 1942)

Kang Imsun 姜任淳
Kim Tongha 金東河
Pang Wǒnch'ǒl 方圓哲
Yi Kigǒn 李奇建
Yun T'aeil 尹泰日

Preparatory Course 豫科 at MMA and Main Course 本科 at JMA
(Graduated from Main Course December 17, 1942)

Ch'oe Ch'angnyun 崔昌崙 (JMA 56)
Ch'oe Ch'angǒn 崔昌彦 (JMA 56)
Cho Yǒngwǒn 趙永遠 (JMA 56)
Kim Min'gyu 金敏圭 (JMA 56)
Kim Yǒngt'aek 金永澤 (JMA Intendance 経理学校)
Pak Imhang 朴林恒 (JMA 56)
Yi Chuil 李周一 (JMA 56)
Yi Sun 李淳 (JMA Intendance 経理学校)

MMA 2
11 KOREANS
(ENTERED APRIL 1940)

Preparatory Course 豫科 and Main Course 本科 at MMA
(Graduated from Main Course May 1, 1944)

An Yǒnggil 安永吉
Ch'oe Ch'angsǒn 崔昌善
Kim Muk 金默
Kim Wǒn'gi 金元起
Yi Chaegi 李再起
Yi Pyǒngju 李丙冑
Yi Sangjin 李尚振

Preparatory Course 豫科 at MMA and Main Course 本科 at JMA
(Graduated from Main Course April 20, 1944)

Kim Chaep'ung 金在豊 (JMA 57)
Pak Chŏnghŭi (Park Chung Hee) 朴正熙 (JMA 57)
Yi Hallim 李翰林 (JMA 57)
Yi Sŏpchun 李燮俊 (JMA 57)

MMA 3
2 KOREANS
(ENTERED APRIL 1941)

Preparatory Course 豫科 at MMA and Main Course 本科 at JMA
(Graduated from Main Course June 17, 1945)

Ch'oe Chujong 崔周種 (JMA 58)
Kang T'aemin 姜泰敏 (JMA 58)

MMA 4
2 KOREANS
(ENTERED MARCH 1942)

Preparatory Course 豫科 and Main Course 本科 at MMA
(Enrolled in Main Course at MMA on August 15, 1945)

Chang Ŭnsan 張銀山
Ye Kwansu 芮琯壽

MMA 5
5 KOREANS
(ENTERED JANUARY 29, 1943)

Preparatory Course 豫科 at MMA and Main Course 本科 at JMA
(Enrolled in Main Course at JMA on August 15, 1945)

Hwang T'aengnim 黃澤林 (JMA 59)
Kang Munbong 姜文奉 (JMA 59)
Kim T'aejong 金泰種 (JMA 59)
Yi X (Given name unknown) 李 某 (JMA 59)
Yi Yongsul 李容述 (JMA 59)

MMA 6
11 KOREANS
(ENTERED APRIL 1944)

Preparatory Course 豫科 at MMA
(Serving Medical and Veterinary Regimental Attachment Duty 隊附勤務 on August 15, 1945)

Andō Takeshi (Korean name unknown) 安藤 猛
Kim Tonghun 金東勳
Niibara X (Japanese given name unknown; Korean name unknown) 新原 某
Yuk Kwoengsu 陸宏修

Preparatory Course 豫科 at MMA and Main Course 本科 at JMA
(Enrolled in Main Course at JMA on August 15, 1945)

Chŏng Chŏngsun 鄭正淳 (JMA 60)
Kim Hangnim 金鶴林 (JMA 60)
Kim Kijun 金基濬 (JMA 60)
Kim Sehyŏn 金世鉉 (JMA 60)
Kim Sŏkkwŏn 金錫權 (JMA 60)
Kim Uch'un 金遇春 (JMA 60)
Kim Yun'gŭn 金潤根 (JMA 60)

MMA 7
4 KOREANS
(ENTERED DECEMBER 1944)

Preparatory Course 豫科 at MMA
(Enrolled in Preparatory Course at MMA on August 15, 1945)

Chŏn Sanghyŏk 田相爀
Han Chinil 韓珍一
Kim Kwangsik 金光植
Kim Yunsŏn 金允善

GLOSSARY OF NAMES AND TERMS

In the following list of Chinese, Japanese, and Korean names and terms appearing in the book, I have generally adhered to the *pinyin*, Hepburn, and McCune-Reischauer romanization systems, respectively, making exceptions for familiar or conventional spellings in English such as Manchukuo, Tokyo, and Park Chung Hee.

Ach'im isŭl　아침이슬

aeguk ŭi ttŭt　愛國의뜻

ai no muchi　愛の鞭

Aizawa Saburō　相沢 三郎

Akasaka　赤坂

akaten　赤店

Akiyama Hiizu　秋山秀

Akiyama Yoshitaka　秋山義隆

Amakasu Masahiko　甘粕正彦

Amaterasu Ōmikami　天照大神

An Yŏnggil　安永吉

Andō Toyosaburō　安藤豊三郎

Anshan　鞍山

Ansŏng (J: Anjō)　安城

Arabian naito　アラビアンナイト

Arakawa Yoshiaki　荒川嘉彰

Araki Sadao　荒木 貞夫

Arikawa Shuichi　有川主一

Ariyoshi Chūichi　有吉忠一

Asahi　朝日

Asaka　朝霞

Asano Hideo　浅野秀雄

Ato ni tsuzuku o shinzu　後に続くを信ず

Atsugi　厚木

Ba Jin　巴金

Bai Guohua　白国华

baka-majime　馬鹿真面目

Banbishan　半壁山

Bandaisan　磐梯山

banzai　万歳

bata　バタ

Benxihu　本溪湖

Binjiang　濱江

binta　びんた (鬢打)

binta kyōiku　びんた教育

bōin bōshoku　暴飲暴食

boku　僕

bōzugari　坊主刈り

bujin no michi, shi no michi　武人の道, 死の道

buka　部下

Bungei shunjū　文藝春秋

bunka seiji　文化政治

buntai (K: *pundae*)　分隊

bushidō　武士道

busu mochi　ブス餅

buyū　武勇

Cai Chongliang　蔡崇樑

chaebŏl (J: *zaibatsu*)　財閥

Chang Chirak　張志樂

Chang Toyŏng　張都英

Changchun　长春

Changch'ungdong　奬忠洞

changgwan　將官

Changsŏng　長城

Changyongwi　壯勇衛

Cheju　濟州

Chiang Kai-shek (Jiang Jieshi)　蔣介石

chikai　誓い

Chikuma　千曲

chimidoro no　血みどろの

Chin Tuhyŏn　陳斗鉉

chinbojŏk 進步的

chinji hage 眞摯하게

Chinmuyŏng 鎭撫營

Chinwidae 鎭衛隊

Ch'inwidae 親衛隊

Cho Kapche 趙甲濟

Cho Usŏk 趙禹錫

Cho Yŏngwŏn 趙永遠

Ch'oe Ch'angŏn 崔昌彦

Ch'oe Chujong 崔周種

Ch'oe Rin 崔麟

chojŏng kwa chido kamdok 調整과 指導監督

chōkei 長兄

chōki enshū 長期演習

chōki sōryokusen no dankai 長期總力戰の段階

ch'ŏkkyŏl 剔抉

Chŏlla 全羅

Chŏng Ilgwŏn 丁一權

Chŏng Naehyŏk 丁來赫

Chŏng Sangsu 鄭祥秀

Chŏng Yagyong 丁若鏞

chŏnggye rŭl chŏnghwa 政界를 淨化

ch'ongjang 總長

Chŏngjo 正祖

Chŏnju 全州

Chosa Sich'altan 朝士視察團

Chōsengun 朝鮮軍

Chōshū 長州

Chosŏn (J: Chōsen) 朝鮮

Chosŏn ilbo 朝鮮日報

chūdan no kamae 中段の構え

chūgi (K: *ch'ungŭi*) 忠義

chūi 注意

chūkaku 中核

chūkonhi   忠魂碑

Ch'unch'ŏn   春川

Ch'ungch'ŏng   忠清

chungdae (J: *chūtai*)   中隊

chungdaejang   中隊長

ch'ungjang   忠壯

Chūō kōron   中央公論

Chūreitō   忠霊塔

chūsetsu   忠節

chūtai   中退

Cui Lifu   崔立夫

daha   打破

-dai   台

dai-go   第五

Dai Manshū Teikoku Rikugun Gunkan Gakkō   大満州帝国陸軍軍官学校

Dai Nihon Teikoku Rikugun Shikan Gakkō   大日本帝国陸軍士官学校

Dai-ni binbō monogatari   第二貧乏物語

daikōri   大行李

Daitō Shinsuke   大東信祐

Daitōjuku   大東塾

Dalian (J: Dairen)   大連

dan   段

danketsu (K: *tan'gyŏl*)   団結

danketsu o kyōkō ni shi   団結を鞏固にし

Datong   大同

Deng Chang   邓昶

dengeki   電撃

deshi   弟子

dokittoshite   ドキッとして

doko made mo kōgeki   何処迄も攻撃

dokudan senkō   独断専行

Dongning   东宁 (東寧)

-dono   殿

dōtoku   同徳

Dōtokudai　同徳台

Enami Shigeru　江波茂

Endō Yoshikazu　遠藤善一

Enoshima　江の島

enryo　遠慮

eppuku　悦服

erabutsu　偉物

Erdaohezi　二道河子

fuhyō　附表

Fuji Takeshi　富士雄

Fujimuro Ryōsuke　藤室良輔

Fujino Ranjō　藤野鸞丈

fukai kanshin　深い関心

Fukaya Tadashi　深谷正

fukkan　副官

Fukui　福井

fukujū no bitoku　服従の美徳

Fukushima　福島

Fukuzawa Yukichi　福沢諭吉

fundoshi　褌

funkotsu-saishin　粉骨砕身

Furuyama Hiroshi　古山浩

fushinban　不寝番

Fushun　抚順

fuzu　附図

Gakushūin　学習院

ganbari　頑張り

Gao Qingyin　高庆印 (高慶印)

gaoliang　高粱

gara　ガラ

gen'an　原案

genchi senjutsu　現地戦術

genjō hakai no shisō　現状破壊の思想

genjū　厳重

genki　元気

Genshinden　原神殿

Gesshō　月照

Go-Ichigo　五・一五

gochō　伍長

gomin　ゴミン

gōrei chōsei　号令調声

gōshi　郷士

gōshi　合祀

gozoku kyōwa　五族協和

Gunjin Chokuyu　軍人勅諭

gunjin no tamashii　軍人の魂

gunkanku (C: *junguanou*)　軍管区

Gunma　群馬

gunseigaku　軍制学

gunshin　軍神

gunsō　軍曹

guntō issen　軍刀一閃

Guo Enlin　郭恩霖

Guo Songling　郭松齢

Guomindang (Kuomintang)　國民黨

Hachiōji　八王子

Hagakure　葉隠

haktodae　學徒隊

hakujaku　薄弱

hakusha o kakete　拍車をかけて

Hamgyŏng　咸鏡

Hamhŭng　咸興

ha'myŏn toe nŭn kŏsida　하면되는것이다

Hanabusa Yoshimoto　花房義質

Han'guk ilbo　韓國日報

hanran　叛乱

hansei　反省

Hansŏng chubo　漢城周報

Hansŏng sunbo 漢城旬報

Harbin 哈尔滨

Harubin/Harupin Gakuin ハルピン/ハルピン 学院

hasagwan 下士官

Hashimoto 橋本

Hata Shinji 秦真次

Hebei 河北

Heihe 黑河

heika 兵科

heiki juyoshiki 兵器授与式

Heilongjiang 黑龙江

Higashikuni (no miya) Toshihiko 東久邇(宮)俊彦

hinkon katei 貧困家庭

Hirabayashi Morito 平林盛人

Hirano Kuniomi 平野國臣

hirō 疲労

Hirohito 裕仁

Hirose Takeo 広瀬武夫

Hiroshima 広島

Hiruma Hiroshi 比留間弘

hisshō no shinnen 必勝の信念

hitotsu-kokoro ni maishin 一つ心に邁進

hittō 筆筒

hōdoku 奉読

hoech'ori 회초리

Hoegyeguk 會計局

Hōjō 北条

hōkoku 報告

Hokushin 北辰

hŏnbyŏngdae 憲兵隊

Hong Kyŏngnae 洪景來

Hong Saik 洪思翊

Hong Tusŭng 洪斗承

Hong Yŏngsik 洪英植

Honjō Shigeru　本庄繁

honka　本科

hooe　號外

Horimoto Reizō　堀本禮造

Hōshu Ikkō　宝珠一幸

hōsō　奉送

Hosokawa Minoru　細川実

hōtai　奉戴

hotondo kawarazu　殆ど変わらず

Howidae　扈衛隊

huangdi　皇帝

Hubei　湖北

hubi　後備

Huifuhui　恢复会

Hullyŏndae　訓錬隊

Hullyŏndae Sagwan Yangsŏngso　訓錬隊士官養成所

Hŭngnam　興南

Hwagyesa　華溪寺

Hwangbo Kyun　皇甫均

Hwanghae　黄海

Hwimun Ŭisuk　徽文義塾

hyakushō　百姓

Hyŏn Chunhyŏk　玄俊赫

Hyŏn Sangyun　玄相允

Hyŏngmyŏng Ilsimhoe　革命一心會

hyŏnyŏk　現役

Ibayashi Kiyonaga　井林清長

Ichigaya　市ヶ谷

Ichigayadai　市ヶ谷台

Ichikawa Ennosuke　市川 猿之助

Ichikawa Kon　市川崑

ichinen okoru to　一念起ると

Iida Shōjirō　飯田祥二郎

Ikeda Kiyoshi　池田清

Ikegami Kunio   池上邦夫

Ilbonsik sagwan kyoyuk   日本式 士官 教育

Im Chihyŏn   임지현

Imamura Hirozumi   今村博純

Inari Teizō   稲荷定三

Inoue Kaoru   井上馨

Inukai Tsuyoshi   犬養毅

inzū   員数

inzū ga awanai   員数が合わない

ipchi   立志

ippen   一変

ishi   意志

ishi no tanren   意志の鍛錬

Ishikawa Seijirō   石河清二郎

Ishiwara Kanji   石原 莞爾

Ishizeki Sakae   石関栄

Isobe Asaichi   磯部浅一

Isobe Kei   磯部圭

isshi gohōkō   一死御奉公

isshin dōtai   一身同体

issho kenmei ni   一所懸命に

Itagaki Seishirō   板垣 征四郎

Itochū   伊藤忠

Iwai Masatoshi   岩井正俊

iyashiku nari   賤しくなり

janku   ジャンク

Jiandao   间岛 (K: Kando   間島)

jidōsha   自動車

jijaku   自若

jiken   事件

jiko   事故

jiko o osame   自己を修め

jiko shūyō   自己修養

Jilin   吉林

jinchi kōchiku　陣地構築

jin'insen　人員戦

Jinzhou　金州

jippei shiki　実兵指揮

jisei　辞世

jishu sekkyoku　自主積極

jōkan　上官

jūdō　柔道

junshi　殉死

junshoku　殉職

jūten sangyō　重点産業

Kabo　甲午

Kabo-Ŭlmi　甲午-乙未

kabuki　歌舞伎

kae tari ch'ulsin　개다리 출신

kaebal tokchae　開發獨裁

kaehwa (J: *kaika*)　開化

Kagawa Yoshio　香川義雄

Kageyama Masaharu　影山正治

Kagoshima　鹿児島

kagyō no taiyō　課業の大要

kaifuku　恢復

Kaigun　海軍

Kaikō　偕行

Kaikōsha　偕行社

kaizen seichō　改善整調

kaizō　改造

kakeashi　駆け足

kakka (K: *kakha*)　閣下

kakoku　苛酷

kakubu　各部

kakumei　革命

kakushin　革新

kamaboko　蒲鉾

Kamakura　鎌倉

kami sama　神様

kamikaze　神風

Kanagawa　神奈川

Kanbe Hajime　神戸肇

kanbu kōhosei　幹部候補生

Kanda Yasunosuke　神田泰之助

Kaneko Tomio　金子富男

Kang Chaeho　姜在浩

Kang Ch'angsǒn　姜昌善

kangai-muryō　感慨無量

Kangde　康徳

Kanghwa　江華

kangp'o　強暴

Kangwǒn　江原

Kan'in (no miya) Kotohito　閑院(宮)載仁

Kanno Hiroshi　菅野弘

kantan　簡単

Kantō　関東

Kantokuen　関特演

Kapsin　甲申

Kashii Kōhei　香椎浩平

Kawakami Hajime　河上肇

Kawanakajima　川中島

Kawashima Yoshiyuki　川島義之

keibigun (C: *jingbeijun*)　警備軍

Keijō　京城

keikaku　計画

kekki (K: *kwǒlgi*)　蹶起

kendai　見台

kendō　剣道

kenkoku　建国

Kenkoku Chūreibyō　建国忠霊廟

Kenkoku Daigaku/Kendai　建国大学/建大

kenzen 健全

kesshi dankō 決死断行

kesshin 決心

kessho (K: *hyŏlsŏ*) 血書

Ketsumeidan 血盟団

ketten 欠点

ki 期

kiai 気合

Kido Kōin 木戸 孝允

Kiguchi Kohei 木口小平

kihap 氣合

Kihara Yoshio 木原義雄

kiken shūkan 危険週間

Kim Chaech'un 金在春

Kim Chaegon 金載坤

Kim Chaehak 金載學

Kim Chaep'ung 金在豊

Kim Chŏngnyŏm 金正濂

Kim Chongp'il 金鍾泌

Kim Chongsin 金鐘新

Kim Dae Jung (Kim Taejung) 金大中

Kim Honam 金浩南

Kim Hongdo 金弘道

Kim Hongjip 金弘集

Kim Hyŏngsŏp (J: Kin Kyōshō) 金亨燮

Kim Il Sung (Kim Ilsŏng) 金日成

Kim Kisu 金綺秀

Kim Ku 金九

Kim Kwangsik (Kim Kwangsic) 金光植

Kim Min'gi 김민기

Kim Muk 金默

Kim Okkyun 金玉均

Kim Sŏgwŏn 金錫源

Kim Tongha 金東河

Kim Tonghun　金東勳

Kim Ujung　金宇中

Kim Yŏnggi　金永驥

Kim Yŏngsu　金泳秀

Kim Yŏngt'aek　金永澤

Kim Yun'gŭn　金潤根

kimi　君

kinenkan　記念館

Kinugasa Teinosuke　衣笠 貞之助

Kirokkuk　記錄局

kisama　貴樣

Kishi Nobusuke　岸信介

Kishi Yonesaku　岸米作

Kita Ikki　北一輝

Kitano Kenzō　北野憲造

Kitsurin Kaidō　吉林街道

Kiyoizumi Nobuo　清泉信男

Kobayashi Tamaki　小林環

Kōbe　神戸

kobushi　古武士

Kodama Gentarō　児玉源太郎

Kōdōha　皇道派

Kōfu　甲府

kōgeki seishin　攻擊精神

kŏgukchŏgin hwansong　擧國的인 歡送

kōhai　後輩

kōhosei　候補生

kōhosha gakuseitai　候補者学生隊

Koiso Kuniaki　小磯国昭

kōjōgun　江上軍

Kojong　高宗

kōka　皇化

kokka　国家

kokka sōdōin keikaku　国家総動員計画

kokō　股肱

Kokoroe　心得

kokorogamae　心構

kokorozashi　志

Koksŏng　谷城

Kokubō no hongi to sono kyōka no teishō　国防の本義とその強化の提唱

kokubō no jishu　国防の自主

kokumin　国民

kokuritsu bunka chiiki　国立文化地域

kokutai　国体

Kōmoto Daisaku　河本大作

Kŏmsaguk　檢査局

Kōno Etsujirō　河野悦次郎

konzetsu　根絶

kōryō　綱領

Koshigoe　腰越

kōtei　皇帝

Kugenuma　鵠沼

Kukka wa hyŏngmyŏng kwa na　國家와 革命과 나

Kumi　龜尾

Kunbu　軍部

kŭndaehwa　近代化

kun'guk segye　軍國世界

kun'gukchuŭi　軍國主義

kun'iku (K: *hunyuk*)　訓育

Kunisada Chūji　國定忠治

kunji　訓示

Kunmuguk　軍務局

Kunmusa　軍務司

kŭnsin　勤愼

kunwa　訓話

Kuroda Shigenori　黒田重徳

Kusabuka Hachirō　草深八郎

Kusumoto Sanetaka　楠本實隆

kutai 区隊

kutaichō 区隊長

kutori 区取

kutsujoku 屈辱

kutta 굳다

Kuwahara Ryōichi 桑原良一

k'waedo 快刀

Kwangju (Chŏlla) 光州

Kwangju (Kyŏnggi) 廣州

Kwangmu 光武

Kwangmyŏng 光明

Kwantung (Kantô) 関東

kyahan 脚絆

kyōdō itchi 協同一致

Kyododae 教道隊

Kyōdōdan 教導団

kyogwandan 教官團

Kyōiku Buchō 教育部長

kyōjubu 教授部

kyōjubuchō 教授部長

kyōko naru ishi 鞏固なる意志

Kyŏnggi 京畿

Kyŏngsang 慶尙

Kyŏngun (Tŏksu) 慶運 (德壽)

kyōrenhan 教練班

Kyōto 京都

kyoyuk 教育

kyūmin 窮民

Kyūshū 九州

Lalatun 拉拉屯

Li Tiancheng 李天成

Liaodong 辽东

Liaoyang 辽阳

Liu Qian 刘前

Liu Qimin   刘启民

Liu Yushan   刘玉善 (劉玉善)

Longshou   龙首

Lü Dianyuan   吕殿元

Lu Wenkong   鲁文孔

Lu Xun   鲁迅

Lüshun   旅顺

machi   町

Maeil sinbo   每日申報

majime   真面目

Manai Tsurukichi   真井鶴吉

Man-chan   満チャン

Manchukuo (Manshūkoku)   満州国

Man'ei   満映

Manjianghong   满江红

Mankei   満系

mankwa   萬科

Manshū shinbun   満州新聞

Mao Dun   茅盾

Maruyama Masao   丸山眞男

Matsui Shigeru   松井滋

Matsui Takurō   松井太久郎

Matsumura Hiroshi   松村弘

Matsuoka Yōsuke   松岡 洋右

Matsuzaki Naoomi   松崎直臣

mattaku dōitsu   全く同一

Mazaki Jinzaburô   真崎甚三郎

mei kudasareta   命下された

meian   名案

Meiji   明治

meikaku naru kito no moto ni   明確なる企図の下に

meirō   明朗

Mejiro   目白

Mikasa (no miya) Takahito   三笠(宮)崇仁

Min Yŏngik　閔泳翊

Minami Jirō　南次郎

minarai shikan　見習士官

Minjok kaejoron　民族改造論

misogi　禊

Mito　水戸

Mitsubishi　三菱

Mitsui Katsuo　三井勝夫

Miura Gorō　三浦梧樓

miya　宮

Miyamoto Masami　宮本正巳

Miyanogahara　宮原

Mizumachi Takezō　水町竹三

mobo　モボ

Mochizuki　望月

mondai　問題

Moriwaki Tameo　森脇為雄

mu　武

muban　武班

Mudanjiang　牡丹江

Mugwan Hakkyo　武官學校

Mukden (Fengtian)　奉天

mun　文

munban　文班

Mun'gyŏng　聞慶

muni-musan　無二無三

munyak　文弱

Muranaka Takaji (Kōji)　村中孝次

musan (J: *musan*)　無産

musanja (J: *musansha*)　無産者

musi musi han　무시무시한

Mutō Yoichi　武藤与一

myŏngnang　明朗

Nagano　長野

Nagasaki　長崎

Nagata Tetsuzan　永田 鉄山

Nagumo Katsurō　南雲克郎

Nagumo Shin'ichirō　南雲親一郎

nagure　殴れ

Nai-Sen ittai　内鮮一体

naimen shidō　内面指導

naimu　内務

Nakahashi Motoaki　中橋基明

Nakajima Kanji　中島莞爾

Nakajima Tadaaki　中島忠秋

Nakano Hidemitsu　中野英光

Nanba Shōroku　難波正六

Nanguan　南关

nanjaku　軟弱

Nanjing　南京

Nanling (J: Nanryō)　南岭

Nanshan　南山

neji　ネジ

nekketsukan　熱血漢

Ni-Niroku　二・二六

Nihon kaizō hōan taikō　日本改造法案大綱

Nihon kokumin　日本国民

Niigata　新潟

Nikkei　日系

nikki　日記

nikudan　肉弾

Nippon Teikoku banzai　日本帝国万歳

Nishida Mitsugi　西田税

Nishigaki Makoto　西垣命

Nishikawa Nobuyoshi　西川順芳

Nishiuchi Masashi　西内雅

Nobi　野火

Noda Hiroshi　野田弘

Nogi Maresuke　乃木希典

Nogizaka　乃木坂

nōmin　農民

Nomonhan　ノモンハン

Nomura Saburō　野村三郎

Nonaka Shirō　野中四郎

Ŏ Chaesun　魚在淳

Ŏ Chaeyŏn　魚在淵

Ŏ Tam (Gyo Tan)　魚潭

O Wŏnch'ŏl　吳源哲

Ŏ Yunjung　魚允中

Obalt'an　誤發彈

Obata Toshishirō　小畑敏四郎

Oda Nobunaga　織田 信長

Odakyū　小田急

Ogasawara Harutsugu　小笠原春次

Ogiwara Ken'ichi　荻原健一

oidashikai　追い出し会

Oikawa Shōji　及川正治

Ōjōjihara　王城寺原

Oka Chōji　岡 長治

Oki Teisuke　沖禎介

Okinajima　翁島

Okinawa　沖縄

Ōkōchi Denjirō　大河内 傳次郎

okonau　行う

Ōkubo Toshimichi　大久保 利通

okuru　贈る

ŏmjunghan ch'wich'e　嚴重한 取締

omohayui　面映い

onna　女

onshi shōkin　恩賜賞金

Ōoka Shōhei　大岡昇平

ore　俺

Origuchi Ryūzō　折口龍三

Ōsaka　大阪

Ōsaka mainichi shinbun　大阪毎日新聞

ōsei　旺盛

Otakebi　雄叫

Otoko da; ganbaruzo　男だ頑張るぞ

otoko no naka no otoko　男の中の男

Ōyama　大山

Paek Nakch'ŏng (Nak-Chung Paik)　白樂 晴

Pak Cheok　朴在玉

Pak Imhang　朴林 恒

Pak Kyusu　朴珪壽

Pak Sanghŭi　朴相熙

Pak Ŭnsik　朴殷植

Pak Yŏnghyo　朴泳孝

Pak Yugwoeng　朴裕宏

Pang Kijung　방기중

Pang Wŏnch'ŏl　方圓哲

Park Chung Hee (Pak Chŏnghŭi)　朴正熙

Park Geun-hye (Pak Kŭnhye)　朴槿惠

p'asijŭm　파시즘

p'asisŭt'ŭ　파시스트

pisŏ silchang　秘書室長

ponggŏn　封建

pojŭngin　保證人

Pujie　溥杰(溥傑)

Pukch'ŏng　北靑

pukhak　北學

pulsu　不數

Pusan　釜山

pusilchang　副室長

Puyi　溥仪(溥儀)

Pyŏlgigun　別技軍

P'yŏngan　平安

pyŏngbŏp 兵法

Pyŏngjo 兵曹

P'yŏngyang (J: Heijō) 平壤

Qing 清

Rai Sanyō 頼 山陽

Rehe 热河 (熱河)

reigi 礼儀

reikō 励行

ren (C: *lian*) 連

renchō (C: *lianzhang*) 連長

riko 利己

rikugun 陸軍

Rikugun Yoka Shikan Gakkō 陸軍予科士官学校

risō 理想

riyō 利用

Roka 蘆花

ryūchō de 流暢で

Ryūgakuseitai 留学生隊

sagam 舍監

Sagami 相模

Sagamihara 相模原

sahoe ŭi konggi 社會의 公器

saigo no saigo made ganbari 最後の最後まで頑張り

Saigō Takamori 西郷隆盛

saikō komon 最高顧問

Saitama 埼玉

Saitō Makoto 斉藤實

Sajima Hiroyuki 佐島博之

Sakai Masao 境正雄

Sakai Naoshi 坂井直

sake 酒

Sakufū banri 朔風万里

Sakuradamon 桜田門

Sakurakai 桜会

Sakusen yōmurei/Sakuyō　作戦要務令/作要

Samch'ŏlli　三千里

Samgunbu　三軍府

samurai　侍

san no san　3 の3

san-pachi shiki hoheijū dono　三八式歩兵銃殿

sangbi　常備

sangmu ŭi chŏngsin　尚武의 精神

sangmujŏk kyoyuk　尚武的教育

Sanjiang　三江

sasage-tsutsu　捧げ銃

Sasaki Sadao　佐々木貞雄

Sasaki Tōichi　佐々木到一

sasara-odori　ササラ踊り

Satō Katsurō　佐藤勝郎

Satō Tetsuo　佐藤哲夫

Satsuma　薩摩

seidai na kangei　盛大な歓迎

Seigunka　精軍課

seikaku　性格

seikan na kihaku　精悍な気魄

seiren　清廉

seishin　精神

seishin kunwa　精神訓話

seishin kyōiku　精神教育

seishinsen　精神戦

seitō　正当

seito　生徒

seiton　整頓

seitondana　整頓棚

seitotai　生徒隊

seitotaichō　生徒隊長

Sejima Ryūzō　瀬島龍三

sekai ishin　世界維新

Sekine Tomiji　関根富司

sekkyokuteki　積極的

seme　攻め

Sendai　仙台

Senjinkun　戦陣訓

senkō gakusei　専攻学生

sen'yūdō　戦友道

seppuku　切腹

sessa-takuma　切磋琢磨

sessakai　切磋会

shaba　娑婆

Shaho (Shahe)　沙河

Shandong　山東

Shanxi　山西

Shenyang　沈阳

Shi Weizhong　史维忠

Shibeiling　石碑岭

Shibuya Saburō　渋谷三郎

shidō seito　指導生徒

shijō　私情

shiki no yōketsu　指揮の要訣

shiko washi　シコワシ

Shimazu　島津

Shimonaga Kenji　下永憲次

shinai　竹刀

shindai gakuyū　寝台学友

shindai sen'yū　寝台戦友

shindai-shūgeki　寝台襲撃

shingi　信義

Shinjuku　新宿

shinkō (K: *sinhŭng*)　新興

shinkoku　神国

shinminzoku　神民族

shinpin　新品

shinrei　神霊

shinshu kisezu　心手期せず

Shintō　神道

shintori　寝取

Shirakami Genjirō　白神源次郎

shishi　志士

shishin o saru　私心を去る

shishin o sutete　私心を捨て

shisso　質素

shiteki seisai　私的制裁

Shixiongdi　十兄弟

shobatsu　処罰

shōbu　尚武

shōi kōhosha　少尉候補者

shokan　所感

shōkōri　小行李

shomin　庶民

shōtai (K: *sodae*)　小隊

Shōwa　昭和

Shōwa no yōkai　昭和の妖怪

shūban shikan　週番士官

shūgō　集合

shugū　殊遇

shuho　酒保

Shuifeng (J: Suihō; K: Sup'ung)　水丰

shuppatsuten　出発点

shūshinsho (K: *susinsǒ*)　修身書

shutō　手套

shutsujin no shiki　出陣の式

Shuzanpo　首山堡

sijo　時調

silchang　室長

silhak　實學

Sin Ch'aeho　申采浩

Sin Hyŏnjun　申鉉俊

Sin Kwanho　申觀浩

Sin Pongmo　申福模

Sin Yongha　愼鏞廈

Sindonga　新東亞

Sinsa Yuramdan　紳士遊覽團

Siwidae　侍衛隊

Sŏ Chaep'il　徐載弼

Sŏ Pyŏngguk　徐炳國

so-a　小我

Sōbudai　相武台

Sōbudai dayori　相武台便り

sŏdang　書堂

soe ppul hwigi　쇠뿔휘기

sōgūsen　遭遇戰

sōgyōdō　創業道

sokoku　祖国

Songhua　松花

Sŏnghwan (J: Seikan)　成歡

Sŏnjo　宣祖

Sŏnsan　善山

sōrōbun　候文

Sōryokusen Kenkyūjo　総力戦研究所

soshiki tōsei　組織統制

sōtei　想定

sōtori　総取

Sŏyu kyŏnmun　西遊見聞

Sudō Tsukasa　須藤司

sugekaeru　スゲカエル

Sugiyama Masayuki　杉山昌之

Sumitomo　住友

Sun Jingda　孫景大

Sun Yat-sen (Sun Yixian)　孫逸仙

Suwŏn　水原

Suzuki Michihiko　鈴木通彦

Suzuki Teruyuki　鈴木照行

Tabohashi Kiyoshi　田保橋潔

tachi-horoboshi　断ち滅ぼし

Tachibana Shūta　橘周太

Tachikawa　立川

Tada Hayao　多田駿

tae-a　大我

taedae　大隊

Taegu　大邱

Taehan Cheguk　大韓帝國

T'aenŭng　泰陵

Taewŏn'gun　大院君

Taewŏnsu　大元帥

tagai ni　互いに

Tahara Kōzō　田原耕三

Tahara Naotake　田原尚武

Tahara Yoshiko　田原由知子

taibatsu　体罰

taihen kinchō　大変緊張

taikan　耐寒

tainetsu　耐熱

tairiku otoko　大陸男

taizuki kinmu　隊付勤務

Takagi Masao　高木正雄

takai kokkashugi, kokuminshugi no shisō　高い国家主義、国民主義の思想

Takaishi Shingorō　高石真五郎

Takamatsu (no miya) Nobuhito　高松(宮)宣仁

Takasugi Shinsaku　高杉晋作

Takayama Toshitake　高山利武

Takebashi　竹橋

Takeda Shingen　武田信玄

Takeshita Yoshiharu　竹下義晴

Takezawa Rikio　竹沢力夫

tami 民

Tanaka Kinuyo 田中絹代

Tang Jirong 唐际荣

tan'gyŏl (J: *danketsu*) 團結

tan'gyŏl ŭi konggoch'i motham 團結의 鞏固치 못함

tantō 短刀

Tanzawa 丹沢

tasukeai 助け合い

tatami 畳

tennō 天皇

Tennō Heika banzai 天皇陛下万歳

Tenri 天理

Tiexueshe 铁血社

Toda Tokuji 戸田徳二

Tōgō Heihachirō 東郷平八郎

Tōhō 東宝

Tōhoku 東北

Tōjō Hideki 東条英機

tokchong 毒種

tokken kaikyū 特権階級

tokkōtai 特攻隊

toku ni taisetsu 特に大切

tokubetsu shitsu 特別室

Tokugawa Bakufu 徳川幕府

Tokugawa Ieyasu 徳川家康

tokui no shokubun 特異の職分

tokumoku 徳目

tokumu kikan 特務機関

Tōmiya Kaneo 東宮鉄男

Tong Zhishan 佟志杉

Tonga ilbo 東亞日報

Tonggyŏng chungdae sagŏn 東京重大事件

Tonghak 東學

Tonghua 通化

T'ongni Kimu Amun　統理機務衙門

T'ongni Kun'guksamu Amun　統理軍國事務衙門

Tongnip Hyǒphoe　獨立協會

Torikai Ikoma　鳥飼生駒

torishimari seito　取締生徒

Tōseiha　統制派

totsugeki　突撃

totsugeki fuseikō　突撃不成功

Toyama　戸山

Toyohashi　豊橋

Toyooka　豊岡

Toyotomi Hideyoshi　豊臣秀吉

tōzen　当然

Tsubokura Tadashi　坪倉正

Tsugiki Hajime　次木一

tsuigeki　追撃

Tsukai Yaichi　塚井弥一

Tsushima　津島

uchite shi yaman　撃ちてし止まむ

Uchiyama Kazuya　内山一弥

udǔngsaeng　優等生

Uesugi Kenshin　上杉兼信

Ugaki Kazushige　宇垣一成

Ŭijǒngbu　議政府

Ŭiju　義州

Umeda Unpin　梅田雲浜

Umezu Yoshijirō　梅津美治郎

Unzen　雲仙

Ushijima Mitsuru　牛島満

utsu　打つ (撃つ)

Wada Toshio　和田俊雄

waikyoku　歪曲

Wakabayashi Tōichi　若林東一

Wang Chengmei　王成美

Wang Jiashan   王家善

Wang Jingyue   汪静岳

Watanabe Akinori   渡辺昭徳

Watanabe Fujio   渡辺富士雄

Watanabe Jōtarō   渡辺 錠太郎

wigwan   尉官

Wŏn Yongdŏk   元容德

Wŏnsu   元帥

Wŏnsubu   元帥府

Wu Zongfang   吴宗方

Xianzhou   仙洲

Xing'an   兴安 (興安)

Xinjing (J: Shinkyō)   新京

Xu Dianxiang   徐殿鄉

Xu Shudong   徐树栋

yaei enshū   野営演習

Yagi Haruo   八木春雄

yakan kōgeki   夜間攻撃

yakan kōgun   夜間行軍

Yamada Otozō   山田乙三

Yamada Tetsujirō   山田鉄二郎

Yamagata Aritomo   山県有朋

Yamamoto Isoroku   山本五十六

Yamamoto Kenjirō   山本健次郎

Yamamoto Tsunetomo   山本常朝

Yamasaki Yasuyo   山崎保代

Yamashita Tomoyuki   山下奉文

Yanbian   延边

Yang Rizhe   杨日哲

Yang Saŏn   楊士彦

yangban   兩班

Yano Yutaka   矢野豊

Yanoi Hiroshi   八野井宏

yashū   夜襲

yasim 野心

Yasuda 安田

Yasuda Yutaka 安田優

Yasukuni 靖国

Yasukuni Kaikō Bunko 靖国偕行文庫

yebi 豫備

Yi Chinho 李軫鎬

Yi Chuil 李周一

Yi Hallim 李翰林

Yi Hyŏnggŭn 李亨根

Yi I (Yulgok) 李珥 (栗谷)

Yi Kwangsu 李光洙

Yi Mun'gŏn 李文楗

Yi Naksŏn 李洛善

Yi Pŏmsŏn 李範宣

Yi Pyŏngju 李丙冑

Yi Sangjin 李尙振

Yi Sŏnggye 李成桂

Yi Sŏngjo 李聖祚

Yi Sŏpchun 李燮俊

Yi Sunsin 李舜臣

Yi T'aejin 李泰鎭

Yi T'aeyŏng 李泰榮

Yi Ŭn 李垠

Yi Wŏnhoe 李元會

Yingkou 营口

Yitong 伊通

yizhi (J: *ishi*; K: *ŭiji*) 意志

yōhaijo 遥拝所

yoka 予科

Yokohama 横浜

Yokokawa Shōzō 横川省三

Yomiuri 読売

yŏndae (J: *rentai*) 聯隊

Yōnen Gakkō　幼年学校

yŏnggwan　領官

Yongsan　龍山

Yŏngjo　英祖

Yŏnmu Kongwŏn　錬武公院

Yoshida Katsusuke　吉田勝助

Yoshida Shōin　吉田松陰

Yoyogi　代々木

Yu Chŭngsŏn (Ryu Chungsun)　柳增善

Yu Hyŏngwŏn　柳馨遠

Yu Hyŏnmok　兪賢穆

Yu Kilchun　兪吉濬

Yu Qinghuai　于请淮

Yu Yangsu (Yoo Yangsoo)　柳陽洙

Yu Yŏngik (Lew Young Ick)　柳永益

Yuan Shikai　袁世凱

Yue Fei　岳飞

yūetsukan　優越感

yūgekitai　遊撃隊

Yuk Yŏngsu　陸英修

Yun Ch'idu　尹致斗

Yun Ch'iho　尹致昊

Yun Haedong　윤해동

Yun T'aeil　尹泰日

Yusin　維新

yūsō na　雄壮な

Zama　座間

zangeki　斬撃

zanshin　残心

zenryō　善良

zettai fukujū　絶対服従

Zhang Lianzhi　张连芝

Zhang Wenshan　张文善

Zhang Xueliang　张学良

Zhang Yousong　張友松

Zhang Zuolin　张作霖

Zhao Guoqi　赵国圻

Zhenyongshe　真勇社

Zhu Huan　朱寰

zuberu　ズベル

zuii jikan　随意時間

BIBLIOGRAPHY

Unpublished Sources

Chŏng Naehyŏk. Letter to author. September 26, 2009.

Fukuchi Akiko (granddaughter of Arikawa Shuichi). Letter to author. January 9, 2004.

Gao Qingyin. Correspondence with Yi Naksŏn. 1962. Courtesy of Gao Qingyin.

Hosokawa Minoru. Hosokawa Minoru Nikki [Hosokawa Minoru diary]. 7 vols. April 3, 1941–May 31, 1942. Courtesy of Hosokawa Minoru (via Suzuki Michihiko).

Kim Kwangsik (Kim Kwangsic). Letters and e-mails to author. 2011–2015.

Kishi Nobusuke Papers. National Diet Library, Tokyo.

Kiyoizumi Nobuo. "Manshūkoku Rikugun Gunkan Gakkō" [The MMA]. N.d. Personal compilation. Courtesy of Kiyoizumi Nobuo.

Nagumo Katsurō (eldest son of Nagumo Shin'ichirō). Letter to author. August 31, 1990.

Origuchi Ryūzō. Letter to author and collection of MMA 2 documents and photographs. Courtesy of Origuchi Ryūzō (via Suzuki Michihiko). November 13, 2003.

Pak Chŏnghŭi (Park Chung Hee). Handwritten letter to Chang Toyŏng. May 16, 1961. Courtesy of Kim Chaech'un (KMA 5).

———. Handwritten letter to Origuchi Ryūzō. December 2, 1961. Courtesy of Origuchi Ryūzō.

Pak Ŭnsik. Pak Ŭnsik chŏ [The works of Pak Ŭnsik]. Edited by Yi Manyŏl. Han'guk kŭndae sasangga sŏnjip 4. Seoul: Han'gilsa, 1980.

Pang Wŏnch'ŏl. "Kwangmyŏng Kodŭng Hakkyo yŏnhyŏk" [History of Kwangmyŏng High School]. Handwritten. Seoul, 1991. Courtesy of Pang Wŏnch'ŏl.

Rikugunshō. "Gunki fūki ni kansuru shiryō" [Documents relating to army and barracks discipline]. Vol. 1, Supplement to summary of remarks by Vice-Minister of War delivered at the assembly of army commanders and general defense commander on April 8, 1943. Secret. Tokyo: Rikugunshō, April 1943. In Selected Japanese Army and Navy Archives, Library of Congress, Washington, DC. Microfilm 5041, Reel 139.

———. "Rikugun Jikan kōen yōshi" [Summary of remarks by Vice-Minister of War]. Delivered at the assembly of army commanders and general defense commander on April 8, 1943. Top Secret. Tokyo: Rikugunshō, April 1943. In Selected Japanese Army and Navy Archives, Library of Congress, Washington, DC. Microfilm 5041, Reel 139.

Rikushikō Honbu. "Rikugun Shikan Gakkō rekishi" [History of the JMA]. Handwritten official history of the JMA through 1945. Bōei Kenkyūjo, Tokyo.

"Sijo." Handwritten collection of traditional Korean poems handed out by TNS English instructor Kim Yŏnggi and compiled by students of the TNS 4 class in the 1930s. Courtesy of Yi Sŏngjo.

Tahara Kōzō. Letters and postcards from Tahara Kōzō to his wife Tahara Yoshiko, and to Mizuno Kazumasa, Yoshiko's brother. July 1944–December 1944. Courtesy of Tahara Naotake, son of Tahara Kōzō.

Yasukuni Kaikō Bunkoshitsu. Kōjin jōhō [Personal database]. Tokyo: Yasukuni Jinja.

Yi Naksŏn. Papers. Courtesy of Cho Kapche.

Yoshida Shōichi. Letter to author (via Matsutani Motokazu). March 13, 2012.

Yu Yangsu. Letters to author. 1997–2006.

Yukkun Kodŭng Hoeŭi. Yukkun Kodŭng Hoeŭi myŏngnyŏng [Orders of the Army High Court]. Ministry of Defense (ROK). In the Chŏnsa Pyŏnch'an Wiwŏnhoe, Seoul. Courtesy of Pak Myŏngnim.

Government and IJA Textbooks and Other Primary Sources (Including MMA, JMA, and JMAP)

Chianbu Kanbō, ed. *Manshūkokugun reiki ruishū* [Regulations by category of the Manchukuo Army]. 2 vols. Shinkyō: Manshū Gyōsei Gakkai, 1942.

Chōsen hantō shusshin no moto Nihongun shōkō meibo [List of Koreans in the former Japanese Army officer corps]. Tokyo: Kōseishō, Hikiage Engo Fukuin Chōsaka, n.d.

Chōsen Sōtokufu. *Chōsen Sōtokufu oyobi shozoku kanshō shokuinroku* [Directory of the Chōsen Government-General and affiliated government offices]. Keijō: Hatsubaijō Chōsen Gyōsei Gakkai, 1940.

——. *Chūtō kyōiku shūshinsho 3* [Morals textbook for secondary education]. Keijō: Chōsen Kyōgaku Tosho, 1940.

——. *Futsū gakkō kokugo tokuhon 10.* [Elementary school national language reader 10]. Keijō: Chōsen Sōtokufu, 1934.

Chōsen Sōtokufu Gakumukyoku. *Chōsen ni okeru kyōiku kakushin no zenbō* [Full picture of the education reforms in Chōsen]. Keijō: Chōsen Sōtokufu Gakumukyoku Gakumuka, 1938.

Kōchō kunjishū (Yoka/Honka/Hohei Gakkō): dai-gojūrokukisei kunren shiryō [Collected lectures of the Superintendent (JMAP, JMA, Infantry School): training materials for the JMA 56 class]. Rikugun Shikan Gakkō, n.d.

Kyōiku Sōkanbu. *Gunjin chokuyu kinkai* [Respectful understanding of the Imperial Rescript to Soldiers and Sailors]. Tokyo: Gunjin Kaikan Toshobu, 1944.

——. *Hohei sentō kyōren* [Infantry combat training]. Kyōiku Sōkanbu, January 1945.

——. *Hohei sōten chūkai* [Infantry manual commentary]. Tokyo, Seibutō, June 20, 1940.

——. "Kyōiku Sōkan shodo junshi yōzu" [Sketch for the Inspector General's first tour of inspection]. Secret: Internal Use Only. Sōkanbu: Revised July 1939.

Kyōiku Sōkanbu, Dai-Nika. *Doitsu haisen to hisshō no shinnen* [The defeat of Germany and the belief in certain victory]. Reproduced for the JMAP. May, 7, 1945.

Kyōiku Sōkanbu, ed. *Kokushi kyōtei: Rikugun Yoka Shikan Gakkō yō* [National history textbook: for JMAP use]. 2 vols. Kyōiku Sōkanbu, n.d.

Manshū Teikoku Chianbu. *Manshūkoku shōkō seito shigansha no tame ni* [On Manchukuo officer and cadet volunteers]. Secret: Internal Use Only. Manshū Teikoku Chianbu, 1939.

Rikugun Shikan Gakkō. *Rikugun Shikan Gakkō sotsugyō jinmeibo: Meiji 30–Shōwa 16 (Dai-ikki-Dai-gojūgoki* [Roster of graduates of the JMA: 1897–1941 (JMA 1-JMA 55)]. N.p.: n.d.

Rikugun Shikan Gakkō kiji (abbreviated *Kiji*) [JMA Bulletin]. 1938–1945.

Rikugun Shikan Gakkō Kōchō Ushijima Mitsuru. *Gunseigaku kyōtei* [Military organization textbook]. Revised edition. 2 vols. 1943–1944.

——. *Senjutsugaku kyōtei 1* [Military tactics textbook 1]. Rikugun Shikan Gakkō, 1943 (November).

——. *Senshi kyōtei 1* [Miliary history textbook 1]. Rikugun Shikan Gakkō, October 1942.

Rikugun Shikan Gakkō Kōchō Yamamuro Munetake. *Kyōikugaku: zen* [Pedagogy: complete]. Rikugun Shikan Gakkō, 1939 (March).

Rikugun Shikan Gakkō seito oyobi gakusei kokoroe (abbreviated *Kokoroe*) [JMA regulations for cadets and students]. Rikugun Shikan Gakkō, 1937 (March).

Rikugunshō. *Chōsa ihō gōgai: 5.15 jiken rikugun gunpō kaigi kōhan kiji* [Investigative report extra issue: proceedings of the public trial of army court martial in connection with the 5.15 incident]. Tokyo: Rikugunshō, 1933.

——. *Kokubō no hongi to sono kyōka no teishō* [The essentials of national defense and a proposal for their strengthening]. Shinbunhan panfuretto. Tokyo: Rikugunshō, October 10, 1934.

——. *Sakusen yōmurei* [Field service regulations]. Tokyo: Ikeda Shoten, 1970. (Reprint of the 1938 edition).

Rikugun Yoka Shikan Gakkō Kōchō Amakasu Jūtarō. *Honpōshi kyōtei: zen* [Our national history: complete]. Rikugun Yoka Shikan Gakkō, 1937.

———. *Seito bunshū: 1927–1937* [Collection of cadet writings]. Rikugun Shikan Gakkō, 1937.

———. *Shinrigaku kari kyōtei (ippan shinri)* [Provisional psychology textbook: general psychology]. Rikugun Yoka Shikan Gakkō, 1937.

Rikugun Yoka Shikan Gakkō Kyōjūbu. *Kōgun hisshō no shinnen* [Belief in certain victory of the Imperial Army]. Rikugun Yoka Shikan Gakkō, 1944 (September 8).

Rikugun Yoka Shikan Gakkō Seitotai. *Seito kun'iku no jissai* [Practicum of cadet moral education]. N.p.: Rikugun Yoka Shikan Gakkō, 1942 (March).

Yamazaki Keiichirō. *Guntai naimu kyōiku* [Instruction in army interior administration]. Tokyo: Takumasha, 1943.

Zheng fu gong bao [Government gazette (Manchukuo)]. N.p.: 1934–1945.

Army, School, and Class Memorabilia
(Albums, Histories, Newsletters, Rosters, and Songbooks)

Byōbō senri: sanju kinen gō [The boundless thousand miles: on the anniversary of our 80th year of age]. 3 vols. Edited by Dōtokudai Yonkiseikai. N.p.: Dōtokudai Yonkiseikai, 2004.

Changchun wenshi ziliao 2 (abbreviated *CWZ*) [Changchun cultural history materials 2]. Edited by Changchun Shi Zhengxie Wenshi Ziliao Weiyuanhui. Changchun: Changchun Shi Zhengxie Wenshi Bangongshi Faxingzu, 1991.

Chiru sakura: Rikushi dai-57-ki senbotsusha kiroku [Fallen cherry blossoms: the record of the fallen soldiers of the JMA 57 class]. Edited by Rikushi 57-ki Kaikō Bunko Taisaku Iinkai Senbotsusha Kiroku Sakuseihan. Tokyo, Rikushi 57-ki Dōkiseikai, 1999.

Dai-yonjūshichikiseikai shi [JMA 47 bulletin]. Issues 1–10. Edited by Rikushi Dai-Yonjūshichiki-seikai.

Dōtoku: Manshūkoku Gunkan Gakkō Dōsōkai Tōgōkai shi [Dōtoku: Combined newsletter of the MMA graduates]. Dōtokudai Dōsōkai.

Dōtokudai dai-shichikisei shi (abbreviated *Dōtokudai*) [History of the MMA 7 class]. Edited by Dōtokudai Dai-Shichikiseikai. Tokyo: Dōtokudai Dai-Shichikiseikai, 1990.

Gojūshichikiseikai tsūshin [The 57th class news]. Tokyo: Rikushi 57-ki Dōkiseikai, Kaikōsha.

Heisei kyūnendo "Take no Kai dayori": seikaban [Heisei Year 9 "Take no Kai news": midsummer edition]. Edited by Take no Kai Kanjikai. N.p.: Rikushi Dai-Yonjūnikisei, 1996 (July 31).

Hohei Dai-Hachijū Rentai shi [History of the 80th Infantry Regiment]. Edited by Hohachi-jūkai. N.p.: Hohachijūkai, 1982.

Hokushin: gunka: Rikugun Gunkan Gakkō [North Star: army songs: MMA]. Edited by Hokushin Henshū Iinkai. Tokyo: Dōtokudai Dōsōkai, 1968.

Kankoku shusshin: Nihon Rikushi-Manshū Gunkō dōsōsei meibo [List of the Korean graduates of the JMA and MMA]. N.p., August 1975.

Manjugukkunji (abbreviated *MKJ*) [Record of the Manchukuo Army]. Edited by Kim Sŏkpŏm (CTS 5). N.p., 1987. Courtesy of Kim Yun'gŭn.

Manshūkokugun (abbreviated *MG*) [The Manchukuo Army]. Edited by Manshūkokugun Kankō Iinkai. Tokyo: Ranseikai, 1970.

Nakajima Toshiyuki. "Shūyō gyōji ichiranhyō: Rikugun Shikan Gakkō: dai-gojūhachikisei: Shōwa 19.5–20.6" [Calendar of important activities: JMA 58: May 1944–June 1945] February 1994. Courtesy of Chŏng Naehyŏk.

———. "Shūyō gyōji ichiranhyō: Rikugun Yoka Shikan Gakkō: dai-gojūhachikisei: dai- 32 chūtai: dai-6 kutai: Shōwa 17.4–18.11 [Calendar of important activities: JMAP 58: 32nd company: 6th section: April 1942–November 1943"] February 1994. Courtesy of Chŏng Naehyŏk.

Nishikawa Nobuyoshi. "Manshūkokugun tenbyō" [An outline of the Manchukuo Army]. Series of 12 monthly articles in *Kaikō* (January–December 2000).

Otakebi [War cry]. Edited by *Otakebi* Henshū Iinkai. Tokyo: Zaidan Hōjin Kaikōsha Jimukyoku, 1960.

Rikugun Shikan Gakkō (abbreviated *RSG*) [The Japanese Military Academy]. Edited by Yamazaki Masao, with the collaboration of the Kaikōsha. 4th ed. Tokyo: Akimoto Shobō, 1984.

Rikugun Shikan Gakkō. *Manshūkoku Gunkan Gakkō dai-nikisei: Shōwa 19-nen 4-gatsu 20-nichi sotsugyō* [The MMA 2 class: graduated April 20, 1944]. MMA 2 Class album. Personal property of Sekine Tomiji. Copy in Yasukuni Kaikō Bunkoshitsu, Tokyo.

———. *Sotsugyō shashinchō: Rikugun Shikan Gakkō dai-gojūshichikisei* [Graduation photo album: JMA 57 class]. Restricted. Rikugun Shikan Gakkō, 1944.

Rikugun Shikan Gakkō dai-rokujūkisei shi [History of the JMA 60 class]. Edited by Rokujūkiseikai. Tokyo: Rokujūkiseikai, 1978.

Rikugun Shikan Gakkō dai-yonjūshichikiseikai kaihō [JMA 47 newsletter]. Rikugun Shikan Gakkō Dai-yonjūshichikiseikai.

Rikugun Shikan Gakkō nijūichikiseikai kaihō [JMA 21 Newsletter]. Rikugun Shikan Gakkō Nijūichikiseikai.

Sakimori no fu: ninkan 40-shūnen kinen gojūniki [Genealogy of soldiers: on the 40th anniversary of the commissioning of the JMA 52 class]. Edited by Rikushi-Kōshi Dai-Gojūnikisei. Rikushi-Kōshi Dai-Gojūnikisei, 1979.

Sakufū banri: Manshūkoku Gunkan Gakkō nikisei no kiroku [The north wind of ten thousand leagues: the record of the MMA 2 class]. Hadano: Dōtokudai Nikiseikai, 1981.

Senku: kaikoroku [Vanguard: memoirs]. Edited by Dōtokudai Ikkiseikai. 2 vols. Tokyo: Dōtokudai Ikkiseikai, 1986–1987.

Sotsugyō kinen shashin: jinjōka dai-4 kai: Kanritsu Taikyū Shihan Gakkō [Graduation commemorative photos: the 4th class of the elementary school department of the Government Normal School of Taegu]. Edited by Taikyū Shihan Gakkō Arubamu Iin. Taegu: Eimei Shashinkan, 1937. Courtesy of Yi Sŏngjo.

Taegu Sabŏm simsanggwaji [History of the elementary school department of Taegu Normal School]. Edited by Han Sŏktong. Taegu: Taegu Sabŏm Simsanggwa Tongmunhoe, 1991. Courtesy of Cho Kapche.

Tairiku no kōbō: Manshūkokugun Nikkei gunkan yonkiseishi [Light of the continent: history of the CTS 4 Nikkei officers of the Manchukuo Army]. 2 vols. Edited by Manshūkokugun Nikkei Gunkan Yonkiseikai. Osaka, Manshūkokugun Nikkei Gunkan Yonkiseikai, 1983.

Tsuioku yonjūshichiki [Reminiscences of the JMA 47 class]. Edited by Rikushi Dai-Yonjūshichikiseikai, Rikushi Yonjūshichikiseikai, 1976.

Chinese Books and Articles

Sheng Ping, ed. *Zhongguo Gongchangdang renming da cidian* [Biographical dictionary of the Chinese Communist Party]. Beijing: Zhongguo Guoji Guangbo Chubanshe, 1991.

Zhongguo renmin da cidian: Dangdai renwu juan [China biographical dictionary: contemporary volume]. Shanghai: Shanghai Cishu Chubanshe, 1992.

Zhonggong renmin lu [Record of Chinese communist figures]. Revised edition. Taibei: Guoli Zhengzhi Daxue Guoji Guanxi Yanjiu Zhongxin, 1978.

Japanese Books and Articles

Asaka Chūtonchi Kōhōhan. *Kinenkan shiori* [Guide to the Memorial Hall]. Asaka: Asaka Chūtonchi Kōhōhan, n.d.

Berunherudi (fon). *Doitsu kōkoku ka metsubō ka* [Germany: world power or downfall]. Translated by Nishimura Jirō. Tokyo: Dōbunkan, 1916.

Chōsen jinji kōshinroku [Chōsen Biographical Directory]. Keijō: Chōsen Shinbunsha: Chōsen Jinji Kōshinroku Hensabu, 1935.

Chōsen toyū taikan [Survey of Chōsen cities and towns]. Keijō: Minshū Jironsha, 1937.

Daitōjuku sanjūnenshi [Thirty-year history of the Daitōjuku]. Edited by Daitōjuku Sanjūnenshi Hensan Iinkai. Tokyo: Daitōjuku Shuppanbu, 1972.

Fukuda Kazuya. *Yamashita Tomoyuki: Shōwa no higeki* [Yamashita Tomoyuki: Shōwa tragedy]. Tokyo: Bungei Shunjū, 2004.

Fukushi Tadashi. *Manshūkoku daigaku-senmon gakkō ryūgaku shiken mondai: zenka kaisetsu* [Manchukuo university and college entrance examination questions: explanations for all subjects]. Mukden: Manshū Tosho Monku Kabushiki Kaisha, 1943.

Gyo Tan (Ŏ Tam). "Gyo Tan Shōshō kaikoroku" [Memoir of Major General Ŏ Tam]. In *Nikkan gaikō shiryŏ*, ed. Ichikawa Masaaki, 10:3–186. Tokyo: Hara Shobō, 1981.

Haraguchi Kenzō, ed. *Rikugun gahō: rinji zōkan* [Army pictorial: special edition]. Tokyo: Rikugun Gahōsha, 1938.

Hatakeyama Seikō. *Tōkyō heidan* [Tokyo division]. 3 vols. Tokyo: Kōfūsha, 1963.

Hayashi Shigeru, ed. *Ni-niroku jiken hiroku.* [Secret record of February 26]. 4 vols. Tokyo: Shōgakkan, 1971–1972.

Hirabayashi Morito. *Waga kaikoroku: uzumaki no naka no zen'i* [Good intentions in the middle of a maelstrom]. Tokyo: Hirabayashi Morito Waga Kaikoroku Kankōkai, 1967.

Hiruma Hiroshi. *Rikugun Shikan Gakkō yomoyama monogatori* (abbreviated *Yomoyama*) [Sundry stories of the JMA]. Tokyo: Kōjinsha, 1983.

Hitora Ādorufu. *Waga tōsō* [My struggle]. Translated by Manabe Ryōichi. Tokyo: Kōfūkan, 1942.

Hittora Adorufu. *Waga tōsō* [My struggle]. Translated by Ōkubo Yasuo. Tokyo: Mikasa Shobō, 1937.

Hōchi Takayuki. *Harubin to Manshūkoku* [Harbin and Manchukuo]. Tokyo: Shinchōsha, 1999.

Jinjō shōgaku shūshinsho 1: jidōyō [Elementary school morals text 1: for children's use]. Tokyo: Monbushō, 1936.

Jōhō Yoshio. *Rikugunshō Gunmukyoku* [War Ministry Military Affairs Section]. Tokyo: Fuyō Shobō, 1979.

Jōhō Yoshio, ed. *Rikugun Daigakkō* [The Army War College]. Tokyo: Fuyō Shobō, 1973.

Jūzenkai, ed. *Ato ni tsuzuku mono o shinzu: Gunshin Wakabayashi chūtaichō tsuitōroku* [Believe that others will follow: Memorial record of the war-god company commander Wakabayashi]. Sakai: Jūnzenkai, 1993.

Kanagawa-ken. *Tōkei Kanagawa kenshi: sengo 20-nen no ayumi* [Statistics of Kanagawa prefectural history: the 20 years after the war]. 2 vols. Yokohama: Kanagawa-ken, 1966.

Kawakami Hajime. *Dai-ni binbō monogatari* [The second tale of poverty]. Introduction by Miyagawa Makoto. Kyōto: San'ichi Shobō, 1948 [1930].

Kendō Wa-Ei jiten [Japanese-English dictionary of *kendō*]. Tokyo: Zen Nihon Kendō Renmei, 2000.

Kin Kyōshō (Kim Hyŏngsŏp), "Kin Kyōshō Taisa kaikoroku" [Memoir of Colonel Kim Hyŏngsŏp]. In *Nikkan gaikō shiryŏ,* edited by Ichikawa Masaaki, 10:189–255. Tokyo: Hara Shobō, 1981.

Kimura Takeo. *Kōmoto Daisaku* [Kōmoto Daisaku]. Tokyo: Tsuchiya Shoten, 1978.

Kishi Toshihiko. *Manshūkoku no bijuaru media: posutā, ehagaki, kitte* [Visual media of Manchukuo: posters, illustrated postcards, postage stamps]. Tokyo: Yoshikawa Kōbunkan, 2010.

Kishi Yonesaku. *Ruten kyōiku rokujūnen* [Constant motion: my 60 years in education]. Privately published, 1982.

Kōno Tsukasa. *Ni-niroku jiken: gokuchū shuki isho* [The 2-26 incident: prison notes and testaments]. Tokyo: Kawade Shōbō Shinsha, 1972.

Mainichi Shinbunsha, ed. *Wakabayashi Tōichi chūtaichō* [Company commander Wakabayashi Tōichi]. Tokyo: Mainichi Shinbunsha, 1944.

Makinami Yasuko. *Gosennichi no guntai: Manshūkoku Gun no gunkan tachi* [The Army of 5,000 days: officers of the Manchukuo Army]. Tokyo: Sōrinsha, 2004.

Makino Kikuo, ed. *Rikushi-Rikuyō: bessatsu ichiokunin no Shōwashi* [Officer and cadet schools: supplement to the Shōwa history of 100 million people]. Nihon no Senshi Betsukan 10. Tokyo: Maininchi Shinbunsa, 1981.

Makiyama Nozomu. *Rikugun chūjō Arikawa Shuichi ryakuden: Okinawa sen, Arikawa ryodan no sentō gaiyō* [Short biography of army lieutenant general Arikawa Shuichi: a summary of the combat of the Arikawa brigade in the battle of Okinawa]. Kagoshima: Kagoshima Ken Okinawa Sen'ekisha Ireikai, 1981.

———. *Rikugun chūjō Arikawa Shuichi shōden* [Brief biography of army lieutenant general Arikawa Shuichi]. Akashi (Hyōgō Ken): Makiyama Nozomu, 1980.

Manchuria Daily News. *Kagayaku Manshū/Kōki no Manshū/Flourishing Manchoukuo*. In Japanese, Chinese, and English. N.p.: Manchuria Daily News, n.d.

Matsuzawa Tetsunari and Suzuki Masasetsu. *Ni-niroku to seinen shōko* [February 26 and the young officers]. Tokyo: San'ichi Shobō, 1974.

Miyata Setsuko. *Chōsen minshū to 'kominka' seisaku* [The Korean people and the imperialization policy]. Tokyo: Miraisha, 1985.

Miyata Setsuko, Kimu Yondaru, and Yan Teho. *Sōshi kaimei* [The name change]. Tokyo: Akashi Shoten, 1992.

Morimatsu Toshio. "Fūsetsu hachinen: Sōbudai no wakazakura: hajime no gojūki kara kuriage shutsujin" [Eight years of wind and snow: the young cherry blossoms of Sōbudai: early dispatch to war beginning with the JMA 50 class]. In *Rikushi-Rikuyō: bessatsu ichiokunin no Shōwashi* [Officer and cadet schools: supplement to the Shōwa history of 100 million people], edited by Makino Kikuo, 188–193. Nihon no Senshi Betsukan 10. Tokyo: Maininchi Shinbunsa, 1981.

———. *Sōryokusen Kenkyūjo* [The Total War Research Institute]. Tokyo: Hakuteisha, 1983.

Morohashi Tetsuji. *Dai Kan-Wa jiten* [Japanese dictionary of Chinese characters]. 13 vols. Tokyo: Taishūkan Shoten, 1989–1990.

Nagata Tetsuzan Kankokai. *Hiroku: Nagata Tetsuzan* [Secret record: Nagata Tetsuzan]. Tokyo: Fūyō Shobō, 1980.

Nanba Kōji. *Uchiteshi yaman: Taiheiyō Sensō to kōkoku no gijutsushatachi* [Never stop fighting: the Pacific War and the engineers of advertising]. Tokyo: Kōdansha, 1998.

Nihon gaikō bunsho [Documents on Japanese foreign relations]. Tokyo: Nihon Kokusai Rengō Kyōkai, 1949.

Nihon Kindai Kyōiku Shi Kankōkai, ed. *Nihon kindai kyōiku shi* [History of Japanese modern education]. Tokyo: Kōdansha, 1973.

Nihon riku-kaigun no seidō soshiki jinji (abbreviated *SSJ*) [System, organization, and personnel of the Japanese army-navy]. Edited by Nihon Kindai Shiryō Kenkyūkai. Tokyo: Tōkyō Daigaku Shuppankai, 1971.

Nihon riku-kaigun sōgō jiten. (abbreviated *SJ*) [Comprehensive dictionary of the Japanese army-navy]. Edited by Hata Ikuhiko. Tokyo: Tokyo Daigaku Shuppankai, 1991.

Nishikawa Hiroshi. *Rappashu no saigo: sensō no naka no minshū* [The bugler's last moment: commoners during the war]. Tokyo: Aoki Shoten, 1984.

Ōe Shinobu. *Tennō no guntai* [Army of the emperor]. Shōwa no rekishi 3. Tokyo: Shōgakkan, 1982.

Ōhama Tetsuya and Ozawa Ikurō, eds. *Teikoku Riku-Kaigun jiten* [Dictionary of the imperial army and navy]. Tokyo: Dōseisha, 1984.

Okuda Kōichirō. *Okinawa Gunshireikan Ushijima Mitsuru* [Okinawa Commanding Officer Ushijima Mitsuru]. Tokyo: Fuyō Shobō, 1985.

Ōtani Eichi. *Kindai Nihon no Nichirenshugi undō* [The Nichrenism movement in modern Japan]. Kyōto: Hōzōkan, 2001.

Otani Tsuyoshi. "Tairiku otoko Matsuoka Gaisō" [Continental man foreign minister Matsuoka]. *Kyōwa: Mantetsu shainkai kikanshi* (August 1940): 2–3.

Riku-kaigun shōkan jinji sōran (abbreviated *SJS*) [Biographical dictionary of army-navy officers]. 2 vols. (Rikugun/Kaigun). Edited by Toyama Misao. Tokyo: Fuyō Shōbō, 1981.

Sakuramoto Tomio. *Uta to sensō: minna ga gunka o utatte ita* [Songs and war: everyone was singing military songs]. 2nd edition. Tokyo: Atene Shobō, 2005.

Sasaki Tōichi. *Aru gunjin no jiden* [Autobiography of a soldier]. Expanded edition. Tokyo: Keisō shobō, 1967.

Sejima Ryūzō. *Ikusanga: Sejima Ryūzō kaisōroku* [Ikusanga: the memoir of Sejima Ryūzō]. Tokyo: Sankei Shinbun Nyūsu Sābisu: Fusōsha, 1995.

Shiino Hattō, ed. *Nihon rikugun rentai sōran: chiiki betsu; hohei hen* [Compendium of Japanese army regiments: classified by region; infantry edition]. Bessatsu rikushi dokuhon dai-24 (123) gō. Tokyo: Shinjinbutsu Ōraisha, 1990.

Shimozawa Kan. *Kunisada Chūji* [Kunisada Chūji]. Tokyo: Kaizōsha, 1933.

Shōji Munemitsu. *Kendō gojūnen* [Fifty years of *kendō*]. Tokyo: Jiji Tsushinsha, 1956.

Tabohashi Kiyoshi. *Kindai Nissen kankei no kenkyō* [Study of Japanese-Korean relations in the modern period]. 2 vols. Tokyo: Bunka Shiryō Chōsakai, 1963–1964.

Takahashi Masae. *Shōwa no gunbatsu* [Army cliques in the Shōwa era]. Tokyo: Chūō Kōronsha, 1969.

Takano Kunio, ed. *Kindai Nihon guntai shiryō shūsei* [Collection of modern Japanese military historical materials]. 12 vols. Tokyo: Kashiwa Shobō, 2004.

Takayama Toshitake. *Yomoyamakatori* [Speaking of this and that]. Privately published by Takayama Toshiyake. 1994.

Tariji Ikuzō. *Shōwa no yōkai: Kishi Nobusuke* [The Monster of Shōwa: Kishi Nobusuke. Tokyo: Gakuyō Shobō, 1979.

Tei Raikaku (Chŏng Naehyŏk). *Watashi no ayunde kita michi: eijoku no nanajūnen* [The path I took: seventy years of honor and shame]. Tokyo: Tendensha, 2003.

Terada Chikao. *Nihon guntai yōgoshū* [Japanese military terms]. 2 vols. Tokyo: Rippū Shobō, 1992.

Tobe Ryōichi et al. *Shippai no honshitsu: Nihongun no soshikironteki ken'kyū* [The essence of failure: an organizational theory analysis of the Japanese military]. Tokyo: Daiyamondosha, 1984.

Tōkei Kanagawa kenshi: sengo 20-nen no ayumi [Statistics of the history of Kanagawa Prefecture: through 20 years after the war]. 2 vols. Yokohama: Kanagawa Prefecture, 1966.

"Toki no hito: sassō/tairiku otoko Itagaki Seishirō." [People of the times: the gallant continental man Itagaki Seishirō]. *Keizai magajin,* July (no year), 2.

Tōmiya Taisa Kinen Jugyō Iinkai. *Tōmiya Kaneo den* [Biography of Tōmiya Kaneo]. 1940. Reprint edition, Tokyo: Ōzorasha, 1997.

Torikai Ikoma. "Kyōgaku Kenkyūjo no rensei jōkyō" [Training at the Educational Research Institute]. *Chōsen* (December 1942): 46–56.

Toshioka Chūka. *Shinjin Yokokawa Shōzō den* [Biography of a true man: Yokokawa Shōzō]. Tokyo: Shinjin Yokokawa Shōzō Den Kankōkai, 1935.

Tsuji Sutezō. *Keihoku taikan* [Encyclopedia of North Kyŏngsŏng]. Taegu: Tsuji Sutezō, 1936.

Utsumi Aiko. *Chōsenjin 'Kōgun' heishitachi no sensō* [The Korean "Imperial Army" soldiers' war]. Tokyo: Iwanami Shoten, 1991.

Yagi Haruo. *Go-ichigo jiken to shikan kōhosei* [The May 15 incident and JMA cadets]. Fukuoka: Fukuoka Keimusho Sagyōka, 1988.

Yamamoto Shichihei. *Kō Shiyoku Chūjo no shokei* [The execution of Lieutenant General Kō Shiyoku]. Tokyo: Bungei Shunjū, 1986.

Yamamoto Tsunetomo. *Hagakure*. 3 vols. Tokyo: Iwanami Shoten, 1940.

Korean Books and Articles

An Chonghwa, ed. and trans. *Ch'odŭng yullihak kyogwasŏ* [Elementary school textbook on morals]. Hwangsŏng (Seoul): Kwanghak Sŏp'ŏ, 1907.

An Taehoe. *Tanwŏn p'ungsokto ch'ŏp* [Genre paintings of Kim Hongdo]. Seoul: Miŭmsa, 2005.

Ch'a Munsŏp. *Chosŏn sidae kunsa kwan'gye yŏn'gu* [Studies on the Chosŏn period military]. Seoul: Tan'guk Taehakkyo Ch'ulp'anbu, 1996.

Chang Hakkŭn. *Haeyang cheguk ŭi ch'imnyak kwa kŭndae Chosŏn ŭi haeyang chŏngch'aek: haeyang chŏngch'aeksa ŭi kyohun* [Imperial naval invasions and Chosŏn naval policy: the lessons of naval policy history]. Seoul: Han'guk Haeyang Chŏllyak Yŏn'guso, 2000.

Chang Tobin. "Chosŏn kŭndaesa sang ŭi muyongjŏn" [Valorous lives of the late Chosŏn]. *Samch'ŏlli* 5, no. 1 (1933): 76–79.

Chin Chunggwŏn. *Ne mudŏm e ch'im ŭl paet'ŭma!* [I will spit on your grave!]. 3 vols. Seoul: Kaemagowŏn, 1998.

Chin Chunggwŏn, "Chugŭn tokchaeja ŭi sahoe" [Society of the dead dictator]. In *Kaebal tokchae wa Pak Chŏnghŭi sidae: uri sidae ŭi chŏngch'i-kyŏngjejŏk kiwŏn* [The era of developmental dictatorship and Park Chung Hee: the political-economic origins of our time], edited by Yi Pyŏngch'ŏn, 339–364. Seoul: Ch'angbi, 2003.

Ch'in-Il Inmyŏng Sajŏn P'yŏnch'an Wiwŏnhoe. *Ch'in-Il inmyŏng sajŏn* (cited in notes as *CIS*) [Pro-Japanese biographical dictionary]. 3 vols. Seoul: Minjok Munje Yŏn'guso, 2009.

Cho Chaegon. "Taehan Chegukki kunsa chŏngch'aek kwa kunsa kigu ŭi unyŏng [Military policy and the functioning of the military structure in the Great Han Empire period]. *Yŏksa wa hyŏnsil* 19 (1996): 100–134.

Cho Ilmun and Sin Pongnyong, eds. *Kapsin chŏngbyŏn hoegorok* [Memoirs of the Kapsin coup]. Seoul: Kŏn'guk Taehakkyo Ch'ulp'anbu, 2006.

Cho Kapche. *Nae mudŏm e ch'im ŭl paet'ora: Cho Kapche kija ka ssŭnŭn kŭndaehwa hyŏngmyŏngga Pak Chŏnghŭi ŭi pijanghan saengae* [Spit on my grave: the resolute life of the modernizing revolutionary Park Chunghee as written by reporter Cho Kapche]. 8 vols. Seoul: Chosŏn ilbosa, 1998.

———. *Pak Chŏnghŭi: han kŭndaehwa hyŏngmyŏngga ŭi pijanghan saengae* [Park Chung Hee: the resolute life of a modernizing revolutionary]. 13 vols. Seoul: Cho Kapche Datk'om, 2006.

Ch'oe Rin. "Chahwasang chungch'ŏp osimnyŏn'gan" [Self-portrait: Fifty years of turbulence]. *Samch'ŏlli*, September 1929, 30–32.

Chŏn T'aekpu. *Han'guk Kidokkyo ch'ŏngnyŏn hoe undongsa (1899–1945)* [Activities of the Korean YMCA 1899–1945]. Seoul: Chŏngŭmsa, 1978.

Chŏng Chaegyŏng, ed. *Pak Chŏnghŭi silgi: haengjŏk ch'orok* [The true record of Park Chung Hee: selected excerpts]. Seoul: Chimmundang, 1994.

Chŏng Ilgwŏn. *Chŏng Ilgwŏn hoegorok* [Memoir of Chŏng Ilgwŏn]. Seoul: Koryŏ Sŏjŏk, 1996.

Chŏng Naehyŏk. *Kyŏkpyŏn ŭi saengae rŭl torabomyŏ: kijŏk ŭi kamyŏ, yŏksa nŭn namŭmyŏ: Chŏng Naehyŏk hoegorok* [Looking back on a tumultuous life: the miracle passes, history remains: the memoir of Chŏng Naehyŏk]. Seoul: Han'guk Sanŏp Yŏn'guwŏn, 2001.

Chŏng Sŏngch'ae. *Sonyŏn ch'ŏkhudan kyobŏm* [Boy Scout handbook]. Kyŏngsŏng (Seoul): Sonyŏn Chŏkhudan Chosŏn Yŏnmaeng, 1931.

Chŏng Sŏnghwa, ed. *Pak Chŏnghŭi sidae yŏn'gu ŭi chaengjŏm kwa kwaje* [Debates and issues in the study of the Park Chung Hee period]. Seoul: Sŏnin, 2005.

Chŏng Yagyong. *Pyŏngjŏn* [On the military]. Translated by Chang Sunbŏm. Minjok munhwa mun'go: Mongmin simsŏ 8. Seoul: Minjok Munhwa Ch'ujinhoe, 1981.

Chŏng Yonghwa. *Munmyŏng ŭi chŏngch'i sasang: Yu Kilchun kwa kŭndae Han'guk* [Civilization and political thought: Yu Kilchun and modern Korea]. Seoul: Munhak kwa Chisŏngsa, 2004.

Chŏngjŏng yŏnp'yo [Diary of government service]: *Ŭmch'ŏngsa* [History cloudy and clear]: *chon* [complete]. Seoul: Kuksa P'yŏnch'an Wiwŏnhoe, 1958.

Chu Chin'o. *Kim Okkyun* [Kim Okkyun]. Seoul: Yŏksa Pip'yŏngsa, 1990.

Chu Unsŏng. "Yŏngung kwa hogŏl ron" [On heroes and great men]. *Samch'ŏlli* (July 1935): 111–113.

Han Sŏkchŏng. *Manju modŏn: 60-nyŏndae Han'guk kaebal ch'eje ŭi kiwŏn* [Manchuria modern: the origins of South Korea's developmental system in the 1960s]. Seoul: Munhak kwa Chisŏng Sa, 2016.

———. *Manjuguk kŏnguk ŭi chaehaesŏk: koeroeguk ŭi kukka hyogwa 1932–1936* [A reinterpretation of the founding of Manchukuo: the state effect of the puppet state]. Revised edition. Pusan Kwangyŏksi: Tong Taehakkyo ch'ulp'anbu, 2007.

Han Yongwŏn. *Ch'anggun* [Creating an army]. Seoul: Pagyŏngsa, 1984.

Hŏ Chaeuk. "Han'guk poisŭk'autt'ŭ undong: ch'ŏngsonnyŏn kyoyuk e mich'in yŏnghyang" [The activities of the Korean Boy Scouts: influence on the education of youth]. M.A. thesis, Koryŏ Taehakkyo Kyoyuk Taehagwŏn, 1971.

Hŏ Tonghyŏn. "1881 Chosŏn Chosa Ilbon Sich'altan e kwanhan il yŏn'gu" [A study of the Chosŏn Courtiers Observation Mission]. *Han'guksa yŏn'gu* 53 (March 1986): 97–151.

———. *Kŭndae Han-Il kwan'gyesa yŏn'gu: Chosa Sich'altan ŭi Ilbon'gwan kwa kukka kusang* [The Courtiers Observation Mission's attitude toward Japan and conception of the state]. Seoul: Kukhak Charyowŏn, 2000.

Hŏ Tonghyŏn, ed. *Chosa Sich'altan kwan'gye ch'aryojip* [Collected documents relating to the Courtiers Observation Mission]. 14 vols. Seoul: Kukhak Charyowŏn, 2000.

Hong Sŏngnyul, Pak Taegyun, Yi Wanbŏm, Yi Chunsik,and Mun Hyŏna, eds. *Pak Chŏnghŭi sidae yŏn'gu* [The Park Chung Hee period]. Seoul: Paeksan Sŏdang, 2002.

Hong Tusŭng. *Han'guk kundae ŭi sahoehak* [Sociology of the Korean military]. Seoul: Nanam, 1993.

Hwimun Ŭisuk P'yŏnjippu, ed. *Chungdŭng susin kyogwasŏ* [Secondary level morals textbook]. Hansŏng (Seoul): Hwimun Ŭisuk Inswaebu, 1906.

Hyŏn Kwangho, "Taehan Chegukki chingbyŏngje nonŭi wa kŭ sŏnggyŏk [On the discussions and character of the conscription system of the Great Han Empire]. *Han'guksa yŏn'gu* 105 (June 1999): 151–187.

Im Chaech'an. "Ku Hanmal Yukkun Mugwan Hakkyo yŏn'gu" [Study of the Late Chosŏn Army Military Academy]. Ph.D. dissertation, History Department, Tonga Taehakkyo, 1989.

Im Chihyŏn. *Uri an ŭi p'asijŭm* [The fascism within us]. Seoul: Samin, 2000.

"In'gan Pak Chŏnghŭi ŭi samuraisik chŏngsin kujo: In'gan Pak Chŏnghŭi chae p'yŏngga: Pak Chŏnghŭi chŏn'gi chakka chŏn Ch'ŏngwadae pisŏgwan Kim Chongsin hoego" [The *samurai* mentality of Park Chung Hee the person: a reconsideration of the person Park Chung Hee: reflections of former Blue House secretary Kim Chongsin on Park Chung Hee's autobiographical work]. *Wŏlgan ŏpsŏbŏ* (October 1991): 187–191.

Kang Chŏngin. *Han'guk hyŏndae chŏngch'i sasang kwa Pak Chŏnghŭi* [Contemporary Korean political thought and Park Chung Hee]. Seoul: Ak'anet, 2014.

Kim Ch'angnam, ed. *Kim Min'gi*. Seoul: Tosŏch'ulp'an Han'ul, 2004.

Kim Chinhwa. *Ilcheha Taegu ŭi ŏllon yŏn'gu* [Studies of the Taegu press under Japanese imperialism]. Taegu: Hwada, 1978.

Kim Chŏngnyŏm. *A, Pak Chŏnghŭi*. [Ah, Park Chung Hee]. Seoul: Chungang M&B, 1997.

———. *Han'guk kyŏngje ch'ŏngch'aek 30-nyŏnsa: Kim Chŏngnyŏm hoegorok* [A thirty-year history of Korean economic policy: the memoirs of Kim Chŏngnyŏm]. Seoul: Chungang Ilbosa, 1995.

Kim Chongsin. *Yŏngsi ŭi hwaetpul: Pak Chŏnghŭi Taet'ongnyŏng ttara ch'illyŏn* [Torch in the midnight hour: seven years with President Park Chung Hee]. Seoul: Hallim Ch'ulp'ansa, 1966.

Kim Kisu. *Iltong kiyu* [Record of a trip to Japan]. Translated and annotated by Yi Chaeho. Pusan: Pusan Taehakkyo Han-Il Munhwa Yŏn'guso, 1962.

Kim Ilyŏng. "Han'guk essŏ palchŏn kukka ŭi kiwŏn, hyŏngsŏng kwa palchŏn kŭrigo chŏnmang" [Origins, formation and development, and future of the developmental state in South Korea]. *Han'guk chŏngch'i oegyo saron ch'ŏng* 23, no. 1 (August 2001): 87–126.

Kim Sŏgwŏn. *Nobyŏng ŭi han: chasŏjŏn* [Lament of an old soldier: autobiography]. Seoul: Yukpŏpsa, 1977.

Kim Sunjŏn, Kim Yonggap, No Hyŏnmi, Sŏ Kijae, Myŏng Hyeyŏng, Pak Chehong, Chang Migyŏng, Chŏng Chumi, Cho Sŏngjin, Pak Kyŏngsu, Sa Hŭiyŏng, eds. *Cheguk ŭi singminji susin: Chosŏn Ch'ongdokpu p'yŏnch'an "susinsŏ" yŏn'gu* [Morals of the imperial colony: studies of "morals textbooks" compiled by the Government-General of Korea]. Seoul: Cheiaenssi, 2008.

Kim Sunjŏn, Mun Ch'ŏlsu, Kim Hyŏnsŏk, Yi Pyŏndam, Chŏng Sŭngun, Kim Yonggap, Sŏ Kijae, and No Hyŏnmi, trans. *Chosŏn Ch'ongtokpu ch'ŏdŭng hakkyo susinsŏ* [Elementary school morals textbooks of the Government-General of Korea]. 5 vols. Seoul: Cheiaenssi, 2006.

Kim Sunjŏn, Mun Ch'ŏlsu, Yi Pyŏngdal, Kim Hyŏnsŏk, Chŏng Sŭngun, Kim Yonggap, Sŏ Kijae, and Pak Chehong, eds. *Chosŏn Ch'ongdokpu ch'odŭng hakkyo susinsŏ: wŏnmun* [The elementary school morals textbooks of the Government-General of Korea: original texts]. 2 vols. Seoul: Cheiaenssi, 2006.

Kim Taejung (Kim Dae Jung). *Kim Taejung chasajŏn* [Autobiography of Kim Dae Jung]. 2 vols. Seoul: Tosŏch'ulp'an Sam'in, 2010.

Kim Yŏnghak. "Han'guk ch'eyuksa yŏngyŏk e ttarŭn kŏmsul mit kŏmdo ŭi paltal kwajŏng e kwanhan yŏn'gu" [The development of the art of the sword and *kendō* in the history of Korean physical education]. Ph.D. dissertation, Myŏngji University, 1999.

Kim Yun'gŭn. *Haebyŏngdae wa 5.16* [The Marine Corps and May 16]. Seoul: Pŏmjosa, 1987.

Kukka Chaegŏn Ch'oego Hoeŭi. *Han'guk kunsa hyŏngmyŏngsa* [The history of the military revolution in South Korea]. 2 vols. Seoul: Kunsa Hyŏngmyŏngsa P'yŏnch'an Wiwŏnhoe, 1963.

Kuksa P'yŏnch'an Wiwŏnhoe, ed. *Susinsa kirok: chŏn* [The complete record of the Japanese missions]. Seoul: T'amgudang, 1971.

Kunsa Hyŏngmyŏngsa P'yŏnch'an Wiwŏnhoe. *Oillyuk kunsa hyŏngmyŏng ŭi chŏnmo* [The complete account of the 5.16 military revolution]. Seoul: Mun'gwangsa, 1964.

Kyŏngsang Puktosa [History of North Kyŏngsang Province]. Taegu: Kyŏngsang Puktosa P'yŏnjip Wiwŏnhoe, 1983.

Miyata Setsuko, Kimu Yondaru, and Yan Teho. *Ch'angssi kaemyŏng* [The name change]. Edited and translated by Chŏng Ŭnhyŏn. Seoul: Hangminsa, 1994.

Na Iltae. "Hyŏn Chunhyŏk ŭi naeryŏk" [The life of Hyŏn Chunhyŏk]. *Sinch'ŏnji* 1, no. 9 (October 1946): 142–143.

Nishino Junya. "Ilbon model essŏ Han'gukchŏk hyŏksin ŭro: 1970 nyŏndae chunghwahak kongŏphwa rŭl tullŏssan chŏngch'aek kwajŏng" [Korean innovation on the Japanese model: policy formation surrounding the 1970s heavy and chemical industrialization]. In *Tet'angt'ŭ wa Pak Chŏnghŭi* [Détente and Park Chung Hee], edited by Sin Ukhŭi, 167–206. Seoul: Nonhyŏng, 2011.

O Wŏnch'ŏl. *Han'guk kyŏngje kŏnsŏl: enjiniŏring ŏp'ŭroch'i* [The economic construction of Korea: an engineering approach]. 7 vols. Seoul: Kia Kyŏngje Yŏn'guso, 1995.

———. *Pak Chŏnghŭi nŭn ŏttŏk'e kangguk mandŭrŏnna: pulgul ŭi tojŏn Hangang ŭi kijŏk* [How Park Chung Hee made a strong country: Never bending to challenge: the miracle on the Han River]. Seoul: Tongsŏ Munhwasa, 2006.

Pak Ch'ansŭng. *Minjok, minjokjuŭi* [Nation, nationalism]. Seoul: Sohwa, 2010.

Pak Chŏnghŭi, *Kukka wa hyŏngmyŏng kwa na* [The country, the revolution, and I]. Seoul: Hyangmunsa, 1963.

———. "Na ŭi sonyŏn sijŏl" [My childhood]. *Wŏlgan Chosŏn*, May 1984, 84–95.

———. *Uri minjok ŭi nagal kil* [Our nation's path]. Seoul: Koryŏ Sŏjŏk Chusik Hoesa, 1965.

Pak Chŏnghŭi Changgun tamhwa munjip [Collected statements of General Park Chung Hee]. Seoul: Taet'ongnyŏng Pisŏsil, 1965.

Pak Chŏnghŭi Taet'ongnyŏng yŏnsŏl munjip [Collected speeches of President Park Chung Hee]. 16 vols. Seoul: Taet'ongnyŏng Pisŏsil, 1965–1979.

Pak T'aegyun. "Pak Chŏnghŭi sigi rŭl t'onghae pon palchŏn kukka e taehan pip'anjŏk siron" [A critical view of developmental state theory by looking at the Park Chung Hee era]. *Yŏksa wa hyŏnsil* 74 (December 2009): 15–43.

Pang Kijung. "Chosŏn chisikin ŭi kyŏngje t'ongjeron kwa 'sin ch'eje' insik: Chung-Il chŏnjaenggi chŏnch'ejuŭi ŭi kyŏngjeron ŭl chungsim ŭro" [The Korean intelligentsia's perceptions of economic controls and the 'new system': the debate on the totalitarian economic system in the period of the Second Sino-Japanese War]. In *Ilcheha chisikin ŭi p'asijŭm ch'eje insik kwa taeŭng* [Perceptions and responses of the intelligentsia toward the fascist system under Japanese imperialism], edited by Pang Kijung. Seoul: Hyean, 2005.

Pang Kijung, ed. *Ilcheha chisikin ŭi p'asijŭm ch'eje insik kwa taeŭng* [Perceptions and responses of the intelligentsia toward the fascist system under Japanese imperialism]. Seoul: Hyean, 2005.

Pang Wŏnch'ol. *Kim Chongp'il ege koham* [Speaking truth to Kim Chongp'il]. Seoul: Sach'o, 1987.

Rŏsia Taejangsŏng. *Ku Hanmal ŭi sahoe wa kyŏngje: yŏlgang kwa ŭi choyak* [Late Chosŏn society and economy: treaties with the great powers]. Translated by Kim Pyŏngnin. Seoul: Yurye Ch'ulp'ansa, 1983.

Sajin ŭro ponŭn Chosŏn sidae: saenghwal kwa p'ungsok [The Chosŏn period through photographs: everyday life and customs]. Text by Cho P'ungyŏn. Seoul: Sŏmundang, 1986.

Sajin ŭro ponŭn tongnip undong [The independence movement through photographs]. 2 vols. Seoul: Sŏmundang, 1987.

Sim Chiyŏn. *Song Namhŏn hoegorok: Kim Kyusik kwa hamkke han kil: minjok chaju wa t'ongil ŭi wihayŏ* [Reminiscences of Song Namhŏn: together with Kim Kyusik: for national independence and unification]. Seoul: Hanul, 2000.

Sin Chubaek. "Ilche malgi Chosŏn'in kunsa kyoyuk, 1942.12–1945" [Korean military education at the end of the Japanese imperial period, 12.1942–1945]. *Han-Il minjok munje yŏn'gu* 9 (2005): 153–186.

———. "Manjugukkun sok ŭi Chosŏnin changgyo wa Hangukkun" [Manchukuo army Korean officers and the South Korean army]. *Yŏksa munje yŏn'gu* 9 (December 2002): 77–132.

Sin Hyŏnjun. *No haebyŏng ŭi hoegorok* [Memoir of an old marine]. Seoul: Katollik Ch'ulp'ansa, 1989.

Sin Ukhŭi, ed. *Tet'angt'ŭ wa Pak Chŏnghŭi* [Détente and Park Chung Hee]. Seoul: Nonhyŏng, 2011.

Sin Yongha. *Han'guk kŭndae sahoe sasangsa yŏn'gu* [Studies of Korean modern social thought]. Seoul: Ilchisa, 1987.

———. *Sin Ch'aeho ŭi sahoe sasang yŏn'gu* [Studies on the social thought of Sin Ch'aeho]. Han'guk Sahoe Yŏn'gu Ch'ongsŏ 1. Seoul: Han'gilsa, 1984.

Sŏ Inhan. *Taehan Cheguk ŭi kunsa chedo* [The military system of the Great Han Empire]. Seoul: Hyean, 2000.

Sŏ Yŏnghŭi. *Taehan Cheguk chŏngch'isa yŏn'gu* [Studies on the political thought of the Great Han Empire. Sŏul Taehakkyo Han'guksa Yŏn'gu Ch'ongsŏ 6. Seoul: Sŏul Taehakkyo, 2005.

Sŏyu kyŏnmun: chŏnmun [Observations on the West: the complete text]. Compiled and edited by Yi Hansŏp, Ch'oe Kyŏngok, Chŏng Yŏngsuk, and Kang Sŏnga. *Sŏyu kyŏnmun* Yŏn'gu Series. Seoul: Pagijŏng, 2000.

Taehan YMCA Yŏnmaeng. *Han'guk YMCA undongsa, 1895–1985* [History of the activities of the Korean YMCA, 1885–1985]. Seoul: No Ch'ulp'an, 1986.

Tanjae Sin Ch'aeho Sŏnsaeng Ki'nyŏm Saŏphoe. *Tanjae Sin Ch'aeho chŏnjip* [The complete works of Tanjae Sin Ch'aeho]. 3 vols. Revised edition. Seoul: Hyŏngsŏl, 1995.

Tanjae Sin Ch'aeho Sŏnsaeng Ki'nyŏm Saŏphoe. *Tanjae Sin Ch'aeho chŏnjip* 4 *(pyŏl)* [The complete works of Tanjae Sin Ch'aeho]. Seoul: Hyŏngsŏl, 1998.

Yamamoto Shichihei. *Hong Saik Chungjang ŭi ch'ŏhyŏng* [The execution of Lieutenant General Hong Saik]. Translated by Yi Myŏngsŏng. Seoul: Tonam Sŏsa, 1986.

Yi Chunsik. "Pak Chŏnghŭi sidae chibae ideollogi ŭi hyŏngsŏng" [Formation of the ruling ideology of the Park Chung Hee period]. In Hong Sŏngnyul, Pak Taegyun, et al., *Pak Chŏnghŭi sidae yŏn'gu*, 173–208.

Yi Hallim. *Segi ŭi kyŏngnang: hoesangnok* [The raging waves of the century: a memoir]. Seoul: P'albogwŏn, 1994.

Yi Hyŏnggŭn. *Kunbŏn 1-bŏn ŭi oegil insaeng: Yi Hyŏnggŭn hoegorok* [The steadfast life of army service number 1: the memoir Yi Hyŏnggŭn]. Seoul: Chungang Ilbosa 1993.

Yi Kidong. *Pigŭk ŭi kun'indŭl: Ilbon Yuksa ch'ulsin ŭi yŏksa* [Soldiers of tragedy: a history of the graduates of the JMA]. Seoul: Ilchogak, 1982.

Yi Kwangnin. *Han'guk kaehwasa yŏn'gu* [Studies in Korean enlightenment history]. Seoul: Ilchogak, 1969.

Yi Kwangsu. *Sosŏl Yi Sunsin* [Novel of Yi Sunsin]. Seoul: Usinsa, 1991.

———. *Yi Kwangsu chŏnjip* [Complete works of Yi Kwangsu]. Edited by Chu Yohan, et al. 20 vols. Seoul: Samjungdang, 1962–1964.

Yi Mun'gŏn. *Yangarok* [Record of child-rearing]. Translated (into Korean) by Yi Sangju. Seoul: T'aehaksa, 1997.

Yi Mi'na. "Taehan Cheguk sidae yukkun changbyŏng pokche chesik kwa taewŏnsu yesangbok e taehayŏ" [Military dress codes in the Great Han Empire and formal and informal dress of the Marshall Commander-in-Chief]. *Hagyeji* 4 (1993): 241–277.

Yi Pŏmsŏn. *Obalt'an* [A stray bullet]. Translated by Mashal P'il (Marshall Pihl). Bilingual text in Korean and English. Pairinggwŏl edisyŏn Han'guk taep'yo sosŏl, vol. 110. Seoul: Asia, 2015.

Yi Pyŏngch'ŏn, ed. *Kaebal tokchae wa Pak Chŏnghŭi sidae: uri sidae ŭi chŏngch'i-kyŏngjejŏk kiwŏn* [The era of developmental dictatorship and Park Chung Hee: the political-economic origins of our time]. Seoul: Ch'angbi, 2003.

Yi Sunsin. *Nanjung ilgi: Yi Ch'ungmu kong chinjung kirok* [War diary: the battle record of Yi Ch'ungmu kong]. Translated by Yi Yongho. Seoul: Tonggwang Munhwasa, 2005.

Yi T'aejin. *Chosŏn hugi ŭi chŏngch'i wa kunyŏngje pyŏnch'ŏn* [Late Chosŏn politics and changes in the system of central military garrisons]. Seoul: Han'guk Yŏn'guwŏn, 1959.

———. *Kojong sidae ŭi chae chomyŏng* [Reilluminating the Kojong era]. Seoul: T'aehaksa, 2000.

Yi T'aejin, Kim Chaeho, et al. *Kojong Hwangje yŏksa ch'ŏngmunhoe* [Inquiry on the history of Emperor Kojong]. Seoul: P'urŭn Yŏksa, 2005.

Yi T'aejin, Kim Kisŏk, Paek Ch'unghyŏn, Yi Kŭngwan, Sin Hyosuk, Yi Yonggwŏn. *Han'guk pyŏnghap ŭi pulbŏpsŏng yŏn'gu* [Studies on the illegality of the annexation of Korea]. Sŏul

Taehakkyo Munhwa Yŏn'guso. Han'gukhak Kongdong Yŏn'gu Ch'ongsŏ, vol. 2. Seoul: Sŏul Taehakkyo Han'guk Munhwa Yŏn'guso, 2003.

Yi Tonghŭi. *Han'guk kunsa chedo ron* [On the Korean military system]. Seoul: Ilchogak, 1982.

Yi Yunsang. "1894–1910 chaejŏng chedo wa unyŏng ŭi pyŏnhwa [Management and changes in the financial system 1894–1910]. Ph.D. dissertation, History Department, Sŏul Taehakkyo Taehagwŏn, 1996.

Yu Kilchun. *Sŏyu kyŏnmun*. Translated by Ch'ae Hun. Seoul: Taeyang Sŏjŏk, 1973.

Yu Yangsu. *Taesa ŭi ilgijang* [Diary of an ambassador]. Seoul: Samsŏng Ch'ulp'ansa: Kong-güpch'ŏ Samsŏng Idea, 1989.

Yu Yŏngik. *Kabo Kyŏngjang yŏn'gu* [Studies on the Kabo reforms]. Seoul: Ilchogak, 1990.

Yukkun Pokchesa P'yŏnjip Wiwŏnhoe, ed. *Yukkun pokchesa* [History of army uniforms]. Seoul: Yukkun Ponbu, 1980.

Yukkun Sagwan Hakkyo Han'guk Kunsa Yŏn'gusil. *Han'guk kunjesa* [History of the military system in Korea]. 2 vols. Seoul: Yukkun Ponbu, 1968–1977.

Yukkun Sagwan Hakkyo samsimnyŏnsa [Thirty-year history of the Korean Military Academy]. Edited by Yuksa Samsimnyŏnsa P'yŏnch'an Wiwŏnhoe. Seoul: Yukkun Sagwan Hakkyo, 1978.

Yun Ch'iho. *Yun Ch'iho ilgi* [Diary of Yun Ch'iho]. 11 vols. Seoul: Kuksa P'yŏnch'an Wiwŏnhoe, 1973–1989.

Yun Haedong. "Singminji insik ŭi 'hoesaek chidae': Ilcheha gongongsŏng kwa kyuyul kwŏllyŏk" [The gray areas of "colonial perception": blank spaces and disciplinary power in Japanese imperialism]. In *Kŭndae rŭl tasi ingnŭnda: Han'guk kŭndae insik ŭi saeroun p'aerodaim ŭi wihayŏ* [Re-reading the modern era: toward a new paradigm of understanding Korea's modern age], edited by Yun Haedong, Ch'ŏn Chŏnghwan, Hŏ Su, Hwang Pyŏngju, Yi Yonggi, and Yun Taesŏk, 1:37–61. Seoul: Yŏksa Pip'yŏngsa, 2006.

Yun Haedong, Ch'ŏn Chŏnghwan, Hŏ Su, Hwang Pyŏngju, Yi Yonggi, and Yun Taesŏk, eds. *Kŭndae rŭl tasi ingnŭnda: Han'guk kŭndae insik ŭi saeroun p'aerodaim ŭi wihayŏ* [Re-reading the modern era: toward a new paradigm of understanding Korea's modern age]. 2 vols. Seoul: Yŏksa Pip'yŏngsa, 2006.

English Books and Articles

Abe, Ikuo. "Muscular Christianity in Japan: The Growth of a Hybrid." In *Muscular Christianity and the Colonial and Post-Colonial World,* edited by John J. Macaloon. New York: Routledge, 2008.

Agamben, Giorgio. *State of Exception*. Translated by Keven Attell. Chicago: University of Chicago Press, 2005.

Agov, Avram Asenov. "Origins of the Annexation of Korea by Japan in 1910: Military and Financial Systems of the Late Choson Dynasty, International Relations, 1895–1905." Master's thesis, Regional Studies East Asia (RSEA) Program, Harvard University, 1995.

Alagappa Muthiah, ed. *Coercion and Governance: The Declining Political Role of the Military in Asia*. Stanford, CA: Stanford University Press, 2001.

Amsden, Alice H. *Asia's Next Giant: South Korea and Late Industrialization*. New York: Oxford University Press, 1989.

Armstrong, Charles K. *The North Korean Revolution 1945–1950*. Ithaca, NY: Cornell University Press, 2003.

The Art of the Warrior. Translated and edited by Ralph D. Sawyer with the collaboration of Mei-chun Lee Sawyer. Boston: Shambhala, 1996.

Awaya Kentarō. "Senjinkun." *Kodansha Encyclopedia of Japan*, 7:65.

Baker, Keith Michael. "A Foucauldian French Revolution?" In *Foucault and the Writing of History,* edited by Jan Goldstein. Oxford: Blackwell, 1994.

Baldwin, Frank Prentiss, Jr. "The March First Movement: Korean Challenge and Japanese Response." Ph.D. dissertation, Columbia University, 1969.

Bargen, Doris G. *Suicidal Honor: General Nogi and the Writings of Mori Ōgai and Natsume Sōseki.* Honolulu: University of Hawaii Press, 2006.

Barnhart, Michael A. *Japan Prepares for Total War: The Search for Economic Security, 1919–1941.* Ithaca, NY: Cornell University Press, 1987.

Barshay, Andrew E. *The Gods Left First: The Captivity and Repatriation of Japanese POWs in Northeast Asia, 1945–1956.* Berkeley: University of California Press, 2013.

Baskett, Michael. "All Beautiful Fascists? Axis Film Culture in Imperial Japan." In *The Culture of Japanese Fascism,* edited by Alan Tansman, 212–234. Durham, NC: Duke University Press, 2009.

Baskett, Michael. *The Attractive Empire: Transnational Film Culture in Imperial Japan.* Honolulu: University of Hawaii Press, 2008.

Bennett, Andrew. *Kendo: Culture of the Sword.* Oakland: University of California Press, 2015.

Bernhardi, Friedrich von. *Germany and the Next War.* Translated by Allen H. Powles. New York: J. S. Ogilvie, n.d.

Bernstein, Gail Lee. *Japanese Marxist: A Portrait of Kawakami Hajime, 1879–1946.* Cambridge, MA: Harvard University Press, 1976.

Berry, Mary Elizabeth. *Hideyoshi.* Cambridge, MA: Council on East Asian Studies, 1982.

Best, Geoffrey. "The Militarization of European Society, 1870–1914." In *The Militarization of the Western World,* edited by John R. Gillis. New Brunswick, NJ: Rutgers University Press, 1989.

Bethell, John T. *Harvard Observed: An Illustrated History of the University in the Twentieth Century.* Cambridge, MA: Harvard University Press, 1998.

Bishop, Donald M. "Shared Failure: American Military Advisors in Korea, 1888–1896." *Transactions of the Royal Asiatic Society, Korea Branch 58* (1983): 53–76.

Bisson, T. A. *Japan's War Economy.* New York: International Secretariat, Institute of Pacific Relations, 1945.

Bolitho, Harold. "The Myth of the Samurai." In *Japan's Impact on the World,* edited by Alan Rix and Ross Mauer, 2–9. Nathan, Australia: Japanese Studies Association of Australia, 1984.

Botsman, Daniel V. *Punishment and Power in the Making of Modern Japan.* Princeton, NJ: Princeton University Press, 2005.

Bourdieu, Pierre. *Distinction: A Social Critique of the Judgement of Taste.* Translated by Richard Nice. Cambridge, MA: Harvard University Press, 1984.

Burchell, Graham, Colin Gordon, and Peter Miller. *The Foucault Effect: Studies in Governmentality.* Chicago: University of Chicago Press, 1991.

Callahan, Mary P. *Making Enemies: War and State Building in Burma.* Ithaca, NY: Cornell University Press, 2003.

Caprio, Mark. *Japanese Assimilation Policies in Colonial Korea, 1910–1945.* Seattle: University of Washington Press, 2009.

Chandra, Vipan. *Imperialism, Resistance, and Reform in Late Nineteenth-Century Korea: Enlightenment and the Independence Club.* Berkeley: Institute of East Asian Studies, University of California, 1988.

Chang, Paul Y. *Protest Dialectics: State Repression and South Korea's Democracy Movement, 1970–1979.* Stanford, CA: Stanford University Press, 2015.

Chartier, Roger. "The Chimera of the Origin: Archeology, Cultural History, and the French Revolution." In *Foucault and the Writing of History,* edited by Jan Goldstein, 167–186. Oxford: Blackwell, 1994.

Choe, Ching Young. *The Rule of the Taewŏn'gun, 1864–1873: Restoration in Yi Korea.* Cambridge, MA: East Asian Research Center, Harvard University, 1972.

Ch'oe, Yŏng-ho. "The Kapsin Coup of 1884: A Reassessment." *Korean Studies 6* (1982): 105–124.

———. "Private Academies and the State in Late Chosŏn Korea." In *Culture and the State in Late Chosŏn Korea,* edited by JaHyun Kim Haboush and Martina Deuchler, 15–45. Cambridge, MA: Harvard University Asia Center, 1999.

Ch'oe Yŏng-ho, Peter H. Lee, and Wm. Theodore de Bary, eds. *Sources of Korean Tradition,* vol. 2, *From the Sixteenth to the Twentieth Centuries.* New York: Columbia University Press, 2000.

Choi, Ellie. "Yi Kwangsu and the Post-World War I Reconstruction Debate." *Journal of Korean Studies* 20, no. 1 (Spring 2015): 33–76.

Citino, Robert M. *Quest for Decisive Victory: From Stalemate to Blitzkrieg in Europe, 1899–1940.* Lawrence: University Press of Kansas, 2002.

Cole, David Chamberlin and Princeton N. Lyman. *Korean Development: The Interplay of Politics and Economics.* Cambridge, MA: Harvard University Press, 1971.

Connaughton, Richard. *Rising Sun and Tumbling Bear: Russia's War with Japan.* London: Cassell, 2003.

Cook, Harold F. *Korea's 1884 Incident: Its Background and Kim Ok-kyun's Elusive Dream.* Seoul: Royal Asiatic Society, Korea Branch, 1972.

Cook, Haruko Taya and Theodore F. Cook. *Japan at War: An Oral History.* New York: The New Press, 1992.

Cook, Theodor Failor, Jr. "The Japanese Officer Corps: The Making of a Military Elite, 1872–1945." Ph.D. dissertation, History Department, Princeton University, 1987.

Coox, Alvin D. *Nomonhan: Japan against Russia, 1939.* Stanford, CA: Stanford University Press, 1985.

Community Relations Office, U.S. Army Garrison, Japan. "The Camp Zama Historical Monument Walking Tour." March 21, 2005.

Cowan, Michael. *Cult of the Will: Nervousness and German Modernity.* University Park: Pennsylvania State University Press, 2008.

Crackel, Theodore J. *West Point: A Bicentennial History.* Lawrence: University Press of Kansas, 2002.

Craig, Albert M. *Chōshū in the Meiji Restoration.* Cambridge, MA: Harvard University Press, 1961.

———. *Civilization and Enlightenment: The Early Thought of Fukuzawa Yukichi.* Cambridge, MA: Harvard University Press, 2009.

Crowley, James B. "Japanese Army Factionalism in the Early 1930s." *Journal of Asian Studies* 21, no. 3 (May 1962): 309–326.

Cumings, Bruce. *Korea's Place in the Sun: A Modern History.* New York: W.W. Norton, 1997.

Dallet, Charles. *Traditional Korea.* New Haven, CT: Human Relations Area Files, 1954. Originally published in French as the introduction to *Histoire de l'Eglise de Corée* (Paris: Victor Palmé, 1874).

De Bary, Wm., Carol Gluck, and Arthur E. Tiedemann, eds. *Sources of Japanese Tradition,* vol. 2, *1600–2000.* 2nd edition. New York: Columbia University Press, 2005.

De Cuester, Koen. "Wholesome Education and Sound Leisure: The YMCA Sports Programme in Colonial Korea." *European Journal of East Asian Studies* 2, no. 1 (2003): 53–88.

Deuchler, Martina. *Confucian Gentlemen and Barbarian Envoys: The Opening of Korea, 1875–1885.* Seattle: University of Washington Press, 1977.

———. "The Practice of Confucianism: Ritual and Order in Chosŏn Dynasty Korea." In *Rethinking Confucianism,* edited by Elman, Duncan, and Ooms, 292–334.

Dini, Jane. "The Art of Selling War: Sargent's World War I Murals for Harvard University." *Harvard University Art Museums Bulletin* 7, no. 1 (Autumn 1999–Winter 2000): 67–84.

Drea, Edward J. *In the Service of the Emperor: Essays on the Imperial Japanese Army.* Lincoln: University of Nebraska Press, 1998.

———. *Japan's Imperial Army: Its Rise and Fall, 1853–1945*. Lawrence: University Press of Kansas, 2009.

———. "The Japanese Army on the Eve of the War." In Peattie, Drea, and Van de Ven, eds., *Battle for China*.

Duara, Prasenjit. *Sovereignty and Authenticity: Manchukuo and the East Asian Modern*. Lanham, MD: Rowman & Littlefield, 2003.

Dupuy, Trevor N. *Evolution of Weapons and Warfare*. New York: Da Capo, 1984.

Duus, Peter. *The Abacus and the Sword: The Japanese Penetration of Korea, 1895–1910*. Berkeley: University of California Press, 1995.

Duus, Peter, Ramon H. Myers, and Mark R. Peattie, eds. *The Japanese Wartime Empire, 1931–1945*. Princeton, NJ: Princeton University Press, 1996.

Eagle and the Serpent: A Journal for Free Spirits and for Spirits Struggling to Be Free. 2 vols. London: 1898–1902.

Eckert, Carter J. "Exorcising Hegel's Ghosts: Toward a Postnationalist Historiography of Korea." In *Colonial Modernity in Korea*, edited by Gi-Wook Shin and Michael Robinson, 363–378. Harvard-Hallym Series on Korean Studies. Cambridge, MA: Harvard University Asia Center, 1999.

———. "A Gentle Voice in the Darkness: The Musical Genius of Kim Min'gi." In *Kim Min'gi*. Seoul, YMB Sŏul Ŭmban, 1994. Translated into Korean and included in *Kim Min'gi*, edited by Kim Ch'angnam, 493–505. Seoul: Tosŏch'ulp'an Han'ul, 2004.

———. *Offspring of Empire: The Colonial Origins of Korean Capitalism, 1876–1945*. Seattle: University of Washington Press, 1991.

———. "Preface." In special issue of *Journal of International and Area Studies* 11, no. 3 (2004): 1–5.

———. "The South Korean Bourgeoisie: A Class in Search of Hegemony." In *State and Society in Contemporary Korea*, edited by Hagen Koo, 95–130. Ithaca, NY: Cornell University Press, 2000.

———. "Total War, Industrialization, and Social Change in Late Colonial Korea." In Duus, Myers, and Peattie, *The Japanese Wartime Empire, 1931–1945*, 3–39.

Eckert, Carter J., Ki-baik Lee, Young Ick Lew, Michael Robinson, and Edward W. Wagner. *Korea Old and New: A History*. Cambridge, MA: Korea Institute, Harvard University, 1995.

Elman, Benjamin A., John B. Duncan, and Herman Ooms, eds. *Rethinking Confucianism: Past and Present in China, Japan, Korea, and Vietnam*. Los Angeles: UCLA Asian Pacific Monograph Series, 2002.

Em, Henry H. *The Great Enterprise: Sovereignty and Historiography in Modern Korea*. Durham, NC: Duke University Press, 2013.

Fitzgerald, F. Scott. *The Great Gatsby*. New York: Charles Scribner's Sons, 1925. Scribner's paperback 2004.

Foucault, Michel. *Discipline and Punish: The Birth of the Prison*. Translated by Alan Sheridan. New York: Vintage Books, 1979.

———. "Governmentality." In Burchell, Gordon, and Miller, *The Foucault Effect: Studies in Governmentality*, 87–104.

———. *The History of Sexuality*, vol. 1. New York: Vintage Books, 1990.

———. "Nietzsche, Genealogy, History." In *The Foucault Reader*, edited by Paul Rabinow, 76–100. New York: Pantheon, 1984.

———. "Technologies of the Self." In *Technologies of the Self: A Seminar with Michel Foucault*, edited by Luther H. Martin, Huck Gutman, and Patrick H. Hutton. Amherst: University of Massachusetts Press, 1988.

Fraleigh, Matthew. "Songs of the Righteous Spirit: 'Men of High Purpose' and Their Chinese Poetry in Modern Japan." *Harvard Journal of Asiatic Studies* 69, no. 1 (June 2009): 109–171.

Goldstein, Jan, ed. *Foucault and the Writing of History*. Oxford: Blackwell, 1994.

Fujitani, T. *Race for Empire: Koreans as Japanese and Japanese as Americans during World War II*. Berkeley: University of California Press, 2011.

Garfield, Brian. *The Thousand-Mile War: World War II in Alaska and the Aleutians*. Garden City, NY: Doubleday, 1969.

Gibbons, Michael, Camille Limoges, Helga Nowotny, Simon Schwartzman, Peter Scott, and Martin Trow. *The New Production of Knowledge: the Dynamics of Science and Research in Contemporary Societies*. London: Sage Publications, 1994.

Glantz, David M. *The Soviet Strategic Offensive in Manchuria, 1945: "August Storm."* London: Frank Cass, 2003.

Gluck, Carol. *Japan's Modern Myths: Ideology in the Late Meiji Period*. Princeton, NJ: Princeton University Press, 1985.

Gordon, Andrew. *A Modern History of Japan: From Tokugawa Times to the Present*. New York: Oxford University Press, 2003.

Gordon, Joel. *Nasser's Blessed Movement: Egypt's Free Officers and the July Revolution*. Cairo: American University in Cairo Press, 1992.

Gosnell, H. H. "The Navy in Korea, 1871." *American Neptune* 7 (April 1947): 107–114.

Gramsci, Antonio. *Selections from the Prison Notebooks*. Edited and translated by Quintin Hoare and Geoffrey Nowell Smith. New York: International, 1971.

Greven, Philip J. *Spare the Child: The Religious Roots of Punishment and the Psychological Impact of Physical Abuse*. New York: Knopf, 1990.

Guldi, Jo and David Armitage. *The History Manifesto*. Cambridge: Cambridge University Press, 2014.

Hackett, Roger F. "Imperial Rescript to Soldiers and Sailors." In *Kodansha Encyclopedia of Japan*. vol. 3, 279–280. Tokyo, New York: Kodansha.

———. *Yamagata Aritomo in the Rise of Modern Japan, 1838–1922*. Cambridge, MA: Harvard University Press, 1971.

Haboush, JaHyun. *The Confucian Kingship in Korea: Yŏngjo and the Politics of Sagacity*. New York: Columbia University Press, 2001.

———. "Constructing the Center: The Ritual Controversy and the Search for a New Identity." In *Culture and the State in Late Chosŏn Korea*, edited by JaHyun Kim Haboush and Martina Deuchler, 46–90. Cambridge, MA: Harvard University Asia Center, 1999.

———, ed. *Epistolary Korea: Letters in the Communicative Space of the Chosŏn, 1392–1910*. New York: Columbia University Press, 2009.

Haggard, Stephan. *Pathways from the Periphery: The Politics of Growth in the Newly Industrializing Countries*. Ithaca, NY: Cornell University Press, 1990.

Hall, Donald E. *Muscular Christianity: Embodying the Victorian Age*. Cambridge Studies in Nineteenth-Century Literature and Culture 2. Cambridge: Cambridge University Press, 1994.

Hall, Robert King. *Shūshin: The Ethics of a Defeated Nation*. New York: Bureau of Publications, Teachers College, Columbia University, 1949.

Han, Suk-Jung. "From Pusan to Fengtian: The Borderline between Korea and Manchukuo in the 1930s." *East Asian History* 30 (December 2005): 91–106.

———. "Puppet Sovereignty: The State Effect of Manchukuo, from 1932 to 1936." Ph.D. dissertation, Sociology Department, University of Chicago, 1995.

Harries, Meirion, and Susie Harries. *Soldiers of the Sun: The Rise and Fall of the Imperial Japanese Army*. London: Heinemann, 1991.

Henry, Todd A. *Assimilating Seoul: Japanese Rule and the Politics of Public Space in Colonial Korea, 1910–1945*. Berkeley: University of California Press, 2014.

High, Peter B. *The Imperial Screen: Japanese Film Culture in the Fifteen Years' War, 1931–1945*. Madison: University of Wisconsin Press, 2003.

Hitler, Adolf. *Mein Kampf.* New York: Reynal and Hitchcock, 1939.

Hobsbawm, E. J. *The Age of Empire 1875–1914.* New York: Pantheon, 1987.

Hooton, E. R. *The Greatest Tumult: The Chinese Civil War: 1936–49.* London: Brassey's, 1991.

Horace. *Odes and Epodes.* Edited and translated by Niall Rudd. Cambridge, MA: Harvard University Press, 2004.

Huer, Jon. *Marching Orders: The Role of the Military in South Korea's "Economic Miracle," 1961–1971.* New York: Greenwood Press, 1989.

Hughes, Thomas. *Tom Brown's School Days.* Boston: Houghton, Mifflin, 1895.

Hull, Isabel V. *Absolute Destruction: Military Culture and the Practices of War in Imperial Germany.* Ithaca, NY: Cornell University Press, 2005.

Humphreys, Leonard A. *The Way of the Heavenly Sword: The Japanese Army in the 1920s.* Stanford, CA: Stanford University Press, 1995.

Hunter, Janet. *Concise Dictionary of Modern Japanese History.* Berkeley: University of California Press, 1984.

Huntington, Samuel P. *Political Order in Changing Societies.* New Haven, CT: Yale University Press, 1968.

Hurst, G. Cameron III. *Armed Martial Arts of Japan: Swordsmanship and Archery.* New Haven, CT: Yale University Press, 1998.

Hwang, Kyung Moon. *Beyond Birth: Social Status in the Emergence of Modern Korea.* Cambridge, MA: Harvard University Asia Center, 2004.

———. *A History of Korea.* New York: Palgrave Macmillan, 2010.

———. *Rationalizing Korea: The Rise of the Modern State, 1894–1945.* Oakland: University of California Press, 2016.

Jager, Sheila Miyoshi. *Narratives of Nation Building in Korea: A Genealogy of Patriotism.* Armonk, NY: M. E. Sharpe, 2003.

Jaisohn, Philip. *My Days in Korea and Other Essays.* Edited by Sun-pyo Hong. Seoul: Institute for Modern Korean Studies, Yonsei University, 1999.

James, William. *Pragmatism and Other Essays.* New York: Washington Square Press, 1963.

Janelli, Roger L., with Dawnhee Yim. *Making Capitalism: The Social and Cultural Construction of a South Korean Conglomerate.* Stanford, CA: Stanford University Press, 1993.

Janowitz, Morris. *The Military in the Development of New Nations: An Essay in Comparative Analysis.* Chicago: University of Chicago Press, 1964.

Janowitz, Morris, and Jacques Van Doorn, eds. *On Military Ideology.* Rotterdam: Rotterdam University Press, 1971.

Jensen, Geoffrey. *Irrational Triumph: Cultural Despair, Military Nationalism, and the Ideological Origins of Franco's Spain.* Reno and Las Vegas: University of Nevada Press, 2002.

Johnson, Chalmers. *MITI and the Japanese Miracle: The Growth of Industrial Policy, 1925–1975.* Stanford, CA: Stanford University Press, 1982.

Jones, F. C. *Manchuria since 1931.* London: Royal Institute of International Affairs, 1949.

Jowett, Philip S. *Rays of the Rising Sun: Armed Forces of Japan's Asian Allies 1931–45*, vol. 1, *China and Manchukuo.* Solihull: Helion, 2004.

Keegan, John. *A History of Warfare.* New York: Vintage, 1993.

Keene, Donald. *Dawn to the West: Japanese Literature in the Modern Era: Fiction.* New York: Holt, Rinehart, and Winston, 1984.

———. *Landscapes and Portraits.* Tokyo: Kodansha International, 1971.

Kershaw, Ian. *Hitler: 1889–1936: Hubris.* New York: W. W. Norton, 1998.

Kidd, Benjamin. *Principles of Western Civilization.* New York: Macmillan, 1902.

Kier, Elizabeth. *Imagining War: French and British Military Doctrine between the Wars.* Princeton, NJ: Princeton University Press, 1997.

Kierman, Frank A., Jr., and John K. Fairbank, eds. *Chinese Ways in Warfare.* Cambridge, MA: Harvard University Press, 1974.

Kim, Byung-Kook and Ezra F. Vogel, eds. *The Park Chung Hee Era: The Transformation of South Korea*. Cambridge, MA: Harvard University Press, 2011.

Kim, Choong Soon. *The Culture of Korean Industry: An Ethnography of Poongsan Corporation*. Tucson: University of Arizona Press, 1992.

Kim, C. I. Eugene, and Han-Kyo Kim. *Korea and the Politics of Imperialism, 1876–1910*. Berkeley: University of California Press, 1967.

Kim, Eun Mee. *Big Business, Strong State: Collusion and Conflict in South Korean Development, 1960–1990*. Albany: State University of New York Press, 1997.

Kim, Hyung-A. *Korea's Development under Park Chung Hee: Rapid Industrialization, 1961–1979*. London: Routledge, 2004.

Kim, Hyung-A and Clark Sorensen, eds. *Reassessing the Park Chung Hee Era 1961–1979: Development, Political Thought, Democracy, and Cultural Influence*. Seattle: University of Washington Press, 2011.

Kim, Michael. "The Aesthetics of Total Mobilisation in the Visual Culture of Late Colonial Korea." *Totalitarian Movements and Political Religions* 8, no. 3–4 (2007): 483–502.

Kim, Se-jin. *The Politics of Military Revolution in Korea*. Chapel Hill: University of North Carolina Press, 1971.

Kim, Sun Joo. "Fathers' Letters Concerning Their Children's Education." In *Epistolary Korea: Letters in the Communicative Space of the Chosŏn, 1392–1910*, edited by JaHyun Haboush, 277–286. New York: Columbia University Press, 2009.

———. *Marginality and Subversion in Korea: The Hong Kyŏngnae Rebellion of 1812*. Seattle: University of Washington Press, 2007.

Kim, Sun Joo and Jungwon Kim, eds. *Wrongful Deaths: Selected Inquest Records from Nineteenth-Century Korea*. Seattle: University of Washington Press, 2014.

Korean Repository (January 1892–December 1898).

Kwon, Insook. "Militarism in My Heart: Militarization of Women's Consciousness and Culture in South Korea." Ph.D. dissertation, Women's Studies, Clark University, 2000.

Kwon, Peter Banseok. "The Anatomy of *Chaju Kukpang*: Military-Civilian Convergency in the Development of the South Korean Defense Industry under Park Chung Hee, 1968–1979." Ph.D. dissertation, History and East Asian Languages, Harvard University, 2016.

Lamb, Malcolm L. *Directory of Officials and Organizations in China*. 2 vols. 3rd edition. Armonk, NY: M.E. Sharpe, 2003.

Larsen, Kirk W. *Tradition, Treaties, and Trade: Qing Imperialism and Chosŏn Korea, 1850–1910*. Cambridge, MA: Harvard University Asia Center, 2008.

Lasswell, Harold D. *The Analysis of Political Behavior: An Empirical Approach*. London: Kegan, Paul, Trench, Trubner, 1947.

Lee, Ki-baik. *A New History of Korea*. Translated by Edward W. Wagner with Edward J. Schultz. Cambridge, MA: Harvard University Press, 1984.

———. "Korea: The Military Tradition." In *The Traditional Culture and Society of Korea: Thought and Institutions*, edited by H. W. Kang, 1–42. Honolulu: Center for Korean Studies, University of Hawaii, 1975.

Lee, Chong-Sik. *The Korean Workers' Party: A Short History*. Stanford, CA: Hoover Institution Press, 1978.

———. *Park Chung-Hee: From Poverty to Power*. Palos Verdes, CA: The KHU Press, 2012.

———. *The Politics of Korean Nationalism*. Berkeley: University of California Press, 1963.

Lee, Hyangjin. *Contemporary Korean Cinema: Identity, Culture, Politics*. Manchester: Manchester University Press, 2000.

Lee, Kwang-rin. "The Role of Foreign Military Instructors in the Later Period of the Yi Dynasty." In *International Conference on the Problems of Modernization in Asia*. Seoul: Asiatic Research Center, Korea University, 1965.

Lee, Peter H. *Poems from Korea: A Historical Anthology.* Compiled and translated by Peter H. Lee. Honolulu: University of Hawaii Press, 1974.

———, ed. *Sourcebook of Korean Civilization*, vol. 2, *From the Sixteenth to the Twentieth Centuries.* New York: Columbia University Press, 1996.

Leon, Philip W. *Bullies and Cowards: The West Point Hazing Scandal, 1898–1901.* Westport, CT: Greenwood Press, 2000.

Levidis, Andrew. "War, Asianism and National Renovation: Kishi Nobusuke and the Politics of Conservatism, 1918–1944." Ph.D. dissertation, Faculty of Law, Kyoto University, 2013.

Lew, Young Ick. "The Reform Efforts and Ideas of Pak Yŏng-hyŏ, 1894–1895." *Korean Studies* 1 (1977): 21–61.

———. "Yüan Shih-k'ai's Residency and the Korean Enlightenment Movement." *Journal of Korean Studies* 5 (1984): 63–107.

Lomsky-Feder and Eyal Ben-Ari, eds. *The Military and Militarism in Israeli Society.* Albany: State University of New York Press, 1999.

Madej, W. Victor, ed. *Japanese Armed Forces Order of Battle.* 2 vols. Allentown, PA: Game Marketing, 1981.

Marshall, Byron K. *Capitalism and Nationalism in Pre-War Japan: The Ideology of the Business Elite, 1868–1941.* Stanford, CA: Stanford University Press, 1967.

Maruyama, Masao. *Thought and Behavior in Japanese Politics.* Expanded edition. Edited by Ivan Morris. London: Oxford University Press, 1969.

Martin, Michel Louis and Ellen Stern McCrate, eds. *The Military, Militarism, and the Polity: Essays in Honor of Morris Janowitz.* New York: The Free Press, 1984.

Matsusaka, Yoshihisa Tak. *The Making of Japanese Manchuria, 1904–1932.* Cambridge, MA: Harvard University Asia Center, 2001.

McGregor, Katharine E. *History in Uniform: Military Ideology and the Construction of Indonesia's Past.* Asian Studies Association of Australia. Honolulu: University of Hawaii Press, 2007.

McNeil, William H. *The Pursuit of Power: Technology, Armed Force, and Society since A.D. 1000.* Chicago: University of Chicago Press, 1982.

McKenzie, F. A. *The Tragedy of Korea.* Seoul: Yonsei University Press, 1969. First published in 1908 by E. P. Dutton.

Menzies, Jackie, ed. *Modern Boy Modern Girl: Modernity in Japanese Art 1910–1935.* Curated by Chiaki Ajioka. Sydney: Art Galley of New South Wales, 1998.

Miller, Stuart Creighton. *Benevolent Assimilation: The American Conquest of the Philippines, 1899–1903.* New Haven, CT: Yale University Press, 1982.

Mitter, Rana. *The Manchurian Myth: Nationalism, Resistance and Collaboration in Modern China.* Berkeley: University of California Press, 2000.

Molony, Barbara. *Technology and Investment: The Prewar Japanese Chemical Industry.* Cambridge, MA: Council on East Asian Studies, Harvard University, 1990.

Moltke, Helmuth. *Moltke on the Art of War: Selected Writings.* Edited by Daniel J. Hughes. Translated by Daniel J. Hughes and Harry Bell. Novato, CA: Presidio, 1993.

Moon, Chung-in, and Byung-joon Jun. "Modernization Strategy: Ideas and Influences." In Kim and Vogel, eds. *The Park Chung Hee Era*, 113–139.

Moon, Seungsook. *Militarized Modernity and Gendered Citizenship in South Korea.* Durham, NC: Duke University Press, 2005.

Moon, Yumi. *Populist Collaborators: The Ilchinhoe and the Japanese Colonization of Korea, 1896–1910.* Ithaca, NY: Cornell University Press, 2013.

Moore, Aaron William. *Writing War: Soldiers Record the Japanese Empire.* Cambridge, MA: Harvard University Press, 2013.

Morse, Edward Sylvester. *Korean Interviews.* New York: D. Appleton, 1897.

Morris, Ivan. *The Nobility of Failure: Tragic Heroes in the History of Japan*. New York: Holt, Rinehart, and Winston, 1975.
Moss, Mark. *Manliness and Militarism: Educating Young Boys in Ontario for War*. Don Mills, ON: Oxford University Press, 2001.
Mussolini, Benito. *My Rise and Fall*. New York: Da Capo Press, 1998.
Nam, Hwasook. *Building Ships, Building a Nation: Korea's Democratic Unionism under Park Chung Hee*. Seattle: University of Washington Press, 2009.
Nietzsche, Friedrich. *On the Genealogy of Morals, Ecco Homo*. Translated and edited by Walter Kaufman. New York: Vintage Books, 1967.
———. *Twilight of the Idols: Or, How to Philosophize with the Hammer*. Translated by Richard Polt. Indianapolis: Hackett, 1997.
Ohnuki-Tierney, Emiko. *Kamikaze, Cherry Blossoms, and Nationalisms: The Militarization of Aesthetics in Japanese History*. Chicago: University of Chicago Press, 2002.
Orbach, Danny. *Curse on This Country: Japanese Military Insubordination and the Origins of the Pacific War, 1860–1936*. Ithaca, NY: Cornell University Press, forthcoming.
Paekpŏm Ilchi: The Autobiography of Kim Ku. Translated, annotated, and introduced by Jongsoo Lee. Lanham, MD: University Press of America, 2000.
Paik, Nak-Chung. "How to Think about the Park Chung Hee Era." In *Reassessing the Park Chung Hee Era 1961–1979: Development, Political Thought, Democracy, and Cultural Influence*, edited by Kim Hyung-A and Clark Sorensen, 85–91. Seattle: University of Washington Press, 2011.
Paine, S. C. M. *The Sino-Japanese War of 1894–1895: Perceptions, Power, and Primacy*. Cambridge: Cambridge University Press, 2003.
Palais, James B. *Confucian Statecraft and Korean Institutions: Yu Hyŏngwŏn and the Late Chosŏn Dynasty*. Seattle: University of Washington Press, 1996.
———. *Politics and Policy in Traditional Korea*. Cambridge, MA: Harvard University Press, 1975.
Palmer, Brandon. *Fighting for the Enemy: Koreans in Japan's War, 1937–1945*. Seattle: University of Washington Press, 2013.
Papacosma, S. Victor. *The Military in Greek Politics: The 1909 Coup d'État*. Kent, OH: Kent State University Press, 1977.
Park, Eugene Y. *Between Dreams and Reality: The Military Examination in Late Chosŏn Korea, 1600–1894*. Cambridge, MA: Harvard University Asia Center, 2007.
Park, Sunyoung. *The Proletarian Wave: Literature and Leftist Culture in Colonial Korea 1910–1945*. Cambridge, MA: Harvard University Asia Center, 2015.
Parker, Geoffrey. *The Military Revolution: Military Innovation and the Rise of the West, 1500–1800*. 2nd edition. Cambridge: Cambridge University Press, 1996.
Payne, Stanley G. *A History of Fascism 1914–45*. Madison: University of Wisconsin Press, 1995.
Peattie, Mark R. *Ishiwara Kanji and Japan's Confrontation with the West*. Princeton, NJ: Princeton University Press, 1975.
Peattie, Mark, Edward Drea, and Hans Van de Ven, eds. *The Battle for China: Essays on the Military History of the Sino-Japanese War of 1937–1945*. Stanford, CA: Stanford University Press, 2011.
Penn, Alan. *Targeting Schools: Drill, Militarism and Imperialism*. London: Woburn Press, 1999.
Plato. *The Republic of Plato*. Translated, with an Introduction, by A. D. Lindsay. New York: E. P. Dutton, 1957.
Porter, Bruce. *War and the Rise of the State: The Military Foundations of Modern Politics*. New York: The Free Press, 1994.
Possner, Roger. *The Rise of Militarism in the Progressive Era, 1900–1914*. Jefferson, NC: McFarland, 2009.

Powell, Ralph L. *The Rise of Chinese Military Power, 1805–1912*. Princeton, NJ: Princeton University Press, 1955.

Presseisen, Ernst L. *Before Aggression: Europeans Prepare the Japanese Army*. Tucson: University of Arizona Press, 1965.

Putney, Clifford. *Muscular Christianity: Manhood and Sports in Protestant America, 1880–1920*. Cambridge, MA: Harvard University Press, 2001.

Rabinow, Paul, ed. *The Foucault Reader*. New York: Pantheon Books, 1984.

Ravina, Mark. *The Last Samurai: The Life and Battles of Saigō Takamori*. Hoboken, NJ: John Wiley and Sons, 2004.

Redbeard, Ragnar. *Might Is Right or the Survival of the Fittest*. New York: Revisionist Press, 1972.

Reischauer, Edwin O. and Albert M. Craig. *Japan: Tradition and Transformation*. Boston: Houghton Mifflin, 1978.

Reynolds, Bruce, ed. *Japan in the Fascist Era*. New York: Palgrave Macmillan, 2004.

Rhyu, Sang-young, and Seok-jin Lew. "Pohang Iron and Steel Company." In *The Park Chung Hee Era: The Transformation of South Korea*, edited by Byung-Kook Kim and Ezra F. Vogel, 322–344. Cambridge, MA: Harvard University Press, 2011.

Richie, Donald. *A Hundred Years of Japanese Film: A Concise History, with a Selective Guide to DVDs and Videos*. Revised edition. Tokyo: Kodansha International, 2005.

Ritter, Gerhard. *The Sword and the Scepter: The Problem of Militarism in Germany*, vol. 1, *The Prussian Tradition 1740–1890*. Translated by Heinz Norden. Coral Gables, FL: University of Miami Press, 1969.

Robinson, Michael Edson. *Cultural Nationalism in Colonial Korea, 1920–1925*. Seattle: University of Washington Press, 1988.

——. *Korea's Twentieth-Century Odyssey: A Short History*. Honolulu: University of Hawaii Press, 2007.

——. "National Identity and the Thought of Sin Ch'aeho: *Sadaejuŭi* and *Chuch'e* in History and Politics." *Journal of Korean Studies* 5 (1984): 121–142.

Ruoff, Kenneth J. *Imperial Japan at Its Zenith: The Wartime Celebration of the Empire's 2,600th Anniversary*. Studies of the Weatherhead East Asian Institute, Columbia University. Ithaca, NY: Cornell University Press, 2010.

Sakurai, Tadayoshi. *Human Bullets: A Soldier's Story of Port Arthur*. Translated by Masujiro Honda. Boston: Houghton, Mifflin, 1907.

Sato, Hiroaki. *Legends of the Samurai*. Woodstock, NY: Overlook Press, 1995.

Sawyer, Robert K. *Military Advisors in Korea: KMAG in Peace and War*. Edited by Walter G. Hermes. Washington, DC: Center of Military History, United States Army, 1988.

Scalapino, Robert A. *The Japanese Communist Movement*. Santa Monica, CA: RAND Corporation, 1966.

Scalapino, Robert A., and Chong-Sik Lee. *Communism in Korea*. 2 vols. Berkeley: University of California Press, 1972.

Schmid, Andre. *Korea between Empires: 1895–1919*. New York: Columbia University Press, 2002.

Sejima, Ryuzo. *Reminiscences: History of Japan from the 1930s to the Outbreak of the Greater East Asia War*. Ryuzo Sejima, 1972.

Selth, Andrew. *Burma's Armed Forces: Power without Glory*. Norwalk, CT: Eastbridge, 2002.

Seow, Victor Kian Giap. "Carbon Technocracy: East Asian Energy Regimes and the Industrial Modern." Ph.D. dissertation, Harvard University, 2014.

Sewell, William H., Jr. *Logics of History: Social Theory and Social Transformation*. Chicago: University of Chicago Press, 2005.

Shillony, Ben-Ami. *Revolt in Japan: The Young Officers and the February 26, 1936 Incident*. Princeton, NJ: Princeton University Press, 1973.

Shimazu, Naoko. *Japanese Society at War: Death, Memory, and the Russo-Japanese War.* New York: Cambridge University Press, 2009.

Shin, Gi-Wook. *Ethnic Nationalism in Korea: Genealogy, Politics, and Legacy.* Stanford, CA: Stanford University Press, 2008.

Shin, Gi-Wook, and Michael Robinson, "Rethinking Colonial Korea." In *Colonial Modernity in Korea,* edited by Gi-Wook Shin and Michael Robinson, 1–18. Harvard-Hallym Series on Korean Studies. Cambridge, MA: Harvard University Asia Center, 1999.

———, eds. *Colonial Modernity in Korea.* Harvard-Hallym Series on Korean Studies. Cambridge, MA: Harvard University Asia Center, 1999.

Sin Yong-Ha. "The Coup d'Etat of 1884 and the Pukch'ŏng Army of the Progressive Party." *Korea Journal* 33, no. 2 (Summer 1993): 5–16.

Shirane, Haruo, ed. *Early Modern Japanese Literature: An Anthology 1600–1900.* New York: Columbia University Press, 2002.

Sugita, Satoshi. "Cherry Blossoms and Rising Sun: A Systematic and Objective Analysis of *Gunka* (Japanese War Songs) in Five Historical Periods (1868–1945)." B.A. thesis, Ohio State University, 1972.

Suh, Dae-Sook. *Documents of Korean Communism, 1918–1948.* Princeton, NJ: Princeton University Press, 1970.

———. *The Korean Communist Movement, 1918–1948.* Princeton, NJ: Princeton University Press, 1967.

Smethurst, Richard J. *A Social Basis for Prewar Japanese Militarism: The Army and the Rural Community.* Berkeley: University of California Press, 1974.

Smith, Henry Dewitt II. *Japan's First Student Radicals.* Cambridge, MA: Harvard University Press, 1972.

Snyder, Jack L. *Ideology of the Offensive: Military Decision Making and the Disasters of 1914.* Ithaca, NY: Cornell University Press, 1984.

Spencer, Herbert. *The Study of Sociology.* International Scientific Series. New York: D. Appleton, 1875.

Stanley, Peter. *White Mutiny: British Military Culture in India.* New York: New York University Press, 1998.

Sumner, William Graham. *War and Other Essays.* Edited with an introduction by Albert Galloway Keller. New Haven, CT: Yale University Press, 1919.

Szpilman, Christopher W. A. "Fascist and Quasi-Fascist Ideas in Interwar Japan, 1918–1941." In *Japan in the Fascist Era,* edited by Bruce Reynolds, 73–106. New York: Palgrave Macmillan, 2004.

———. "Kita Ikki and the Politics of Coercion." *Modern Asian Studies* 36, no. 2 (2002): 467–490.

Tankha, Brij. *Kita Ikki and the Making of Modern Japan: A Vision of Empire.* Folkestone, UK: Global Oriental, 2006.

Tanner, Harold Miles. "Guerrilla, Mobile, and Base Warfare in Communist Military Operations in Manchuria, 1945–1947." *Journal of Military History* 67, no. 4 (October 2003): 1177–1222.

Tansman, Alan, ed. *The Culture of Japanese Fascism.* Durham, NC: Duke University Press, 2009.

Tilly, Charles. *Coercion, Capital, and European States, AD 990–1992.* Revised edition. Malden, MA: Blackwell, 1992.

Tipton, Elise K. *The Japanese Police State: The Tokkō in Interwar Japan.* Honolulu: University of Hawaii Press, 1990.

Tokeshi, Jinichi. *Kendo: Elements, Rules, and Philosophy.* Honolulu: University of Hawaii Press, 2003.

Totten, George Oakley, III. *The Social Democratic Movement in Prewar Japan*. New Haven, CT: Yale University Press, 1966.

Townshend, Charles, ed. *The Oxford History of Modern War*. Oxford: Oxford University Press, 2000.

Tsunoda, Ryusaku, Wm. Theodore de Bary, and Donald Keene, eds. *Sources of Japanese Tradition*. New York: Columbia University Press, 1958.

Tucker, David Vance. "Building 'Our Manchukuo': Japanese City Planning, Architecture, and Nation-Building in Occupied Northeast China, 1931–1945." Ph.D. dissertation, History Department, University of Iowa, 1999.

Tucker, Robert C., ed. *The Marx-Engels Reader*. New York: W. W. Norton, 1972.

Turfan, M. Naim. *Rise of the Young Turks: Politics, the Military and Ottoman Collapse*. London: I. B. Tauris, 2000.

Uchida, Jun, *Brokers of Empire: Japanese Settler Colonialism in Korea, 1876–1945*. Cambridge, MA: Harvard University Asia Center, 2011.

U.S. War Department. *Handbook on Japanese Military Forces*. New introduction by David Isby and afterword by Jeffrey Ethell. Baton Rouge: Louisiana State University Press, 1991.

Wagner, Edward Willett. *The Literati Purges: Political Conflict in Early Yi Korea*. Cambridge, MA: East Asian Research Center, 1974.

Wald, Royal Jules. "The Young Officers Movement in Japan, ca. 1925–1937: Ideology and Actions." Ph.D. dissertation, History Department, University of California, 1949.

Wales, Nym [Helen Foster Snow], and Kim San. *Song of Arian: A Korean Communist in the Chinese Revolution*. San Francisco: Ramparts Press, 1941.

Walraven, Boudewijn. "Reader's Etiquette, and Other Aspects of Book Culture in Chosŏn Korea." In *Books in Numbers: Seventy-Fifth Anniversary of the Harvard Yenching Library: Conference Papers,* edited by Wilt Idema. Cambridge, MA: Harvard Yenching Library, 2007.

Warner, Denis, and Peggy Warner. *The Tide at Sunrise: A History of the Russo-Japanese War, 1904–1905*. London: Angus and Robertson, 1975.

Warner, Peggy, and Sadao Seno. *The Coffin Boats: Japanese Midget Submarine Operations in the Second World War*. London: Leo Cooper, 1986.

Weber, Max. *Economy and Society*. 2 vols. Edited by Guenther Roth and Claus Wittich. Berkeley: University of California Press, 1968.

———. *The Protestant Ethnic and the Spirit of Capitalism*. Translated and updated by Stephen Kalberg. New York: Oxford University Press, 2011.

Wells, Kenneth M. *New God, New Nation: Protestants and Self-Reconstruction Nationalism in Korea, 1896–1937*. Honolulu: University of Hawaii Press, 1990.

Wilkinson, William Henry. *The Corean Government: Constitutional Changes, July 1894 to October 1895*. Shanghai: Statistical Department of the Inspectorate General of Customs, 1897.

Woo, Jung-en. *Race to the Swift: State and Finance in Korean Industrialization*. New York: Columbia University Press, 1991.

Woo-Cumings, Meredith, ed. *The Developmental State*. Ithaca, NY Cornell University Press, 1999.

Yamamoto Tsunetomo, *Hagakure: The Book of the Samurai*. Translated by William Scott Wilson. Tokyo: Kodansha International, 1979.

Yamamuro Shin'ichi. *Manchuria under Japanese Dominion*. Translated by Joshua A. Fogel. Philadelphia: University of Pennsylvania Press, 2006.

Young, Louise. *Japan's Total Empire: Manchuria and the Culture of Wartime Imperialism*. Berkeley: University of California Press, 1998.

Books and Articles in Other Languages

Afanas'ev. *Sovremennoe sostoianie vooruzhhennykh sil Korei* [Current state of Korean armed forces]. Vladivostok: Tip. T-va Sushchinskii I KO, 1903.

[Meckel, Jakob.] *Befehlsführung und Selbstständigkeit, von einem alten Truppenoffizier* [Command leadership and independence, by an old troop officer]. Berlin: Mittler und Sohn, 1885.

Russia, Ministerstvo Finansov, *Opisanie Korei* [Description of Korea]. 3 vols. St. Petersburg: Tip. Lu. N. Erlikh, 1900.

Newspapers

Asahi shinbun
Chosŏn ilbo
Chungang ilbo
Han'guk ilbo
Independent
Kyunghyang sinmun
Manshū nichi-nichi shinbun
Maeil sinbo
Manshū shinbun
Nihon keizai shinbun
Renmin ribao
Tonga ilbo
Tongnip sinmun

Interviews

Cai Chongliang (MMA 2)
Cho Kapche
Cho, Lee-Jay
Chŏng Naehyŏk (JMA 58)
Daitō Shinsuke
Fujimori Shin'ichi (MMA 6/JMA 60)
Fujimoto Shigemi (MMA 2/JMA 57)
Gao Qingyin (MMA 2)
Hiratsuka Hisano (MMA 7)
Hwangbo Kyun (TNS 4)
Kaneko Tomio (MMA 2/JMA 57)
Kim Chaech'un (KMA 5)
Kim Chŏngnyŏm
Kim Chongp'il (KMA 8)
Kim Kwangsik (MMA 7)
Kim Min'gyu (MMA 1)
Kim Muk (MMA 2)
Kim Tonghun (MMA 6)
Kim Yŏngt'aek (MMA 1)
Kim Yun'gŭn (MMA 6/JMA 60)
Kiyoizumi Nobuo (MMA 2/JMA 57)
Millett, Allan R.
Nishikawa Nobuyoshi (MMA 7)
O Wŏnch'ŏl
Origuchi Ryūzō (MMA 2/JMA 57)

Origuchi Ryūzō et al. (Origuchi and others: Hiratsuka, Fujimori. Fujimoto, Sekine, and Takeshita)
Paek Sŏnyŏp (CTS 9)
Pak Sanggil
Pang Wŏnch'ŏl (MMA 1)
Sekine Tomiji (MMA 2/JMA 57)
Shiraishi Hiroshi
Sŏ Pyŏngguk (TNS 6)
Suzuki Michihiko
Takeshita Morio (MMA 2/JMA 57)
Takezawa Rikio (MMA 2/JMA 57)
Wang Jingyue (MMA 6)
Xu Shudong (MMA 2)
Yi Hallim (MMA 2/JMA 57)
Yi Sŏngjo (TNS 4)
Yi T'aeyŏng
Yu Chŭngsŏn
Yu Yangsu (KMA Special 7)
Yun Ch'idu (TNS 4)
Zhu Huan (MMA 6)

SOURCES AND ACKNOWLEDGMENTS

Researching and writing this book has been a great adventure. With many unanticipated personal and professional interruptions along the way, it has taken much longer than I ever imagined. But even though there were moments when I felt as if I had been conscripted for life into one or more of the military units I was studying, I was continually fascinated by the new and at first very alien world that was opening up to me, with its own regulations, rituals, language, and even music, and the implications that these practices held for the larger story I wanted to tell.

The project all began about twenty years ago with a deceptively simple question: How had Park Chung Hee's military background, including his formative years as a cadet and officer in the Manchukuo Army, shaped his thinking and approach to South Korean development? I knew the research would be challenging, but in my enthusiasm for the question, and my sense that an answer to it would expand our understanding of both Park and South Korea and perhaps even our ways of thinking about modern Korean history, I plunged in without hesitation, and only gradually came to realize the scope of the task. Painfully, I came to grasp how little documentary evidence existed about Park himself during this period, especially subjective materials such as personal letters and diaries that might allow one a deeper insight into his personality. I also came to realize the extent to which the records of the Manchurian Military Academy (MMA) and the Manchukuo Army more generally had been lost, many destroyed at the end of the Pacific War on the orders of the Imperial Japanese Army, along with other government and military documents in Japan itself. But by that time I was well into the work, and there was no alternative to a long and arduous piecemeal collection of data and documents from whatever sources I could identify and access. This quest led me to many diverse places and people in South Korea, Japan, China, and the United States, including, quite unexpectedly, Las Vegas, where I spent a full day interviewing one of Park Chung Hee's closest Chinese MMA classmates. I am pleased to report that in this case what happened in Vegas did not stay in Vegas, but has been incorporated into the book.

Throughout the period of research and writing I have been extraordinarily blessed. Over time a veritable army of colleagues, students, friends, acquaintances, and even initial strangers have aided and abetted me in my endeavors, often coming to my rescue just at the moment when I needed a vital piece of information or a critical primary source. Wherever possible, I have tried to acknowledge such collegiality and kindness in my notes and bibliography, but there is unfortunately no way I can do justice here to the countless numbers of people who have contributed to this book in one way or another. Even so, you know who you are, and I hope you know how very appreciative I am. I am especially grateful to the former MMA cadets, Korean, Japanese, and Chinese, who agreed to meet and share their experiences and thoughts with me through many hours and sometimes even days of interviews; many of them continued afterward to keep in touch and respond to further inquiries. When other documentation was absent, their testimonies proved especially valuable, and even when other documentation did exist, their testimonies brought that material to life and endowed it with what the French medievalist Marc Bloch liked to call the true quarry of the historian, "the scent of human flesh." Already quite elderly when I interviewed them, many of these men, indeed most, are no longer with us, and for that reason their testimonies are all the more precious as part of the historical record.

In South Korea, I am indebted above all to the late Yu Yangsu, to whom this book is dedicated, and whose knowledge and experience of both the Imperial Japanese Army and the Republic of Korea Army (ROKA), as well as his close association with Park Chung Hee, beginning in the late 1940s, informed and enhanced my research in manifold ways over the years and opened doors to key people and places that otherwise might have remained closed. I learned much from my conversations with Kim Chŏngnyŏm and the late Yi Hallim, and both were also helpful in arranging otherwise unobtainable interviews with important figures; their memoirs of course remain essential sources for the Park era. I am also deeply obliged to Professor Kim Kwangsik, a former MMA 7 cadet and later the head of the MMA Alumni Association in South Korea, who freely and generously shared his vast store of MMA history and lore with me and never failed to respond as I continued time and again, especially in the last several years, to disturb him with questions and requests for more information and clarifications. I also want to thank Cho Kapche, whom I met just as he was beginning his own research for a series of articles that would eventually become a major biography of Park Chung Hee. Although we approached Park from different perspectives and disciplines, we enjoyed many fruitful conversations and shared various materials we had each uncovered along the way, and Cho's work has been a valuable reference for my own. I am grateful also to the ROKA Korean Military Academy at T'aenŭng for opening its archives to me and allowing me, together with Ambassador Yu (Yangsu), to spend a full residential week on its premises observing and participating in everyday academy life from reveille to taps and interviewing cadets and faculty. At an early and formative stage in the research process, I was also the recipient of a grant from the Korea Foundation.

In the case of Japan, I must begin by thanking Daitō Shinsuke and Shiraishi Hiroshi, successive directors of the Yasukuni Archive (Yasukuni Kaikō Bunko), who not only unfailingly met my innumerable requests for information and documents but also allowed me to go inside the archive itself and browse through materials as I wished. Researchers and staff of the National Institute for Defense Studies (Bōei Kenkyūjo), another key archive for this book, were helpful and generous to a fault, not least of all Shōji Jun'ichirō. Suzuki Michihiko, a retired general in the Japan Self-Defense Forces whom I met when he was a senior fellow at Harvard's Asia Center, played a central role in arranging interviews with a number of Park Chung Hee's former Japanese MMA classmates and helping me acquire a copy of Hosokawa Minoru's cadet diary, from which I quote extensively in the book, as well as photographs from Hosokawa's cadet album. My former student Matsutani Motokazu, now a professor at Tōhoku Gakuin University, was a true and dedicated collaborator in the final stages of the research. Embracing the project as if it were his own, he checked facts and sources, contacted key people, assisted in interviews, and accompanied me on trips to important sites and archives. When I look back on the years of research for this book, some of my fondest memories are of the time I spent working and traveling with Moto in Japan. I must also express my gratitude to the U.S. embassy in Japan for arranging a trip to Camp Zama, and to the officers and staff of the camp for their hospitality, including Colonel Craig Agena and Stephen Lowell.

For an illuminating and unforgettable research trip to China I owe virtually everything to Sun Qi Lin of Northeast Normal University in Changchun. Professor Sun scheduled interviews for me with a number of Chinese MMA graduates, including Park Chung Hee's former classmates, and provided me with important local reference material on the academy and its graduates that I could not have obtained elsewhere. Through Professor Sun's extensive network of colleagues, including officers in the People's Liberation Army (PLA), I was also given rare permission to tour the former MMA in the Lalatun area just east of the city, then as during the Manchukuo period a restricted military school. In fact, when I visited the site in 1992, it still looked much the same as it had in photographs from the 1940s; even the remains of the former Japanese shrine, burned by the departing cadets in

1945, had been preserved as a reminder (and caution) to the PLA of the school's earlier history.

In the United States from beginning to end I have been buoyed by the enthusiasm and support of many friends, colleagues, and students, including some who, I am sad to say, have passed away, most notably my former teacher James Palais and close personal friends David Grose and Alice Amsden, whose conversations with me about the work were always lively and challenging. At Harvard, friends and colleagues in the Department of East Asian Languages and Civilizations and at the Korea Institute have provided a warm and stimulating environment, and the great resources of the Harvard Yenching Library, both material and human, have been central to the completion of this work. I especially want to thank Chung-Nam Yoon and Mikyung Kang, successive librarians of the Korean collection, and Kuniko McVey, librarian of the Japanese collection, for their unstinting assistance and infinite patience in responding to my never-ending questions and requests for obscure materials—which, miraculously, they somehow always managed to track down and acquire. Throughout the research and writing—and, indeed, throughout all of my years at Harvard—Ezra Vogel has been a cherished colleague and champion, always willing to bend an ear or lend a helping hand. I also benefited immensely from a sabbatical year as a fellow at the Woodrow Wilson International Center for Scholars in Washington, D.C., where I first had the good fortune to meet Professor Allan Millett, whose knowledge of U.S. sources on both American and South Korean military matters has no parallel. The people of Harvard University Press, especially Kathleen McDermott, executive editor for history, have been excellent professional partners, always attentive to my concerns and ready with helpful suggestions.

Finally, I must thank Sun Ho Kim, who has not only shared my life for the past three decades but also joined in the work on the book at crucial moments, checking translations, videotaping and transcribing interviews, and frequently acting as a sounding board for my ideas, based on his own experiences of growing up in the Park Chung Hee era and serving in the South Korean military. In the end, it was Sun Ho's love and encouragement that took me across the finish line.

INDEX